THE BARBOUR COLLECTION
OF CONNECTICUT TOWN
VITAL RECORDS

THE BARBOUR COLLECTION
OF CONNECTICUT TOWN
VITAL RECORDS

NEW LONDON 1646–1854

Compiled by

Nancy E. Schott

General Editor
Lorraine Cook White

INTRODUCTION

As early as 1640 the Connecticut Court of Election ordered all magistrates to keep a record of the marriages they performed. In 1644 the registration of births and marriages became the official responsibility of town clerks and registrars, with deaths added to their duties in 1650. From 1660 until the close of the Revolutionary War these vital records of birth, marriage, and death were generally well kept, but then for a period of about two generations until the mid-nineteenth century, the faithful recording of vital records declined in some towns.

General Lucius Barnes Barbour was the Connecticut Examiner of Public Records from 1911 to 1934 and in that capacity directed a project in which the vital records kept by the towns up to about 1850 were copied and abstracted. Barbour previously had directed the publication of the Bolton and Vernon vital records for the Connecticut Historical Society. For this new project he hired several individuals who were experienced in copying old records and familiar with the old script.

Barbour presented the completed transcriptions of town vital records to the Connecticut State Library where the information was typed onto printed forms. The form sheets were then cut, producing twelve small slips from each sheet. The slips for most towns were then alphabetized and the information was then typed a second time on large sheets of rag paper, which were subsequently bound into separate volumes for each town. The slips for all towns were then interfiled, forming a statewide alphabetized slip index for most surviving town vital records.

The dates of coverage vary from town to town, and of course the records of some towns are more complete than others. There are many cases in which an entry may appear two or three times, apparently because that entry was entered by one or more persons. Altogether the entire Barbour Collection--one of the great genealogical manuscript collections and one of the last to be published--covers 137 towns and comprises 14,333 typed pages.

ABBREVIATIONS

ae. -------------- age
b. ----------------born, both
bd.----------------buried
B.G.--------------Burying Ground
d.----------------died, day, or daughter
decd.------------deceased
f.---------------- father
h.----------------hour
J.P.--------------Justice of Peace
m.---------------married or month
res.--------------resident
s. ----------------son
st. ----------------stillborn
w. ----------------wife
wid. ------------widow
wk. -------------week
y. ---------------year

THE BARBOUR COLLECTION
OF CONNECTICUT TOWN
VITAL RECORDS

NEW LONDON VITAL RECORDS
1646- 1854

	Vol.	Page
ABBERT, Mary, m. Hezekiah **DART**, Jan. 24, 1821, by Elijah Hedding	4	5
ABB[E]Y, Lydia, d. Abiel & Lydia, b. May 28, 1795	3	137
ABEL, ABELL, Caleb, of Norwich, m. Mary **LOOMER**, June 25, 1701	1	26
Elijah, of Bozrah, m. Mary **TUBBS**, of New London, Oct. 5, 1829, by Rev. Abel McEwen	4	37
Margaret, m. Richard **DOUGLASS**, Dec. 7, 1704	1	66
Ralph G., of Norwich, m. Lucretia S. **HARRIS**, of New London, Mar. 30, 1848, by Rev. Jabez S. Swan	4	138
ABRAM, Sarah, of Haddam, m. John **TAYLOR**, of New London, Jan. 15, 1701/2	1	26
ADAMS, Alexander Pygan, s. [Pygan & Anne], b. Sept. 6, 1747; lost at sea in 1782	3	74
Anne, d. [Pygan & Anne], b. Apr. 30, 1749	3	74
Charles Edwin, s. [David, Jr. & Elisabeth], b. Apr. 3, 1827	3	206
Daniel, Jr., m. Lucretia **SHERMAN**, b. of [New London], Jan. 8, 1849, by Rev. M. P. Alderman	4	144
David, Jr., b. Apr. 9, 1787; m. Elisabeth **BOLLES**, Dec. 29, 1812	3	206
David, Jr., d. Oct. 6, 1826, at Norfolk	3	206
David Franklin, s. [David, Jr. & Elisabeth], b. Nov. 19, 1824	3	206
Delia W., of New London, m. Lieut. Edward **WHITE**, of U. S. Army, Apr. 18, 1832, by Rev. B. Judd	4	48
Eliza Ann, of New London, m. Matthias **CORWIN**, of New York, June 3, 1832, by Rev. Alpheus Hayden	4	47
Eliza Ann Stark, d. [David, Jr. & Elisabeth], b. Nov. 22, 1814	3	206
Elisabeth, d. [Pygan & Anne], b. Dec. 21, 1752	3	74
Elisabeth, d. Pygan & Anne, m. Thomas **POOL**, s. John & Sarah, of Rariton, N.J., Oct. 19, 1775	3	74
Frances Culver, d. [David, Jr. & Elisabeth], b. Sept. 10, 1819	3	206
Frances H., m. Nathaniel **CHAPMAN**, Feb. 22, 1818, by Rev. Abel McEwen	3	238
James, m. Eliza **MOXLEY**, Nov. 11, 1847, by Rev. M. P. Alderman	4	135
John, m. Sarah **GREEN**, June 15, 1716	1	49
John Latham, s. [David, Jr. & Elisabeth], b. May 10, 1822	3	206
Leander, s. [David, Jr. & Elisabeth], b. Sept. 1, 1816	3	206
Lydia, d. Eliphalet & Lydia, b. Feb. [ ], 1720/21	1	57
Lydia, d. Eliphalet & Lydia, d. July 17, 1721	1	58
Lydia, d. [Pygan & Anne], b. July 5, [1751]; d. Sept. 11, 1751	3	74
Lydia, d. [Pygan & Anne], b. Dec. 21, 1752	3	74

	Vol.	Page
ADAMS (cont.)		
Lydia, m. Robert **HALLAM**, Sept. 17, 1779	3	59
Mary, d. Eliphalet & Lydia, b. Mar. 15, 1713/4	1	43
Mary, m. Jonathan **GARDINER**, Nov. 13, 1733	2	31
Mary Harper, of [New London], m. James P.		
KIRKWOOD, of Edinburgh Scotland, Nov. 9,		
1835, by Rev. Abel McEwen	4	63
Patrick, m. Martha **McBURNAY**, b. of New London,		
Oct. 11, 1849, by Rev. Jared R. Avery	4	147
Pygan, s. Eliphalet & Lydia, b. Mar. 27, 1712	1	43
Pygan, s. Eliphalet & Lydia, b. Mar. 27, 1712	3	74
Pygan, m. Anne **RICHARDS**, June 7, 1744	3	74
Samuel, s. Eliphalet & Lydia, b. Aug. 11, 1717	1	49
Samuel, s. Eliphalet & Lydia, b. Aug. 11, 1717; d.		
Jan. 21, 1718/19	1	57
Thomas, s. [Pygan & Anne], b. Jan. 15, 1761	3	74
William, s. Eliphalet & Lydiah, b. Oct. 7, 1710	1	43
William, s. Eliphalet & Lydia, b. Oct. 7, 1710; d.		
Aug. 30, 1798	3	74
William, s. [Pygan & Anne], b. Nov. 20, 1745; d.		
Apr. 2, 1777, in West Indies	3	74
ADGATE, Ruth, m. [Jam]es **HAUGHTON**, June 6, 1782	3	2
AGENS, John, m. Margaret **PAYNE**, b. of New London,		
Mar. 4, 1832, by Rev. Abel McEwen	4	45
ALBERTSON, James Monroe, s. [William], b. July 4,		
1831	3	269
Louisa Ellen, d. [William], b. Mar. 22, 1829	3	269
Louisa Ellen, m. Simeon Spencer **BASSETT**, of		
Washington City, July 23, 1850, by Rev. James		
W. Dennis	4	155
ALDEN, Abigail, d. Prince & Mary, b. Aug. 11, 1753	2	21
Andrew Stanford, s. Prince & Mary, b. May 5, 1766	2	21
Lydia, d. Prince & Mary, b. Oct. 31, 1758	2	21
Mary, d. Prince & Mary, b. Dec. 1, 1747	2	21
Mason Fitch, s. Prince & Mary, b. Oct. 25, 1750	2	21
Prince, s. Prince & Mary, b. Mar. 14, 1762	2	21
Sarah, d. Prince & Mary, b. Feb. 6, 1756	2	21
ALDERSTIEN, Herman, m. Martha **CHAPMAN**, June		
13, 1847, by Rev. Thomas J. Greenwood	4	132
ALLEN, ALLIN, [see also **ALLYN**], Abigail, m.		
Christopher **STUBBENS**, s. Daniel [&		
Bethiah], Dec. 22, 1720	2	102
Abigail, of New London, m. Daniel **RUDD**, of		
Norwich, Dec. 7, 1780, by David Jewit[t]	3	151
Amelia, d. [Thomas, Jr. & Amelia], b. July 10, 1795,		
on Fisher's Island	3	76
Anna, b. Aug. 25, 1754; m. Jonathan **BISHOP**, Dec.		
21, 1775	3	122
Betty, d. Jason, Jr. & Lydia, b. Oct. 23, 1768	3	49

Vol. Page

ALLEN, ALLIN (cont.)

Clarrissa S., of N. Kingston, R.I., m. William H.
AUSTIN, of Newport, R.I., May 2, 1848, by
Rev. Nicholas T. Allen ... 4 ... 138

Cynthia, see under Synthia

Elizabeth, d. [Thomas, Jr. & Amelia], b. Nov. 23,
1779 ... 3 ... 76

Ellen, of [New London], m. William **WEEVER***, of
Buffalo, N.Y., Sept. 13, 1847, by Rev. Robert
A. Hallam *(Perhaps **MINER**) ... 4 ... 135

Fanny Taber, d. [Thomas, Jr. & Amelia], b. Mar. 21,
1787 ... 3 ... 76

Frances E., of N[ew] London, m. Albigence W,
TUCKER, of Walworth, N.Y., May 9, 1832,
by Rev. B. Judd ... 4 ... 49

Frances Elizabeth, d. [Lewis & Mary D.], b. Jan. 21,
1811, at Fisher's Island ... 3 ... 252

Frances T., m. Jesse D. **SMITH**, July 26, 1815 ... 3 ... 252

Frederick Lee, s, [Lewis & Mary D.], b. May 30,
1820 ... 3 ... 252

George, s. Jason, Jr. & Lydia, b. June 8, 1771 ... 3 ... 49

George, s. [Thomas, Jr. & Amelia], b. Sept. 23, 1793,
on Fisher's Island ... 3 ... 76

Hannah, d. Samuel, late of West Town, decd., m.
James **COMSTOCK**, of New London, s.
Daniel, Mar. 23, 1737/8 ... 2 ... 44

Harriet, m. Ansel D. **CADY**, b. of [New London],
Dec. 21, 1841, by Rev. Robert A. Hallam ... 4 ... 98

Harriet Amelia, d. [Lewis & Mary D.], b. Sept. 25,
1813, at Groton ... 3 ... 252

Henry Nelson, s. [Thomas, Jr. & Amelia], b. May 27,
1799, on Fisher's Island ... 3 ... 76

Hester, m. Samuel **FOX**, Aug.9, 1715 ... 1 ... 44

Jane C., of [New London], m. Worthington B.
BUTTON, of Boston, Mass., May 8, 1847, by
Rev. Robert A. Hallam ... 4 ... 140

Jason, Jr., s. Jason, m. Lydia **ALLEN**, d. John, all of
New London, Apr. 21, 1763 ... 3 ... 49

John, of New London, s. Samuel, m. Caron **FOX**, d.
Samuel, of New London, Feb. 24, 1742/3 ... 2 ... 79

John, s, [Thomas, Jr. & Amelia], b. May 18, 1797, on
Fisher's Island ... 3 ... 76

John H., of New Bedford, Mass., m. Harriet **WEBB**,
d. Daniel, Feb. 11, 1838, by Rev. Daniel Webb ... 4 ... 75

Lewis, s. [Thomas, Jr. & Amelia], b. May 2, 1783 ... 3 ... 76

Lewis, m. Mary D. **SMITH**, Sept. 18, 1805, at
Groton ... 3 ... 252

Lewis D., s. [Lewis & Mary D.], b. Aug. 10, 1806, at
Groton ... 3 ... 252

Lewis D., of Buffalo, N.Y., m. Lucretia **ISHAM**, of
New London, July 25, 1837, by Rev. Robert A.
Hallam ... 4 ... 72

	Vol.	Page
ALLEN, ALLIN (cont.)		
Lydia, d. Gideon, of Killingworth, m. Eben[eze]r		
HARRIS, s. Sam[ue]ll, of New London, decd.		
Mar. 25, 1729	2	58
Lydia, d. John & Caron, b. June 20, 1744	2	79
Lydia, d. John, m. Jason **ALLEN**, Jr., all of New		
London, Apr. 21, 1763	3	49
Lyman, of Springfield, Mass., m. Emma **TURNER**,		
of New London, June 5, 1825, by Rev. Abel		
McEwen	4	23
Mary, d. Jason, Jr., & Lydia, b. Apr. 22, 1764	3	49
Mary S., d. [Lewis & Mary D.], b. July 7, 1808, at		
Fisher's Island	3	252
Mary S., d. Lewis, m. Enoch V. **STODDARD**, May		
9, 1832	3	181
Mary S., m. Enoch V. **STODDARD**, b. of New		
London, May 9, 1832, by Rev. B. Judd	4	49
Nancy, m. John G. **SWEET**, b. of Groton, Apr. 18,		
1823, by Rev. Abel McEwen	4	13
Nathaniel, s. [Thomas, Jr. & Amelia], b. June 23,		
1791	3	76
Samuel, s. Jason, Jr. & Lydia, b. June 17, 1766	3	49
Samuel Taber, s. [Thomas, Jr. & Amelia], b. Oct. 11,		
1789	3	76
Sarah, d. Rob[er]t, m. George **GEARES**, Feb. 17,		
[1658]	1	3
Sarah A., m. Enoch V. **STODDARD**, b. of New		
London, Jan. 15, 1849, by Rev. Robert A.		
Hallam	4	144
Sarah Ann, d. [Lewis & Mary D.], b. May 4, 1817, at		
Groton	3	252
Synthia, m. Archabold **ROBERTSON**, s. Patrick &		
Elisabeth, Feb. 23, 1775	3	72
Thomas, Jr., m. Amelia **TABER**, Apr. 23, 1778	3	76
Thomas, s. [Thomas, Jr. & Amelia], b. June 18, 1781	3	76
Thomas G., of Nashville, Tenn., m. Adelaide		
BICKNELL, of [New London], Dec. 1, 1833,		
by Daniel Wildman	4	52
William, s. [Thomas, Jr. & Amelia], b. Mar. 13, 1785	3	76
ALLENDER, Henry, s. [John & Elizabeth], b. Feb. 25,		
1835	3	290
James, s. [John & Elizabeth], b. May 30, 1844	3	290
John, s. [John & Elizabeth], b. Oct. 11, 1840	3	290
John, m. Elizabeth **JAMES**, [ ], at Arston		
Church, Birmingham, Warwickshire, England	3	290
Thomas, s. [John & Elizabeth], b. Nov. 10, 1836	3	290
William, [s. John & Elizabeth], b. Apr. 8, 1839	3	290
ALLY, Samuel, m. Arletta **PAGE**, May 8, 1836, by		
Daniel Huntington	4	97
ALLYN, [see also **ALLEN**], Ann L., m. Thomas W.		
WILLIAMS, b. of New London, July 14, 1831,		
by Rev. Abel McEwen	4	43

	Vol.	Page

ALLYN (cont.)

Betsey, d. [Pardon, a negro, & Betsey], b. Apr. 23, 1810 — 3 — 240

Charlotte H., of Groton, m. James **CHAPMAN**, Jr., of [New London], Feb. 15, 1852, by Rev. Jabez S. Swan — 4 — 172

Elizabeth, d. John & Elizabeth, b. Dec. 24, [1669] — 1 — 6

Fanny, m. Jason **ROGERS**, May 29, 1783 — 3 — 130

Hanson, s. [Pardon, a negro, & Betsey], b. Mar. 23, 1808 — 3 — 240

John, s. Robert, m. Elizabeth, d. John **GADGER**, of Norwich, Dec. 24, [1668] — 1 — 6

Mary, d. Robert, m. Thomas **PARKER**, s. Thomas, Jan. 4, [1672] — 1 — 8

Pardon, a negro, m. Betsey **FOG**, June 23, 1803 — 3 — 240

Rebecca, of New London, m. Lucius C. **FOOT[E]**, of Nunda, N.Y., Oct. 12, 1824, by Rev. Abel McEwen — 4 — 20

Robert, s. John & Elizabeth, b "about the middle of Sept.", [1671] — 1 — 8

ALMY, W[illia]m E., m. Ann B. **FRINK**, b. of [New London], July 11, 1844, by Rev. Abel McEwen — 4 — 115

William T., of Norwich, m. Sarah W. **TIBBITTS**, of [New London], Oct. 13, 1851, by Rev. Abel McEwen — 4 — 165

AMES, [see also **EAMES**], Elisabeth, m. Cruttenden **WARD**, June 25, 1780 — 3 — 125

Enoch D., m. Abby S. **HOLT**, b. of New London, Feb. 5, 1832, by Rev. B. Judd — 4 — 48

Henry O., of New Orleans, m. Caroline L. **HEMPSTE[A]D**, of New London, Oct. 3, 1837, by Rev. Abel McEwen — 4 — 74

John, of New London, m. Eliza **BEEBE**, of New London, Aug 12, 1827, by James Rogers, J.P. — 4 — 31

Joseph S., m Eliza Ann **COMSTOCK**, b. of New London, Mar 6, 1831, by Rev. Daniel Wildman — 4 — 41

Leona, m. Thomas **STERRY**, b. of New London, June 24, 1849, by Rev. Jabez S. Swan — 4 — 146

Nancy M., m. John O. **WHEELER**, b. of [New London], Sept. 9, 1844, by Rev. Abel McEwen — 4 — 113

Sally, m. Samuel **PLUMBE**, Aug. 27, 1785 — 3 — 23

Samuel, m. Lydia **LESTER**, b. of New London, Sept. 4, 1831, by Rev. Daniel Wildman — 4 — 43

AMY, Celia, d. [Jack & Seela], b. Sept. 5, 1804 (Negroes) — 3 — 47

Jack, a negro, m. Seela **SHAW**, Feb. 22, 1800 — 3 — 47

John, s. [Jack & Seela], b. Aug. 11, 1802 (Negroes) — 3 — 47

ANDERSON, Alexander B., m. Mary H. **PERKINS**, d. Ebenezer, Feb. 21, 1805, by Rev. Charles Seabuary — 3 — 199

Alice, d. Sonne & Susan[n]ah, b. Mar. 1, 1772, (Black persons) — 3 — 56

Benjamin, s. [Scipio & Genny], b. Jan. 1, 1804 — 3 — 104

	Vol.	Page
ANDERSON (cont.)		
Celinda D., d. [William & Celinda Dunham], b. Sept. 26, 1846	3	282
Daniel, s. Sonne & Susan[n]ah, black persons, b. Feb. 2, 1765	3	56
Ebenezer Perkins, s. [Alexander B. & Mary H.], b. June 23, 1807	3	199
Eliza, m. Jacob **FREEMAN**, Oct. 13, 1833, by Rev. I. W. Hallam	4	52
Maria Perkins, d. [Alexander B. & Mary H.], b. Dec. 6, 1805	3	199
Mary, d. [Scipio & Genny], b. Dec. 28, 1807	3	104
Mary, of New London, m. Uriah W. **PELHAM**, of Norwich, Oct. 24, 1844, by Rev. S. Benton	4	114
Mary Harris, d. [William & Celinda Dunham], b. Mar. 20, 1837	3	282
Rebecca, d. Sonne & Susan[n]ah, b. May 24, 1769 (Black persons)	3	56
Robert, m. Rebecca **KELLY**, b. of [New London], May 4, 1843, by Rev. Robert A. Hallam	4	117
Rosannah, m. Samson **CATO**, Feb. 20, 1782	3	65
Sarah Jane, d. [William & Celinda Dunham], b. Apr. 23, 1835	3	282
Scipio, servant of Guy **RICHARDS**, m. June, Mar. 21, 1779	3	104
Scipio, m. Genny **SMITH**, Jan. 1, 1803	3	104
Sonne, m. Susan[n]ah **FREEMAN**, Mar. 13, 1775* (Black persons) *Corrected to Nov. 1, 1763	3	56
Sonne, s. Sonne & Susan[n]ah, b. Dec. 8, 1767 (Black persons)	3	56
Sophronia, d. [Alexander B. & Mary H.], b. Nov. 29, 1809	3	199
William, s. [Scipio & Genny], b. Apr. 8, 1805	3	104
William, m. Celinda Dunham **HARRIS**, May 21, 1834	3	282
William Harris, s. [William & Celinda Dunham], b. Oct. 20, 1839	3	282
ANDRES, Hannah, m. Robert **GANTER**, Sept. 8, 1719	1	57
ANDREWS, John, of [New London], m. Hannah **PHILIPS**, of Plainfield, July 12, 1847, by Rev. M. P. Alderman	4	133
Lavina, of [New London], m. William **CARTER**, of Charlestown, Mass., Aug. 11, 1847, by Rev. Abel McEwen	4	133
Warren, m. Emeline **MERRITT**, b. of New London, Apr. 16, 1833, by Chester Tilden	4	50
ANGELL, Almira Powers, d. [Nathan S. & Sophia H.], b. June 3, 1815	3	247
Almy, d. William & Almy, b. Oct. 24, 1739	2	98
Amy, w. W[illia]m, d. Aug. 7, 1750, ae 39 y.	2	98
Ann Elizabeth, d. [Nathan S. & Sophia H.], b. May 8, 1816	3	247

	Vol.	Page
ANGELL (cont.)		
Anne, d. [James & Hannah], b. July 12, 1776	3	2
Christopher, s. [James & Hannah], b. July 24, 1783	3	2
Elisabeth, d. [James & Hannah], b. May 13, 1772; d. May 26, 1772	3	2
Elisabeth, d. [James & Hannah], b. June 22, 1773; d. Apr. 30, 1775	3	2
George Washington, s. [Nathan S. & Sophia H.], b. Sept. 17, 1818	3	247
Hannah, d. [James & Hannah], b. July 31, 1778	3	2
James, s. William & Almy, b. June 12, 1736	2	98
James, father of William, d. July 29, 1742	2	98
James, s. William, of New London, m. Anna **JENKINS**, d. John, late of Warwick, R.I., Feb. 23, (21?), 1760. by Rev. Joshua Morse	3	12
James, m. Hannah **SAGE**, Nov. 11, 1771	3	2
James, s. [James & Hannah], b. May 9, 1781	3	2
Jemima, d. William & Amy, b. May 21, 1733	2	97
Mary, d. William & Almy, b. Oct. 7, 1744	2	98
Mary, mother of William, d. July 6, 1749, ae 69 y.	2	98
Nathan S., m. Sophia H. **POWERS**, July 8, 1811, at New Haven	3	247
Nathan Sage, s. [James & Hannah], b. Nov. 8, 1792	3	2
Sylvanus Pinckham, s. [James & Hannah], b. Jan. 15, 1788	3	2
Thomas, d. William & Almy, b. Nov. 5, 1747	2	98
William, s. James, of Warwick, m. Amy **HARDING**, d. of Stephen, of Warwick, Aug. 31, 1732	2	97
William, s. William & Almy, b. May 27, 1742	2	98
ANNABAL, ANNABLE, Ann, twin with William W., [d. Joseph & Ann], b. Feb. 8, 1802	3	142
Asenath, d. John, of Millington, m. William **WOODWORTH**, Oct. 3, 1802	3	43
James, s. [Joseph & Ann], b. Mar. 6, 1808	3	142
John, s. [Joseph & Ann], b. July 14, 1805	3	142
Joseph, s. [Joseph & Ann], b. Sept.* 26, 1797 *(First written "October")	3	142
Levi C., s. [Joseph & Ann], b. Feb. 3, 1800	3	142
William W., twin with Ann, [s. Joseph & Ann], b. Feb. 8, 1802	3	142
ANNOLA, Charles, m. Lucretia Ann **FORD**, b. of [New London], Nov. 12, 1837, by Rev. Abel McEwen	4	74
ANTHONY, Ellen, m. Edward **JORDON**, b. of [New London], Aug. 20, 1851, by Rev. Samuel Fox	4	164
Nicholas, m. Lydia Ann **SPENCER**, June 30, 1830, by Rev. B. Judd	4	41
ANTONIA, Francis, m. Lucinda **GARDINER**, b. of New London, Mar. 13, 1832, by Rev. Abel McEwen	4	45
ANTONY, ANTONE, Filema, m. James **MITCHEL**, (negroes), Aug. 1, 1808	3	14

	Vol.	Page
ANTONY, ANTONE (cont.)		
George, of Cape de Verds, m. Clara **MORTON**, of		
Schenectady, N.Y., May 18, 1847, by Rev.		
Jabez S. Swan	4	131
ANSART, Charles Burroughs, s. [Felix & Mary Elizabeth		
Shannon], b. Feb. 5, 1839	3	164
Felix, m. Mary Elizabeth Shannon **PRESCOTT**, Jan.		
13, 1834, in Portsmouth, N.H.	3	164
Felix, s. [Felix & Mary Elizabeth Shannon], b. Jan.		
28, 1837	3	164
Lewis Henry, s. [Felix & Mary Elizabeth Shannon],		
b. Aug. 21, 1842	3	164
Mary Elizabeth, d. [Felix & Mary Elizabeth		
Shannon], b. Apr. 9, 1835, at Fort Constitution,		
N.H.	3	164
APHIN*, Junies, m. Nancy **HALLADAY**, b. of [New		
London], May 13, 1850, by Aaron E. Stone,		
J.P. *(Perhaps "**UPHIN**")	4	153
APPLETON, Ann, d. Joshua & Jane, b. July 29, 1721	2	2
Benj[ami]n, s. Joshua & Jane, b. July 18, 1723	2	2
Daniel, s. Joshua & Jane, b. Mar. 10, 1731/1	2	2
Elizabeth, d. Joshua & Jane, b. Sept. 8, 1729	2	2
Jane, d. Joshua & Jane, b. Sept. 15, 1719	2	2
Jane, d. Joshua, of New London, m. Daniel		
WHITTEMORE, s. Daniel, of Boston, Nov. 5,		
1738	2	56
Joshua, m. Elizabeth **HUBBEL[L]**, Nov. 5, 1713	1	41
Joshua, m. Jane **SHAPLEY**, Feb. 5, 1716	1	50
Mary, d. Joshua & Jane, b. Dec. 23, 1717	1	50
William, s. Joshua & Jane, b. May 5, 1726	2	2
ARMSTRONG, Mary, of Norwich, m. Charles		
WOODWORTH, of Montville, Feb. 7, 1848,		
by Rev. Jabez S. Swan	4	137
Mary, m. Patrick **BRENNAN**, b. of New London,		
Jan. 7, 1849, by Rev. Robert A. Hallam	4	144
ARNOLD, Albert, m. Charlotte **CHAPMAN**, b. of N[ew]		
London, Dec. 24, 1833, by Rev. D. Wildman	4	54
Chauncey, m. Sally **OWEN**, d. John, Sept. 24, 1803	3	218
Chauncey, s. [Chauncey & Sally], b. Oct. 31, 1808	3	218
Edmon, s. [Chauncey & Sally], b. Oct. 30, 1806	3	218
Edmund O., m. Harriet **BROWN**, b. of New London,		
Jan. 2, 1831, by Rev. Abel McEwen	4	40
Fanny D., m. Henry **SMITH**, b. of New London,		
Dec. 16, 1825, by Rev. Abel McEwen	4	25
Fanny L., m. Henry **SMITH**, Dec. 16, 1825	3	267
John, late of Boston, m. Mercy **FOSDICK**, wid.,		
Dec. 6, 1703	1	29
John, d. Aug. 26, 1725	2	1
Lucretia, d. John & Mercy, b. Aug. 26, 1706	1	31
Mercy, d. Nov. 28, 1725	2	1
Ruhamah, d. John & Mercy, b. Sept. 7, 1704	1	30
Sally, d. [Chauncey & Sally], b. Feb. 18, 1805	3	218

	Vol.	Page
ARNOLD (cont.)		
We[a]lthy, d. Capt. John, m. Ezra **CHAPPELL**,		
Sept. 10, 1804	3	200
ARTHUR, ARTHER, Abby Jane, m. Charles S.		
MILLER, of [New London], Mar. 3, 1845, by		
Rev. S. Benton	4	117
Lucy A., of New London, m. Isaac C. **BRAGAW**,		
May 7, 1845, by Rev. S. Benton	4	119
Prudence, m. George **HARRISON**, b. of New		
London, June 12, 1837, by Daniel Huntington	4	70
ASH, Benjamin F., m. Lucretia A. **COMSTOCK**, Oct. 31,		
1832, by James Porter	4	48
Horace T., of Springfield, Ill., m. Martha P.		
MUSSEY, d. Thomas, of [New London], Sept.		
4, 1850, by Rev. T. Edwards	4	155
ASHBY, Lydia, m. George B. **CONGDON**, Oct. 7, 1827	3	269
ASHCRAFT, Charlotte, d. [William & Sarah], b. Sept. 24,		
1794	3	99
Fanny, d. [William & Sarah], b. Apr. 25, 1793	3	99
Fanny, of New London, m. William **HENDERICK**,		
of New York, Apr. 27, 1823, by Thomas W.		
Tucker, Elder	4	13
John, s. [William & Sarah], b. Jan. 16, 1787	3	99
Mary, d. [William & Sarah], b. Nov. 1, 1784	3	99
Peter, s. [William & Sarah], b. Aug. 5, 1788	3	99
Stephen, s. [William & Sarah], b. Dec. 24, 1790	3	99
William, m. Sarah **STRICKLING**, d. Peter, Feb. 12,		
1784	3	99
ATWELL, Benjamin, s. Richard & Elizabeth, b. July 25,		
1705; d. May 3, 1708	1	31
Benjamin, s. Benjamin & Mary, b. July 24, 1707	1	37
Benjamin, s. Richard & Joannah, b. Oct. 18, 1719	2	1
Caroline, of Lyme, m. Nelson **HUNTLEY**, of		
Colchester, Apr. 17, 1827, by Rev. Abel		
McEwen	4	29
Elizabeth, d. Richard & Elizabeth, b. Mar. 25, 1708	1	35
Elizabeth, d. Thomas & Mary, b. Mar. 25, 1708	1	41
Joannah, d. Richard & Joannah, b. Aug. 10, 1716	2	1
Joannah, m. Culbert **BLYTH**, Aug. 24, 1733	2	4
John, s. Benjamin & Mary, b. May 19, [1675]	1	10
John, s. Richard & Joannah, b. Jan. 19, 1718	2	1
Joseph, s. Benjamin & Mary, b. Mar. 10, [1677]	1	12
Joseph, s. Benjamin & Mary, b. June 26, 1710	1	37
Mary, d. Benjamin & Mary, b. Oct. 19, [1672]	1	8
Mary, d. Benjamin & Mary, b. Oct. 11, 1703	1	37
Mary, d. Thomas & Mary, b. Jan. 8, 1705	1	41
Patience, d. Richard & Joannah, b. Apr. 26, 1721	2	1
Richard, s. Benjamin & Mary, b. Mar. 1, [1679]	1	14
Richard, m. Elizabeth **BAKER**, Mar. 11, 1703	1	29
Richard, s. Richard & Elizabeth, b. Oct. 19, 1709.		
Entered at his mother's request Mar. 28, 1728	2	1
Richard, d. Oct. 15, 1727	2	2

10 BARBOUR COLLECTION

	Vol.	Page
ATWELL (cont.)		
Samuell, s. Benjamin & Mary, b. Apr. 23, [1682]	1	16
Sam[ue]ll, s. Richard & Joannah, b. July 8, 1723; d. May 13, 1725	2	2
Samuel H., m. Harriet **CHURCH**, b. of Montville, Sept. 25, 1844, by Rev. Abel McEwen	4	114
Thomas, s. Benjamin & Mary, b. Aug. 10, [1670]	1	7
Thomas, m. Sarah **LEWIS**, July 24, 1704	1	30
Thomas, m. Anne **MORGAN**, Sept. 7, 1714	1	42
Thomas, s. Thomas & Sarah, b. June 21, 1731	2	2
William, s. Benjamin & Mary, b. Apr. 17, 1674	1	10
AUGUSTUS, Peter, m. Ann **BRAMBLE**, b. of New London, Apr. 14, 1831, by Rev. Abel McEwen	4	41
AUSTIN, Edmond, m. Mary Elizabeth **LEWIS**, b. of [New London], Sept. 17, 1838, by Rev. C. C. Williams	4	79
Elias, m. Jane **STEPHENS**, b. of [New London], Dec. 1, 1834, by Rev. Ebenezer Blake	4	59
Harry, of New York, m. Mary **SALTONSTALL**, of New London, Oct. 10, 1838, by Rev. Robert Hallam	4	80
Mary, m. Comstock **BROWN**, Apr. 4, 1771	3	69
Mercy Ann Beebe, m. Henry **HUGHES**, Dec. 2, 1832, by Rev. Francis Darrow	4	49
Rebecca, m. Charles **DANIELS**, b. of Waterford, Mar. 20, 1836, by Rev. Squire B. Hascall	4	84
William H., of Newport, R.I., m. Clarrissa S. **ALLEN**, of N. Kingston, R.I., May 2, 1848, by Rev. Nicholas T. Allen	4	138
AVERY, Aaron, s. [Amos & Prudence], b. Sept. 27, 1771	3	46
Abell, s. Abner & Amy, b. May 29, 1745	3	3
Abigail, d. Jno. & Abigail, b. Jan. 15, [1676]	1	11
Abigail, d. John & Abigail, d. July 18, [1677]	1	12
Abigail, d. John & Abigail, b. Jan. 18, [1679]	1	14
Abner, m. Amy **FOX**, b. of New London, May 22, 1740	3	3
Abraham, m. Jane **HILL**, Mar. 14, 1727	2	1
Abraham, s. Abraham & Jane, b. July 18, 1744	2	2
Amos, s. Abner & Amy, b. Mar. 10, 1758	3	3
Amy, d. Abner & Amy, b. July 25, 1747	3	3
Ann, m. Samuel **GRIFFING**, Nov. 16, 1727	2	30
Anna Maria, d. [Thomas L. & Lucretia], b. Nov. 3, 1820	3	276
Anne, d. Thomas & Anne, b. Nov. 12, 1707	1	33
Anne, wid., m. Jonathan **ROFFE**, Nov. 21, 1712	1	44
Betsey, of Groton, d. Jasper, m. John **BOLLES**, s. Samuel, Apr. 1, 1792	3	153
Cavon*, d. Abner & Amy, b. July 3, 1743 *(Perhaps Caron)	3	3
Christopher, d. very near the death of the mother	1	67
Christopher, s. James & Joan, b. Apr. 30, [1661]	1	3
Christopher, s. James & Deborah, b. Jan. 23, [1679]	1	14

	Vol.	Page
AVERY (cont.)		
Christopher, s. James & Deborah, b. Jan. 23, 1679	1	68
Deborah, d. James & Debora[h], b. Aug. 10, [1671]	1	7
Ebenezer, s. James & Debora[h], b. May 1, [1678]	1	12
Edward, s. James & Debora[h], b. Mar. 20 [1675]	1	10
Edward, s. [Joshua & Hannah], b. Dec. 10, 1806	3	216
Egbert H., of Groton, m. Sarah **COGSHALL**, of [New London], Nov. 9, 1840, by Rev. Abel McEwen	4	92
Elihu, s. Abner & Amy, b. Mar. 25, 1748	3	3
Elijah, s. [Amos & Prudence], b. Sept. 21, 1783	3	46
Elizabeth, d. Capt. Elijah, of Groton, b. Dec. 1, 1771; m. William **ELDREDGE**, [s. Charles of Groton], Sept. 14, 1794	3	197
Eunice Williams, d. [Amos & Prudence}, b. June 20, 1774	3	46
George, s. [George Dolbeare & Mary], b. Jan. 23, 1791	3	116
George Dolbeare, s. William & Mary, of Groton, m. Mary **CHAMPLIN**, wid. of Capt. Lodowick Champlin, & dau. of Guy & Elizabeth **RICHARDS**, Apr. 1, 1790	3	116
Gilbert, m. Lucy **OLCOTT**, July 21, 1799	3	137
Gurdon, of Waterford, m. Maria **GARDNER**, of New London, Apr. 14, 1822, by Elias Sharp, Elder	4	3
Hannah, d. James & Joan, b. Oct. 11, 1644. (Not born in New London)	1	1
Han[n]ah, d. James & Deborah, b. Mar. 24, 1685	1	17
Hannah, d. Abraham & Jane, b. Oct. 31, 1732	2	2
Hannah, d. William, of Groton, m. Benjamin **BUTLER**, Dec. 11, 1791	3	178
Henry Thomas, s. [Thomas L. & Lucretia], b. June 8, 1827	3	276
Isaac A., of Groton, m. Emeline **MINER**, of [New London], Dec. 1, 1830, by Rev. Leonard B. Griffing	4	40
James, s. James & Joan, b. Dec. 15, 1646	1	1
James, Jr., s. James, Sr., m. Deborah, d. Edward **STALLION**, Feb. 20, [1669]	1	6
James, s. James & Debora[h], b. Apr. 20, [1673]	1	9
James, s. [Joshua & Hannah], b. Mar. 5, 1804	3	216
Jane, d. Abraham & Jane, b. Dec. 3, 1727	2	1
Jane, w. Abraham, d. July 26, 1744	2	2
Jefferson, of New London, m. Esther **HOLT**, Oct. 27, 1844, by Rev. G. Thompson	4	115
John, s. James & Joan, b. Feb. 10, [1653]	1	2
John, s. Capt. James, m. Abigail, d. Samuel **CHEESEBOROUGH**, Nov. 29, [1675]	1	10
John Coit, s. [Thomas L. & Lucretia], b. Oct. 3, 1822	3	276
Jonathan, s. James & Joan, b. Jan. 5, [1658]	1	3

	Vol.	Page
AVERY (cont.)		
Jonathan, s. Capt. James, d. "in ye month of August",		
[1681]	1	15
Jonathan, s. James, d. Aug. [ ], 1681	1	67
Jonathan, s. James & Deborah, b. 8ber. [ ], 1681	1	68
Johnathan, s. James & Debora[h], b. Nov. 1, [1681]	1	15
Jonathan, s. Abraham & Jane, b. June 22, 1737	2	2
Jonathan, s. Abner & Amy, b. Sept. 10, 1755	3	3
Joseph Manwaring, s. [Thomas L. & Lucretia], b.		
Nov. 3, 1828	3	276
Joshua, m. Hannah **AVERY**, d. Thomas, Apr. 1,		
1798	3	216
Katharine, of Groton, d. of Ebenezer, of Groton, m.		
Daniel **DENISON**, of New London, s. Daniel,		
late of New London, decd. July 1, 1756, in		
Groton, by Rev. Daniel Kirtland	2	121
Lavina, of New London, m. Sandford **MORGAN**, of		
Groton, Oct. 2, 1821, by Abel McEwen	4	6
Lavinea, d. [Joshua & Hannah], b. Dec. 18, 1801	3	216
Lucretia, d. [Thomas L. & Lucretia], b. July 15, 1825	3	276
Lucretia, w. Thomas L., d. Oct. 25, 1833	3	276
Lucy, of Groton, d. Eben[eze]r, of Groton, m. George		
COLFAX, of New London, s. John, Apr. 13,		
1749, old style	3	21
Margaret, d. James & Deborah, b. Feb. 7, [1674]	1	9
Margarett, d. Abner & Amy, b. Dec. 15, 1750	3	3
Mary, d. James & Joan, b. Feb. 19, 1648	1	1
Mary, d. Abraham & Jane, b. Sept. 15, 1729; d. Oct.		
3, [1729]	2	1
Mary, wid. of Ichabod Avery, of Groton, & dau. of		
James **FORSYTH**, of Groton, m. John		
BISHOP, Jr., s. John, of New London, June 16,		
1751	2	91
Mary, m. Simeon **SMITH**, Sept. 11, 1792	3	151
Mary Holt, d. [Thomas L. & Lucretia], b. Dec. 11,		
1830	3	276
Mercy, d. James & Deborah, b. Feb. 4, [1683]	1	17
Nathan, s. Abraham & Jane, b. May 8, 1741	2	2
Orlando, s. [Joshua & Hannah], b. Jan. 1, 1799	3	216
Prudence, d. [Amos & Prudence], b. Sept. 18, 1777	3	46
Rebecca, d. Capt. James, of New London, m.		
William **POTTS**, of Newcastle, Old England,		
Aug. 5, [1678]	1	13
Rebecca, d. James & Joan, b. Oct. 6, [1756]*		
*([1656] written in pencil)	1	2
Rebeckah, d. Elisha, of Stonington, m. Samuel		
DOUGLASS, Feb. 26, 1781	3	185
Robert Austin, Deac., of Groton, m. Lucina		
TOPLIFF, of Willington, Ct., Jan. 7, 1846, by		
Rev. L. Geo[rge] Leonard	4	124

	Vol.	Page
AVERY (cont.)		
Russel H., of Norwich, m. Elizabeth **MINER**, of New London, Aug. 31, 1825, by Christopher Griffing, J.P.	4	31
Ruth, d. Abraham & Jane, b. July 1, 1735	2	2
Samuel, s. James & Joan, b. Aug. 14, [1664]	1	2
Samuel, s. Thomas & Hannah, b. Nov. 15, [1680]	1	14
Samuel, s. Thomas & Hannah, b. Nov. 15, 1680	1	67
Samuel, of Saybrook, m. Elizabeth **RANSFORD**, d. Jonathan, decd., sometime of Boston, June 23, 1702	1	27
Samuel, s. Abner & Amy, b. Sept. 11, 1753	3	3
Sarah, d. James & Deborah, b. May 10, 1688	1	18
Thomas, s. James & Joan, b. May 6, 1651	1	1
Thomas, s. Capt. James, m. Hanna[h], d. Thomas **MINER**, of Stonington, Oct. 22, [1677]	1	12
Thomas, s. Thomas & Hanna[h], b. Apr. 20, [1679]	1	13
Thomas, m. Hannah **BUCKLEY**, b. of New London, Mar. 13, [1693], in Wethersfield, by John Chester, J.P.	1	21
Thomas, m. Ann **SHAPLEY**, July 12, 1704	1	30
Thomas, s. Thomas & Ann, b. Mar. 31, 1705	1	30
Thomas, s. Abraham & Jane, b. Oct. 16, 1730	2	1
Thomas J., m. Sarah R. **SMITH**, June 1, 1836, by Rev. Francis Darrow	4	84
Thomas L., m. Lucretia **MANWARING**, Jan. 31, 1819	3	276
Thomas L., m. Maria **MANWARING**, Nov. 27, 1834	3	276
William, s. Abraham & Jane, b. Mar. 7, 1738/9	2	2
William, s. [George Dolbeare & Mary], b. Nov. 29, 1793; d. Mar. 30, 1794	3	116
William, s. [George Dolbeare & Mary], b. Jan. 24, 1796	3	116
AYRES, AYRE, Catharine, m. Nathaniel S. **CHIPMAN**, b. of [New London], Sept. 29, 1844, by Rev. S. Benton	4	114
Daniel S., of Lyme, m. Tacy **KNIGHT**, of [New London], Feb. 27, 1831, by Rev. Leonard B. Griffing	4	40
Daniel Smith, of New London, m. Abby Ann **SMITH**, of Montville, Feb. 3, 1842, by Rev. R. W. Allen	4	97
Ellen Maria, m. Christian **ISOPH***, Apr. 7, 1850, by Rev. James W. Dennis *(Perhaps "LSOPH")	4	152
Frances A., m. Charles O. **HARRIS**, Apr. 13, 1851, by Rev. Charles Willett	4	161
Lucretia M., m. Benjamin F. **BARKER**, b. of New London, Nov. 3, 1844, by Rev. J. Blain	4	115
BABCOCK, Alfred, of Lyme, m. Julia **COMSTOCK**, of Groton, Sept. 2, 1837, by Rev. Daniel Webb	4	73

	Vol.	Page

BABCOCK (cont.)

Ephraim, s. [Ehraim H. & Mary Ann], b. May 10,
1820 — 3 — 258

Ephraim H., m. Mary Ann **POTTER**, Jan. 13, 1811 — 3 — 258

Francis M., s. [Ephraim H. & Mary Ann], b. Dec. 24,
1811 — 3 — 258

John, twin with William, [s. Ephraim H. & Mary
Ann], b. May 1, 1816 — 3 — 258

Mary Ann, d. [Ephraim H. & Mary Ann], b. Aug. 29,
1813 — 3 — 258

Mary Ann, of N[ew] London, m. Samuel
McCLINTOCK, of Portsmouth, N.H., Dec. 13,
1833, by Rev. Abel McEwen — 4 — 54

Orren F., of Lyme, m. Ann Maria **HUNTINGTON**,
of N[ew] London, Mar. 12, 1837, by Rev.
Squire B. Hascall — 4 — 68

Orville, m. Almira **TILLOTSON**, b. of Lyme, July
3, 1837, by Rev. Abel McEwen — 4 — 72

Sarah H., d. [Ephraim H. & Mary Ann], b. May 13,
1818 — 3 — 258

Sylvia, m. Philo **PECKHAM**, b. of Lyme, Dec. 5,
1822, by Rev. Abel McEwen — 4 — 11

William, twin with John, [s. Ephraim H. & Mary
Ann], b. May 1, 1816 — 3 — 258

William, m. Emily A. **GREEN**, b. of [New London],
May 23, 1847, by Rev. L. Geo[rge] Leonard — 4 — 131

BACKUS, Harriet, m. John **McLELLAN**, Aug. 25, 1833,
by Rev. Abel McEwen — 4 — 53

BACON, Alexander, s. Cato & Fame, b. June 20, 1810 — 3 — 164

Hannah, m. Ebenezer **WILLIAMS**, Apr. 11, 1717 — 1 — 48

BADET, BADETT, Edward, s. [Thomas S. & Betsey], b.
Feb. 19, 1817 — 3 — 234

Edward, m. Eunice **WILLIAMS**, b. of New London,
Apr. 17, 1842, by Rev. Lemuel Covell — 4 — 99

Edward, m. Nancy **CHURCH**, b. of [New London],
Sept. 2, 1851, by Rev. Abel McEwen — 4 — 164

Francis, s. [Thomas S. & Betsey], b. Nov. 25, 1814 — 3 — 234

Harriet Butler, [d. Thomas S. & Betsey, b.] June 23,
1825 — 3 — 234

Henry, s. [Thomas S. & Betsey], b. Dec. 2 ,1819 — 3 — 234

Peter, m. Hannah **PALMS**, June 6, 1784, by Rev.
Samuel Buel. Witnesses: Tho[ma]s Shaw,
Lucy Prentis — 3 — 16

Thomas P., m. Harriet A. **LEWIS**, b. of [New
London], Oct. 26, 1848, by Rev. Abel McEwen — 4 — 142

Thomas Pierce, s. [Thomas S. & Betsey], b. Feb. 12,
1812 — 3 — 234

Thomas S., m. Betscy **BUTLER**, May 12, 1811 — 3 — 234

Thomas Shaw, s. [Peter & Hannah], b. Apr. 21, 1790 — 3 — 16

William, [s. Thomas S. & Betsey, b.] June 6, 1822 — 3 — 234

	Vol.	Page
BADGLEY, Samuel L., of Hudson, N.Y., m. Ann M.		
BAKER, of New London, Dec. 3, 1850, by		
Rev. James W. Dennis	4	157
BAGNALL, Mary, d. Thomas W. & Polly Tucker, b. Jan.		
8, 1824	3	194
BAILEY, BALEY, BAYLEY, BAYLAY, BAILY,		
Abigail, d. [Nathan, Jr. & Mary], b. Oct. 5,		
1785	3	80
Ann Maria, d. Giles & Meribah, b. Sept. 20, 1826	3	225
Ann Maria, d. [Giles & Meribah], b. Sept. 20, 1826;		
d. Oct. 13, 1830	3	299
Anthony, m. Eliza Ann **LATHROP**, May 19, 1830,		
by Rev. B. Judd	4	41
Augusta Maria, d. [Giles & Meribah], b. July 8,		
1839; d. Sept. 29, 1853	3	299
Betsey, d. [Nathan, Jr. & Mary], b. Mar. 23, 1778	3	80
Charles W., of Groton, m Elizabeth **FRINK**, of		
Stonington, Apr. 24, 1836, by Rev. Squire B.		
Hascall	4	83
Deborah, of Groton, d. John, m. James		
HOUGHTON, of New London, s. Sampson, of		
New London, Jan. 4, 1748/9	2	45
Deborah, d. [Nathan, Jr. & Mary], b. Sept. 14, 1789	3	80
Eliza, d. Nathan, m. Amos **WOODWARD**, Feb. 26,		
1792	3	147
Eliza J., m. Caleb H. **RICE**, b. of [New London],		
Apr. 10, 1851, by Rev. Abel McEwen	4	161
Emeline Merritt, d. [Giles & Meribah], b. July 3,		
1828; d. Sept. 28, 1829	3	299
Emely, of New London, m. Lucius L. **BUTLER**, of		
Stonington, May 22, 1842, by Rev. Lemuel		
Covell	4	99
Esther, m. Frances **HARRIS**, Mar. 30, 1785	3	135
Giles, m. Meribah **MERRITT**, June 27, 1824, in		
Groton	3	299
Giles, Jr., s. [Giles & Meribah], b. Feb. 19, 1834; d.		
Sept. 18, 1836	3	299
Hannah, of New London, m. Orlenzo **LOMBARD**,		
of Lebanon, Ct., May 6, 1832, by Chester		
Tilden	4	46
Harriot, d. [Nathan, Jr. & Mary], b. Dec. 4, 1795	3	80
Henry, s. [Nathan, Jr. & Mary], b. Oct. 28, 1792	3	80
James, s. Thomas & Lydya, b. Sept. 26, [1666]	1	5
Jerusha, m. Robert G. **DAWSON**, Jan. 28, 1813*, by		
Rev. Peter Griffing. *(So in the copy.		
Probably 1831)	4	40
John, s. Thomas & Lydia, b. Apr. [, 1661]	1	3
John, s. [Nathan, Jr. & Mary], b. May 11, 1781	3	80
Lydia, wid. of Thomas, m. William **THORN**, of		
Dorsetshire, Old England, July 26, [1676]	1	11
Mary, d. Thomas & Lydia, b. Feb. 14, [1756]*		
*([1656] written in pencil)	1	2

	Vol.	Page

BAILEY, BALEY, BAYLEY, BAYLAY, BAILY (cont.)

Mary Ann, m. Alfred W. **CHAPMAN**, b. of New
London, Jan. 13, 1833, by Chester Tilden — 4 — 49

Nancy, m. Charles **CHAPMAN**, b. of New London,
Sept. 21, 1823, by Rev. Abel McEwen — 4 — 15

Nancy L., m. Edward P. **DEW[E]Y**, May 18, 1831,
by Rev. Daniel Wildman — 4 — 42

Nathan, Jr., m. Mary **WARD**, May. 2, 1777 — 3 — 80

Nathan, s. [Nathan, Jr. & Mary], b. July 31, 1779 — 3 — 80

Polly, d. [Nathan, Jr. & Mary], b. July 17, 1784 — 3 — 80

Prudence, of Groton, d. John, m. Jedidiah
DARROW, of New London, s. Christopher,
Mar. 27, 1752 — 3 — 9

Sally, d. [Nathan, Jr. & Mary], b. Jan. 13, 1791 — 3 — 80

Terrey, s. [Nathan, Jr. & Mary], b. Oct. 2, 1782 — 3 — 80

Thomas, m. Lydda, d. of James **REDFIN**, Jan. 20,
[1655] — 1 — 2

Thomas, s. Thomas & Lydia, b. Mar. 5, [1658] — 1 — 3

William, s. Thomas & Lydia, b. Apr. 27, [1664] — 1 — 4

William, s. [Nathan, Jr. & Mary], b. Aug. 23, 1787 — 3 — 80

William, of Groton, m. Jane **LEEDS**, of New
London, Mar. 3, 1836, by Rev. John G.
Wightman — 4 — 65

BAILIS, Jane, m. Denison **BECKWITH**, of Waterford,
Mar. 9, 185[1], by Rev. Jabez S. Swan — 4 — 163

BAIN, John, formerly of London, Great Britain, now of
New London, m. Sarah **FORSYTH**, of New
London, June 28, 1829, by Rev. Nehemiah
Dodge — 4 — 36

BAKER, Abell, s. Stephen & Elisabeth, b. Jan. 13, 1753,
old style — 3 — 11

Agnes, m. John **DANIELS**, Dec. 3, [1685] — 1 — 17

Alexander, s. Joshua & Hanna[h], b. Dec. 16, [1679] — 1 — 14

Alexander, m. Mary **PEMBERTON**, Apr. 27, 1707 — 1 — 32

Alexander, d. Jan. 15, 1724/5 — 1 — 64

Alexander, s. Joshua & Hannah, b. Dec. 16, [ ] — 1 — 67

Ann, d. Joshua, of New London, m. Noah
HAMMOND, of New London, s. Isaac, of
New London, Nov. 9, 1738 — 2 — 46

Ann M., of New London, m. Samuel L. **BADGLEY**,
of Hudson, N.Y., Dec. 3, 1850, by Rev. James
W. Dennis — 4 — 157

Anna, d. Joshua & Meriam, b. May 28, 1716 — 1 — 55

Anna, d. John & Rachel, b. Apr. 23, 1758 — 3 — 4

Charles, m. Henrietta **HAMMELL**, d. Jacob &
Regina, all of [New London], Sept. 27, 1847,
by Rev. T. Edwards — 4 — 134

Charlotte E., of New London, m. John T.
DICKINSON, of Stonington, [ ] 4, [1847?],
by Rev. T. Edwards — 4 — 129

David, s. Stephen & Elisabeth, b. Oct. 9, 1750 — 3 — 11

Desire, d. John & Rachel, b. Sept. 25, 1756 — 3 — 4

	Vol.	Page
BAKER (cont.)		
Elias, s. John & Rachel, b. Apr. 14, 1768	3	4
Elisha, s. John & Rachel, b. Oct. 14, 1763	3	4
Elisha A., of Groton, m. Laura **TAYLOR**, of		
Colchester, Aug. 30, 1825, by Rev. Abel		
McEwen	4	24
Elizabeth, d. Joshua & Hanna[h], b. May 9, [1676]	1	11
Elizabeth, wid., m. Peter **HARKLY**, July 31, 1699	1	25
Elizabeth, m. Richard **ATWELL**, Mar. 11, 1703	1	29
Elizabeth, d. Joshua & Meriam, b. Apr. 24. 1709	1	55
Elizabeth, d. Alexander & Mary, b. Mar. 4, 1713/14	1	47
Francis E., m. Abby Ann **ROGERS**, b. of [New		
London], Nov. 13, 1848, by Rev. L. G. Leonard	4	143
Gideon, s. Joshua & Meriam, b. Nov. 27, 1711	1	55
Gideon, m. Harriet L. **LOOMIS**, b. of New London,		
Jan. 1, 1843, by L. Covell	4	101
Hanna[h], twin with Sarah, d. Joshua & Hanna[h], b.		
Jan. 18, [1683]	1	17
Hannah, d. Alexander & Mary, b. Jan. 24, 1707	1	33
Hurlbut, s. John & Rachal, b. Dec. 25, 1759	3	4
James, s. Joshua & Meriam, b. Mar. 17, 1714	1	55
John, s. Joshua, late of New London, decd., m		
Rachel **SCOVEL**, d. of Arthur Scovell, of		
Colchester, Mar. 14, 1754	3	4
John, s. John & Rachel, b. Apr. 14, 1755	3	4
John, s. [Joshua & Hannah], b. Dec. 24, [ ]	1	67
Joseph, s. Alexander & Mary, b. Sept. 12, 1721	1	64
Joshua, s. Alexander, of Boston, m. Hanna[h], widow		
of Trustram **MINTER**, Sept. 13, [1674]	1	9
Joshua, s. Joshua & Hanna[h], b. Jan. 5, [1677]	1	12
Joshua, m. Merriam **HURLBUTT**, Mar. 27, 1705	1	55
Joshua, s. Joshua & Merriam, b. May 3, 1706	1	55
Joshua, of New London, d. Dec. 27, 1717	1	49
Lucy, d. Stephen & Elisabeth, b. Oct. 13, 1746	3	11
Lydia, d. Joshua & Meriam, b. June 12, 1712; d. Nov.		
21, 1712	1	55
Lydia, d. Alexander & Mary, b. July 24, 1725	2	3
Manuel, of Spain, m. Diana **DENCE**, of Stonington,		
Mar. 20, 1831, by Rev. B. Judd	4	42
Mary, d. Alexander & Mary, b. Apr. 30, 1710	1	35
Mary, m. Jason **CHAPMAN**, July 15, 1786	3	99
Mary, of Groton, m. Leonard **CULVER**, of Hebron,		
Aug. 30, 1825, by Rev. Abel McEwen	4	24
Pemberton, s. Alexander & Mary, b. Mar. 24, 1716	1	47
Precillia, of New London, m. Joshua **BECKWITH**,		
of Bozrah, Mar. 4, 1823, by T. W .Tucker,		
Elder	4	13
Rachel, d. John & Rachel, b. Nov. 16, 1761	3	4
Rhoda, d. John & Rachel, b. Apr. 11, 1766	3	4
Samuel, s. Joshua & [Meriam], b. Aug. 24, 1707	1	55
Sarah, twin with Hanna[h], d. Joshua & Hanna[h], b.		
Jan. 18, [1683]	1	17

	Vol.	Page

BAKER (cont.)

Sarah, m. Andrew **DAVIS**, Dec. 9, 1708	1	34
Sarah, d. Alexander & Mary, b. Dec. 3, 1718	1	64
Sarah, d. Joshua & Meriam, b. May 14, 1721	1	55
Sarah, d. Alexander, decd., d. June 17, 1738	2	5
Sarah, d. Joshua, of New London, decd., m. John MAPLES, s. Ste[phe]n of New London, May 12, 1743	2	65
Sibbell, d. Stephen & Elizabeth, b. Jan. 19, 1759, new style	3	11
Stephen, s. Joshua & Meriam, b. Mar. 17, 1719	1	55
Stephen, s. Joshua, late of New London, decd., m. Elisabeth **COMSTOCK**, d. Kingland Comstock, late of New London, decd., Nov. 13, 1745	3	11
Stephen Hurlburt, s. Stephen & Eliza[beth], b. Oct. 29, 1748	3	11
Susannah, m. William **HATCH**, Oct. 13, 1726	2	37
Sybil, see under Sibbell		
Zebadiah C., m. Mary **KIMBALL**, b. of New London, May 14, 1823, by Rev. Abel McEwen	4	15
Zebediah C., m. Mercy **CRANDALL**, b. of [New London], Sept. 14, 1835, by Rev. Abel McEwen	4	62

BALDEUF, Frederick, m. Ann **DOYLE**, July 7, 1849, by
Rev. William Logan .... 4 ... 150

BALDWIN, Maria F., m Savillion **HALEY**, Oct. 6, 1833,
by Daniel Wildman .... 4 ... 52

| Thomas, m. Elizabeth Jane **BECKWITH**, b. of
Waterford, July 19, 1837, by Rev. Daniel Webb | 4 | 73 |
| William, m. Delia **CROCKER**, Nov. 16, 1834, by
Rev. Alvin Ackley | 4 | 58 |

BALL, Van R., of Stonington, m. Amanda **COBB**, of
Noank (Groton), Oct. 27, 1850, by Rev. E. R.
Warren .... 4 ... 156

BANISTER, Mary A. M., m. George B. **LINCOLN**, Dec.
28, 1841, at Brookfield, Mass. .... 3 ... 295

BANKS, Susan A., of Groton, m. Christopher A. **POTTS**,
of New London, Aug. 1, 1830, by Rev. Abel
McEwen .... 4 ... 38

BARBER, Anna Prentis, d. [Benjamin & Bridget], b. Aug.
17, 1790 .... 3 ... 96

Benjamin, m. Bridget **PRENTIS**, Sept. 5, 1786	3	96
Horace, m. Nancy **MORRIS**, b. of [New London], Mar. 16, 1845, by Rev. Abel McEwen	4	118
John, m. Abby **WATSON**, b. of New London, June 8, 1845, by Rev. Jabez S. Swan	4	119
Nancy, m. Henry **HEMPSTEAD**, Aug. 7, 1808	3	256
Noyes C., of Ovill, N.Y., m. Jane E. [ ], of [New London], June 19, 1837, by Rev. Abel McEwen	4	71

	Vol.	Page
BARKER, [see also **BARTER**], Alvira D., m. Robert **GOODWIN**, b. of New London, Mar. 2, 1851, by Rev. Jabez S. Swan	4	163
Ann Connand Pitnam, d. [Oliver Dutton & Pheby], b. Aug. 27, 1811	3	57
Benjamin F., m. Lucretia M. **AYRES**, b. of New London, Nov. 3, 1844, by Rev. J. Blain	4	115
Edward L., m. Catharine **TRACY**, b. of New London, Apr. 6, 1852, by Rev. Robert A. Hallam	4	167
Elizabeth Holt Young, d. [Oliver Dutton & Pheby], b. Oct. 3, 1812	3	57
Frances A., m. Joseph T. **HOWARD**, b. of New London, July 17, 1842, by Rev. R. W. Allen	4	100
Hannah, d. [Phineas & Grace], b. Oct. 25, 1803	3	111
Henry L., m. Mary Ann **DARROW**, b. of [New London], Jan. 1, 1838, by Rev. Daniel Webb	4	75
Jonathan, m. Lydia **HARRIS**, b. of [New London], Apr. 24, 1831, by Rev. Daniel Wildman	4	41
Joseph Alyan, s. [Oliver Dutton & Pheby], b. Sept. 18, 1810	3	57
Oliver, s. [Oliver Dutton & Pheby], b. Oct. 17, 1807	3	57
Pheby, relict. of Oliver, dau. of Joseph **HOLT**, m. Oliver Dutton **BEEBE**, Oct. 30 1806	3	57
Phineas, m. Grace **BECKWITH**, Oct. 14, 1802	3	111
William P., m. Martha Ann **HALL**, b. of New London, Dec. 30, 1832, by Chester Tilden	4	49
BARNES, BARNS, Abba, m. Joseph **REEVES**, b. of [New London], Oct. 27, 1839, by J. Lovejoy	4	87
Harriet, of [New London], m. Frank **VINCENT**, of New York, Aug. 11, 1845, by Rev. Abel McEwen	4	120
Oliver S., m. Eliza **HARRINGTON**, Apr. 21, 1821, by Elijah Hedding	4	5
Samuel, m. Abby **BEEBE**, d. George, Dec. 11, 1807	3	236
Samuel, m. Abby **FISH**, b. of New London, Dec. 16, 1834, by Th[oma]s S. Perkins, J.P.	4	59
Samuel Devenport, s. [Samuel & Abby], b. Aug. 10, 1809	3	236
William H., m. Lucretia J. **DENNIS**, b. of [New London], Jan. 19, 1846, by Rev. Abel McEwen	4	123
BARNET, John, m. Bridget **CODY**, Feb. 8, 1852, by Rev. J. Stokes. Witnesses: Henry Bell, Anne Coda	4	169
BARR, Betsey, d. John & Elizabeth, m. William **GALE**, May 23, 1801	3	183
Elisabeth, d. [John & Elisabeth], b. Dec. 2, 1781	3	100
Elisabeth, m. Daniel **GREEN**, Apr. 17, 1785	3	100
John, m. Elisabeth **JAMES**, Sept. 6, 1778	3	100
John, s. [John & Elisabeth], b. Apr. 28, 1779	3	100
John, d. [ ]	3	100

	Vol.	Page
BARROS, Francis, of Rio Hache, m. Mary **SHERMAN**, of Waterford, May 8, 1831, by Rev. Daniel Wildman	4	41
BARROW, Esther, m. John **HOWARD**, Sept. 10, 1774	3	78
Polly, m. Hallam **HEMPSTE[A]D**, June 29, 1784, by Joseph Harris, J.P.	3	97
Sarah Ann, of New London, m. James F. **GORMAN**, of St. Johns, New Brunswick, N.S., Feb. 9, 1845, by Rev. S. Benton	4	117
BARRY, Caroline A., of [New London], m. Charles B. **HUNTINGTON**, of New York, May 10, 1849, by Rev. T. Edwards	4	145
James, m. Ann **SHACKETT**, Oct. 28, 1849, by Rev. William Logan	4	151
BARTER [see also **BARKER**], Polly, m. Paul **ROGERS**, Oct. 4, 1787	3	107
William, s. Henry & Sarah, b. Mar. 15, 1766. Recorded at his desire Dec. 1792	3	120
BARTHOLOMEW, Emanuel, m. Carroline **SPENCER**, b. of [New London], June 20, 1838, by Rev. Abel McEwen	4	77
George, of New London, m. Laura A. **BROCKWAY**, of Lyme, Nov. 11, 1832, by Rev. Abel McEwen	4	48
BASCOM, Flavel, of Lebanon, m. Ellen P. **CLEAVELAND**, of New London, Apr. 30, 1833, by Rev. Abel McEwen	4	50
BASSETT, Helen P., of [New London], m. Edward **RAWSON**, of Akron, Ohio, Nov. 8, 1848, by Rev. Tryon Edwards	4	143
Lucretia S., of New London, m. Gustavus W. **SMITH**, of U. S. Corps of Engineers, Oct. 3, 1844, by Rev. Abel McEwen	4	114
Simeon Spencer, of Washington City, m. Louisa Ellen**ALBERTSON**, July 23, 1850, by Rev. James W. Dennis	4	155
BATES, Elizabeth J., of Glastonbury, m. John W. **SMITH**, of Durham, July 4, 1848, by Rev. Giles H. Deshon, of Glastonbury	4	140
Jane, m. James B. **LYMAN**, Jr., of New London, Sept. 24, 1848, by Rev. Tho[ma]s J. Greenwood	4	142
BATTELL, Sally B., d. William, of Torrington, m. Rev. Abel **McEWEN**, Jan. 21, 1807	3	227
BAXTER, Bartholomew Crannall, s. [James & Catharine], b. Mar. 8, 1800	3	115
Catharine, d. [James & Catharine], b. Oct. 10, 1793, on Island of Hispaniola	3	115
James, m. Catharine **CRANNELL**, d. Capt. Robert & Joanna, of New York, Feb. 8, 1785	3	115
James, s. [James & Catharine], b. July 14, 1788	3	115
James had slave Labosiere, s. to Mary, a negro, & Labosiere, a Frenchman, b. Aug. 7, 1799	3	128

	Vol.	Page
BAXTER, (cont.)		
Joanna, d. [James & Catharine], b. Dec. 6, 1786	3	115
Mary Catharine Josephine, d. [James & Catharine], b. Mar. 11, 1791, on Island of Hispaniola	3	115
Sally Agnis Griswold, d. [James & Catharine], b. Sept. 12, 1796, at Easthampton, L.I.	3	115
Sophia Vandike, d. [James & Catharine], b. Apr. 10, 1802	3	115
Thomas, of St. Helena, m. Grace B. **ROUSE**, of New London, May 31, 1842, by Rev. R. W. Allen	4	98
BAYWOOD, John C., of New York City, m. Fanny **HOBRON**, of [New London], June 23, 1837, by Rev. Abel McEwen	4	71
BEACH, Benjamin, m. Anne **PARSONS**, May 14, 1828, by Rev. Rob[er]t Bowzer	4	35
Chauncey E., m. Hannah E. **McLEAN**, b. of [New London], July 9, 1846, by Rev. Tryon Edwards	4	127
Elizabeth S., m. Oliver A. **MUDGE**, b. of [New London], Oct. 18, 1841, by Rev. Able McEwen	4	97
Elvira L., m. Benjamin W. **DART**, Sept. 23, 1839, by James M. Macdonald	4	88
Mary E., m. Albert **McLEAN**, b. of N[ew] London, Mar. 5, 1833, by Rev. Abel McEwen	4	51
BEAMIS, Rebeckah, d. James, m. Tobias **MINTER**, s. Ezra, of New Foundland, Apr. 3, [1672]	1	8
BEAUMIS, John, m. Elizabeth **MINER**, b. of New London, May 2, 1851, by Rev. Jabez Swan	4	163
BECKET, Mary, d. of Thomas & Sarah, of Lyme, m. Thomas **HARRIS**, s. Richard & Lucy, of New London, Dec. 5, 1744	2	78
BECKLY, Benjamin, of Wethersfield, m. Meriam **STEVENS**, Nov. 12, 1702	1	27
BECKWITH, Alanson, m. Elizabeth **SQUIRES**, b. of [New London], Feb. 19, 1832, by Rev. Chester Tilden	4	45
Albert, m. Lucy **SPRAGUE**, Jan. 14, 1830, by Daniel Wildman	4	37
Allen W., of New London, m. Mary A. C. **WILKINSON**, of Bath, Me., Oct. 7, 1851, by Rev. E. R. Warren	4	166
Amia, m. Daniel **HOWARD**, Jan. 22, 1769	3	105
Amy, see Amy **DARROW**		
Amy, d. John & Elisabeth, b. June 23, 1747	3	27
Angeline, m. Calvin **PEMBER**, Aug. 22, 1852, by Rev. C. Willett	4	171
Bathshea, m. Nathaniell **DANIELLS**, Oct. 4, 1716	1	46
Bathsheba, of New London, m. Nathaniel **DANIELS**, of New London, Oct. 30, 1716	2	90
Benjamin F., m. Eunice D. **EDGAR**, b. of [New London], June 25, 1838, by Rev. Abel McEwen	4	78
Caleb, s. John & Elisabeth, b. Dec. 16, 1763	3	27
Caleb, s. [Caleb & Joanna], b. Nov. 4, 1788	3	111

	Vol.	Page
BECKWITH (cont.)		
Caleb, m. Joanna **BEEBE**, [ ], 1788	3	111
Carlos S., m. Susan J. **PIMER**, b. of New London,		
Nov. 6, 1851, by Rev. Robert A. Hallam	4	165
Charles, s. [Noah & Anna], b. Feb. 18, 1786	3	109
Charles, m. Elizabeth Y. **GRACE**, b. of New		
London, Dec. 1, 1850, by Rev. Jabez S. Swan	4	157
Denison, s. [Caleb & Joanna], b. Sept. 27, 1795	3	111
Denison, of Waterford, m. Jane **BAILIS**, Mar. 9,		
185[1], by Rev. Jabez S. Swan	4	163
Desire, of [New London], m. Lyman **BEEBE**, of		
Waterford, Nov. 8, 1835, by Rev. Abel		
McEwen	4	63
Ebenezer, s. [John, Jr. & Hannah], b. Nov. 4, 1780	3	109
Eldredge, m. Margaret F. **HARRIS**, Dec. 11, 1834,		
by Rev. Alvan Ackley	4	59
Elisha, s. [Jason & Elisabeth], b. Oct. 24, 1786	3	106
Elisabeth, d. John & Elisabeth, b. Oct. 25, 1745	3	27
Elisabeth, of Lyme d. Jonathan, 2d, of Lyme, m.		
Joseph **STUBBINS**, of New London, s.		
Clem[en]t, May 31, 1764	3	36
Elisabeth, d. [Noah & Anne], b. Sept. 16, 1779	3	109
Elizabeth, m. James **CARROL**, b. of New London,		
May 5, 1822, by Roswell Burrows, Admr.	4	4
Elizabeth B., m. Daniel G. **KEENEY**, b. of New		
London, July 31, 1844, by Rev. Jabez S. Swan	4	113
Est[h]er, d. John & Elisabeth, b. Apr. 12, 1762	3	27
Esther, m. Nehemiah **CROCKER**, Oct. 11, 1785	3	107
Francis D., m. Nancy A. **HOWE**, b. of New London,		
Nov. 4, 1832, by Chester Tilden	4	49
Frederick, s. John & Elisabeth, b. Feb. 13, 1758	3	27
Frederick, m. Lydia **MOSHER**, Apr. 3, 1783	3	49
Grace, m. Phineas **BARKER**, Oct. 14, 1802	3	111
Hannah, d. [John, Jr. & Hannah], b. June 5, 1784	3	109
Harriet A., of East Lyme, m. Nicholas L. **SMITH**, of		
New London, Jan. 3, 1847, by Rev. Jabez S.		
Swan	4	129
Henry, of Waterford, m. Miranda **BECKWITH**, of		
New London, Nov. 9, 1847, by Nathaniel		
Chapman, J.P.	4	135
Hester, d. [Seth & Esther], b. Oct. 16, 1782	3	109
Jane, m. Thomas **BALDWIN**, b. of Waterford, July		
19, 1837, by Rev. Daniel Webb	4	73
Jane E., of East Lyme, m. John S. **MORGAN**, of		
Waterford, Feb. 17, 1850, by Rev. Abel		
McEwen	4	152
Jason, m. Elisabeth **CROCKER**, May 19, 1785	3	106
Jason, Jr., m. Harriet F. **SISSON**, b. of New London,		
Apr. 12, 1849, by Rev. Edwin R. Warren	4	148
John, s. John, m. Elisabeth **DART**, d. Daniel, Nov. 8,		
1744	3	27
John, s. John & Elisabeth, b. Sept. 10, 1754	3	27

	Vol.	Page
BECKWITH (cont.)		
John, Jr., m. Hannah **DARROW**, Jan. 27, 1780	3	109
John, s. [Noah & Anna], b. Nov. 28, 1781	3	109
John, s. [John, Jr. & Hannah], b. Jan. 19, 1788	3	109
John Leland, s. [Caleb & Joanna], b. Aug. 21, 1793	3	111
Joseph, s. [Seth & Esther], b. Jan. 25, 1785	3	109
Joshua, of Bozrah, m. Precillia **BAKER**, of New London, Mar. 4, 1823, by T. W. Tucker, Elder	4	13
Julia E., m. John **PEARCE**, b. of Waterford, Sept. 6, 1846, by John Howson	4	130
Lucinda, d. [John, Jr. & Hannah], b. Apr. 26, 1786	3	109
Lucretia, d. [Noah & Anna], b. Feb. 15, 1774	3	109
Lucretia, m. Asahel **STEWARD**, Nov. 6, 1796	3	134
Lucretia A., d. Charles, m. Chauncey R. **CROCKER**, June 4, 1837	3	284
Lucretia A., m. Chauncey R. **CROCKER**, b. of [New London], June 4, 1837, by Rev. Nathan Wildman	4	71
Lydia, d. John & Elisabeth, b. Aug. 6, 1760	3	27
Mary, m. Joseph **WEEKS** [ ]	3	30
Mary A., of Waterford, m. Silas E. **BURROWS**, of New London, Jan. 4, 1852, by Rev. Samuel Fox	4	167
Mary Ann, of Waterford, m. Albert **STILLMAN**, of New London, Apr. 5, 1835, by Alvan Ackley	4	60
Mary B., m. William **JOYCE**, Feb. 19, 1823, by Lodowick Fosdick, J.P.	4	12
Mary Billings, d. [Samuel & Amey], b. Nov. 26, 1801	3	166
Mehetable, m. Robert **CANNON**, Jan. 22, 1784	3	224
Mirack, m. Harriet M. **CROCKER**, Feb. 22, 1842, by H. R. Knapp	4	101
Miranda, of New London, m. Henry **BECKWITH**, of Waterford, Nov. 9, 1847, by Nathaniel Chapman, J.P.	4	135
Nancy, d. [Caleb & Joanna], b. Mar. 3, 1791	3	111
Nancy P., m. Lyman **HARRIS**, b. of New London, Aug. 29, 1836, by Rev. Alvan Ackley	4	83
Nelson B., of New York, m. Lucretia H. **SPRAGUE**, of New London, Apr. 3, 1836, by Rev. Alvan Ackley	4	65
Noah, s. John & Elisabeth, b. Sept. 18, 1752	3	27
Noah, m. Anna **BROOKS**, July 8, 1773	3	109
Noah, s. [Noah & Anna], b. Oct. 10, 1775	3	109
Phebe, d. [Noah & Anna], b. Feb. 22, 1784; d. Feb. 20, 1786	3	109
Polly, d. [John, Jr. & Hannah], b. Aug. 10, 1782	3	109
Polly, d. [Frederick & Lydia], b. June 11, 1786	3	49
Polly, d. Nathan, of Lyme, m. Jesse **MOORE**, Mar. 19, 1795	3	184
Prudence, m. Roger **DART**, July 24, 1717	2	13
Rebecca, m. Richard **COMSTOCK**, Mar. [ ], 1809	3	262
Richard, s. [Noah & Anna], b. Sept. 19, 1777	3	109

	Vol.	Page

BECKWITH (cont.)

Roxy, of New London, m. George **DANIELS**, Jr., of Waterford, Aug. 19, 1832, by Th[omas] S. Perkins, J.P. — 4 — 47

Roxy, of [New London], m. Joseph **YOUNG**, of Wind[h]am, [Jan. 1836], by Rev. Alvan Ackley — 4 — 64

Russel[l], s. [Seth & Esther], b. Dec. 27, 1788 — 3 — 109

Sabra, d. John & Elisabeth, b. Sept. 13, 1750 — 3 — 27

Sally, d. [Frederick & Lydia], b. July 18, 1784 — 3 — 49

Sally, d. Frederick, b. July 18, 1784; m. Pardon **LEWIS**, Jan. 20, 1805 — 3 — 204

Sally, m. Allen **DARROW**, Nov. 24, 1822, by Rev. Francis Darrow — 4 — 12

Samuel, m. Amey **SLATER**, d. Zorobabel, Nov. 20, 1800 — 3 — 166

Samuel C., m. Almira **GORTON**, Sept. 25, 18334, by Rev. Francis Darrow — 4 — 57

Sarah, of Waterford, m. Lyman **WADE**, of Lyme, Feb. 21, 1836, by Rev. Squire B. Hascall — 4 — 83

Seth, s. John & Elisabeth, b. Aug. 28, 1756 — 3 — 27

Seth, m. Esther **LEACH**, Nov. 14, 1781 — 3 — 109

Silas, s. [Noah & Anna], b. Feb. 14, 1788 — 3 — 109

Susan, m. Joshua **POTTER**, b. of [New London], Jan. 7, 1827, by Rev. B. Judd — 4 — 29

Susan B., of [New London], m. Samuel H. **BEEBE**, Oct. 28, 1827, by La Roy Sunderland — 4 — 32

Timothy, m. Maranda **CALVERT**, b. of New London, Apr. 7, 1851, by Rev. Jabez S. swan — 4 — 163

William, of Waterford, m. Miranda **COLVERT**, of [New London], June 11, 1845, by John Grace, J.P. — 4 — 120

Zorobabel Slator, s. [Samuel & Amey], b. Dec. 12, 1807 — 3 — 166

-----, d. [Samuel & Amey], b. July 5, 1809 — 3 — 166

BEDINGTON, James, of Wallington, N.Y., m. Charlotte **COLFAX**, of [New London], June 8, 1835, by Rev. Abel McEwen — 4 — 61

BEEBE, Aaron, s. Jeduthan & Lucretia, b. Mar. 14, 1765 — 2 — 63

Abby, d. George, m. Samuel **BARNES**, Dec. 11, 1807 — 3 — 236

Abell, s. [Othniel & Johanna], b. May 3, 1775 — 2 — 121

Abel, m. Sally **LESTER**, Jan. 12, 1794 — 3 — 129

Abel, s. [Abel & Sally], b. Apr. 20, 1795 — 3 — 129

Abigail, d. Stephen & Mary, b. July 20, 1723 — 2 — 4

Abigail, d. Joseph, m. Josiah **SMITH**, s. John, all of New London, Sept. [ ], 175[ ] — 2 — 120

Abigail, d. Daniel & Ann, b. Apr. 28, 1769 — 3 — 38

Abraham, s. Hezekiah & Hannah, b. June 24, 1734 — 2 — 5

Adin, s. [Reuben & Mary], b. Dec. 7, 1764 — 3 — 13

Adin, m. Lucy **CROCKER**, Sept. 6, 1787 — 3 — 24

Adin, s. [Adin & Lucy], b. May 11, 1788 — 3 — 24

	Vol.	Page
BEEBE (cont.)		
Alexander Mullen, s. Daniel & Anna, b. July 19,		
1773	3	38
Alfred, s. [Jethro & Martha], b. Nov, 8, 1792	3	12
Amos, s. Stephen & Mary, b. July 3, 1730	2	4
Amos, s. Sam[ue]l, Jr. & Anne, b. Aug. 29, 1739	2	6
Amos, s. [Reuben & Mary], b. June 19, 1760	3	13
Amos, s. W[illia]m & Hannah], b. June 28, 1777	3	19
Amy, d. [William, Jr. & Hannah], b. July 5, 1779	3	19
Ann, d. William, Jr. & Jerusha, b. July 3, 1727; d.		
Feb. 23, 17[ ]	2	4
Ann, d. Samuel & Ann, b. Jan. 1, 1728/9	2	4
Ann, m. Elisha **PHILIPS**, b. of New London, July 4,		
1845, by Rev. Jabez S. Swan	4	120
Ann E., m. George **SHEPARD**, b. of New London,		
Apr. 22, 1827, by Rev. Abel McEwen	4	30
Anna, d. Daniel & Anne, b. June 6, 1771	3	38
Anna, d. Will[ia]m, Jr. & Hannah, b. June 26, 1773	3	19
Anne, d. Samuel, Sr., m. Thomas **CROCKER**, Apr.		
23, [1700]	1	25
Asa, s. Hezekiah & Hannah, b. June 5, 1732	2	5
Asa, s. Hezekiah, m. Mary **NEWBURY**, d.		
Nath[anie]l, the 2d, b. of New London, Mar. 20,		
1758	3	5
Bailey, s. [Jason & Betsey], b. Sept. 3, 1787	3	12
Bethshua, [d. Samuel & Elizabeth], b. Mar. 16, 1688	1	16
Betsey, whose maiden name was **CRIST**, was b.		
June 7, 1764	3	42
Betsey, m. Jason **BEEBE**, Jan. 19, 1784	3	12
Betsey, m. Griswold **HARRIS**, Dec. 20, 1795	3	136
Betsey, m. Eliphalet **HARRIS**, Mar. 10, 1797	3	42
Betsey, m. Henry **OSBORN**, b. of New London,		
May 9, 1824, by Rev. B. Judd	4	18
Caroline, of New London, m. John L. **KEABLES**, of		
Stonington, Apr. 19, 1836, by Rev. Squire B.		
Hascall	4	83
Catharine, m. Edward H. **MASON**, b. of New		
London, Nov. 21, 1847, by Rev. L. G. Leonard	4	138
Catharine H. E., m. Daniel C. **CHAPMAN**, b. of		
New London, Sept. 4, 1849, by Rev. Jabez S.		
Swan	4	147
Charles, m. Laura Ann **BEEBE**, b. of Waterford,		
June 29, 1822, by Thomas W. Tucker, Elder	4	15
Charles H., of New London, m. Sarah Ann		
HUMPHREY, of Hartford, Dec. 8, 1844, by		
Rev. Jabez S. Swan	4	115
Daniel, s. William* & Sarah, b. Dec. 11, 1716		
*(Probably Samuel)	1	52
Daniel, s. Samuel & Sarah, b Dec. 11, 1716	2	19
Daniel, s. Jonathan, of East Haddam, m. Hannah		
BEEBE, d. of Ezekiel, of New London, Jan. 10,		
1751	2	77

	Vol.	Page
BEEBE (cont.)		
Daniel, s. Daniel & Hannah, b. Oct. 4, 1751	2	77
Daniel, m. Ann **MULLIN**, b. of New London, July		
18, 1768, by David Sprague, Elder	3	38
Daniel, m. Hannah Wheeler **McGAWREY**, b. of		
New London, Apr. 5, 1835, by Rev. Alvan		
Ackley	4	60
David, m. Hannah **BROOKS**, d. James, Nov. 16,		
1795	3	215
David, m. Nancy **STEWARD**, b. of New London,		
July 17, 1831, by Rev. Daniel Wildman	4	43
Edward, s. Will[iam, Jr.] & Hannah, b. Apr. 18, 1775	3	19
Edward Hempste[a]d, s. [Elijah & Sally], b. July 15,		
1809	3	209
Elijah, s. [Jethro & Martha], b. Sept. 24, 1785	3	12
Elijah, m. Sally **HEMPSTE[A]D**, d. Stephen, Sept.		
13, 1808	3	209
Eliphalet, s. Samuel & Ann, b. Dec. 27, 1723	2	3
Eliphalet, s. Samuel, drowned, Sept. 12, 1745	2	84
Eliza, of New London, m. John **AMES**, of New		
London, Aug. 12, 1827, by James Rogers, J.P.	4	31
Elizabeth, [d. Samuel & Elizabeth], b. Oct. 27, 1684	1	16
Elizabeth, d. Samuel & Ann, b. Oct. 13, 1719	2	3
Elizabeth, d. Samuel, of Plumb Island, m. William		
KING, s. William, of Oyster Pond, Southold,		
L.I., July 26, 1738	2	60
Elisabeth, d. [Reuben & Mary], b. Apr. 28, 1762	3	13
Elisabeth, d. Othniel & Johanna, b. Feb. 19, 1768	2	121
Elisabeth, d. [Ephraim & Elisabeth], b. Feb. 20, 1783	3	64
Elisabeth, d. [Paul & Mary], b. May 15, 1783; d. May		
30, 1794	3	123
Elisabeth, m. Ezekiel **TINKER**, Feb. 19, 1786	3	104
Elisabeth, d. [Paul & Mary], b. Mar. 29, 1795	3	123
Elizabeth, d. [Jethro & Martha], b. June 9, 1795	3	12
Elizabeth, d. [David & Hannah], b. May 29, 1801	3	215
Elnathan, s. Samuel & Ann, b. Oct. 25, 1725	2	3
Ely, s. Daniel & Hannah, b. Apr. 21, 1753	2	77
Eley, m. Mary **SMITH**, Oct. 18, 1807	3	153
Emeline M., m. Joseph T. **ECCLESTON**, Dec. 28,		
1851, by Rev. Charles Willett	4	166
Ephraim, s. Joseph & Mehetable, b. May 5, 1712	1	45
Ephraim, s. Jeduthan & Lucretia, b. Aug. 15, 1756	2	63
Ephraim, m. Elisabeth **BROWN**, JAN. 7 ,1778	3	64
Ephraim, S. [Ephraim & Elisabeth], b. Nov. 24, 1791	3	64
Esther, d. [Jethro & Martha], b. Mar. 18, 1787	3	12
Eunice, d. [Paul & Mary], b. Mar. 18, 1805	3	123
Ezekiel, m. Hannah **ROGERS**, Nov. 13, 1729	2	3
Ezekiel, s. Ezekiel & Hannah, b. Jan. 24, 1734/5	2	5
Ezekiel T., m. Mary **CRANDALL**, b. of Waterford,		
Jan. 9, 1823, by Lodowick Fosdick, J.P.	4	11
Ezra, s. Asa & Mary, b. Jan. 23, 1759	3	5

	Vol.	Page

BEEBE (cont.)

George, of New London, m. Elizabeth Ann
    POWERS, of Lebanon, Oct. 5, 1834, by Rev.
    Ebenezer Blake | 4 | 57

George G., m. Sally **BEEBE**, b. of New London,
    Oct. 27, 1824, by Rev. George W. Fairbanks | 4 | 19

Gideon, s. William* & Sarah, b. Dec. 4, 1713
    *(probably Samuel) | 1 | 52

Gideon, s. Samuel & Sarah, b. Dec. 4, 1713 | 2 | 19

Gilbert, s. [Nathan & Sally], b. June 18, 1809 | 3 | 162

Gilbert, of [New London], m. Martha **KEENEY**, of
    Groton, Mar. 30, 1851, by Rev. Abel McEwen | 4 | 161

Grace, d. [Nathaniel & Grace], b. Oct. 28, 1763; d.
    Dec. 28, 1765 | 3 | 96

Grace, d. [Nathaniel & Grace], b. May 3, 1766 | 3 | 96

Grace, d. [Nathaniel & Grace], b. Oct. 28, 1773; d.
    Dec. 28, 1775 (Entry crossed out) | 3 | 88

Grace, d. [William, Jr. & Hannah], b. Mar. 23, 1784 | 3 | 19

Grace, m. Samuel **RYON**, July 28, 1785 | 3 | 89

Grace, d. [Nathaniel & Grace], b. May 3, 17[ ]
    (Entry crossed out) | 3 | 88

Gurdon, s. [David & Hannah], b. Oct. 12, 1796 | 3 | 215

Guy, s. William, Jr. & Hannah, b. Mar. 6, 1769 | 3 | 19

Hannah, [d. Samuel & Elizabeth], b. Apr. 5, 1695 | 1 | 16

Hannah, m. John **HOUGH**, Jan. 16, 1698/9 | 1 | 24

Hannah, m. David **CROCKER**, Dec. 3, 1722 | 1 | 62

Hannah, d. Samuel & Ann, b. Aug. 23, 1727; d. Oct.
    23, 1736 | 2 | 3

Hannah, d. Ezekiel & Hannah, b. Nov. 27, 1730 | 2 | 4

Han[n]ah, d. Samuel, Jr. & Anne, b. June 12, 1736 | 2 | 6

Hannah, d. Ezekiel, of New London, m. Daniel
    BEEBE, s. Jonathan, of East Haddam, Jan. 10,
    1751 | 2 | 77

Hannah, d. Daniel & Hannah, b. Feb. 14, 1755 | 2 | 77

Hannah, d. William, Jr. & Hannah, b. Aug. 10, 1764 | 3 | 19

Hannah, m. Daniel **COLVER**, Sept. 19, 1764 | 3 | 119

Hannah, w. Daniel, d. Mar. 26, 1768 | 3 | 28

Hannah, d. Zadoc & Sarah, b. Aug. 13, 1768 | 3 | 30

Harriet, of N[ew] London, m. John F. **PAGE**, Apr.
    14, 1834, by Rev. Ebenezer Blake | 4 | 55

Harriet, m. Joseph **EAMES**, Jan. 14, 1839, by Rev.
    Abraham Holway | 4 | 85

Harriet, m. W. G. **CHAPPELL**, b. of [New London],
    Dec. 25, 1849, by Rev. James W. Dennis | 4 | 152

Henry H., of South Hold, L.I., m. Esther P.
    PACKER, of New London, Aug. 31, 1823, by
    Ebenezer Loomis | 4 | 16

Hester, m. John **PIERCE**, Apr. 20, 1839, by Rev.
    Abraham Holway | 4 | 85

Hezekiah, s. William* & Sarah, b. May 1, 1711
    *(Probably Samuel) | 1 | 52

Hezekiah, s. Samuel & Sarah, b. May 1, 1711 | 2 | 19

	Vol.	Page
BEEBE (cont.)		
Hezekiah, m. Hannah **TINKER**, Aug. 25, 1729	2	5
Hezekiah, s. Hezekiah & Hannah, b. Sept. 27, 1730	2	5
Hopestill, twin with Patience, [d. Samuel &		
Elizabeth], b. Feb. 25, 1691/2	1	16
Isaac, s. Ephraim [& Elisabeth], b. Nov. 5, 1779	3	64
Isaiah, s. Jeduthan & Lucretia, b. May 16, 1771	2	63
Isaiah, m. Amy **BROOKS**, Aug. 9, 1794	3	63
Isaiah, of Waterford, m. Pamela **KEENEY**, of New		
London, June 28, 1821, by Tho[ma]s Shaw		
Perkins, J.P.	4	6
Jabez, s. William, Jr. & Jerusha, b. Sept. 18, 1729	2	4
Jabez, s. William, Jr., of New London, m. Eunice		
NEWBURY, d. Nathaniel, of New London,		
Oct. 11, 1747	2	62
Jabez, s. Jabez & Eunice, b. Jan. 18, 1759	2	62
Jabez, of New London, s. William, decd., m. Patience		
BEEBE, of New London, d. Theophilus Beebe,		
decd., June 16, 1799, by David Rogers, Elder	3	2
James, [s. Samuel & Elizabeth], b. Oct. 10, 1701	1	16
James, s. Ezekiel & Hannah, b. Feb. 17, 1740/1	2	6
James H., of New London, m. Mary B. **PERKINS**,		
of Groton, Feb. 13, 1825, by Rev. Abel		
McEwen	4	21
Jared, s. Othniel & Joanna, b. May 28, 1758	2	121
Jason, s. Othniel & Johanna, b. Jan. 16*, 1763		
*(Perhaps Jan. 10)	2	121
Jason, m. Betsey **BEEBE**, Jan. 19, 1784	3	12
Jasper, s. William* & Sarah, b. May. 7, 1718/19		
*(Probably Samuel)	1	52
Jasper, s. Samuel & Sarah, b. Mar. 7, 1718/19	2	19
Jeduthan, s. William & Jerusha, b. Sept. 10, 1734	2	5
Jeduthan, s. William, of New London, m. Lucretia		
DATON, d. of Ephraim, of New London,		
decd., Dec. 27, 1753	2	63
Jeduthan, s. Jeduthan & Lucretia, b. Oct. 27, 1754	2	63
Jemima, d. Ezekiel & Hannah, b. Jan. 25, 1732/3	2	5
Jemima, twin with Jerusha, d. Samuel & Anne, b.		
Dec. 8, 1743	2	84
Jemima, d. Ezekiel, of New London, m. Samuel		
BEEBE, 3d of East Haddam, Apr. 6, 1757	2	49
Jemima, d. Daniel & Hannah, b. July 10, 1761	2	77
Jerusha, d. William, Jr. & Jerusha, b. Mar. 12,		
1725/6; d. July 25, 1730	2	3
Jerusha, d. Ezekiel & Hannah, b. Aug. 19, 1743	2	110
Jerusha, twin with Jemima, d. Samuel & Anne, b.		
Dec. 8, 1743	2	84
Jerusha, d. Jabez & Eunice, b. June 4, 1752	2	62
Jerusha, d. Jeduthan & Lucretia, b. Oct. 3, 1773	2	63
Jerusha, m. James **MILLS**, Feb. 17, 1791	3	129
Jethro, s. Othniel & Joanna, b. June 20, 1752	2	121
Jethro, m. Martha **STEWARD**, Jan. 14, 1779	3	12

	Vol.	Page
BEEBE (cont.)		
Jethro, s. [Jethro & Martha], b. Aug. 6, 1801	3	12
Joanna, m. Caleb **BECKWITH**, [ ], 1788	3	111
Johanna, d. Othniel & Johanna, b. Aug. 18, 1770	2	121
John, s. Jeduthan & Lucretia, b. Aug. 10, 1758	2	63
John, s. [Nathaniel & Grace], b. June 3, 1769	3	96
Johns, [Richard & Elizabeth], b. May 3, 1797	3	171
John, s. [Peter & Nancy], b. Jan. 26, 1803	3	180
Jonathan, s. Joseph & Mehetable, b. Mar. 2, 1709	1	45
Jonathan, s. William & Hannah, b. Sept. 7, 1766	3	19
Jonathan, s. Daniel & Anna, b. Dec. 27, 1778	3	38
Jonathan, m. Elizabeth **GRAVES**, Dec. 26, 1706	1	32
Joseph, s. Joseph & Mehetable, b. Dec. 4, 1707	1	45
Joseph, of New London, m. Azubah **SMITH**, d.		
Josiah Smith, of Lyme, Dec. 27, 1789, in Lyme,		
by Andrew Griswold, J.P.	2	123
Joshua, s. Boanerges & Elisabeth, b. Aug. 6, 1768	3	116
Katharine, d. Jeduthan & Lucretia, b. Apr. 16, 1769	2	63
Laura, m. Nathan **NEWBURY**, b. of New London,		
Jan. 12, 1851, by Rev. Jabez S. Swan	4	162
Laura Ann, m. Charles **BEEBE**, b. of Waterford,		
June 29, 1822, by Thomas W. Tucker, Elder	4	15
Lavinia, m. David **BRANCH**, b. of New London,		
Dec. 31, 1843, by Rev. S. Benton	4	110
Leonard, m. Charlotte **FAIRFIELD**, b. of New		
London, Sept. 14, 1845, by Rev. Abel McEwen	4	121
Lois, m. James E. **MEDCALF**, b. of New London,		
Feb. 22, 1846, by Rev. L. Geo[rge] Leonard	4	124
Love, d. Capt. Abijah, m. Clement **FOSDICK**, Jan.		
6, 1789	3	105
Lucinda, m. Oliver **GEER**, b. of Norwich, Mar. 11,		
1829, by Rev. Abel McEwen	4	36
Lucretia, d. Samuel & Ann, b. Dec. 27, 1732	2	4
Lucretia, d. Samuel of Plumbe Island, m. Thomas		
LESTER, of New London, s. Daniel, late of		
New London, decd. May 30, 1756	3	12
Lucretia, d. Jeduthan & Lucretia, b. Jan. 23, 1761	2	63
Lucretia, d. [Ephraim & Elisabeth], b. Aug. 11, 1789	3	64
Lucretia, of Waterford, m. Samuel **STROUD**, of		
New London, May 19, 1822, by Rev. Abel		
McEwen	4	7
Lydia, d. Samuel & Annah, b. Oct. 9, 1748	2	19
Lydia, d. [Jeduthan], b. Jan. 2, 1776	3	64
Lyman, of Waterford, m. Desire **BECKWITH**, of		
[New London], Nov. 8, 1835, by Rev. Abel		
McEwen	4	63
Marian, of New London, m. Seth **CHAPMAN**, of		
Waterford, Mar. 25, 1833, by Rev. Abel		
McEwen	4	50
Martha, d. [Jethro & Martha], b. Apr. 28, 1780	3	12
Martha, of [New London], m. William **HOLLAND**,		
Aug. 14, 1843, by Rev. S Benton	4	107

	Vol.	Page
BEEBE (cont.)		
Sally, m. George G. **BEEBE**, b. of New London,		
Oct. 27, 1824, by Rev. George W. Fairbanks	4	19
Sally Smith, d. [Eley & Mary], b. July 25, 1808	3	154
Samuel, s. Samuel, of New London, m. Elizabeth		
ROGERS, d. James, Sr., Feb. 9, 1681/2	1	16
Samuel, [s. Samuel & Elizabeth], b. July 16, 1697	1	16
Samuel, s. William, m. Sarah **TUBBS**, May 29, 1710	1	52
Samuel, s. William, m. Sarah **TUBBS**, d. Samuel,		
May 29, 1710	2	19
Samuel, s. Samuel, m. Ann **LESTER**, Jan. 1, 1717/8	2	3
Samuel, s. Samuel & Ann, b. Nov. 21, 1721	2	3
Samuel, m. Annah **HARRIS**, d. Asa, May 14, 1739	2	19
Samuel, 3d., of East Haddam, m. Jemima **BEEBE**, d.		
Ezekiel, of New London, Apr. 6, 1757	2	49
Samuel, s. [William, Jr. & Hannah], b. Sept. 11, 1787	3	19
Samuel H., m. Susan B. **BECKWITH**, of [New		
London], Oct. 28, 1827, by La Roy Sunderland	4	32
Sarah, d. Sam[ue]l & Sarah, b. Mar. 29, 1726	2	3
Sarah, d. Samuel & Sarah, b. Mar. 29, 1726	2	19
Sarah, w. Samuel, d. Nov. 21, 1738	2	19
Sarah, d. Ezekiel & Hannah, b. July 25, 1749	2	110
Sarah, d. Daniel & Hannah, b. July 31, 1763	2	77
Sarah, d. Zadock & Sarah, b. Apr. 27, 1770	3	30
Sarah, d. [Ephraim & Elisabeth], b. Nov. 23, 1787	3	64
Sarah, d. Joab, m. James **JEFFREY**, May 11, 1795	3	190
Sarah, m. Richard **COOPER**, b. of [New London],		
May 17, 1840, by Rev. Abel McEwen	4	89
Sarah, of New London, m. Green **ROGERS**, of		
Waterford, Aug. 30, 1845, by Rev. Jabez S.		
Swan	4	121
Silas, s. Samuel & Ann, b. Nov. 11, 1734	2	5
Stephen, s. Joseph & Mehetable, b. July 13, 1714	1	45
Stephen, m. Mary **LEACH**, Nov. 16, 1716	2	4
Stephen, s. Samuel & Sarah, b. Dec. 20, 1728	2	4
Stephen, s. Samuel & Sarah, b. Dec. 20, 1728	2	19
Susan, d. [David & Hannah], b. Nov. 16, 1803	3	215
Tathyer, d. Samuel, m. George **NEWCOMBE**, Mar.		
1, 1799	3	52
Temperance, d. Jeduthan & Lucretia, b. Mar. 11,		
1763	2	63
Theophilus, s. Sam[ue]l & Ann, b. Jan. 31, 1730/1	2	4
William, Jr., m. Jerusha **ROGERS**, June 9, 1720	2	3
William, s. William & Jerusha, b. Sept. 19, 1731	2	4
William, 3d, s. William, 2d, of New London, m.		
Rachel **SMITH**, d. Mat[t]hew, of Lyme, Apr.		
16, 1749	2	72
William, s. Jabez & Eunice, b. Aug. 4, 1754	2	62
William, Jr., s. William, m. Hannah **LESTER**, d.		
Jonathan, all of New London, May 7, 1761	3	19
William, s. William, Jr. & Hannah, b. Aug. 4, 1762	3	19

	Vol.	Page
BEEBE (cont.)		
William C., m. Mary E. **PACHEY**, b. of Waterford,		
Aug. 8, 1850, by Rev. T. Edwards	4	154
William Davis, s. [Moses & Mary], b. Aug. 3, 1803	3	141
William Rogers, s. [Paul & Mary], b. Mar. 31, 1792	3	123
Zadock, s. Ezekiel & Hannah, b. Nov. 29, 1745	2	110
Zadock, m. Sarah **LEACH**, Dec. 11, 1764	3	30
Zadock, s. Zadock & Sarah, b. June 30, 1772	3	30
Zerviah, d. Daniel & Hannah, b. Apr. 5, 1757	2	77
BEENEY, Stephen, of Sag Harbor, N.Y., m. Harriet A.		
JEROME, of [New London], Aug. 3, 1851, by		
Rev. J. M. Eaton	4	164
BEETS, BEETZ, Fanny, of New London, m. Peter		
STOUT, of Key West, Florida, July 30, 1837,		
by Rev. Robert A. Hallam	4	72
John, m. Fanny **SMITH**, b. of New London, Dec. 3,		
1826 by Rev. Bethel Judd	4	28
BELCHER, Ann W., d. [Nathan & Ann P.], b. Dec. 28,		
1842	3	293
Charles, of St. Louis, Mo., m. Jane **WILSON**,		
of [New London], Oct. 29, 1849, by Rev. Abel		
McEwen	4	147
Nathan, m. Ann P. **WILSON**, Oct. 20, 1841	3	293
Nathan, m. Ann P. **WILSON**, b. of [New London],		
Oct. 20, 1841, by Rev. Abel McEwen	4	97
William, s. [Nathan & Ann P.], b. Feb. 27, 1845	3	293
BELDEN, BELDING, Daniel, s. Samuel & Sarah, b. Dec.		
23, 1769	3	13
Daniel, s. [Samuel & Sarah], b. Dec. 15, 1789	3	13
Esther, d. [Samuel & Sarah], b. June 7, 1775; d. Nov.		
[ ], 1775	3	13
Hiluh Ann, m. John **GRACE**, Dec. 22, 1834	3	155
Hilah Ann, m. John **GRACE**, b. of [New London],		
Dec. 22, 1834, by Rev. Abel McEwen	4	59
Margarett, d. Samuel & Sarah, b. Oct. 30, 1751	3	13
Mary, d. Samuel & Sarah, b. Dec. 17, 1771	3	13
Matilda, m. Giles **DART**, b. of New London, July 5,		
1837, by Rev. Daniel Webb	4	73
Mehetabel, d. Samuel & Sarah, b. Mar. 11, 1763	3	13
Mehetabel, d. [Samuel & Sarah], d. Jan. 20, 1801	3	13
Nathan, s. Ste[phe]n & Obedience, b. Nov. 27,		
1736	2	6
Nathaniel, s. Samuel & Sarah, b. June 15, 1766	3	13
Richard, s. [Samuel & Sarah], b. Sept. 11, 1773	3	13
Samuel, m. Sarah **COIT**, d. Nathaniel, all of New		
London, June 17, 1759	3	13
Sam[ue]l, s. Samuel & Sarah, b. Dec. 16, 1764	3	13
Samuel, s. Samuel & Sarah, d. Jan. 8, 1767	3	13
Samuel, s. Samuel & Sarah, b. May 3, 1768	3	13
Samuel, had servant Susannah, b. Jan. 28, 1781	3	13
Sarah, d. Samuel & Sarah, b. Mar. 28, 1760; d. Nov.		
26, 1776	3	13

	Vol.	Page

BELDEN, BELDING (cont.)

    Sarah, d. [Samuel & Sarah], b. Dec. 27, 1776   3   13

BELL, Sarah, m. Abel **BINGHAM**, of East Haddam, Dec.

    9, 1850, by Rev. James W. Dennis   4   157

BELLOWS, Dexter, m. Sarah A. **DARROW**, Apr. 14,

    1841, by H. R. Knapp   4   94

    George Lyman, of Ogdensburg, N.Y., m. Charlotte

    Louisa **STODDARD**, of New London, Dec. 10,

    1829, by Rev. Abel McEwen   4   38

BEMENT, Asa B., of Evansville, Ind., m Ann P. **LAW**, of

    [New London], Oct. 26, 1847, by Rev. Abel

    McEwen   4   135

BENJAMIN, George D., of St. Helena, m. Elsie **HULL**,

    of [New London], Apr. 23, 1851, by Rev. T.

    Edwards   4   161

    Mary, of Preston, m. George W. **CRANDALL**, of

    [New London], July 19, 1852, by Rev. Thomas

    Ely   4   171

    William P., m. Mary L. **TURNER**, July 20, 1834, by

    Rev. Alvan Ackley   4   56

BENNET[T], BENETT, Cornelius W. B., of Providence,

    R.I., m. Emely R. **DABOLL**, of [New London],

    May 4, 1840, by John Lov[e]joy   4   90

    Micahel, m. Eliza **KING**, May 2, 1852, by Rev. J.

    Stokes. Witnesses: Peter McCaffery, Catharine

    King   4   170

    Peter R., of New York City, m. Maria

    SALTONSTALL, of New London, Aug. 17,

    1835, by Rev. Robert A. Hallam   4   61

    Sarah, m. Mathias **RYLY**, July 8, 1731   2   94

    -----, w. James, d. May 7, [1690]   1   20

BENSON, Sarah Ann, of London, England, m. Milo

    DAVIS, of Montville, Oct. 4, 1839, by James

    H. Lanman, J.P.   4   87

BENTLEY, BENTLY, Anna, d. Elisha & Sarah, b. Jan.

    30, 1754   2   11

    Benjamin, m. Mary **RYON**, d. James, Mar. 28, 1798   3   187

    Charles A., m. Harriet N. **RIXFORD**, b. of New

    London, July 8, 1846, by Rev. Tryon Edwards   4   127

    James, s. [Benjamin & Mary], b. Sept. 22, 1807   3   187

    John, s. [Benjamin & Mary], b. Apr. 21, 1805   3   187

    Marcy, d. [Benjamin & Mary], b. Jan. 4, 1810   3   187

    Mary, m. John **CHAMPLAIN**, Oct. 15, 1748   2   96

    Mary, d. [Benjamin & Mary], b. Dec. 13, 1802   3   187

    William, s. [Benjamin & Mary], b. Sept. 26, 1801   3   187

    William, m. Hannah **PHILLIPS**, Dec. 21, 1823, by

    Rev. Thomas W. Tucker   4   17

BENTON, Henry, of Hartford, m. Lucy Ann P. **STARR**,

    of New London, May 3, 1827, by Rev. Abel

    McEwen   4   30

BEQUET, James, s. Mat[t]hew & Eliza, b. June 1, [1671]   1   7

    Jona, s. Mat[t]hew & Elizabeth, b. Dec. 27, [1673]   1   9

	Vol.	Page
BEQUET (cont.)		
Prudence, d. Mat[t]hew & Elizabeth, b. Aug. 22, [1676]	1	11
BERRY, William S., m. Emily L. **CRANDALL**, Feb. 4, 1838, by Rev. Francis Darrow	4	70
BETTY, Rachel, d. of Mrs., d. July 8, [1689], ae 15 y.	1	69
BIBER, Nathaniel, s. John & Johanna, b. Feb. 6, 1719/20	1	57
BICKNELL, Adelaide, of [New London], m. Thomas G. **ALLEN**, of Nashville, Tenn., Dec. 1, 1833, by Daniel Wildman	4	52
BILL, BILLS, Bazilla, of New York, m. Harriet **CHAPMAN**, of New London, Jan. 8, 1832, by Rev. Daniel Wildman	4	45
Christopher, m. Mary **SKINNER**, b. of [New London], Feb. 6, 1827, by Rob[er]t Bowzer	4	29
Daniel, s. Samuel & Martha, b. Dec. 1, 1755	2	28
David, s. Samuel, Jr. & Martha, b. Oct. 2, 1751	2	28
Elizabeth, d. Samuel, Jr. & Martha, b. Oct. 17, 1749; d. Apr. 3, 1756	2	28
Elisabeth, m. Nathaniel **DICKINSON**, Nov. 22, 1778	3	68
John, s. Samuel, Jr. & Martha, b. Apr. 7, 1741; d. Nov. 27, 1744	2	28
John, s. Samuel, Jr. & Martha, b. Mar. 13, 1747; d. June 19, 1756	2	28
John, s. Samuel, Jr. & Martha, b. Sept. 14, 1759	2	28
Marcy, d. Samuel & Hannah, m. Daton **SMITH**, May 11, 1746	2	109
Margaret, d. Philip, Jr., d. Aug. 12, [1689], ae 3 y.	1	69
Martha, d. July 21, 1785	3	88
Mary, d. Samuel, Jr. & Martha, b. Aug. 5, 1742	2	28
Mary, m. John **HEMPSTE[A]D**, Jr., Nov. 1, 1767	3	88
Mercy, of New London, d. James **CHAPMAN**, of New London, m. Jonathan **BROOKS**, of New London, s. Nathan, of Weborn, Mass., Dec. 3, 1766	3	53
Phillip, Sr., d. July 8, [1689]	1	69
Rebecca D., m. Thomas A. **GREEN**, b. of Windham, Ct., Apr. 22, 1832, by Chester Tilden	4	46
Samuel, Jr., s. Sam[ue]l, of New London, m. Martha **WHEELER**, d. John, of East Hampton, N.Y., May 10, 1737	2	28
Samuel, s. Sam[ue]l, Jr. & Martha, b. Apr. 12, 1738	2	28
Samuel, d. Mar. 5, 1779	3	88
Samuel P., m. Mary J. **HOLT**, b. of M[as]s., Sept. 6, 1846, by Rev. Jabez S. Swan	4	127
BILLINGS, Abigail, d. Capt. Benj[amin] & Abigail, b. Sept. 3, 1751	2	121
Abigail, d. Capt. Benj[amin] & Abigail, m. John **SPENCER**, of Island of Bermudas, Sept. 8, 1779	2	121

	Vol.	Page
BILLINGS (cont.)		
Ann, m. Coddington **BILLINGS**, July 18, 1819, in Stonington, by Rev. Ira Hart. She was his 2d wife.	3	290
Ann, d. Coddington & Ann, b. May 14, 1821, at Stonington	3	290
Ann, of [New London], m. Calvin G. **WILLIAMS**, of Stonington, Oct. 25, 1841, by Rev. Abel McEwen	4	96
Benjamin, m. Lament **BLAKE**, Nov. 16, 1762	2	122
Benjamin, s. [Benjamin & Lament], b. Aug. 28, 1763	2	122
Benjamin, Sr., d. Jan. 15, 1780	2	122
Benjamin, Jr., [s. Benjamin & Lament], d. July 22, 1784	2	122
Benjamin, s. [William & Mary], b. Jan. 23, 1786	2	121
Coddington, m. his 2d w. Ann **BILLINGS**, July 18, 1819, in Stonington, by Rev. Ira Hart	3	290
Coddington, s. Coddington & Ann, b. Feb. 8, 1834	3	290
Elisabeth, m. Richard **STROUD**, Nov. 25, 1765	3	101
Elizabeth, d. [Benjamin & Lament], b. May 23, 1771	2	122
Elizabeth, m. George **CHAPMAN**, Nov. 13, 1791	3	175
Eunice W., of New London, m. Ralph **FARNSWORTH**, of Norwich, Nov. 25, 1828, by Rev. Abel McEwen	4	36
Frances, d. [Benjamin & Lament], b. Mar. 18, 1773	2	122
Hannah, m. Henry E. **JACOBS**, b. of [New London], Feb. 4, 1849, by Rev. Abel McEwen	4	145
Harriet, 2d d. Coddington & Ann, b. June 16, 1832	3	290
James, m. Susan **STEB[B]INS**, Sept. 22, 1835, by Rev. Alvan Ackley	4	62
Mary, d. [Benjamin & Lament], b. Oct. 14, 1765	2	122
Mary, m. William **HAMILTON**, Oct. 19, 1783	2	121
Prudence, d. [Benjamin & Lament], b. May 28, 1779	2	122
Prudance, m. George **CHAPMAN**, Jan. 29, 1804	3	175
Rebecah, d. [Benjamin & Lament], b. Apr. 21, 1776	2	122
Sally, [d. Benjamin & Lament], d. Nov. 17, 1786	2	122
Sarah, d. [Benjamin & Lament], b. Dec. 25, 1768	2	122
Zip[p]orah, m. Thomas **STRICKLAIN**, Mar. 16, 1714	1	62
BINDLOSS, Jane Palmer, of Liverpool, England, m. Leander **KNIGHT**, of New London, Apr. 9, 1843, by L. Covell	4	101
Jane Palmer, of Liverpool, England, m. Leander **KNIGHT**, of New London, Apr. 9, 1843, by Rev. Lemuel Covel	3	295
Margaret Ann, m. George **ELLIOTT**, b. of [New London], [Aug.] 7, 1848, by Rev. Robert A. Hallam	4	141
Margaret Ann, of Liverpool, England, m. George **ELLIOTT**, of New London, Aug. 9, 1848, by Rev. Robert A. Hallam	3	296

	Vol.	Page
BINDLOSS (cont.)		
Mary, m. Joseph **SCROGGIE**, b. of [New London],		
Dec. 6, 1849, by Rev. Robert A. Hallam	4	151
BINGHAM, Abel, of East Haddam. m Sarah **BELL**, Dec.		
9, 1850, by Rev. James W. Dennis	4	157
Charles Mortimer, s. [Nathan & Elizabeth], b. Feb.		
22, 1804	3	203
George Edwin, s. [Nathan & Elizabeth], b. Apr. 8,		
1806	3	203
Lucy M., of East Haddam, m. William C. **SEGUR**,		
of N[ew] London, July 12, 1846, by Rev. L.		
Geo[rge] Leonard	4	129
Milinda, d. Elijah, m. Thomas H. **RAWSON**, Feb.		
19, 1792	3	149
Nathan, m. Elizabeth **LEE**, d. Abner, of Lyme, July		
29, 1801	3	203
Silas, s. [Nathan & Elizabeth], b. May 23, 1802	3	203
BIRCH, [see also **BURCH**], Jenney, m. George		
LOWDEN, free negroes, Aug. 6, 1803	3	18
Nancy, d. [William & Jinney, free negroes], b. Mar.		
28, 1786	3	18
Nancy, m. Richard Easton **FREEMAN**, people of		
color, Mar. 25, 1802	3	46
Silve, d. [William & Jinney, free negroes], b. May 9,		
1785	3	18
BIRD, Mary Frances, m. J. Franklin **WILLIS**, Sept. 1,		
1847, by Rev. Tho[ma]s Greenwood	4	136
BISHOP, Ann, d. John, Jr. & Mary, b. Jan. 31, 1754	2	91
Anna, d. Eleazer & Susannah, b. Aug. 4, 1754	3	43
Anna, d. [Jonathan & Anna], b. June 2 1780	3	122
Catharine D., m. Gilbert **BISHOP**, b. of New		
London, Dec. 24, 1845, by Rev. L. Geo[rge]		
Leonard	4	123
Charles, s. John, Jr. & Mary, b. Dec. 3, 1758	2	91
Charles, of New London, m. Cynthia **DAVISON**, of		
Norwich, Nov. 12, 1837, by Rev. Alvan Ackley	4	80
Chester R., of Danielsonville, s. Gurdon & Lucy, of		
Chesterfield, m. Ellen C. **HOLT**, d. of the late		
Robert & Ann of [New London], Sept. 6, 1847,		
by Tryon Edwards, Minister	4	134
Ebenezer, m. Sally **PIERPOINT**, May 9, 1776	3	113
Ebenezer, s [Ebenezer & Sally], b. Mar. 3, 1780	3	113
Ebenezer, d. Jan. 3, 1782	3	113
Eleazer, m. Sarah **DART**, June 22, 1704	1	29
Eleazer, Jr., s. Eleazer, b. Apr. 11, 1727; m. Susannah		
WHIPPLE, d. Silas, Apr. 15, 1750	3	43
Eleazer, s. Eleazer & Susannah, b. June 15, 1766	3	43
George Dolbear, s. Eleazer & Susannah, b. Aug. 7,		
1770	3	43
Gilbert, m. Catharine D. **BISHOP**, b. of New		
London, Dec. 24, 1845, by Rev. L. Geo[rge]		
Leonard	4	123

	Vol.	Page
BOILING, Ann, of Ireland, m. Frederick **ROATH**, of Wurtemburg, Germany, Feb. 4, 1849, by Rev. Edwin R. Warren	4	148
BOLLES, BOLLS, Aaron, s. [Isaiah & Elizabeth], b. Feb. 17, 1786	3	143
Abigail, d. Isaiah & Lydia, b. Aug. 18, 1741	2	86
Alpheas, s. Joshua & Jaonna, b. Oct. 4, 1752	2	42
Amos, s. Thomas & Mary, b. May 15, 1739	2	68
Andrew, s. [John & Betsey], b Apr. 24, 1796	3	153
Ann Eliza, m. Allen **RICHARDS**, b. of [New London], June 11, 1848, by Rev. M. P. Alderman	4	139
Asa, s. Enoch & Hannah, b. Dec. 26, 1746	2	47
Avery, s. [John & Betsey], b. Dec. 14, 1792; d. Jan. 11, 1793	3	153
Avery, s. [John & Betsey], b. Feb. 16, 1794	3	153
Bathsheba, d. Isaiah & Lydia, b. Feb. 24, 1743; d. July 18, 1747	2	86
Bathsheba, d. Isaiah & Lydia, b. Apr. 20, 1751; d. Aug. 30, 1753	2	86
Benjamin F., m. Elizabeth C. **HOBRON**, Mar. 18, 1838, by Rev. James M. Macdonald	4	76
Betty, m. Ebenezer **MINER**, of New London, s. Clement, Aug. 23, 1750	2	45
Calvin, s. [Samuel & Margaret], b. Dec. 18, 1777	3	98
Charles, m. Mary Ann **GALE**, b. of [New London], Nov. 18, 1823, by Rev. Thomas W. Tucker	4	17
Charles, m. Ann M. **DERTIN**, b. of New London, Mar. 15, 1848, by Rev. Abel McEwen	4	138
Charles Owen, s. [Enoch & Nancy], b. Jan. 13, 1807	3	201
Christian, d. John & Elizabeth, b. Mar. 5, 1738/9	2	5
Dan, s. [Isaiah & Elizabeth], b. Apr. 1, 1782; d. Aug. 1, 1784	3	143
Daniel, s. Tho[ma]s & Mary, b. May 4, 1736	2	68
David, s. Enoch & Hannah, b. Jan. 14, 1743	2	47
Delight Rogers, [d. Hezekiah & Anna], b. Sept. 13, 1796; d. Dec. 2, 1825 at Hampton	3	303
Ebenezer, s. John & Sarah, b. July 12, 1708	1	41
Ebenezer, s. John, of New London, m. Mary **ROGERS**, d. John, of New London, Nov. 29, 1744	2	114
Ebenezer, s. Joshua & Joanna, b. July 13, 1764	2	43
Edgcombe, s. Joseph, 3d, & Lydia, b. July 23, 1767	3	54
Elijah, twin with Elisha, s. Joshua & Joanna, b. Oct. 15, 1754	2	42
Elijah, of Montville, m. Nancy **CORNELL**, of [New London], Oct. 15, 1827, by Rev. Robert Bowzer	4	32
Elijah, Jr., of Waterford, m. Abby **SWAINEY**, of Lyme, July 8, 1832, by Rev. Abel McEwen	4	47
Elisha, twin with Elijah, s. Joshua & Joanna, b. Oct. 15, 1754	2	42
Eliza, [d. Hezekiah & Anna], b. Nov. 25, 1791	3	303

	Vol.	Page
BOLLES, BOLLS (cont.)		
Elisabeth, d. John & Eliz[abeth], b. Mar 5, 1742/3	2	6
Elisabeth, m. John **ROGERS**, s. Sam[ue]l, Apr. 24,		
1763, by Pygan Adams, Esq.	3	64
Elizabeth, d. [Samuel & Margaret], b. Sept. 5, 1772;		
d. Nov. 12, 1774	3	98
Elizabeth, d. [Samuel & Margaret], b. Feb. 27, 1776	3	98
Elizabeth, d. [Isaiah & Elizabeth], b. Feb. 22, 1784	3	143
Elisabeth, b. May 29, 1792; m. David **ADAMS**, Jr.,		
Dec. 29, 1812	3	206
Elizabeth R., m. Gains P. **POMEROY**, b. of [New		
London], Dec. 5, 1848, by Rev. Abel McEwen	4	143
Ellen E., of New London, m. Samuel		
McCLINTOCK, of New York, Mar. 1, 1829,		
by Rev. Abel McEwen	4	35
Emeline, of New London, m. Robert H. **SMITH**, of		
Portland, Me., Mar. 11, 1832, by Rev. Abel		
McEwen	4	45
Enoch, s. John & Sarah, b. Oct. 20, 1715	1	49
Enoch, s. John & Sarah, b. Oct. 20, 1715	2	5
Enoch, s. John, m. Hannah **MOOR[E]**, d. Joshua, b.		
of New London, Nov. 2, 1738	2	47
Enoch, s. Enoch & Hannah, b. July 19, 1739	2	47
Enoch, s. [Isaiah & Elizabeth], b. Mar. 11, 1778	3	143
Enoch, m. Nancy **OWEN**, d. John, June 16, 1802	3	201
Ephraim, s. [Isaiah & Elizabeth], b. Jan. 14, 1780	3	143
Esther, d. Joseph, 3d, & Lydia, b. Mar. 17, 1762	3	54
Ezra, s. Joshua & Joanna, b. June 18, 1744	2	42
Fanny, d. [Joseph & Lydia], b. Feb. 4, 1779	3	54
Fanny, d. [Isaiah & Elizabeth], b. Feb. 26, 1790	3	143
Francis, s. [Samuel & Margaret], b. Aug. 12 ,1783	3	98
Francis E., of Livonia, N.Y., m. William		
HUNTLEY, of Waterford, Oct. 5, 1846, by		
Rev. Abel McEwen	4	128
Gilbert, s. Joseph, 3d, & Lydia, b. Sept. 22, 1769	3	54
Giles, s. [Samuel & Margaret], b. Nov. 27, 1781	3	98
Giles, s. [Samuel & Margaret], d. Sept. 26, 1787	3	98
Hannah, m. Jeremiah **ROGERS**, Dec. 11, 1791	3	140
Hezekiah, twin with Jeremiah, s. Joshua & Joanna, b.		
Dec. 15, 1759	2	43
Hezekiah, s. Joshua Bolles & Joanna **WILLIAMS**,		
m. Anna **ROGERS**, d. John Rogers & Delight		
GREENE, Feb. 1, 1791	3	303
Isaac, s. [Stephen & Sukey], b. Oct. 9, 1787	3	95
Isaiah, s. John, m. Lydia **POWERS**, d. of Joseph, all		
of New London, [ ], 1735	2	86
Isaiah, s. Enoch & Hannah, b. May 26, 1754, new		
style	2	47
Isaiah, s. Joseph, 3d, & Lydia, b. Oct. 30, 1763	3	54
Isa[i]ah, m. Elizabeth **TILLASON**, d. Abraham		
Tillason, of Hebron, July 1, 1776	3	143
Isaiah, s. [Enoch & Nancy], b. June 26, 1804	3	201

	Vol.	Page

BOLLES, BOLLS (cont.)

Jeremiah, twin with Hezekiah, s. Joshua & Joanna, b.
Dec. 15, 1759   2   43

Jesse, s. Enoch & Hannah, b. Mar. 31, 1749   2   47

Joanna, d. Tho[ma]s & Mary, b. Feb. 7, 1733   2   68

Joanna Williams, [d. Hezekiah & Anna], b. Jan. 25,
1805; d. Jan. 11, 1841   3   303

John, m. Sarah **EDGECOMB**, July 3, 1699   1   25

John, m. Sarah **EDGECOMB**, July 3, 1699   1   41

John, s. John & Sarah, b. Oct. 22, 1702   1   41

John, Jr., s. John, m. Lydia **STARR**, d. Ben[jamin],
July 20, 1727   2   17

John, Jr., m. Lydia **STAR[R]**, July 20, 1727   2   4

John, s. John & Lydia, b. July 8, 1728   2   4

John, s. John & Lydia, b. July 8, 1728   2   17

John, of New London, m. Elizabeth **WOOD**, of
Groton, May 26, 1736, at her father's house in
Groton, by Joshua Hempstead, J.P.   2   5

John, s. Enoch & Hannah, b. Feb. 3 ,1752   2   47

John, m. Merriam **DILLAMORE**, July 26, 1758   2   18

John, s. [Samuel & Margaret], b. Aug. 17, 1767   3   98

John, s. Samuel, m. Betsey **AVERY**, of Groton, d.
Jasper Avery, Apr. 1, 1792   3   153

John, s. [Isaiah & Elizabeth], b. June 30, 1795; d. Jan.
3, 1796   3   143

John Hempstead, s. [John Rogers & Mary], b. Jan.
13, 1854   3   303

John Rogers, [s. Hezekiah & Anna], b. Aug. 13,
1810; m. Mary **HEMPSTEAD**, d. Joshua, May
30, 1839   3   303

Jonathan, s. Enoch & Hannah, b. Oct. 27, 1740; d.
[   ]   2   47

Jonathan, s. Enoch & Hannah, b. Nov. 1, 1744   2   47

Joseph, s. John & Sarah, b. Mar. 1, 1701   1   41

Joseph, s. Jos[eph] & Martha, b. 17 of 2d month,
1732   2   114

Joseph, s. Isaiah & Lydia, b. Mar. 24, 1736   2   86

Joseph, Jr., s. Joseph, of New London, m. Deborah
ROGERS, d. of Samuel, of New London, Dec.
30, 1753   2   107

Joseph, m. Nancy **RICE**, d. Thomas, Aug. 10, 1804   3   214

Joshua, s. John & Sarah, b. Aug. 5, 1717; d. Sept. 19,
1800   1   49

Joshua, s. John & Sarah, b. Aug. 5, 1717   2   5

Joshua, s. Joshua & Joanna, b. Dec. 26, 1746   2   42

Joshua, [s. Hezekiah & Anna], b. Jan. 21 ,1808; d.
May 22, 1857   3   303

Joshua, m. S. **HARRIS**, b. of harbour's mouth, New
London, Jan. 12, 1839, by Rev. C. C. Williams   4   82

Josiah, s. John & Sarah, b. Oct. 11, [1715]   1   44

Lucy, d. Tho[ma]s & Mary, b. Oct. 1, 1737   2   68

Lydia, d. Jos[eph], 3d, & Lydia, b. July 29, 1765   3   54

	Vol.	Page
BOLLES, BOLLS (cont.)		
Margaret, d. Isaiah & Lydia, b. Feb. 12, 1738	2	86
Margaret, d. Jos[eph], 3d, & Lydia, b. Apr. 3, 1772	3	54
Margaret, d. [Samuel & Margaret], b. Mar. 27, 1774	3	98
Mariah, d. [John & Betsey], b. Sept. 4, 1798	3	153
Martha, d. Joseph & Martha, b. 31 of 10th month, 1738	2	114
Martin, s. [Samuel & Margaret], b. Nov. 21, 1770	3	98
Mary, d. John & Elizabeth, b. Apr. 11, 1737	2	5
Mary, d. Thomas & Mary, b. June 1, 1741	2	68
Mary, d. Ebenezer & Mary, b. Oct. 7, 1745	2	114
Mary, w. Ebenezer, d. Nov. 9, 1745	2	114
Mary, d. Joshua & Joanna, b. July 19, 1758	2	43
Mary, d. Ebenezer, late of New London, decd., m. Joseph **HURLBUT**, Jr., s. Capt. Jos[eph], of New London, July [ ], 1762	3	46
Mary, d. Joseph & Lydia, b. Sept. 27, 1776. She was born with her right ear "cropt"	3	54
Mary, d. [Samuel & Margaret], b. Mar. 22, 1788	3	98
Mary Ann, m. Levi **CASE**, Apr. 13, 1825	3	266
Mary Ann, m. Levi **CASE**, b. of New London, Apr. 13, 1825, by Rev. Abel McEwen	4	22
Mary Ann, m. Slvanus H. **GIBSON**, July 14, 1840	3	302
Mary Ann, m. Sylvanus H. **GIBSON**, b. of [New London], July 14, 1840, by Rev. Abel McEwen	4	91
Mary Lydia, d. [John Rogers & Mary], b. June 13, 1840	3	303
Nancey, d. [Isaiah & Elizabeth], b. June 30, 1792	3	143
Nathan, s. Enoch & Hannah, b. Jan. 7, 1757	2	48
Nathan, s. [Isaiah & Elizabeth], b. Feb. 17, 1786	3	143
Patience, d. John & Sarah, b. Nov. 26, 1709	1	41
Patience, m. Thomas **TURNER**, Nov. 23, 1727	2	112
Patience, d. John & Lydia, b. Jan. 9, 1734/5	2	18
Patience, of New London, d. John, Jr., of New London, m. Stephen **CLAY**, of Boston, s. Jonas, of Boston, Jan. 6, 1754	2	29
Patience, twin with Zipporah, d. Joshua & Joanna, b. June 19, 1762	2	43
Ralph, s. [Isaiah & Elizabeth], b. Mar. 7, 1777	3	143
Rebecca, d. [Samuel & Margaret], b. Mar. 16, 1769	3	98
Richard, s. Enoch & Hannah, b. Apr. 14, 1759	2	48
Samuell, s. John & Sarah, b. Apr. 22, 1707	1	41
Samuel, s. John & Lydia, b. Dec. 29, 1730; d. Jan. 30, 1766	2	17
Samuel, s. Joshua & Joanna, b. Dec. 7, 1740	2	42
Samuel, s. John & Eliz[abeth], b. 10th day of 3rd month, 1744	2	6
Samuel, m. Margaret **MOOR[E]**, Dec. 18, 1766	3	98
Samuel, s. [Samuel & Margaret], b. June 18, 1785	3	98
Sarah, d. Tho[ma]s & Mary, b. Feb. 4, 1729	2	68
Sarah, d. Joseph & Martha, b. 31 of 10th month, 1736	2	114
Sarah, d. Joshua & Joanna, b. July 30, 1742	2	42

	Vol.	Page

BRANDEGEE (cont.)

Mary I., of New London, m. Theodore T. **WOOD**, of
Morristown, N.J., Oct. 5, 1843, by Rev. Robert
A. Hallam | 4 | 107

BRAYTON, [see under **BRAITON**] | 4 | 150

BRENNAN, Ann, m. John **MALAY**, Oct. 28, 1849, by
Rev. William Logan | 4 | 150

Patrick, m. Mary **ARMSTRONG**, b. of New
London, Jan. 7, 1849, by Rev. Robert A.
Hallam | 4 | 144

BREWSTER, Albert, m. Mary **BEEBE**, b. of [New
London], Oct. 1, 1848, by Rev. M. P. Alderman | 4 | 142

Charles A., of Stonington, m. Mary E. **FORSYTH**,
of New London, Nov. 23, 1831, by Rev. Abel
McEwen | 4 | 44

Grace, d. of Jonathan & Grace, of New London, m.
Danyell **WITHERELL**, s. William, of
Scituate, New England, Aug. 4, [1659] | 1 | 3

Hannah, d. Jon[atha]n, m. Samuel **STARR**, Dec. 23,
[1664] | 1 | 4

John, m. Ann Eliza **NICHOLS**, b. of Norwich, Oct.
5, 1844, by Rev. Jabez S. Swan | 4 | 114

BRICKLEY, William, m. Mary **MAID**, May 21, 1846, by
Rev. John Brady | 4 | 126

BRIGGS, Charles, m. Eliza **MILLER**, May 7, 1822, by
Rev. Francis Darrow | 4 | 8

Fanny, d. [William & Fanny], b. Aug. 10, 1783 | 3 | 76

Jerome, s. [William & Fanny], b. Sept. 11, 1787 | 3 | 76

Phebe, m. Tho[ma]s **CROCKER**, of New London,
Sept. 3, 1741 | 2 | 12

Phebe Ann, m. W[illia]m W. **KINGLSEY**, b. of New
London, June 12, 1845, by Rev. Tho[ma]s J.
Greenwood | 4 | 124

Philip, of Colchester, m. Paulina Louisa **GILLETT**,
of [New London], Sept. 4, 1848, by Rev. T.
Edwards | 4 | 141

Sally, d. William, m. Henry **DENNIS**, June 21, 1807 | 3 | 234

William, m. Fanny **SMITH**, Feb. 14, 1782 | 3 | 76

William, s. [William & Fanny], b. Sept. 2, 1785 | 3 | 76

BRISTOL, Louis, s. William & Sarah, m. Mary D.
CLEAVELAND, d. William P. & Mary, May
29, 1844, at Springfield, Mass. | 3 | 297

Louis Bacon, s. [Louis & Mary D.], b. Dec. 30, 1847 | 3 | 297

William Cleaveland, s. [Louis & Mary D.], b. Mar.
10, 1845 | 3 | 297

BROCKFIELD, [see under **BROOKFIELD**]

BROCKWAY, Abigail, d. Rich[ar]d, of Lyme, m.
Benjamin **FOX**, Jr., of New London, s. of
Benjamin, Nov. 7, 1745 | 2 | 18

Horace B., m. Janette C. **GREENFIELD**, b. of
Lyme, Nov. 21, 1847, by Rev. L. G. Leonard | 4 | 138

	Vol.	Page
BROCKWAY (cont.)		
Laura A. of Lyme, m. George **BARTHOLOMEW**, of New London, Nov. 11, 1832, by Rev. Abel McEwen	4	48
Mary Ann, m. Jeremiah **SHAW**, b. of New London, Dec. 28, 1845, by Rev. L. Geo[rge] Leonard	4	123
BRODERICK, Francis, m. Margaret **DOLAN**, Nov. 29, 1851, by Rev. J. Stokes. Witnesses: Patrick Greeley, Bridget Kelley	4	169
BROMEFIELD, BROMSFIELD, Hannah, m. Richard **WYAT[T]**, Dec. 28, 1704	1	30
John, m. Hannah **PARKER**, Jan. 16, 1698/9	1	24
BRONNER, Eliza, m George Bernard **KEHR**, b. of Norwich, Aug. 18 1839, by Rev. Robert A. Hallam	4	86
BROOKFIELD, BROCKFIELD, Charles, s. William & Katharine, b. July 27, 1726	2	6
Charles, s. William & Katharine, b. July 27, 1726	2	29
Elizabeth, d. William & Katharine, b. July 31, 1728	2	29
Stephen, s. William & Katharine, b. Aug. 30, 1724	2	6
Stephen, s. William & Katharine, b. Aug. 30, 1724	2	29
Uriah, s. William & Katharine, b. May 7, 1722	1	60
Uriah, s. William & Katharine, b. May 7, 1722	2	6
Uriah, s. William & Katharine, b. May 7, 1722	2	29
William, m. Katharine **ROGERS**, Apr. 10, 1720	1	60
William, s. William, of Elizabethtown, in the Province of Jerseys, m. Katharine **ROGERS**, d. Jonathan, of New London, Apr. 15, 1720	2	29
BROOKS, Abby, d. Thaddeus, m. Amos **LEEDS**, Apr. 23, 1797	3	175
Abby Leeds, d. [Hubbel & Lydia], b. Nov. 21, 1801	3	170
Abigail, d. [Thaddeus & Abigail], b. Nov. 26, 1778	3	73
Aliss, d. Josiah & Bathsua, b. Oct. 16, 1745	2	113
Aliss, m. William **MELOY**, Aug. 1, 1779	3	53
Alice, m. John **NORCUTT**, Aug. 8, 1782	3	136
Amy, d. William & Amy, b. Apr. 10, 1762	3	125
Amy, m. Isaac **CROCKER**, July 3, 1763	3	107
Amy, d. [Stephen & Ede], b. May 25, 1776	3	63
Amy, m. Isaiah **BEEBE**, Aug. 9, 1794	3	63
Anna, d. Samuel & Mary, b. Jan. 16, 1754, old style	3	6
Anna, m. Noah **BECKWITH**, July 8, 1773	3	109
Anna, m. John **SKINNER**, s. Elizabeth, Feb. 3, 1800	3	199
Bathshua, d. Josiah & Bathshua, b. Jan. 19, 1743/4	2	113
Benj[amin], s. Josiah & Bathshua, b. Sept. 3, 1740	2	113
Betsey, d. [Jeremiah & Abigail], b. Oct. 18, 1791	3	110
Betty, m. Dyer **COMSTOCK**, Feb. 19, 1792	3	131
Charlotte, d. Richard & Rebecca, b. July 21, 1799	3	240
Charlotte, m. Charles **HARRIS**, b. of New London, Dec. 21, 1823, by Rev. Ebenezer Loomis	4	16
Clarissa, d. Richard & Rebecca, b. Jan. 3, 1805	3	240
David, s. Samuel & Mary, b. Sept. 8, 1757	3	6
David, s. [Jeremiah & Abigail], b. Nov. 29, [ ]	3	110

	Vol.	Page
BROOKS (cont.)		
Elizabeth, d. Josiah & Bathshua, b. July 28, 1749	2	114
Elisabeth, d. [Thaddeus & Abigail], b. May 4, 1782	3	73
Elizabeth P., of New London, m. Samuel S.		
HOPKINS, of Providence, Sept. 30, 1824, by		
Rev. Abel McEwen	4	19
Elizabeth Proctor, d. [Hubbel & Lydia], b. Jan. 10,		
1808	3	170
Ezekiel, s. Samuel & Mary, b. Apr. 9, 1736	3	6
Fanny, d. [Hubbel & Lydia], b. Jan. 23, 1804	3	170
Hannah, of New London, d. Comfort, of New		
London, m. Allen CHADWICK, of New		
London, s. James, of Lyme, decd., Jan. 30, 1767	3	41
Hannah, d. [William & Amy], b. Jan. 11, 1774	3	125
Hannah, d. James, m. David BEEBE, Nov. 16, 1795	3	215
Henry, s. Rich[ar]d & Rebecca, b. Dec. 9, 1807	3	240
Hubbil, s. [Thaddeus & Abigail], b. Nov. 24, 1776	3	73
Hubbel, m. Lydia CLARK, d. John, Dec. 19, 1798	3	170
Jabez, m. Christina Ann JENNINGS, b. of [New		
London], June 21, 1848, by Rev. Robert A.		
Hallam	4	141
Jane, m. John DANFORTH, b. of [New London],		
Oct. 1, 1848, by Rev. Abel McEwen	4	142
Jeremiah, m. Abigail FOX, May 13, 1784	3	110
John, s. [Jonathan & Mercy], b. May 21, 1776	3	53
John s. [Thaddeus & Abigail], b. Feb. 18, 1785; d.		
Sept. 11, 1786	3	73
John, s. [Thaddeus & Abigail], b. Jan. 20, 1787; d.		
Apr. 28, 1787	3	73
John, m. Levine FREEMAN, Sept. [ ], 1808		
(Negroes)	3	8
John Clark, s. [Hubbel & Lydia], b. Dec. 5, 1805	3	170
Jonathan, of New London, s. Nathan, of Weborn,		
Mass., m. Mercy BILL, of New London, d.		
James CHAPMAN, of New London, Dec. 3,		
1766	3	53
Jonathan, s. Jonathan & Mercy, b. Aug. 29, 1767	3	53
Jonathan, of New London, m. Jane DOUGLASS, of		
Enfield, Mass., Aug. 29, 1837, by Rev. Robert		
A. Hallam	4	72
Joseph, s. Elizabeth, b. Aug. 24, 1773	3	8
Josiah, s. Henry, of New London, m. Bathshua		
FARGO, d. of Moses, Jr., of New London,		
Nov. 3, 1738	2	113
Josiah, s. Josiah & Bathshua, b. June 9, 1739	2	113
Lucretia, d. [Jeremiah & Abigail], b. Dec. 13, 17[ ]	3	110
Lucretia, d. Rich[ar]d & Rebecca, b. Apr. 11, 1801	3	240
Lucretia H., m. Thomas FINGERS, May 7, 1826, by		
Rev. Francis Darrow	4	26
Lydia, m. Daniel DRISCOLL, [ ]	2	106
Lydia C., m. Jeremiah H. GODDARD, b. of New		
London, Feb. 26, 1832, by Rev. Abel McEwen	4	45

	Vol.	Page
BROOKS (cont.)		
Lydia Clark, d. [Hubbel & Lydia], b. Apr. 11, 1813	3	170
Mahala, of Waterford, m. Samuel C. **KEENEY**, of		
New London, Aug. 6, 1832, by Rev. Abel		
McEwen	4	48
Mary, d. [Thaddeus & Abigail], b. Sept. 15, 1783; d.		
Oct. 2, 1784	3	73
Mary, d. [Hubbel & Lydia], b. Mar. 21, 1811	3	170
Mary, m. John W. **BROWN**, b. of New London, May		
9, 1830, by Rev. Abel McEwen	4	37
Nathan, s. [Jonathan & Mercy], b. Jan. 15, 1774	3	53
Prudence, formerly Prudence **CHAMPLAIN**, m.		
William **HARRIS**, Apr. 7, 1763	3	31
Ransom, s. [William & Amy], b. Nov. 22, 1769	3	125
Rebecca, m. Christopher **MINER**, May 7, 1790	3	119
Richard, s. Samuel & Mary, b. Oct. 10, 1744	3	6
Richard, s. [Stephen & Ede], b. Sept. 9, 1777	3	63
Samuel, ae 22 y., s. Henry, m. Mary **CALKINS**, ae		
19 y., d. John, all of New London, Dec. 9, 1734	3	6
Samuel, s. Samuel & Mary, b. Oct. 15, 1737	3	6
Sarah, d. Jonathan & Mercy, b. Oct. 9 ,1769; d. Sept.		
30, 1770	3	53
Sarah, d. Jonathan & Mercy, b. July 12, 1771	3	53
Stephen, s. Samuel & Mary, b. Apr. 15, 1750	3	6
Stephen, m. Ede [ ]	3	63
Susan C., of New London, m. Samuel A. **COOK**, of		
Norwich, Dec. 25, 1842, by Rev. Robert A.		
Hallam	4	104
Susan Smith, d. [Hubbel & Lydia], b. Aug. 11, 1816	3	170
Thaddeus, m. Abigail **SMITH**, Mar. 10, 1776	3	73
Thaddeus, s. [Thaddeus & Abigail], b. Sept. 3, 1780	3	73
Thaddeus, Jr., of New London, m. Elizabeth		
LANPHERE, of New London, Jan. 1, 1823, by		
Rev. Abel McEwen	4	11
Thomas, s. Josiah & Bathshua, b. Aug. 30, 1747	2	113
Thomas, s. Aliss, b. June 28, 1770	3	53
Thomas Hubbel, s. [Hubbel & Lydia], b. May 23,		
1800	3	170
Tiffany, s. [Jeremiah & Abigail], b. July 8, 1789	3	110
William, s. [Hubbel & Lydia], b. May 7, 1815	3	170
BROWER, Abraham, s. Garrot, of Fredericksburg, N.Y.,		
b. Oct. 25, 1778, m. Hannah **SPARROW**, relict		
of Timothy & dau. of Sperry **DOUGLASS**,		
June 1, 1806	3	216
Spearry D., s. [Abraham & Hannah], b. Oct. 21, 1808	3	216
Thomas H., s. [Abraham & Hannah], b. Feb. 24,		
1807	3	216
BROWN, Ab[b]y H., of New London, m. James		
MORGAN, of Groton, Aug. 5, 1826, by Rev.		
John G. Wightman	4	26
Adaline Maranda, d. [Dyar* & Fanny], b. Oct. 11,		
1809 *(Note says it should be Jedediah)	3	221

	Vol.	Page
BROWN (cont.)		
Jedidiah, m. Mary **CROCKER**, Mar. 7, 1782	3	26
Jedidiah, d. May 31, 1782	3	114
Jedidiah, s. [Jedidiah & Mary], b. Jan. 16, 1783	3	26
Jedediah, s. [Dyar* & Fanny], b. June 29, 1819		
*(Note says should be Jedediah)	3	221
Jedediah, m. Matilda **CHAPEL**, Apr. 1, 1825, by		
Ebenezer Loomis	4	21
Jedediah, m. Sarah **STUBBINS**, [ ]	3	114
John, m. Ruth **ROGERS**, d. Adam, Aug. 8, 1734	2	5
John, s. [John & Mary], b. June 1, 1788	3	9
John, m. Bridget **MAY**, Nov. 27, 1851, by Rev. J.		
Stokes. Witnesses: James Brown, Johanna		
Cullin	4	169
John F., of Waterford, m. Sarah C. **FOX**, of		
Montville, Jan. 3, 1847, by Rev. T. Edwards	4	128
John Newton, s. [Charles & Hester], b. June 29, 1803	3	230
John W., m. Mary **BROOKS**, b. of New London,		
May 9, 1830, by Rev. Abel McEwen	4	37
John Wheeler, s. [Benjamin & Hannah], b. Dec. 24,		
1807	3	204
Jonathan Comstock, s. [Comstock & Mary], b. Jan. 3,		
1785	3	69
Louisa Amelia, d. [Benjamin & Hannah], b. Dec. 10,		
1819	3	204
Lucretia, d. [Jedediah & Sarah], b. Sept. 20, 1770	3	114
Lucretia, d. [John & Mary], b. July 19, 1778, in		
Groton	3	9
Lucretia, d. [Christopher & Grace], b. Mar. 24, 1799	3	109
Lucretia F., of Waterford, m. Jedidiah B.		
CHAPMAN, of N[ew] London, Mar. 11, 1834,		
by Chester Tilden	4	55
Lydia, d. [Jedediah & Sarah], b. Mar. 3, 1779	3	114
Lydia, d. [Charles & Sarah], b. Jan. 20, 1785	3	50
Lydia C., m. James M. **DOWSITT**, b. of Norwich,		
Oct. 23, 1848, by Rev. Jabez S. Swan	4	142
Martha, d. Benjamin & Deborah, b. Jan. 27, 1749	3	131
Martha, m. Caleb **COMSTOCK**, Jan. 2, 1767	3	131
Mary, m. Samuel **DANIELS**, July 20, 1760	3	14
Mary, d. [Comstock & Mary], b. Feb. 5, 1772	3	69
Mary, d. [Jedidiah & Mary], b. Apr. 29, 1786	3	26
Mary, m. Edward **SHAW**, b. of N[ew] London, July		
31, 1834, by Rev. Ebenezer Blake	4	56
Mary Ann, d. [Benjamin & Hannah], b. Sept. 23,		
1805	3	204
Mary Ann, of New London, m. Lucius		
BLYDENBURGH, of New York, Apr. 30,		
1823, by Rev. Abel McEwen	4	13
Mary E., d. [William R. & Mary A.], b. Jan. 25, 1839	3	294
Mehetibel, d. [Jedediah & Sarah], b. Sept. 30, 1756	3	114
Nancy, m. John **CURRE**, Mar. 13, 1839, by Rev.		
Abraham Holway	4	85

	Vol.	Page
BROWN (cont.)		
Nancy W., m. Joseph **LAWRENCE**, July 19, 1817, in Waterford	3	157
Noise, s. [Dyar* & Fanny], b. Oct. 11, 1805 *(Note says should be Jedediah)	3	221
Patty, d. [Christopher & Grace], b. Jan. 23, 1788	3	109
Phebe, m. Elias L. **COIT**, Nov. 12, 1812	3	198
Rebeckah, d. [Jedediah & Sarah], b. Feb. 19, 1775	3	114
Rebeckah, d. [Jedidiah & Mary], b. Feb. 17, 1789	3	26
Reuel, s. Rachel **FOX**, d. Sam[ue]l Fox, b. Feb. 4, 1739/40	2	24
Richard, s. Charles & Sarah, b. June 17, 1772	3	50
Robert, s. [Charles & Sarah], b. Dec. 7, 1782	3	50
Robert, m. Eliza **CHAP[P]EL[L]**, b. of Waterford, Mar. 5, 1826, by Rev. Abel McEwen	4	26
Sally, d. Charles, m. Nathaniel **CANADA**, Nov. 6, 1796	3	159
Sally, d. [Charles & Hester], b. Sept. 28, 1799	3	230
Sarah, m. John **CLOTHIER**, Dec. 27, 1703	1	29
Sarah, d. [Jedediah & Sarah], b. Sept. 13, 1764	3	114
Sarah, d. [Charles & Sarah], b. Mar. 19, 1774	3	50
Sarah, m. Daniel **LESTER**, Feb. 2, [ ]	2	55
Sarah, m. Richard **CHAPEL**, Oct. 23, [ ]	3	133
Sarah A., m. Henry **SMITH**, b. of [New London], Oct. 25, 1847, by Rev. Abel McEwen	4	135
Sarah A., m. Christopher A. **WEAVER**, b. of New London, Nov. 24, 1847, by Rev. Jabez S. Swan	4	136
Sarah Scott, d. [Benjamin & Hannah], b. Dec. 1, 1817; d. Sept. 11, 1821	3	204
Sarah Scott, d. [Benjamin & Hannah], b. Jan. 2, 1822	3	204
Sarah W., m. Orrin **BRUMLEY**, b. of New London, May 4, 1845, by Rev. Jabez S. Swan	4	119
Silas, s. [Charles & Sarah], b. Dec. 23, 1780	3	50
Sophrona, m. Edwin **FOWLER**, Dec. 22, 1840, by H. R. Knapp	4	93
Susannah, d. [Jedediah & Sarah], b. Nov. 28, 1754	3	114
Theresa H., of New London, m. John H. **BUTLER**, of New Bedford, Mass., Feb. 22, 1832, by Rev. Abel McEwen	4	45
Theressa Hannah, d. [Benjamin & Hannah], b. Jan. 6, 1814	3	204
Thomas Fitch, s. [William R. & Mary A.], b. Feb. 9, 1837; d. Apr. 10, 1842	3	294
Wealthy, d. [John & Mary], b. Sept. 24, 1780, in Groton	3	9
Wealthy Ann, m. John **McGINLEY**, Apr. 25, 1800	3	242
William, m. Nancy **STEBBINS**, b. of New London, Jan. 9, 1825, by Rev. Daniel Dorchester	4	20
William B., s. [William R. & Mary A.], b. May 31, 1842	3	294
William R., m. Mary A. **SMITH**, Feb. 7, 1834	3	294

	Vol.	Page

BROWN (cont.)

William R., m. Mary A. **SMITH**, b. of New London, Feb. 7, 1834, by Rev. Abel McEwen   4   54

William W., m. Emma O. **CRANDALL**, of Westerly, R.I., Jan. 10, 1842, by Lemuel Cavell   4   95

-----, m. Ann **DART**, b. of East Lyme, Feb. 6, 1846, by Rev. L. Geo[rge] Leonard   4   124

BROWNING, Susannah, of Conn., m. Stephen **COLE**, of R.I., Nov. 21, 1794, by G. Williams, J.P.   3   75

BRUMLEY, Orrin, m. Sarah W. **BROWN**, b. of New London, May 4, 1845, by Rev. Jabez S. Swan   4   119

BUCKINGHAM, Martha E., m. Jesse **RICH**, Oct. 11, 1847, by Rev. Tho[ma]s Greenwood   4   136

BUCKMASTER, Elisabeth, m. Samuel **COLVER**, Nov. 3, 1774   3   78

BUDDINGTON, BUDINGTON, Belinda, m. Solomon **MORGAN**, b. of New London, [   ], by Christopher Griffing, J.P.   4   25

Tabathy, of Ledyard, m. Timothy W. **TURNER**, of Uncasville, Oct. 11, 1842, by L. Covel   4   103

BULKLEY, Charles, s. Charles, decd., m. Elisabeth **HALLAM**, d. Nicholas, Dec. 14, 1779   3   66

Charles H., s. [Charles & Elisabeth], b. Sept. 28, 1780   3   66

Elisabeth, d. Charles & Ann, b. May 26, 1760   3   30

Francis H., s. [Charles & Elisabeth], b. July 12, 1789   3   66

Hannah, m. Thomas **AVERY**, b. of New London, Mar. 13, [1693], in Wethersfield, by John Chester, J.P.   1   21

Harriet, d. [Charles & Elisabeth], b. June 13, 1783   3   66

Jonathan, s. Charles & Ann, b. Oct. 30, 1756   3   30

Leonard H., s. [Charles & Elisabeth], b. Dec. 22, 1791   3   66

Sophia M., m. Jonathan A. **CHAP[P]EL[L]**, b. of [New London], May 20, 1846, by Rev. Abel McEwen   4   126

Thomas H., s. [Charles & Elisabeth], b. July 4, 1786   3   66

BULL, Edward, of Lebanon, m. Eliza Ann **HALLAM**, of New London, Nov. 3, 1825, by Rev. Abel McEwen   4   24

BULLFINCH, Betsey, m. Reuben **GODFREY**, Nov. 11, 1776   3   140

BUMP, Sarah, d. Lydia **GREEN**, alias Bump, b. Dec. 10, 1762   2   16

BUNCE, Hannah, wid. of Paris, m. James **FLETCHER**, Feb. 12, 1808   3   58

BUNDY, Hiram, of Hartford, m. Mary **SEARS**, of Greenwich, May 22, 1825, by Lodowick Fosdick, J.P.   4   22

BUNNELL, Abigail, d. Samuel & Abigail, b. Jan. 9, 1758   3   14

	Vol.	Page
BUNNELL (cont.)		
Charles A., of Middlebury, Ohio, m. Emmeline **VAN**		
NAPP, of New London, Sept. 13, 1849, by		
Rev. T. Edwards	4	147
Lydia, of Groton, m. Harvey **NICHOLS**, of New		
London, Aug. 15, 1830, by Rev. Abel McEwen	4	39
Mercy, d. Samuel & Abigail, b. Sept. 3, 1755	3	14
Samuel, m. Abigail **HAINES**, d. James, Feb. [ ],		
1754	3	14
BURBECK, Charlotte Augusta, [d. Henry & Lucy], b.		
Mar. 8, 1818	3	243
Henry, m. Lucy **CALDWELL**, Dec. 16, 1813	3	243
Henry William, [s. Henry & Lucy], b. May 31, 1819	3	243
John Cathcart, [s. Henry & Lucy], b. Feb. 9, 1825	3	243
Mary E., of New London, m. Chandler **SMITH**, of		
New York, Apr. 22, 1851, by Rev. Robert A.		
Hallam	4	161
Mary Elizabeth, [d. Henry & Lucy], b. Mar. 7, 1821	3	243
Susan H., of New London, m. Lieut. Epaphras		
KIBBY, of U. S. Army, June 9, 1835, by Rev.		
Robert A. Hallam	4	61
Susan Henrietta, d. [Henry & Lucy], b. Sept. 23,		
1815	3	243
William Henry, [s. Henry & Lucy], b. Oct. 2, 1823	3	243
BURCH, [see also **BIRCH**], Edward, s. Richard &		
Elizabeth, b. Aug. 18, 1714	1	43
Elizabeth, d. Richard & Elizabeth, b. May 17, 1716	1	48
Elizabeth, d. Richard, of New London, m. William		
CARDWELL, Sept. 4, 1747	2	22
Gibson, s. Richard & Elizabeth, b. Oct. 12, 1719	1	64
Lydia, d. Richard & Elizabeth, b. Apr. 7, 1723	1	64
Lydia, d. Richard, of New London, m. Joshua		
HEMPSTEAD, Jr., of New London, s.		
Nathaniel, decd., Nov. 3, 1743	2	43
Mary, d. Richard & Elizabeth, b. Oct. 20, 1721	1	64
Richard, m. Elizabeth **HARRIS**, Oct. 16, 1713	1	41
Richard, m. Elizabeth **HARRIS**, Oct. 18, 1713	1	42
BURCHIN, George, m. Isabella **DOWNING**, May 10,		
1716	1	46
BURDEN, BURDON, Lavinia, of Norwich, m. William		
DAVIS, of New London, Aug. 31, 1843, by		
Rev. S. Benton	4	108
Mary, m. William **COLVER**, s. David & Elizabeth,		
Nov. 2, 1748	2	84
BURDICK, Desire, of Stonington, m. Andrew **CULVER**,		
of Groton, Aug. 31, 1828, by Nehemiah Dodge	4	35
Frances, m. Horace **COOLEY**, b. of Norwich, June		
16, 1850, by Rev. Jabez S. Swan	4	154
Gilbert Russel[l], s. [Henry W. & Abba], b. Jan. 17,		
1842	3	159
Henry W., m. Abba **MOORE**, Apr. 9, 1837	3	159

	Vol.	Page

BURDICK (cont.)

John, of Portugal, m. Susan **RAYMOND**, of New
    London, Mar. 13, 1831, by Rev. B. Judd | 4 | 42

Lafayette, m. Laura A. **SKINNER**, Oct. 11, 1847, by
    Rev. Tho[ma]s Greenwood | 4 | 136

Pheby, d. [William Clark & Sarah], b. Dec. 15, 1804 | 3 | 61

Phebe, m. Meritt **ROCKWELL**, May 2, 1824, by
    Rev. Thomas W. Tucker | 4 | 18

Phebe, m. Mer[r]it **ROCKWELL**, May 31, 1824 | 3 | 141

Robert, m. Rebecca **FOSTER**, Jan. 4 ,1700 | 1 | 26

Rubey, d. [William Clark & Sarah], b. Apr. 15, 1806 | 3 | 61

Sarah Seabury, d. [Henry W. & Abba], b. Mar. 18,
    1840, at Norwich | 3 | 159

William Clark, m. Sarah **WAY**, Apr. 5, 1804 | 3 | 61

William Clark, s. [William Clark & Sarah], b. Nov. 6,
    1808 | 3 | 61

BURDON, [see under **BURDEN**]

BURGESS, Albert T., m. Cynthia S. **CHIPMAN**, b. of
    New London, Apr. 2, 1847, by Rev. Jabez S.
    Swan | 4 | 130

James, m. Abby **MAY**, Feb. 11, 1849, by Rev.
    William Logan | 4 | 150

John, of Plymouth, Mass. ,m. Eliza **CHIPMAN**, of
    New London, Aug. 31, 1842, by L. Covel | 4 | 103

BURKE, Mary, m. James **CARLIN**, Dec. 28, 1848, by
    Rev. William Logan | 4 | 150

BURNS, [see also **BYRNE**], Elizabeth, m. Michael
    FORD, b. of New London, Dec. 10, 1843, by
    Rev. Lemuel Covell | 4 | 109

Francis, m. Caroline Louisa **SIMMONS**, b. of [New
    London], b. Feb. 28, 1836, by Rev. Abel
    McEwen | 4 | 64

Frank, m. Mary **KELLEY**, b. of New London, July
    30, 1839, by Rev. Daniel Webb | 4 | 73

Matthias, of Portland, m. Sarah D. **POOL**, of New
    London, June 27, 1830, by Rev. B. Judd | 4 | 41

Patrick H., m. Rosanna **COOGAN**, b. of [New
    London], Mar. 3, 1844, by Rev. Robert A.
    Hallam | 4 | 110

BURR, [E]unis, d. George, of Hartford, m. John **STARR**,
    Oct. 22, 1796 | 3 | 201

Sally, d. George, of Hartford, m. Francis **SISTARE**,
    July 30, 1809 | 3 | 231

BURRINGTON, Walter, d. [Sept. ?] 17, [1689] | 1 | 69

BURROWS, Abiga[i]ll, d. Jno. & Mary, b. Aug. 10,
    [1682] | 1 | 16

Asahel, of Groton, m. Mary Ann **SMITH**, of [New
    London], Jan. 1, 1824, by Tho[ma]s W. Tucker,
    Minister | 4 | 17

Dennison, of Groton, m. Sally **MIDDLETON**, of
    New London, July 16, 1822, by Rev. Abel
    McEwen | 4 | 9

	Vol.	Page

BURROWS (cont.)

Hannah, d. John & Mary, b. Dec. 15, 9th year [sic]
[1674] — 1 — 10

John, s. Robert, of New London, m. Mary
CULLVER, d. Jno. of N[ew] London ,Dec. 14,
[1670] — 1 — 7

John, s. John & Mary, b. Sept. 2, [1671] — 1 — 8

Margaret, d. John & Mary, b. Oct. 5, [1677] — 1 — 12

Mary, d. John & Mary, b. Dec. 14, [1672] — 1 — 8

Robert, s. John & Mary, b. Sept. 9, [1681] — 1 — 16

Samuel, s. Jno.* & Mary, b. Aug. 5, [1679]   *(First
written "Geo." Corrected by L. B. B.) — 1 — 14

Silas E., of New London, m. Mary A. **BECKWITH**,
of Waterford, Jan. 4, 1852, by Rev. Samuel Fox — 4 — 167

-----, w. Robert, d. [, 1672] — 1 — 8

BURT, John, m. Catharine **WELCH**, June 7, 1851, by
Jno. J. Brandigee — 4 — 162

BURTON, Benjamin, m. Betsey **WILLIAMS**, b. of New
London, May 14, 1832, by Rev. Abel McEwen — 4 — 47

BURTWELL, Eliza, d. [James & Love], b. Sept. 23, 1795;
d. Oct. 8, 1796 — 3 — 158

George Henry, s. [James & Love], b. July 17, 1808 — 3 — 158

James, m. Love **ROGERS**, d. George, Jan. 20, 1793 — 3 — 158

James, s. [James & Love], b. July 22, 1799 — 3 — 158

John, s. [James & Love], b. May 22, 1797 — 3 — 158

Mary, d. [James & Love], b. Nov. 5, 1793 — 3 — 158

BUSH, Anson, of Canterbury, m. Marian **BUSH**, of New
London, Sept. 4, 1823, by Rev. Abel McEwen — 4 — 15

Charles A., m. Eliza Mary **LEWIS**, b. of [New
London], Oct. 23, 1848, by Rev. L. G. Leonard — 4 — 142

Charles Anson, [s. Anson & Mary Ann], b. Nov. 19,
1828 — 3 — 259

Lucy Ann, d. Anson & Mary Ann, b. Feb. 8, 1826 — 3 — 259

Marian, of New London, m. Anson **BUSH**, of
Canterbury, Sept. 4, 1823, by Rev. Abel
McEwen — 4 — 15

Mary Ann, [d. Anson & Mary Ann], b. June 20, 1827 — 3 — 259

T. Clifford, m. Frances **PRINCE**, b. of New London,
Dec. 31, 1851, by Rev. Samuel Fox — 4 — 167

William G., m. Eliza Ann **GREEN**, b. of New
London, Mar. 14, 1832, by Rev. Abel McEwen — 4 — 45

BUTLER, Abigail, d. John, of New London, m. Allen
MULLENS, s. Dr. Alexander Mullens, of
Galway, Ireland, Apr. 8, 1725 — 2 — 87

Amos, s. Thomas & Sarah, b. Sept. 15, 1757 — 3 — 8

Anna, m. Samuel **WATERHOUSE**, s. Elijah, b. of
New London, Dec. 27, 1787, by Andrew
Griswold, J.P. — 2 — 123

Benjamin, m. Hannah **AVERY**, d. William, of
Groton, Dec. 11, 1791 — 3 — 178

Benjamin, s. [Benjamin & Hannah], b. Mar. 4, 1800;
d. June 13, 1800 — 3 — 178

	Vol.	Page
BUTLER (cont.)		
Betsey, m. Thomas S. **BADET**, May 12, 1811	3	234
Catharine, m. William **HOLT**, Jan. 7, 1713/14	1	55
Charles, b. Mar. 21, 1779; m. Sally **CROCKER**,		
Nov. 9, 1802	3	261
Charles, s. [Charles & Sally], b. Sept. 2, 1803	3	261
Charles, m. Hannah **POTTER**, Apr. 26, 1808	3	261
Courtland, s. [William & Amelia], b. Oct. 34, 1819	3	173
Daniel, s. Thomas & Sarah, b. Mar. 13, 1755	3	8
Evelina, d. [Charles & Hannah], b. Aug. 15, 1819	3	261
Evelyn, of [New London], m. Theodore F. **HULL**,		
of Marietta, Ohio, Sept. 9, 1850, by Rev. Abel		
McEwen	4	155
Ezekiel, s. Tho[ma]s & Sarah, b. Oct. 23, 1744		
(Written "**BULLER**")	3	8
Frances, d. [Charles & Hannah], b. Jan. 2, 1815	3	261
Frances, of [New London], m. Charles S. **POTTER**,		
of Brooklyn, N. Y., [June, 1838], by Rev. Abel		
McEwen	4	77
Franklin, s. [William & Emelia], b. Sept. 19, 1816	3	173
George, s. [Charles & Hannah], b. Nov. 11, 1812	3	261
Hannah, d. Walter & Hannah, b. June 16, 1757	2	58
Hannah, d. [Charles & Hannah], b. Feb. 15, 1817	3	261
Hannah, m. Samuel R. **TURNER**, b. of New		
London, May 16, 1837, by Daniel Huntington	4	70
Hannah Potter, [d. Charles & Hannah], b. Nov. 29,		
1783	3	261
Harriet E., m. Michael **YORK**, Apr. 21, 1850, by		
Rev. Charles Willett	4	153
Henry William, s. [William & Emelia], b. June 20,		
1811	3	173
Jane, m. William R. **CHAMPLIN**, b. of N[ew]		
London, May 10, 1846, by Rev. John Howson	4	126
John, s. Walter & Mary, b. Nov. 22, 1723	1	63
John, s. [Charles & Hannah], b. Jan. 22, 1822	3	261
John G., of Saybrook, m. Lucretia **MANWARING**,		
of Waterford, Sept. 13, 1835, by Rev. Robert A.		
Hallam	4	62
John H., of New Bedford, Mass., m. Theressa H.		
BROWN, of New London, Feb. 22, 1832, by		
Rev. Abel McEwen	4	45
Julia, d. [Benjamin & Hannah], b. June 13, 1794	3	178
Lucius L., of Stonington, m. Emely **BAILEY**, of		
New London, May 22, 1842, by Rev. Lemuel		
Covell	4	99
Lucretia, d. [Thomas & Jemima], b. Sept. 6, 1770	3	70
Lucretia, d. [Charles & Hannah], b. Sept. 26, 1810	3	261
Lydia, d. [Thomas & Jemima], b. Apr. 5, 1772	3	70
Lydia, d. Thomas, m. Joseph **YOUNG**, Aug. 8, 1791	3	172
Martha, m. Henry G. **WILSON**, b. of [New London],		
Dec. 3, 1843, by Rev. Abel McEwen	4	108

	Vol.	Page
BUTLER (cont.)		
Mary, d. Robert* & Mary, b. Aug. 29, 1714		
*(Walter in the margin)	1	43
Mary, d. Walter & Hannah, b. Nov. 20, 1755	2	58
Mary, d. [Benjamin & Hannah], b. Jan. 8, 1797	3	178
Mary A., of Waterford, m. George W. **CROWELL**, of New London, Oct. 14, 1849, by Rev. Jabez S. Swan	4	147
Sally, d. [Charles & Sally], b. Apr 12, 1805	3	261
Sally, w. Charles, d. Sept. 2, 1806	3	261
Sally, d. Charles & Sally, d. June 23, 1820	3	261
Sarah, d. Thomas & Sarah, b. Nov. 9, 1749	3	8
Sarah E., m. Humphrey P. **HORTON**, b. of [New London], May 4, 1847, by Rev. Abel McEwen	4	131
Thomas, s. Walter & Mary, b. Jan. 31, 1715/6	1	45
Thomas, s. Thomas & Sarah, b. May 18, 1747 (Written **BULLER**)	3	8
Thomas, d. Dec. 20, 1759	3	8
Thomas, m. Jemima **LANPHEAR**, Mar. 22, 1770	3	70
Thomas, Jr., s. Thomas, m. Sarah **LEWIS**, d. Moses, all of New London, | | (written Thomas **BULLER**)	3	8
Thomas Harris, s. [William & Emelia], b. Nov. 22, 1812	3	173
Walter, s. Lieut. Walter & Mary, b. May 27, 1718	1	49
Walter, s. Thomas & Sarah, b. July 11, 1752	3	8
Walter, s. Thomas, m. Hannah **CROCKER**, d. of Capt. David, all of New London, Jan. 28, 1755	2	58
William, s. [Charles & Hannah], b. Feb. 20, 1809	3	261
William, m. Emelia **HARRIS**, Sept. 11, 1810	3	173
-----, d. John, d. Aug. 13, [1689]	1	69
BUTTON, BUTTIN, John, of Bona Vista, m. Francis **HOWARD**, of [New London], b. Sept. 28, 1850, by Rev. Abel McEwen	4	155
Worthington B., of Boston, Mass., m. Jane C. **ALLEN**, of [New London], May 8, 1847, by Rev. Robert A. Hallam	4	140
BUTTS, Henry L., m. Sarah A. **RICHARDS**, Dec. 3, 1849, by Rev. Charles Willett	4	151
BYINGTON, William, m. Ruth Ann **BEEBE**, b. of New London, Jan. 30, 1845, by Rev. S. Benton	4	117
BYRNE, [see also **BURNS**], Betsey, d. [John & Anne], b. Nov. 11, 1785	3	3
John, m. Anne **POWERS**, Nov. 16, 1784	3	3
Sally, d. [John & Anne], b. Mar. 28, 1787	3	3
Samuel Hazard, s. [John & Anne], b. Feb. 8, 1789	3	3
CADY, Ansel C., m. Harriet **ALLEN**, b. of [New London], Dec. 21, 1841, by Rev. Robert A. Hallam	4	98
Ebenezer Pemberton, m. Elizabeth **SMITH**, d. Luther, of Plainfield, Mar. 18, 1806	3	191

	Vol.	Page
CALKINS, CAULKINS (cont.)		
Pember, m. Joanna **PERKINS**, Jan. 6, 1780	3	42
Peter, s. David & Mary, b. Oct. 9, [1681]	1	15
Peter, s. [David & Mary], b. Oct. 9 [ ]	1	67
Phebe, d. William & Mary, b. June 23, 1751, old style	3	22
Rebeckah, m. Lemuel **DARROW**, Nov. 16, 1775	3	91
Richard, s. [Samuel & Lydia], b. Mar. 17, 1780	3	95
Ruth, d. Amos & Jedidiah, b. Mar. 16, 1766	3	124
Ruth, m. David **CROCKER**, Dec. 9 ,1790	3	124
Sally, d. [Jonathan & Anna], b. Dec. 30, 1792	3	111
Samuel, alias William, s. John & Frances, b. May 7, 1728	2	8
Samuel, m. Lydia **CALKINS**, Aug. 17, 1760	3	95
Samuel, s. [Samuel & Lydia], b. Aug. 19, 1771	3	95
Samuel, m. Grace **CALKINS**, Nov. 15, 1785	3	95
Samuel W., s. [Jonathan & Anna], b. Mar. 31, 1798	3	111
Sarah, d. Jonathan & Sarah, b. July 17, 1703	1	61
Sarah, w. Jonathan, d. Aug. 15, 1718/19	1	61
Sarah, d. [Jonathan & Lydia], b. Mar. 3, 1785	3	37
Silas, s. Pember & Abigail, b. May 9, 1770	3	42
Temperance, d. William & Mary, b. Apr. 22, 1758	3	22
Thomas, s. Jonathan & Sarah, b. July 29, 1713	1	61
Thomas, s. [Samuel & Lydia], b. May 19, 1764	3	95
William, s. Joseph & Lucretia, b. Apr. 18, 1724	2	6
William, alias Samuel, s. John & Frances, b. May 7, 1728	2	8
William, s. Joseph, m. Mary **PRENTISS**, d. Stephen, Jr., decd., all of New London, May 20, 1746, old style	3	22
William, d. Oct. 31, 1762	3	22
William, s. William & Mary, b. Feb. 25, 1763	3	22
William, s. [Pember & Abigail], b. Nov. 13, 1773; d. July 18, 1774	3	42
William, s. [Pember & Abigail], b. Jan. 24, 1777; d. July 21, 1777	3	42
CALLANAN, Patrick, m. Mary **SHEA**, June 27, 1852, by Rev. J. Stokes. Witnesses: Daniel Shea, Julia Shea	4	171
CALVERT, Fanny A., m. Charles B. **TOBEY**, b. of [New London], Mar. 10, 1850, by Rev. Abel McEwen	4	152
Maranda, m. Timothy **BECKWITH**, b. of New London, Apr. 7, 1851, by Rev. Jabez S. Swan	4	163
Pheebe, m. William **TALMAN**, Aug. 14, 1797, by Rev. Charles Seabury	3	129
CALVIN, Polly, d. Gabriel, m. David **PERRY**, Dec. [ ], 1802	3	112
CAMP, CAMPE, Ann, m. Jonathan **HAMBLETON**, May 2, 1732	2	39
Anne, d. James, m. John **CROCKER**, s. John, decd., May 18, 1758, by Rev. David Jewett	3	17
Bathshua, m. Samuel **WILLIAMS**, July 14, 1713	1	41

	Vol.	Page
CAMP, CAMPE (cont.)		
Jacob A., of Sandusky, Ohio, m. Fanny S.		
PERKINS, of [New London], Oct. 22, 1850,		
by Rev. T. Edwards	4	156
William, m. Abigaill **WILLOUBE**, Mar. 26, 1713	1	40
CAMPELL, Caroline H., m. Henry F. **FORSYTH**, b. of		
New London, Apr. 22, 1849, by Rev. Jabez S.		
Swan	4	145
CANADA, Caroline Thompson, d. [Nathaniel & Sally], b.		
Aug. 6 ,1805	3	159
Charles Brown, s. [Nathaniel & Sally], b. Aug. 27,		
1797	3	159
George William, s. [Nathaniel & Sally], b. Dec. 19,		
1809	3	159
Nathaniel, m. Sally **BROWN**, d. Charles, Nov. 6,		
1796	3	159
Phebe Whiting, d. [Nathaniel & Sally], b. Jan. 1,		
1800	3	159
CANELL, Henry, m. Mary **SMITH**, b. of New London,		
May 7, 1830, by Rev. Abel McEwen	4	38
CANNON, Charles William, s. [Robert & Mehetable], b.		
Dec. 13, 1797	3	224
Mary Nelson, d. [Robert & Mehetable], b. Sept. 7,		
1804	3	224
Robert, m. Mehetable **BECKWITH**, Jan. 22, 1784	3	224
Robert, s. [Robert & Mehetable], b. Apr. 24, 1785	3	224
Thomas, s. [Robert & Mehetable], b. May 22, 1787	3	224
CAPRON, Eunice, m. Elisha **MINER**, Feb. 12, 1792	3	126
John S., of Norfolk, Va., m. Amy Jane **WHIPPLE**,		
of Waterford, Oct. 13, 1843, by Rev. Abel		
McEwen	4	107
CAPWELL, Randall, of R.I., m. Mary Ann **DERRY**, of		
Groton, Ct., May 14, 1843, by Rev. Lemuel		
Covell	4	109
CARDER, Elizabeth, d. Richard & Martha, b. Dec. 2,		
1707	1	46
CARDWELL, Andrew, s. William & Dorcas, b. Jan. 26,		
1744	2	22
Dorcas, d. William & Dorcas, b. Sept. 30, 1745	2	22
Dorcas, w. William, d. Apr. 18, 1747	2	22
John, s. William & Elizabeth, b. Dec. 5, 1752	2	22
Mary, d. William & Elizabeth, b. Jan. 16, 1757	2	22
Nathaniel, s. William & Elizabeth, b. May 11, 1755	2	22
Rebecca, d. William & Elizabeth, b. Apr. 6, 1751	2	22
Samuel, s. William & Elizabeth, b. Aug. 27, 1748	2	22
William, formerly of the Parish of Zebulon, County		
of Cornwell, now of New London, m. Dorcas		
HORSKINS, of Win[d]sor, Jan. 19, 1738/9	2	22
William, m. Elizabeth **BURCH**, d. Richard, of New		
London, Sept. 4, 1747	2	22
William, s. William & Elizabeth, b. Feb. 19, 1750	2	22

	Vol.	Page
CAREW, Palmer, of Norwich, m. Hannah HILL, of New London, d. Charles, late of New London, decd., June 1, 1730	3	20
CAREY, Abigaill, m. Solomon COIT, Nov. 16, 1715	1	46
CARLIN, James, m. Mary BURKE, Dec. 28, 1848, by Rev. William Logan	4	150
CARPENTER, Elizabeth, m. John PENDALL, June 19, 1704	1	29
Hannah, m. John LESTER, Apr. 8, 1702	1	27
Hannah, m. John LESTER, Apr. 8, 1702	1	34
Lucy B., m. Everett L. SWEET, b. of Attleborow, Mass., Mar. 6, 1851, by Rev. George M. Carpenter	4	160
Sarah, wid., m. William STEPHENS, of Kenellworth, Nov. 24, 1703	1	29
Sarah, m. Alexander HOSSACK, b. of New London, Nov. 13, 1842, by Eld. L. Covell	4	103
CARRINGTON, John, m. Marcella KENNEDY, Sept. 9, 1849, by Rev. William Logan	4	150
CARROLL, CAREL, CARROL, CARRELL, Almyra L., of [New London], m. Abel G. PAYNE, of Waterford, May 21, 1848, by Rev. L. G. Leonard	4	138
Elizabeth, m. Rodolphus A. GIFFORD, b. of N[ew] London, Mar. 20, 1836, by Rev. Squire B. Hascall	4	83
James, s. [John & Eliner], b. July 13, 1791	3	159
James, m. Elizabeth BECKWITH, b. of New London, May 5, 1822, by Roswell Burrows, Admr.	4	4
John, m. Eliner RYON, d. James, Apr. 5, 1786	3	159
John, s. [John & Eliner], b. Jan. 15, 1790	3	159
Lucretia, m. Frederick HULL, b. of [New London], Aug. 12, 1838, by Rev. Abel McEwen	4	78
Mary, d. [John & Eliner], b. Dec. 9 ,1798	3	159
Mary, m. John MATSON, May 26, [18]50, [by Peter J. Blenkinsop]. Witnesses: John Fahy, Mary Guinness	3	306
Mary, m. John MATSON, May 26, 1850. Witnesses: John Failey, Mary Guinness	4	159
Mary E., m. William M. CHAPPELL, b. of [New London], May 18, 1847, by Rev .M. P. Alderman	4	131
Michael, m. Mary MALROONY, Oct. 27, [18]50, [by Peter J. Blenkinsop]. Witnesses: John Power, Ellen Phelan	3	306
Michael, m. Mary MALOONEY, Oct. 27, 1850. Witnesses: John Power, Ellen Pheloir	4	159
Thomas, m. Mary MAHONEY, Oct. 28, 1849, by Rev. William Logan	4	150
Thomas B., m. Almira L. HARRIS, Nov. 15, 1840, by H. R. Knapp	4	93

	Vol.	Page
CARROLL, CAREL, CARROL, CARRELL (cont.)		
William, s. [John & Elinor], b. July 7, 1797	3	159
William G., m. Ellen **LEOPARD**, b. of New		
London, Nov. 13, 1842, by Eld[er] L. Covell	4	103
CARTER, James, of Hartford, m. Eder Ann **SHAW**, of		
New London, July 7, 1840, by Rev. Robert A.		
Hallam	4	90
Martha A., of Bristol, Me., m. John P. **DAVIS**, of		
New London, Nov. 3, 1844, by Rev. J. Blain	4	115
Mary W., formerly of Bristol, Me., m. Luther		
DAVISON, of New London, May 22, 1842, by		
Rev. Lemuel Covell	4	99
Melissa B., of Bristol, m. William H. **DAVIS**, of		
New London, Dec. 18, 1850, by Rev. Jabez S.		
Swan	4	158
William, of Charlestown, Mass., m. Lavina		
ANDREWS, of [New London], Aug. 11, 1847,		
by Rev. Abel McEwen	4	133
CASE, Ann E., m. William H. **LEWIS**, b. of [New		
London], Oct. 18, 1849, by Rev. Abel McEwen	4	147
Ann Elizabeth, d. [Levi & Mary Ann], b. Feb. 12,		
1827	3	266
Joseph, m. Clarrissa **MARDELAINE**, Jan. 1, 1829,		
by Rev. Samuel West	4	35
Levi, m. Mary Ann **BOLLES**, Apr. 13, 1825	3	266
Levi, m. Mary Ann **BOLLES**, b. of New London,		
Apr. 13, 1825, by Rev. Abel McEwen	4	22
CASEY, Lucius H., of Norwich, Ct., m. Mary Ann		
HUBBARD, of New London, Mar. 19, 1842,		
by Rev. R. W. Allen	4	99
CATO, Betsey, d. [John & Darkis], b. Feb. [ ], 1787		
(Negroes)	3	47
George, s. [John & Darkis], b. May 3, 1785		
(Negroes)	3	47
John, m. Darkis **PALMES**, Apr. 16, 1783 (Negroes)	3	47
John, s. [John & Darkis], b. Apr. 12, 1784 (Negroes)	3	47
Samson, m. Rosannah **ANDERSON**, Feb. 20, 1782	3	65
Samson, s. [Samson & Rosannah], b. Sept. 15, 1792;		
d. July 20, 1793	3	65
Susannah, d. [Samson & Rosannah], b. July 15, 1791	3	65
CATON, Elizabeth, m. John **LAWRENCE**, b. of New		
London, Apr. 10, 1823, by Rev. Abel McEwen	4	21
CAULKINS, [see under **CALKINS**]		
CAVANA[U]GH, Anastasia, m. Murray M. **CLARK**, b.		
of [New London], May 30, 1849, by Rev.		
Robert A. Hallam	4	146
CAVARRE, Mary, m. Maurice **CONNORS**, Apr. 24,		
1852, by Rev. J. Stokes. Witnesses: John		
Bigley, Ellen Lynch	4	170
CAVERLY, Cornelia, of Lyme, m. Thomas T. **TABOR**,		
Apr. 9, 1838, by Rev. James M. Macdonald	4	76

	Vol.	Page

CAVERLY (cont.)

Sarah, d. Grenfield, m. John **FOX**, of Concord, June 28, [1687]. [Corrected to Sarah **LARABY** by L. B. B.] — 1 — 12

CEGANE, James, native of Marsailles, France, m. Lydia **DESHON**, Sept. 10, 1789 — 3 — 120

Lydia, d. [James & Lydia], b. May 21, 1791 — 3 — 120

CHADWICK, Abigail, d. R[e]uben, of Lyme, m. Samuel **WAIT**, Apr. 8, 1799 — 3 — 178

Allen, of New London, s. James, of Lyme, decd., m. Hannah **BROOKS**, of New London, d. Comfort, of New London, Jan. 30, 1767 — 3 — 41

Catherine, of New London, m. Peter **STUPUY**, a French gentleman from the W. Indies, then residing in New London, June 20, 1784, by Rev. Aaron Kinne, of Groton — 3 — 20

James, s. Allen & Hannah, b. Sept. 4, 1767 — 3 — 41

John M., of Lyme, m. Ursula **RAYMOND**, of Pine, Mass., Sept. 29, 1828, by Rev. Abel McEwen — 4 — 34

Roxana, of Waterford, m. Daniel S. **FARNHAM**, of New London, Oct. 2, 1837, by Rev. Abel McEwen — 4 — 73

William, s. Allen & Hannah, b. Feb. 13 ,1769 — 3 — 41

CHAMPION, Lucinda, m. Frederick **COATS**, Jan. 3, 1789 — 3 — 130

CHAMPLIN, CHAMPLAIN, CHAMPLEN, Anna, d. Samuel, b. Dec. 30, 1750, on Block Island — 3 — 189

Bridget, d. [Samuel & Elisabeth], b. Oct. 30, 1759 — 3 — 32

Charles, m. Sarah G. **LATHROP**, b. of [New London], May 6, 1845, by Rev. S. Benton — 4 — 119

Charles, m. Abby **WOODWARD**, b. of [New London], Apr. 15, 1852, by Rev. J. M. Eaton — 4 — 167

Daniel, s. [Samuel & Elisabeth], b. Oct. 31, 1773 — 3 — 32

Eliza W., of New London, m. Edward C. **RILEY**, of New York, Sept. 10, 1826, by Rev. B. Judd — 4 — 30

Eliza Way, d. [George W. & Eliza], b. Mar. 29, 1797 — 3 — 230

Elizabeth, d. John, of Lyme, m. John **HARRIS**, s. Lieut. Joseph, of New London, Mar. 31, 1737 — 2 — 27

Elisabeth, d. [Samuel & Elisabeth], b. June 1, 1766 — 3 — 32

Elizabeth, [w. George W. (?)], d. Oct. 25, 1825 — 3 — 230

Elizabeth, see Elizabeth **HUNTINGTON** — 3 — 155

Frances, m. Gilbert **PENDLETON**, Mar. 3, 1839, by Rev. Abraham Holway — 4 — 85

Frederick A., m. Mary L. **HARRIS**, b. of New London, May 29, 1842, by Rev. Lemuel Covell — 4 — 99

George, s. John & Mary, b. Sept. 17, 1750 — 2 — 96

George, of Lebanon, Ct., m. Lucina H. **THOMPSON**, of New London, Apr. 29, 1849, by Rev. Geo[rge] M. Carpenter — 4 — 145

George Oliver, s. [George W. & Eliza], b. Oct. 17, 1795 — 3 — 230

	Vol.	Page
CHAMPLIN, CHAMPLAIN, CHAMPLEN (cont.)		
George W., m. Eliza **WAY**, d. Ebenezer, Nov. 2,		
1794	3	230
G[eorge] W., d. Apr. 21, 1820	3	230
George Whitfield, s. [Samuel & Elisabeth], b. Nov. 7,		
1771	3	32
Guy, s. [Lodowick & Mary], b. Aug. 5, 1785	3	99
Hannah, d. John & Mary, b. Mar. 8, 1754	2	96
John, m. Mary **BENTLEY**, Oct. 15, 1748	2	96
John, s. John & Mary, b. Jan. 27, 1757	2	96
John L., m. Martha L. **HARRIS**, b. of New London,		
Jan. 5, 1851, by Rev. Abel McEwen	4	158
Lodowick, s. [Samuel & Elisabeth], b. July 13,		
1762; d. Jan. [ ], 1781	3	32
Lodowick, m. Mary **RICHARDS**, June 19, 1778	3	99
Lodowick, s. [Lodowick & Mary], b. Sept. 3, 1781	3	99
Lodowick, Capt., d. Mar. 20, 1786	3	99
Martha T., m. Daniel S. **KEENEY**, b. of New		
London, Oct. 9, 1849, by Rev. Edwin R.		
Warren	4	149
Mary, wid. of Capt. Lodowick **CHAMPLIN** & dau.		
of Guy & Elizabeth **RICHARDS**, m. George		
Dolbeare **AVERY**, s. William & Mary, of		
Groton, Apr. 1, 1790	3	116
Oliver, s. [Samuel & Elisabeth], b. Sept. 30, 1769	3	32
Prudence, d. [Samuel & Elisabeth], b. Dec. 28, 1760	3	32
Prudence, see Prudence **BROOKS**	3	31
Rebeckah, d. [Samuel & Elisabeth], b. Sept. 26, 1775	3	32
Samuel, m. Elisabeth **HARRIS**, July 12, 1759	3	32
Samuel, Sr., s. Samuel, lost at sea, [ ], 1782	3	32
Samuel, s. [Lodowick & Mary], b. May 16, 1783	3	99
Samuel, s. [George W. & Eliza], b. Aug. 22, 1800	3	230
William, s. [George W. & Eliza], b. Aug. 17, 1802	3	230
William C., of Colchester, m. Rebecca		
PENHALLAM, Sept. [ ], 1842, by Rev. D. W.		
Allen	4	94
William Harris, s. [Samuel & Elisabeth], b. Feb. 21,		
1768; d. Feb. 11, 1779	3	32
William Harris, s. [Samuel & Elisabeth], b. Apr. 5,		
1779	3	32
William R., m. Jane **BUTLER**, b. of N[ew] London,		
May 10, 1846, by Rev. John Howson	4	126
CHANDLER, John, s. John & Mary, b. Oct. 13, [1693]	1	22
Joshua, s. John & Mary, b. Feb. 9, 1695/6	1	22
Mary, d. John & Mary, b. Apr. 20, 1700	1	25
William, s. John & Mary, b. Nov. 3, 1698	1	24
CHANEY, CHANY, Abiga[i]l, d. [Jacob & Elizabeth], b.		
Dec. 16, 1803	3	34
Eliza, d. [Samuel, Jr. & Rebecca], b. Aug. 13, 1805	3	177
Elizabeth, d. [Jacob & Elizabeth], b. Sept. 29, 1793	3	34
Gurdon, s. [Jacob & Elizabeth], b. Dec. 1, 1805	3	34

	Vol.	Page

CHANEY, CHANY (cont.)

Jacob, m. Elizabeth **HOLMES**, d. James, Jan. 1, 1792 — 3, 34

Jacob, s. [Samuel, Jr. & Rebecca], b. May 9, 1795 — 3, 177

James, s. [Jacob & Elizabeth], b. Oct. 9 ,1801 — 3, 34

John Owen, s. [Samuel, Jr. & Rebecca], b. Aug. 2, 1802 — 3, 177

Mary, d. [Jacob & Elizabeth], b. Oct. 2, 1795 — 3, 34

Mary Ann, d. [Samuel, Jr. & Rebecca], b. Dec. 14, 1800; d. June 8, 1806 — 3, 177

Mary S., of [New London], m. Eli **GATES**, of Salem, Ct., Apr. 23, 1826, by Rev. Isaac Stoddard — 4, 26

Rebecca, d. [Samuel, Jr. & Rebecca], b. July 30, 1797 — 3, 177

Ryal, s. [Samuel, Jr. & Rebecca], b. Dec. 30, 1808 — 3, 177

Samuel, Jr., b. Apr. 21, 1770; m. Rebecca **STACY**, Oct. 23, 1791 — 3, 177

Samuel, 3d, s. [Samuel, Jr. & Rebecca], b. May 20, 1792; d. Sept. 8, 1793 — 3, 177

Samuel, s. [Jacob & Elizabeth], b. Mar. 18, 1798 — 3, 34

CHANNING, Alexander Stewart, s. [Henry & Sally], b. Oct. 3, [1797]; d. Oct. 9, 1797, twin with Walter — 3, 136

Edwin, s. [Henry & Sally], b. Feb. 9, 1795 — 3, 136

Henry, of New London, s. John & Mary, of Newport, R.I., m. Sally **McCURDY**, of Lyme, Sept. 25, 1787 — 3, 136

Henry William, s.[Henry & Sally], b. Aug. 5, 1788 — 3, 136

John McCurdy, s. [Henry & Sally], b. Jan. 19, 1796 — 3, 136

Mary Ann, d. [Henry & Sally], b. May 11, 1791; d. Aug. 2 ,1791 — 3, 136

Sally, w. Henry, d. Sept. 6, 1798 — 3, 136

Thomas Shaw, s. [Henry & Sally], b. Oct. 25, 1789 — 3, 136

Walter, twin with Alexander Stewart, [s. Henry & Sally], b. Oct. 3, [1797]; d. Oct. 11, 1797 — 3, 136

Walter McCurdy, [s. Henry & Sally], b. Oct. 27, 1792; d. Aug. 29, 1793 — 3, 136

William, s. [Henry & Sally], b. Jan. 31, 1794 — 3, 136

CHAPIN, Emma, m. John **McMORIN** (?), Dec. 9, 1838, by Rev. Abraham Holway — 4, 85

CHAPMAN, Abigail, d. [James & Mary], b. June 4, 1803 — 3, 245

Abigail, m. Merchant **TINKER**, b. of New London, Dec. 20, 1825 — 4, 25

Alfred W., m. Mary Ann **BAILEY**, b. of New London, Jan. 13, 1833, by Chester Tilden — 4, 49

Anna, of Lyme, m. George **SMITH**, Jr., of New London, Mar. 3, 1793, by Andrew Griswold, J.P., in Lyme — 2, 124

Ann, d. [Jason & Mary], b. Oct. 19, 1804, in Waterford — 3, 99

Bathiah, d. Sam[ue]l & Bathiah, b. Apr. 6, 1711 — 1, 61

	Vol.	Page
CHAPMAN (cont.)		
Bethiah, d. Samuel & Dinah, b. Feb. 10, 1739/40	2	16
Betsey, d. [John, Jr. & Susannah], b. Feb. 11, 1788	3	22
Betsey, d. [Daniel & Mehetable], b. Apr. 22, 1792	3	174
Catharine, d. Ezekiel & Elizabeth, b. Apr. 27, 17490	2	69
Charles, s. [James & Mary], b. Jan. 9, 1809	3	245
Charles, m. Nancy **BAILEY**, b. of New London,		
Sept. 21, 1823, by Rev. Abel McEwen	4	15
Charlotte, d. [Jason & Mary], b. Mar. 29, 1790	3	99
Charlotte, m. Albert **ARNOLD**, b. of N[ew] London,		
Dec. 24, 1833, by Rev. D. Wildman	4	54
Comfort, s. Samuel & Dinah, b. Jan. 23, 1735/6	2	16
Daniel, b. Apr. 9, 1761; m. Mehetable **TREBBY**,		
Dec. 26, 1784	3	174
Daniel, s. [Daniel & Mehetable], b. Nov. 2, 1794	3	174
Daniel, m. Mary **TRUMAN**, Dec. 18, 1796	3	174
Daniel, s. [Jason & Mary], b. Apr. 8, 1800	3	99
Daniel C., m. Catharine H. E. **BEEBE**, b. of New		
London, Sept. 4, 1849, by Rev. Jabez S. Swan	4	147
Daniel H., m. Rebecca **GETCHEL**, b. of New		
London, Aug. 22, 1852, by Rev. Jabez S. Swan	4	174
David, twin with Jonathan, s. William & Hannah, b.		
Feb. 22, [1693]	1	21
Desire, m. John **CHURCH**, of Waterford, June 30,		
1839, by Rev. Abraham Holway	4	85
Dinah, d. Samuel & Dinah, b. July 20, 1734	2	16
Dowglass, s. John & Elisabeth, b. Oct. 17, 1764	3	32
Edmond, s. [John, Jr. & Susannah], b. July 4, 1786	3	22
Eliphalet, m. Rebecca **DOYAL**, Feb. 12, 1786	3	99
Elizabeth, d. Jeremiah & Hannah, b. Nov. 22, 1702	1	32
Elizabeth, d. Samuel & Dinah, b. Apr. 7, 1731	2	16
Elizabeth, d. Ezekiel & Elizabeth, b. Apr. 13, 1733	2	7
Elizabeth, m. John **SILLIVAN**, Feb. 21, 1756, by		
Mather Byles	2	103
Elizabeth, d. [James & Mary], b. Oct. 17, 1798	3	245
Elizabeth, [w. George], d. Sept. 15, 1802	3	175
Elizabeth, m. George R. **COMSTOCK**, b. of New		
London, Jan. 19, 1823, by Rev. Abel McEwen	4	12
Ellen, of [New London], m. Edwin R. **FELLOWS**,		
Jan. 6, 1845, by Rev. S. Benton	4	116
Esther, d. [Jason & Mary], b. Sept. 29, 1788	3	99
Esther, d. [Ire & Patience], b. July 22, 1804; d. June		
16, 1807	3	93
Esther W., m. William **NEWMAN**, Aug. 29, 1841,		
by Peter D. Irish, J.P.	4	96
Eunice, m. Absalam **HARRIS**, June 15, 1773	3	112
Ezekiel, s. Jeremiah & Hannah, b. Sept. 9, 1706	1	32
Ezekiel, m. Elizabeth **CHAPPELL**, Nov. 23, 1730	2	7
Frederick, m. Frances **POTTS**, Mar. 31, 1831, by		
Rev. Leonard B. Griffing	4	41
George, s. John & Elisabeth, b. Mar. 1, 1770	3	32
George, m. Elizabeth **BILLINGS**, Nov. 13, 1791	3	175

	Vol.	Page

CHAPMAN (cont.)

	Vol.	Page
George, s. [Jason & Mary], b. June 17, 1802, in Waterford	3	99
George, m. Prudence **BILLINS**, Jan. 29, 1804; d. [ ]	3	175
George, m. Elizabeth **HALLAM**, relict of John, June 23, 1807	3	175
George Prentice, s. [George & Elizabeth], b. Mar. 30, 1808	3	175
Gideon, s. Jeremiah & Hannah, b. Nov. 1, 1704	1	32
Gideon, s. John & Elisabeth, b. Jan. 2 ,1762	3	32
Gideon, s. [John, Jr. & Susannah], b. Nov. 29, 1784	3	22
Giles P., m. Electia R. **LYON**, b. of Waterford, May 16, 1842, by H. R. Knapp	4	100
Hannah, d. William & Hannah, b. July 24, [1695]	1	22
Hanna[h], d. Jeremiah & Hannah, b. July 30, 1700	1	32
Hannah, m. John **PRESTON**, Sept. 9, 1718	1	50
Hannah, w. Samuel, formerly wife of Thomas **DOUGLASS**, d. Nov. 4, 1758	2	9
Hannah, d. [Ire & Patience], b. June 7, 1806	3	93
Harriet, of New London, m. Bazilla **BILLS**, of New York, Jan. 8, 1832, by Rev. Daniel Wildman	4	45
Hezekiah, s. Samuel & Dinah, b. Apr. 17, 1726	2	16
Ire, m. Patience **BEEBE**, Sept. 14, 1802	3	93
Ire, s. [Ire & Patience], b. June 14, 1803	3	93
James, s. Jeremiah & Hannah, b. Feb. 18, 1708/9	1	66
James, b. Oct. 23, 1762; m. Mary **HOLT**, Dec. 25, 1784	3	245
James, s. [James & Mary], b. Aug. 22, 1790	3	245
James, of Waterford, m. Amelia **DAVIS**, of Waterford, Feb. 18, 1838, by Rev. Abel McEwen	4	81
James, Jr., of [New London], m. Charlotte H. **ALLYN**, of Groton, Feb. 15, 1852, by Rev. Jabez S. Swan	4	172
Jane, d. Ezekiel & Elizabeth, b. Apr. 5, 1738; d. May 12, 1771	2	69
Jared Miner, s. [John Jr. & Susannah], b. July 7, 1797	3	22
Jason, m. Mary **BAKER**, July 15, 1786	3	99
Jason, s. [Jason & Mary], b. Nov. 16, 1794	3	99
Jedediah, s. Ezekiel & Elizabeth, b. Feb. 2, 1755	2	69
Jedediah B., of N[ew] London, m. Lucretia F. **BROWN**, of Waterford, Mar. 11, 1834, by Chester Tilden	4	55
Jeremiah, s. Jeremiah & Hannah, b. Jan. 23, 1695/6	1	32
Jeremiah, s. [James & Mary], b. Aug. 24, 1794	3	245
Jesse, s. [John, Jr. & Susannah], b. Mar. 4, 1794	3	22
Joanna, d. Samuel, b. July 4, 1697	1	23
Joanna, d. Sam[ue]l & Dinah, b. Nov. 11, 1737	2	16
John, s. James, m. Elisabeth **DOWGLASS**, d. William, Sept. 17, 1758	3	32
John, s. John & Elisabeth, b. June 16, 1760	3	32

	Vol.	Page
CHAPMAN (cont.)		
John, Jr., m. Susannah **MINER,** Jan. 4, 1784	3	22
John, s. [Jason & Mary], b. Oct. 6, 1792	3	99
Jonathan, twin with David, s. William & Hannah, b. Feb. 22, [1693]	1	21
Jonathan, of Waterford, m. Anna **CONGDON**, of Montville, May 28, 1826, by Rev. Abel McEwen	4	26
Joseph, s. Samuel, b. June 20, 1694	1	23
Joseph, s. Sam[ue]l & Dinah, b. Dec. 10, 1722	1	62
Joseph, s. Sam[ue]l & Dinah, b. Dec. 10, 1722	2	16
Joseph, s. [James & Mary], b. Nov. 24, 1796	3	245
Louis, d. Capt. Joseph, of Norwich, m. John P. **TROT[T]**, Dec. 11, 1796	3	144
Lucy, d. Ezekiel & Elizabeth, b. Apr. 27, 1744; d. Feb. 25, 1711	2	69
Lucy, d. [John, Jr. & Susannah], b. Mar. 26, 1792	3	22
Lucy, d. [James & Mary], b. Nov. 11, 1805	3	245
Lucy, m. John **COMSTOCK**, b. of New London, Oct. 3, 1826, by Rev. Abel McEwen	4	27
Lydia, m. Jeremiah **HARDING**, Aug. 30, 1787	3	10
Lyman, s. [Ire & Patience], b. Jan. 2, 1808	3	93
Martha, m. Herman **ALDERSTIEN**, June 13, 1847, by Rev. Thomas J. Greenwood	4	132
Mary, d. Samuel & Dinah, b. Sept. 3, 1727	2	16
Mary, of New London, m. William **DART**, of New London, Nov. 24, 1761	3	58
Mary, d. James, m. Thomas **HEMPSTEAD**, of New London, s. Stephen, all of New London, Oct. 28, 1764	3	31
Mary, d. [Jason & Mary], b. Apr. 20, 1797	3	99
Mary, d. [John, Jr. & Susannah], b. Mar. 21, 1801	3	22
Mary, of Norwich, m. John **CHARLETON**, Nov. 24, 1837, by Rev. Alvan Ackley	4	75
Mary A., of East Lyme, m. John **KELLEY**, of [New London], Oct. 20, 1850, by Rev. Abel McEwen	4	156
Mary Spaulding, d. [William H. & Sarah W.], b. Apr. 4, 1846	3	291
Mehetable, d. [Daniel & Mehetable], b. Mar. 13, 1790	3	174
Mehetable, w. Daniel, d. Dec. 3, 1794	3	174
Nath[anie]l, s. Samuel & Dinah, b. Dec. 26, 1724	2	16
Nathaniel, m. Frances H. **ADAMS**, Feb. 22, 1818, by Rev. Abel McEwen	3	238
Noah, s. [Eliphalet & Rebecca], b. Feb. 15, 1788	3	99
Olive, of [New London], m. George **RATHBONE**, of Salem, Oct. 25, 1835, by Daniel Huntington	4	63
Peter, s. Samuel, b. May 13, 1700	1	26
Polly, d. [James & Mary], b. Sept. 15, 1792	3	245
Rebeckah, d. Samuell & Bathia, b. Dec. 16, 1704	1	30

	Vol.	Page
CHAPMAN (cont.)		
Rebecca, d. of Samuel, of New London, m. Ebenezer **SIMONS**, s. of Robert, late of Ipswich, County of Essex, Mass., then of Wenham, Mass., Mar. 7, 1733/4	2	35
Rebeckah, d. Samuel & Dinah, b. Jan. 10, 1741/2	2	16
Rebeckah, m. Spearry **DOUGLASS**, May 8, 1768	3	95
Robert, s. Samuel, b. Oct. 21, 1691	1	20
Sally, d. [James & Mary], b. Aug. 21, 1787	3	245
Samuel, s. Samuel & Dinah, b. June 27, 1689	1	19
Sam[ue]l, m. Dinah **HATCH**, Mar. 8, 1722	1	62
Samuel, Jr., s. Sam[ue]l, m. Dinah **HATCH**, d. William, Mar. 8, 1722	2	16
Samuel, s. Samuel & Dinah, b. Sept. 7, 1729	2	16
Sarah, d. Jeremiah & Hannah, b. Sept. 20, 1711	1	40
Sarah, d. Ezekiel & Elizabeth, b. Apr. 27, 1736	2	32
Sarah, d. Ezekiel, of New London, m. Samuel **SIMMONS**, b. in London, now of New London, Feb. 24, 1756	2	33
Sarah, m. Nathan **HOWARD**, May 30, 1762	3	108
Sarah, d. [Jason & Mary], b. Mar. 15, 1787	3	99
Sarah E., of New London, m. Abel S. **LORD**, of Boston, June 27, 1848, by Rev. L. G. Leonard	4	140
Sarah E., m. Reuben R. **LAMB**, Dec. 16, 1851, by Rev. Jabez S. Swan	4	172
Seth, of Waterford, m. Marian **BEEBE**, of New London, Mar. 25, 1833, by Rev. Abel McEwen	4	50
Sophia, of [New London], m. Mark **COMSTOCK**, June 12, 1837, by Rev. Daniel Wildman	4	85
Sukey, d. [John, Jr. & Susannah], b. Jan. 18, 1790	3	22
Susannah, m. Nathaniel **HEMPSTE[A]D**, 3d, July 2, 1783	3	86
Thomas, s. Samuel, b. June 5, 1702	1	28
Wealthy A., m. Enoch **POWERS**, b. of New London, May 19, 1844, by Rev. Tho[ma]s J. Greenwood	4	111
William, m. Hannah **LESTER**, Mar. 27, [1690]	1	20
William, s. William & Hannah, b. Mar. 29, 1691	1	20
William, m. Lydia **LINCKHOME**, Aug. 11, 1702	1	27
William, s. [Eliphalet & Rebecca], b. Sept. 17, 1786	3	99
W[illia]m, of Norwich, m. Eliza **PENDLETON**, of New London, Sept. 2, 1834, by Daniel Huntington	4	57
William H., m. Sarah W. **HUTCHINS**, Sept. 13, 1843	3	291
William H., of New York, m. Lucy **FOWLER**, of [New London], May 18, 1847, by Rev. L. Geo[rge] Leonard	4	131

	Vol.	Page
CHAPPELL, CHAPEL, CHAPPEL, CHAPELL,		
CHAAPEL, CHAPLE, CHAPPLE, [see also		
CHEAFELL], Abby D., of New London, m. Burr		
SISTARE, May 29, 1831, by Rev. Abel		
McEwen	4	42
Abigail, d. Jonathan & Elizabeth, b. June 28, 1761	2	17
Abigail, d. [Isaac, 2d, & Elizabeth], b. May 7, 1785	3	238
Abigail, m. Frederick **SHEPARD**, Mar. 13, 1826, by		
Ebenezer Loomis	4	21
Aden, s. [William & Lydia], b. Sept. 15, 1784	3	33
Amanda, d. [Samuel, Jr. & Lucy], b. Nov. 25, 1804	3	255
Andrew, m. Bathsheba **DART**, Mar. [ ], 1757	3	24
Andrew, d. [ ]	3	24
Ann, d. John & Hannah, b. Aug. 13, 1738	2	88
Ann E., of Waterford, m. Henry F. **JONES**, of		
Salem, Nov. 8, 1848, by Rev. Abel McEwen	4	143
Anna, d. [Andrew & Bathsheba], b. Apr. 5, 1775; d.		
ae 4 m. 8d.	3	24
Anne, d. Walter & Anne, b. Aug. 8, 1754	2	80
Bethiah, d. Joseph, of New London, m. Stutely		
SCRANTON, of Newport, R.I., s. John, of		
Warwick, decd., Jan. 3, 1735	2	30
Bethia, d. Jonathan & Elizabeth, b. Sept. 10, 1758	2	17
Bethiah, m. Thomas **HARDING**, Jr., Mar. 16, 1769	3	108
Betsey H., d. [Samuel, Jr. & Lucy], b. Nov. 1, 1818	3	255
Caleb, s. George & Margaret, b. Oct. 7, [1671]	1	7
Caleb, s. [Andrew & Bathsheba], b. Aug. 20, 1770	3	24
Catherine Coit, d. [Richard & Chloe Bates], b.		
June 29, 1827	3	265
Charles, m. Mary A. **MAYNARD**, Oct. 20, 1834, by		
Rev. Francis Darrow	4	58
Charlotte C., m. Avery **LAMB**, b. of New London,		
May 27, 1832, by Chester Tilden	4	47
Christian, d. W[illia]m & Christian, b. end of		
February, [1680]	1	14
Christian, d. [William & Christian], b. Feb. [ ], 1680	1	67
Christian, m. Edward **STALLION**, Mar. 16, [1692/3]	1	21
Christian, d. Jonathan & Elizabeth, b. July 14, 1751	2	17
Christopher, s. [Andrew & Bathsheba], b. Jan. 20,		
1763; d. Sept. 29, 1782	3	24
Comstock, s. Jonathan & Elisabeth, b. Mar. 9, 1768	3	24
Cornelia, d. [Ezra & Welthy], b. May 11, 1808	3	200
Cynthia B., d. [Samuel, Jr. & Lucy], b. Apr. 17, 1821	3	255
Daniel, s. Walter & Anne, b. June 12, 1757	2	80
Delia, m. Jeremiah L. **DAVIS**, May 8, 1836, by Rev.		
Alvan Ackley	4	65
Ebenezer, s. Jonathan & Elizabeth, b. Mar. 22,		
1748/9	2	17
Edward, s. [Ezra & Welthy], b. Nov. 4, 1815	3	200
Edwin F., m. Eliza Jane **CHAPPELL**, b. of		
Montville, Apr. 13, 1845, by Rev. Abel		
McEwen	4	118

	Vol.	Page
CHAPPELL, CHAPEL, CHAPPEL, CHAAPEL, **CHAPLE, CHAPPLE** (cont.)		
Eleazer, s. Nathaniell & Hope, b. Sept. 15, 1702	1	27
Eleazer, m. Rachel **CROCKER**, Nov. 4, 1729	2	7
Eleazer, twin with Jonathan, s. Jonathan & Elizabeth, b. Jan. 29, 1756; d. June 3, 1756	2	17
Eliza, m. Robert **BROWN**, b. of Waterford, Mar. 5, 1826, by Rev. Abel McEwen	4	26
Eliza Jane, m. Edwin F. **CHAP[P]EL[L]**, b. of Montville, Apr. 13, 1845, by Rev. Abel McEwen	4	118
Elizabeth, d. John & Sarah, b. Aug. 20, 1708	1	45
Elizabeth, d. John & Eliza[bet]h, b. Oct. 16, 1719* *(Date seems to conflict with the birth of Jno.)	1	54
Elizabeth, m. Ezekiel **CHAPMAN**, Nov. 23, 1730	2	7
Elizabeth, d. Jno. & Elizabeth, b. Nov. 16, 1753	2	17
Elizabeth, d. George & Margaret, b. Aug. 30, [1756]* *("[1656]" written in)	1	2
Elisabeth, d. Jonathan, m. Jonathan **LATIMER**, Jr., (formerly 3d), s. Jonathan, Aug. 3, 1775	3	60
Elizabeth, d. [Isaac, 2d, & Elizabeth], b. Oct. 18, 1800	3	238
Elizabeth, of New London, m. Richard R. **MORGAN**, of Waterford, Dec. 29, 1826, by Rev. Abel McEwen	4	28
Emily, d. [Samuel, Jr. & Lucy], b. Mar. 22, 1807	3	255
Emily, m. William **TINKER**, Apr. 11, 1825, by Rev. Francis Darrow	4	22
Esther, d. Eleazer & Rachel, b. Nov. 9, 1731	2	7
Esther, d. Jonathan & Elisabeth, b. [ ], 1765; d. Aug. 15, 1769	3	24
Ezekiel, of Waterford, m. Lucy **PENNIMAN**, of New London, Jan. 13, 1827, by Rev. Abel McEwen	4	28
Ezra, m. We[a]lthy **ARNOLD**, d. Capt. John, Sept. 10, 1804	3	200
Fanny, d. [Ezra & Welthy], b. July 28, 1817	3	200
Frances, m. Denison **HEMPSTEAD**, of New London, July 18, 1844, by Rev. R. A. G. Thompson	4	113
Frances C., of New London, m. Thomas **PARSONS**, of New York, Mar. 18, 1822, by Rev. Abel McEwen	4	3
Francis, m. Eunice **DAVIS**, b. of Montville, Oct. 10, 1841, by Rev. R. W. Allen	4	96
Franklin, s. [Ezra & Welthy], b. Oct. 13, 1813	3	200
Franklin H., s. [Samuel, Jr. & Lucy], b. Sept. 13, 1809	3	255
Franklin H., s. [Samuel, Jr. & Lucy], d. Sept. 24, 1811	3	255
George, s. George & Margary, b. Mar. 17, [1653]	1	2
George, s. Geo[rge], m. Alise **WAYS**, Oct. 3, [1676]	1	11

	Vol.	Page
CHAPPELL, CHAPEL, CHAPPEL, CHAPELL,		
CHAAPLE, CHAPLE, CHAPPLE (cont.)		
George, s. Geo[rge] & Alse, b. Sept. 9, [1678]	1	13
George, s. George, d. Sept. 23, [1678]	1	13
George, b. Dec. 3, 1722; m. Sarah **DANIELS**, June		
[ ], 1744	3	90
George, s. [Isaac, 2d & Elizabeth], b. May 6, 1793	3	238
Grace, d. [Jonathan & Eunice], b. Sept. 21, 1753	3	103
Grace, m. Christopher **BROWN**, Aug. 5, 1781	3	109
Guy, s. [Jonathan & Eunice], b. Aug. 23, 1755	3	103
Guy, [s. Jonathan & Eunice], d. June 18, 1782	3	103
Hannah, d. John & Sarah, b. July 17, 1704	1	45
Hannah, d. John & Hannah, b. Mar. 12, 1735	2	88
Hannah, d. [George & Sarah], b. July 22, 1749	3	90
Hannah, d. Walter & Anne, b. Dec. 3, 1758	2	80
Hannah, [d. Andrew & Bathsheba], b. Mar. 3, 1768	3	24
Hannah, d. [Isaac & Mary], b. Aug. 30, 1772; d.		
[ ], 1785	3	105
Hannah, m. Stedman **NEWBURY**, Dec. 21, 1772	3	103
Hannah L., d. [Ezra & Welthy], b. Jan. 27, 1810	3	200
Harriet, d. [Richard & Sarah], b. Sept. 28, 1793	3	133
Harriet E., of New London, m. Cornelius **MASON**,		
of Waterford, Sept. 6, 1846, by Rev. L.		
Geo[rge] Leonard	4	129
Henry, s. [Isaac, 2d, & Elizabeth], b. Feb. 6, 1796	3	238
Hester, d. George & Margaret, b. Apr. 15, [1662]	1	3
Hope, m. Thomas **BOOL***, Sept. 13, 1717		
*(**BOLLES**. See Caulkins' History)	1	53
Isaac, s. John & Hannah, b. June 17, 1743	2	88
Isaac, s. [George & Sarah], b. Jan. 10, 1766	3	90
Isaac, m. Lucy **WHIPPLE**, Feb. [ ], 1763	3	105
Isaac, m. Mary **DART**, Mar. [ ], 1766	3	105
Isaac, 2d, m. Elizabeth **KING**, Nov. [ ], 1783	3	238
Isaac, s. [Isaac, 2d, & Elizabeth], b. Mar. 19, 1789	3	238
Jabez, s. Jabez & Ann, b. Jan. 11, 1752	2	113
James, m. Mary Thankful **TEFT**, b. of New London,		
Sept. 5, 1830, by Rev. Chester Colton, of Lyme	4	39
James Carrol, s. Jed[idiah], Jr. & Theody, b. Apr. 17,		
1767	3	33
Jedidiah, Jr., of New London, s. Jed[idiah], m.		
Theody **SWADDLE**, d. William, Jan. 17, 1765	3	33
Jesse, s. John & Hannah, b. Apr. 3, 1748	2	88
Jesse, s. [Jonathan & Eunice], b. Aug. 5 ,1768	3	103
John, s. [William & Christian], b. Feb. [ ], 1671	1	67
John, s. W[illia]m & Christian, b. Feb. 28, [1671]		
(Note says "d. Mar. 22, 1657 [sic]")	1	8
John, m. Elizabeth **CURTICE**, Feb. 18, 1716/17	1	48
Jno., s. Jno. & Elizabeth, b. Sept. 14, 1719 [sic]*		
*(Date seems to conflict with the birth of		
Elizabeth)	1	54

	Vol.	Page
CHAPPELL, CHAPEL, CHAPPEL, CHAPELL,		
CHAAPEL, CHAPLE, CHAPPLE (cont.)		
John, s. John, of New London, m. Hannah		
EDGECOMBE, dau. of John, of New London,		
Mar. [ ], 1726	2	88
John, s. John & Hannah, b. Feb. 28, 1728; d. in		
Jamaica	2	88
John, s. [Jonathan & Eunice], b. Nov. 9, 1750; d. in		
1750, ae 9 m.	3	103
John, s. [Jonathan & Eunice], b. Apr. 1, 1772	3	103
John G., m. Jane **TISDALE**, b. of New London, July		
18, 1852, by Rev. Jabez S. Swan	4	175
Jonathan, s. John & Hannah, b. Aug. 30, 1730	2	88
Jonathan, s. John, b. Aug. 30, 1730	3	103
Jonathan, s. Joseph, of New London, m. Elizabeth		
COMSTOCK , d. Peter, of New London, Mar.		
25, 1742	2	17
Jonathan, m. Eunice **LEECH**, Aug. [ ], 1750	3	103
Jonathan, twin with Eleazer, s. Jonathan & Elizabeth,		
b. Jan. 29, 1756	2	17
Jonathan, s. [Isaac, 2d, & Elizabeth], b. Feb. 22, 1787	3	238
Jonathan A., m. Sophia M. **BULKLEY**, b. of [New		
London], May 20, 1846, by Rev. Abel		
McEwen	4	126
Joseph, s. John & Sarah, b. Feb. 1, 1706	1	45
Joseph, s. John & Hannah, b. Nov. 9, 1740	2	88
Joseph, s. Jonathan & Elizabeth, b. Dec. 10, 1745	2	17
Joshua, s. John & Hannah, b. Dec. 13, 1733	2	88
Joshua, s. [Isaac & Mary], b. Nov. 13, 1774	3	105
Julia, d. [Ezra & Welthy], b. Feb. 20, 1812	3	200
Julia, of [New London], m. Elisha O. **JONES**, of		
Hartland, Sept. 7, 1835, by Rev. Abel McEwen	4	62
Juliet, d. [Samuel, Jr. & Lucy], b. Aug. 19, 1814	3	255
Lucinda, m. James **LAWSON** (?), Nov. 29, 1842, by		
Henry R. Knapp	4	103
Lucretia, d. Walter & Anne, b. Sept. 27, 1765	2	80
Lucretia, d. [Richard & Sarah], b. May 2, 1791	3	133
Lucretia, of New London, m. Sanford **KEENEY**, of		
New York, Sept. 4, 1829, by Rev. Abel		
McEwen	4	36
Lucy, d. [Jonathan & Eunice], b. Jan. 26, 1760	3	103
Lucy, d. [Isaac & Lucy], b. Apr. [ ], 1764	3	105
Lucy, w. Isaac, d. May [ ], 1764	3	105
Lucy, d. [William & Abigail], b. July 29, 1786	3	38
Lucy, d. [Samuel, Jr. & Lucy], b. May 3, 1812	3	255
Lydia, d. [Andrew & Bathsheba], b. Feb. 5, 1759	3	24
Lydia, d. [William & Lydia], b. Mar. 26, 1777	3	33
Lydia, d. [Isaac, 2d, & Elizabeth], b. Mar. 10, 1804	3	238
Lydia, m. John **DENNIS**, b. of New London, July 20,		
1822, by Rev. Abel McEwen	4	9

	Vol.	Page
CHAPPELL, CHAPEL, CHAPPEL, CHAPELL,		
CHAAPEL, CHAPLE, CHAPPLE (cont.)		
Maria A., of New London, m. Joseph		
WHITTLESEY, of Stonington, Oct. 11, 1831,		
by Rev. Abel McEwen	4	44
Mariah Arnold, d. [Ezra & Welthy], b. Oct. 30, 1806	3	200
Martha, d. Jonathan & Elizabeth, b. Sept. 11, 1758	2	17
Martha, of Montville, m. Elijah **FENTON**, of		
Norwich, Nov. 26, 1846, by John Howson	4	130
Mary, d. Geo[rge], m. John **DANYELL**, Jan. 19,		
[1664]	1	4
Mary, d. W[illia]m & Christiana, b. "Latter end		
February", [1668]	1	6
Mary, d. W[illia]m & Christian, b. Feb. 14, 1668	1	67
Mary, d. Joseph, of New London, m. Daniel		
COMSTOCK, s. Kingsland, of New London,		
July 7, 1736	2	102
Mary, d. Jabez & Ann, b. June 2, 1746	2	113
Mary, m. Jethro **WEEKS**, Sept. 10, 1759	3	15
Mary, d. [Andrew & Bathsheba], b. Mar. 29, 1766	3	24
Mary, d. [Isaac & Mary], b. Aug. 24, 1766; d. Oct. 7,		
1771	3	105
Mary, d. [Isaac & Mary], b. Oct. 15, 1779	3	105
Mary, d. Isaac, m. Elisha **TUBBS**, June 1, 1803	3	234
Mary C., m. Franklin F. **SMITH**, b. of New London,		
May 23, 1830, by Rev. Abel McEwen	4	38
Matilda, m. Jedediah **BROWN**, Apr. 1, 1825, by		
Ebenezer Loomis	4	21
Mehetable, d. [George & Sarah], b. Apr. 29, 1762	3	90
Mehetable, m. Edward **HAY[E]S**, [ ], 1783	3	90
Moses, s. [Samuel, Jr. & Lucy], b. Oct. 28, 1816	3	255
N. G., m. Harriet **BEEBE**, b. of [New London], Dec.		
25, 1849, by Rev. James W. Dennis	4	152
Nancy, d. [Isaac, 2d, & Elizabeth], b. May 15, 1798	3	238
Nathaniel, s. George & Margaret, b. May 21, [1668]	1	5
Nathaniel, s. Nathaniell & Hopestill, b. Dec. 23,		
[1694]	1	22
Nathaniel, s. Eleazer & Rachel, b. Nov. 25, 1730; d.		
Dec. 5, 1730	2	7
Nathaniel, s. Eleazer & Rachel, b. Oct. 15, 1733	2	7
Peter, s. Jonathan & Elizabeth, b. Feb. 26, 1742/3	2	17
Peter, s. Jabez & Ann, b. July 21, 1753	2	113
Phebe, d. [George & Sarah], b. Mar. 21, 1745	3	90
Phebe, d. [Andrew & Bathsheba], b. Dec. 21, 1760	3	24
Phebe, of New London, d. George, m. James		
HAINES, of New London, s. James, decd.,		
Nov. 30, 1767	3	37
Phebe, d. [William & Lydia], b. Dec. 19, 1786	3	33
Polly, d. James Chappel & Ann **STEBBINS**, b. Sept.		
23, 1773. Recorded at the desire of Nathan		
Fox	3	121
Polly, d. [William & Abigail], b. Feb. 13, 1784	3	38

	Vol.	Page
CHAPPELL, CHAPEL, CHAPPEL, CHAPELL,		
CHAAPEL, CHAPLE, CHAPPLE (cont.)		
Polly, m. Nathan **FOX**, June 26, 1791	3	121
Prudence, d. Jno. & Eliz[abeth], b. Dec. 3, 1746	2	17
Prudence, d. Jonathan, m. Thomas **STICKLAND**, s.		
Peter, all of New London, Jan. 12 ,1770	3	47
Rebeckah, d. [Andrew & Bathsheba], b. Aug. 18,		
1772	3	24
Rebecca, d. [Isaac & Mary], b. Apr. 9, 1777	3	105
Rhoda, d. [Jonathan & Eunice], b. Jan. 15, 1758	3	103
Richard, s. [Jonathan & Eunice], b. Nov. 25, 1766	3	103
Richard, s. [Richard & Sarah], b. Jan. 19, 1792	3	133
Richard, m. Chloe Bates **ELLIOTT**, June 14, 1824,		
at Thompson, Conn.	3	265
Richard, s. [Richard & Chloe Bates], b. Nov. 7, 1825;		
d. July 7, 1826	3	265
Richard, m. Sarah **BROWN**, Oct. 23, [ ]	3	133
Ruth, d. [George & Sarah], b. Jan. 30, 1758	3	90
Ruth, d. [Isaac & Mary], b. May 20, 1768	3	105
Ruth, m. Daniel **LEECH**, Sept. 6, 1787	3	105
Sally, d. [Richard & Sarah], b. Sept. 29, 1789	3	133
Sally Rockwell, d. [Ezra & Welthy], b. July 2, 1805;		
d. July 27, 1806	3	200
Samuell, s. Nathaniell & Hopestill, b. Dec. 21, 1699	1	25
Samuell, s. John & Sarah, b. May 30, 1709	1	45
Samuel, s. [George & Sarah], b. Mar. 17, 1755	3	90
Samuel, Jr., m. Lucy **JEWETT**, Dec. 15, 1803	3	255
Sarah, d. George & Margaret, b. Feb. 14, [1665] [A		
note says "died Nov. 24, 1660", perhaps meant		
for 1666]	1	4
Sarah, d. Nathaniel & Hopestill, b. June 20, [1697]	1	23
Sarah, d. John & Hannah, b. Oct. 23, 1726	2	88
Sarah, d. Eleazer & Rachel, b. Jan. 23, 1735/6	2	8
Sarah, d. [George & Sarah], b. Apr. 16, 1752	3	90
Sarah, d. Walter & Anne, b. Oct. 23, 1761	2	80
Sarah, d. Jona[than], & Elizabeth, b. Sept. 7, 1763	3	24
Susannah, d. [Isaac & Mary], b. Sept. 8, 1770	3	105
Temperance, d. Jabez & Ann, b. Dec. 8, 1748	2	113
Temperance, d. [Jonathan & Eunice], b. Apr. 21,		
1764	3	103
Walter, s. George, of New London, m. Anne		
WATERHOUSE, d. of William, of New		
London, Nov. 18, 1756	2	80
Walter, s. Walter & Anne, b. Feb. 12, 1774	2	80
Wealthy, d. [William & Lydia], b. Jan. 25, 1779	3	33
William, s. W[illia]m & Christian, b. "ye mid[dle] of		
September", [1677]	1	12
William, s. [William & Christian], b. [ ],		
1677	1	67
William, s. [George & Sarah], b. Mar. 21, 1747	3	90
William, s. Walter & Anne, b. June 20, 1762	2	80
William, m. Lydia **CROCKER**, Dec. 22, 1772	3	33

	Vol.	Page
CHAPPELL, CHAPEL, CHAPELL, CHAPPEL,		
CHAAPEL, CHAPLE, CHAPPLE (cont.)		
William, s. [Jonathan & Eunice], b. Feb. 13, 1775	3	103
William, s. [William & Lydia], b. Nov. 26, 1781	3	33
William, s. Abigail **MOORE**, Oct. 19, 1783	3	38
William, m. Rachel **LEE**, b. of New London, Oct. 3,		
1793, by Andrew Griswold, J.P.	2	124
William, of Middletown, m. Eloisa **YOUNG**, of New		
London, Mar. 24, 1846, by Rev. L. Geo[rge]		
Leonard	4	125
William M., m. Mary E. **CARRELL**, b. of [New		
London], May 18, 1847, by Rev. M. P.		
Alderman	4	131
CHARLETON, John, m. Mary **CHAPMAN**, of Norwich,		
Nov. 24, 1837, by Rev. Alvan Ackley	4	75
CHASE, David S., of New Bedford, m. Isabella		
GETCHELL, of Salem, May 22, 1844, by		
Rev. G. Thompson	4	112
CHEAFELL, [see also **CHAPPELL**], John, m. Sarah		
LEWIS, Aug. 26, 1708 (Perhaps		
CHAPPELL)	1	33
CHECKEROUGH*, Margaret, m. John **McPHERSON**,		
b. of New London, June 30, 1850, by Rev.		
George M. Carpenter *(Perhaps		
"CHESBEROUGH")	4	153
CHEENEY, John, m. Sally **SHEPPARD**, d. John, Sept. 3,		
1804	3	146
Mary, d. [John & Sally], b. July 29, 1805	3	146
CHELDS, CHEILDS, Hannah, m. Lott **DEMMET**, Oct.		
26, 1807	3	116
Mary, d. Joseph, m. Aaron **LYNN**, June 8, 1806, by		
Guy Richards	3	186
CHELES, Hannah, m. Joseph **GRIFFING**, Nov. 7, 1791	3	115
CHESEBROUGH, CHEESEBOROUGH,		
CHESEBOROUGH, Abigail, d. Samuel, m. John		
AVERY, s. Capt. James, Nov. 29, [1675]	1	10
Abigail, d. Amos & Mary, b. Jan. 26, 1761	2	3
Alfred, s. [Ephraim & Hannah Pickett], b. Sept. 15,		
1816	3	207
Amos, of Stonington, m. Mary **CHRISTOPHERS**,		
of New London, Jan. 23, 1735, by Rev.		
Mat[t]hew Graves	2	3
Augustus, s. [Ephraim & Hannah Pickett], b. Sept.		
12, 1834; d. May 6, 1835	3	207
Desire, d. Amos & Mary, b. Feb. 4, 1759	2	3
Elam, of Bozrah, m. Betsey M. **HUNTINGTON**, of		
Norwich, Feb. 19, 1823, by Lodowick Fosdick,		
J.P.	4	12
Elias Perkins, s. [Ephraim & Hannah Pickett], b. Jan.		
2, 1820	3	207
Ellen Elizabeth, d. [Ephraim & Hannah Pickett], b.		
Dec. 18, 1818; d. Jan. 5, 1819	3	207

	Vol.	Page
CHESEBROUGH, CHEESEBOROUGH, CHESEBOROUGH (cont.)		
Ellen Louisa, d. [Ephraim & Hannah Pickett], b. Jan. 7, 1822	3	207
Ephraim, m. Hannah Pickett **LATIMER**, July 20, 1815	3	207
Hannah Pickett, w. Ephraim, d. July 28, 1839	3	207
John Mulford Latimer, s. [Ephraim & Hannah Pickett], b. Feb. 10, 1830	3	207
Julius, s. [Ephraim & Hannah Pickett], b. Mar. 29, 1832	3	207
Lucretia Latimer, d. [Ephraim & Hannah Pickett], b. Nov. 9, 1825; d. Jan. 23, 1829	3	207
Margaret, m. John **McPHERSON**, b. of New London, June 30, 1850, by Rev. George M. Carpenter (Perhaps Margaret **CHECKEROUGH**)	4	153
Mary, d. Amos & Mary, b. Mar. 30, 1757	2	3
Matilda Wright, d. [Ephraim & Hannah Pickett], b. Jan. 25, 1828	3	207
Richard, Christophers, s. Amos & Mary, b. Feb. 20, 1763	2	3
Robert, s. [Ephraim & Hannah Pickett], b. Mar. 21, 1836	3	207
William Picket[t], s. [Ephraim & Hannah Pickett], b. Jan. 21, 1824; d. Jan. 2, 1825	3	207
CHESTER, Caroline Elizabeth, m. Capt. Thomas **LONG**, b. of [New London], Aug. 14, 1845, by Rev. John Howson	4	121
Frances G., m. Henry L. **PERKINS**, b. of [New London], Apr. 4, 1847, by John Howson	4	130
George F., of New York City, m. Jane P. **WINTHROP**, of [New London], Sept. 8, 1852, by Rev. Robert C. Hallam	4	173
John F., of Colchester, m. Caroline **WOOD**, of New London, Sept. 19, 1825, by Rev. Abel McEwen	4	24
Joseph, Jr., of New London, m. Elizabeth **LEE**, of Lyme, Sept. 22, 1785, by Andrew Griswold, J.P.	2	123
Josiah, m. Frances **McLEAN**, b. of [New London], Oct. 8, 1851, by Rev. Samuel Fox	4	167
Mary, d. William, m. Lambert **WILLIAMS**, Sept. 29, 1795	3	224
Sarah A., of New London, m. Harris **PENDLETON**, of Stonington, Apr. 3, 1844, by Rev. S. Benton	4	111
CHEW, Colby, m. Frances **LEARNED**, d. Amasa, Nov. 17, 1796	3	45
Colby, d. Sept. [ ], 1802, at sea	3	45
Colby, s. [Colby & Frances], b. Nov. 17, 1802	3	45
Coleby, m. Mary C. **LAW**, b. of New London, Oct. 11, 1832, by Rev. Abel McEwen	4	48

	Vol.	Page

CHEW (cont.)

Fanny, d. Joseph, m. Gabriel **SISTARE**, Aug. 3, 1786 — 3, 156

Francis A., of N[ew] London, m. Leonard **COIT**, of New York, Apr. 3, 1834, by Rev. Abel McEwen — 4, 55

Frances Ann, d. [Colby & Frances], b. Nov. 25, 1800 — 3, 45

Mary C., m. William C. **CRUMP**, b. of [New London], Oct. 21, 1852, by Rev. Abel McEwen — 4, 174

CHILDS, [see under **CHELDS**]

CHIPMAN, Cynthia S., m. Albert T. **BURGESS**, b. of New London, Apr. 2, 1847, by Rev. Jabez S. Swan — 4, 130

Eliza, of New London, m. John **BURGESS**, of Plymouth, Mass., Aug. 31, 1842, by L. Covel — 4, 103

Emeline, m. John **GRACE**, June 13, 1827*   *(First written 1727) — 3, 155

Emeline, m. John **GRACE**, b. of New London, June 13, 1827, by Rob[er]t Bowzer — 4, 31

Francis Amanda, m. Egbert **DECKER**, b. of New London, Oct. 31, 1842, by Eld. I.. Covell — 4, 103

John S., of Waddington, N.Y., m. Sarah R. **STODDARD**, of [New London], Sept. 25, 1848, by Rev. Abel McEwen — 4, 142

Lucretia, relict of Samuel Chipman, & d. of Samuel **CHESTER**, m. Benjamin **TITMAN**, Dec. 14, 1799 — 3, 36

Nathaniel S., m. Catharine **AYRES**, b. of [New London], Sept. 29, 1844, by Rev. S. Benton — 4, 114

Orlando, m. Harriet **LEE**, b. of New London, May 27, 1824, by Ebenezer Loomis — 4, 18

Phebe, m. Walter **HARRIS**, b. of New London, Aug. 17, 1828, by Rev. Abel McEwen — 4, 34

Sarah, m. John M. **SKINNER**, b. of [New London], Dec. 5, 1847, by Rev. M.P. Alderman — 4, 136

CHITTENDEN, Frederick J., of Killingworth, m. Mary **WILLIAMS**, of New London, Oct. 18, 1848, by H. Brownson, V. D.M. — 4, 144

CHRISTANY, Antona, m. Bridget **LYER**, b. of [New London], June 13, 1847, by Rev. M. P. Alderman — 4, 132

CHRISTIE, Alexander, m. Catharine **GOFF**, b. of [New London], Apr. 2, 1845, by Rev. Abel McEwen — 4, 118

CHRISTOPHERS, CHRISTOPHER, Abagail, [d. Peter & Abigail, b. [   ], 1784; d. 1784 ae 3 m. — 3, 232

Abagail, w. Peter, d. May [ ], 1791 — 3, 232

Ann Saltonstall, d. [Peter & Rebecca], b. Aug. 31, 1796 — 3, 232

Ann Saltonstall, of New London, m. George **JONES**, of Boston, [   ], by Rev. B. Judd — 4, 42

Christopher, s. Richard & Lucretia, b. Dec. 2, 1683 — 1, 17

	Vol.	Page

CHRISTOPHERS, CHRISTOPHER (cont.)

	Vol.	Page
Christopher, s. Richa[r]d & Lucretia, b. Dec. 2, [1683]	1	17
Christopher, m. Sarah **PROUT**, at New Haven, Jan. 22, 1711/12	1	43
Christopher, s. Christopher & Sarah, b. Oct. 10, 1717; d. Oct. 25, 1775	1	48
Christ[ophe]r, Capt. had an Indian woman named Juno who died Feb. 11, 1719/20	1	57
Eliza, d. Richard & Mary, b. Dec. 24, 1735; d. Mar. 11, 1798	2	47
Elizabeth, d. John & Elizabeth, b. Feb. 15, 1698/9	1	24
Elizabeth, m. John **PICKETT**, Oct. 21, 1706	1	32
Elizabeth, d. Richard & Elizabeth, b. Sept. 13, 1714	1	44
Elizabeth, m. Joshua **RAYMOND**, Aug. 31, 1719	1	51
Elizabeth, m. John **SHACKMAPLE**, Aug. 31, 1732	2	104
Elisabeth, m. Ebenezar **HOLT**, Jr., June 12, 1786	3	161
Elisabeth, see Elisabeth **HINMAN**	3	66
Est[h]er, m. Thomas **MANWARING**, Feb. 14, 1721/22	1	61
Geoffrey, Jr., d. May 17, [1690]	1	20
Grace, d. Richard & Grace, b. Oct. 14, 1698	1	24
Grace, d. Richard & Grace, b. Nov. 14, 1698	2	56
Grace, m. John **COIT**, July 2, 1718	1	58
Grace, m. John **COIT**, July 2, 1719	2	56
Grace, d. June 1, 1734	2	8
Hester, d. John & Elizabeth, b. June 20, 1703	1	29
Jane, w. Jeffrey*, Sr., d. June 7, [1690] *(Perhaps Geoffrey)	1	20
Joann, d. Richard & Grace, b. Mar. 19, 1706	1	32
Johanna, d. Geofry, m. John Ma[y]hew, of Devonshire, old England, Dec. 25, [1676]	1	11
John, s. Richard & Lucretia, b. Mar. 15, 1689/90	1	19
John, m. Elizabeth, d. Capt. **MULLFORD**, of Long Island, July 28, 1696	1	22
John, s. John & Elizabeth, b. May [ ], 1701	1	26
John, Lieut., d. Feb. 3, 1702/3, in Barbadoes	1	27
John, Lieut., d. Feb. 3, 1702/3, in Barbadoes	1	28
John, s. Christopher & Sarah, b. Feb. 27, 1718/19	1	50
John, of New London, s. Christ[ophe]r, m. Jerusha **GARDINER**, of New London, d. John, of New London, decd., Mar. 7, 1741/2	2	72
John, s. John & Jerusha, b. Feb. 14, 1743/4	2	72
John, s. [Peter & Abigail], b. Mar. [ ], 1779; d. Apr. 2, 1784	3	232
John, s. [Peter & Abigail], b. Aug. 8, 1788	3	232
Jonathan, s. Richard & Grace, b. Sept. 19, [1696]; d. Oct. 12, [1696]	1	22
Joseph, s. Richard & Grace, b. July 14, 1692	1	21
Joseph, s. Richard & Elizabeth, b. Nov. 30, 1722	1	62
Katharine, d. Richard & Elizabeth, b. Jan. 5, 1724/5	1	65
Lucretia, w. Richard, d. Jan. 7, [1690]	1	20

	Vol.	Page
CHRISTOPHERS, CHRISTOPHER (cont.)		
Lucretia, d. Christopher & Sarah, b. June 24, 1721	1	58
Lucretia, m. John Henry **BRADICK**, June 19, 1726	2	3
Lucretia, d. Richard, of New London, m. John		
BRADDICK, s. John, late of London, June 19,		
1726	2	24
Lucretia, of New London, d. of Christopher, late of		
New London, decd., m. Edward **PALMER**, of		
New London, s. Andrew, of New London, Oct.		
19, 1740	2	71
Lucretia, d. John & Jerusha, b. Jan. 19, 1749/50	2	73
Lucy, m. Jonathan **DOUGLASS**, Aug. 3, 1731	2	14
Lucy, d. [Peter & Abigail], b. Sept. 18, 1780	3	232
Lucy, d. Peter, m. Orlando **HALLAM**, June 22, 1806	3	192
Lydia, d. Richard & Grace, b. Aug. 10, 1701	1	26
Lydia, m. Daniel **COIT**, May 9, 1721	1	58
Lydia, of New London, dau. of Richard, of New		
London, m. Daniel **COIT**, of New London, s.		
William, of New London, decd., May 9, 1721	2	74
Lydia, d. Christopher & Sarah, b. June 21, 1723; d.		
July 2, [1723]	1	62
Margaret, d. Christopher & Sarah, b. Mar. 7, 1724/5	2	65
Margaret, d. Christopher & Sarah, d. Aug. 23, 1725	2	6
Mary, d. Christopher, m. Peter **BRADLEY**, s. Peter,		
of New London, May 9, [1678]	1	13
Mary, d. Richard & Grace, b. Sept. 18, 1694	1	22
Mary, d. Christopher & Sarah, b. Aug. 25, 1714	1	43
Mary, d. Richard & Elizabeth, b. Dec. 17, 1716	1	47
Mary, d. Richard & Mary, b. May 23, 1734	2	47
Mary, of New London, m. Amos		
CHESEBOROUGH, of Stonington, Jan. 23,		
1735, by Rev. Mat[t]hew Graves	2	3
Mary, wid. of Richard, 3rd, of New London, & dau.		
of John **PICKETT**, m. Nath[anie]l **GREEN**, s.		
Dea. Timothy, Jan. 17, 1738/9	2	57
Mary, d. John & Jerusha, b. May 10, 1746	2	73
Mary, d. [Peter & Abigail], b. Nov. 19, 1790	3	232
Mary, m. Joseph C. **SISTARE**, May 2, 1824	3	147
Mary, m. Joseph S. **SISTARE**, b. of New London,		
May 2, 1824, by Rev. B. Judd	4	18
Peter, s. Richard & Lucretia, b. July 18, [1687]	1	18
Peter, s. Christopher & Sarah, b. Aug. 28, 1713; d.		
Aug. 30, 1713	1	43
Peter, s. John & Jerusha, b. Jan. 6, 1747/8	2	73
Peter, m. Abigail **MILLER**, d. Capt. John, Feb. 9,		
1777	3	232
Peter, m. Rebecca **SALTONSTALL**, d. Winthrop,		
Apr. 2 ,1792	3	232
Richard, s. Christopher, m. Lucretia, d. Peter		
BRADLEY, of New London, Jan. 26, 1681	1	16
Richard, m. Lucretia **BRADLEY**, Jan. 26, 1681	1	16
Richard, s. Richard & Lucretia, b. Dec. 10, [1685]	1	17

	Vol.	Page
CHRISTOPHERS, CHRISTOPHER (cont.)		
Richard, m. Grace **TURNER**, of Scituate, Sept. 3, 1691	1	20
Richard, m. Elizabeth **SALTONSTALL**, Aug. 14, 1710	1	39
Richard, s. Richard & Elizabeth, b. July 29, 1712	1	39
Richard had a negro man named Quash, who d. Dec. 6 or 7, 1717	1	57
Richard, d. June 9, 1726	2	6
Richard, Jr., s. Richard, m. Mary **PICKETT**, d. John, b. of New London, [ ], 1734	2	47
Richard, d. Sept. 28, 1736	2	47
Richard, s. John & Jerusha, b. Dec. 18, 1744	2	72
Richard Peter, s. [Peter & Rebecca], b. Jan. 7, 1793	3	232
Ruth, d. Richard & Grace, b. Sept. 26, 1705	1	31
Ruth, m. Daniel **DISHON**, Oct. 4, 1724	2	12
Sally, d. [Peter & Abigail], b. Mar. 21, 1782	3	232
Samuel, s. John & Elizabeth, b. July 24, [1697]	1	23
Sarah, d. Richard & Elizabeth, b. Dec. 6, 1719	1	57
Sarah, d. Christopher & Sarah, b. Mar. 10, 1719/20	1	57
CHUBB, Benjamin, s. [Joseph & Sarah], b. Oct. 29, 1793; d. Sept. 21, 1805	3	121
Electa, d. [Joseph & Sarah], b. Sept. 6, 1797	3	121
Joseph, m. Sarah **TINKER**, Nov. 23, 1779	3	121
Joseph, s. [Joseph & Sarah], b. Sept. 21, 1780	3	121
Lucretia, d. [Joseph & Sarah], b. Apr. 24, 1791	3	121
Phebe, d. [Joseph & Sarah], b. May 20, 1785	3	121
Polly, d. [Joseph & Sarah], b. Jan. 10, 1788	3	121
Sarah, d. [Joseph & Sarah], b. Aug. 4, 1782	3	121
Sarah, w. [Joseph], d. Nov. 3, 1805	3	121
CHURCH, Amy, m. James **COMSTOCK**, Aug. 2, 1773	3	74
Betsey B., of Montville, m. Joseph L. **WATERMAN**, of Norwich, Nov. 15, 1844, by Rev. Abel McEwen	4	114
Catherine, m. Adam **FILES**, Dec. [ ], 1783	3	220
Cato, m. Jane **CHURCH**, Aug. 6, 1794 (Negroes)	3	8
Edwin, m. Sarah F. **ROGERS**, b. of Montville, Oct. 15, 1850, by Rev. Geo[rge] M. Carpenter	4	156
Elizabeth, of Waterford, m. Antone F. **JACKSON**, of [New London], July 23, 1845, by Rev. John Howson	4	121
Hannah, d. Singleton & Margaret, b. Sept. 13, 1757	2	111
Hannah, of Waterford, m. Emanuel **ENOS**, of [New London], Nov. 16, 1845, by Rev. John Howson	4	122
Harriet, m. Samuel H. **ATWELL**, b. of Montville, Sept. 25, 1844, by Rev. Abel McEwen	4	114
Jane, m. Cato **CHURCH**, Aug. 6, 1794 (Negroes)	3	8
John, of Waterford, m. Desire **CHAPMAN**, June 30, 1839, by Rev. Abraham Holway	4	85
Lodowich, s. Singleton & Margaret, b. Apr. 16, 1761	2	111
Margaret, m. Patrick **ROBERTSON**, Nov. 14, 1769	3	72

	Vol.	Page

CHURCH (cont.)

Nancy, m. Edward **BADETT**, b. of [New London],
    Sept. 2, 1851, by Rev. Abel McEwen | 4 | 164

Rebecca, m. Thomas **JONES**, Dec. 25, 1776 | 3 | 139

CHURCHILL, George, of Chatham, m. Sally **PECK**, of
    New London, June 1, 1830, by Rev. Abel
    McEwen | 4 | 38

William, Capt., m. Jane **SQUIRE**, Aug. 2, 1852, by
    Rev. Charles Willett | 4 | 171

CHURCHWOOD, Hannah, d. Josia[h], of Wethersfield,
    m. Samuel **ROYCE**, s. Robert, Jan. 9, [1666] | 1 | 5

CLARK, CLARKE, Abigail, d. of Rev. Thomas, late of
    Clemsford, Mass., m. Samuel **GREEN**, s.
    Timothy, Nov. 12, 1733 | 2 | 30

Abraham, m. Mary **MULLEIN**, Mar. 1, 1698/9 | 1 | 24

Amanda, d. [Isaac & Mary], b. Sept. 25, 1806 | 3 | 180

Amasa B., of New London, m. Nancy N. **DART**, of
    Waterford, Mar. 23, 1845, by Rev. S. Benton | 4 | 118

Andrew Jackson, s. [Arnold & Sophia], b. Mar. 5,
    1815; d. May 21, 1821 | 3 | 158

Arnold, m. Sophia **HOLT**, d. Stephen, Oct. 11, 1804,
    by Rev. H. Channing | 3 | 158

Arnold, supposed to have been lost in the Gulf
    Stream in his passage from Cuba, Sept. 3, 1821 | 3 | 158

Charles A., of N[ew] York, m. Elizabeth **ROGERS**,
    of New London, Apr. 14, 1837, by Rev. Squire
    B. Hascall | 4 | 68

Charles Arnold, s. [Arnold & Sophia], b. Mar. 5,
    1813 | 3 | 158

Christopher Culver, s. [Ebenezer & Susan], b. Sept.
    16, 1843 | 3 | 235

Eben, s. [Ebenezer & Susan], b. Jan. 19, 1840 | 3 | 235

Ebenezer, m. Catherine **CODNER**, d. William, Feb.
    3, 1799 | 3 | 233

Ebenezer, s. [Ebenezer & Catherine], b. Apr. 23,
    1813 | 3 | 233

Ebenezer, m. Susan **CULVER**, Feb. 27, 1839 | 3 | 235

Ebenezer, m. Susan **CULVER**, b. of N[ew] London,
    Feb. 27, 1839, by Rev. C. C. Williams | 4 | 82

Eliza, d. [Ebenezer & Catherine], b. Sept. 26, 1801 | 3 | 233

Eliza, of New London, m. Elbridge G. **PEASE**, of
    Edgartown, Mass., June 27, 1825, by Rev. B.
    Judd | 4 | 23

Elisabeth, d. [John & Elisabeth], b. Aug. 14, 1773 | 3 | 79

Elisabeth, wid., m. Abel **PROCTER**, Oct. 5, 1788 | 3 | 79

Elizabeth, d. [Isaac & Mary], b. Nov. 17, 1790 | 3 | 180

Elizabeth, of Lyme, m. Samuel **DART**, of New
    London, Aug. 6, 1791, in Lyme, by Andrew
    Griswold, J.P. | 2 | 123

Elizabeth, d. Josiah & Bridget, b. Dec. 7, 1802 | 3 | 189

Elizabeth, d. [John & Lucy], b. Dec. 28, 1804 | 3 | 210

	Vol.	Page
CLARK, CLARKE (cont.)		
Elizabeth, d. Isaac, m. Samuel **COIT**, Jr., Dec. 6, 1807	3	230
Elizabeth Downer, d. [Arnold & Sophia], b. Feb. 15, 1808	3	158
Elizabeth P., of New London, m. David G. **STRATTON**, of Millford, June 30, 1844, by Rev. Jabez S. Swan	4	112
Ellen, d. [Ebenezer & Catherine], b. Apr. 3, 1810	3	233
Ellen Louisa, d. [Ebenezer & Susan], b. Sept. 20, 1841	3	235
Emeline, d. [Ebenezer & Catherine], b. Nov. 21, 1803	3	233
Fanny, d. [Josiah & Bridget], b. Oct. 17, 1798	3	189
Frances B., d. [James J. & Frances], b. Jan. 2, 1835	3	292
Frances Bridget, d. [James & Frances], b. Jan. 2, 1835	3	179
Francis, of Waterford, m. Susan **CLARK**, of [New London], Mar. 2, 1845, by Rev. S. Benton	4	117
George, s. [John & Lucy], b. July 6, 1808	3	210
George, s. [Isaac & Mary], b. Aug. 27, 1808	3	180
George, s. [James J. & Frances], b. Aug. 7, 1840	3	292
Harriet, d. [Isaac & Mary], b. Mar. 30, 1804	3	180
Hester, d. [Isaac & Mary], b. Dec. 7, 1797	3	180
Isaac, m. Mary **DARROW**, d. Elder Zadock Darrow, Dec. 6, 1787	3	180
Isaac, of Waterford, m. Sally **SMITH**, Mar. 24, 1831, by Rev. Leonard B. Griffing	4	40
James, s. [Ebenezer & Catherine], b. Nov. 28, 1805	3	233
James, m. Frances **POTTER**, Mar. 19, 1834	3	179
James, m. Frances **POTTER**, b. of N[ew] London, Mar. 19, 1834, by Rev. Abel McEwen	4	55
James, m. Mary Ann **JOHNSON**, b. of N[ew] London, July 28, 1851, by Rev. J. M. Eaton	4	164
James J., m. Frances **POTTER**, b. of New London, d. Joshua, Mar. 19, 1834	3	292
James J., s. [James J. & Frances], b. Sept. 14, 1836	3	292
James Josiah, s. [James & Frances], b. Sept. 18, 1836	3	179
Jane W., m. James H. **TURNER**, Nov. 25, 1841, by Rev. A. Bois	4	102
John, m. Elisabeth **WORTHYLAKE**, Nov. 5, 1772	3	79
John, s. [John & Elisabeth], b. Aug. 3, 1775	3	79
John was killed at Fort Griswold, in Groton, Sept. 6, 1781	3	79
John, s. [Josiah & Bridget], b. Apr. 9 ,1795	3	189
John, m. Lucy **TINKER**, d. Daniel, Dec. 31, 1803	3	210
John, s. [John & Lucy], b. Sept. 7, 1806	3	210
John, m. Margaret **POLLOCK**, b. of New London, July 19, 1848, by Rev. Jabez S. Swan	4	141
John O., m. Nancy **CLARK**, Oct. 26, 1817	3	233
Joseph, s. [Isaac & Mary], b. Mar. 29, 1793	3	180

	Vol.	Page
CLARK, CLARKE (cont.)		
Josiah, m. Bridget **NEWSON**, d. Robert Newson,		
Mar. [ ], 1794	3	189
Julia, d. [Josiah & Bridget], b. Apr. 22, 1805	3	189
Julia, of New London, m. Benjamin **FERNELL**, of		
Boston, Mass., July 17, 1825, by Rev. B. Judd	4	23
Julia, m. Joseph **FRANCIS**, b. of N[ew] London,		
Mar. 23, 1834, by Chester Tilden	4	55
Lester, s. William & Hannah, b. Jan. 4, 1771	3	140
Louisa W., d. [Ebenezer & Catherine], b. Oct. 26,		
1819	3	233
Lucy Ann, d. [Arnold & Sophia], b. Aug. 8, 1805	3	158
Lucy Ann, of [New London], m. William F.		
WELLMAN, of Portland, Me., May 23, 1836,		
by Rev. Alvan Ackley	4	65
Lydia, d. [John & Elisabeth], b. June 14, 1778	3	79
Lydia, d. John, m .Hubbel **BROOKS**, Dec. 19, 1798	3	170
Lydia A., m. Isaac **CLEMENS**, b. of [New London],		
Feb. 28, 1847, by John Howson	4	130
Martha Holt, d. [Ebenezer & Catherine], b. Nov. 26,		
1807	3	233
Mary, m. Eleazer **TRUMAN**, Oct. 19, 1727	2	79
Mary, d. [Isaac & Mary], b. Dec. 9, 1788	3	180
Mary, m. Jeremiah **TINKER**, b. of New London,		
Dec. 19, 1824, by Rev. B. Judd	4	2
Mary, d. John, of New London, m. Giles L. **SMITH**,		
of Essex, Aug. 2, [1847], by Rev. Tryon		
Edwards	4	133
Murray M., m. Anastasia **CAVANAGH**, b. of [New		
London], May 30, 1849, by Rev. Robert A.		
Hallam	4	146
Nancy, d. [Josiah & Bridget], b. Dec. 29, 1796	3	189
Nancy, m. John O. **CLARK**, Oct. 26, 1817	3	233
Nancy, d. [John O. & Nancy], b. July 23, 1818	3	233
Nancy, m. William H. **YOUNG**, b. of New London,		
Jan. 22, 1820, by Rev. Nehemiah Dodge	4	2
Polly, d. [Josiah & Bridget], b. Nov. 7, 1800	3	189
Rogers, m. Emily **SPENCER**, b. of New London,		
Oct. 2, 1832, by Rev. Daniel Wildman	4	43
Sally, d. [John & Elisabeth], b. Oct. 31, 1780	3	79
Sarah M., of Ledward*, Ct., m. Richard H.		
WILLIAMS, July 28, 1841, by Rev. R. W.		
Allen *(Probably "Ledyard")	4	98
Sarah P., d. [James P. & Frances], b. Jan. 16, 1843	3	292
Sophia, [w. Arnold], d. Oct. 13, 1827	3	158
Sophia D. C., d. [Arnold & Sophia], b. Jan. 18, 1818	3	158
Susan, of [New London], m. Francis **CLARK**, of		
Waterford, Mar. 2, 1845, by Rev. S. Benton	4	117
Thomas Douglas, s. [Arnold & Sophia], b. Feb. 21,		
1822	3	158

	Vol.	Page
CLARK, CLARKE (cont.)		
William, m. Mary Ann **DOWSETT**, b. of New London, Aug. 23, 1846, by Rev. L. Geo[rge] Leonard	4	129
William Codner, s. [Ebenezer & Catherine], b. Nov. 19, 1799;' d. Nov. 25, 1802	3	233
William H., Capt., m. Susan **POTTER**, Feb. 3, 1822, by V. R. Osborn, V. D. M.	4	7
William Howland, s. [Ebenezer & Catherine], b. May 9, 1816	3	233
CLAXTON, George W., of Philadelphia, Pa., m. Eliza J. **MIDDLETON**, of [New London], June 24, 1846, by John Howson	4	130
CLAY, Daniel, s. [Stephen & Patience], b. Sept. 10, 1770	2	29
John Allen, s. [Stephen & Patience], b. Oct. 13, 1759	2	29
Lydia, d. [Stephen & Patience], b. Dec. 2, 1756	2	29
Mary, d. [Stephen & Patience], b. June 9, 1762	2	29
Mary, m. William **WILSON**, Jan. 27, 1793, by Walter King	3	186
Sally, d. Capt. Stephen, b. Feb. 22, 1773; m. Alexander **MORGAN**, Sept. 21, 1794	3	173
Sarah, d. [Stephen & Patience], b. Feb. 22, 1773	2	29
Stephen, of Boston, s. Jonas, of Boston, m. Patience **BOLLES**, of New London, d. John, Jr., of New London, Jan. 6, 1754	2	29
Stephen, s. Stephen & Patience, b. Oct. 3, 1754	2	29
Stephen, s. [Stephen & Patience], b. Jan. 6, 1765	2	29
CLEAVELAND, CLAVELAND, Abby, d. [William P. & Abby], b. Sept. 22, 1817	3	50
Abby, of N[ew] London, m. William B. **McEWEN**, of Norwalk, Ohio, July 5, 1838, by Rev. Abel McEwen	4	78
Caroline, d. W[illiam] P. & Mary, b. Aug. 15, 1799; d. Feb. 28, 1800	3	50
Eliza C., m. Frederick W. **KIRTLAND**, b. of [New London], May 25, 1837, by Rev. Abel McEwen	4	70
Eliza Crump, d. [William P. & Abby], b. June 24, 1813	3	50
Ellen P., of New London, m. Flavel **BASCOM**, of Lebanon, Apr. 30, 1833, by Rev. Abel McEwen	4	50
Ellen Payne, d. [William P. & Abby], b. Oct. 28, 1810	3	50
George Payne, s. [William P. & Abby], b. July 27, 1808; d. Oct. 21, 1808	3	50
Guy Richards, s. [William P. & Abby], b. May 24, 1815; d. Mar. [ ], 1816	3	50
Harriet Lewis, d. [William P. & Abby], b. Nov. 2, 1806	3	50
Jennette Richards, d. [William P. & Abby], b. Aug. 16, 1809	3	50
Mary, w. William P., d. Jan. 27, 1801	3	50

	Vol.	Page
CLEAVELAND, CLAVELAND (cont.)		
Mary D., d. William P., & Mary, m. Louis		
BRISTOL, s. William & Sarah, May 29, 1844,		
at Springfield, Mass.	3	297
Mary Dwight, d. [William P., Jr. & Mary], b. Oct. 17,		
1824	3	264
William Bacon, s. [William P., Jr. & Mary], b. June		
18, 1829	3	264
W[illiam] P., m. Abby **RICHARDS**, Jan. 15, 1806	3	50
William P., Jr., of New London, m. Mary **DWIGHT**,		
of Springfield, Mass., d. James S., decd., Feb.		
19, 1824	3	264
CLEFFORD, [see under **CLIFFORD**]		
CLEMENS, Isaac, m. Lydia A. **CLARK**, b. of [New		
London], Feb. 28, 1847, by John Howson	4	130
CLEVELAND, [see under **CLEAVELAND**]		
CLIFFORD, CLEFFORD, Eliza Ann, d. Silvester		
Clefford, m. David **LEACH**, Feb. 29, 1807	3	48
Franklin, m. Mary Ann **SIMMONS**, Feb. 6, 1835, by		
Abel T. Sizer, J.P.	4	59
CLINE, Catharine, m. Thomas **FARRELL**, Sept. 20,		
1849, by Rev. William Logan	4	150
CLINTON, Charles S., m. Elizabeth A. **GLOVER**, b. of		
[New London], Nov. 29, 1846, by John		
Howson	4	130
CLOTHIER, John, m. Sarah **BROWN**, Dec. 27, 1703	1	29
COATS, Charles, s. [Frederick & Lucinda], b. Nov. 25,		
1799	3	130
Frances M., m. Braddock M. **TINNIE**, b. of New		
London, Nov. 23, 1831, by Rev. Abel McEwen	4	44
Frederick, m. Lucinda **CHAMPION**, Jan. 3, 1789	3	130
Frederick, s. [Frederick & Lucinda], b. Nov. 30, 1789	3	130
Frederick, s. Charles & Electa, b. Apr. 25, 1821	3	233
Harriet, m. Timothy **CONE**, Sept. 29, 1828	3	280
Harriet Cynthia, d. [Frederick & Lucinda], b. Sept. 8,		
1805	3	130
Maria, d. [Frederick & Lucinda], b. Feb. 7, 1801	3	130
Maria, of [New London], b. George		
GREETHURST, of England, Jan. 3, 1836, by		
Rev. Alvan Ackley	4	64
Martin, s. [Frederick & Lucinda], b. Sept. 7, 1792	3	130
Martin, s. [Frederick & Lucinda], b. June 2, 1809	3	130
Martin S., of [New London], m. Amelia J.		
MARSHALL, of East Haddam, Mar. 19, 1846,		
by Rev. John Howson	4	126
Nancy, d. [Frederick & Lucinda], b. Aug. 7, 17971	3	130
William, s. [Frederick & Lucinda], b. Mar. 20, 1795	3	130
COBB, Amanda, of Noank, (Groton), m. Van R. **BALL**,		
of Stonington, Oct. 27, 1850, by Rev. E. R.		
Warren	4	156
George, m. Grace **LESCETER**, Oct. 14, 1821, by V.		
R. Osborn, V. D. M.	4	6

	Vol.	Page

COBB (cont.)

Mary Ann, m. William **PACKER**, b. of [New
    London], Mar. 12, 1846, by Rev. L. Geo[rge]
    Leonard   4   124

Zabediah Austin, m. Caroline **TILOTSON**, b. of
    Lyme, Feb. 26, 1822, by Rev. B. Judd   4   5

COCHRAN, [see also **CORCORAN**], John W., m. Mary
    E. **HALL**, b. of New London, Oct. 27, 1851, by
    Rev. Jabez S. Swan   4   173

CODNER, Catherine, d. William & Catherine, b. July 17,
    1775   3   58

Catherine, d. William, m. Ebenezer **CLARK**, Feb. 3,
    1799   3   233

Martin, s. Lawrence & Sarah, b. Jan. 20, [1673]   1   9

Martin, s. Lawrence & Sara[h], d. Sept. 11, [1676]   1   11

Sarah, d. Lawrence & Sara[h], b. Mar. 1, [1672]   1   8

Thomas, s. Lawrence & Sarah, b. Feb. 11, [1675]   1   10

Thomas, s. Lawrence & Sara[h], d. Dec. 12, [1676]   1   11

William, of Middletown, m. Catherine **HOLT**, of
    New London, July 3, 1774   3   58

William, d. Dec. 15, 1776   3   58

CODY, Bridget, m. John **BARNET**, Feb. 8, 1852, by Rev.
    J. Stokes. Witnesses: Henry Bell, Anne Coda   4   169

COFFIN, Richard, of Nantucket, Mass., m. Elizabeth
    WHEAT, of New London, Dec. 5, 1825, by
    Rev. Abel McEwen   4   25

COFFMAN, Fanny, m. Henry **MARTINS**, b. of [New
    London], Feb. 9, 1840, by Rev. Abel McEwen   4   89

COGGESHALL, COGGSHALL, COGSHALL, Eliza
    G., of [New London], m. G. C. **HAZZARD**, of
    Newport, R.I., Dec. 15, 1846, by Rev. Abel
    McEwen   4   128

Harriet L., of [New London], m. Benjamin F.
    CRAGIN, of New York, June 14, 1852, by
    Rev. T. Edwards   4   168

Sarah, of [New London], m. Egbert H. **AVERY**, of
    Groton, Nov. 9, 1840, by Rev. Abel McEwen   4   92

COGSWELL, Mary, d. [   ], of East Hampton, N.Y., m.
    John **PICKETT**, s. John, of New London, Jan.
    3, 1738/9   2   52

COIT, COITE, Abigail, d. [Thomas & Abigail], b. Mar.
    5, 1757; d. June 21, 1757   3   98

Abigail, d. [Thomas & Abigail], b. Aug. 10, 1761   3   98

Abigail, w. Thom[a]s, d. Aug. 19, 1761   3   98

Abigail, d. Dr. Thomas & Abigail, m. George
    HALLAM, s. Nicholas & Grace, Nov. 3, 1784   3   59

Abigail (**RICHARDS**), w. Dr. Thomas, d. Aug. 19,
    1761   3   108

Alfred, s. [Robert & Charlotte], b. May 23, 1835   3   263

Ann, d. William & Sarah, b. Mar. 30, 1770   3   28

	Vol.	Page

COIT, COITE (cont.)

Ann, of New London ,m. John **MILLER**, of Waterford, Dec. 19, 1824, by Geo[rge] W. Fairbank	4	20
Ann Barrowdale, d. [Robert & Charlotte], b. Mar. 5, 1827	3	263
Ann Wanton, d. [Thomas, Jr. & Mary Wanton], b. Nov. 29, 1789*; d. Aug. 30, 1794 *(Conflicts with date of parents' marriage)	3	176
Augusta D., m. Daniel **DESHON**, Jr., May 25, 1820	3	182
Augusta Dudley, [d. Thomas, Jr. & Mary Wanton], b. Mar. 31 ,1797	3	176
Betsey, d. [David & Betsey], b. Oct. 28, 1802	3	176
Boradil, d. Capt. Nathaniel, m. Stephen Greenhef **THATCHER**, Oct. 31, 1798	3	195
Charles, s. [Thomas & Mary], b. Feb. 9, 1776	3	98
Charlotte, d. [David & Betsey], b. May 22, 1798	3	176
Charlotte, m. Robert **COIT**, Oct. 16, 1821	3	263
Charlotte, m. Robert **COIT**, b. of New London, Oct. 16, 1821, by Abel McEwen	4	6
Charlotte, d. [Robert & Charlotte], b. May 27, 1825	1	263
Christopher, s. [Samuel, Jr. & Silvia], b. Nov. 6, 1793	3	20
Danyell, s. Joseph & Martha, b. Dec. 8, [1677]	1	12
Da[n]iell, s. William & Sarah, b. Oct. 25, 1698; d. July 19, 1773	1	24
Daniel, m. Lydia **CHRISTOPHERS**, May 9, 1721	1	58
Daniel, of New London, s. William, of New London, decd., m. Lydia **CHRISTOPHERS**, of New London, dau. of Richard, of New London, May 9, 1721	2	74
Daniel, m. Mehetable **HOOKER**, of Hartford, dau. of Samuel, of Farmington, decd., Jan. 21, 1741/2	2	74
Daniel, s. Daniel & Mehetable, b. Oct. 13, 1751; d. Sept. 1, 1753	2	75
D[aniel] had servants Flora, b. May 7, 1760; Dinah, b. May 9, 1762; Cato, b. July 17, 1765; Zip, b. Nov. 24, 1768	2	75
Daniel, m. Elizabeth **JEFFRAY**, of Groton, dau. of Capt. Jonathan **STARR**, decd., Dec. 16, 1764	2	75
Daniel, s. William & Sarah, b. Aug. 6, 1768	3	28
Daniel, d. July 19, 1773, of consumption	2	75
Daniel Lathrop, s. Joseph & Lydia, b. Sept. 20, 1754	2	72
David, s. [Thomas & Mary], b. May 3, 1769	3	98
David, m. Betsey **CAULKINS**, d. Pember Caulkins, Apr. 28, 1797	3	176
David, s. [John & Lucy], b. Sept. 21, 1808	3	156
David, 2d, m. Mary Ann **ROGERS**, b. of [New London], Sept. 17, 1838, by Rev. C. C. Williams	4	79
David Gardiner, s. [David & Betsey], b. Dec. 28, 1800	3	176

	Vol.	Page

COIT, COITE (cont.)

Desire, d. John & Hannah, b. Oct. 15, 1749	2	57
Ebenezer Rogers, s. [Samuel, Jr. & Silvia], b. Feb. 16, 1800	3	20
Edward, of Norwich, m. Elizabeth B. **COIT**, of [New London], Feb. 13, 1835, by Rev. Abel McEwen	4	60
Elias L., m. Phebe **BROWN**, Nov. 12, 1812	3	198
Elias Lewis, s. [Samuel, Jr. & Silvia], b. May 25, 1789	3	20
Elias W., [s. Elias L. & Phebe], b. Sept. 1, 1813	3	198
Elizabeth, d. John & Mehetable, b. Mar. 22, 1704	1	30
Elizabeth, w. Solomon, d. Mar. 25, 1715	1	46
Elizabeth, d. John & Grace, b. Dec. 31, 1724; d. Apr. 25, [1725]	2	56
Elizabeth, d. Joseph & Lydia, b. Apr. 5, 1743	2	72
Elizabeth, d. Samuel & Elizabeth, b. Nov. 25, 1754	2	83
Elisabeth, d. [Thomas & Abigail], b. Sept. 16, 1759	3	98
Elizabeth, d. Samuel, m. Joseph **FOX**, s. Benjamin, all of New London, Jan. 16, 1772	3	55
Elisabeth, m. Nathan **RICHARDS**, Jan. 22, 1784	3	85
Elizabeth, d. [Samuel, Jr. & Silvia], b. Sept. 15, 1791	3	20
Elizabeth, d. William, m. Joseph **BECAGE**, a native of Paris, Nov. 9, 1796	3	239
Elizabeth, w. David, d. May* 25, 1808, ae 33 y. *(First written August)	3	176
Elizabeth B., of [New London], m. Edward **COIT**, of Norwich, Feb. 13, 1835, by Rev. Abel McEwen	4	60
Elizabeth Richards, d. [Thomas, Jr. & Mary Wanton], b. May 25, 1806	3	176
Ellen, d. [Robert & Charlotte], b. Nov. [ ], 1837	3	263
Esther, d. Daniel & Mehetable, b. Feb. 18, 1749/50; d. Mar. 25, 1750	2	75
Esther, d. William & Sarah, b. Jan. 15, 1767	3	28
Fanny, d. [Joshua & Nancy], b. Feb. 11, 1792	3	81
Fanny, d. [Robert & Charlotte], b. Feb. 16, 1823	3	263
George Washington, s. [Samuel, Jr. & Silvia], b. July 6, 1796	3	20
Grace, d. John & Mary, b. Aug. 27, 1744	2	59
Grace, w. John, d. Nov. 9, 1745	2	56
Gurdon Saltonstall, s. [Thomas, Jr. & Mary Wanton], b. Oct. 28, 1808	3	176
Hannah Saltonstall, d. [Thomas, Jr. & Mary Wanton], b. June 18, 1795; d. Aug. 23, 1796	3	176
Henry, s. [Thomas & Mary], b. Oct. 21, 1780	3	98
Henry , s. [John & Lucy], b. May 11, 1804	3	156
Henry, m. Nancy **HEMPSTEAD**, b. of New London, May 16, 1830, by Rev. Abel McEwen	4	38
Hortha, [child of Thomas, Jr. & Mary Wanton], b. Mar. 13, 1802; d. Mar. 17, 1802	3	176
James, s. [Thomas & Mary], b. Jan. 31, 1786	3	98
James L., [s. Elias B. & Phebe], b. July 29, 1815	3	198

	Vol.	Page

COIT, COITE (cont.)

	Vol.	Page
Jane E., m. Albert R. **HARRIS**, Jan. 16, 1838, by Rev. Nathan Wildman	4	85
Jerusha, d. Joseph & Lydia, b. June 21, 1756	2	72
John, h. of Mary, d. Aug. 29, [1659]	1	3
John, s. Joseph & Martha, b. Dec. 1, [1670]	1	7
John, m. Mehetable **CHANDLER**, June 25, 1695	1	22
John, s. John & Mehetable, b. May 25, 1696	1	23
John, s. John & Mehetabel, b. May 25, 1696	2	56
John, m. Grace **CHRISTOPHER**, July 2, 1718	1	58
John, s. John & Grace, b. Apr. 7, 1719	1	58
John, m. Grace **CHRISTOPHERS**, July 2, 1719	2	56
John, s. John & Grace, b. Apr. 7, 1720	2	56
John, s. John & Grace, m. Mary, d. Robert & Ann **PIERCE**, June 13, 1742	2	59
John, drowned Mar. 26, 1745, near Middletown	2	56
John, drowned Mar. 26, 1745, at Middletown	2	59
John, s. John & Mehetable, m. Hannah **POTTER**, wid. of Thomas, of Newport, & dau. of Henry **GARDINER**, of N. Kingstown, June 20, 1748	2	57
John, s. John & Hannah, b. Oct. 10, 1752	2	57
John, m. Lucy **SMITH**, d. James, Dec. 3, 1789	3	156
John, s. [John & Lucy], b. July 31, 1790; d. Aug. 9, 1790	3	156
John, s. [John & Lucy], b. Sept. 7, 1794	3	156
John B., of Philadelphia, m. Maria **HOBRON**, d. Thomas, of [New London], [June] 18, [1845], by Rev. Edwards	4	124
John Caulkins, s. [David & Betsey], b. July 27, 1799	3	176
John Wolf, s. [Russell & Lucretia], b. July 29, 1803	3	132
Jonathan, s. [Thomas & Mary], b. Aug. 6, 1771	3	98
Joseph, s. John & Martha, m. Martha, d. William **HARRIS**, of Wethersfield, July 17, [1667]	1	5
Joseph, s. Joseph & Martha, b. Apr. 4, [1673]	1	9
Joseph, s. John & Mehitable, b. Nov. 15, 1698	1	24
Joseph, Deac., d. Mar. 27, 1704	1	20
Joseph, s. John & Grace, b. Oct. 3, 1728	2	56
Joseph, s. John & Mehetable, m. Lydia **LOTHROP**, d. Tho[ma]s & Lydia, of Norwich, Jan. 9, 1739/40	2	72
Joseph, s. Joseph & Lydia, b. Sept. 23, 1750	2	72
Joseph, s. [Samuel, Jr. & Silvia], b. Feb. 20, 1785	3	20
Joseph, m. Sally **MASON**, d. Noah, Dec. 6, 1807	3	200
Joshua, s. Joseph & Lydia, [ ], 1758	2	72
Joshua, of New London, m. Nancy **HALLAM**, of [New London], Jan. 2 1785, by Timo[thy] Green, J.P.	3	81
Joshua, s. [Robert & Charlotte], b. Feb. 4, 1832	3	263
Julia, d. [David & Betsey], b. Mar. 4, 1805; d. Dec. 8, 1805	3	176
Julia, d. [David & Betsey], b. Apr. 22, 1808; d. Oct. 5, 1808	3	176

	Vol.	Page
COIT, COITE (cont.)		
Leonard, s. [Joshua & Nancy], b. Nov. [ ], 1789	3	81
Leonard, of New York, m. Francis A. **CHEW**, of		
N[ew] London, Apr. 3, 1834, by Rev. Abel		
McEwen	4	55
Lorey, of New London, m. Eber **WEST**, of Tolland,		
Sept. 16, 1823, by Rev. B. Judd	4	16
Love, d. [Russell & Lucretia], b. Nov. 2, 1794; d.		
Aug. 21, 1795	3	132
Love, d. [Russell & Lucretia], b. Nov. 19, 1798	3	132
Lucretia, d. Joseph & Lydia, b. Apr. 10, 1748; d. Oct.		
16, 1751	2	72
Lucretia, d. [John & Lucy], b. Sept. 28, 1792	3	156
Lucretia, d. Samuel, m. Henry **YOUNG**, Oct. 8, 1796	3	61
Lucy, d. Joseph & Lydia, b. July 2, 1746	2	72
Lucy, d. [John & Lucy], b. July 31, 1801	3	156
Lucy, w. John, d. Dec. 3, 1808	3	156
Lucy S., m. Euclid **ELLIOTT**, b. of New London,		
Apr. 21, 1822, by Rev. Abel McEwen	4	8
Lydia, d. Joseph & Lydia, b. June 17, 1741	2	72
Lydia, w. Daniel, d. Jan. 22, 1748/9	2	74
Lydia, m. Joshua **POTTER**, May 4, 1780	3	15
Lydia, d. [Joshua & Nancy], b. Dec. [ ], 1787	3	81
Mabel, w. Daniel, d. Nov. 17, 1763	2	75
Margaret, d. Nath[anie]l & Margaret, b. Feb. 8,		
1742/3; d. Sept. 4, 1746	2	70
Margaret, w. Nathaniel, d. July 17, 1752	2	70
Marion, d. [Elias L. & Phebe], b. July 23, 1814; d.		
Sept. 25, 1814	3	198
Martha, d. Jno., m. Hugh **MOULD**, of Barnstable,		
June 11, [1662]	1	3
Martha, d. John & Mehetable, b. Apr. 1, 1706	1	32
Martha, w. Deac. Joseph, d. July 14, 1713	1	20
Martha, m. Daniel **HUBBARD**, Aug. 18, 1731	2	38
Martha, d. Richard & Abigail, b. Oct. 9, 1744	2	20
Martha, m. John **HOLT**, Jr., Nov. 21, 1771	3	88
Mary, w. John, d. Jan. 2, [1676], ae 80 y.	1	11
Mary, d. Solomon & Mary, b. June 30, 1713	1	20
Mary, w. Solomon, d. July 7, 1713	1	20
Mary, d. Nath[anie]l & Margaret, b. Nov. 10, 1740;		
d. Feb. 5, 1742/3	2	70
Mary, d. Nathaniel & Margaret, b. Aug. 2, 1747	2	70
Mary, wid. of John, Jr., m. James **COLVER**,		
formerly of Groton, Jan. 22, 1756	2	35
Mary, d. [Thomas & Mary], b. Oct. 13, 1773; d. Dec.		
29, 1774	3	98
Mary, d. [Thomas & Mary], b. May 9, 1778	3	98
Mary, d. Dr. Thomas, m. Benjamin **RICHARDS**,		
Dec. 18, 1795	3	182
Mary, d. [Russell & Lucretia], b. Sept. 4, 1796	3	132
Mary Gardiner, d. [Thomas, Jr. & Mary Wanton], b.		
Apr. 28, 1792	3	176

	Vol.	Page
COIT, COITE (cont.)		
Mehetable, d. Daniel & Mehetable, b. Feb. 18, 1745/6	2	75
Mehetable, d. John & Hannah, b. June 16, 1755	2	57
Mehetabel, d. William & Sarah, b. Aug. 10, 1765	3	28
Nancy, d. [Joshua & Nancy], b. June 10, 1795	3	81
Nancey, d. [John & Lucy], b. July 26, 1800; d. Aug. 7, 1800	3	156
Nancy, d. [Russell & Lucretia], b. Feb. 21, 1801	3	132
Nancy, d. [John & Lucy], b. Apr. 3, 1806	3	156
Nancy, d. [Samuel, Jr. & Elizabeth], b. Oct. 23, 1808	3	230
Nancy, m. Edward **LEARNED**, Nov. 24, 1814	3	179
Nathaniell, s. Sollomon & Mary, b. May 30, 1711	1	39
Nathaniel, m. Margaret **DOUGLASS**, Nov. 6, 1735	2	8
Nathaniel, s. Solomon, m. Margaret **DOUGLASS**, d. Capt. Rich[ar]d, b. of New London, Nov. 6, 1735	2	70
Nathaniel, s. Nath[anie]l & Margaret, b. Dec. 1, 1738	2	70
Nathaniel, m. Mary **BRADDICK**, wid. of Capt. John, late of New London, & dau. of Richard **CHRISTOPHERS**, 2d, of New London, July 13, 1754	2	70
Nathaniel, s. [Samuel, Jr. & Silvia], b. Dec. 28, 1786	3	20
Nathaniel, s. [Russell & Lucretia], b. Aug. 13, 1792	3	132
Rhoda, d. Samuel & Elizabeth, b. Apr. 1, 1757	2	84
Richard, s. John & Grace, b. July 8, 1722	1	59
Richard, s. John & Grace, b. July 8, 1722	2	56
Richard, s. John, Jr., of New London, m Abigail **BRADDICK**, of New London, d. Capt. John, late of Southold, L.I., decd., Oct. 12, 1743, by Rev. Eliphalet Adams	2	20
Richard, d. Oct. 3, 1745	2	20
Richard, s. [John & Lucy], b. Nov. 6, 1796	3	156
Richard H., of Norwich, m. Caroline L. **MASON**, of [New London], Mar. 17, 1846, by Rev. Abel McEwen	4	125
Robert, s. [Joshua & Nancy], b. Nov [ ], 1785	3	81
Robert, m. Charlotte **COIT**, Oct. 16, 1821	3	263
Robert, m. Charlotte **COIT**, b. of New London, Oct. 16, 1821, by Abel McEwen	4	6
Robert, s. [Robert & Charlotte], b. Apr. 26, 1830	3	263
Russel[l], m. Lucretia **WOLF**, Nov. 19, 1791	3	132
Sally Mason, d. [Joseph & Sally], b. Sept. 15, 1808	3	200
Samuell, s. John & Mehetable, b. Feb. 18, 1700	1	26
Samuel, s. John & Grace, b. Oct. 14, 1726	2	56
Samuel, s. John & Grace, b. Oct. 14, 1726; m. Elizabeth **RICHARDS**, Feb. 18, 1753	2	83
Samuel, twin with William, s. Nathaniel & Margaret, b. July 1, 1752	2	70
Samuel, s. Samuel & Elizabeth, b. Feb. 22, 1755; d. Sept. 10, 1756	2	84
Samuel, Jr., m. Silvia **LEWIS**, Nov. 28, 1782	3	20

	Vol.	Page
COIT, COITE (cont.)		
Samuel, s. [Samuel, Jr. & Silvia], b. Aug. 12, 1783	3	20
Samuel, Jr., m. Elizabeth **CLARK**, d. Isaac, Dec. 6, 1807	3	230
Sarah, m. John **GARDNER**, Sept. 2, 1708	1	33
Sarah, d. Daniel & Lydia, b. Apr. 26, 1726; d. Mar. 22, 1730	2	6
Sarah, d. Daniel & Lydia, b. Apr. 26, 1726; d. Mar. 22, 1729/30	2	74
Sarah, d. Daniel & Lydia, d. Mar. 22, 1730	2	8
Sarah, d. Nath[anie]l & Marg[a]rett, b. July 18, 1736	2	8
Sarah, d. Nath[anie]l & Margaret, b. July 18, 1736	2	70
Sarah, d. Daniel & Mehetable, b. May 30, 1744	2	75
Sarah, d. Nathaniel, m. Samuel **BELDEN**, all of New London, June 17, 1759	3	13
Sarah, d. Daniel, m. Robinson **MUMFORD**, s. James, Feb. 1, 1761	3	16
Sarah, d. William & Sarah, b. Apr. 27, 1764	3	28
Sarah A., m. Frederick W. **TREADWAY**, Nov. 4, 1839, by James M. Macdonald	4	88
Solomon, s. Joseph & Martha, b. Nov. 29, [1679]	1	14
Sollomon, m. Mary **STOW[E]**, Dec. 24, 1706	1	32
Sollomon, s. Sollomon & Mary, b. June 28, 1710; d. about 3 weeks later	1	39
Solomon, m. Elizabeth **SHORTT**, Aug. 8, 1714	1	20
Solomon, m. Abigaill **CAREY**, Nov. 16, 1715	1	46
Solomon, s. Nathaniel & Margaret, b. Feb. 15, 1744/5	2	70
Susan, of New London, m. Ebenezer **KELLOGG**, of Williamstown, Mass., June 2, 1826, by Rev. Abel McEwen	4	26
Susannah, d. [Thomas & Mary], b. July 11, 1783	3	98
Thomas, s. John & Mehetable, b. June 1, 1702	1	28
Thomas, m. Mary **PRENTICE**, Nov. 5, 1723	1	63
Thomas, s. Joseph & Lydia, b. July 11, 1752	2	72
Thomas, m. Abigail **RICHARDS**, d. John, May 23, 1756	3	98
Thomas, s. [Thomas & Abigail], b. Aug. 5, 1758; d. Sept. 16, 1758	3	98
Thomas, m. Mary **GARDINER**, d. David, Jan. 12, 1764	3	98
Thomas, s. [Thomas & Mary], b. Apr. 2, 1767	3	98
Thomas, Jr., m. Mary Wanton **SALTONSTALL**, Nov. 29, 1789* *(Conflicts with date of birth of dau. Ann Wanton Coit)	3	176
Thomas, d. June 5, 1811, ae 86 y.	3	98
Thomas Winthrop, s. [Thomas, Jr. & Mary Wanton], b. June 28, 1803	3	176
William, s. Joseph & Martha, b. Jan. 25, [1675]	1	10
William, s. Daniel & Mehetable, b. Nov. 26, 1742	2	74
William, twin with Samuel, s. Nathaniel & Margaret, b. July 1, 1752; d. July 9, 1752	2	70

	Vol.	page
COIT, COITE (cont.)		
William, s. Daniel, m. Sarah **PRENTISS**, d. Capt.		
John, decd., all of New London, [ ],		
1763	3	28
William, s. William & Sarah, b. Nov. 19, 1771	3	28
William, s. [John & Lucy], b. Feb. 24, 1798	3	156
William Avery, s. [Russell & Lucretia], b. Oct. 30,		
1806	3	132
William E., of Norwich, m. Jane Maria **SIZER**, of		
New London, June 13, 1842, by Rev. A. Boies	4	100
-----, s. Sollomon & Mary, b. Feb. 18, 1708/9; d.		
within 2 hours	1	39
-----, d. stillborn, Daniel & Mehetable, Sept. 23, 1747	2	75
-----, s. Stillborn, Daniel & Mehetable, Jan. 17,		
1748/9	2	75
COLBERT, Elizabeth, m. Isaac **DELONG**, b. of New		
London, Feb. 27, 1841, by Rev. Squire B.		
Hascall	4	93
Maurice, m. Anne **LAMB**, Jan. 6, 1852, by Rev. J.		
Stokes. Witnesses: Bartholomew Lynch,		
Bridget Donahue	4	169
COLBY, Edward, m. Rachel **SCOVEL**, b. of [New		
London], May 14, 1845, by Rev. Abel McEwen	4	119
COLE, COLES, Elizabeth, d. John, m. James		
STEWART, Oct. 10, 1798	3	237
Stephen, of R.I., m. Susannah **BROWNING**, of		
Conn., Nov. 21, 1794, by G. Williams, J.P.	3	75
COLFAX, Ann, d. John & Ann, b. May 16, 1730	2	7
Ann, d. George & Lucy, b. Apr. 12, 1760	3	21
Ann, d. George, of New London & Lucy, m.		
Ebenezer **LESTER**, s. Eliphalet, of New		
London & Sarah, July 5, 1778	3	71
Ann, d. [George & Mary], b. Mar. 27, 1783	3	62
Ann, d. George, m. Robert **COLFAX**, Jr., Nov. 16,		
1807	3	187
Anna, d. John*, m. Jonathan **DOUGLASS**, s.		
William, all of New London, Apr. 29, 1767		
*(First written "George")	3	60
Charlotte, d. [George & Mary], b. Feb 4, 1790	3	62
Charlot[te], d. George, m. Ralph **STODDARD**, Feb.		
1, 1808	3	206
Charlotte, d. [Robert, Jr. & Ann], b. Sept. 15,		
1818	3	187
Charlotte, of [New London], m. James		
BEDINGTON, of Walington, N.Y., June 8,		
1835, by Rev. Abel McEwen	4	61
Charlotte, d. [William P. & Elizabeth Ann], b. Dec.		
23, 1836	3	285
Ebenezer, s. George & Lucy, b. Sept. 15, 1753	3	21
Ebenezer, m. Lucretia **HEMPSTE[A]D**, May 19,		
1776	3	87
Ebenezer, s. [Ebenezer & Lucretia], b. Sept. 21, 1781	3	87

	Vol.	Page
COLFAX (cont.)		
Ebenezer, m. Lydia **POTTER**, d. Joshua, Sept. 25,		
1803	3	114
Ebenezer, s. [Ebenezer & Lydia], b. July 7, 1804	3	114
Ebenezer, Sr., lost at sea, [ ]	3	87
Elizabeth, d. [Jonathan & Elizabeth], b. Mar. 3, 1789	3	171
Elisabeth, d. [George & Mary], b. June 6, 1797	3	62
Elizabeth, m. Robert **COLFAX**, June 24, 1803	3	27
Elizabeth, m. Thomas **HUNTINGTON**, Oct. 21,		
1818, in New York	3	156
Frances C., m. Everard **HOLT**, b. of [New London],		
Nov. 2, 1834, by Rev. Abel McEwen	4	58
Frances Curtis, d. [Robert, Jr. & Ann], b. Mar. 18,		
1813	3	187
George, s. John & Ann, b. Dec. 5, 1727	2	7
George, of New London, s. John, m. Lucy **AVERY**,		
of Groton, d. Eben[eze]r Avery, of Groton,		
Apr. 13, 1749, old style	3	21
George, s. George & Lucy, b. Feb. 9, 1751/2, old		
style	3	21
George, of New London, m. Mary **ROBBINS**, of		
Wethersfield, Oct. 2, 1777	3	62
George, s. [Robert & Sarah], b. Nov. [ ], 1783	3	27
George, s. [George & Mary], b. May 16, 1794	3	62
George, s. [William P. & Elizabeth Ann], b. Dec. 18,		
1838	3	285
George Robbins, s. [George & Mary], b. May 27,		
1786	3	62
Harriet, d. [Robert & Sarah], b. Feb. 28, 1789	3	27
Harriet Ann, d. [Ebenezer & Lydia], b. Dec. 28, 1807	3	114
John, s. [George & Lucy], b. Nov. 21, 1763	3	21
John, s. [George & Mary], b. Sept. 26, 1784	3	62
Jonathan, s. George & Lucy, b. Mar. 12, 1758	3	21
Jonathan, m. Elizabeth **WILLSON**, d. Thomas		
Willson, Dec. 15, 1783	3	171
Jonathan, s. [Jonathan & Elizabeth], b. Jan. 15, 1785	3	171
Jonathan, d. Jan. [ ], 1790, at Auxey's	3	171
Lucretia, d. [Ebenezer & Lucretia], b. Jan. 28, 1777	3	87
Lucretia, wid., m. Kimbell **PRIME**, Feb. 19, 1784	3	87
Lucy, d. George & Lucy, b. Mar. 21, 1755	3	21
Lucy, m. Christopher **PRINCE**, Jan. 11, 1778	3	59
Lucy, d. [George & Mary], b. Aug. 3, 1778	3	62
Lucy, d. George, m. Joshua **STARR**, Jr., Apr. 19,		
1798	3	193
Maria, d. [Robert & Sarah], b. July [ ], 1785	3	27
Maria Ward, d. [Robert, Jr. & Ann], b. Nov. 8, 1814	3	187
Mary, d. [George & Lucy], b. Jan. 8, 1766	3	21
Mary, of New London, m. Alexander **RICHARDS**,		
of New London, May 15, 1788, by Rev. Henry		
Channing	3	100
Mary, d. [George & Mary], b. Oct. 1, 1791	3	62
Mary Ann, d. [Robert, Jr. & Ann], b. May 1, 1810	3	187

	Vol.	Page
COLFAX (cont.)		
Richard, s. [Jonathan & Elizabeth], b. Nov. 18, 1787	3	171
Robert, s. George & Lucy, b. Dec. 26, 1761	3	21
Robert, s. George & Lucy, m. Sarah **WILLSON**, d.		
Capt. Thomas & Sarah, [ ], 1781	3	27
Robert, s. [Robert & Sarah], b. Feb. 10, 1782	3	27
Robert, m. Elizabeth **COLFAX**, June 24, 1803	3	27
Robert, Jr., m Ann **COLFAX**, d. George, Nov. 16,		
1807	3	187
Sarah, d. George & Lucy, b. Jan. 30, 1750, old style	3	21
Sarah, d. [George & Mary], b. May 15, 1780	3	62
Sarah, d. Dec. 1, 1801	3	27
Sarah, d. [Robert, Jr. & Ann], b. July 29, 1821	3	187
William, s. George & Lucy, b. July 3, 1756	3	21
William, s. [George & Mary], b. Oct. 8, 1787	3	62
William, s. [Robert & Sarah], b. Apr. [ ], 1791	3	27
William, s. [Ebenezer & Lydia], b. Oct. 26, 1805	3	114
William P., m. Elizabeth Ann **HOLT**, Oct. 25, 1834	3	285
William P., m. Elizabeth Ann **HOLT**, b. of New		
London, Oct. 25, 1834, by Rev. Abel McEwen	4	58
COLLINS, COLLIN, COLINS, [see also **CULLINS**],		
Charlotte, d. [James & Grace], b. May 21, 1822	3	210
Charlotte L., m. Enoch **CRANDALL**, b. of [New		
London], June 8, 1845, by Rev. L. Geo[rge]		
Leonard	4	123
Daniel, m. Alice **PELL**, Feb. 22, 1730/1	2	7
Daniel, s. Daniel & Alice, b. Jan. 15, 1737/8	2	8
Elizabeth, d. [James & Grace], b. July 20, 1814	3	210
Elizabeth, m. Patrick **KENNENY**, Apr. 16, 1852, by		
Rev. J. Stokes. Witnesses: Timothy Lynch,		
Mary Forrest	4	170
Elizabeth C., of N[ew] London, & George R.		
SLATE, of Lyme, Apr. 25, 1837, by Rev.		
Squire B. Hascall	4	69
Ellen, m. William B. **SMITH**, Aug. 1, 1850, by Rev.		
Charles Willett	4	154
James, of New London, m. Grace **TINKER**, of		
Waterford, Mar. 27, 1814	3	210
Jane, d. [James & Grace], b. May 27, 1819	3	210
Johanna, m. Rodger **McGRATH**, Sept. 22, [18]50,		
[by Peter J. Blenkinsop]. Witnesses: John		
McNerny, Elizabeth Collins	3	306
Johannah, m. Rodger **McGRATH**, Sept. 22, 1850.		
Witnesses: John McNerny, Elizabeth Collins	4	159
John, m. Mary **DUNBAR**, b. of New London, May		
29, 1831, by Rev. Abel McEwen	4	42
John P., m. Mary M. **BLIVEN**, Aug. 19, 1850, by		
Rev. Charles Willett	4	156
Lucretia, d. Daniel & Alice, b. Apr. 22, 1736	2	8
Martha, d. Daniel & Alice, b. Dec. 22, 1731	2	7
Mary, d. Daniel & Alice, b. Mar. 25, 1734	2	8
Mary, d. Joseph, m. Andrew **MASON**, Jan. 1, 1801	3	169

	Vol.	Page

COLLINS, COLLIN, COLINS (cont.)

	Vol.	Page
William, s. [James & Grace], b. Feb. 5, 1817	3	210
COLT, Ama, of Lyme, m. Pardon T. **TABER**, of New London, Nov. 26, 1789, by Rev. David Higgins	3	114
COLVER, [see also **CULVER**], Abiah, d. [Samuel & Elisabeth], b .May 26, 1776	3	78
Absalom, s. [Daniel & Hannah], b. Mar. 21, 1767	3	119
Ann, d. William & Mary, b. Apr. 14, 1753	2	84
Caleb, twin with Charles, s. [Christopher & Phebe], b. Apr. 13, 1786; d. Sept. 7, 1787	3	91
Caleb, s. [Christopher & Phebe], b. July 4, 1797	3	91
Charles, twin with Caleb, [s. Christopher & Phebe], b. Apr. 13, 1786; d. Aug. 16, 1787	3	91
Charles, s. [Christopher & Phebe], b. Mar. 10, 1788	3	91
Christopher, m. Phebe **HOLT**, Dec. 14, 1779	3	91
Christopher, s. [Christopher & Phebe], b. Oct. 13, 1782; d. May 10, 1783	3	91
Christopher, s. [Christopher & Phebe], b. Mar. 13, 1784	3	91
Daniel, m. Hannah **BEEBE**, Sept. 19, 1764	3	119
Daniel, s. [Daniel & Hannah], b. Jan. 14, 1770	3	119
Edwin, of Groton, m. Mary W. **MANWARING**, of N[ew] London, Mar. 6, 1836, by Rev. Squire B. Hascall	4	83
Elisabeth, d. [Samuel & Elisabeth], b. Apr. 18, 1782; d. [ ], 1785 (?)	3	78
Elisabeth, d. [Samuel & Elisabeth], b. Oct. 14, [1785]	3	78
George, s. [Samuel & Elisabeth], b. Apr. 13, 1780	3	78
Grace, d. William & Mary, b. Sept. 25, 1755	2	84
Grace, m. Nathaniel **BEEBE**, Oct. 28, 1762	3	96
Hannah, m. Harry **MILLER**, Feb. 29, 1787	3	119
James, formerly of Groton, m. Mary **COIT**, wid., of John, Jr., Jan. 22, 1756	2	35
James, s. James & Mary, b. Sept. 25, 1757	2	35
Jerusha, d. [Samuel & Elisabeth], b. Feb. 31, 1778 [sic]	3	78
John, s. [Christopher & Phebe], b. June 11, 1799	3	91
John Wait*, s. Hannah, b. Aug. 22, 1778 *(Daniel, his father?)	3	119
Joseph, s. [Daniel & Hannah], b. Aug. 13, 1765* *(First written Mar. 21, 1765)	3	119
Lucretia, d. [Daniel & Hannah], b. May 11, 1771	3	119
Martha, d. Daniel & Elizabeth, m. John **ROGERS**, May 15, 1738	2	110
Mary, d. [Christopher & Phebe], b. July 19, 1781; d. May 14, 1783	3	91
Mary, d. [Christopher & Phebe], b. Jan. 14, 1791	3	91
Nancy, d. [Christopher & Phebe], b. Mar. 15, 1793	3	91
Richard, s. [Daniel & Hannah], b. Dec. 6, 1774	3	119
Samuel, m. Elisabeth **BUCKMASTER**, Nov. 3, 1774	3	78
Samuel, s. [Samuel & Elisabeth], b. June 8, 1789	3	78

	Vol.	Page
COLVER (cont.)		
Tabitha, m. William **PERKINS**, July 18, 1765	3	10
William, s. David & Elizabeth, m. Mary **BURDEN**,		
Nov. 2, 1748	2	84
William, s. William & Mary, b. Apr. 16, 1750	2	84
William, s. [Samuel & Elisabeth], b. Feb. 16, 1795	3	78
COLVERT, Grace, m. Nathaniel **BEEBE**, Dec. 28, 1772		
(Entry crossed out)	3	88
Jane, d. [William & Deborah], b. Apr. 7, 1767	3	89
Jane, m. James **PETTRIE**, Sept. 2, 1782	3	121
John, s. [William & Deborah], b. Nov. 24, 1780	3	89
John, m. Francess **COMBS**, b. of New London, Mar.		
19, 1842, by Rev. R. W. Allen	4	99
Ma[t]thew, s. [William & Deborah], b. Feb. 18, 1779	3	89
Miranda, of [New London], m. William		
BECKWITH, of Waterford, June 11, 1845, by		
John Grace, J.P.	4	120
Phebe, d. [William & Deobrah], b. Aug. 18, 1775	3	89
Temperance, d. [William & Deborah], b. July 15,		
1764	3	89
Thomas, s. [William & Deborah], b. Jan. 4, 1785	3	89
William, m. Deborah **DAYTON**, July 22, 1762	3	89
William, s. [William & Deborah], b. Apr. 5, 1769	3	89
COLWELL, Elizabeth F., m. William **O'BRIEN**, b. of		
New London, Apr. 4, 1852, by Rev. Seth		
Chapin	4	166
COMSTOCK, Abby E., of New London, m. Henry M.		
THOMPSON, of Vermont, May 18, 1849, by		
Rev. Geo[rge] M. Comstock	4	145
Adeline, m. George **HOLMES**, b. of New London,		
Jan. 26, 1845, by Rev. Jabez S. Swan	4	116
Amy, d. Ransford & Katharine, b. July 28, 1762	3	51
Amy, d. James & Amy, b. Oct. 28, 1776	3	74
Andrew J., m. Mary C. **TINKER**, b. of New		
London, June 6, 1852, by Rev. Jabez S. Swan	4	173
Anna, d. Lancaster & Mary, b. July 9, 1759	3	5
Anna, d. [Peter & Elizabeth], b. Apr. 6, 1767	3	75
Asa, 2d, of Montville, m. Sarah **STRICKLAND**, of		
Waterford, Mar. 22, 1833, by Rev. Abel		
McEwen	4	50
Bethiah, d. Zeb[adiah], & Bethiah, b. June 10, 1744	2	100
Betty Brooks, [d. Caleb & Martha], b. June 8, 1777	3	131
Caleb, s. Sam[ue]l, b. [ ], 1712	1	56
Caleb, m. Martha **BROWN**, Jan. 2, 1767	3	131
Charles, s. [Richard & Rebecca], b. Apr. 10, 1819	3	262
Charlotte, s. Ransford & Katharine, b. Apr. 8, 1765	3	51
Charlot[te], d. John, m. Silas **CRANDALL**, May 29,		
1808	3	56
Christopher, s. Sam[ue]l & Sarah, b. Jan. 1 ,1703	1	55
Christopher C., m. Ursula **HARRIS**, Aug. 11, 1830,		
by Rev. Francis Darrow	4	39
Daniel, m. [ ] **PRENTICE**, May 23, 1700	1	54

	Vol.	Page
COMSTOCK (cont.)		
Daniel, s. Daniel, b. Sept. 22, 1703	1	54
Daniel, s. Kingsland, of New London, decd., m. Mary		
CHAPLE, d. Joseph, of New London, July 7,		
1736	2	102
Daniel, d. Apr. 24, 1746	2	9
Daniel, s. Daniel & Mary, b. Dec. 14, 1750	2	102
Deborah, d. [Dyer & Betty], b. Dec. 21, 1795	3	131
Desire, d. Daniel & Mary, b. Nov. 24, 1744	2	102
Desire, d. Lancaster & Mary, b. Nov. 16, 1763	3	5
Desire, of Montville, m. Zebadiah **MINER**, of		
Norwich, May 13, 1827, by C. Griffing, J.P.	4	30
Desire A., m. Leonard **STRICKLAND**, b. of [New		
London], Nov. 1, 1846, by John Howson	4	130
Dyer, s. [Caleb & Martha], b. Nov. 20, 1767	3	131
Dyer, m. Betty **BROOKS**, Feb. 19, 1792	3	131
Ebenezer, s. Daniel & Mary, b. July 12, 1742	2	102
Edmund, s. [Richard & Rebecca], b. Jan. 1, 1821	3	262
Elisha, s. Daniel & Mary, b. May 31, 1737	2	102
Eliza Ann, m. Joseph S. **AMES**, b. of New London,		
Mar. 6, 1831, by Rev. Daniel Wildman	4	41
Elizabeth, m. Joseph **MYNOR**, Mar. 12, 1689	1	38
Elizabeth, d. Daniel, b. Aug. 2, 1717	1	54
Elizabeth, d. Kinsland & Rachel, b. Nov. 20, 1727	2	8
Elizabeth, d. Peter, of New London, m. Jonathan		
CHAPPELL, s. Joseph, of New London, Mar.		
25, 1742	2	17
Elisabeth, d. Kinsland Comstock, late of New		
London, decd., m. Stephen **BAKER**, s. Joshua,		
late of New London, decd., Nov. 13, 1745	3	11
Elizabeth, d. [Peter & Sarah], b. Sept. 8, 1775	3	75
Elisabeth, d. [Nathan & Mary], b. Aug. 14, 1783	3	73
Elizabeth, of Montville, d. Jason, m. Henry		
CORNELL, of New London, Dec. 1, 1811	3	184
Elizabeth, w. Peter, d. [ ]	3	75
Ellen, d. [Richard & Rebecca], b. Oct. 22, 1822	3	262
Ellen, m. William B. **TATE**, b. of [New London],		
[ ], 13, [1847?], by Rev. T. Edwards	4	129
Emblem, d. [Peter & Elizabeth], b. July 25, 1769	3	75
Fitch, s. [Peter & Elizabeth], b. Apr. 3, 1771	3	75
Frances, of Uncasville, m. Thomas J. **WEST**, of		
Colchester, Apr. 5, 1846, by Rev. Jabez S.		
Swan	4	125
Franklin, s. [Richard & Rebecca], b. Feb. 11, 1815	3	262
George, s. [Peter & Elizabeth], b. July 2, 1763	3	75
George R., m. Elizabeth **CHAPMAN**, b. of New		
London, Jan. 19, 1823, by Rev. Abel McEwen	4	12
Gideon, s. Sam[ue]l, b. [ ], 1708	1	55
Grace, d. [Peter & Sarah], b. Aug. 1, 1778	3	75
Hannah, d. Gideon, late of New London, decd., m.		
John **FORSYTH**, s. James, late of New		
London, decd., June 6, 1771	3	48

	Vol.	Page
COMSTOCK (cont.)		
Henry N., m. Nancy E. **LYNCH**, b. of New London, Apr. 23, 1848, by Rev. Jabez S. Swan	4	138
Henry S., m. Caroline S. **LYMAN**, b. of [New London], July 14, 1847, by Rev. M. P. Alderman	4	133
Horace T., m. Jane E. **HUNTLEY**, June 4, 1845, by Rev. Francis Darrow	4	122
Huldah, d. William & Lucy, b. Nov. 10, 1765	3	46
James, s. Daniel, b. June 18, 1712	1	54
James, of New London, s. Daniel, m. Hannah **ALLEN**, d. Samuel, late of West Town, decd., Mar. 23, 1737/8	2	44
James, s. James & Hannah, b. Sept. 19, 1745	2	44
James, m. Amy **CHURCH**, Aug. 2, 1773	3	74
James, s. James & Amy, b. May 7, 1774	3	74
James N., m. Mary M. **CONE**, b. of New London, Mar. 30, 1845, by Rev. S. Benton	4	118
Jason, s. James & Hannah, b. May 2, 1739	2	44
Jemima, d. Daniel & Mary, b. Apr. 8, 1749	2	102
Jesse, s. Ransford & Katharine, b. Aug. 30, 1769	3	51
John, s. Daniel, b. Sept. 12, 1705	1	54
John, s. Kinsland & Rachel, b. Oct. 20, 1722	2	8
John, m. Lucy **CHAPMAN**, b. of New London, Oct. 3, 1826, by Rev. Abel McEwen	4	27
John, of Montville, m. Emma **LOVERAGE**, of East Lyme, Nov. 16, 1845, by Sandford Benton, Minister	4	133
John, of New York, m. Charlotte C. **HAGERMAN**, of [New London], July 26, 1849, by Rev. Jabez S. Swan	4	147
Jonathan, s. Daniel, b. July 28, 1714	1	54
Jonathan, s. [Peter & Sarah], b. June 8, 1781	3	75
Joseph, s. Kinsland & Rachel, b. Aug. 13, 1725	2	8
Joseph, s. Joseph & Stephen, b. June 4, 1749	2	103
Joseph, s. Kingsley, the younger, decd., m. Alethea **BLISS**, d. Peletiah, all of New London, [ ]	2	103
Julia, of Groton, m. John **DAY**, of New London, May 24, 1835, by Rev. Abel McEwen	4	61
Julia, of Groton, m. Alfred **BABCOCK**, of Lyme, Sept. 2, 1837, by Rev. Daniel Webb	4	73
Julia Ann, m. Benjamin F. **SKINNER**, b. of New London, Apr. 2, 1843, by Rev. R. W. Allen	4	102
Katharine, w. Ransford, d. [ ]	3	51
Kingsland, m. Rachell **CROCKER**, Sept. 18, 1717	1	54
Lancaster, s. Gideon, decd., m Mary **SMITH**, d. Jethro Smith, of New London, May 2, 1754	3	5
Leonard, of Montville, m. Lucy **TUCKER**, of [New London], Mar. 10, 1833, by James Porter	4	52
Lucretia A., m. Benjamin F. **ASH**, Oct. 31, 1832, by James Porter	4	48

	Vol.	Page
COMSTOCK (cont.)		
Lucretia Ann, d. [Richard & Rebecca], b. Feb. 10, 1817	3	262
M. M., m. Ellen M. **CULVER**, b. of New London, Oct. 1, 1834, by Rev. Alvan Ackley	4	57
Margarett, m. Joseph **PRENTIS**, Mar. [ ], 1759	3	112
Mark, m. Sophia **CHAPMAN**, of [New London], June 12, 1837, by Rev. Daniel Wildman	4	85
Martha, d. Sam[ue]l, b. [ ], 1716	1	56
Martha, d. Zeb[adiah], & Bethiah, b. Jan. 8, 1748/9	2	100
Martha, d. [Peter & Elizabeth], b. July 28, 1757	3	75
Mary, d. Kingsland & Rachel, b. Sept. 8, 1718	1	54
Mary, m. Philip **WANT**, May 25, 1721	2	117
Mary, d. Daniel & Mary, b. Apr. 7, 1740	2	102
Mary, d. Zeb[adiah], & Bathiah], b. Mar. 23, 1745/6	2	100
Mary, m. James **ROGERS**, of Mamcock, July 22, 1764	3	63
Mary, of New London, d. Caleb, m. Eliphalet **HARRIS**, of New London, s. Henry, decd., Oct. 31, 1765	3	42
Mary, d. [Nathan & Mary], b. Mar. 15, 1785	3	73
Nancy, d. [Ransford & Azuba], b. June 9, 1785	3	51
Nathan, Jr., m. Mary **ROGERS**, Feb. 14, 1782	3	73
Nath[anie]l, s. Sam[ue]l, b. [ ], 1706	1	55
Obedience, d. Ransford & Katharine, b. June 26, 1767	3	51
Peregreen, s. Lancaster & Mary, b. Nov. 11, 1757	3	5
Peter, s. Daniel, b. Mar. 4, 1702	1	54
Peter, m. Elizabeth **FITCH**, Sept. [ ], 1756	3	75
Peter, m. Sarah **MIRICK**, May 12, 1774	3	75
Peter, s. [Peter & Sarah], b. Dec. 5, 1779	3	75
Phebe Ann, m. Robert B. **JACKSON**, b. of New London, Sept. 23, 1849, by Rev. Edwin R. Warren	4	149
Rachel, d. Kinsland & Rachel, b. Aug. 20, 1720	2	8
Ransford, s. Peter, late of New London, decd., m. Katharine **VIBER**, d. John, of New London, Dec. 13, 1761	3	51
Ransford, m. Azuba **DAVIS**, May 2, 1782	3	51
Ransford, s. [Ransford & Azuba], b. Apr. 25, 1783	3	51
Rebecca, d. Dan[ie]ll, m. Danyell **STEB[B]INS**, s. John, of N[ew] London, May 31, [1675]	1	10
Richard, m. Rebecca **BECKWITH**, Mar. [ ], 1809	3	262
Richard, s. [Richard & Rebecca], b. Dec. 26, 1810	3	262
Richard, m. Betsey **SMITH**, b. of New London, Dec. 6, 1838, by Rev. C. C. Williams	4	81
Robert William, s. William & Lucy, b. July 16, 1762	3	46
Samuel, m. Sarah **DOUGLASS**, [ ], 1699	1	55
Samuel, m. Sarah **DOUGLASS**, June 22, [1699]	1	25
Sam[ue]l, s. Sam[ue]l & Sarah, b. June 22, 1701	1	55
Sam[ue]l, m. [ ] **WHITTLECY**, May 22, 1705	1	55
Sarah, first w. of Sam[ue]l, d. Apr. 1, 1704	1	56

	Vol.	Page
COMSTOCK (cont.)		
Sarah, d. Sam[ue]l, b. [ ], 1714; d. Aug. 15, 1714	1	56
Sarah, d. Joseph & Sarah, b. May 25, 1725	2	111
Sarah, m. Daniel **TUTHILL**, Mar. [ ], 1728	2	111
Sarah, d. James & Hannah, b. Nov. 7, 1743	2	44
Sarah, d. Nath[anie]ll, m. Jonathan **SMITH**, Jr., s. Jonathan, b. of New London, Nov 13, 1755	3	39
Sarah, d. [Peter & Sarah], b. Feb. 24, 1777	3	75
Solomon, s. William & Lucy, b. Oct. 2, 1767	3	46
Thomas, s. Daniel, b. Mar. 25, 1710	1	54
Tho[ma]s, s. Lancaster & Mary, b. Mar. 13, 1766	3	5
William, s. James & Hannah, b. Nov. 2 ,1741	2	44
William, s. James, of New London, m. Lucy **DAVIS**, d. Benajah, Feb. 12, 1861* *("1761" written in)	3	46
Zebadiah, s. Sam[ue]l, b. [ ], 1710	1	56
Zebadiah, of New London, m. Bethiah **PRENTISE**, of New London, July 11, 1743	2	100
Zebadiah, s. Zeb[adiah], & Bethiah, b. Dec. 15, 1751	2	100
CONDLON, Jane Maria, of Southhampton, N.Y., m. John **HARRISON**, of Southhold, N.Y., Sept. 16, 1840, by Rev. Abel McEwen	4	91
CONE, Ebenezer Young, s. [Samuel & Mary], b. Dec. 8, 1820	3	164
Fame, d. Ceaser & Phillis, slave of John Hallam, b. Feb. 28, 1789	3	128
Francis Lucinda, d. [Timothy & Harriet], b. Oct. 9, 1832	3	280
Frederick Augustus, s. [Timothy & Harriet], b. Sept. 10, 1829	3	280
James, of New London, m. Edah **TOCKER**, of Haddam, Sept. 25, 1836, by Rev. Squire B. Hascall	4	68
Mary Ann, d. [Samuel & Mary], b. June 19, 1818	3	164
Mary Ann, m. Joseph F. **JOHN**, b. of New London, July 7, 1844, by Rev. Robert A. Hallam	4	112
Mary M., m. James N. **COMSTOCK**, b. of New London, Mar. 30, 1845, by Rev. S. Benton	4	118
Nancy, of [New London], m. Gad **SMITH**, of East Haddam, Jan. 31, 1838, by Rev. James M. Macdonald	4	75
Oliver M., of Lyme, m. Louisa **ELLIOT**, Dec. [ ], 1850, by Frederick R. Chapman, J.P.	4	160
Samuel, [m.] Mary [ ]	3	164
Timothy, m. Harriet **COATS**, Sept. 29, 1828	3	280
William P., m. Ann **WAY**, b. of New London, Aug. 17, 1845, by Rev. Jabez S. Swan	4	121
CONGDON, Anna, of Montville, m. Jonathan **CHAPMAN**, of Waterford, May 28, 1826, by Rev. Abel McEwen	4	26

	Vol.	Page

CONGDON (cont.)

Caroline, of Lyme, m. Cyrus **WILLIAMS**, of New
    London, Aug. 22, 1844, by Rev. Rob[er]t A.
    Hallam — 4 — 113

Clarissa, of Franklin, m. Rodman **LATHROP**, of
    New London, Apr. 17, 1830, by Abel McEwen — 4 — 37

Elisha, s. John, Jr. & Mehetable, b. Aug. 5, 1740 — 2 — 97

Eliza, m. Henry **CONGDON**, b. of Lyme, Aug. 17,
    1851, by Rev. Jabez S. Swan. (The name
    "Eliza **COULINE**" follows) — 4 — 173

Eunice, d. John, Jr. & Mehetable, b. Apr. 14, 1738 — 2 — 97

George R., m. Lydia **ASHBY**, Oct. 7, 1827 — 3 — 269

Harriet E., d. [George R. & Lydia], b. Sept. 14,
    1828 — 3 — 269

Henry, m. Eliza **CONGDON***, b. of Lyme, Aug. 17,
    1851, by Rev. Jabez S. Swan   *(Eliza
    COULINE follows this name) — 4 — 173

Jeremiah, s. John, Jr. & Mehetable, b. Aug. 27, 1736 — 2 — 96

John, Jr., of New London, m. Mehetable
    GARDINER, d. of Stephen, of Norwich — 2 — 96

Martha, d. Jeremiah, of New London, m. Joseph
    ROGERS, s. Jona[than], of New London,
    North Parish, Jan. 23, 1754 — 3 — 35

Mehetable, d. John, Jr. & Mehetable, b. Nov. 3, 1742 — 2 — 97

Sarah, d. [George R. & Lydia], b. Nov. 26, 1829; d.
    Aug. 14, 1830 — 3 — 269

Sarah Ashby, d. [George R. & Lydia], b. Apr. 26,
    1831 — 3 — 269

Stephen, s. [William & Hannah], b. May 12, 1807 — 3 — 111

Susanna, d. Jeremiah, of New London, m. James
    ROGERS, s. Jona[than], of New London,
    North Parish, Mar. 12, 1751 — 3 — 39

Timothy, s. John, Jr. & Mehetable, b. Apr. 15, 1739 — 2 — 97

William, s. John, b. Nov. [ ], 1723. Recorded Feb. 8,
    1742/3 — 2 — 9

William, m. Hannah **MALONA**, d. William, Feb. 16,
    1805 — 3 — 111

William, s. [William & Hannah], b. Apr. 13, 1806 — 3 — 111

William G., of Southington, R. I., m. Eliza Jane
    DUCE, of N[ew] London, Aug. 18, 1842, by L.
    Covel — 4 — 103

CONKLIN, Daniel F., m. Eliza **TINKER**, June 22, 1823,
    by Thomas W. Tucker, Elder — 4 — 14

Johanna, m. Jeremiah O'Donovan, Sept. 22, [18]50,
    [by Peter J. Blenkinsop]. Witnesses: James
    Young, Julia O'Donovan — 3 — 306

CONNORS, Maurice, m. Mary **CAVARRE**, Apr. 24,
    1852, by Rev. J. Stokes. Witnesses: John
    Bigley, Ellen Lynch — 4 — 170

COOGAN, Rosanna, m. Patrick H. **BURNS**, b. of [New
    London], Mar. 3, 1844, by Rev. Robert A.
    Hallam — 4 — 110

	Vol.	Page

COOK, Mary, m. Jared **STARR**, Jan. 25, 1768, on Long
    Island   3   84
    Rebecca L., m. Peirce H. **OGDEN**, b. of [New
    London], Mar. 23, 1845, by Rev. Abel McEwen   4   118
    Sally A., m. George **WAIDE**, b. of New London,
    Mar. 21, 1833, by James Porter   4   50
    Samuel A., of Norwich, m. Susan C. **BROOKS**, of
    New London, Dec. 25, 1842, by Rev. Robert A.
    Hallam   4   104
COOLEDGE, Jemima, m. Stephen **SMITH**, Feb. 4, 1781   3   107
COOLEY, Horace, m. Frances **BURDICK**, b. of
    Norwich, June 16, 1850, by Rev. Jabez S. Swan   4   154
COOMBS, Abiga[i]ll, m. Stephen **SMITH**, Jan. 2 ,1798   3   171
    Francess, m. John **COLVERT**, b. of New London,
    Mar. 19, 1842, by Rev. R. W. Allen   4   99
    Jeremiah, s. [Joseph & Abiga[i]ll, b. Dec. 12, 1796   3   171
    Joseph, m. Abiga[i]ll **LEACH**, Aug. 22, 179[ ]   3   171
COONEY, COONY, Bridget, m. Michael **FORD**, Jan. 7,
    1838, by Rev. Francis Darrow   4   70
    Hannah, m. Richard **GOONY**, Sept. 21, [18]50, [by
    Peter J. Blenkinsop]. Witnesses: Timothy
    Maxwell, Catherine Igo   3   306
    Hannah, m. Richard **GOONY**, Sept. 21, 1850.
    Witnesses: Timothy Maxwell, Catharine Igo   4   159
COOPER, Elisha, m. Ele[a]nor **BROWN**, Apr. 30, 1801,
    by Rev. Charles Seabuery   3   50
    Richard, m. Sarah **BEEBE**, b. of [New London],
    May 17, 1840, by Rev. Abel McEwen   4   89
COPELAND, Catharine Epes, m. Eldrige **TUFTS**, Jan.
    24, 1848, by Rev. Tho[ma]s J. Greenwood   4   137
COPP, Anne, [d. Joseph & Rachel], b. May 25, 1766; d.
    June 11, 1766   3   58
    Daniel, s. [Joseph & Rachel], b. Aug. 4, 1770   3   58
    David, s. Samuel & Elizabeth, b. Aug. 10, 1752   2   107
    Elisabeth, d. [Joseph & Rachel], b. Nov. 12, 1758   3   58
    Elisabeth, m. Benjamin **HEMPSTE[A]D**, June 10,
    1779   3   13
    Isabell, d. John & Isabell, b. Nov. 17, 1747   2   101
    John, m. Issable **DIXSON**, b. of New London, North
    Parish, Nov. 7, 1744, by Rev. David Jewet[t]   2   101
    John, s. Jonathan & Esther, b. June 25, 1748   2   35
    Jonathan, s. Jonathan, of Stonington, m. Esther
    SEABURY, d. of James **ROGERS**, late of
    New London, then of Norwalk, decd., May 30,
    1747   2   35
    Jonathan, s. Samuel & Elizabeth, b. Nov. 7, 1749   2   107
    Jonathan, s. [Joseph & Rachel], b. Aug. 27, 1767   3   58
    Jonathan, [s. Joseph & Rachel], d. Jan. 2, 1774
    (First written Oct. 7th)   3   58
    Jonathan Shipley, [s. Joseph & Rachel], b. Feb. 13,
    1778   3   58
    Joseph, m. Rachel **DENISON**, Dec. 11, 1757   3   58

	Vol.	Page
COPP (cont.)		
Joseph, s. [Joseph & Rachel], b. June 25, 1760	3	58
Katharine, d. John & Issable, b. Aug. 12, 1745; d.		
May 29, 1747	2	101
Katharine, d. [Joseph & Rachel], b. Oct. 7, 1775	3	58
Lois, d. Samuel & Elizabeth, b. Dec. 31, 1754	2	107
Margaret, [d. Joseph & Rachel], b. Nov. 19, 1764; d.		
Dec. 7, 1765	3	58
Peggy, d. [Joseph & Rachel], b. July 13, 1773	3	58
Prudence, d. Samuel & Elizabeth, b. Apr. 5, 1746	2	107
Rachel, d. [Joseph & Rachel], b. July 21, 1762	3	58
Samuel, s. Dea. Jonathan, of New London, m.		
Elizabeth **LEFFINGWELL**, d. Daniel, of		
Norwich, Mar. 7, 1745	2	107
Samuel, s. Samuel & Elizabeth, b. Nov. 22, 1747	2	107
CORCORAN, [see also **COCHRAN**], John, m. Elizabeth		
MULHALL, May 16, 1852, by Rev. J. Stokes.		
Witnesses: Francis Keefe, Anne Drumm	4	170
COREY, CORY, Charles W., m. Cynthia A. **LEEDS**,		
Oct. 13, 1850, by Rev. James W. Dennis	4	156
Daniel, m. Mary **WEEKS**, Sept. [ ], 1779* *(First		
written 1794)	3	129
Daniel, s. [Daniel & Mary], b. July 15, 1780*		
*(First written 1795)	3	129
CORNELL, CORNEL, Abby, d. [Samuel & Hannah], b.		
July 14, 1805	3	215
Almor, m. George **PELLEY**, Apr. 9, 1827, by C.		
Griffing, J.P.	4	30
Ann Elizabeth, of New London, m. Henry **NOTT**,		
June 2, 1842, by H. R. Knapp	4	100
Charles Lee Smith, s. [John Valentine & Zerviah], b.		
Nov. 5, 1796	3	137
Eliza, d. [John Valentine & Zerviah], b. Mar. 7, 1801	3	137
Elizabeth, d. Job, m. Daniel **HULL**, Oct. 3, 1784	3	146
Ellenore, of Griswold, m. Thomas **WOOD**, of R.I., a		
soldier stationed at Fort Trumbull, Oct. 9, 1822,		
at New London, by Lodowick Fosdick, J.P.	4	10
George W., m. Abby H. **GRAY**, b. of New London,		
May 20, 1844, by Rev. Tho[ma]s J.		
Greenwood	4	111
Helen, of [New Haven], m. James L. **HICKOX**, of		
Durham, June 21, 1852, by Rev. T. Edwards	4	168
Henry, of New London, m. Elizabeth **COMSTOCK**,		
of Montville, d. Jason, Dec. 1, 1811	3	184
John Valentine, m. Zerivah **SMITH**, Mar. 19, 1796	3	137
Mariah, d. [Samuel & Hannah], b. July 2, 1799	3	215
Maria, m. Lewis **DARROW**, b. of New London,		
June 11, 1820, by Rev. B. Judd	4	1
Mary, d. [Samuel & Hannah], b. Mar. 11, 1801	3	215
Mary, d. Job, m. William **POOL**, Dec. 25, 1804	3	224
Nancy, d. [Samuel & Hannah], b. June 14, 1803	3	215

	Vol.	Page

CORNELL, CORNEL (cont.)

Nancy, of [New London], m. Elijah **BOLLES**, of
Montville, Oct. 15, 1827, by Rev. Robert
Bowzer — 4 — 32

Nancy, m. Benjamin **VOLENTINE**, May 25, 1833,
by James Porter — 4 — 50

Samuel, m. Hannah **DAVIS**, d. John, Sept. 23, 1798 — 3 — 215

William, s. [John Valentine & Zerviah], b. May 10,
1799 — 3 — 137

William, s. [John Valentine & Zerviah], b. May 18,
1804 — 3 — 137

CORNING, Charles R., of New London, m. Mary
FAIRFIELD, of New London, May 21, 1848,
by Rev. John Howson — 4 — 137

CORNWALL, CORNWELL, Eliza, m. Samuel
FREEMAN, b. of [New London], May 10,
1835, by Rev. Abel McEwen — 4 — 61

Henry, s. Job & Mary, b. Mar. 1, 1787 — 3 — 59

John J., of Norwich, m. Eliza a. **GARDINER**, of
New London, Aug. 3, 1830, by Rev. Abel
McEwen — 4 — 39

Mary, m. Ichabod **RU**, b. of New London, Dec. 30,
1827, by Rev. B. Judd — 4 — 33

Nancy H., m. Sip **LEWEY**, Sept. 25, 1832, by James
Porter — 4 — 48

CORPREW, George W., of U. S. Army, m. Martha
Newton **LINDSEY**, of New London, Oct. 22,
1830, by Rev. B. Judd — 4 — 41

CORWIN, Matthias, of New York, m. Eliza Ann
ADAMS, of New London, June 3, 1832, by
Rev. Alpheus Hayden — 4 — 47

CORY, [see under **COREY**]

COTTERELL, Edward, s. [James & Rosamond], b. July
16, 1790 — 3 — 84

Elizabeth, [d. James & Rosamond], b. Sept. 22, 1806 — 3 — 84

Fanny, d. [James & Rosamond], b. Feb. 21, 1800 — 3 — 84

James, m. Rosamond **POWERS**, July 2, 1786 — 3 — 84

James Wickham, s. [James & Rosamond], b. Oct. 19,
1788 — 3 — 84

Julia, d. [James & Rosamond], b. Mar. 8, 1792 — 3 — 84

Maria, of [New London], m. Oliver **LUKE**, of
Tiverton, R.I., Feb. 22, 1838, by James M
Macdonald — 4 — 75

Mary Ann, d. [James & Rosamond], b. Feb. 20, 1794 — 3 — 84

Rebecca, d. [James & Rosamond], b. July 16, 1787 — 3 — 84

Rosamond, d. [James & Rosamond], b. Aug. 7, 1802 — 3 — 84

Sally, d. [James & Rosamond], b. Dec. 15, 1797 — 3 — 84

COTTON, Henry, of New London, m. Elizabeth
HUMPRHEY, of Hartford, June 1, 1845, by
Rev. L. Geo[rge] Leonard — 4 — 123

COUGHY, Thomas, m. Bridget **MAGINNESS**, Sept. 9,
1849, by Rev. William Logan — 4 — 150

	Vol.	Page
COULINE*, Eliza, m. Henry CONGDON, b. of Lyme, Aug. 17, 1851, by Rev. Jabez S. Swan *(The name Eliza CONGDON preceded this.)	4	173
CRAGIN, Benjamin F., of New York, m. Harriet L. COGGSHALL, of [New London], June 14, 1852, by Rev. T. Edwards	4	168
CRAIG, CRAGUE, Abby Jane, d. [Alexander & Abby], b. Dec. 10, 1819; d. Oct. 2, 1820	3	283
Alexander, m. Abby LYMAN, d. Elisha, of New London, Oct. 22, 1815	3	283
Alexander, s. [Alexander & Abby], b. Sept. 21, 1823	3	283
Charles, s. [Alexander & Abby], b. Dec. 9, 1834	3	283
Elisah Lyman, s. [Alexander & Abby], b. June 24, 1816	3	283
George, m. Mary HEWIT[T], b. of [New London], Feb. 4, 1836, by Rev. Able McEwen	4	64
John, m. Zerivah FRENCH, Oct. 21, 1778	3	67
John, s. [John & Zerviah], b. Dec. 1, 1780	3	67
Lucretia McKINSTREL, [d. Alexander & Abby], b. Oct.25, 1830; d. Oct. 13, 1831	3	282
Lucretia McKinstrel, d. [Alexander & Abby], b. Oct. 9, 1832	3	283
Mary, of New London, m. Antone LOPES, Aug. 23, 1843, by Rev. S. Benton	4	107
Mary Ann, d. [Alexander & Abby], b. June 18, 1826	3	283
Robert, s. [Alexander & Abby], b. June 21, 1828; d. July 22, 1835	3	283
Robert, s. [Alexander & Abby], b. Apr. 29, 1838	3	283
CRANDALL, CRANDELL, Annie*, [d. Joshua & Emeline], b. [ ] *(Written in pencil)	3	279
Bathsheba, d. Enoch, m. Lewis CRANDALL, Feb. 20, 1805	3	238
Charles, s. [Silas &Charlotte], b. July 7, 1809	3	56
Charles W., s. [Joshua & Emeline], b. Apr. 5, 1845	3	279
Cynthia E., m. William W. WILLIS, b. of New London, June 13, 1852, by. Rev. Jabez S. Swan	4	174
Emily L., m. William S. BERRY, Feb. 4, 1838, by Rev. Francis Darrow	4	70
Emma, d. [Joshua &Emeline], b. July 27, 1853	3	279
Emma O. of Westerly, R. I., m. William W. BROWN, Jan. 10, 1842, by Lemuel Cavell	4	95
Enoch, m. Charlotte L. COLLINS, b. of [New London], June 8,1845, by Rev. L. Geo[rge] Leonard	4	123
Francess, of New London, m. Erastus GILBERTS, of South Lyme, July 1, 1852, by Rev. Edward R. Warren	4	171
George W., m, Eliza M. BLAKE, b. of New London, Oct. 1, 1840, by Rev. Ebenezer Blake, of Norwich	4	92

	Vol.	Page

CRANDALL, CRANDELL (cont.)

	Vol.	Page
George W., of [New London], m. Mary **BENJAMIN**, of Preston, July 19, 1852, by Rev. Thomas Ely	4	171
Germond, of White Plaine, N. Y., m. Susannah A. **SMITH**, of New London, Dec. 26, 1848, by Rev. Tryon Edwards	4	143
Hannah, of Hopkinton, m. Nathan **ROGERS**, of New London, Sept. 1, 1757, in Westerly, by Rev. John Maxon, of Newport, R.I.	3	1
Janet, d. [Joshua & Emeline], b. Apr. 21, 1842	3	279
Joshua, s. [Lewis & Bathsheba], b. Jan. 14, 1807	3	238
Joshua, m. Emeline **TINKER**, July 20, 1834	3	279
Joshua, m. Emeline **TINKER**, b. of [New London], July 20, 1834, by Rev. Ebenezer Blake	4	56
Lewis, m. Bathsheba **CRANDALL**, d. Enoch, Feb. 20, 1805	3	238
Lewis, s. [Lewis & Bathsheba], b. Jan. 12, 1809	3	238
Lorenzo, s. [Lewis & Bathsheba], b. Nov. 3, 1805	3	238
Lorenzo, m. Emily L. **STEBBINS**, b. of New London, Dec. 5, 1830, by Rev. Abel McEwen	4	39
Louisa, d. [Joshua & Emeline], b. June 12, 1839	3	279
Mary, m. Ezekiel T. **BEEBE**, b. of Waterford, Jan. 9, 1823, by Loddowick Fosdick, J.P.	4	11
Mary Ann, m. Samuel **GREEN**, Apr. 28, 1839, by Rev. Abraham Holway	4	85
Mercy, m. Zebediah C. **BAKER**, b. of [New London], Sept. 14, 1835, by Rev. Abel McEwen	4	62
Silas, m. Charlot[te] **COMSTOCK**, d. John, May 29, 1808	3	56
William, s. [Joshua & Emeline], b. July 29, 1840	3	279
William H., m. Sarah Ann **HAMBLEY**, b. of [New London], Oct. 28, 1834, by Rev. Ebenezer Blake	4	58

CRANE, Oliver R., of East Windsor, m. Ann H. **LEWIN**, of [New London], Mar. 15, 1840, by John Lovejoy | 4 | 89 |

CRANNALL, CRANNELL, CRANELL, Catharine, d. Capt. Robert & Joanna, of New York, m. James **BAXTER**, Feb. 8, 1785 | 3 | 115 |

	Vol.	Page
Charlotte L., of New London, m. Israel **MINOR**, of New York, June 4, 1837, by Rev. Robert A. Hallam	4	70
Charlotte Louisa, d. [Isaac Van Hook & Sarah], b. Aug. 27, 1809	3	165
Elizabeth, d. [Isaac Van Hook & Sarah], b. June 24, 1794	3	165
Emeline, m. William **TATE**, Jr., b. of New London, Oct. 14, 1824, by Rev. B. Judd	4	20
Emeline Richards, d. [Isaac Van Hook & Sarah], b. Dec. 10, 1804	3	165

	Vol.	Page

CRANNALL, CRANNELL, CRANELL (cont.)

Fanny Maria, d. [Isaac Van Hook & Sarah], b. Feb.
28, 1796 — 3 — 165

Harriet, d. [Isaac Van Hook & Sarah], b. Mar. 16,
1814 — 3 — 165

Isaac Van Hook, m. Sarah **TURNER**, d. John, Dec.
24, 1789 — 3 — 165

Isaac Van Hook, s. [Isaac Van Hook & Sarah], b.
Feb. 26, 1803 — 3 — 165

Joanna, d. [Isaac Van Hook & Sarah], b. Aug. 14,
1807 — 3 — 165

Joanna, m. William **MORGAN**, b. of [New London],
May 18, 1840, by Rev. William Warland, of
Say Brook, Ct. — 4 — 90

John Turner, s. [Isaac Van Hook & Sarah], b. Dec.
25, 1815 — 3 — 165

Robert, s. [Isaac Van Hook & Sarah], b. May 18,
1798 — 3 — 165

Sally Turner, d. [Isaac Van Hook & Sarah], b. July
16, 1800 — 3 — 165

Sarah, w. Isaac V[an] H[ook], d. Apr. 19, 1816 — 3 — 165

Sarah T., [d. Isaac Van Hook & Sarah], d. Sept. 7,
1821 — 3 — 165

CRARY, Christabell, d. Peter & Christabell, b. "ye latter
end of Feb." [1678] — 1 — 13

Mary Ann, m. Clarke **DANIELS**, b. of New London,
Dec. 24, 1843, by Rev. Lemuel Covell — 4 — 109

Peter, m. Christobel **GALLUP**, Dec. [, 1677] — 1 — 12

CRAWFORD, Morris, of Fairfield, Ct., m. Sally
ELLIOTT, of New London, May 15, 1846, by
Rev. John Howson — 4 — 126

CRENTTENTON, [see also **CRUTTENDEN**], Irene, of
Guilford, m. John **WARD**, of New London,
Feb. 18, 1747/8 — 2 — 114

CRIST, Betsey, see Betsey **BEEBE** — 3 — 42

CROCKER, Abby C., m. Nathaniel **MIDDLETON**, b. of
New London, Apr. 5, 1830, by Rev. Abel
McEwen — 4 — 37

Amey, m. David **MAL[L]ARY**, Feb. 23, 1778 — 3 — 8

Andrew, m. Sarah **LEECH**, Sept. 10, 1706 — 1 — 31

Andrew, s. John & Jerusha, b. Mar. 28, 1743/4 — 2 — 9

Betsey, d. [John & Elisabeth], b. Apr. 22, 1779 — 3 — 34

Betsey, d. [Jonathan, Jr. & Betsey], b. July 15, 1804 — 3 — 26

Billy, s. [John & Elisabeth], b. May 27, 1775 — 3 — 34

Catherine, d. [Elihu & Catharine], b. Apr. 3, 1802 — 3 — 82

Catharine M., m. James M. **DANIELS**, b. of New
London, June 15, 1845, by Rev. Jabez S. Swan — 4 — 120

Charles, s. [Jonathan & Jane], b. Aug. 1, 1781; d.
Oct. 12, 1782 — 3 — 31

Cha[rle]s, b. [   ] — 3 — 304

Charles Z., s. James W. & Henrietta A., b. May 19,
1846 — 3 — 158

	Vol.	Page
CROCKER (cont.)		
Charles Z., s. James, of [New London], b. May 19, 1846. Affidavit of N. S. Perkins, M.D., made Oct. 16, 1862	3	158
Chauncey R., m. Lucretia A. **BECKWITH**, d. Charles, June 4, 1837	3	284
Chauncey R., m. Lucretia A. **BECKWITH**, b. of [New London], June 4, 1837, by Rev. Nathan Wildman	4	71
Daniel, s. [Moses & Lucretia], b. Sept. 11, 1807	3	85
Daniel, m. Anna **STRANGE**, b. of Norwich, Aug. 22, 1844, by Rev. I. Blain	4	113
David, s. Thomas & Mary, b. Nov. 19, 1697; d. Apr. 11, 1772	1	23
David, m. Hannah **BEEBE**, Dec. 3, 1722	1	62
David, s. David & Hannah, b. Feb. 20, 1733/4	2	8
David, s. [Jonathan & Jane], b. Nov. 1, 1767	3	31
David, m. Ruth **CALKINS**, Dec. 9, 1790	3	124
David, s. [David & Ruth], b. Sept. 26, 1792	3	124
David, s. [Oliver & Mary], b. Dec. 2, 1793	3	134
Delia, m. William **BALDWIN**, Nov. 16, 1834, by Rev. Alvin Ackley	4	58
Edwin R., b. Dec. 11, 1849	3	304
Elihu, m. Catharine **SMITH**, Nov. 16, 1799	3	82
Elihu, s. [Elihu & Catharine], b. Apr. 22, 1804	3	82
Eliphalet M., m. Catharine **HARRIS**, b. of New London, Feb. 14, 1848, by Rev. Jabez S. Swan	4	137
Eliza, d. [Daniel & [E]unice], b. Oct. 6, 1800	3	186
Elizabeth, d. William & Sarah, b. Feb. 24, 1709/10	1	43
Elizabeth, d. Thomas, Jr. & Joannah, b. Mar. 22, 1724; d. Nov. 29, 1725	2	7
Elizabeth, d. Thomas, Jr. & Joanna, b. Mar. 22, 1724; d. Nov. 29, 1725	2	21
Elizabeth, d. of John, decd., m. Ezekiel **DANIELS**, s. John, Jr., decd., [ ], 1731	2	35
Elizabeth, d. John, of New London, decd., m. Ezekiel **DANIELS**, s. John, Jr. late of New London, decd., Oct. 27, 1731	2	50
Elizabeth, d. William, of New London, decd., m. William **MORGAN**, s. Benjamin, of New London, decd., Jan. 13, 1732	2	108
Elisabeth, d. [Isaac & Amy], b. Nov. 2, 1765	3	107
Elisabeth, m. Joseph **HOLT**, July 30, 1766	3	32
Elisabeth, d. [Freeman & Lucy], b. Aug. 14, 1775	3	102
Elisabeth, m. Jason **BECKWITH**, May 19, 1785	3	106
Emma Ann, m. Thomas Isaac Benjamin **PENHALLOW**, b. of [New London], May 22, 1847, by Rev. L. Geo[rge] Leonard	4	131
Francis, s. [Daniel & [E]unice], b. June 6, 1793	3	186
Freeman, m. Lucy **TABER**, July 26, 1767	3	102
Freeman, s. [Freeman & Lucy], b. July 4, 1781	3	102
Gertrude F., b. Aug. 7, 1853	3	304

	Vol.	Page

CROCKER (cont.)

	Vol.	Page
Giles, s. [Jonathan & Jane], b. Feb. 19, 1783	3	31
Grace, d. William & Sarah, b. Dec. 24, 1711	1	43
Gurdon, s. [Nehemiah & Esther], b. July 16, 1786	3	107
Hannah, d. David & Han[nah], b. Sept. 23, 1727	2	6
Hannah, d. of Capt. David, m. Walter **BUTLER**, s. Thomas, all of New London, Jan. 28, 1755	2	58
Hannah, d. [Jonathan & Jane], b. May 12, 1764; d. Nov. 2 ,1764	3	31
Hannah, d. Stephen, m. Joseph **WEEKS**, Jan. 8, 1801	3	153
Harriet M., m. Mirack **BECKWITH**, Feb. 22, 1842, by H. R. Knapp	4	101
Ichabod, s. [Jonathan & Jane], b. Aug. 31 ,1785	3	31
Isaac, m. Amy **BROOKS**, July 3, 1763	3	107
Isaac, s. [Nehemiah & Esther], b. Jan. 14, 1788	3	107
James, s. [Thomas, Jr. & Susanna], b. Feb. 21, 1768	2	10
James, s. [Jonathan, Jr. & Betsey], b. Dec. 7, 1794	3	26
James, m. Henrietta A. **TUTTLE**, b. of New London, Apr. 30, 1843, by Rev. Lemuel Covell	4	109
Ja[me]s F., b. June 8, 1857	3	304
Jeremiah, twin with Tabor, s. [Freeman & Lucy], b. Mar. 9, 1778	3	102
Johanna, d. Tho[ma]s, Jr. & Susanna, b. Apr. 25, 1758	2	10
John, s. Jno. & Mercy, b. Jan. 19, 1704/5	1	53
John, m. Jerusha **LAR[R]ABEE**, Mar. 20, 1733/4	2	8
John, s. John & Jerusha, b. Jan. 12, 1734/5	2	8
John, s. John, decd., m. Anne **CAMP**, d. James, b. of New London, May 18, 1758, by Rev. David Jewett	3	17
John, s. William, m. Elisabeth **HOLT**, d. William, 2d, all of New London, Nov. 24, 1765	3	34
John, s. John & Elisabeth, b. Mar. 4, 1767	3	34
John H., m. Lucy A. **MORGAN**, Mar. 20, 1843, by H. R. Knapp	4	104
Jonathan, s. David & Hannah, b. Dec. 21, 1736	2	8
Jonathan, m. Jane **MINER**, Mar. 1, 1762	3	31
Jonathan, s. [Jonathan & Jane], b. Mar. 3 ,1772	3	31
Jonathan, Jr., m. Betsey **KELLY**, Dec. 18, 1792	3	26
Joseph, s. John & Jerusha, b. Mar. 18, 1735/6	2	8
Joseph, s. John & Anne, b. Mar. 21, 1759	3	17
Joseph, s. [Jonathan, Jr. & Betsey], b. Apr. 5, 1793	3	26
Lodowick F., m. Marion A. **TIFFANY**, June 2, 1850, by Rev. Charles Willett	4	154
Lucretia, m. Jacob **POOL**, b. of [New London], Apr. 5, 1835, by Rev. Ebenezer Blake	4	60
Lucretia A., w. Chauncey R., d. Jan. 23, 1840	3	284
Lucy, d. [Jonathan & Jane], b. Sept. 21, 1765; d. Oct. 23, 1782	3	31
Lucy, d. [Freeman & Lucy], b. May 5, 1770	3	102
Lucy had son David **LEECH**, b. Jan. 26, 1787. Recorded at desire of Daniel Shaw	3	6

	Vol.	Page
CROCKER (cont.)		
Lucy, m. Adin **BEEBE**, Sept. 6, 1787	3	24
Lucy, m. Edmund A. **RAYMOND**, b. of New		
London, July 3, 1831, by Rev. Abel McEwen	4	43
Lydia, m. William **CHAPPEL**, Dec. 22, 1772	3	33
Marcy, d. Thomas, Jr. & Joannah, b. Oct. 29, 1729; d.		
Apr. [ ], 1736	2	7
Martha, m. William **HOWARD**, s. Eben[eze]r, June		
6, 1768	3	78
Mary, d. Thomas & Rachel, b. Mar. 4, [1668]	1	6
Mary, m. Thomas **LEACH**, Dec. 4, 1706	1	32
Mary, d. David & Hannah, b. Feb. 15, 1724	1	63
Mary, d. John & Jerusha, b. Mar. 14, 1738	2	8
Mary, d. [Jonathan & Jane], b. June 8, 1762	3	31
Mary, m. Jedidiah **BROWN**, Mar. 7, 1782	3	26
Mary, m. Stephen **MINER**, Mar. 3, 1790	3	77
Mary, d. [Daniel & [E]unice], b. Jan. 19, 1795	3	186
Mary C., of New London, m. Mat[t]hew **TOWN**, of		
Philadelphia, Apr. 13, 1845, by Rev. Jabez S.		
Swan	4	118
Mary Warring, d. [Elihu & Catharine], b. July 28,		
1800	3	82
Mercy, m. Thomas **LEECH**, Dec. 24, 1706/9 [sic]	1	53
Mercy, d. Thomas, Jr. & Joanna, b. Oct. 29, 1729	2	21
Mercy, d. Tho[mas] & [Joanna], d. Apr. [ ], 1736	2	21
Mercy, d. John & Jerusha, b. Mar. 2, 1739/40	2	8
Mercy, d. John, late of New London, decd., m.		
Nathaniel **WATERHOUSE**, Mar. 22, 1762	2	98
Mercy, d. [Freeman & Lucy], b. Sept. 1, 1772	3	102
Moses, m. Lucretia **MASON**, d. Samuel, Aug. 18,		
1805	3	85
Naomi, d. [Thomas, Jr. & Susanna], b. Aug. 18, 1765	2	10
Naomi, m. Jesse **EDGECOMBE**, Nov. 6, 1785	3	11
Nathan, s. Thomas & Joannah, b. May 17, 1722	2	7
Nathan, s. Thomas, Jr. & Joannu, b. May 17, 1722	2	21
Nehemiah, s. [Isaac & Amy], b. Nov. 25, 1763	3	107
Nehemiah, m. Esther **BECKWITH**, Oct. 11, 1785	3	107
Oliver, s. [Thomas, Jr. & Susanna], b. June 12, 1770	2	10
Oliver, m. Mary **POWERS**, Jan. 13, 1793	3	134
Peter, s. Thomas, Jr. & Joanna, b. Mar. 20, 1735/6	2	21
Phebe, d. John & Jerusha, b. Feb. 16, 1741/2	2	8
Polly, d. [Oliver & Mary], b. Feb. 3, 1798	3	134
Rachel, m. Eleazer **CHAPPELL**, Nov. 4, 1729	2	7
Rebecca, d. [Jonathan & Jane], b. Nov. 7, 1769	3	31
Rebecca, m. Daniel **ROGERS**, s. Ebenezer, Jan. 28,		
1790	3	132
Rebecca, d. [Oliver & Mary], b. Dec. 11, 1795	3	134
Richard, s. [Jonathan & Jane], b. May 25, 1774	3	31
Richard, s. [Daniel & [E]unice], b. Sept. 8, 1804	3	186
Richard C., m. Mary L. **FENNER**, July 16, 1843, by		
Rev. Allen Darrow	4	106
Sally, d. [John & Elisabeth], b. Dec. 21, 1780	3	34

	Vol.	Page
CROCKER (cont.)		
Sally, b. June 20, 1782; m. Charles **BUTLER**, Nov. 9, 1802	3	261
Sally, m. James **MORRIS**, b. of New London, Dec. 25, 1827, by Rev. Abel McEwen	4	33
Samuel, s. Tho[mas] & Rachell, b. July 27, [1677]	1	11
Samuel, s. Tho[mas] & Phebe, b. July 11, 1742	2	12
Sarah, d. William & Sarah, b. Oct. 19, 1714	1	43
Sarah, d. Thomas, Jr. & Joannah, b. Apr. 16, 1727	2	7
Sarah, d. Thomas, Jr. & Joanna, b. Apr. 16, 1727	2	21
Sarah, d. [Jonathan & Jane], b. Apr. 20, 1777	3	31
Simeon, s. [John & Elisabeth], b. Sept. 22, 1782	3	34
Susannah, d. p[Thomas, Jr. & Susanna], b. July 16, 1773	2	10
Tabor, twin with Jeremiah, s. [Freeman & Lucy], b. Mar. 9, 1778	3	102
Tacy, m. James **SHELLY**, b. of Waterford, Dec. 31, 1843, by Rev. Abel McEwen	4	110
Theoda, d. [Jonathan & Jane], b. Mar. 26, 1779	3	31
Thomas, s. Tho[ma]s & Rachel, b. Sept. 1, [1670]	1	6
Thomas, s. Thomas & Mary, b. Dec. 12, 1699	1	25
Thomas, m. Anne **BEEBE**, d. Samuel, Sr. Apr. 23, [1700]	1	25
Thomas, Jr., m. Joannah **HACKLEY**, June 22, 1721	2	7
Thomas, Jr., s. Thomas, m. Joanna **HACKLEY**, d. of Peter, June 22, 1721	2	21
Thomas, s. Thomas, Jr. & Joannah, b. Nov. 20, 1732	2	7
Thomas, s. Thomas, Jr. & Joanna, b. Nov. 20, 1732	2	21
Tho[ma]s, of New London, m. Phebe **BRIGGS**, Sept. 3, 1741	2	12
Thom[as], d. Mar. 28, 1754, ae 83 y. 7 m.	2	9
Thomas, Jr., s. Thomas, m. Susannah **DAVIS**, d. John, Jan. 30, 1757	2	10
Thomas, s. Thomas, Jr. & Susannah, b. June 14, 1761; d. Dec. 30, 1779	2	10
William, s. Tho[ma]s & Rachel, b. Jan. 10, [1674]	1	9
William, s. William & Sarah, b. Aug. 13, 1707	1	43
William, m. Lydia **MOORE**, Feb. 17, 1792	3	169
W[illia]m, b. Feb. 10, 1844	3	304
William Chaunc[e]y, s. [Chauncey R. & Lucretia], b. June 11, 1839	3	284
W[illia]m T., m. Catharine **HAMMEL**, Feb. 19, 1843, by H. R. Knapp	4	104
CROSBY, Christopher, m. Rebecca **STONE**, Mar. 8, 1803	3	237
Christopher, m. Julia Ann **MILLER**, b. of New London, Apr. 19, 1832, by Chester Tilden	4	46
Elinor, d. [Christopher & Rebecca], b. Feb. 1806; d. [　　　], 1807	3	237
Elisha, m. Mary **SPENCER**, b. of [New London], May 13, 1834, by Rev. Abel McEwen	4	56
Emeline, m. Nathaniel **HOPKINS**, Jan. 1, 1832, by		

	Vol.	Page

CROSBY (cont.)

Emeline, m. Nathaniel **HOPKINS**, Jan. 1, 1832, by
    Rev. Nathan Wildman   4   45

Frances B., m. Caleb **HOWARD**, Mar. 4, 1822, by
    V. R. Osborn   4   3

James, s. [Christopher & Rebecca], b. Mar. [ ], 1808;
    d. Aug. [ ], 1808   3   237

Mary, of N[ew] London, m. Jared **LEWIS**, of
    Manchester, Oct. 15, 1831, by Rev. Daniel
    Wildman   4   44

Mary, m. Michael **DWIRE**, Apr. 9, 1849, by Rev.
    William Logan   4   150

Mary Ann, d. [Christopher & Rebecca], b. Mar. 3,
    1809   3   237

Nancy, d. [Christopher & Rebecca], b. Oct. 14, 1804   3   237

Nancy, m. Charles **MILLER**, b. of New London,
    May 13, 1822, by William Stockman, J.P.   4   8

CROSS, Betsey Sewell, m. Frederick **KIRTLAND**, b. of
    [New London], Jan. 5, 1843, by Rev. Abel
    McEwen   4   104

CROSSMAN, CROSMAN, Bartholomew, s. John &
    Elizabeth, b. Feb. 28, 1730/1, at Lyme   2   31

Dan, s. John & Lydia, b. Nov. 5, 1740   2   31

Eliza[bet]h, w. John, d. Dec. 18, 1736   2   31

Elizabeth, d. John & Lydia, b. Nov. 4, 1746   2   31

John, s. Bartholomew, of England & Elizabeth
    GRAVES, d. of Thomas, of Lyme, m. Apr. 2,
    1725   2   31

John, s. John & Eliz[abeth], b. Jan. 3, 1725/6   2   31

Lydia, d. John & Lydia, b. Aug. 1, 1744   2   31

Pavilla, of New London, m. Henry **JONES**, of
    Hamburg, France, May 8, 1832, by Chester
    Tilden   4   46

Sarah, d. John & Eliz[abeth], b. July 8, 1734, at
    Lyme   2   31

Thomas, s. John & Eliz[abeth], b. Aug. 5, 1728, at
    Lyme   2   31

CROSWELL, James, m. Mary **TAYLOR**, Mar. 25, 1734   2   8

CROW, Catharine, of London, m. William **BOSTON**, of
    London, Aug. 3, [1657]   1   2

CROWELL, George W., of New London, m. Mary A.
    BUTLER, of Waterford, Oct. 14, 1849, by
    Rev. Jabez S. Swan   4   147

Hannah E., of Groton, m. Charles D. **SWANEY**, of
    Lyme, Feb. 18, 1849, by Rev. H. R. Knapp   4   145

CRUMB, Jesse B., m. Mary **HALL**, b. of Charleston, R.I.,
    Jan. 11, 1835, by Rev. Alven Ackley   4   59

Joseph P. of Charleston, R.I., m. Abby Jane
    DARROW, of N[ew] London, Mar. 16, 1834,
    by Rev. Ebenezer Blake   4   55

William C., m. Mary C. **CHEW**, b. of [New
    London], Oct. 21, 1852, by Rev. Abel McEwen   4   174

	Vol.	Page
CRUMYER, Arnold of North Stonington, m. Lucinda **LANPHEAR**, of Westerly, R.I., Jan. 3, 1826, by Christopher Griffing, J.P.	4	25
CRUTTENDEN, [see also **CRENTTENTON**], Irene, m. John **WARD**, Feb. 18, 1748	3	79
CUFFEE, Jerry, m. Sarah **MITCHEL**, b. of New London, Jan. 8, 1832, by Rev. B. Judd	4	48
Rachel B., m. Scipio **LOUIS** b. of [New London], May 29, 1834, by Rev. Abel McEwen	4	57
Sarah A., of Groton, m. John **PINER**, of [New London], Mar. 14, 1850, by Rev. Abel McEwen	4	152
CULLINS, CULLIN, [see also **COLLINS**], Anna, m. Patrick **McGARRY**, Feb. 23, 1852, by Rev. J. Stokes. Witnesses: Walter Brown, Mary McGarry	4	169
Johanna, m. Jeremiah **ODONOVAN**, Sept. 22, 1850. Witnesses: James Young, Julian O'Donovan	4	159
Johanna, m Edmond **SWEENEY**, Feb. 24, 1852, by Rev. J. Stokes. Witnesses: Garrett May, Honora O'Donnely	4	170
CULVENS, Frances, of New Orleans, m. Mary **TURNER**, of New London, May 24, 1831, by Rev. Abel McEwen	4	42
CULVER, CULLVER, [see also **COLVER**], Abiah, of Groton, m. Abraham **WYER**, of Oyster Bay, Long Island, N.Y., Nov. 25, 1716	1	47
Albert D., of New London, m. Cloe S. **ROOT**, of Wilkesbarre, Pa., Sept. 5, 1852, by Rev Jabez S. Swan	4	175
Andrew, of Groton, m. Desire **BURDICK**, of Stonington, Aug. 31, 1828, by Nehemiah Dodge	4	35
Charles C., m. Rhoda **DABOLL**, b. of [New London], Sept. 11, 1834, by Rev. Ebenezer Blake	4	83
Christopher, m. Ellen **HARRIS**, b. of New London, Sept. 25, 18345, by Rev. Jabez S. Swan	4	122
David, m. Elizabeth **KEENEY**, Oct. 7, 1708	1	34
David, s. David & Elizabeth, b. June 26, 1709	1	44
David, s. David & Elizabeth, b. June 26, 1709; d. Nov. 22, 1790	1	66
David, m. Eliza **MOORE**, Nov. 17, 1833, by Rev. Daniel Wildman	4	84
Elizabeth, d. David & Elizabeth, b. Sept. 20, 1711	1	44
Elizabeth, m. Clement **LEACH**, Oct. 25, 1725	2	53
Ellen M., m. M. M. **COMSTOCK**, b. of New London, Oct. 1, 1834, by Rev. Alvan Ackley	4	57
Enock Bolles, s. [George & Susan], b. Dec. 30, 1805	3	197
Frances, d. [Samuel & Hannah], b. Nov. 15, 1819	3	278
George, b. Apr. 13, 1780; m. Susan **BOLLES**, d. Enock, Sept. 26, 1802	3	197
George, s. [George & Susan], b. Sept. 26, 1804; d. Feb. 5 ,1805	3	197

	Vol.	Page
CULVER (cont.)		
George Buckmaster, s. [George & Susan], b. Sept. 8, 1807	3	197
George H., s. [Samuel & Hannah], b. Apr. 20, 1814, at Middletown	3	278
Hannah, d. [Samuel & Hannah], b. Oct. 4, 1827, at Colchester	3	278
Jonathan, s. David & Elizabeth, b. July 19, 1714	1	44
Leonard, of Hebron, m. Mary **BAKER**, of Groton, Aug. 30, 1825, by Rev. Abel McEwen	4	24
Lucy Ann, d. [Samuel & Hannah], b. Nov. 26, 1825, at Colchester	3	278
Martha Freeman, d. [Samuel & Hannah], b. Sept. 10, 1821	3	278
Mary, d. Jno. of N[ew] London, m. John **BURROWS**, s. Robert, of New London, Dec. 14, [1670]	1	7
Mary, d. [George & Susan], b. July 6, 1803	3	197
Mary Ann, m. Francis Henry **DOUGLASS**, Dec. 20, 1832	3	271
Mary Ann, m. Francis H. **DOUGLASS**, b. of New London, Dec. 20, 1832, by Chester Tilden	4	49
Mary L., m. Ira **THOMPSON**, Dec. 30, 1845, by Rev. H. R. Knapp	4	122
Nathan, m. Lucretia **MANWARING**, b. of N[ew] London, Mar. 23, 1834, by Re. Ebenezer Blake	4	55
Olive Sizer, d. [Samuel & Hannah], b. Sept. 8, 1823, at Colchester	3	278
Sally Ann, of New London, m. Charles **LOYD**, Apr. 25, 1833, by Chester Tilden	4	50
Samuel, s. Samuel, b. June 8, 1789; m. Hannah **MINER**, June 20, 1813	3	278
Sarah Ann, d. [Samuel & Hannah], b. Oct. 19, 1815, at Middletown	3	278
Susan, m. Ebenezer **CLARK**, Feb. 27, 1839	3	235
Susan, m. Ebenezer **CLARK**, b. of N[ew] London, Feb. 27, 1839, by Rev. C. C. Williams	4	82
W[illia]m, s. David & Elizabeth, b. Aug. 13, 1723	2	9
William, s. [Samuel & Hannah], b. Sept. 7, 1817	3	278
William, of Hebron, m. Olive **SIZER**, of New London, June 1, 1823, by Thomas W. Tucker, Elder	4	14
CUMMINGS, Margaret, m. Tomas **FAHY**, Aug. 25 [18]50, [by Peter J. Blenkinsop}. Witnesses: Michael Quany, Ann Barrett	3	306
Margarett, m. Thomas **FAHY**, Aug. 25, 1850. Witnesses: Michael Tuany, Ann Barrett	4	159
CURRE, John, m. Nancy **BROWN**, Mar. 13, 1839, by Rev. Abraham Holway	4	85
CURTICE, [see under **CURTIS**]		
CURTIN, Catharine, m. Andrew **MAHER**, July 16, 1848, by Rev. John Brady	4	141

	Vol.	Page
CURTIS, CURTICE, Ann, m. Michael **DWYER**, Nov. 6, 1849, by Rev. Robert A. Hallam	4	148
Elizabeth, m. John **CHAP[P]ELL**, Feb. 18, 1716/17	1	48
Margaret, m. John **ROBINSON**, b. of [New London], Aug. 4, 1845, by Rev. Abel McEwen	4	120
CUTTER, John, of New London, m. Abby A. **MILLER**, of Waterford, Mar. 11, 1850, by Rev. Jabez S. Swan	4	152
DABOLL, Celaden, of Groton, m. Phebe **DABOLL**, of New London, July 3, 1843, by Rev. Erastus Denison	4	105
Charles M., m. Jerusha T. **GRAY**, b. of New London, July 2, 1846, by Rev. Tho[ma]s J. Greenwood	4	127
Emely R., of [New London], m. Cornelius W. B. **BENNET**, of Providence, R.I., May 4, 1840, by John Lov[e]joy	4	90
Esther P., m. Charles A. **PACKSON**, b. of [New London], Oct. 7, 1851, by Rev. Samuel Fox	4	167
Ezra, of Noank (Groton), m. Ann M. **FOWLER**, of New London, Jan. 1, 1847, by Rev. L. Geo[rge] Leonard	4	129
Phebe, of New London, m. Celaden **DABOLL**, of Groton, July 3, 1843, by Rev. Erastus Denison	4	105
Rachel, m. Thomas S. **HOXIE**, Nov. 15, 1835, by Rev. Squire B. Hascall	4	83
Rhoda, m. Charles C. **CULVER**, b. of [New London], Sept. 11, 1834, by Rev. Ebenezer Blake	4	83
Sarah P., m. Leonard **HEMPSTEAD**, Sept. 14, 1835, by Rev. Alven Ackley	4	62
Timothy S., m. Florinell F. **THOMPSON**, b. of [New London], Jan. 12, 1846, by Rev. T. Edwards	4	123
DALY, John, m. Bridget **DIFFLIN**, Dec. 27, 1848, by Rev. William Logan	4	150
DANFORTH, John, m. Caroline B. **PRENTIS**, b. of New London, Sept. 7, 1823, by Rev. Abel McEwen	4	15
John, m. Jane **BROOKS**, b. of [New London], Oct. 1, 1848, by Rev. Abel McEwen	4	142
DANIELS, DANYELL, DANNIELLS, DANNELS, DANIELLS, Abigail, d. Eben[eze]r & Mary, b. June 28, 1730	2	13
Albert, s. [Joseph & Hannah], b. Mar. 1, 1801	3	229
Alfred, of New London, lost overboard from a sloop bound from New London to New York, on or about Feb. 15, 1845. Body was found on Fisher's Island Mar. 1845, and buried there. Affidavit of Nancy L. Daniels	3	301
Amy, m. George **GETCHER**, b. of Waterford, July 1, 1832, by Tho[mas] S. Perkins, J.P.	4	47

	Vol.	Page

DANIELS, DANYELL, DANNIELLS, DANNELS,
DANIELLS (cont.)

Ann, m. William **HOLT**, b. of New London, Aug. 3,
    1823, by Thomas W. Tucker, Elder   4   15

Anna, d. [Joseph & Hannah] b. July 16, 1793   3   229

Bathsheba, d. Nath[anie]ll & Bathsheba, b. Jan. 11,
    1733/4   2   90

Bathsheba, m. Richard **DART**, June 9, 1752   3   24

Benjamin, s. Eben[eze]r & Mary, b. Nov. 11, 1739   2   15

Benjamin, s. [Samuel & Mary], b. June 20, 1772   3   14

Charles, m. Rebecca **AUSTIN**, b. of Waterford, Mar.
    20, 1836, by Rev. Squire B. Hascall   4   84

Christian, d. Jno. & Mary, b. Mar. 3, [1671]   1   8

Clarke, m. Mary Ann **CRARY**, b. of New London,
    Dec. 24, 1843, by Rev. Lemuel Covell   4   109

Constant F., of Chatham, m. Mary **PRENTICE**, of
    New London, Dec. 30, 1821, by Rev. B. Judd   4   7

Daniel, s. [Samuel & Mary], b. July 10, 1774   3   14

David, s. Nath[anie]l & Bathsheba, b. Mar. 4,
    1729/30   2   90

Eben[eze]r, s. John & Agnes, b. Feb. 15, 1702/3   1   28

Ebenezer, m. Mary **GRAVES**, Oct. 21, 1724   2   13

Ed[war]d, s. Eben[eze]r & Mary, b. Feb. 17, 1735   2   15

Edward Keeney, s. [Joseph & Hannah], b. Nov. 9,
    1807   3   229

Eliza, d. Ezekiel & Elizabeth, b. Dec. 23, 1732; d.
    Feb. 26, 1732/3   2   50

Elisabeth, b. Jan. 26, 1720; m. John **TINKER**, Dec.
    19, 1740   3   54

Elizabeth, d. Ezekiel & Elizabeth, b. Mar. 8, 1738/9   2   50

Elizabeth, d. Ezekiel & Elizabeth, b. [   ],
    173[ ]; d.   2   25

Elizabeth, d. Noah & Elizabeth, b. July 24, 1753   2   9

Elizabeth, d. Jasper, m. Robert **DOUGLASS**, Apr. 4,
    1807   1   214

Ellen, of Groton, m. George A. **MAY**, of New
    London, [   ], by Rev. R. W. Allen   4   98

Emily M., m. Warren **FISH**, b. of [New London],
    Dec. 29, 1839, by Rev. Abel McEwen   4   88

Emma, m. Leonard **KNIGHT**, b. of Waterford, Mar.
    27, 1839, by Rev. Abel McEwen   4   82

Esther, of New London, d. John, Jr., of New London,
    m. Caleb **MOOR[E]**, of New London, s.
    Joseph, of South Hampton, Mar. 2, 1734/5   2   109

Esther, d. [Samuel & Mary], b. Dec. 5, 1765   3   14

Esther, m. Thomas **PEMBER**, Apr. 8, 1789   3   112

Esther, m. John **LEONARD**, of New London, Dec.
    31, 1845, by G. Thompson   4   122

Ezekiel, s. John & Mary, b. Dec. 27, 1708   1   35

Ezekiel, s. John, Jr., late of New London, decd., m.
    Elizabeth **CROCKER**, d. John, of New
    London, decd., Oct. 27, 1731   2   50

	Vol.	Page

DANIELS, DANYELL, DANNIELLS, DANNELS, DANIELLS (cont.)

	Vol.	Page
Ezekiel, s. John, Jr., decd., m. Elizabeth **CROCKER**, d. of John, decd., [ ], 1731	2	25
Ezekiel, s. Ezekiel & Elizabeth, b. Sept. 5, 1736	2	25
Ezekiel, s. Ezekiel & Elizabeth, b. Sept. 5, 1736	2	50
Fanny, m. Richard **MALLOR**, b. of New London, Apr. 3, 1845, by Rev. S. Benton	4	118
George, Jr., of Waterford, m. Roxy **BECKWITH**, of New London, Aug. 19, 1832, by Tho[mas] S. Perkins, J.P.	4	47
Hannah[h], d. John & Mary, b. Apr. 20, [1674]	1	9
Hannah, d. John & Agnes, b. Sept. 15, 1706	1	31
Hannah, m. Jabez **RICHARDS**, Oct. 15, 1777	3	57
Hester, d. John & Mary, b. Aug. 4, 1715	1	46
Isaac, s. [Samuel & Mary], b. Feb. 5, 1768	3	14
James, s. John & Agnes, b. Aug. 31, 1708	1	34
James, s. [Joseph & Hannah], b. Dec. 13, 1803	3	229
James, m. Fanny **KEEN[E]Y**, b. of New London, Oct. 7, 1827, by Rev. Robert Bowzer	4	32
James M., m. Catharine M. **CROCKER**, b. of New London, June 15, 1845, by Rev. Jabez S. Swan	4	120
Jasper, of New London, m. Phebe **HODGE**, late of Stonington, Feb. 15, 1789, by Andrew Griswold, J.P.	2	123
John, m. Mary, d. Geo[rge] **CHAPPELL**, Jan. 19, [1664]	1	4
John, s. Jno. & Mary, b. Jan. 19, [1665]	1	4
John, m. Agnes **BAKER**, Dec. 3, [1685]	1	17
John, s. John & Agnes, b. Oct 22, [1686]	1	18
John, s. Eben[eze]r & Mary, b. Nov. 9, 1739	2	15
John C., m. Abba F. **DARROW**, Mar. 27, 1843, by H. R. Knapp	4	105
Jonathan, s. Jno. & Mary, b. Oct. 15, [1682]	1	16
Jonathan, s. John & Agnes, b. Mar. 22, 1692/3	1	21
Jonathan, m. Rebecka **GRAVES**, Dec. 12, 1706	1	32
Jona[than], m. Mary **POTTS**, Jan. 1, 1717/18	1	56
Joseph, s. [Samuel & Mary], b. Mar. 15, 1770	3	14
Joseph, m. Hannah **KEENEY**, d. Samuel, Aug. [ ], 1791	3	229
Joseph, s. [Joseph & Hannah], b. Jan. 2, 1796	3	229
Lucy, d. John & Mary, b. June 29, 1713	1	38
Lydia, m. Bradley **HARRIS**, Dec. 29, 1827, by Rev. Robert Bowzer	4	32
Mariah, d. Ebenezer & Mary, b. Aug. 31, 1733	2	14
Mary, d. John & Mary, b. Oct. 12, [1667]	1	5
Mary, m. Samuell **WALLER**, Dec. 26, 1685	1	68
Mary, d. John & Agnis, b. Feb. 24, [1694/5]	1	22
Mary, m. Jonathan **FOX**, Oct. 23, 1713	1	41
Mary, d. Nath[anie]ll & Bathsheba, b. July 3, 1717	2	90
Mary, d. Ebenezer & Mary, b. Apr. 29, 1737	2	15
Mary, d. Noah & Elizabeth, b. Apr. 19, 1755	2	9

	Vol.	Page
DANIELS, DANYELL, DANNIELLS, DANNELS,		
DANIELLS (cont.)		
Mary, of New London, m. William W. **HUBBARD**,		
of Middletown, Jan. 20, 1822, by Rev. B. Judd	4	7
Mary Ann, m. John H. **FULLER**, b. of New London,		
May 7, 1843, by Rev. Lemuel Covell	4	109
Naomi, m. William **MORGAN**, b. of New London,		
May 7, 1789, by Andrew Griswold, J.P.	2	123
Nathan, s. Nath[anie]ll & Bathsheba, b. Jan. 10,		
1735/6	2	90
Nathaniel, s. John & Agnes, b. June 20, [1697]	1	23
Nathaniell, m. Bathsheba **BECKWITH**, Oct. 4, 1716	1	46
Nathaniel of New London, m. Bathsheba		
BECKWITH, of New London, Oct. 30, 1716	2	90
Peter, s. John & Mary, b. Dec. 27, 1710	1	38
Peter, s. Nath[anie]ll & Bathsheba, b. Apr. 23, 1738	2	90
Rachell, d. Jno. & Mary, b. Feb. 27, [1676]	1	11
Rachal, d. Nath[anie]ll & Bathsheba, b. Feb. 14,		
1719/20	2	90
Rebecca, d. Noah & Elizabeth, b. Nov. 22, 1759	2	9
Rhoda, d. Ezekiel & Elizabeth, b. July 5, 1735, d.		
Oct. 8, 1735	2	50
Rhadia, d. Ezekiel & Elizabeth, b. [ ], 173[ ];		
d. [ ]	2	25
Rocksey, d. [Joseph & Hannah], b. June 20, 1799	3	229
Ruth, d. Nath[aniel]l & Bathsheba, b. Apr. 9, 1722	2	90
Samuell, s. John & Agnes, b. Nov. 29, [1688]	1	18
Samuel, s. Ezekiel & Elizabeth, b. Dec. 31, 1737	2	50
Samuel, m. Mary **BROWN**, July 20, 1760	3	14
Samuel, s. [Samuel & Mary], b. Apr. 2, 1762	3	14
Sarah, d. John & Mary, b. Feb. 10, [1679]	1	14
Sarah, m. Miles **MOORE**, Dec. 28, 1698	1	24
Sarah, d. Nath[anie]l & Bathsheba, b. Apr. 16, 1724	2	90
Sarah, m. George **CHAPPEL**, June [ ], 1744	3	90
Silah, of Lyme, m. Earles P. **GARDNER**, June 11,		
1822, by W[illia]m Stockman, J.P.	4	9
Starlin, s. Eben[eze]r & Mary, b. Mar. 6, 1738	2	13
Stephen, s. Nath[anie]ll & Bathsheba, b. June 12,		
1743	2	90
Susanna, d. John & Agnes, b. Apr. 9, 1705	1	31
Thomas, s. Jno. & Mary, b. Dec. 31, [1669]	1	6
Thomas, s. John & Agnes, b. Jan. 22, [1689/90]	1	19
Thomas, m. Gemima [ ] Dec. 11, 1702	1	27
William, s. John & Agnes, b. Sept. 1, [1699]	1	25
William, d. Dec. 25, 1717	1	57
William, s. Jona[than] & Mary, b. Feb. 19, 1718/19	1	56
William, s. [Samuel & Mary], b. Oct. 12, 1763	3	14
William, m. Cynthia **MAYNARD**, b. of Waterford,		
Mar. 11, 1832, by Rev. Abel McEwen	4	45
DARBY, Daniel R., m. Mary Ann **JOY**, of Norwich, Nov.		
14, 1843, by Rev. Sanford Benton	4	110
DARROW, Abi, d. [Zadock & Hester], b. May 28, 1770	2	1

	Vol.	Page

DARROW (cont.)

Abba F., m. John C. **DANIELS**, Mar. 27, 1843, by
   H. R. Knapp — 4, 105

Abby Jane, twin with George Henry, [d. Nicholas &
   Sally], b. July 20, 1813 — 3, 154

Abby Jane, of N[ew] London, m. Joseph P. **CRUMB**,
   of Charleston, R.I., Mar. 16, 1834, by Rev.
   Ebenezer Blake — 4, 55

Abby T., d. [Nicholas, Jr. & Lucy], b. Nov. 9, 1821 — 3, 214

Allen, m. Sally **BECKWITH**, Nov. 24, 1822, by
   Rev. Francis Darrow — 4, 12

Ambrose, s. [Nicholas, Jr. & Lucy], b. Nov. 11, 1817 — 3, 214

Amy, m. Anson **SMITH**, May 4, 1817 (Amy
   "Beckwith" written in pencil) — 3, 245

Catharine, d. [Nicholas & Sarah], b. Oct. 8, 1776 — 3, 70

Cha[rle]s T., m. Amanda **HEMPSTEAD**, b. of New
   London, Jan. 5, 1845, by Rev. T. Edwards — 4, 116

Christopher, m. Elizabeth **PACKER**, June 27, 1701 — 1, 26

Christopher, s. Christopher & Elizabeth, b. Oct. 22,
   1702 — 1, 66

Christopher, s. Jedidiah & Prudence, b. Dec. 25, 1752 — 3, 9

Daniel, s. [Nicholas & Sarah], b. Aug. 10, 1792 — 3, 70

Daniel B., m. Sally **ELLIOTT**, Feb. 16, 1840, by
   Rev. James M. Macdonald — 4, 88

Eben[eze]r, s. Christopher & Elizabeth, b. Aug. 12,
   1704 — 1, 66

Ebenezer, s. [Zadock & Hester], b. June 19, 1761 — 2, 1

Ebenezer, m. Naomi **CALKINS**, Jan. 1, 1786 — 3, 30

Ebenezer, s. [Ebenezer & Naomi], b. Apr. 7, 1788 — 3, 30

Edward M., m. Elizabeth **THORP**, b. of [New
   London], Sept. 3, 1845, by Rev. Abel McEwen — 4, 121

Ele[a]nor, d. [Nicholas & Sally], b. Aug. 4, 1792 — 3, 154

Elias L., m. Mary **TINKER**, b. of New London, Jan.
   5, 1845, by Rev. John Blain — 4, 117

Elizabeth, d. Christopher & Elizabeth, b. June 27,
   1719 — 1, 63

Elizabeth, d. Christ[ophe]r, m. Dan[ie]l **LESTER**, s.
   Benj[amin], decd., b. of New London, Sept. 25,
   1739 — 2, 65

Elizabeth, d. Nicholas & Mary, b. June 7, 1752 — 2, 47

Elizabeth, of New London, dau. of Eben[eze]r, m.
   Ephraim **STORRY**, of Groton, s. John, of
   Groton, Feb. 7, 1754 — 2, 78

Francis, s. [Lemuel & Rebeckah], b. June 24, 1779 — 3, 91

George, of N[ew] London, m. Elizabeth
   MARSHALL, of Hartford, Aug. 10, 1702 — 1, 27

George, s. Christopher & Elizabeth, b. Mar. 17, 1712 — 1, 41

George B., of Providence, R.I., m. Clarretta B.
   HARRIS, of New London, Mar. 31, 1845, by
   Rev. Jabez S. Swan — 4, 118

George Henry, twin with Abby Jane, [s. Nicholas &
   Sally], b. July 20, 1813 — 3, 154

	Vol.	Page

DARROW (cont.)

Giles, m. Nancy **WELLS**, Mar. 2, 1841, by H. R.
Knapp | 4 | 94
Hannah, d. Zadock & Hester, b. Aug. 24, 1758 | 2 | 1
Hannah, m. John **BECKWITH**, Jr., Jan. 27, 1780 | 3 | 109
Harriet, d. [Nicholas & Sally], b. July 26, 1806 | 3 | 154
Hester, d. [Zadock & Hester], b. Sept. 15, 1779 | 2 | 1
Hester, d. [Lemuel & Rebeckah], b. Oct. 27, 1784 | 3 | 91
Hester, d. Zadock, m. Charles **BROWN**, Oct. 11,
1798 | 3 | 230
Ic[h]abod, s. Christopher & Elizabeth, b. June 20,
1723 | 1 | 63
James, s. Nicholas & Mary, b. Jan. 21, 1741/2 | 2 | 15
James, Jr., of New London, m. Hepsibah
STERLING, of Lyme, Nov. 10, 1790 | 3 | 101
Jason, s. [Lemuel & Rebeckah], b. Oct. 9, 1776 | 3 | 91
Jedediah, s. Christopher & Elizabeth, b. Aug. 10,
1721 | 1 | 63
Jedidiah, of New London, s. Christopher, m.
Prudence **BA[I]LEY**, of Groton, d. John, Mar.
27, 1752 | 3 | 9
John, s. Christopher & Elizabeth, b. Aug. 11, 1706 | 1 | 66
John, s. Jed[idia]h & Prudence, b. Oct. 1, 1754 | 3 | 9
John, s. [Nicholas & Sarah], b. Apr. 16, 1781 | 3 | 70
John, Jr., m. Mary Elizabeth **PEMBER**, Oct. 25,
1835, by Rev. Alvan Ackley | 4 | 63
Joseph, s. [Zadock & Hester], b. Oct. 18, 1773 | 2 | 1
Joseph, s. [Nicholas & Sarah], b. Oct. 7, 1782 | 3 | 70
Lemuel, s. Christopher & Elizabeth, b. Apr. 9, 1717 | 1 | 49
Lemmuel, s. Christopher & Elizabeth, b. Apr. 10,
1717 | 1 | 63
Lemuel, s. Zadock & Hester, b. Feb. 1, 1756 | 2 | 1
Lemuel, m. Rebeckah **CALKINS**, Nov. 16, 1775 | 3 | 91
Leonard, s. [Nicholas & Sally], b. Mar. 22, 1808; d.
Dec. 13, 1808, ae 1 y. 8 m | 3 | 154
Lewis, m. Maria **CORNELL**, b. of New London,
June 11, 1820, by Rev. B. Judd | 4 | 1
Lucy, d. [James, Jr. & Hepsibah], b. July 27, 1791 | 3 | 101
Lucy, m. Francis S. **HUNTER**, b. of New London,
June 26, 1844, by Rev. I. Blain | 4 | 112
Lucy Vernet, d. [Nicholas, Jr. & Lucy], b. Sept. 6,
1816 | 3 | 214
Lydia, m. Peter **HACKLY**, Aug. 3, 1708 | 1 | 33
Lydia, d. Christopher & Elizabeth, b. Aug. 3, 1708 | 1 | 66
Mary, d. Nicholas & Mary, b. Aug. 10, 1738 | 2 | 15
Mary, d. [Zadock & Hester], b. Sept. 15, 1764 | 2 | 1
Mary, d. [Nicholas & Sarah], b. Feb. 14, 1778 | 3 | 70
Mary, d. Elder Zadock Darrow, m. Isaac **CLARKE**,
Dec. 6, 1787 | 3 | 180
Mary, d. [Nicholas & Sally], b. Jan. 29, 1801 | 3 | 154
Mary, m. John **EDGERTON**, b. of [New London],
Nov. 26, 1822, by T. W Tucker, Elder | 4 | 11

	Vol.	Page
DARROW (cont.)		
Mary, m. Edward **MERRELL**, b. of [New London],		
Nov. 16, 1823, by Rev. Thomas W. Tucker	4	17
Mary A., m. John **RICHARDS**, b. of New London,		
Dec. 20, 1842, by Eld[er] L. Covell	4	103
Mary Ann, m. Henry L. **BARKER**, b. of [New		
London], Jan. 1, 1838, by Rev. Daniel Webb	4	75
Millicent, d. Nicholas & Mary, b. June 14, 1744	2	47
Nicholas, m. Mary **GRIFFING**, Dec. 9, 1731	2	14
Nicholas, s. Nicholas & Mary, b. July 16, 1750	2	47
Nicholas, s. Peter, b. Jan. 29, 1769; m. Sally		
WEEKS, [d. James], b. July 15, 1773	3	154
Nicholas, m. Sarah **ROGERS**, Nov. 12, 1773	3	70
Nicholas, s. [Nicholas & Sarah], b. Oct. 5, 1789	3	70
Nicholas, drowned Apr. 1, 1792, in Conn. River	3	70
Nicholas, Jr., m. Lucy **TINKER**, Jan. 10, 1813	3	214
Orrin, of Waterford, m. Abby Jane **MASON**, of New		
London, Sept. 2, 1833, by Chester Tilden	4	52
Orrin, of [New London], m. Charlotte F.		
GLEASON, of Manchester, Ct., June 27, 1847,		
by Rev. L. Geo[rge] Leonard	4	132
Pearce, m. Sally **HARRIS**, d. Benjamin, Jan. 14,		
1809	3	212
Peter, s. Nicholas & Mary, b. Apr. 6, 1736	3	15
Peter, s. [Nicholas & Sally], b. May 1, 1796	3	154
Polly, d. [Lemuel & Rebeckah], b. June 5, 1787	3	91
Rebeckah, d. Nicholas & Mary, b. Apr. 6, 1740	2	15
Rebekah, d. [Lemuel & Rebeckah], b. May 6, 1782	3	91
Rebekah, d. [Nicholas & Sarah], b. Oct. 17, 1786	3	70
Rebec[c]a Ann, [d. Nicholas & Sally], b. Sept. 12,		
1816	3	154
Sally, d. [Nicholas & Sarah], b. Dec. 17, 1784	3	70
Sally, d. [Nicholas & Sally], b. Nov. 18, 1793; d.		
May 15, 1794	3	154
Sally, d. [Nicholas & Sally], b. Nov. 9, 1798	3	154
Samuell, s. Christopher & Elizabeth, b. Jan. 29, 1713	1	42
Samuel Harris, s. [Nicholas & Sally], b. July 22,		
1803	3	154
Sarah, d. Nicholas & Mary, b. June 4, 1734	2	15
Sarah A., m. Dexter **BELLOWS**, Apr. 14, 1841, by		
H. R. Knapp	4	94
Sarah Ann, d. [Nicholas, Jr. & Lucy], b. Dec. 11,		
1819	3	214
Sidney Leonard, [s. Nicholas & Sally], b. Sept. 23,		
1810	3	154
Silas, s. Jed[idia]h & Prudence, b. Feb. 9, 1757	3	9
Turner S., m. Mary A. **WHALEY**, b. of Norwich,		
Dec. 16, 1847, by Rev. Jabcz S. Swan	4	136
William, s. Christopher & Elizabeth, b. Aug. 30,		
1715	1	45
Zadock, s. Eben[eze]r & Abi, m. Hester **LEE**, d.		
Joseph, of Lyme, Apr. 1, 1755	2	1

	Vol.	Page
DARROW (cont.)		
Zadock, s. [Zadock & Hester], b. June 11, 1768	2	1
-----, d. Nicholas & Mary, b. Jan. 6, 1732/3; d. the same day	2	14
DART, DARTT, Abiah, d. Daniell & Elizabeth, b. Dec. 2, 1701	1	40
Algin, m. Mary **BEEBE**, b. of New London, Mar. 11, 1829, by Rev. Abel McEwen	4	35
Amey, d. [Ebenezer & Elisabeth], b. June 19, 1777	3	6
Ann, d. Richard & Bethyra, b. Feb. 14, [1674]	1	9
Ann, m. [ ] **BROWN**, b. of East Lyme, Feb. 6, 1846, by Rev. L. Geo[rge] Leonard	4	124
Anne, m. John **MORGAN**, [ ], 1699	1	46
Anne, d. Roger & Prudence, b. May 31, 1724	2	13
Bathsheba, m. Andrew **CHAPPEL**, Mar. [ ], 1757	3	24
Belinda, m. Stephen **WELSH**, b. of New London, Jan. 10, 1827, by Rev. Abel McEwen	4	28
Benjamin M., m. Elvira L. **BEACH**, Sept. 23, 1839, by James M. Macdonald	4	88
Bethya, d. Richard & Bethya, b. July 30, [1677]	1	11
Bethiah, d. Ebenezer & Mary, b. Dec. 12, 1709	1	50
Caleb, m. Margaret **BRADDICK**, Apr. 9, 1780	3	110
Caleb, s. [Caleb & Margaret], b. Dec. 7, 1787	3	110
Charles, s. [William, Jr. & Betsey], b. Oct. 31, 1787	3	8
Charlotte, m. Benjamin **HAMILTON**, b. of [New London], Nov. 6, 1823, by Rev. Thomas W. Tucker	4	16
Christian, d. [Ebenezer & Elisabeth], b. Oct. 5, 1774	3	6
Danyell, s. Richard & Bethiah, b. May 3, [1666]	1	5
Daniell, m. Elizabeth **DOUGLASS**, Aug. 4, 1686	1	40
Daniell, s. Daniell & Elizabeth, b. Aug. 31, 1691	1	40
David, s. [Ebenezer & Elisabeth], b. Feb. 5, 1761	3	6
David Marvin, s. [Leonard & Ellen S.], b. Apr. 17, 1840	3	289
Dealer, d. [Ebenezer & Elisabeth], b. Oct. 0, 1700	3	6
Dynah, d. Richard & Bethya, b. Jan. 13, [1664]	1	4
Ebenezer, s. Richard & Bethyea, b. Feb. 18, [1672]	1	8
Ebenezer, s. Daniell & Elizabeth, b. May 16, 1698	1	40
Ebenezer, s. John & Ruth, b. Oct. 26, 1736	2	64
Ebenezer, m. Elisabeth **MINER**, May 14, 1759	3	6
Ebenezer, s. [Ebenezer & Elisabeth], b. Oct. 10, 1765	3	6
Edwin Fenno, s. [Leonard & Ellen S.], b. Mar. 6, 1843	3	289
Elizabeth, d. Rich[ar]d & Bethia, b. Dec. 15, [1679]	1	14
Elizabeth, d. Daniell & Elizabeth, b. Oct. 14, 1689	1	40
Elizabeth, d. Thomas & Elizabeth, b. Mar. 17, 1718	1	62
Elizabeth, d. Richard, of New London, m. Jonathan **WHIPPLE**, s. David, of New London, Feb. 28, 1726/7	2	115
Elisabeth, d. Daniel, m. John **BECKWITH**, s. John, Nov. 8, 1744	3	27

	Vol.	Page
DART, DARTT (cont.)		
Emma Salina, d. [Leonard & Ellen S.], b. June 18, 1844	3	289
Eunice, d. [Ebenezer & Elisabeth], b. Aug. 15, 1763	3	6
Franklin, of Waterford, m. Sally **LOYD**, of [New London], Mar. 28, 1841, by John Lovejoy	4	94
Giles, m. Matilda **BELDEN**, b. of New London, July 5, 1837, by Rev. Daniel Webb	4	73
Hannah, d. Roger & Prudence, b. July 25, 1735	2	46
Harriet, m. Perry **DOUGLASS**, b. of New London, Jan. 9, 1828, by Rev. Abel McEwen	4	33
Harriet B., w. Leonard, d. June 5, 1830, ae 24 y 14 d.	3	289
Harriet B., m. Christopher H. **FOX**, b. of New London, Nov. 26, [1843], by Rev. Lemuel Covell	4	109
Harriet E., m. John **UPWARD**, b. of [New London], June 1, 1847, by Rev. Abel McEwen	4	132
Harriet Ellen, d. [Leonard & Ellen S.], b. Dec. 17, 1832	3	289
Harvey F., of New London, m. Mary Jane **WHITE**, Nov. 29, 1843, by Rev. R. A. G. Thompson	4	109
Hezekiah, m. Mary **ABBERT**, Jan. 24, 1821, by Elijah Hedding	4	5
Jabez, s. Daniell & Elizabeth, b. Mar. 12, 1708	1	41
Job, s. John & Ruth, b. Dec. 30, 1734	2	64
Job, m. Lydia **HADLOCK**, Dec. 2, 1787	3	2
John, s. Daniell & Elizabeth, b. Dec. 2, 1693	1	40
John, s. Ebenezer & Mary, b. Oct. 11, 1707	1	50
John, s. Mary **LEACH**, b. July 5, 1731. Father John Dart	2	54
John, s. John & Ruth, b. Sept. 14, 1743	2	64
John, s. Eben[eze]r, late of New London, decd., m. Ruth **MOOR[E]**, d. Joshua, of New London, [ ]	2	64
Jonathan, s. [William & Mary], b. May 29, 1767	3	58
Joshua, s. John & Ruth, b. Oct. 26, 1736	2	64
Joshua, s. [Ebenezer & Elisabeth], b. Nov. 4, 1778	3	6
Joshua, s. [Caleb & Margaret], b. Feb. 17, 1781	3	110
Leonard, m. Harriet B. **WATROUS**, Nov. 27, 1827	3	289
Leonard, m. Ellen S. **DOWNER**, Oct. 30, 1831	3	289
Leonard, m. Mary **HOLMES**, b. of New London, Aug. 28, 1836, by Rev. Squire B. Hascall	4	68
Leonard Watrous, s. [Leonard & Harriet B.], b. Feb. 13, 1829	3	289
Lois, d. [Ebenezer & Elisabeth], b. Oct. 23, 1769	3	6
Lucretia, d. [Caleb & Margaret], b. Aug. 8, 1785	3	110
Lucy, d. Roger & Prudence, b. May 10, 1722	2	13
Lucy, d. [Ebenezer & Elisabeth], b. July 8, 1767	3	6
Lydia, d. Daniell & Elizabeth, b. Nov. 4, 1703	1	40
Lydia N., of Waterford, m. John L. **DEARBORN**, of New London, Apr. 6, 1845, by Rev. S. Benton	4	119
Marah, d. Daniell & Elizabeth, b. Nov. 13, 1695	1	40

	Vol.	Page
DART, DARTT (cont.)		
Marcinda, of New London, m. James **STANLEY**, of Norfolk, Va., July 10, 1825, by Rev. Abel McEwen	4	23
Margaret, d. Roger & Prudence, b. Mar. 1, 1737	2	46
Mary, d. Rich[ar]d, d. July 19, [1689], ae 4 y.	1	69
Mary, d. Ebenezer & Mary, b. Aug. 19, 1711	1	50
Mary, d. John & Ruth, b. Feb. 23, 1740/1	2	64
Mary, m. Isaac **CHAPEL**, Mar. [ ], 1766	3	105
Mary, d. [William & Mary], b. July 1, 1769	3	58
Mary, d. [William, Jr. & Betsey], b. June 6, 1790	3	8
Mary, m. Elijah **REXFORD**, b. of New London, Oct. 25, 1823, by Rev. Abel McEwen	4	16
Mercy W., m. Thomas W. **FOX**, b. of New London, Apr. 1, 1843, by L. Covell	4	101
Nancy N., of Waterford, m. Amasa B. **CLARK**, of New London, Mar. 23, 1845, by Rev. S. Benton	4	118
Oliver W., m. Francess M. **JEFFREY**, b. of [New London], Sept. 21, 1851, by Rev. Tryon Edwards	4	165
Peter, s. Richard & Elizabeth, b. Apr. 9, 1709	2	15
Prudence, d. Roger & Prudence, b. Dec. 5, 1732	2	14
Rebeckah, d. Capt. John & Ruth, m. William **RYON**, s. James & Bashuba, Oct. 3, 1778	3	70
Richard, s. Richard & Bethia, b. May 7, [1667]	1	5
Richard, m. Elizabeth **STICKLAND**, June 22, [1699]	1	25
Richard, s. Roger & Prudence, b. Dec. 20, 1728	2	13
Richard, m. Bathsheba **DANIELS**, June 9, 1752	3	24
Richard, s. [Richard & Bathsheba], b. Dec. 21, 1754	3	24
Richard, Sr., d. [ ]	3	24
Robert, s. Richard & Bethia, b. Nov. 22, [1670]	1	7
Roger, m. Prudence **BECKWITH**, July 24, 1717	2	13
Roger, s. Roger & Prudence, b. July 14, 1726	2	13
Ruth, of New London, m. Eliakim **ROOT**, of Hartford, Apr. 11, 1825, by Rev. Abel McEwen	4	22
Ruth, d. Daniell & Elizabeth, b. Aug. 26, 1711	1	41
Ruth, d. John & Ruth, b. Dec. 2, 1746	2	64
Samuell, s. Daniell & Elizabeth, b. Dec. 12, 1705	1	40
Samuel, of New London, m. Elizabeth **CLARK**, of Lyme, Aug. 6, 1791, by Andrew Griswold, J.P., in Lyme	2	123
Sarah, d. Rich[ar]d & Bethiah, b. June 16, [1681]	1	15
Sarah, d. Richard & Bethia, b. June 10, 1681	1	67
Sarah, m. Eleazer **BISHOP**, June 22, 1704	1	29
Sarah, d. [Richard & Bathsheba], b. May 15, 1753	3	24
Sarah, d. [William, Jr. & Betsey], b. May 5, 1789	3	8
Sarah, of Waterford, m. Amos **HALLAM**, of Groton, Sept. 23, 1837, by Rev. Abel McEwen	4	73
Sarah Ann, d. [Leonard & Ellen S.], b. Oct. 31, 1837	3	289
Solomon, s. Roger & Prudence, b. Apr. 10, 1739	2	46
Stedman, s. [William & Mary], b. Oct. 9, 1764	3	58

	Vol.	Page
DART, DARTT (cont.)		
Stedman, m. Sally **WHEELER**, Jan. 20, 1791	3	119
Thomas, s. Daniell & Elizabeth, b. July 8, 1687	1	40
Thomas, s. [William & Mary], b. Mar. 6, 1773	3	58
William, s. Roger & Prudence, b. Dec. 12, 1730	2	14
William, of New London, m. Mary **CHAPMAN**, of New London, Nov. 24, 1761	3	58
William, s. [William & Mary], b. Sept. 21, 1762	3	58
William, Jr., m. Betsey **THOMPSON**, Jan. 28, 1787	3	8
William Henry, s. [Leonard & Ellen S.], b. May 11, 1835	3	289
DAVENPORT, Jared, s. [James & Welthey], b. Aug. 31, 1786	3	129
Russell, s. [James & Welthey], b. May 3, 1784	3	129
Sarah A., of New London, m. Edmund **HUNTLEY**, of Norwich, Aug. 12, 1849, by Rev. Edwin R. Warren	4	148
DAVIS, Abigail, d. [Reuben & Catharine], b. Dec. 6, 1785	3	130
Albert W., of Norwich, Ct., m. Leonora **GRANT**, Mar. 8, 1842, by Rev. Edwin C. Brown	4	97
Amelia, of Waterford, m. James **CHAPMAN**, of Waterford, Feb. 18, 1838, by Rev. Abel McEwen	4	81
Andrew, m. Sarah **BAKER**, Dec. 9, 1708	1	34
Ann, m. William **WEST**, b. of New London, July 17, 1851, by Rev. J. M. Eaton	4	164
Azuba, m. Ransford **COMSTOCK**, May 2, 1782	3	51
Benajah, m. Zerviah **SMITH**, b. of [New London], Sept. 15, 1785, by Jason Lee, Elder, of Lyme	3	80
David, s. John, 2d & Bethiah, b. Mar. 13, 1748/9	2	111
Edward, m. Bridget **HENRIGHT**, June 18, 1848, by Rev. John Brady	4	139
Elias, m. Julia Ann **WILCOX**, b. of Stonington, Apr. 16, 1850, by Rev. Jabez S. Swan	4	153
Eunice, m. Francis **CHAPPEL**, b. of Montville, Oct. 10, 1841, by Rev. R. W. Allen	4	96
Frances O., m. Robert **BOADWELL**, July 17, 1842, by H. R. Knapp	4	100
Hannah, d. John, 2d, & Bathiah, b. Sept. 16, 1744, at Stonington	2	110
Hannah, d. [Reuben & Catharine], b. May 11, 1794; d. July 23, 1798	3	130
Hannah, d. John, m. Samuel **CORNELL**, Sept. 23, 1798	3	215
Hannah, d. [Reuben & Catharine], b. Dec. 7, 1801	3	130
Hannah, of New London, m. Charles **PECK**, of New York, Sept. 6, 1826, by Rev. Newel S. Spaulding	4	27
Hannah H., of New Bedford, Mass., m. Benjamin **RICHARDSON**, of Providence, R.I., Aug. 8, 1844, by John Grace, J.P.	4	116

	Vol.	Page

DAVIS (cont.)

Harriet S., of New London, m. John T. **FLAGG**, of
  Boylston, Mass., Nov. 30, 1848, by Rev. Tryon
  Edwards — 4 — 143

James, s. [Reuben & Catharine], b. Aug. 28, 1788 — 3 — 130

Jeremiah L., m. Delia **CHAP[P]EL[L]**, May 8, 1836,
  by Rev. Alvan Ackley — 4 — 65

John P., of New London, m. Martha A. **CARTER**, of
  Bristol, Me., Nov. 3, 1844, by Rev. J. Blain — 4 — 115

Lavina, m. Antonia **LOPER**, [May] 13, [1847], by
  Rev. Robert A. Hallam — 4 — 131

Lucy, d. Benajah, m. William **COMSTOCK**, s.
  James, of New London, Feb. 12, 1861 — 3 — 46

Margaret, d. Samuel & Sarah, b. Dec. 6, 1730 — 2 — 13

Martha, d. John, b. of Stonington, m. Nathan
  ROGERS, s. Capt. Jona[than], b. of New
  London, Dec. 17, 1740 — 3 — 1

Mary, d. [Reuben & Catharine], b. Aug. 15, 1791 — 3 — 130

Mary, d. William, m. Moses **BEEBE**, s. Jeduthan,
  Dec. 16, 1797 — 3 — 141

Milo, of Montville, m. Sarah Ann **BENSON**, of
  London, England, Oct. 4, 1839, by James M.
  Lanman, J.P. — 4 — 87

Reuben, s. Philip & Abigail, b. Mar. 13, 1762, in
  Darby, Ct. — 3 — 130

Reuben, m. Catharine **THORP**, Mar. [ ], 1784 — 3 — 130

Reuben, s. [Reuben & Catharine], b. Oct. 7, 1796 — 3 — 130

Robert S., of Boston, m. Mary H. **SHANNON**, of
  New London, Sept. 4, 1837, by Rev. Robert A.
  Hallam — 4 — 73

Saltonstall, s. Samuel & Sarah, b. Sept. 12, 1729 — 2 — 13

Samuel, m. Sarah **GARDENER**, Jan. 1, 1727 — 2 — 13

Sarah, of [New London], m. James **McDERMOTT**,
  of Rochester, N.Y., Nov. 12, 1845, by Rev. L.
  Ph.[ilip?] Lemont — 1 — 100

Susannah, d. John, m. Thomas **CROCKER**, Jr., s.
  Thomas, Jan. 30, 1757 — 2 — 10

William, d. June 19, 1725 — 2 — 13

William, s. John, 2d, & Bethiah, b. May 14, 1747 — 2 — 110

William, of New London, m. Lavinia **BURDON**, of
  Norwich, Ct., Aug. 31, 1843, by Rev. S.
  Benton — 4 — 108

William, m. Sarah **SMITH**, b. of New London, Apr.
  28, 1845, by Rev. L. Geo[rge] Leonard — 4 — 123

William A., m. Susan **MAYNARD**, b. of New
  London, Apr. 4, 1832, by Rev. Abel McEwen — 4 — 46

William H., of New London, m. Melissa B.
  CARTER, of Bristol, Dec. 18, 1850, by Rev.
  Jabez S. Swan — 4 — 158

Williamina, of Philadelphia, m. Isaac G. **PORTER**,
  Sept. 12, 1833 — 3 — 237

	Vol.	Page
DAVISON, Cynthia, of Norwich, m. Charles **BISHOP**, of New London, Nov. 12, 1837, by Rev. Alvan Ackley	4	80
James, m. Lucey **SMITH**, d. Josiah, May 22, 1808	3	204
Jonathan Brooks, s. [James & Lucey], b. May 16, 1809	3	204
Luther, of New London, m. Mary W. **CARTER**, formerly of Bristol, Me., May 22, 1842, by Rev. Lemuel Covell	4	99
DAWSON, Robert G., m. Jerusha **BAILEY**, Jan. 28, 1813*, by Rev. Peter Griffing *(So in the copy. Probably 1831)	4	40
DAY, Abigail Hinman, d. [James & Hannah], b. June 9, 1813	3	253
James, m. Hannah **HINMAN**, d. Capt. Elisha, [ ]	3	253
James Ingersoll, s. [James & Hannah], b. Mar. 5, 1812	3	253
John, m. Cinderilla **HEWLET**, b. of New London, May 5, 1833, by Rev. Abel McEwen	4	51
John, of New London, m. Julia **COMSTOCK**, of Groton, May 24, 1835, by Rev. Abel McEwen	4	61
John, m. Lydia **LATHAM**, b. of New London, Apr. 4, 1837, by Daniel Huntington	4	70
Malvina, m. Edwin **OSBORN**, b. of New London, May 14, 1830, by Rev. Abel McEwen	4	38
Mary Sherwood, d. [James & Hannah], b. Nov. 28, 1814, twin with William Sherwood	3	253
Peter, m. Sally **PARKER**, June 20, 1802	3	21
Peter, s. [Peter & Sally], b. May 17, 1803	3	21
Polly Lucretia, d. [Peter & Sally], b. Nov. 26, 1806	3	21
Thomas David, s. [James & Hannah], b. June 27, 1820	3	253
William Sherwood, s. [James & Hannah], b. Nov. 28, 1814, twin with Mary Sherwood; d. Aug. [ ], 1815	3	253
DAYNES, Abraham, of N. Yarmouth, m. Sarah, d. William **PECKE**, of New London, Dec. 27, [1671]	1	7
Johanna, d. Abraham & Sarah, b. Feb. 2, [1671]	1	8
DAYTON, DATON, [see also **DEIGHTON**], Angerro C., of New London, m. Dominico **STARR**, "of the Rev. Cutter"*, Nov. 5, [1844], by Rev. J. Blain *(So in the original)	4	115
Deborah, b. Jan. 4, 1746;' m. William **COLVART**, July 22, 1762	3	89
Ellen S., m. Thomas F. **PERRY**, Aug. 22, 1852, by Rev. Jabez S. Swan	4	174
Ephraim, m. Abiga[i]ll **WILLOBE**, Oct. 27, 1720	1	57
Louisa Jane, m. William F. **MASON**, b. of [New London], Mar. 22, 1847, by Rev. L. G. Leonard	4	129

	Vol.	Page

DAYTON, DATON (cont.)
  Lucretia, d. Ephraim, of New London, decd., m.
    Jeduthan **BEEBE**, s. William, of New London,
    Dec. 27, 1753 — 2 — 63
  Phebe, m. David **GOODFAITH**, Mar. 5, 1786 — 3 — 115
DEARBORN, John, m. Eliza **MOORE**, b. of [New
    London], Mar. 28, 1841, by John Lovejoy — 4 — 94
  John L., of New London, m. Lydia N. **DART**, of
    Waterford, Apr. 6, 1845, by Rev. S. Benton — 4 — 119
DECAMP, John, of the U.S. Navy, m. Mary Augusta
    GREEN, of [New London], Sept. 9, 1835, by
    Rev. Robert A. Hallam — 4 — 62
  Sarah Canfield, m. John **BRANDEGEE**, Mar. 21,
    1836, by Rev. Robert A. Hallam — 4 — 65
DECKER, Egbert, m. Francis Amanda **CHIPMAN**, b. of
    New London, Oct. 31, 1842, by Eld. L. Covell — 4 — 103
DEE, Joseph, of Hartford, m. Theresa **GUY**, of
    Jamesborough, Ms., Nov. 18, 1847, by Rev.
    Jabez S. Swan — 4 — 136
DEGNEW, Matilda, m. Joseph **STANDISH**, b. of [New
    London], May 29, 1850, by Rev. Robert A.
    Hallam — 4 — 154
DEIGHTON, [see also **DAYTON**], Deborah, m. John
    ROGERS, s. Joseph, Feb. 1, 1718/19 — 1 — 56
DELAMORE, Henry, m. Johanna **EDGECOMBE**, Feb.
    14, 1716/17 — 1 — 51
DELANEY, Edwin A., m. Harriet A. **HOWARD**, Nov. 1,
    1850, by Rev. James W. Dennis — 4 — 157
DELARROY, Daniel, of Norwich, m. Amanda F.
    STROUD, of [New London], May 25, 1844, by
    Rev. Abel McEwen — 4 — 114
DELONG, Isaac, m. Eunice **SMITH**, b. of New London,
    Dec. 25, 1830, by Rev. Abel McEwen — 4 — 40
  Isaac, m. Elizabeth **COLBERT**, b. of New London,
    Feb. 27, 1841, by Rev. Squire B. Hascall — 4 — 93
DEMMET, Lott, m. Hannah **CHELDS**, Oct. 26, 1807 — 3 — 116
  Sally, d. [Lott & Hannah], b. Dec. 31, 1808 — 3 — 116
DENCE, Diana, of Stonington, m. Manuel **BAKER**, of
    Spain, Mar. 20, 1831, by Rev. B. Judd — 4 — 42
DENEEFE, Richard, m. Catharine **MURPHY**, Oct. 14,
    1849, by Rev. William Logan — 4 — 150
DENISON, Andrew, s. Maj. Robert, m. Mary
    THOMPSON, d. Isaac, b. of New London,
    [   ] — 3 — 3
  Ann, d. George & Mary, b. Aug. 11, 1707 — 1 — 33
  Ann, m. Jabez **HOUGH**, Jan. 7, 1724/5 — 1 — 64
  Ann, d. Daniel & Rachel, b. Sept. 8, 1743 — 2 — 16
  Borradill, d. George & Mary, b. May 17, 1701 — 1 — 26
  Barradill, m. Jonathan **LATTIMORE**, Apr. 6, 1721 — 1 — 57
  Danniell, s. George & Mary, b. June 27, 1703 — 1 — 29
  Daniel, m. Rachel **STAR[R]**, Nov. 14, 1726 — 2 — 13
  Daniel, s. Daniel & Rachel, b. Dec. 16, 1730 — 2 — 14

	Vol.	Page
DENISON (cont.)		
Daniel, of New London, s. Daniel, late of New London, decd., m. Katharine **AVERY**, of Groton, d. of Ebenezer, of Groton, July 1, 1756, in Groton, by Rev. Daniel Kirtland	2	121
Daniel, s. Daniel & Katharine, b. Sept. 26, 1758	2	121
Deborah, d. Rob[er]t & Deborah, b. Dec. 9, 1722	2	12
Deborah, d. Capt. Robert, of New London, m. Christopher **MANWARING**, s. Richard, of New London, Jan. 31, 1745	3	80
Ebenezer Avery, s. Daniel & Katharine, b. Jan. 26, 1760	2	121
Elizabeth, d. Rob[er]t & Deborah, b. Feb. 28, 1722/3; d. Mar. 16, 1722/3	2	12
Elizabeth, d. Rob[er]t & Deborah, b. Sept. 10, 1726	2	13
Elizabeth, d. Daniel & Rachel, b. Nov. 19, 1748	2	19
Elizabeth, d. Elisha, of Stonington, m. Nathaniel **LEDYARD**, Feb. 20, 1795	3	151
Elizabeth H., m. William H. **MILLER**, b. of New London, Jan. 13, 1851, by Rev. George M. Carpenter	4	158
Esther, d. Wetherell & Lydia, b. Mar. 16, 1734/5	2	106
Esther, d. Wetherill, m. Rupert **SANDIFORTH**, s. John, Mar. 27, 1758	3	21
George, s. John & Phebe, of Stonington, b. Mar. 28, 1671	1	8
George, d. Jan. 20, 1719/20	1	59
George, s. Wetherell & Lydia, b. Jan. 16, 1729/30	2	13
Grace, d. George & Mary, b. Jan. 4, 1694/5	1	22
Grace, m. Edw[ar]d **HALLAM**, July 30, 1713	2	36
Grace, d. Wetherell & Lydia, b. Feb. 8, 1727/3	2	13
Hannah, d. George & Mary, b. Mar. 28, 1698/99	1	25
Hannah, m. John **HOUGH**, Sept. 4, 1718	1	51
Hannah, d. Daniel & Rachel, b. Jan. 2, 1738/9	2	15
Hannah, m. Henry **JEPSON**, Jan. [ ], 1769	3	41
Isaac, s. Andrew & Mary, b. Dec. 20, 1753	3	3
James, s. Daniel & Rachel, b. Apr. 18, 1746	2	19
John, s. Andrew & Mary, b. Sept. 16, 1755	3	3
Katharine, d. Daniel & Katharine, b. July 24, 1757	2	121
Lucy, d. Wetherell & Lydia, b. May 5, 1739	2	106
Lydia, d. Wetherell & Lydia, b. Aug. 1, 1731	2	14
Mary, w. George, d. Aug. 22, 1711	1	37
Mary, d. Daniel & Rachel, b. Aug. 19, 1728	2	14
Mary, d. of Daniel, late of New London, decd., m. Samuel **DOUGLASS**, of New London, s. Capt. Richard, decd., Nov. 2, 1749	2	99
Mary, d. Andrew & Mary, b. June 21, 1757	3	3
Mary A., m. James M. **WILLIAMS**, b. of [New London], May 14, 1848, by Rev. M. P. Alderman	4	139
Matilde, d. Elisha, of Stonington, m. Samuel **HURLBUT**, June 2, 1796	3	156

	Vol.	Page
DENISON (cont.)		
Phebe, d. George & Mary, b. Mar. 3, 1696/7	1	23
Phebe, m. Gibson HARRIS, Jan. 12, 1720	1	58
Phebee, d. Daniel & Rachel, b. [ ]	2	16
Rachel, d. Daniel & Rachel, b. Sept. 20, 1734	2	15
Rachel m. Joseph COPP, Dec. 11, 1757	3	58
Robert, m. Deborah GRISWOLD, Oct. 19, 1721	2	12
Rob[er]t, s. Rob[er]t & Deborah, b. Mar. 5, 1724; d. May 16, 1724	2	12
Robert, s. Andrew & Mary, b. Dec. 22, 1749	3	3
Samuel, s. Daniel & Rachel, b. Nov. 9, 1736	2	15
Sarah, d. George & Mary, b. June 20, 1710	1	36
Sarah, m. William DOUGLASS, Mar. 4, 1730/1	2	14
Sarah, d. George & Joannah, b. Sept. 8, 1733	2	14
Sarah, d. Wetherell & Lydia, b. May 31, 1743	2	106
Thomas, s. Daniel & Rachel, b. Nov. 4, 1732	2	14
Wetherell, s. George & Mary, b. Aug. 24, 1705	1	30
Wetherell, m. Lydia MORE, Nov. 9, 1726	2	13
William, m. Nancy MASON, b. of [New London], June 3, 1824, by Rev. Thomas W. Tucker	4	19
DENNIS, DENNESS, Abba M., d. [Henry G. & Abby M.], b. Dec. 27, 1837,	3	218
Ann, d. Eben[eze]r, late of New London, decd., m. Nathan DOUGLASS, s. Thomas, of New London, decd., Dec. 22, 1745	2	74
Ann, m. Mark EDGAR, Apr. 18, 1813, at Norwich	3	234
Ann E., d. [Henry G., & Abby M.], b. July 7, 1840	3	218
Augustus, s. [Henry G., & Abby M.], b. Dec. 27, 1836	3	218
Betsey, m. Felix DURGEE, b. of Norwich, Mar. 28, 1824, by Rev. Abel McEwen	4	17
Charles, s. [Henry & Sally], b. Jan. 26, 1821	3	234
Deborah, m. Merrit ROCKWELL, Aug. 10, 1782	3	138
Ebenezer, s. George & Elizabeth, b. Oct. 23, [1682]	1	16
Eben[eze]r, m. Sarah HOUGH, Feb. 20, 1706/7	1	53
Eben[eze]r, m. Deborah ELY, Nov. 19, 1717	1	53
Edgar, s. [Henry & Sally], b. Aug. 12, 1823	3	234
Eliza E., m. Charles REDFIELD, b. of [New London], Sept. 28, 1846, by Rev. Abel McEwen	4	127
Elizabeth, d. Eben[eze]r & Sarah, b. Aug. 14, 1708	1	53
Elizabeth, d. May 1, 1712	1	53
Elizabeth, d. Feb. 16, 1714/5	1	53
Esther, d. Eben[eze]r & Sarah, b. Oct. 23, 1711	1	53
Ezra Hiram, s. [John & Lydia], b. Jan. 13, 1799	3	155
Fanny Dorr, d. [Henry & Sally], b. May 4, 1809; d. Jan. 27, 1825	3	234
Frances Jane, d. [Henry & Sally], b. Dec. 8, 1831	3	234
Francis B., s. [Henry G. & Abby W.], b. May 30, 1855	3	218
George, of Long Island, m. Elizabeth, wid. of Joshua RAYMOND, Jan. 26, [1681]	1	16

	Vol.	Page
DENNIS, DENNESS (cont.)		
George, s. Eben[eze]r & Deborah, b. Oct. 19, 1718	1	53
Henry, s. [John & Lydia], b .Mar. 14, 1794; d. Oct. 28, 1795	3	155
Henry, m. Sally **BRIGGS**, d. William, June 21, 1807	3	234
Henry, s. [Henry G. & Abby M.], b. Apr. 30, 1842	3	218
Henry G., m. Abby M. **HOLT**, d. Robert, Nov. 2, 1834	3	218
Henry G., m. Abby M. **HOLT**, b. of [New London], Nov. 2, 1834, by Rev. Abel McEwen	4	58
Henry Gallup, s. [Henry & Sally], b. Mar. 5, 1813	3	234
John, m. Lydia **MAYNARD**, d. Andrew, Aug. 24, 1788	3	155
John, m. Nancy **HULL**, relict of John, May 21, 1797	3	222
John, s. [John & Nancy], b. Apr. 27, 1799	3	222
John, m. Lydia **CHAPEL**, b. of New London, July 20, 1822, by Rev. Abel McEwen	4	9
John Andrew, s. [John & Lydia], b. Dec. 24, 1795	3	155
Lodowick Fosdick, s. [Henry & Sally], b. Mar. 26, 1826; d. Oct. 30, 1827	3	234
Lodowick Fosdick, s. [Henry & Sally], b. Sept. 30, 1828	3	234
Lucretia J., m. William H. **BARNES**, b. of [New London], Jan. 19, 1846, by Rev. Abel McEwen	4	123
Lydia, d. [John & Lydia], b. Feb. 14, 1790	3	155
Lydia, d. John, m. Elisha **SWAN**, Mar. 26, 1806	3	37
Lydia, w. John, d. [ ]	3	155
Mary, [d. Ebenezer & Sarah], b. Apr. 5, 1713	1	53
Mary Elizabeth, d. [Henry & Sally], b. Mar. 16, 1836	3	234
Nancy, relict, of John, m. Ebenezer **SMITH**, July 22, 1803	3	222
Samuel, s. [Henry & Sally], b. Jan. 6, 1819	3	234
Sarah, d. Eben[eze]r & Sarah, b. June 30, 1710	1	53
Sarah, w. Eben[eze]r, d. Feb. 19, 1714/5	1	53
Sarah Ann, d. [Henry & Sally], b. Feb. 27, 1811	3	234
Sarah B., d. [Henry G. & Abby M.], b. Nov. 9, 1848	3	218
William Briggs, s. [Henry & Sally], b. Sept. 14, 1816	3	234
William Henry, s. [John & Lydia], b. Feb. 13, 1797	3	155
-----, young child of Eben[eze]r [& Sarah], d. Feb. 19, 1714/15 about an hour after its birth	1	53
DENOIR, Mary, m. Henry **FORESTALL**, Aug. 11, 1850. Witnesses: John Curran, Catharine Reilly	4	159
Mary, m. Henry **FORESTELL**, Aug. 11, [18]50, [by Peter J. Blenkinsop]. Witnesses: John Curran, Catharine Reilly	3	306
DERRY, George, of East Haddam, m. Hannah **VANDEVORT**, of New London, Oct. 24, 1825, by Rev. Abel McEwen	4	24
Mary Ann, of Groton, Ct., m. Randall **CAPWELL**, of R.I., May 14, 1843, by Rev. Lemuel Covell	4	109

	Vol.	Page
DERTIN, Ann M., m. Charles **BOLLES**, b. of New London, Mar. 15, 1848, by Rev. Abel McEwen	4	138
DESANT, Antonia, of Bonavista, m. Diana **CAGER**, of New London, Sept. 18, 1842, by Rev. Robert A. Hallam	4	101
DESHON, DISHON, Abby Emely, d. [Daniel & Sally], b. Mar. 7, 1804	3	135
Augusta Coit, d. [Daniel, Jr. & Augusta D.], b. Mar. 13, 1821	3	182
Christopher, s. [Richard & Mary], b. Nov. 12, 1766	3	150
Daniel, m. Ruth **CHRISTOPHERS**, Oct. 4, 1724	2	12
Daniel, s. Daniel & Ruth, b. Nov. 10, 1725	2	13
Daniel, s. Henry & Bathsheba, m. Mary Ann **PACKWOOD**, d. William & Abigail, Dec. 9, 1784	3	135
Daniel, s. [Daniel & Mary Ann], b. Aug. 6, 1785	3	135
Dan[ie]l, Capt., had servant Quam Joe, s. Eunice, b. Sept. 7, 1796	3	104
Daniel, Capt. had negro slave Quam Joe, s. Eunice, b. Sept. 7, 1796	3	128
Daniel, m. Fanny **ROGERS**, Aug. 22, 1798* *(Incorrect date?)	3	135
Daniel, m. Sally **ROBINSON**, Jan. 31, 1799	3	135
Daniel, Jr., m. Augusta D. **COIT**, May 25, 1820	3	182
Eader, m. Ce[a]sar **SHAW**, (negroes), May [ ], 1779	3	16
Fanny, [w. Daniel], d. Oct. 3, 1798	3	135
Frances Boureon, d. [Daniel & Sally], b. Mar. 17, 1802	3	135
Frances E., of [New London], m. Benjamin B. **THURSTON**, of Hopkinton, R.I., Mar. 12, 1834, by Rev. Isaac W. Hallam	4	55
Giles Buonaparte, s. [Daniel & Mary Ann], b. Jan. 9, 1797	3	135
Grace, d. Daniel & Ruth, b. Aug. 13, 1733	2	15
Grace, d. Henery, m. James **LAMPHERE**, May 27, 1776	3	155
Harriet Eliza, d. [Daniel & Sally], b. Sept. 3, 1807	3	135
Henry, s. Daniel & Ruth, b. Dec. 28, 1729	2	14
Henry, s. [Daniel & Mary Ann], b. Jan. 11, 1790	3	135
James, s. [Daniel & Mary Ann], b. May 19, 1795	3	135
John, s. Daniel & Ruth, b. Dec. 25, 1727; d. June 29, 1794	2	13
John, s. Daniel & Ruth, m. Sarah **STARR**, d. Benj[amin] & Lydia, Aug. 25, 1751	2	1
John Prentice, s. [Richard & Mary], b. Oct. 29, 1770	3	150
Joseph, s. Daniel & Ruth, b. Dec. 27, 1728	2	14
Joseph, s. Daniel & Ruth, b. Sept. 27, 1731	2	14
Joseph, s. [Richard & Mary], b. Apr. 7, 1779	3	150
Lucy, d. [Richard & Mary], b. Oct. 17, 1774	3	150
Lucy, d. Col. Richard, m. William **LEEDS**, Oct. 20, 1797	3	193

	Vol.	Page
DESHON, DISHON (cont.)		
Lydia, m. James **CEGANE**, native of Marsailles,		
France, Sept. 10, 1789	3	120
Mary Ann, d. [Daniel & Mary Ann], b. Aug. 16,		
1793; d. Sept. 2, 1798	3	135
[Mary Ann, w. Daniel], d. Sept. 3, 1798*		
*(Incorrect date?)	3	135
Mary Ann, d. [Daniel & Sally], b. Dec. 3 ,1799	3	135
Mary Ann, of New London, m. John **BRANDEGEE**,		
of New Orleans, July 4, 1821, b Rev. B. Judd	4	6
Peter, s. [Richard & Mary], b. July 13, 1772	3	150
Richard, s. Daniel & Ruth, b. Oct. 13, 1733	2	14
Richard, m. Mary **HARRISS**, d. Capt. John		
PRENTICE, Oct. 2, 1763	3	150
Richard, s. [Richard & Mary], b. Aug. 7, 1764	3	150
Sarah, d. John & Sarah, b. Apr. 27, 1752	2	1
Sarah, d. [Richard & Mary], b. Oct. 18, 1776	3	150
Susan, d. Col. Richard, m. Christopher **GRIFFING**,		
Apr. 25, 1795	3	178
Susannah, d. [Richard & Mary], b. Nov. 10, 1768	3	150
William, s. [Daniel & Mary Ann], b. Mar. 21, 1787;		
d. Oct. 31, 1787	3	135
William, s. [Daniel & Mary Ann], b. July 26, 1788	3	135
DESMOND, Ellen, m. Richard **HIGGINS**, Dec. 8, [18]50,		
[by Peter J. Blenkinsop]. Witnesses: John		
Halpin, Mary Reordan	3	306
DESTIN, Andrew, s. [George & Fanny], b. June 16, 1828	3	221
Ann, d. [George & Fanny], b. Apr. 15, 1825	3	221
Fanny, d. [George & Fanny], b. Mar. 25, 1816	3	221
Fanny, of New London, m. Charles G. **EVERETT**,		
of Northampton, Pa., Mar. 26, 1837, by Rev.		
Squire B. Hascall	4	68
George, m. Fanny **ROGERS**, d. Nathan, Feb. 19,		
1807	3	221
George, s. [George & Fanny], b. Aug. 12, 1808	3	221
Jane, d. [George & Fanny], b. May 25, 1821	3	221
Leonard, s. [George & Fanny], b. Aug. 31, 1813	3	221
Nathan, s. [George & Fanny], b. Nov. 20, 1818	3	221
William, s. [George & Fanny], b. Nov. 25, 1810	3	221
DEVRO, Ann Elizabeth, m. William **MILLER**, Nov. 8,		
1826	3	202
DEWEY, DEWY, Abiga[i]l, m. Elisha **LYMAN**, Oct. 1,		
1835, by Rev. Alvan Ackley	4	63
Edward P., m. Nancy L. **BAILEY**, May 18, 1831, by		
Rev. Daniel Wildman	4	42
Erastus, s. [Erastus & Caroline], b. Jan. 20, 1804	3	62
Patty, d. Erastus & Caroline, d. Oct. 5, 1803	3	62
DeWOLF, DeWOLFE, Edward, of Lyme, m. Susannah		
DOUGLASS, Nov. 4, 1708	1	34
Lucretia, m. Jeremiah **HARRIS**, Mar. 10, 1850, by		
Rev. Charles Willett	4	152

	Vol.	Page

DeWOLF, DeWOLFE (cont.)

Mary A., m. Henry W. **HAYNES**, July 3, 1839, by
James M. Macdonald — 4 — 86

DIBBLE, Alvira L., m. John **HUDSON**, Sept. 4, 1839, by
Rev. James M. Macdonald — 4 — 89

DICKERMAN, Jairus, of Troy, N.Y., m. Catharine E.
NOYES, of [New London], May 9, 1841, by
Rev. Abel McEwen — 4 — 95

DICKINSON, David Bill, s. [Nathaniel & Elisabeth], b.
Sept. 3, 1787 — 3 — 68

Elisabeth, d. [Nathaniel & Elisabeth], b. Jan. 20,
1782 — 3 — 68

Jerome Chapman, s. [Nathaniel & Elisabeth], b. Nov.
27, 1785 — 3 — 68

John, m. Mary S. **ISHAM**, d. Jirah, [   ] — 3 — 268

John T., of Stonington, m. Charlotte E. **BAKER**, of
New London, [   ] 4, [1847?], by Rev. T.
Edwards — 4 — 129

Martha, d. [Nathaniel & Elisabeth], b. Jan. 28, 1784 — 3 — 68

Nathaniel, m. Elisabeth **BILL**, Nov. 22, 1778 — 3 — 68

Nathaniel, s. [Nathaniel & Elisabeth], b. Jan. 8, 1780;
d. July 25, 1781 — 3 — 68

Thomas, m. Nancy **HAYSE**, June 17, 1805 — 3 — 95

Thomas, s. [Thomas & Nancy], b. Sept. 9 ,1807 — 3 — 95

William, s. [John & Mary S.], b. July 26, 1831 — 3 — 268

DICKSON, [see under **DIXON**]

DIFFLIN, Bridget, m. John **DALY**, Dec. 27, 1848, by
Rev. William Logan — 4 — 150

DILLAMORE, Merriam, m. John **BOLLES**, July 26,
1758 — 2 — 18

DILMAN, Peter, m. Nancy **POMEROY**, b. of New
London, Nov. 14, 1830, by Rev. Abel McEwen — 4 — 39

DINON Thomas, m. Eder **SHAW**, b. of New London,
July 11, 1830, by Rev. D. Judd — 4 — 41

DIXON, DICKSON, Abigail, d. [Luke & Naomi], b.
Sept. 11, 1803 — 3 — 47

David, s. [Luke & Naomi], b. Nov. 2, 1791 — 3 — 47

Issable, m. John **COPP**, b. of New London, North
Parish, Nov. 7, 1744, by Rev. David Jewet[t] — 2 — 101

John, s. [Nathan & Elizabeth], b. Sept. [   ], 1808 — 3 — 225

Luke, m. Naomi **EDGECOMB**, Jan. 18, 1791 — 3 — 47

Nathan, m. Elizabeth **YENTON**, d. Ezekiel, Feb. [ ],
1807 — 3 — 225

DOBBS, Mary, of New York, m. Charles **HOLT**, Aug. 10,
1800, in New York, by Rev. John McKnight — 3 — 46

Oliver R., of Danbury, Ct., m. Mary
WHITTEMORE, of [New London], Jan. 28,
1848, by Rev. M. P. Alderman — 4 — 140

DODGE, Abigail, m. Benjamin **GREEN**, Jan. 11, 1775 — 3 — 108

Daniel, s. [Ezra & Elisabeth], b. Nov. 2, 1791 — 3 — 119

Elizabeth, m. John **ROGERS**, s. John, Jan. 28,
1722/3, by Ephraim Woodbridge — 1 — 60

	Vol.	Page
DODGE (cont.)		
Elizabeth, d. Nathaniel Hempster, m. Asa		
SPENCER, Nov. 1, 1801	3	44
Ezra, m. Elisabeth **HEMPSTE[A]D**, Sept. 26, 1790;		
d. Aug. [ ], 1798	3	119
Ezra, s. [Ezra & Elisabeth], b. June 13, 1795	3	119
Ezra, m. Elizabeth **MARRAT**, Oct. 5, 1820, at New		
York	3	171
Ezra Spencer, s. [Ezra & Elizabeth], b. Dec. 3, 1821	3	171
John, s. [Nehemiah, Jr. & Mary Ann], b. Oct. 20,		
1825, in New York	3	251
Lucy Smith, d. [Nehemiah, Jr. & Mary Ann], b. Dec.		
21, 1823	3	251
Mary Ann, d. [Nehemiah, Jr. & Mary Ann], b. Mar.		
19, 1822	3	251
Mercy A., of New London, m. John **WOODWARD**,		
of South Hampton, L.I., N.Y., Aug. 2, 1827, by		
Rev. Nehemiah Dodge	4	31
Nehemiah, m. Lucy **SMITH**, June 15, 1794	3	127
Nehemiah, Jr., m. Mary Ann **PAYNE**, Nov. 16, 1820	3	251
Nehemiah, Jr., m. Mary Ann **PAYNE**, b. of New		
London, Nov. 16, 1820, by Rev. Nehemiah		
Dodge	4	3
Samuel, s. [Ezra & Elisabeth], b. Oct. 12, 1797	3	119
DOHERY, DOUGHERTY, Jane, of [New London], m.		
John **JARMAN**, of New Orleans, Nov. 30,		
1846, by Rev. Abel McEwen	4	128
Rosanna, m. Richard **MURPHY**, Apr. 8, 1849, by		
Rev. William Logan	4	150
DOLAN, Margarit, m. Francis **BRODERICK**, Nov. 29,		
1851, by Rev. J. Stokes. Witnesses: Patrick		
Greeley, Bridget Kelley	4	169
DOLBEARE, Abigail, m. Elisha **HINMAN**, Mary 24,		
1777	3	76
George Benjamin, s. George & Mary, b. Dec. 25,		
1753	3	22
Hannah, d. George & Mary, b. Nov. 26, 1751, old		
style	3	22
Hannah, m. Guy **RICHARDS**, June 17, 1773	3	74
DOOLEY, Johanna, m. Thomas **ROWE**, Nov. 23, 1851,		
by Rev. J. Stokes. Witnesses: Patrick Rowe,		
Ellen Tuohy	4	169
DONOVAN, DONOVEN, Alice, m. James **FINIGAN**,		
June 19, 1848, by Rev. John Brady	4	139
Ann, m. Bartholomew **JONES**, Sept. 9, 1849, by		
Rev. William Logan	4	150
Bridget, m. Michael **MORGAN**, Nov. 26, 1848,		
by Rev. William Logan	4	150
DORRY, Lydia, m. Ebenezer **WAY**, Dec. 21, 1783	3	147
DOSETT, [see under **DOWSETT**]		
DOUGLASS, DOUGLAS, DOWGLASS, Abell, s. John		
& Esther, b. June 27, 1770	2	100

	Vol.	Page
DOUGLASS, DOUGLAS, DOWGLASS (cont.)		
Abia*, d. William & Abial, b. Apr. 2, [1671] *(Or		
Sarah)	1	7
Abia, d. Will[ia]m & Abia, b. Aug. 18, [1675]	1	10
Abiah, d. William & Sarah, b. Jan. 5, 1741/2	2	51
Abiah, d. [George & Elisabeth], b. May 25, 1775	3	67
Abigail, d. [Ebenezer & Abigail], b. Oct. 11, 1775	3	120
Abiga[i]l, w. Richard, 2d., d. Mar. 24, 1799	3	212
Albert G., of Waterford, m. Lucy A. **FOX**, of [New		
London], Oct. 10, 1849, by Rev. Abel McEwen	4	147
Alexander, s. [Richard & Anne], b. Oct. 3, 1778	3	65
Alexander, s. [Richard & Ann], b. Oct. 3, 1778	3	189
Alexander, Jr., of Aron, N.Y., m. Eliza R. **BROWN**,		
of New London, Mar. 2, 1831, by Rev. Abel		
McEwen	4	40
Alfred, s. [Richard, 2d & Lucy], b. Jan. 15, 1807	3	212
Ann, d. Robert & Mary, b. Dec. 25, [1669]	1	6
Ann, d. William & Abiah, b. May 24, [1680]	1	14
Ann, d. Nathan & Ann, b Apr. 7, 1749	2	74
Ann, d [John & Mary], b. May 24, 1806	3	139
Archabald T., m. Delia A. **LATHAM**, Dec. 25, 1850,		
by Rev. Charles Willett	4	158
Artemas G., of N[ew] London, m. Lucretia B.		
THOMPSON, of Norwich, Nov. 16, 1834, by		
Daniel Huntington	4	60
Benjamin, s. [Ebenezer & Abigail], b. Mar. 3, 1781;		
d. Sept. 9, 1783	3	120
Benjamin, s. [Daniel & Lydia], b. Mar. 14, 1785	3	9
Caleb, s. John & Esther, b. Feb. 12, 1756	2	99
Caleb, m. Grace **MORGAN**, Feb. 20, 1787	3	38
Catharine C., m. Jacob **SPOONER**, b. of New		
London, Nov. 9, 1845, by Rev. Jabez Swan	4	124
Charles, s. Nathan & Ann, b. Dec. 13, 1768	2	74
Charles, s. [Richard & Ann], b. July 20, 1792	3	189
Charles, s. [Henry & Harriot], b. Apr. 16, 1832	3	235
Christopher, s. [George & Elisabeth], b. Feb. 14,		
1783	3	67
Christopher, s. [Daniel & Lydia], b. Feb. 22, 1787	3	9
Christopher George, s. [Daniel & Lucy], b. Sept. 30,		
1801	3	147
Clarissa, d. [Richard & Anne], b. July 6, 1781	3	65
Clarrassa, d. [Richard & Ann], b. July 6, 1781	3	189
Clarrisse, d. Richard, m. Palmer **PECK**, May 26,		
1802	3	189
Colbey, s. [John & Mary], b. Nov. 29, 1809	3	139
Cornelia C., of [New London], m. Thomas		
McKINSTREY, of Hartford, Mar. 18, 1836, by		
Rev. Abel McEwen	4	65
Cornelia Chappell, d. [Henry & Harriet], b. Mar. 26,		
1815	3	235
Daniel, s. Thomas & Hannah, b. Sept. 8, 1713	1	52
Daniel, s. Robert & Sarah, b. May 22, 1752	2	99

	Vol.	Page
DOUGLASS, DOUGLAS, DOWGLASS (cont.)		
Daniel, s. John & Esther, b. Feb. 12, 1768	2	100
Daniel, m. Lydia **DOUGLASS**, Apr. 23, 1778	3	9
Daniel, m. Lucy **DOUGLASS**, d. George, [ ]	3	147
Daniel, m. Melia **DOUGLASS**, d. George, [ ]	3	147
Daniel Wetherell, s. [Daniel & Lydia], b. Apr. 14, 1794	3	9
Daniel William, s. [Daniel & Lucy], b. Aug. 8, 1799	3	147
David, s. John & Esther, b. May 2, 1758	2	100
Deborah, d. Nathan & Ann, b. Oct. 18, 1753	2	74
Deborah, m. Judah P. **SPOONER**, Sept. 10, 1770	3	25
Earl, s. [Richard, 2d, & Lucy], b. May 27, 1805	3	212
Ebenezer, s. Nathan & Ann, b. Feb. 24, 1746/7	2	74
Ebenezer, s. Nathan & Anne, m. Abigail **BAILEY**, d. Nathan & Elizabeth, June 3, 1773	3	120
Ebenezer, s. [Ebenezer & Abigail], b. July 14, 1774; d. Nov. 5, 1776	3	120
Eb[eneze]r, Capt. d. Sept. 3, 1798	3	120
Edmond, s. [Daniel & Lydia], b. Mar. 11, 1779	3	9
Edwin Lucas, s. [Daniel & Lucy], b. June 10, 1805	3	147
Elijah, s. John & Esther, b. Dec. 1, 1762; d. [ ]	2	100
Elisha, s. [Samuel & Rebeckah], b. Feb. 7, 1782	3	185
Elisha, s. Mary **KNAPP**, b. Nov. 2, 1800	3	40
Elisha, m. Lydia **HOLMAN**, b. of New London, Aug. 2, 1823, by Thomas W Tucker, Elder	4	15
Elisha, m. Caroline **LEWIS**, b. of [New London], Mar. 31, 1852, by Rev. Jabez S. Swan	4	172
Eliza, d. [John & Mary], b. May 13, 1799	3	139
Elizabeth, d. W[illia]m & Abyah, b. Feb. 25, [1668]	1	6
Elizabeth, d. Robert & Mary, b. Apr. 26, [1677]	1	12
Elizabeth, m. Daniell **DARTT**, Aug. 4, 1686	1	40
Elizl[abet]h, d. William & Sarah, b. Nov. 26, 1733	2	15
Elisabeth, d. William, m. John **CHAPMAN**, s. James, Sept. 17, 1758	3	32
Elizabeth, d. Nathan & Ann, b. June 21, 1759	2	74
Elizabeth, d. [George & Elisabeth], b. Jan. 23, 1768	3	67
Elizabeth, d. [John & Esther], b. May. 29, 1776	2	100
Elisabeth, d. [Ebenezer & Abigail], b. July 8, 1790	3	120
Elizabeth Dickinson, d. [Henry & Harriot], b. July 16, 1823	3	235
Ellen M., m. William **LYON**, b. of [New London], May 12, 1844, by Rev. Abel McEwen	4	111
Ephraim Harris, s. [Henry & Harriot], b. Apr. 12, 1817	3	235
Esther, d. John & Esther, b. Dec. 11, 1750	2	99
Eunice, d. [George & Elisabeth], b. Sept. 16, 1771	3	67
Eunice, m. Picket **LATIMER**, Jan. 13, 1791	3	120
Fanney, d. [Richard & Ann], b. Jan. 15, 1784	3	189
Fanny, d. Richard, m. Jeremiah **MINER**, Mar. 1, 1801	3	189
Febbee, d. Robert & Mary, b. Jan. 26, [1681]	1	15

	Vol.	Page
DOUGLASS, DOUGLAS, DOWGLASS (cont.)		
Ferdinand, s. [Francis Henry & Mary Ann], b. June		
30, 1845	3	271
Francis, s. [Ebenezer & Abigail], b. Mar. 27, 1783	3	120
Francis H., m. Mary Ann **CULVER**, b. of New		
London, Dec. 20, 1832, by Chester Tilden	4	49
Francis H., s. [Francis Henry & Mary Ann], b. July		
24, 1835	3	271
Francis Henry, s. [Henry & Harriot], b. Sept. 11,		
1808	3	235
Francis Henry, m. Mary Ann **CULVER**, Dec. 20,		
1832	3	271
Francis Henry, s. [Francis Henry & Mary Ann], d.		
Apr. 9, 1838	3	271
George, s. William & Sarah, b. July 16, 1739	2	15
George, m. Elisabeth **LUCAS**, Feb. 3, 1765	3	67
George, s. [Jonathan & Anna], b. Jan. 17, 1776	3	60
George, s. [George & Elisabeth], b. Mar. 18, 1781	3	67
George, s. [John & Mary], b. Apr. 5, 1795	3	139
George, s. [Daniel & Melia], b. May 29, 1807	3	147
Gilbert, s. [Daniel & Lydia], b. Jan. 22, 1783	3	9
Grace, d. John & Esther, b. Apr. 8, 1753	2	99
Grace, d. [George & Elisabeth], b. Feb. 3, 1766	3	67
Gurdon, s. [Daniel & Lucy], b. Dec. 29, 179[ ]	3	147
Hannah, d. Robert & Mary, b. May 14, [1673]	1	9
Hannah, d. William, Jr. & Hannah, b. Oct. 23 ,1703	1	35
Hannah, d. Robert & Sarah, b. June 5, 1732	2	15
Hannah, d. Nathan & Ann, b. Sept. 9, 1751	2	74
Hannah, w. Thomas, later Hannah Chapman, w.		
Samuel, d. Nov. 4, 1758	2	9
Hannah, d. Capt. Nathan, m. Stephen **HOLT**, Sept.		
17, 1775	3	163
Hannah, d. [Spearry & Rebeckah], b. July 20, 1776	3	95
Harriet, d. [Henry & Harriot], b. Dec. 4, 1812	3	235
Harriet Harris, d. [Francis Henry & Mary Ann], b.		
Nov. 14, 1847	3	271
Henery, s [Spearry & Rebeckah], b. Dec. 16, 1780	3	95
Henry, m. Harriot **HARRIS**, d. Francis, Dec. 6 ,1807	3	235
Henry, s. [Francis Henry & Mary Ann], b. Aug. 27,		
1842	3	271
Hiram, s. W[illia]m, m. Abigail, d. William		
HOUGH, Dec. 18, 1667	1	5
Isaac, s. John & Esther, b. July 4, 1773	2	100
Isaac, s. [John & Mary], b. Apr. 24, 1801	3	139
Isabella, d. [Henry & Harriot], b. May 16, 1828	3	235
James, s. Thomas & Hannah, b. Apr. 5, 1710	1	52
Jane, of Enfield, Mass., m. Jonathan **BROOKS**, of		
New London, Aug. 29, 1837, by Rev. Robert A.		
Hallam	4	72
Jeremiah, s. [Spearry & Rebeckah], b. Oct. 11, 1774;		
d. Feb. 9, 1803, at Demarra	3	95
John, s. Robert & Mary, b. July 17, [1671]	1	8

	Vol.	Page
DOUGLASS, DOUGLAS, DOWGLASS (cont.)		
John, s. William, Jr. & Hannah, b. Nov. 4, 1701	1	35
John, s. Thomas & Hannah, b. Sept. 7, 1704	1	52
John, s. Thomas & Hannah, b. Apr. 8, 1724	1	64
John, s. Thomas, decd., m. Esther **LEACH**, d.		
Clement, b. of New London, May 11, 1746	2	99
John, s. John & Esther, b. Apr. 21, 1747; d. Apr. 4,		
1748	2	99
John, s. John & Esther, b. Jan. 18, 1748/9	2	99
John, s. Jona[than], & Ann[a], b. Jan. 15, 1770	3	60
John, m. Mary **HOLMES**, Aug. 12, 1791	3	139
John, s. [John & Mary], b. Dec. 18, 1793	3	139
John, m. Mary **SIZER**, Dec. 9, 1826, by Robert		
Bowzer	4	27
John Woodward, s. [Ebenezer & Abigail], b. Oct. 12,		
1788	3	120
Jonathan, s. Richard & Margaret, b. Oct. 30, 1705	1	66
Jonathan, m. Lucy **CHRISTOPHERS** Aug. 3, 1731	2	14
Jonathan, s. William & Sarah, b. July 4, 1737	2	15
Jonathan, s. William, m. Anna **COLFAX**, d. John*,		
all of New London, Apr. 29, 1767 *(First		
written "George")	3	60
Jonathan, s. [John & Anna], b. Aug. 19, 1771	3	60
Jonathan, m. Sally **WORTHINGTON**, Apr. 20,		
1787	3	143
Jonathan, s. [Jonathan & Sally], b. Mar. 10, 1795	3	143
Jonathan, the elder, d. Mar. 6, 1800	3	143
Joseph, s. Robert & Sarah, b. June 1, 1750	2	99
Joseph, s. [Jonathan & Anna], b. July 30, 1778; d.		
Sept. 3, 1798	3	60
Joseph Chapman, s. [Henry & Harriot], b. May 13,		
1810	3	235
Josephine, d. [Francis Henry & Mary Ann], b. Oct.		
18, 1837	3	271
Joshua, s. William, Jr. & Hannah, b. June 2, 1708	1	35
Joshua, s. John & Esther, b. Sept. 5, 1760	2	100
Josiah, of New London, m. Mary **GRISWOLD**, of		
Lyme, Aug. 20, 1798, in Lyme, by Andrew		
Griswold, J.P.	2	124
Josiah, s. [Daniel & Lucy], b. Sept. 21, 1803	3	147
Louisa, m. Franklin **STARR**, b. of [New London],		
Nov. 16, 1835, by Rev. Abel McEwen	4	64
Lucy, d. Jonathan & Lucy, b. Jan. 4 ,1732/3	2	14
Lucy, wid. of Jno., late of New London, decd., m.		
Guy **PALMER**, of New London, s. Andrew,		
decd., Mar. 6, 1736/7	2	45
Lucy, d. William & Sarah, b. Nov. 27, 1743	2	51
Lucy, d. Nathan & Ann, b. Sept. 22, 1755	2	74
Lucy, d. William, m. Daniel **STARR**, Jr., s. Capt.		
Daniel, Jan. 5, 1764	3	32
Lucy, d. [George & Elisabeth], b. June 25, 1773	3	67
Lucy, d. [Ebenezer & Abigail], b. July 29, 1777	3	120

	Vol.	Page
DOUGLASS, DOUGLAS, DOWGLASS (cont.)		
Lucy, d. [Daniel & Lucy], b. Apr. 11, 179[ ]	3	147
Lucy, w. Daniel, d. [ ]	3	147
Lucy, d. George, m. Daniel **DOUGLASS**, [ ]	3	147
Luke, s. [Richard & Ann], b. Nov. 30, 1788	3	189
Lydia, d. [George & Elisabeth], b. Apr. 25, 1777	3	67
Lydia, m. Daniel **DOUGLASS**, Apr. 23, 1778	3	9
Lydia, d. [Daniel & Lydia], b. Dec. 10, 1780	3	9
Margaret, d. William & Sarah, b. Oct. 4, 1735	2	15
Margaret, m. Nathaniel **COIT**, Nov. 6, 1735	2	8
Margaret, d. Capt. Rich[ar]d, m. Nathaniel **COIT**, s.		
Solomon, b. of New London, Nov. 6, 1735	2	70
Margaret, d. William, m. John **BRADDICK**, s. John		
& Lucretia, b. of New London, Dec. 20, 1753	2	79
Margaret, d. William & Mary, b. Feb. 19, 1755	2	87
Mariah Ann, d. [Robert & Elizabeth], b. Mar. 4, 1810	3	234
Mary, see Mary **GODDARD**	3	149
Mary, d. Robert & Mary, b. June 13, [1668]	1	5
Mary, d. Thomas & Hannah, b. Feb. 13, 1715/16	1	52
Mary, d. Robert & Sarah, b. Dec. 4, 1742	2	98
Mary, d. Caleb & Mary, b. Dec. 18, 1745	2	51
Mary, d. Samuel & Mary, b. July 29, 1750	2	99
Mary, d. William & Mary, b. Dec. 25, 1757	2	87
Mary, d. Nathan & Ann, b. Mar. 12 ,1765	2	74
Mary, d. Caleb, of New London, decd., m. John		
OWEN, of New London, s. Rev. John Owen,		
of Groton, decd., June 21, 1767	3	41
Mary, m. Thomas Henry **GODDARD**, Feb. 22, 1786	3	90
Mary, d. [Richard & Ann], b. Dec. 20, 1794; d. Aug.		
22, 1795	3	189
Mary, d. [Jonathan & Sally], b. May 1, 1796	3	143
Mary, d. [John & Mary], b. Jan. 25, 1797	3	139
Mary Adelaide, d. [Francis Henry & Mary Ann], b.		
Mar. 22, 1840	3	271
Mary Ann, d. [Francis Henry & Mary Ann], b. Sept.		
22, 1833; d. June 1, 1840	3	271
Mehetable, d. Robert & Sarah, b. Sept. 8, 1747	2	98
Mehetable, m. Benjamin **GORTON**, Sept. 28, 1769	3	75
Melia, d. [George & Elisabeth], b. Feb. 4, 1779	3	67
Melia, d. George, m. Daniel **DOUGLASS**, [ ]	3	147
Mercy, d. William, Jr. & Hannah, b. Nov. 4, 1705	1	35
Michael, s. [Jonathan & Anna], b. Oct. 19, 1773	3	60
Michael, s. [Jonathan & Sally], b. Apr. 12, 1800	3	143
Nancy, d. [Richard & Anna], b. Jan. 18, 1780	3	65
Nancy, d. [Richard & Ann], b. Jan. 18, 1780	3	189
Nancy, d. Jonathan, m. Asa **NOWLAND**, Jan. 31,		
1808	3	235
Nathan, s. Thomas & Hannah, b. Apr. 15, 1721	1	64
Nathan, s. Thomas, of New London, decd., m. Ann		
DENNESS, d. Eben[eze]r, late of New London,		
decd., Dec. 22, 1745	2	74
Nathan, s. Nathan & Ann, b. Sept. 6, 1757	2	74

	Vol.	Page
DOUGLASS, DOUGLAS, DOWGLASS (cont.)		
Nathan, s. [Ebenezer & Abigail], b. Jan. 31, 1787	3	120
Nelson P., of Norwich, m. Eunice **SKINNER**, of New London, June 30, 1844, by Rev. Thomas J. Greenwood	4	116
Oliver P., of Waterford, m. Eliza **GARDAN**, of [New London], Apr. 30, 1840, by Rev. Abel McEwen	4	89
Orry, of Norwich, m. Laura **LEWIS**, of [New London], Dec. [ ], 1835, by Rev. Abel McEwen	4	64
Patty, d. [Ebenezer & Abigail], b. Mar. 3, 1779	3	120
Perry, m. Harriet **DART**, b. of New London, Jan. 9, 1828, by Rev. Abel McEwen	4	33
Perry Mumford Haskel, s. [John & Mary], b. July 20, 1803	3	139
Peter, s. [Richard & Ann], b. June 28, 1796	3	189
Peter, m. Lucy W. **STOW**, b. of New London, June 10, 1821, by Abel McEwen	4	5
Phebe, see under Febbee		
Polly, d. [Ebenezer & Abigail], b. Dec. 28, 1784	3	120
Rebecca, d. W[illia]m & Abia, b. June 14, [1678]	1	12
Rebeckah, d. Caleb & Mary, b. Apr. 2, 1741	2	51
Rebeckah, d. [Spearry & Rebeckah], b. Sept. 10, 1772	3	95
Rebecca, m. Samuel **JENISON**, Nov. 20, 1791	3	122
Rebeckah, d. [Samuel & Rebeckah], b. Mar. 29, 1795	3	185
Rebecca, w. [Spearry, Sr.], d. Oct. 16, 1826, at Troy, N.Y.	3	95
Richard, s. W[illia]m & Abia, b. July 19, 1681	1	68
Richard, s. William & Abia, b. July 19, [1682]	1	16
Richard, m. Margaret **ABELL**, Dec. 7, 1704	1	66
Richard, s. Stephen, b. Aug. 8, 1746, old style	3	189
Richard, s. Richard, b. Oct. 10, 1777. Recorded at desire of Ephraim Beebe	3	65
Richard, m. Anne **JENNINGS**, Nov. 9, 1777	3	65
Richard, m. Wid. Ann **JINNINGS**, d. Samuel **CHAMPLIN**, Nov. 9, 1777	3	189
Richard, s. [Jonathan & Anna], b. Mar. 10, 1781	3	60
Richard, s. [Richard & Ann], b. Sept. 10, 1785	3	189
Richard, s. [Jonathan & Sally], b. Feb. 10, 1709	3	143
Richard, 2d, m. Abiga[i]ll **STARR**, d. Daniel & Elizabeth, Oct. 28, 1790	3	212
Richard, 2d, m. Lucy **PALMES**, relict of Samuel & dau. of John **WAY**, Sept. 2, 1804	3	212
Richard, of Waterford, m. Sarah C. **MORGAN**, of New London, Oct. 1, 1846, by Rev. Robert A. Hallam	4	128
Robert, s. William & Mary, d. Robert **HEMPSTEAD**, Sept. 28, [1665]	1	4
Robert, s. Thomas & Hannah, b. Dec. 28, 1705	1	52
Robert, d. Jan. 15, 1715/16	1	52
Robert, m. Sarah **EDGECOMBE**, Aug. 5, 1731	2	15

	Vol.	Page
DOUGLASS, DOUGLAS, DOWGLASS (cont.)		
Robert, s. Robert & Sarah, b. Aug. 7, 1740	2	98
Robert, s. [Samuel & Rebeckah], b. Dec. 19, 1785	3	185
Robert, m. Elizabeth **DANIELS**, d. Jasper, Apr. 4,		
1807	3	234
Russell, s. Nathan & Ann, b. Mar. 18, 1767	2	74
Sally, twin with William, d. [Jonathan & Sally], b.		
Dec. 20, 1791	3	143
Samuel, s. Robert & Sarah, b. Feb. 26, 1744/5	2	98
Samuel, of New London, s. Capt. Richard, decd., m.		
Mary **DENISON**, d. of Daniel, late of New		
London, decd., Nov. 2, 1749	2	99
Samuel, m. Rebeckah **AVERY**, d. Elisha, of		
Stonington, Feb. 26, 1781	3	185
Samuel, s. [Caleb & Grace], b. June 6, 1787	3	38
Samuel, s. [Jonathan & Sally], b. Apr. 25, 1788	3	143
Sarah, d. William, m. John **KENNEY**, s. William,		
"in ye month of October", [1661]	1	3
Sarah*, d. William & Abial, b. Apr. 2, [1671] *(Or		
Abia))	1	7
Sarah, d. Robert & Mary, b. Dec. 2, [1674]	1	10
Sarah, m. Samuell **COMSTOCK**, June 22, [1699]	1	25
Sarah, m. Samuel **COMSTOCK**, [ ], 1699	1	55
Sarah, d. Robert & Sarah, b. July 15, 1738	2	98
Sarah, d. William & Sarah, b. Feb. 7, 1745/6	2	51
Sarah, m. Edward **RAYMOND**, Feb. 14, 1758, by		
Rev. Mather Boyles	3	28
Sarah, d. [George & Elisabeth], b. Nov. 16, 1769	3	67
Sarah, d. [Daniel & Lydia], b. Apr. 14, 1791	3	9
Sarah, d. May 12, 1797	2	51
Sarah, d. [Robert & Elizabeth], b. Jan. 3, 1808	3	234
Sarah Ann, m. John William **GENT**, b. of New		
London, June 7, 1825, by Rev. B. Judd	4	23
Spearry, m. Rebeckah **CHAPMAN** *, May 8, 1768		
*(First written Douglass and crossed out)	3	95
Spearry, s. [Spearry & Rebeckah], b. Jan. 8, 1770	3	95
Spearry, Sr., d. Apr. 27, 1816	3	95
Stephen, s. Thomas & Hannah, b. May 18, 1719	1	52
Stephen, s. Thomas & Hannah, b. May 28, 1719	1	64
Stephen, s. John & Esther, b. Aug. 26, 1765	2	100
Stephen, s. [Spearry & Rebeckah], b. Nov. 1, 1768	3	95
Susannah, m. Edward **DeWOLF**, of Lyme, Nov. 4,		
1708	1	34
Thomas, s. Robert & Mary, b. May 15, [1679]	1	14
Thomas, m. Hannah **SPERRY***, Nov. 25, 1703		
*(Perhaps **SPENCER**?)	1	52
Thomas, s. Thomas & Hannah, b. Feb. 18, 1707	1	52
Thomas, Jr., d. Feb. 25, 1724/5	1	64
Thomas, Sr., d. Mar. 3, 1724/5	1	64
Thomas, s. Robert & Sarah, b. Aug. 1, 1734	2	15
Thomas, s. [Nathan & Ann], b. Aug. 5, 1771	2	74
William, s. Robert & Mary, b. Nov. 11, [1666]	1	5

	Vol.	Page
DOUGLASS, DOUGLAS, DOWGLASS (cont.)		
William, s. W[illia]m & Abia, b. Feb. 19, [1672]	1	8
William, Sr., d. July 26, [1682], ae [ ] y.	1	16
W[illia]m, s. [William & Abia], d. July 26, 1682	1	68
William, s. Richard & Margaret, b. Jan. 1, 1708	1	66
William, s. William, Jr. & Hannah, b. June 29, 1710	1	35
William, s. William & Sarah, b. Feb. 7, 1731/2	2	14
William, m. Sarah **DENISON**, Mar. 4, 1730/1	2	14
William, s. William & Sarah, of New London, m.		
Mary **LUCAS**, d. Jerry & Mary, May 31, 1752	2	87
William, s. William & Mary, b. Sept. 29, 1753	2	87
William, d. Nov. 13, 1787	2	51
William, s. [Daniel & Lydia], b. Apr. 1, 1789	3	9
William, twin with Sally, s. [Jonathan & Sally], b.		
Dec. 20, 1791	3	143
William, s. [Daniel & Melia], b. Mar. 17, 1809	3	147
William Prentiss, s. [Henry & Harriot], b. Mar. 2,		
1826	3	235
-----, d. W[illia]m, d. Aug. 12, [1689], ae 14 y.	1	69
-----, m. Thomas, d. Dec. 26, 1711	1	52
-----, d. [Richard & Ann], b. Oct. 8, 1790; lived a few		
hours	3	189
DOWNER, Ellen S., m. Leonard **DART**, Oct. 30, 1831	3	289
DOWNING, Isabella, m. George **BURCHIN**, May 10,		
1716	1	46
DOWSETT, DOWSITT, DOSETT, Abby, m. Russell		
HARDING, b. of Lyme, Oct. 18, 1821, by		
Abel McEwen	4	6
James M., m. Lydia C. **BROWN**, b. of Norwich, Oct.		
23, 1848, by Rev. Jabez S. Swan	4	142
Mary Ann, m. William **CLARK**, b. of New London,		
Aug. 23, 1846, by Rev. L. Geo[rge] Leonard	4	129
Sila M., m. Nelson T. **WILBUR**, b. of New London,		
Nov. 7, 1847, by Rev. Jabez S. Swan	4	135
Washington, m. Philenia **TILLOTSON**, May 17,		
1852, by Rev. J. M. Eaton	4	168
DOYLE, DOYAL, Ann, m. Frederick **BALDEUF**, July 7,		
1849, by Rev. William Logan	4	150
Ellen, m. James **MAHER**, Sept. 9, 1849, by Rev.		
William Logan	4	150
Rebecca, m. Eliphalet **CHAPMAN**, Feb. 12, 1786	3	99
DRISCOLL, Daniel, m. Lydia **BROOKS**, [ ]	2	106
Ele[a]nor, d. Daniel & Lydia, Mar. 13, 1743	2	106
Elias, s. Daniel & Lydia, b. Aug. 19, 1745	2	016
Lydia, d. Daniel & Lydia, b. Mar. 6, 1744	2	106
DUCE, [see under **DUCY**]		
DUCY, DUCE, Eliza Jane, of N[ew] London, m. William		
G. **CONGDON**, of Southington, R.I., Aug. 18,		
1842, by L. Covel	4	103
John, m. Ann **FEGAN**, Feb. 11, 1849, by Rev.		
William Logan	4	150
DUMMER, Mary, m. John **BLOYD**, Mar. 29, 1760	3	21

	Vol.	Page
DUNBAR, Mary, m. John **COLLINS**, b. of New London, May 29, 1831, by Rev. Abel McEwen	4	42
Sarah, m. Francis **JOHNSON**, b. of New London, May 14, 1846, by Rev. L. Geo[rge] Leonard	4	129
Sarah E., m. Albert B. **NEWBURY**, b. of New London, May 23, 1852, by Rev. Jabez S. Swan	4	173
DUNCKIN, Ellen, d. [Henry & Betsey], b. Mar. 15, 1820	3	174
Henry, m. Betsey **HOLT**, d. Jonathan, Dec. 22, 1805	3	174
Henry, s. [Henry & Betsey], b. Jan. 29, 1813	3	174
Jane, d. [Henry & Betsey], b. Aug. 18, 1810; d. Dec. 24, 1812	3	174
Jane, twin with William, s. [Henry & Betsey], b. Apr. 20, 1815	3	174
Mariah, d. [Henry & Betsey], b. Oct. 3, 1806	3	174
Martha, d. [Henry & Betsey], b. July 23, 1808	3	174
William, twin with Jane, s. [Henry & Betsey], b. Apr. 20, 1815; d. Aug. 20, 1815	3	174
William, s. [Henry & Betsey], b. May 16, 1817	3	174
DUNHAM, Phebe, m. Jacob **FENK**, Apr. 19, 1773	3	113
DUNN, Mary, m. Edmund **PEGASH**, b. of New London, July 10, 1850, by Rev. Geo[rge] M. Carpenter	4	154
William, m. Cath **SEXTINE**, Oct. 13, [18]50, [by Peter J. Blenkinsop]. Witnesses: John Curran, Maria Caldwell	3	306
William, m. Catharine **SEXTINE**, Oct. 13, 1850. Witnesses: John Curran, Maria Caldwell	4	159
DUNTON, Abiah, d. Ebenezer, m. Jonathan **HOLT**, Oct. 24, 1784	3	152
Mary Ann, of [New London], m. Salisbury **JACKSON**, of Wilmington, Del., Nov. 11, 1842, by Rev. Abel McEwen	4	103
Sukey, m. Stephen **BOLLES**, Jan. 1 ,1787	3	95
William H., m. Lucy Ann **LANE**, b. of New London, June 21, 1849, by Rev. Abel McEwen	4	146
DURFEY, DURPHY, Christopher, s. Richard & Sarah, b. Dec. 25, 1742	2	48
Richard, m. Sarah **PALMER**, Feb. 25, 1738/9	2	48
Richard, s. Richard & Sarah, b. Apr. 20, 1740	2	48
Sarah, d. Richard & Sarah, b. June 3, 1740	2	48
Thomas, s. Richard & Sarah, b. Nov. 5, 1744. Recorded May 2, 1758, at desire of Mrs. Sarah Durfey	2	48
Thomas, m. Rebecca **MANWARING**, Oct. 23, 1776	3	59
DURGEE, Felix, m. Betsey **DENNIS**, b. of Norwich, Mar. 28, 1824, by Rev. Abel McEwen	4	17
DUTTON, Asa, m. Clarrissa **FITCH**, d. Ammi, of Lebanon, Apr. 27, 1794	3	198
Charles Chauncey, s. [Asa & Clarrissa], b. June 4, 1807	3	198
Clarrissa, d. [Asa & Clarrissa], b. Nov. 27, 1798	3	198
Clarrissa, of New London ,m. Enoch **NOYES**, of Lyme, June 28, 1820, by Rev. Abel McEwen	4	1

	Vol.	Page

DYMOND, DYMAN (cont.)

Thomas, of Hartford, m. Elizabeth **BRADLEY**, d.
  Peter & Elizabeth, Sept. 22, 1670 — 1 — 7

Thomas, s. Thomas & Elizabeth, b. July 22, 1675 — 1 — 10

EAMES, EMS, [see also **AMES**], Elizabeth, d. John &
  Abigail, b. May 24, 1704 — 1 — 29

Emanuel, m. Margaret **FERRIS**, b. of New London,
  June 7, 1846, by Rev. John Howson — 4 — 126

John, m. Abigail **MORGAN**, Feb. 1, 1698/9 — 1 — 24

John, s. John & Abigail, b. Aug. 15, 1701 — 1 — 27

Joseph, m. Harriot **BEEBE**, Jan. 14, 1839, by Rev.
  Abraham Holway — 4 — 85

Mary, d. Joseph & Mary, b. Feb. 7, 1705/6.
  Recorded Aug. 23, 1733 and witnessed by
  Daniel Polly and Daniel Palmeter — 2 — 22

Robert, s. John & Abigaill, b. Apr. 1, 1707 — 1 — 33

ECCLESTON, Joseph T., m. Emeline M. **BEEBE**, Dec.
  28, 1851, by Rev. Charles Willett — 4 — 166

EDEY, Patience, m. John **STONE**, Sept. 24, 1769 — 3 — 116

EDGAR, Ann Elisabeth, d. [Thomas & Mary], b. Sept. 26,
  1783 — 3 — 55

Eunice D., m. Benjamin F. **BECKWITH**, b. of [New
  London], June 25, 1838, by Rev. Abel McEwen — 4 — 78

Eunice Dennis, d. [Mark & Ann], b. June 11, 1816 — 3 — 234

George, s. [Mark, & Ann], b. July 30, 1814 — 3 — 234

Mark, s. [Thomas & Mary], b. Dec. 3, 1779 — 3 — 55

Mark, m. Ann **DENNIS**, Apr. 18, 1813; at Norwich — 3 — 234

Thomas, of Newcastle upon "Tine", Great Britain, m.
  Mary **LATIMER**, Nov. 9, 1777 — 3 — 55

EDGECOMBE, EDGECOMB, EDGECOMB, Amy
  Ransom, d. [Jesse & Naomi], b. Jan. 14, 1793 — 3 — 11

Ebenhaley, s. John & Sara[h], b. Jan. 23, 1681 — 1 — 68

Elizabeth, d. John & Hannah, m. David
  RICHARDS, Jr., s. David, Apr. 3, 1733 — 2 — 118

Elisabeth, d. [Jesse & Naomi], b. June 29, 1706 — 2 — 11

Grace, [d. John & Hannah, b.] Mar. 16, 1712/13.
  Recorded May 28, 1736, at the request of the
  mother — 2 — 22

Hannah, d. Jno. & Hannah, b. Sept. 9, 1704 — 2 — 22

Hannah, d. of John, of New London, m. John
  CHAAPEL, s. John, of New London, Mar. [ ],
  1726 — 2 — 88

James L., of Groton, m. Sarah L. **FORSYTH**, of
  New London, Oct. 15, 1844, by Rev. J. Blain — 4 — 117

Jane O., of Groton, m. William N. **WILBER**, of
  Stonington, July 18, 1852, by Rev. Jabez S.
  Swan — 4 — 175

Jesse, s. John & Hannah, b. Mar. 27, 1721 — 2 — 22

Jesse, m. Naomi **CROCKER**, Nov. 6, 1785 — 3 — 11

Jesse, d. May 7, 1792 — 3 — 11

Johanna, d. John & Sarah, b. Mar. 3, [1679] — 1 — 14

Johanna, m. Henry **DELAMORE**, Feb. 14, 1716/17 — 1 — 51

	Vol.	Page

EDGECOMBE, EDGECOMB, EDGCOMB (cont.)

John, s .Nicholas, of Plymouth, Old England, m.

Sarah **STALON**, d. Edward, Feb. 9, [1673]	1	9
John, s. John & Sarah, b. Nov. 14, [1675]	1	10
John, m. Hannah **HEMPSTEAD**, Feb. 28, [1699]	1	25
John, s. John & Hannah, b. Nov. 29, 1700	2	22
Lydia, see Lydia **WHEELER**		
Lydia, d. [Jesse & Naomi], b. July 29, 1787	3	11
Naomi, m. Luke **DICKSON**, Jan. 18, 1791	3	47
Nicholas, s. Jno. & Sarah, b. Jan. 23, [1681]	1	15
Nicholas, s. John & Hannah, b. Aug. 10, 1702	2	22
Samuel, m. Elizabeth **PRENTICE**, Nov. 24, 1720	1	57
Sam[ue]l, d. Feb. 26, 1786	3	11
Samuel, s. [Jesse & Naomi], b. Apr. 25, 1789	3	11
Sarah, d. John & Sarah, b. July 29, [1678]	1	13
Sarah, m. John **BOLLES**, July 3, 1699	1	25
Sarah, m. John **BOLL[E]S**, July 3, 1699	1	41
Sarah, [d. John & Hannah, b.], Mar. 20, 1710/11. Recorded May 28, 1736, at the request of the mother	2	22
Sarah, m. Robert **DOUGLASS**, Aug. 5, 1731	2	15
Sara[h] Eliz[abeth], [d. John & Hannah], b. Sept. 25, 1708. Recorded May 28, 1736, at the request of the mother	2	22

EDGERTON, Albert Hyde, s. [James & Catharine], b.

Feb. 9, 1791	3	124
Caroline Matilda, d. [James & Catharine], b. Sept. 18, 1808	3	124
Catherine, of [New London], m. Joseph **NOYES**, of Lyme, Oct. 15, 1835, by Rev. Abel McEwen	4	63
Catharine Elizabeth, d. [James & Catharine], b. Jan. 25, 1803	3	124
Cortlandt, s. [James & Catharine], b. Mar. 16, 1798	3	124
Ellin, d. [James & Catharine], b. Nov. 21, 1804	3	124
James, m. Catharine **HINMAN**, May 29, 1788	3	124
James, s. [James & Catharine], b. June 13, 1789	3	124
John, m. Mary **DARROW**, b. of [New London], Nov. 26, 1822, by T. W. Tucker, Elder	4	11
Loisa, of [New London], m. John A. **HART**, of Sagg Harbor, N.Y., June 17, 1839, by Rev. Abel McEwen	4	86
Sarah, m. Edward H. **LEARNED**, b. of [New London], Jan. 12, 1837, by Rev. Abel McEwen	4	67
Urbon, s. [James & Catharine], b. Oct. 8, 1793	3	124

EDWARDS, Mary of New London, m. Lucius P.

MAYNARD, of Waterford, Apr. 2, 1828, by Rev. Abel McEwen	4	34
Mary, m. Lucius P. **MAYNARD**, Apr. 14, 1828	3	279
Samuel H., of Portland, Ct., m. Harriet L. **MARSHALL**, of East Haddam, Ct., Sept. 13, 1849, by Rev. James W. Dennis	4	152

	Vol.	Page
EDWARDS (cont.)		
Tryon, m. Catharine B. **HUGHES**, youngest d.		
Samuel & Catharine, of Maryland, May 29,		
1843, in Philadelphia, by Rev. H. A. Boardman	3	293
Tryon, s. [Tryon & Catharine B.], b. Feb. 26, 1846	3	293
EGARD, Ellen, m. Alfred **MORELAND**, b. of New		
London, Nov. 3, 1831, by Rev Abel McEwen	4	44
ELDERKIN, Mary, d. James, of Norwich, m. Joshua		
HOWARD, Mar. 29, 1795	3	119
ELDREDGE, ELDRIDGE, ELDRIGE, Abigail, d.		
Charles, of Groton, b. May 11, 1761; m.		
Nicoll **FOSDICK**, Jan. 19, 1784	3	152
Elisabeth, m. Eleazer **GRANT**, May 4, 1760	3	62
Frances Eliza, d. [William & Elizabeth], b. Dec. 10,		
1806	3	197
William, s. Charles, of Groton, b. Dec. 14, 1769; m.		
Elizabeth **AVERY**, [d. Capt. Elijah], b. Sept.		
14, 1794	3	197
ELLIOTT, ELLIOT, Chloe Bates, m. Richard		
CHAPPELL, June 14, 1824, at Thompson,		
Conn.	3	265
Clark, d. July* 11, 1793 *(Aug. written in pencil)	3	78
Clark, s. [Euclid & Abigail], b.Oct. 12, 1796	3	78
Desiah, [w. Clark], d. Mar. 10, 1799	3	78
Ellen, d. [George & Margaret Ann], b. Jan. 26, 1850	3	296
Euclid, m. Abiga[i]ll **STARR** ,d. William, of		
Middletown, May 11, 1794	3	78
Euclid, the elder, d. Sept. 30, 1798	3	78
Euclid, s. [Euclid & Abigail], b. Oct. 9, 1798	3	78
Euclid, m. Lucy S. **COIT**, b. of New London, Apr.		
21, 1822, by Rev. Abel McEwen	4	8
George, m. Margaret Ann **BINDLOSS**, b. of [New		
London, Aug.] 7, 1848, by Rev. Robert A.		
Hallam	4	141
George, of New London, m. Margaret Ann		
BINDLOSS, of Liverpool, England, Aug. 9,		
1848, by Rev. Robert A. Hallam	3	296
Louisa, m. Oliver M. **CONE**, of Lyme, Dec. [ ],		
1850, by Frederick R. Chapman, J.P.	4	160
Rebecca, b. Nov. 21, 1822; m. William W. **GREEN**,		
Apr. 4, 1841, by Mr. Williams* *(Mr.		
Williams written in pencil)	3	195
Sally, m. Daniel B. **DARROW**, Feb. 16, 1840, by		
Rev. James M. Macdonald	4	88
Sally, of New London, m. Morris **CRAWFORD**, of		
Fairfield, Ct., May 15, 1846, by Rev. John		
Howson	4	126
Zimri, of Cleaveland, Ohio, m. Louisa **KNIGHT**, of		
[New London], b Feb. 21, 1843, by Rev. Abel		
McEwen	4	102
ELLIS, Abby, m. Anthony **MARKS**, June 14, 1842, in		
Providence, by J. Dowling, of Providence, R.I.	3	197

	Vol.	Page

ELLIS (cont.)

Abby, m. Anthony **MARKS**, June 14, 1842, at
    Providence, R.I., by J. Dowling, of Providence 4 175

William, of Plymouth, England, m. Abby Frances
    GOODWIN, of New London, Mar. 17, 1833,
    by Rev. Abel McEwen 4 51

ELY, Deborah, m. Eben[eze]r **DENNISS**, Nov. 19, 1717 1 53

EMANUEL, Sophia, m. Emanuel **JOSEPH**, July 1, 1850,
    by Rev. James W. Dennis 4 155

EMERSON, Edward, m. Bridget **McCRIB**, of Groton,
    July 9, 1851, by Rev. Jabez S. Swan 4 172

Polly, d. Joseph & Mary, b. Sept. 25, 1787 3 101

ENOS, Antone, of New London, m. Harriet **HARRIS**,
    Apr. 10, 1848, by Rev. Tho[ma]s J. Greenwood 4 140

Emanuel, of [New London], m. Hannah **CHURCH**,
    of Waterford, Nov. 16, 1845, by Rev. John
    Howson 4 122

Joseph, m. Hannah **HART**, b. of [New London], Jan.
    27, 1846, by Rev. John Howson 4 126

ENSWORTH, Jedediah, m. Sophia **ENSWORTH**, b. of
    Coventry, Sept. 9, 1825, by Rev. Abel McEwen 4 24

Sophia, m. Jedediah **ENSWORTH**, b. of Coventry,
    Sept. 9, 1825, by Rev. Abel McEwen 4 24

EVANS, Frances T., m. Seraphine **LASSALL**, b. of New
    London, Apr. 15, 1847, by Rev. Jabez S. Swan 4 131

John, of New London, m. Susan **TULL**, of Groton,
    Jan. 8, 1837, by Rev. Squire B. Hascall 4 68

EVERETT, Charles G., of Northampton, Pa., m. Fanny
    DESTIN, of New London, Mar. 26, 1837, by
    Rev. Squire B. Hascall 4 68

EWEN, Charlotte R., of New London, m. Geo[rge] G.
    GATES, of Moodus, July 16, 1848, by Rev. L.
    G. Leonard 4 140

Frances, of New London, m. Julius **TAYLOR**, of
    Albion, N.Y., July 16, 1848, by Rev. L. G.
    Leonard 4 140

Harriet, m. Josiah **ROGERS**, b. of [New London],
    Jan. 7, 1835, by Rev. Alvin Ackley 4 59

Isaac S., of New London, m. Fanny **WILSON**, of
    Norwich, Dec. 26, 1847, by Rev. L. G. Leonard 4 138

Susan, m. George **ROGERS**, b. of N[ew] London,
    Oct. 17, 1838, by Rev. C. C. Williams 4 81

FAGE, Mary L., m. Elias F. **LEWIS**, b. of New London,
    Mar. 24, 1833, by Chester Tilden 4 50

FAGIN, [see under **FEGAN**]

FAHY, Thomas, m. Margaret **CUMMINGS**, Aug. 25,
    [18]50, [by Peter J. Blenkinsop]. Witnesses:
    Michael Quany, Ann Barrett 3 306

Thomas, m. Margarett **CUMMINGS**, Aug. 25, 1850.
    Witnesses: Michael Tuany, Ann Barrett 4 159

FAIRBANKS, Barachrah, m. Margaret **HALL**, b. of [New
    London], Nov. 12, 1834, by Daniel Huntington 4 60

	Vol.	Page
FAIRFIELD, Charles, of Norwich, m. Fanny A.		
WHEELER, of New London, May 26, 1850,		
by Rev. E. R. Warren	4	153
Charlotte, m. Leonard **BEEBE**, b. of New London,		
Sept. 14, 1845, by Rev. Abel McEwen	4	121
Mary, of New London, m. Charles R. **CORNING**, of		
New London, May 21, 1848, by Rev. John		
Howson	4	137
FANNING, FANING, Bathsheba, m. Edward **JONES**, b.		
of New London, June 9, 1822, by Rev. Abel		
McEwen	4	9
Benjamin R., of Chatham, m. Mehitable P. **GATES**,		
of Chatham, Aug. 29, 1836, by Rev. Alvan		
Ackley	4	66
Dennis, m. Bathsheba **HAY[E]S**, June 10, 1806	3	192
Eleanor, d. [Dennis & Bathsheba], b. Mar. 11, 1809	3	192
Elizabeth, d. Jonathan & Elizabeth, b. Apr. 23, 1716	1	46
Jonathan, m. Elizabeth **WAY**, May 17, 1714	1	42
Jonathan, s. Jonathan & Elizabeth, b. Oct. 28, 1717	1	49
Jonathan, s. Jonathan, [ ]	1	49
Mary Bridget, d. [Dennis & Bathsheba], b. Mar. 11,		
1807	3	192
FARGO, FERGO, FIRGO, FARGOE, [see also		
FURZE], Aaron, s. Moses [& Sarah], b. Dec. 9,		
1702	1	37
Aaron, s. Aaron & Sarah, b. Feb. 5, 1729/30	2	23
Amey, d. Robert, Jr. & Prudence, b. Sept. 13, 1758	3	2
Ann, d. Moses [& Sarah], b. Mar. 2, 1684/5	1	37
Anna, d. [Thomas & Mercy], b. Mar. 22, 1780	3	106
Bathshua, d. Moses, Jr., of New London, m. Josiah		
BROOKS, s. Henry, of New London, Nov. 3,		
1738	2	113
Daniel, s. [Moses & Hannah], b. Mar. 9, 1764	3	128
Elizabeth, d. [Moses & Hannah], b. Aug. 10, 1774	3	128
Elisabeth, d. [Moses & Hannah], b. Jan. 1, 1781	3	128
Elizabeth, d. [John & Sally], b. May 20, 1804	3	172
Esther, d. [Moses & Hannah], b. July 1, 1783	3	128
Hannah, d. [Moses & Hannah], b. Apr. 1, 1771	3	128
Harriet, d. [John & Sally], b. Nov. 8, 1811	3	172
Jabez, s. Moses, 2d, & Mercy, b. June 27, 1763	3	23
Jason, s. [Thomas & Mercy], b. Feb. 17, 1782	3	106
John, m. Sally **PATTERSON**, July 9, 1803	3	172
John Nicholas, s. [John & Sally], b. Sept. 11, 1806	3	172
Lucy, d. Zachariah, m. John **HINES**, Oct. 18, 1795	3	224
Lydia, d. [Moses & Hannah], b. Nov. 12, 1776	3	128
Mary, d. Moses [& Sarah], b. Jan. 1, 1681/2	1	37
Mary, d. [Moses & Hannah], b. Aug. 16, 1767	3	128
Mary E., m. Mark D. **KING**, b. of New London, Apr.		
7, 1833, by Rev. Abel McEwen (Perhaps		
Mary E. **FURZE**?)	4	50
Matthew, s. [Moses & Hannah], b. Nov. 3, 1765	3	128
Mercy, m. Joseph **SMITH**, Nov. 2, 1775	3	106

	Vol.	Page
FARGO, FERGO, FIRGO, FARGOE (cont.)		
Mercy, w. Thomas, d. Dec. 19, 1788	3	106
Moses, s. Moses [& Sarah], b. Apr. 9, 1691	1	37
Moses, 2d, s. Robert, late of New London, decd., m.		
Mercy **TURNER**, d. Thomas, of New London,		
Feb. 14, 1762	3	23
Moses, m Hannah **LANPHE[A]R**, [ ], 1763	3	128
Moses, s. Moses, 2d, & Mercy, b. Sept. 16, 1767	3	23
Moses, s. [Moses & Hannah], b. June 13, 1773	3	128
Nancy, d. [Moses & Hannah], b. June 9, 1769	3	128
Patience, d. Moses [& Sarah], b. May 9, 1688	1	37
Ralph, s. Moses [& Sarah], b. Aug. 18, 1693	1	37
Robert, s. Moses [& Sarah], b. Sept. 30, 1696	1	37
Robert, Jr., s. Robert, of New London, m. Prudence		
STANTON, d. Tho[ma]s, late of Groton, decd.,		
July 1, 1756	3	2
Samuel, s. Moses, 2d, & Mercy, b. Nov. 6, 1765	3	23
Sarah, d. Moses [& Sarah], b. June 19, 1680	1	37
Sarah, d. Robert, Jr. & Prudence, b. Apr. 25, 1757	3	2
Thomas, s. Moses [& Sarah], b. Nov. 9, 1699	1	37
Thomas, s. Moses, 2d & Mercy, b. May 19, 1769	3	23
Thomas, m. Mercy **SMITH**, Mar. 25, 1779	3	106
William, s. [John & Sally], b. Feb. 14, 1809	3	172
FARLEY, Rose, m. James **O'BRION**, Nov. 8, 1851, by		
Rev. J. Stokes. Witnesses: Owen Clifford, Ann		
Farley	4	169
FARNHAM, Daniel G., of New London, m. Roxana		
CHADWICK, of Waterford, Oct. 2, 1837, by		
Rev. Abel McEwen	4	73
Edgar E., m. Lydia H. **THOMPSON**, [ ]	3	295
Henry M., s. [Edgar & Lydia H.], b. Aug. 10, 1845	3	295
William P., s. [Edgar E. & Lydia H.], b. Oct. 17,		
1847	3	295
FARNSWORTH, Ralph, of Norwich, m. Eunice W.		
BILLINGS, of New London, Nov. 25, 1828,		
by Rev. Abel McEwen	4	36
FARRELL, Thomas, m. Mary **McGHOUGHLIN**, Aug.		
22, 1847, by Rev. John Brady	4	133
Thomas, m. Catharine **CLINE**, Sept. 23, 1849, by		
Rev. William Logan	4	150
FASSET, Charles, of New London, m. Henrietta		
SEYMOUR, of Norwich, July 14, 1851, by		
Rev. Abel McEwen	4	164
FEGAN, Ann, m. John **DUCY**, Feb. 11, 1849, by Rev.		
William Logan	4	150
FELLOWS, Charles H., m. Abby **MALLORY**, b. of		
[New London], Jan. 24, 1841, by John Lovejoy	4	93
Edwin R., m. Ellen **CHAPMAN**, of [New London],		
Jan. 6, 1845, by Rev. S. Benton	4	116
Elizabeth, d. Isaac & Mary, b. July 2, 1756; d. July		
25, 1757	2	27
Elizabeth, d. Isaac & Mary, b. Apr. 8, 1759	2	27

	Vol.	Page
FELLOWS (cont.)		
Hannah, d. Isaac & Mary, b. Aug. 26, 1763	2	27
Isaac, m. Mary **WANT**, Sept. 13, 1742	2	26
Isaac, s. Isaac & Mary, b. Oct. 13, 1745	2	26
Joseph, s. Isaac & Mary, b. May 1, 1754	2	27
Lucretia, d. Isaac & Mary, b. Feb. 13, 1761	2	27
Mary, d. Isaac & Mary, b. July 7, 1743	2	26
Pryington, s. Isaac & Mary, b. Jan. 7, 1749	2	26
Sarah, d. Isa[ac] & Mary, b. July 13, 1766; d. Sept. 24, 1767	2	27
Thomas, s. Isaac & Mary, b. Mar. 11, 1752; d. Aug. 4, 1753	2	26
William, s. Isaac & Mary, b. Oct. 6, 1747	2	26
FENGAR, FENGARR, FANGER, Christopher C., m. Charlotte **HARRIS**, Sept. 21, 1852, by Rev. Charles Willett	4	172
Fanny, m. Joseph **MASON**, Oct. 30, 1841, by Abel T. Sizer, J.P.	4	96
Morinda, m. George **TILLER**, Feb. 28, 1828, by Rev. La Roy Sunderland	4	33
Richard B., m. Olive P. **MINER**, b. of New London, Nov. 18, 1849, by Rev. Edwin R. Warren	4	149
Ursula H., m. Henry **GOO[D]RICH**, June 20, 1852, by Rev. Charles Willett	4	168
FENK, Catharine, d. [Jacob & Phebe], b. May 8, 1783	3	113
Jacob, m. Phebe **DUNHAM**, Apr. 19, 1773	3	113
Olive, d. [Jacob & Phebe], b. Dec. 15, 1773	3	113
Olive, m. Hugh **WARNER**, May 5, 1789	3	139
Phebe, d. [Jacob & Phebe], b. Oct. 2, 1776	3	113
FENNER, Mary L., m. Richard C. **CROCKER**, July 16, 1843, by Rev. Allen Darrow	4	106
FENTON, Elijah, of Norwich, m. Martha **CHAPPELL**, of Montville, Nov. 26, 1846, by John Howson	4	130
FERGO, [see under **FARGO**]		
FERGUSON, Julia M., of Stafford, Ct., m. Charles H. **TYLER**, of Springfield, Mass., June 10, 1852, by Rev. Thomas Fly	4	168
Margaret, m. James **KILDOFF**, Oct. 14, 1849, by Rev. William Logan	4	150
William P., of New York, m. Priscilla A. **SMITH**, of New London, Dec. 20, 1846, by Rev. Jabez S. Swan	4	128
FERNELL, Benjamin, of Boston, Mass., m. Julia **CLARK**, of New London, July 17, 1825, by Rev. B. Judd	4	23
FERRIS, Margaret, m. Emanuel **EAMES**, b. of New London, June 7, 1846, by Rev. John Howson	4	126
FETTERMAN, George, of U. S. Army, m. Ann Maria Chandler **JUDD**, of New London, [ ], by Rev. B. Judd	4	42

	Vol.	Page
FICKETT, Stillman H., of Portland, Me., m. Harriet **ROATH**, of [New London], June 21, 1842, by Rev. Abel McEwen	4	99
FIELDING, Moses, s. Timothy & Ann Hill, b. Aug. 5, 1775, the day the Sons of Liberty burned a barrel of tea (See Hill, Moses)	3	128
FIELDS, George, m. Mary **YOUNG**, Nov. 26, 1849, by Rev. W[illia]m Logan	4	151
FILES, Adam, m. Catherine **CHURCH**, Dec. [ ], 1783	3	220
Amy, d. [Adam & Catherine], b. Aug. 10, 1790	3	220
John, s. [Adam & Catherine], b. May 7, 1788	3	220
Lucretia, d. [Adam & Catherine], b. Aug. 3 ,1796	3	220
Lydia, d. [Adam & Catherine], b. Aug. 8, 1792	3	220
Mary, d. [Adam & Catherine], b. July 29, 1793	3	220
Sarah, d. [Adam & Catherine], b. Feb. 3, 1785	3	220
Sarah, d. Adam, m. Frances **VANARP**, Dec. 25, 1801	3	220
FINE, George, m. Isabella **McHUGO**, Mar. 10, 1852, by Rev. Robert A. Hallam	4	166
FINGER, FINGERS, [see also **FENGAR**], George, m. Fanny **BOLTON**, Mar. 23, 1823, by Tho[ma]s Shaw Perkins, J.P.	4	13
Oliver, m. Mary **McGOWAN**, July 23, 1849, by Rev. William Logan	4	150
Sarah G., of New London, m. Emmanuel **FRANCIS**, (Portugee), July 1, 1844, by Rev. R. A. G. Thompson	4	113
Thomas, m. Lucretia H. **BROOKS**, May 7, 1826, by Rev. Francis Darrow	4	26
FINIGAN, James, m. Alice **DONOVEN**, June 19, 1848, by Rev. John Brady	4	139
FIRGO, [see under **FARGO**]		
FISH, Abby, m. Samuel **BARNES**, b. of New London, Dec. 16, 1834, by Tho[oma]s S. Perkins, J.P.	4	59
Seaberry, m. Hannah **HALL**, Sept. 9, 1787	3	7
Warren, m. Emily M. **DANIELS**, b. of [New London], Dec. 29, 1839, by Rev. Abel McEwen	4	88
FISHER, Enoch, m. Serena **MARBURY**, b. of N[ew] London, July 20, 1833, by Rev. Abel McEwen	4	53
FISK, Sarah, d. Capt. Ebenezer & Sarah, of Southington, m. James **ROGERS**, 3d, s. James, of G. Neck, Dec. 9, 1783	3	84
FITCH, FICH, Clarrissa, d. Ammi, of Lebanon, m. Asa **DUTTON**, Apr. 27, 1794	3	198
Elizabeth, m. Peter **COMSTOCK**, Sept. [ ], 1756	3	75
Elizabeth C., m. Francis H. **FITCH**, b. of [New London], Oct. 11, 1837, by Rev. Abel McEwen	4	74
Francis H., m. Elizabeth C. **FITCH**, b. of [New London], Oct. 11, 1837, by Rev. Abel McEwen	4	74
James, Jr., m. Betsey **LATHAM**, b. of [New London], May 31, 1848, by Rev. L. G. Leonard	4	139

	Vol.	Page

FITCH, FICH (cont.)

Mary, m. Rev. James **HILLHOUSE**, s. John, decd.,
of Freehall, County of Londonderry, Ireland,
Jan. 18, 1725/6, in New London — 2 — 38

Patty, m. Thomas **HARVEY**, Oct. 7, 1785 — 3 — 17

Samuel P., m. Mary **WILSON**, May 16, 1798 — 3 — 186

Sarah, d. Capt. Adonijah, of New London, m.
Thomas **ROGERS**, s. Daniel, Apr. 7, 1751, by
Rev. Jewett — 3 — 48

Sarah, d. Gideon, m. Stephen **MAYNARD**, [s.
David & Rebeckah], b. Jan. 11, 1764 — 3 — 107

Thomas, 2d, m. Abby Ann **SMITH**, b. of [New
London], Oct. 15, 1836, by Rev. Abel McEwen — 4 — 76

FITZGERALD, FITSGERALD, FITCHGERALD,

Ann, m. William **CAHILL**, Jan. 14, 1852, by
Rev. J. Stokes. Witnesses: William &
Johanna Lawton — 4 — 169

Mary, m. John **SULLIVAN**, July 13, [18]50, [by
Peter J. Blenkinsop]. Witnesses: Daniel
Sullivan, Alice Fitzgerald — 3 — 306

Mary, m. John **SULLIVAN**, July 13, 1850.
Witnesses: Daniel Sullivan, Alice Fitzgerald — 4 — 159

Mary, m. Daniel **LYON**, Feb. 10, 1852, by Rev. J.
Stokes. Witnesses: John Begley, Mary
Kennedy — 4 — 169

FITZMAURICE, Michael, m. Mary **TURNULTY**, Feb.
11, 1849, by Rev. William Logan *(Perhaps
"**TUMULTY**") — 4 — 150

FLAGG, Charles, of Boston, m. Harriet **SISSON**, of New
London, Sept. 23, 1828, by Rev. Abel McEwen — 4 — 34

John T., of Boylston, Mass., m. Harriet S. **DAVIS**, of
New London, Nov. 30, 1848, by Rev. Tryon
Edwards — 4 — 143

FLETCHER, James, m. Hannah **BUNCE**, wid. of Peris,
Feb. 12, 1808 — 3 — 58

FLINN, Maria, m. James **WHITE**, b. of New London,
Nov. 3, 1844, by Rev. J. Blain — 4 — 115

FLOOD, John, m. Bridget **NOTT**, Aug. 11, [18]50, [by
Peter J. Blenkinsop]. Witnesses: Pat Meillen,
Sarah Campbell — 3 — 306

John, m. Bridget **NOTT**, Aug. 11, 1850. Witnesses:
Pat Meiller, Sarah Campbell — 4 — 159

FLORENCE, John J., of Floras Western Islands, m.
Josephine **PARKER**, of New London, Oct. 10,
1850, by Rev. Geo[rge] M. Carpenter — 4 — 156

FLYNN, [see under **FLINN**] — 4 — 156

FOG, Betsey, m. Pardon **ALLYN**, a negro, June 23, 1803 — 3 — 240

William, s. Betsey, B. Aug. 14, 1793 — 3 — 240

FOLEY, Terry, m. Catharine **FRANCIS**, June 15, 1852,
by Rev. J. Stokes. Witnesses: Patrick Sheehan,
Johanna Lynch — 4 — 171

	Vol.	Page
FOLLETT, FOLLET, Bartlett, s. Joseph & Annah, b. Jan. 12, 1735/6	2	12
George, s. Joseph & Annah, b. Apr. 30, 1732	2	12
Joseph, m. Annah **TONGUE**, of New London, Mar. 6, 1730/1	2	12
FOOTE, FOOT, Isaac, s. Pascho, late of New London, decd., on Mar. 7, 1714/15, made record that he was thereafter to be known as Isaack, alias Stallion Foote	1	44
Lucius C., of Nunda, N.Y., m. Rebecca **ALLYN**, of New London, Oct. 12, 1824, by Rev Abel McEwen	4	20
FORD, David, s. John & Ann, b. Feb. 27, 1742/3	2	24
John, m. Ann **HOLLOWAY**, May 26, 1729	2	24
John, s. John & Ann, b. Oct. 4, 1732; d. Nov. 28, 1732	2	24
Lucretia Ann, m. Charles **ANNALA**, b. of [New London], Nov. 12, 1837, by Rev. Abel McEwen	4	74
Mary, d. John & Ann, b. Aug. 18, 1730; d. Nov. 3, 1732	2	24
Michael, m. Bridget **COONEY**, Jan. 7, 1838, by Rev. Francis Darrow	4	70
Michael, m. Elizabeth **BURNS**, b. of New London, Dec. 10, 1843, by Rev. Lemuel Covell	4	109
Sarah, d. John & Ann, b. Jan. 21, 1733/4	2	24
FORDHAM, Augustus D., of Sag Harbor, m. Ellen **WHITTEMORE**, Sept. 1, 1845, by Rev. G. Thompson	4	121
FORESTALL, FORESTELL, Henry, m. Mary **DENOIR**, Aug. 11, [18]50, [by Peter J. Blenkinsop]. Witnesses: John Curran, Catharine Reilly	3	306
Henry, m. Mary **DENOIR**, Aug. 11, 1850. Witnesses: John Curran, Catharine Reilly	4	159
FORSEY, Mary, d. Benjamin & Mary, b. Mar. 1, 1766	3	9
FORSYTH, Anna, d. Timothy & Ruth, b. Apr. 21, 1754	3	9
Charlotte, d. [John & Hannah], b. Feb. 12, 1783; d. May 21, 1788	3	48
David, s. Timothy & Ruth, b. Apr. 21, 1756	3	9
Delia, d. [John & Hannah], b. Jan. 19, 1786	3	48
Elisabeth, twin with William, d. Timothy & Ruth, b. July 20, 1758	3	9
Elizabeth, m. Chapman **SIMMONS**, May 25, 1780	3	281
Elizabeth, d. [James & Betsey], b. Sept. 12, 1806	3	232
Esther, d. Timothy & Ruth, b. Aug. 4, 1748	3	9
Eunice, d. [John & Hannah], b. Apr. 14, 1772; d. Jan. 4, 1776	3	48
Gideon Comstock, s. [John & Hannah], b. May 4, 1780	3	48
Hannah, d. [John & Hannah], b. Dec. 21, 1791	3	48

	Vol.	Page
FORSYTH (cont.)		
Henry F., m. Caroline H. **CAMP[B]ELL**, b. of New London, Apr. 22, 1849, by Rev. Jabez S. Swan	4	145
Hobart, s. [John & Hannah], b. Feb. 7, 1789; d. Dec. 24, 1793	3	48
James, s. [John & Hannah], b. Oct. 13, 1775	3	48
James, m. Betsey **LEE**, d. Seth, June 12, 1800	3	232
James, s. [James & Betsey], b. Oct. 19, 1808	3	232
John, s. James, late of New London, decd., m. Hannah **COMSTOCK**, d. Gideon, late of New London, decd., June 6, 1771	3	48
John, s. [John & Hannah], b. Apr. 9, 1778	3	48
Jonathan, s. [John & Hannah], b. Dec. 10, 1795	3	48
Joseph Sill, s. [James & Betsey], b. May 26, 1802	3	232
Lee L., m. Frances **GODDARD**, b. of New London, Apr. 4, 1824, by Rev. B. Judd	4	18
Lemuel, s. [John & Hannah], b. Nov. 10, 1773	3	48
Mary, d. [John & Hannah], b. Nov. 27, 1784	3	48
Mary E., of New London, m. Charles A. **BREWSTER**, of Stonington, Nov. 23, 1831, by Rev. Abel McEwen	4	44
Richard, s. [James & Betsey], b. July 30, 1804; d. Sept. 25, 1805	3	232
Sarah, of New London, m. John **BAIN**, formerly of London, Great Britain, now of New London, June 28, 1829, by Rev. Nehemiah Dodge	4	36
Sarah L, of New London, m. James L. **EDGECOMB**, of Groton, Oct. 15, 1844, by Rev. J. Blain	4	117
Susan E., of New London, m. John **BOTTOM**, of Stonington, May 15, [1843], by Rev. Lemuel Covell	4	109
Thomas, s. Timothy & Ruth, b. May 11, 1752, old style	3	9
Timothy, s. Timothy & Ruth, b. Apr. 20, 1750, old style	3	9
William, twin with Elisabeth, s. Timothy & Ruth, b. July 20, 1758	3	9
FOSDICK, Abigail, d. [Nicoll & Abigail], b. Mar. 8, 1790	3	152
Annah, d. Samuel & Mercy, b. Dec. 8, 1691	1	21
Anna, d. [Richard & Phebe], b. Feb. 23, 1803	3	135
Anne, m. Thomas **LATHAM**, Mar. 13, 1715/16	1	45
Charles, s. [Nicholl & Abigail], b. Jan. 19, 1793	3	152
Clarine, [w. Clement], d. Apr. 8, 1787	3	105
Clarine, d. [Clement & Love], b. Nov. 8, 1795; d. Aug. 21, 1796	3	142
Clement, s. Thomas & Grace, b. Sept. 23, 1756	2	24
Clement, m. [E]unice **WAY**, d. Lieut. Thomas Way, Oct. 14, 1778	3	105
Clement, m. Clarine **SMITH**, d. Capt. Stephen Smith, Oct. 22, 1786	3	105

	Vol.	Page

FOSDICK (cont.)

Clement, m. Love **BEEBE**, d. Capt. Abijah Beebe,
Jan. 6, 1789 — 3 — 105

Clement Way, s. [Clement & [E]unice], b. Dec. 15,
1785 — 3 — 105

Edward, s. [Clement & Love], b. Oct. 9, 1799 — 3 — 142

Esther, d. Thomas & Esther, b. Apr. 30, 1722 — 1 — 60

Eunice, [w. Clement], d. Dec. 21, 1785 — 3 — 105

Eunice, d. [Clement & Love], b. Feb. 18, 1793 — 3 — 142

Fanney, d. [Clement & Love], b. July 31, 1791 — 3 — 142

Frances, d. [Clement & [E]unice], b. May 22, 1783;
d. Mar. 1, 1785 — 3 — 105

Frances E., m. George **JONES**, b. of [New London],
Oct. 5, 1834, by Rev. Abel McEwen — 4 — 58

Frances Eliza, d. [Nicoll & Abigail], b. Jan. 28, 1801 — 3 — 152

Gloriana, d. [Nicoll & Abigail], b. Oct. 17, 1798; d.
Oct. 27, 1800 — 3 — 152

Gloriana, d. [Nicoll & Abigail], b. Jan. 22, 1803 — 3 — 152

Henry, s. [Clement & Love], b. July 10, 1801 — 3 — 142

Henry Nicoll, s. [Richard & Phebe], b. Sept. 21,
1808 — 3 — 135

James, s. Sam[ue]l & Susannah, b. Nov. 20, 1716 — 1 — 62

John, s. Sam[ue]ll & Mercy, b. Feb. 1, 1693/4 — 1 — 21

Katharine, d. Thomas & Esther, b. Feb. 7, 1726/7 — 2 — 23

Katharine, d. Dea. Thomas, m. George **RICHARDS**,
Jr., s. Capt. Geo[rge], b. of New London, Dec.
21, 1747 — 2 — 102

Lodowick, s. [Clement & [E]unice], b. Apr. 3, 1781 — 3 — 105

Lodowick, s. [Nicoll & Abigail], b. Feb. 27, 1788 — 3 — 152

Lodowick, m. Elizabeth Turner **SMITH**, May 12,
1811, by Rev. Charles Seabury — 3 — 241

Marcy, d. Samuell & Marcy, b. Nov. 30, [1686] — 1 — 18

Mary, d. Samuell & Mercy, b. July 7, 1699 — 1 — 25

Mary, of N[ew] London, m. Thomas **JIGGLES***, of
Boston, Nov. 17, 1708. *(Arnold copy gives
the name "**JOGGLES**". See Caulkins' History
for correction) — 1 — 34

Mary Ann, d. [Nicoll & Abigail], b. Aug. 19, 1796 — 3 — 152

Mary Ann, d. Capt. Nicoll Fosdick, m. Thomas
MUSSEY, May 16, 1817 — 3 — 230

Mercy, wid., m. John **ARNOLD**, late of Boston, Dec.
6, 1703 — 1 — 29

Mercy, d. Sam[ue]l & Susannah, b. Mar. 28, 1708 — 1 — 62

Nicoll, s. [Thomas & Anna], b. Apr. 18, 1750; m.
Abigail **ELDRIDGE**, Jan. 19, 1784 — 3 — 152

Nicoll, s. [Nicoll & Abigail], b. Nov. 9, 1785 — 3 — 152

Nicoll, the elder, d. Jan. 1, 1821, at North Stonington — 3 — 152

Rhoda, d. Ezekiel, of Wethersfield, m. Samuel
WHITTEMORE, Nov. 1, 1775 — 3 — 183

Richard, m. Phebe **L'HOMMEDIEU**, Oct. 20,
[1796], by Aaron Woolworth, V.D.M., of Sag
Harbor — 3 — 135

	Vol.	Page
FOSDICK (cont.)		
Richard, s. [Clement & Love], b. Sept. 10, 1797	3	142
Ruth, d. Samuel & Mercy, b. June 27, 1689	1	19
Ruth, d. Sam[ue]l & Susannah, b Jan. 25, 1713/14	1	62
Samuel, s. John, of Charlestown, N. England,		
m. Mary **PICKETT**, d. John & Ruth, Nov. 1,		
[1682]	1	16
Samuell, s. Samuell & Marcy, b. Aug. 16, [1683]; d.		
Nov. 18, [1683]	1	17
Samuell, s. Samuell & Marcy, b. Sept. 18, [1684]	1	17
Sam[ue]l, m. Susannah **TURNER**, July 13, 1706	1	62
Samuel, s. Sam[ue]l & Susannah, b. Mar. 11, 1710	1	62
Samuel, s. Thomas & Grace, b. Dec. 29, 1757	2	24
Samuel, s. [Clement & Love], b. Sept. 9, 1789	3	142
Samuel, s. [Richard & Phebe], b. Mar. 21, 1801	3	135
Sarah, d. Thomas & Esther, b. Apr. 9, 1731	1	24
Sylvester L'Hommedieu, s. [Richard & Phebe], b.		
May 6, 1799	3	135
Thomas, s. Sam[ue]l & Mercy, b. Aug. 20, 1696	1	22
Thomas, m. Est[h]er **UPDIKE**, June 29, 1720	1	58
Thomas, s. Thomas & Esther, b. Apr. 30, 1725	1	65
Thomas, s. Thomas & Esther, b. Apr. 30, 1725	2	23
Tho[ma]s, s. Samuel & Mercy, m. Grace, d.		
Clement & Martha **MINOR**, Sept. 2, 1755	2	24
Thomas, d. July 17, 1774, ae 79 y.	2	24
Thomas, s. [Clement & [E]unice], b. July 14, 1779	3	105
Thomas, s. [Nicoll & Abigail], b. Jan. 19, 1795; d.		
Sept. 26, 1795	3	152
Thomas Richard, s. [Richard & Phebe], b. June 22,		
1797	3	135
William, s. Sam[ue]l & Susannah, b. Feb. 4, 1712	1	62
FOSTER, FORSTER, Benjamin, m. Eunice **POWERS**,		
wid., Jan. 22, 1785	3	91
Edward, s. Tho[ma]s & Susanna, b. & d. Aug. 5,		
[1677]	1	12
Elizabeth, m William **LEWIS**, b. of New London,		
Aug. 7, 1843, by Rev. J. Benton	4	107
Jonathan, s. Tho[ma]s & Susanna, b. Aug. 17, [1673]	1	9
Jonathan, m. Elizabeth **BROWN**, June 11, 1707	1	32
Mary, d. Tho[ma]s & Susanna, b. June 14, [1675]	1	10
Rebecca, m. Robert **BURDICK**, Jan 4, 1700	1	26
Samuel, s. Tho[ma]s & Susanna, b. Sept. 22, [1678]	1	13
Susannah, d. Thomas & Susanna, b. Mar. 4, [1666]	1	5
Susannah, m. Carey **LATHAM**, Dec. 26, 1688	1	18
Thomas, s. John J., of Kingsware, m. Susanna, d.		
Ralph **PARKER**, Mar. 27, [1665]	1	4
Thomas, s. Thomas & Susanna, b. Feb. 26, [1668]	1	6
FOWLER, Abby, m. James **LESTER**, Mar. 20, 1831, by		
Nathan Wildman	4	40
Ann M., of New London, m. Ezra **DABOLL**, of		
Noank (Groton), Jan. 1, 1847, by Rev. L.		
Geo[rge] Leonard	4	129

	Vol.	Page

FOWLER (cont.)

Edwin, m. Sophrona **BROWN**, Dec. 22, 1840, by H.
R. Knapp — 4 — 93

Emma, m. Edward **GILBERTS**, Oct. 6, 1850, by
Rev. Charles Willett — 4 — 155

John, s. Morris & Elisabeth, b. Jan. 9, 1760 — 3 — 14

Lucy, of [New London], m. William H. **CHAPMAN**,
of New York, May 18, 1847, by Rev. L.
Geo[rge] Leonard — 4 — 131

Lydia H., m. George N. **WOODWARD**, b. of [New
London], Mar. 31, 1847, by Rev. L. Geo[rge]
Leonard — 4 — 129

Mary, d. Morris & Elisabeth, b. Feb. 24, 1757 — 3 — 14

Morris, m. Elisabeth **LESTER**, b. of New London,
Sept. 10, 1754 — 3 — 14

Sarah G., m. Harris **LESTER**, Oct. 5, 1851, by Rev.
Charles Willett — 4 — 165

Thomas, s. Morris & Elisabeth, b. Oct. 10, 1755 — 3 — 14

FOX, Abigail, m. Charles **HILL**, Aug. 28, 1701 — 1 — 26

Abigail, m. Jeremiah **BROOKS**, May 13, 1784 — 3 — 110

Amy, m. Abner **AVERY**, b. of New London, May
22, 1740 — 3 — 3

Ann, d. Sam[ue]l & Mary, b. Oct. 6, [1678] — 1 — 13

Bathsua, d. Sam[ue]l & Rachel, b. Aug. 11, 1727 — 2 — 23

Bathshua, d. Sam[ue]l & Rachel, b. Aug. 31, 1733 — 2 — 24

Benjamin, m. Naomie **ROGERS**, Feb. 25, 1707/8 — 1 — 33

Benjamin, Jr., b. Aug. 29, 1715 — 2 — 18

Benjamin, Jr., of New London, s. of Benjamin, m.
Abigail **BROCKWAY**, d. Rich[ar]d, of Lyme,
Nov. 7, 1745 — 2 — 18

Caron, d. Samuel, of New London, m. John **ALLEN**,
of New London, s. Samuel, Feb. 24, 1742/3 — 2 — 79

Christopher H., m. Harriet B. **DART**, b. of New
London, Nov. 26, [1843], by Rev. Lemuel
Covell — 4 — 109

Ebenezer, s. Ebenezer & Jane, b. Feb. 8, 1720/21 — 1 — 57

Elizabeth, d. Sam[ue]l & Mary, b. Nov. 5, [1677] — 1 — 12

Elizabeth, d. Benj[amin] & Abigail, b. Sept. 28, 1746 — 2 — 18

Elizabeth, d. Joseph & Elizab[et]h, b. June 11, 1773 — 3 — 55

Ezekiel Turner, s. Ezekiel & Susan, b. Dec. 6, 1800 — 3 — 127

Francis, m. Margaret **KEENEY**, b. of New London,
Apr. 5, 1846, by Rev. Jabez S. Swan — 4 — 127

Hannah, d. Thomas, m. Danyell **LESTER**, s.
Andrew, Aug. 11, [1669] — 1 — 6

Han[n]ah, d. Sam[ue]l, s. Sam[ue]l, b. May 4, 1717 — 1 — 59

Hannah, d. Samuell, 2d, m. David **LESTER**, s.
Benjamin, Apr. 13, 1737 — 2 — 11

James, s. Sam[ue]l, s. Sam[ue]l, b. July 21, 1722 — 1 — 59

Jane, m. David **ROBARTS**, Nov. 20, 1776 — 3 — 67

Jeremiah, s. Isaac, of Colchester, b. Mar. 16, 1712.
Recorded Mar. 22, 1726/7 — 2 — 23

Jeremy, s. [Samuel & Esther], b. Feb. 26, 1790 — 3 — 104

	Vol.	Page
FOX (cont.)		
Johanna, w. Sam[ue]ll, d. Oct. [ ], [1689]	1	69
John, of Concord, m. Sarah, d. Grenfield		
CAVERLY*, June 28, [1678] *(Corrected to		
"**LARABY**", by L. B. B.)	1	12
John, s. John & Sarah, b. June 1, [1680]	1	14
John, of Willington, m. Jemima **ROGERS**, d. Adam,		
of New London, Feb. 24, 1742/3, by Rev.		
Eliphalet Adams	2	19
John, s. Benjamin, of New London, decd., m. Mary		
PIERCE, d. William, of S. Kingston, decd.,		
Mar. 19, 1745/6	2	52
Jonathan, m. Mary **DANIELLS**, Oct. 23, 1713	1	41
Jonathan, s. Samuell, s. Sam[ue]l, b. Oct. 5, 1715	1	59
Joseph, s. Benjamin, m. Elizabeth **COIT**, d. Samuel,		
all of New London, Jan. 16, 1772	3	55
Joseph, s. [Joseph & Elizabeth], b. Mar. 30, 1775	3	55
Lois, d. [Nathan & Polly], b. Sept. 20, 1791	3	121
Lucy, d. [Benjamin & Abigail], b. Sept. 26, 1752	2	18
Lucy, had d. Anna **SCRANTON**, b. July 30, 1782.		
Father was George Scranton	3	38
Lucy, d. John, of Chatham, m. Chester **KIMBALL**,		
Nov. 8, 1786	3	51
Lucy A., of [New London], m. Albert G.		
DOUGLASS, of Waterford, Oct. 10, 1849, by		
Rev. Abel McEwen	4	147
Mary, d. John & Mary, b. Jan. 10, 1746/7	2	52
Nancy, d. Joseph, m. Peter **BEEBE**, Mar. 1, 1801	3	180
Naomi, d. Sam[ue]l & Rachel, b. Apr. 21, 1731	2	24
Nathan, s. [Benjamin & Abigail], b. Sept. 8, 1766	2	18
Nathan, m. Polly **CHAPPEL**, June 26, 1791	3	121
Rachel, d. Sam[ue]l, s. Sam[ue]l & Hester*, b. May		
24, 1724. *(First written "Rachel". Changed		
by L. B. B.)	1	64
Rachel, m. David **LESTER**, Feb. 19, 1734/5	2	11
Rachel, d. Sam[ue]l Fox, 2d, had s. Reuel **BROWN**,		
b. Feb. 4, 1739/40	2	24
Rachel, d. Sam[ue]l, 2d, had s. Ichabod **BROWN**, b.		
June 7, 1746	2	24
Rachel Wright, d. Ezekiel, m. Increase **WILSON**,		
Jan. 1, 1810	3	236
Sally, d. [Samuel & Esther], b. Dec. 6, 1791	3	104
Samuel, s. Tho[ma]s, m. Mary **LESTER**, d. Daniel,		
Jr., Mar. 31, [1675]	1	10
Samuel, s. Sam[ue]l & Mary, b. Apr. 24, [1681]	1	16
Samuell, m. Mary **STEEVENS**, Mar. 25, 1703	1	27
Samuel, m. Hester **ALLEN**, Aug. 9, 1715	1	44
Sam[ue]l, s. Sam[ue]l, s. Sam[ue]l, b. June 29, 1719	1	59
Samuel, s. [Benjamin & Abigail], b. Nov. 1, 1762	2	18
Samuel, m. Esther **LESTER**, Nov. 30, 1788	3	104
Sarah, of New London, m. Joseph **HURLBUT**, of		
Boston, Apr. 15, 1823, by Rev. Abel McEwen	4	13

	Vol.	Page

FOX (cont.)

Sarah C., of Montville, m. John F. **BROWN**, of
Waterford, Jan. 3, 1847, by Rev. T. Edwards — 4 — 128

Susan F., m. Gilbert **POTTER**, Oct. 26, 1817 — 3 — 196

Thomas W., m. Mercy W. **DART**, b. of New
London, Apr. 1, 1843, by L. Covell — 4 — 101

FRANCESCO, FRANCISCO, Charles, m. Mary
JOSEPH, b. of New London, July 7, 1850, by
Rev. George M. Carpenter — 4 — 155

John, m. Mary Ann **TILLINGHAST**, b. of Norwich,
July 24, 1824, by Rev. Abel McEwen — 4 — 19

FRANCIS, Antonie, m. Fanny **TINKER**, b. of [New
London], Feb. 7 ,1841, by John Lovejoy — 4 — 93

Catharine, m. Terry **FOLEY**, June 15, 1852, by Rev.
J. Stokes. Witnesses: Patrick Sheehan,
Johanna Lynch — 4 — 171

Emmanuel, (Portugee), m. Sarah G. **FINGERS**, of
New London, July 1, 1844, by Rev. R. A. G.
Thompson — 4 — 113

Fanny, m. Chauncey **GATT**, b. of New London, May
11, 1846, by Rev. John Howson — 4 — 126

Joseph, m. Eliza **HAVENS**, b. of New London, June
26, 1831, by Rev. Abel McEwen — 4 — 43

Joseph, m. Julia **CLARK**, b. of N[ew] London, Mar.
23, 1834, by Chester Tilden — 4 — 55

Joseph, m. Ann **KNIGHT**, b. of [New London],
Sept. 30, 1846, by Rev. T. Edwards — 4 — 128

Simeon, m. Eliza **RAMSEY**, b. of New London,
Dec. 5, 1820, by Rev. Abel McEwen — 4 — 4

Simeon, m. Eliza **RUMSEY**, d. Benjamin & Mary,
Dec. 6, 1820 — 3 — 220

FREEMAN, Andrew, s. [Richard Easton & Nancy, people
of color], b. June 25, 1808 — 3 — 46

Clarry, d. [Richard Easton & Nancy, people of color],
b. July 13, 1806 — 3 — 46

Dinah, d. [Providence & Betsey], b. July 25, 1800 — 3 — 104

Eliza, m. Henry **TREADWAY**, b. of [New London],
July 8, 1838, by Rev. Robert Hallam — 4 — 78

George, of New London, m. Nancy **MORRIS**, of
Groton, Aug. 25, 1839, by J. Lovejoy — 4 — 87

Harriet, of [New London], m. Joseph **MARTIN**, of
Island of Martinico, Apr. 21, 1841, by Rev.
Abel McEwen — 4 — 94

Hoitson, s. Providence & Dinah, negroes, b. May 21,
1775 — 3 — 104

Jacob, m. Eliza **ANDERSON**, Oct. 13, 1833, by Rev.
I. W. Hallam — 4 — 52

Jane, m. Ce[a]ser **SHAW**, Oct. 8, 1809   (negroes) — 3 — 16

Levine, m. John **BROOKS**, Sept. [ ], 1808 (negroes) — 3 — 8

Martha P., m. Peter A. **HULL**, b. of [New London],
Jan. 14, 1847, by Rev. Robert A. Hallam — 4 — 129

	Vol.	Page
FREEMAN (cont.)		
Providence, s. [Providence & Dinah], b. Feb. 24, 1778	3	104
Providence, m. Betsey **STEP**, negroes, [ ], 179[ ]	3	104
Richard Easton, m. Nancy **BIRCH**, people of color, Mar. 25, 1802	3	46
Robert, m. Silva **PEMBLETON**, (negroes), Nov. 6, 1806	3	10
Samuel, m. Eliza **CORNWALL**, b. of [New London], May 10, 1835, by Rev. Abel McEwen	4	61
Susan[n]ah, m. Sonne **ANDERSON**, Mar. 13, 1775*, black persons. *(Corrected to Nov. 1, 1763)	3	56
Thomas, s. Robert & Silva (negroes), b. Dec. 30, 1808	3	10
FRENCH, Ann S., of New London, m. Charles H. **SMITH**, of Stonington, Oct. 3, 1844, by Rev. Tho[ma]s J. Greenwood	4	116
Ann Sheffield, [d. John, 2d, & Betsey], b. Dec. 25, 1836	3	208
Charles, s. [John, 2d, & Betsey], b. July 3, 1808	3	208
Charles, m. Elizabeth **HARRIS**, b. of [New London], May 5, 1830, by Rev. Daniel Wildman	4	39
Elizabeth, d. [John, 2d, & Betsey], b. Nov. 26, 1809	3	208
John, b. Sept. 17, 1762	3	149
John, m. Mary **GODDARD**, d. Capt. Nathan **DOUGLASS**, Apr. 8, 1794	3	149
John, m. Betsey **HYDE**, d. Ebenezer, of Lebanon, July 22, 1804	3	149
John, m. Betsey **HYDE**, d. Ebenezer, of Lebanon, July 22, 1804* *(First written 1808. Corrected by L. B. B.)	3	208
John, 2d, m. Betsey **ROGERS**, d. Benjamin, Oct. 13, 1807	3	208
John F., m. Abby S. **MINER**, b. of New London, Nov. 20, 1849, by Rev. Robert A. Hallam	4	147
John Francis, s. [John, 2d, & Betsey], b. Jan. 28, 1821	3	208
Lucretia, d. [John, 2d, & Betsey], b. Nov. 22, 1811	3	208
Lucretia H., of New London, m. Benjamin F. **WRIGHT**, of New York, Nov. 28, 1832, by Rev. J. W. Hallam	4	48
Mary, d. [John & Mary], b. Apr. 4, 1795	3	149
Mary, w. John, d. Feb. 6, 1804	3	149
Mary, m. Andrew **LAWRENCE**, Oct. 13, 1836, by Rev. Alvin Ackley	4	84
Zerviah, m. John **CRAIG**, Oct. 21, 1778	3	67
Zerviah, m. John **PRESTON**, [ ]	2	85
FRINK, Abigail, d. [David & Dezier], b. July 27, 1785	3	157
Adom, s. [David & Dezier], b. July 4, 1780	3	157
Andrew Miner, s. [David & Dezier], b. June 29, 1793	3	157

	Vol.	Page

FRINK (cont.)

Ann B., m. W[illia]m E. **ALMY**, b. of [New
   London], July 11, 1844, by Rev Abel McEwen — 4 — 115

Daniel, s. [David & Dezier], b. Sept. 18, 1791 — 3 — 157

David, m. Dezier **MINER**, d. Ephra[i]m, June 2,
   1773 — 3 — 157

Elizabeth, of Stonington, m. Charles W. **BAILIEY**,
   of Groton, Apr. 24, 1836, by Rev. Squire B.
   Hascall — 4 — 83

Elizabeth, m. Sevel **WILLIAMS**, b. of [New
   London], Dec. 23, 1838, by Rev. C. C.
   Williams — 4 — 81

Ephra[i]m Miner, s. [David & Dezier], b. Feb. 1,
   1777. (Perhaps Ephraim Minor who died in
   1802) — 3 — 157

Eunice, d. [David & Dezier], b. Apr. 23, 1774 — 3 — 157

Eunice, m. John **PRENTIS**, Nov. 1, 1795 — 3 — 250

Fan[n]y, d. [David & Dezier], b. Mar. 22, 1788 — 3 — 157

John, s. [John H. & Ann], b. Oct. 4, 1807 — 3 — 206

John H., s. [David & Dezier], b. Mar. 6, 1783 — 3 — 157

John H., m. Ann **KILBOURN**, d. Freeman Kilbourn,
   of Hartford, Dec. 17, 1806 — 3 — 206

Julia, of [New London], m. Henry G. **LOPER**, of
   Charleston, S.C., Sept. 17, 1847, by Rev. Abel
   McEwen — 4 — 134

Robert, of North Stonington, m. Mary **HEWITT**, of
   New London, Aug. 8, 1832, by Rev. Abel
   McEwen — 4 — 47

Stiles, of Stonington, m. Eliza **JONES**, of East
   Haddam, Jan. 18, 1835, by Rev. Alven Ackley — 4 — 59

FROWD, Robert, m. Grace **STARR**, Oct. 23, 1734 — 2 — 24

FULLER, Desire, late of Barnstable, m. John **TAYLOR**,
   June 11, 1703 — 1 — 28

John H., m. Mary Ann **DANIELS**, b. of New
   London, May 7, 1843, by Rev. Lemuel Covell — 4 — 109

Samuell, of Malshamesdas (?), m. Nam(?)
   ROWLEE, June 11, 1703 — 1 — 28

FULTON, John, s. [John A. & Mehetable], b. May 8, 1791 — 3 — 147

John A., formerly of Boston, m. Mehetable **OWEN**,
   d. John, Jan. 9, 1789 — 3 — 147

John A., m. Mary **POWERS**, b. of [New London],
   Mar. 15, 1837, by Rev. Robert A. Hallam — 4 — 67

Mehetable, d. [John & Mehetable], b. Mar. 16, 1790 — 3 — 147

Mehittable, m. Thomas **BRADLEY**, 2d, of Boston,
   July 25, 1814 — 3 — 240

Salley Bradley, d. [John A. & Mehetable], b. Sept.
   19, 1798 — 3 — 147

Sarah B., m. Jeremiah H. **GODDARD**, b. of New
   London, Jan. 30, 1825, by Rev. B. Judd — 4 — 2

FURZE, [see also **FARGO**], Mary E., m. Mark D. **KING**,
   b. of New London, Apr. 7, 1833, by Rev. Abel
   McEwen — 4 — 50

	Vol.	Page
GADGER, Elizabeth, d. John, of Norwich, m. John		
ALLYN, s. Robert, Dec. 24, [1668]	1	6
GAF[F]NEY, Mary, m. James **WILLIAMS**, May 12,		
1849, by Rev. William Logan	4	150
GAFFREY, Michael, m. Bridget **GANERN**, June 22,		
1846, by Rev. John Brady	4	127
GAFFY, Rose, m. James **SHARKEY**, July 22, 1849, by		
Rev. William Logan	4	150
GAGER, Rebecca, d. of Sam[ue]l, of Norwich, m.		
William **MANWARING**, s. Oliver, of New		
London, Nov. 5, 1735	2	51
GALE, Betsey, d. [William & Betsey], b. Feb. 13, 1802	3	183
Charles Turner, s. [Luther & Lucretia], b. Dec. 21,		
1791; d. Jan. 18, 1792	3	153
Elizabeth, m. Nathaniel **RICHARDS**, Jr., of New		
London, May 12, 1825, by Rev. Abel McEwen	4	22
Fanney, d. [Luther & Lucretia], b. Feb. 21, 1796	3	153
John, s. [Luther & Lucretia] b. Mar. 14, 1794	3	153
Leonard, s. [Luther & Lucretia], b. Jan. 19, 1798	3	153
Luther, b. Jan. 3, 1764, in Princetown, County of		
Worcester, Mass.; m. Lucretia **TURNER**, June		
21, 1790, by Rev. Henry Channing	3	153
Mariah, d. [Luther & Lucretia], b. Dec. 24, 1800	3	153
Mary Ann, d. [William & Betsey], b. June 15, 1805	3	183
Mary Ann, m. Charles **BOLLES**, b. of [New		
London], Nov. 18, 1823, by Rev. Thomas W.		
Tucker	4	17
Sally Edgerton, d. [William & Betsey], b. Sept. 21,		
1810	3	183
Sarah E., m. Samuel **LOYD**, b. of New London,		
Aug. 15, 1833, by Rev. Isaac Stoddard	4	52
William, m. Betsey **BARR**, d. John & Elizabeth,		
May 23, 1801	3	183
GALLOP, [see under **GALLUP**]		
GALLOWAY, Andrew, s. Andrew & Thankful, b. Aug.		
19, 1748	2	106
Mary, d. Andrew & Thankful, b. Apr. 5, 1739	2	106
Prudence, d. Andrew & Thankful, b. June 1, 1742	2	106
GALLUP, GALLOP, Betsey, m. Josiah **ROGERS**, of		
[New London], Sept. 20, 1838, by Rev. C. C.		
Williams	4	81
Christobel, m. Peter **CRARY**, Dec. [, 1677]	1	12
Lorenzo D., b. at Glastonbury, m. Eliza Jane		
MAXON, July 12, 1843, by R. A. G.		
Thompson	4	106
GAM[M]ON, Catherine, d. Thomas, m. Thomas		
JOANES, June 25, [1677]	1	11
Katharine, d. Thomas, of New Foundland, m.		
Thomas **JONES**, June 25, 1677	1	67
GANERN, Bridget, m. Michael **GAFFREY**, June 22,		
1846, by Rev. John Brady	4	127

	Vol.	Page
GANTER, Ann, twin with Esther, d. Robert & Hannah, b.		
June 6, 1720	1	57
Ann, d. Robert & Hannah, d. July 16, 1721	1	59
Ann, d. Robert & Hannah, b. Apr. 24, 1722	1	59
Esther, twin with Ann, d. Robert & Hannah, b. June		
6, 1720	1	57
Robert, m. Hannah **ANDRES**, Sept. 8, 1719	1	57
Samuel, s. Robert & Hannah, b. Mar. 20, 1725/6	2	30
GARDINER, GARDNER, GARDAN, GARDENER,		
Abigail, b. May 1, 1724, old style; m. Samuel		
GARDINER, May 22, 1746, by Rev. Nathaniel		
Hunting, of East Hampton	2	71
Abigail, dau. of William & Elizabeth, of Newport,		
R.I., m. Matthew **STEWART**, formerly of		
Ireland, Oct. 19, 1735, by Rev. Honeyman, of		
Rhode Island	2	73
Abigail, d. Samuel & Abigail, b. Aug. 1, 1747	2	71
Ann J., m. John C. **LAMB**, b. of New London, July		
13, 1851, by Rev. Jabez S. Swan	4	171
Benjaman, m. Phebe **HARRIS**, d. Daniel, Mar. 15,		
1795	3	177
Benjaman, s. [Benjaman & Phebe], b. Jan. 26, 1801	3	177
Christopher, s. [Rufus & Lydia], b. Aug. 28, 1795	3	160
Christopher*, s. [Rufus & Lydia], *(Written in		
pencil and no date given)	3	160
David, Jr., of the Isle of Wight, Province of New		
York, s. of David of Isle of Wight, m. Elizabeth		
GARDENER, of New London, dau. of Capt.		
Samuel, late of East Hampton, Province of New		
York, decd., Mar. 29, 1741	2	70
David, s. David & Elizabeth, b. Mar. 18, 1749/50	2	70
Desire, [d. Christopher], b. Feb. 22, 1762	3	165
Desire, d. Christopher, m. Henry **NORRIS**, Jr., Oct.		
14, 1786	3	165
Douglass W.*, s. [Rufus & Lydia], *(Written in		
pencil and no data given)	3	160
Earles P., m. Sila **DANIELS**, of Lyme, June 11,		
1822, by W[illia]m Stockman, J.P.	4	9
Eliza, of [New London], m. Oliver P. **DOUGLASS**,		
of Waterford, Apr. 30, 1840, by Rev. Abel		
McEwen	4	89
Eliza A., of New London, m. John J. **CORNWALL**,		
of Norwich, Aug. 8, 1830, by Rev. Abel		
McEwen	4	39
Elizabeth, of New London, dau. of Capt. Samuel,		
decd., late of East Hampton, Province of New		
York, m. David **GARDENER**, Jr., of the Isle of		
Wight, Province of New York, s. of David, of		
Isle of Wight, Mar. 29, 1741	2	70
Elizabeth, d. David & Elizabeth, b. Oct. 15, 1744; d.		
Aug. 6, 1747	2	70

	Vol.	Page

GARDINER, GARDNER, GARDAN, GARDENER
(cont.)

	Vol.	Page
Fanny, of New London, m. Elias **SHARP**, of Lyme,		
May 24, 1820, by Elder Lester Rogers	4	3
Francis, d. [Benjamin & Phebe], b. Nov. 27, 1795	3	177
Franklin, of New York, m. Abby **LEEDS**, of New		
London, June 12, 1831, by Rev. Abel McEwen	4	42
George W., of Bristol, R.I., m. Elizabeth **MORGAN**,		
of New London, May 12, 1822, by Rev. B. Judd	4	4
Hannah, d. Peregreen & Susanna, b. Dec.10, 1745	2	87
Hannah, d. Samuel & Abigail, b. July 26, 1749	2	71
Harriet, d. [Rufus & Lydia], b. Jan. 22, 1803	3	160
Henry, s. Chris[tophe]r & Marcy, b. Feb. 8, 1769	3	137
Henry, m. Etherlinda **RICHARDS**, Aug. 25, 1789	3	137
Henry, s. [Henry & Etherlinda], b. Feb. 18, 1792	3	137
Henry, s. [Rufus & Linda], b. Feb. 26, 1798	3	160
Henry, the elder, d. Oct. 16, 1806	3	137
Henry, of New London, m. Mary **MINER**, of		
Waterford, May 16, 1824, by Ebenezer Loomis	4	18
Jedidiah, s. [Henry & Etherlinda], b. Jan. 24, 1795	3	137
Jerusha, d. John & Sarah, b. Oct. 7, 1721; d. Feb. 7,		
1721/2	1	61
Jerusha, d. John & Sarah, b. Oct. 6, 1723	1	62
Jerusha, of New London, d. John, of New London,		
decd., m. John **CHRISTOPHERS**, s.		
Christ[ophe]r, Mar. 7, 1741/2	2	72
John, m. Sarah **COITE**, Sept. 2, 1708	1	38
John, m. Sarah **SALTONSTALL**, May 6, 1716	1	46
John, s. John & Sarah, b. Apr. 9, 1720; d. May 27,		
1720	1	61
John, s. Jonathan & Mary, b. Oct. 7, 1734	2	31
John, s. Peregreen & Susanna, b. May 9, 1737	2	87
John, s. [Benjamin & Phebe], b. Feb. 23, 1797	3	177
Jonathan, m. Mary **ADAMS**, Nov. 13, 1733	2	31
Joseph, s. David & Elizabeth, b. Apr. 17, 1753	2	70
Lucinda, m. Francis **ANTONIA**, b. of New London,		
Mar. 13, 1832, by Rev. Abel McEwen	4	45
Lucretia, d. David & Elizabeth, b. Apr. 18, 1755	2	70
Lucy, d. [Rufus & Lydia], b. Mar. 13 ,1800	3	160
Lydia, d. [Rufus & Lydia], b. May 21 ,1790	3	160
Marcy, d. [Rufus & Lydia], b. Dec. 24, 1787	3	160
Maria, d. [Benjamin & Phebe], b. July 29, 1799	3	177
Maria, of New London, m. Gurdon **AVERY**, of		
Waterford, Apr. 14, 1822, by Elias Sharp, Elder	4	3
Mary, d. Peregreen & Susanna, b. Mar. 14, 1735	2	87
Mary, d. David & Elizabeth, b. Mar 12, 1747, old		
style	2	70
Mary, d. David, m. Thomas **COIT**, Jan. 12, 1764	3	98
Mehetable, d. Samuel & Abigail, b. Jan. 8, 1753, new		
style	2	71
Mehetable, d. Stephen, of Norwich, m. John		
CONGDON, Jr., of New London, [ ]	2	96

	Vol.	Page

GARDINER, GARDNER, GARDAN, GARDENER
(cont.)

Melvin H., of Sag Harbour, N.Y., m. Belinda
  WELCH, of [New London], June 5, 1835, by
  Rev. Abel McEwen .... 4 ... 61

Nathaniel, of New Bedford, m. Jane **KEENEY**, of
  New London, July 29, 1824, by Rev. Abel
  McEwen .... 4 ... 19

Peregreen, s. Peregreen & Susanna, b. Mar. 12 ,1739 ... 2 ... 87

Robinson, s. Peregreen & Susanna, b. Nov. 27, 1743 ... 2 ... 87

Rosetta J., of New London, m. Benjamin C.
  NORTHROP, of Norwich, Jan. 24, 1848, by
  Rev. L. G. Leonard .... 4 ... 137

Rowland B., m. Eunice **HARRIS**, Mar. 5, 1837, by
  Rev. Alvan Ackley .... 4 ... 67

Rufus, m. Lydia **HARRIS**, May 11, 1786 ...... 3 ... 160

Rufus, s. [Rufus & Lydia], b. Jan. 23, 1793 ... 3 ... 160

Ruth, d. Peregreen & Susanna, b. Oct. 25, 1742 ... 2 ... 87

Sally, m. Jeremiah Gates **BRAINARD**, Dec. 10,
  1783 .... 3 ... 80

Samuel, b. Feb. 25, 1723/4, old style; m. Abigail
  GARDINER, May 22, 1746, by Rev. Nathaniel
  Hunting, of East Hampton .... 2 ... 71

Samuel, s. David & Elizabeth, b Feb. 4, 1741/2 ... 2 ... 70

Samuel, s. Samuel & Abigail, b. Oct. 10, 1758 ... 2 ... 71

Sarah, d. John & Sarah, b. Aug. 26, 1717 ...... 1 ... 49

Sarah, d. John & Sarah, b. Aug. 26, 1717 ...... 1 ... 61

Sarah, m. Samuel **DAVISS**, Jan. 1, 1727 ..... 2 ... 13

Sarah, of South Kingston, m. Jonathan **SMITH**, Aug.
  24, 1732 .... 2 ... 104

Sarah, of South Kingston, m. Jonathan **SMITH**, Aug.
  24, 1732 .... 2 ... 105

Sarah, d. Peregreen & Susanna, b. Apr. 1, 1733 ... 2 ... 87

Stephen, s. Peregreen & Susanna, b. Aug. 1, 1734 ... 2 ... 87

Thomas, s. David & Elizabeth, b. Nov. 5, 1757 ... 2 ... 71

William, s. Peregreen & Susanna, b. Aug. 13, 1747 ... 2 ... 87

William H., m. Emily **LEWIS**, b. of New London,
  Sept. 14, 1826, by Rev. N. S. Spaulding ... 4 ... 27

GARRETT, Alexander, of Kentucky, m. Jane W.
  STARR, of [New London], Sept. 29, 1833, by
  Daniel Huntington .... 4 ... 54

Henry, m. Sarah **McEWEN**, b. of [New London],
  June 5, 1838, by Rev. Abel McEwen .... 4 ... 77

GARRY, Michael, m. Honora **BOYLE**, Nov. 26, 1848, by
  Rev. William Logan .... 4 ... 150

GARVIN, Rosana, of New London, m. Lewis
  PEARSALL, June 3, 1847, by Rev. Thomas J.
  Greenwood .... 4 ... 132

GASERS, Christopher, d. June 25, 1689. Drowned.
  Foreigner .... 1 ... 69

	Vol.	Page
GATELEY, Edward, m. Anna **TIGHE**, May 23, 1852, by		
Rev. J. Stokes. Witnesses: Michael Maxwell,		
Catharine Murphy	4	170
Michael, m. Ann **CAIN**, Aug. 26, 1849, by Rev. P. J.		
Blinkensop	4	151
GATES, Eli, of Salem, Ct., m. Mary S. **CHAN[E]Y**, of		
[New London], Apr. 23, 1826, by Rev. Isaac		
Stoddard	4	26
Geo[rge] G., of Moodus, m. Charlotte R. **EWEN**, of		
New London, July 16, 1848, by Rev. L. G.		
Leonard	4	140
Mehitable P., of Chatham, m. Benjamin R.		
FANNING, of Chatham, Aug. 29, 1836, by		
Rev. Alvan Ackley	4	66
Noah, of East Haddam, m. Eliza **BROWN**, Sept. 12,		
1827, by Robert Bowzer, Pastor	4	33
Sally, d. [Caleb & Anna, of East Haddam], b. Oct. 3,		
1802	3	182
GATT, Chauncey, m. Fanny **FRANCIS**, b. of New		
London, May 11, 1846, by Rev. John Howson	4	126
GEE, W[illia]m, Jr., of Lyme, m. Delight **TINKER**, of		
Lemster, N.H., Mar. 9, 1834, by Chester Tilden	4	54
GENT, John William, m. Sarah Ann **DOUGLASS**, b. of		
New London, June 7, 1825, by Rev. B. Judd	4	23
GERE, GEARES, GEER, George, m. Sarah, d. Rob[er]t		
ALLEN, Feb. 17, [1658]	1	3
Jonathan, s. George & Sarah, b. May 26, [1662]		
*(First written "Jonathan **GRAVES**")	1	3
Jonathan Joseph, see Jonathan Joseph **GRAVES**		
Oliver, m. Lucinda **BEEBE**, b. of Norwich, Mar. 11,		
1829, by Rev. Abel McEwen	4	36
Robert, s. George & Sarah, b. Jan. 2, [1675]		
*(Originally written "**GRAVES**")	1	10
Sarah, d. Sarah & George, b. Feb. 27, [1659]	1	3
GERISH, Samuel, [see under **SEWALL**, Stephen]		
GESTIN, Betsey, m. Hugh **HENRY**, b. of New London,		
Nov. 12, 1796, by Andrew Griswold, J.P.	2	124
GETCHEL, GETCHELL, GETCHER, Abigail, m.		
Warren G. **WATROUS**, b. of New London,		
Sept. 17, 1832, by Rev. Abel McEwen	4	47
Elizabeth, m. Mark W. **SMITH**, Sept. 10, 1835, by		
Rev. Alven Ackley	4	62
Isabella, of Salem, m. David S. **CHASE**, of New		
Bedford, May 22, 1844, by Rev. G. Thompson	4	112
Lester, of New London, m. Mary **GETCHEL**, of		
Montville, June 6, 1852, by Rev. Jabez S. Swan	4	173
Mary, of Montville, m. Lester **GETCHEL**, of New		
London, June 6, 1852, by Rev. Jabez S. Swan	4	173
Rebecca, m. Daniel H. **CHAPMAN**, b. of New		
London, Aug. 22, 1852, by Rev. Jabez S. Swan	4	174

	Vol.	Page

GETCHEL, GETCHELL, GETCHER (cont.)
Sarah Ann, of Waterford, m. George H.
    WILLIAMS, of Saybrook, Apr. 1, 1844, by
    Rev. G. Thompson — 4 — 111
GETHCER, George, m. Amy **DANIELS**, b. of
    Waterford, July 1, 1832, by Th[omas] S.
    Perkins, J.P. — 4 — 47
GIBBONS, John, Capt. of Island of St. Croix, m. Esther
    RICHARDS, of New London, Jan. 31, 1781,
    by Timo[thy] Green, J.P. — 3 — 80
John William, s. Capt. John & Esther, b. Nov. 19,
    1781 — 3 — 80
GIBSON, [see also **GIPSON**], Ann L., d. Sylvanus H. &
    Mary Ann, b. Apr. 23, 1842 — 3 — 302
George, s. Roger & Love, b. Sept. 21, 1757 — 3 — 10
Hannah, d. Roger & Love, b. Mar. 8, 1759 — 3 — 10
Love, d. [Roger & Love], b. Dec. 23, 1765 — 3 — 10
Love, w. Roger, d. Sept. 16, 1787 — 3 — 10
Roger, s. William, of Edinburgh, North Britain,
    Notary Public, & Margaret, m. Love
    MANWARING, d. Richard, of New London &
    Elenor, Feb. [ ], 1754 — 3 — 10
Sylavnus H., m. Mary Ann **BOLLES**, July 14, 1840 — 3 — 302
Sylvanus H., m. Mary Ann **BOLLES**, b. of [New
    London], July 14, 1840, by Rev. Abel McEwen — 4 — 91
GIFFORD, Charles, m. Abby Ann **KINGSLEY**, b. of
    New London, Feb. 26, 1843, by L. Covell — 4 — 101
Rodolphus A., m. Elizabeth **CARROLL**, b. of N[ew]
    London, Mar. 20, 1836, by Rev. Squire B.
    Hascall — 4 — 83
Surviah, d. Justice **GIFFORD**, m. William
    MANWARING, Sept. 9, 1798 — 3 — 221
Warren, of New York, m. Lucy Ann **HARRIS**, of
    New London, Oct. 15, 1827, by Henry
    Wightman — 4 — 32
GILBERT, GILBERTS, Ann, d. Philip & Abigail, b. Feb.
    17, 1728/9 — 2 — 30
Edward, m. Emma **FOWLER**, Oct. 6, 1850, by Rev.
    Charles Willet — 4 — 155
Erastus, of South Lyme, m. Francess **CRANDALL**,
    of New London, July 1, 1852, by Rev. Edward
    R. Warren — 4 — 171
Francis, of Meriden, m. Lydia **HOWARD**, of
    Waterford, Nov. 8, 1846, by Rev. L. Geo[rge]
    Leonard — 4 — 129
Horace S., of Lyme, m. Harriet **MIDDLETON**, of
    N[ew] London, Sept. 8, 1833, by Rcv. Ebenezer
    Blake — 4 — 53
Marcy, m. Joseph **PRENTICE**, May 2, 1727 — 2 — 81
Mary, m. John S. **SMITH**, Nov. 14, 1838, by Rev.
    Abraham Holway — 4 — 85

	Vol.	Page
GILBERT, GILBERTS (cont.)		
Patience, d. Sylvester, of Hebron, m. Reuben		
LANGDON, Sept. 18, 1803	3	199
GILDERSLEEVE, Thomas, of Coldspring, N.Y., m.		
Maria L. **SHARON**, of New London, Mar. 3,		
1846, by Rev. S. Benton	4	125
GILLETT, [see also **JILLET**], Anson, of Hebron, m.		
Anna **PEASE**, of [New London], Nov. 18,		
1849, by Rev. Abel McEwen	4	151
Paulina Louisa, of [New London], m. Philip		
BRIGGS, of Colchester, Sept. 4, 1848, by Rev.		
T. Edwards	4	141
GILSON, Mary, m. James **NORRIS**, b. of New London,		
Oct. 3, 1836, by Rev. Squire B. Hascall	4	68
GIPSON, [see also **GIBSON**], Elizabeth, m. Samuell		
HARRIS, Aug. 5, 1687	1	19
GLASS, William, m. Harriet **LATHROP**, Apr. 7, 1839,		
by Rev. Abraham Holway	4	65
GLEASON, Charlotte F., of Manchester, Ct., m. Orrin		
DARROW, of [New London], June 27, 1847,		
by Rev. L. Geo[rge] Leonard	4	132
GLOVER, Elizabeth A., m. Charles S. **CLINTON**, b. of		
[New London], Nov. 29, 1846, by John		
Howson	4	130
GODDARD, Charlotte, m. James S. **WILLIAMS**, Jan. 12,		
1840, by James M. Macdonald	4	88
Eben Henfield, s. [Ebenezer, Jr. & Charlotte], b. Mar.		
5, 1809	3	233
Ebenezer, s. Ebenezer, b. Dec. 7, 1757; m. Lydia		
HURLBUT, [d. Daniel], Sept. 18, 1782	3	154
Ebenezer, s. [Ebenezer & Lydia], b. Sept. 2, 1783	3	154
Ebenezer, Jr., m. Charlotte **TREBY**, d. Isaac, Oct.		
12, 1806	3	198
Ebenezer, Jr., m. Charlotte **TRIBBY**, d. Isaac, Oct.		
12, 1806	3	233
Eben[eze]r Henfield, s. [Ebenezer, Jr. & Charlotte],		
b. Mar. 5, 1809	3	198
Elizabeth, d. [Ebenezer & Lydia], b. Feb. 27, 1793	3	154
Frances, m. Lee L. **FORSYTH**, b. of New London,		
Apr. 4, 1824, by Rev. B. Judd	4	18
Frances Mary Hurlbut, d. [Ebenezer & Lydia], b. July		
11, 1806	3	154
George, s. [Ebenezer & Lydia], b. June 18, 1788; d.		
June 25, 1795	3	154
George Henry, s. [Ebenezer & Lydia], b. June 4,		
1795; d. July 10, 1797	3	154
Isaac Treby, s. [Ebenezer, Jr. & Charlotte], b. Sept.		
21, 1807	3	198
Isaac Tribby, s. [Ebenezer, Jr. & Charlotte], b. Sept.		
21, 1807	3	233
James Edward, s. Hezekiah [& Eunice], b. June 14,		
1817	3	119

	Vol.	Page

GODDARD (cont.)

Jeremiah H., m. Sarah B. **FULTON**, b. of New
London, Jan. 30, 1825, by Rev. B. Judd — 4 — 2

Jeremiah H., m. Lydia C. **BROOKS**, b. of New
London, Feb. 26, 1832, by Rev. Abel McEwen — 4 — 45

Jeremiah H., m. Amelia **TOY**, [, 1851], by
Rev. Robert A. Hallam — 4 — 167

John Calvin, s. Hez[ekia]h & Eunice, b. Feb. 3, 1815 — 3 — 119

Joseph, s. [Ebenezer & Lydia], b. July 18, 1797 — 3 — 154

Levi H., of Mariet[t]a, Ohio, m. Mary W. **PERKINS**,
of [New London], May 12, 1835, by Rev. Abel
McEwen — 4 — 61

Lydia, d. [Ebenezer & Lydia], b. Nov. 21, 1790 — 3 — 154

Lydia, m. Joseph H. **HENFIELD**, of Salem, Dec. 24,
1809 — 3 — 239

Mary, d. Capt. Nathan **DOUGLASS**, m. John
FRENCH, Apr. 8, 1794 — 3 — 149

Paulina, m. John **MASON**, 2d, b. of New London,
June 28, 1824, by Rev. Abel McEwen — 4 — 19

Polly, b. May 15, 1759; m. John **THOMPSON**, Nov.
11, 1779 — 3 — 132

Thomas, s. [Ebenezer & Lydia], b. Sept. 28, 1785; d.
Oct. 25, 1797 — 3 — 154

Thomas Henry, m. Mary **DOUGLASS**, Feb. 22,
1786 — 3 — 90

Thomas Henry, s. [Thomas Henry & Mary], b. Mar.
16, 1787 — 3 — 90

William, s. [Ebenezer & Lydia], b. Jan. 3, 1800 — 3 — 154

GODFREY, Benjamin, s. [Reuben & Betsey], b. Dec. 10,
1781 — 3 — 140

Jennettee, d. [Reuben & Betsey], b. Apr. 16, 1785 — 3 — 140

Mary, of Cape Cod, m. Thomas **HAMPTON**, of
North Carolina, August, [ ], 1774, in Nantucket — 3 — 120

Polly, d. [Reuben & Betsey], b. Oct. 21, 1777 — 3 — 140

Reuben, m. Betsey **BULLFINCH**, Nov. 11, 1776 — 3 — 140

Reuben, s. [Reuben & Betsey], b. Oct. 10, [ ] — 3 — 140

William, s. [Reuben & Betsey], b. Apr. 16, 1791 — 3 — 140

GOFF, [see also **GOUGH**], Catharine, m. Alexander
CHRISTIE, b. of [New London], Apr. 2, 1845,
by Rev. Abel McEwen — 4 — 118

Ephraim, of Wethersfield, m. Lucy, d. Stephen &
Lucy **POTTER**, of New London, Sept. 25,
1757 — 2 — 30

Laura P., m. Andrew J. **HOBRON**, b. of New
London, Sept. 5, 1852, by Rev. Jabez S. Swan — 4 — 175

Naomy, m. Samuel **WESTCOTE**, May [ ], 17[ ] — 2 — 117

Phoebe M., of New London, m. Charles W.
MORGAN, of Poughkeepsie, N.Y., May 6,
1843, by Rev. R. W. Allen — 4 — 117

GOOD, Abby, d. [William & Abigail], b. July 4, 1794 — 3 — 131

Abby, d. [William & Abigail], b. July 4, 1794 — 3 — 133

	Vol.	Page
GOOD (cont.)		
Edward Latham, s. [William & Abigail], b. July 8, 1788	3	133
Joseph Cambri[d]ge, s. [William & Abigail], b. June 11, 1798	3	133
Lavina, d. [William & Abigail], b. Aug. 10, 1792	3	133
Lavinia, d. William & Abigail, b. Aug. 20, 1792	3	131
William, m. Abigail **LATHAM**, d. Capt. Edward Latham, of Groton, June 24, 1787	3	133
William Whiting, s. [William & Abigail], b. June 22, 1796	3	131
William Whiting, s. [William & Abigail], b. June 22, 1796	3	133
GOODFAITH, David, m. Phebe **DATON**, Mar. 5, 1786	3	115
James, s. [David & Phebe], b. Apr. 14, 1787	3	115
GOODING, Sophia, m. Archibald **HALL**, b. of New London, Apr. 12, 1835, by Rev. Hiram Walden	4	60
GOODRICH, GOORICH, Ellen, m. Charles **SMITH**, Apr. 7, 1849, by Rev. Charles Willett	4	145
Henry, m. Ursula H. **FENGARR**, June 20, 1852, by Rev. Charles Willett	4	168
GOODWIN, Abby Ann, d. [Robert & Eunice], b. Apr. 25, 1816	3	196
Abby Frances, of New London, m. William **ELLIS**, of Plymouth, England, Mar. 17, 1833, by Rev. Abel McEwen	4	51
Eleanor, d. [Robert & Eunice], b. Feb. 27, 1820	3	196
Eunice, m. James M. **PERKINS**, b. of New London, June 2, 1851, by Rev. Jabez S. Swan	4	164
Lydia, d. [Robert & Eunice], b. Feb. 1, 1818	3	196
Robert, of Dresden, Maine, m. Eunice **JEFFERY**, July 23, 1815	3	196
Robert, m. Alvira D. **BARKER**, b. of New London, Mar. 2, 1851, by Rev. Jabez S. Swan	4	163
GOONY, Richard, m. Hannah **COONY**, Sept. 21, [18]50, [by Peter J. Blenkinsop]. Witnesses: Timothy Maxwell, Catharine Igo	3	306
Richard, m. Hannah **COONY**, Sept. 21, 1850. Witnesses: Timothy Maxwell, Catharine Igo	4	159
GORDON, GORDINS, [see also **GORTON**], Abram, m. Betsey **GORHAM**, b. of New London, Aug. 23, 1832, by Chester Tildon	4	49
Austin Rob[b]ins, s. [John & Lucy], b. Feb. 8, 1798	3	72
Car[o]line, d. [John & Lucy], b. July 2, 1801; d. Sept. 10, 1802	3	72
Charles, s. [John & Lucy], b. Dec. 5, 1785	3	72
Frank, s. [John & Lucy], b. Aug. 15, 1793	3	72
Gennet, d. John, m. Daniel **KEENEY**, 3d, Jan. 1, 1804	3	188
George, s. [John & Lucy], b. Dec. 10, 1787	3	72
George, s. [John & Experience], b. June* 7, 1788 *(First written "July")	3	239

	Vol.	Page
GORDON, GORDINS (cont.)		
Henry, s. [John & Lucy], b. Sept. 19, 1791	3	72
Jane, d. [John & Experience], b. Apr. 26, 1786, in Norwich	3	239
Jennet, see under Gennet		
John, b. Apr. 28, 1759; of New London, m. Lucy **ROBBINS**, of Wethersfield, Apr. 4 ,1782	3	72
John, s. Ann **LATIMER**, b. Apr. 28, 1759	3	81
John, s. [John & Lucy], b. Jan. 7, 1784	3	72
John, m. Experiance **YOUNG**, relict of William Young, [ ]	3	239
Lucey, d. [John & Lucy], b. Dec. 13, 1795	3	72
Nancy, d. [John & Lucy], b. Oct. 26, 1782; d. Mar. 20, 1783	3	72
Nancey, d. [John & Lucy], b. Feb. 2, 1789; d. Sept. 2, 1789	3	72
Prudence M., of [New London], m. Nelson **STERRY**, of Groton, Mar. 29, 1836, by Rev. Abel McEwen	4	65
GORHAM, Betsey, m. Abram **GORDON**, b. of New London, Aug. 23, 1832, by Chester Tilden	4	49
Charles M., m. Sarah S. **HOLT**, b. of [New London], Apr. 19, 1852, by Rev. Tryon Edwards	4	167
GORMAN, James F., of St. Johns, New Brunswick, N.S., m. Sarah Ann **BARROW**, of New London, Feb. 9, 1845, by Rev. S. Benton	4	117
GORMAS, John, m. Lucinda **JEROME**, b. of [New London], Feb. 9, 1849, by Rev. Abel McEwen	4	145
GORTON, [see also **GORDON**], Almira, m. Samuel C. **BECKWITH**, Sept. 25, 1834, by Rev. Francis Darrow	4	57
Benjamin, m. Mehetable **DOUGLASS**, Sept. 28, 1769	3	75
Fanny, d. [Benjamin & Mehetable], b. Feb. 25, 1789	3	75
John, s. William, late of New London, decd., m. Mary **MANWARING**, d. Oliver, of New London, Feb. 2, 1764	3	29
Lydia, d. John & Mary, b. June 5, 1765	3	29
Mary, m. Reuben **BEEBE**, Jan. 19, 1759	3	13
Mary, m. Jedidiah **CALKINS**, Apr. 26, 1763	3	29
Mehitabel, d. [Benjamin & Mehetable], b. Jan. 27, 1785	3	75
Richard, s. [Benjamin & Mehetable], b. Mar. 16, 1779	3	75
Robert, s. [Benjamin & Mehetable], b. Dec. 19, 1776	3	75
Sarah, d. William, late of New London, decd., m. Charles **BROWN**, s. Benjamin, of New London, Jan. 4, 1770	3	50
Sarah, d. [Benjamin & Mehetable], b. Jan. 29, 1775	3	75
Stephen, Rev., b. Mar. 21, 1703/4	2	30
Thomas, s. [Benjamin & Mehetable], b. July 27, 1770	3	75

	Vol.	Page
GORTON (cont.)		
William, s. [Benjamin & Mehetable], b. July 22,		
1782	3	75
GOUGH, [see also **GOFF**], Ann, d. Alexander & Ann, b.		
Feb. 26, 1722	2	84
Ellen, m. Timothy **McLAUGHLIN**, Aug. 12, 1849,		
by Rev. William Logan	4	150
Rebeccah, d. Alexander & Ann, b. Apr. 17, 1725	2	84
William, s. Alexander & Ann, b. Sept. 28, 1726	2	84
GOVE, Sarah, m. Nathan **MINER**, May 22, 1786	3	181
GRACE, Abigaile, d. [Walter & Abigaiel], b. Feb. 19,		
1807	3	174
Charles, m. Pamelia **LESTER**, of New London, May		
20, 1823, by Thomas W. Tucker, Elder	4	14
Elizabeth Y., m. Charles **BECKWITH**, b. of New		
London, Dec. 1, 1850, by Rev. Jabez S. Swan	4	157
Emeline, d. [John & Emeline], b. Dec. 1, 1828	3	155
Emeline, w. John, d. [ ]	3	155
George M., m. Lucretia G. **MILLER**, b. of New		
London, June 24, 1830, by Rev. Abel McEwen	4	38
John, s. [Walter & Abigaiel], b. Mar. 27, 1803	3	174
John, m. Emeline **CHIPMAN**, June 13, 1827*		
*(First written 1727)	3	155
John, m. Emeline **CHIPMAN**, b. of New London,		
June 13, 1827, by Rob[er]t Bowzer	4	31
John, s. [John & Emeline], b. Jan. 21, 1831	3	155
John, m. Hiluh Ann **BELDEN**, Dec. 22, 1834	3	155
John, m .Hilah Ann **BELDEN**, b. of [New London],		
Dec. 22, 1834, by Rev. Abel McEwen	4	59
Lucretia, of New London, m. W[illia]m		
WILLIAMS, of New York, Apr. 20, 1845, by		
Rev. John Blain	4	119
Mary Ann, d. [Walter & Abigaiel], b. Sept. 18, 1805	3	174
Thomas, s. [Walter & Abigaiel], b. Aug. 14, 1801	3	174
Walter, m. Abigaiel **BLACKLEY**, Aug. 31, 1800	3	174
William, s. [Walter & Abigaiel], b. July 19, 1804; d.		
July 14, 1806	3	174
William, s. [John & Emeline], b. Nov. 5, 1827; d.		
Sept. 10, 1828	3	155
GRAHAM, Mary, m. John **O'HARE**, Nov. 16, 1845, by		
Rev. John Brady	4	122
GRANT, Eleazer, m. Elisabeth **ELDRIDGE**, May 4, 1760	3	62
Elisabeth, d. [Eleazer & Elisabeth], b. Mar. 4, 1761	3	62
Elisabeth, m. Joseph **WEEKS**, Nov. 18, 1764	3	62
Elisabeth, m. John **THOMAS**, Feb. 18, 1786	3	18
Leonora, m. Albert W. **DAVIS**, of Norwich, Ct.,		
Mar. 8, 1842, by Rev. Edwin C. Brown	4	97
GRAVES, GREAVES, Elizabeth, m. Joseph **BEEBE**,		
Dec. 26, 1706	1	32
Elizabeth, d. of Thomas, of Lyme, m. John		
CROS[S]MAN, s. Bartholomew, of England,		
Apr. 2 ,1725	2	31

	Vol.	Page

GRAVES, GREAVES (cont.)

Elizabeth, d. Maboth & Irene, b. Nov. 13, 1738 — 2 — 31

Hannah, d. George & Sarah, b. Feb. 27, [1665] — 1 — 4

Isa[a]ck, s. George & Sarah, b. Mar. 26, [1681] — 1 — 15

Jane, d. George & Sarah, b. Jan. 6, [1679] — 1 — 14

Jonathan, s. George & Sarah, b. May 26, [1662]
("GERE" written in brackets) — 1 — 3

Jonathan Joseph, s. George & Sarah, b. Oct. 14,
[1664], at Nahantick ("Perhaps "GERE"?) — 1 — 4

Margaret, d. George & Sarah, b. Feb. [ ], 1669 — 1 — 6

Mary, d. George & Sarah, b. Mar. 26, [1671] — 1 — 8

Mary, m. Ebenezer **DANIELS**, Oct. 21, 1724 — 2 — 13

May, d. Naboth & Irene, b. Sept. 10, 1729 — 2 — 30

Naboth, m. Irene **PRENTICE**, May 13, 1725 — 2 — 30

Rebecka, m. Jonathan **DANNIELLS**, Dec. 12, 1706 — 1 — 32

Robert, s. George & Sarah, b. Jan. 2, [1675]
("GERE" written in margin) — 1 — 10

GRAY, GREY, Abby H., m. George W. **CORNELL**, b.
of New London, May 20, 1844, by Rev.
Tho[ma]s J. Greenwood — 4 — 111

Emeline, of [New London], m. George **SWEET**,
(Not American), Aug. 25, 1844, by Rev.
George Thompson — 4 — 113

Harriet, of New London, m. Henry W.
WASHBURN, of Sag Harbor, Apr. 6, 1851, by
Rev. James W. Dennis — 4 — 162

Jerusha T., m. Charles M. **DABOLL**, b. of New
London, July 2, 1846, by Rev. Tho[ma]s J.
Greenwood — 4 — 127

John B., m. Lucretia **LANPHERE**, May 6, 1847, by
Rev. Charles Willett — 4 — 146

Lydia, m. Joseph **MILLER**, [ ], 1803 — 3 — 170

Mary, d. Ebenezer & Mary, of Newport, m. Russell
HUBBARD, s. Daniel & Martha, Jan. 30, 1755 — 2 — 26

Samuel, of Boston, m. Lucy **PALMER**, Apr. 2, 1707 — 1 — 32

Susannah, m. John **RICHARDS**, s. John & Ann, July
7, 1765 — 3 — 108

GREEN, GREENE, Abby Ann, m. John P.
HEMPSTEAD, b. of [New London], June 19,
1844, by Rev. Abel McEwen — 4 — 112

Abigail, d. Samuel & Abigail, b. Aug. 9, 1734 — 2 — 30

Abigail, d. Samuel, of New London, m. James
PITMAN, formerly of Rhode Island, Feb. 22,
1757 — 3 — 70

Alexander, s. Jonas & Jane, b. Jan. 13, 1702/3 — 1 — 27

Ann, d. Benjamin, m. John **ROGERS**, s. Samuel, all
of New London, Oct. 17, 1759 — 3 — 8

Ann W., d. Deac. Timothy, m. Stephen **PECK**, May
13, 1806 — 3 — 191

Anna, d. [Benjamin & Abigail], b. Mar. 5, 1783 — 3 — 108

Anne, d. Samuel & Abigail, b. Feb. 19, 1741/2 — 2 — 72

	Vol.	Page

GREEN, GREENE (cont.)

Anne, twin with John, [d. Timothy & Rebeckah], b.
June 12, 1779 — 3 — 23

Benjamin, m. Abigail **DODGE**, Jan. 11, 1775 — 3 — 108

Catharine, m. Noble **HINMAN**, Oct. 16, 1760
*(First written Catharine Hinman and crossed
out) — 3 — 5

Clifton, m. Sophia **NAIL**, b. of New London, May
14, 1837, by Rev. Nathan Wildman — 4 — 69

Daniel, m. Elisabeth **BARR**, Apr. 17, 1785 — 3 — 100

Delight, d. of Capt. Benjamin, of New London, m.
John **ROGERS**, of New London, s. John,
decd,. late of New London, who lived in
Mamecock, Jan. 2, 1755 — 2 — 95

Eliza, d. Samuel & Abigail, b. Nov. 23, 1738 — 2 — 31

Eliza Ann, m. William G. **BUSH**, b. of New London,
Mar. 14, 1832, by Rev. Abel McEwen — 4 — 45

Emily A., m. William **BABCOCK**, b. of [New
London], May 23, 1847, by Rev. L. Geo[rge]
Leonard — 4 — 131

Fanny, d. [Benjamin & Abigail], b. Sept. 9, 1796 — 3 — 108

Harriet, m. James **THOMPSON**, May 20, 1847, by
Rev. Robert A. Hallam — 4 — 131

Henry, [s. Timothy & Rebeckah], b. Feb. 9, 1782 — 3 — 23

Henry, of Nantucket, Mass., m. Esther J.
HEMPSTEAD, of [New London], July 31,
[1745], by Rev. John Howson — 4 — 121

Henry P., m. Lucy **ROGERS**, Sept. 10, 1823, by
Rev. Thomas W. Tucker — 4 — 19

Isaac, s. Jonas* & Jane, b. Jan. 9, [1695]   *(First
written Isaac. Corrected by L.B.B.) — 1 — 22

James*, m. Jane **PYGAN**, Mar. 29, [1694]
*(Corrected to "Jonas" by L.B.B.) — 1 — 22

James M., m. Mary **LYON**, b. of [New London],
June 8, 1847, by Rev. Abel McEwen — 4 — 132

Jane, twin with Joseph, d. Jonas & Jane, b. Sept. 28,
[1705] — 1 — 30

Jared Starr, s. [Samuel & Mary], b. May 27, 1804 — 3 — 162

John, s. Timothy & Mary, b. May 25, 1719 — 1 — 51

John, twin with Anne, [s. Timothy & Rebeckah], b.
June 12, 1779 — 3 — 23

Jonas*, m. Jane **PYGAN**, Mar. 29, [1694]   *(First
written James. Corrected by L. B. B.) — 1 — 22

Joseph, twin with Jane, s. Jonas & Jane, b. Sept. 28,
[1705] — 1 — 30

Joseph, [twin with Jane, s. Jonas & Jane], d. Nov. 7,
1705 — 1 — 31

Joseph, s. Lydia, b. Nov. 11, 1767 — 2 — 16

Judeth, of Hopkinton, m. David **ROGERS**, Sept. 12,
1771 — 2 — 86

Katharine, d. Nath[anie]l & Mary, b. June 5, 1740 — 2 — 57

Lucy, d. Samuel & Abigail, b. Apr. 22, 1740 — 2 — 31

	Vo;/	Page
GREEN, GREENE (cont.)		
Lydia, d. Jonas & Jane, b. May 1, 1714	1	45
Lydia, d. Nath[anie]l & Mary, b. Apr. 22, 1742	2	57
Lydia, m. Samuel **LATIMER**, Nov. 9, 1793	3	82
Margaret, d. Samuel & Abigail, b. Dec. 18, 1749	2	72
Margarett, d. [Benjamin & Abigail], b. July 27, 1779	3	108
Mary, d. Timothy & Mary, b. July 7, 1722	1	59
Mary, d. Samuel & Abigail, b. July 26, 1746	2	72
Mary, w. Dea. Timothy & dau. of Capt. John **FLINT**, of Concord, d. May 24, 1748, ae 68 y.	2	57
Mary, w. Nathaniel, d. May 11, 1754	2	57
Mary Augusta, of [New London], m. John **DECAMP**, of the U.S. Navy, Sept. 9, 1835, by Rev. Robert A. Hallam	4	62
Milla, m. Jonathan **ROGERS**, Oct. [ ], 1781	3	93
Nancy, d. [Daniel & Elisabeth], b. Sept. 24, 1786	3	100
Nath[anie]l, s. Dea. Timothy, of New London, m. Mary **CHRISTOPHERS**, wid. of Richard, 3rd, of New London, & dau. of John **PICKETT**, Jan. 17, 1738/9	2	57
Rebeckah, d. Timothy & Rebeckah, b. Apr. 30, 1773	3	23
Robert, m. Sarah A. **WINGROVE**, b. of New London, Feb. 12, 1851, by Rev. Edwin R. Warren	4	160
Robert Starr, s. [Samuel & Mary], b. Dec. 31, 1808	3	162
Sally Elizabeth, d. [Samuel & Mary], b. Dec. 10, 1806	3	162
Sally Field, w. S[amuel], d. Mar. 16, 1801	3	162
Samuell, s. Jonas & Jane, b. May 21, [1699]	1	25
Samuel, s. Timothy, m. Abigail **CLARKE**, d. of Rev. Thomas, late of Clemsford, Mass., Nov. 12, 1733	2	30
Samuel, s. Samuel & Abigail, b. Nov. 23, 1743	2	72
Samuel, s. [Benjamin & Abigail], b. Dec. 30, 1784	3	108
Samuel, s. Timothy & Rebecca, b. Feb. 28, 1768	3	23
Samuel, m. Sally Field **POOL**, d. Thomas Pool, Jan. 4, 1798	3	162
Samuel, m. Mary **STARR**, d. Jared, Feb. 14, 1803	3	162
Samuel, m. Mary Ann **CRANDALL**, Apr. 28, 1839, by Rev. Abraham Holway	4	85
Sarah, d. Jonas & Jane, b. Oct. 19, 1696, at Saybrook	1	22
Sarah, m. John **ADAMS**, June 15, 1716	1	49
Sarah, d. Lydia **GREEN**, alias **BUMP**, b. Dec. 10, 1762	2	16
Sarah, d. [Benjamin & Abigail], b. Sept. 2, 1777	3	108
Sarah, m. Zebulon **ROGERS**, Jan. 9, 1783	3	93
Stephen, s. [Benjamin & Abigail], b. Feb. 1, 1794	3	108
Thomas, s. Timothy & Mary, b. Jan. 31, 1715	1	46
Thomas, s. Samuel & Abigail, b. Aug. 25, 1735	2	30
Thomas A., m. Rebecca D. **BILL**, b. of Windham, Ct., Apr. 22, 1832, by Chester Tilden	4	46

	Vol.	Page
GREEN, GREENE (cont.)		
Thomas Clark, s. Timothy & Rebecca, b. May 14, 1765	3	23
Timothy, s. Samuel & Abigail, b. Apr. 2, 1737	2	31
Timothy, Dea., m. Abigail **HILL**, d. Capt. Charles, formerly of New London, decd., Mar. 26, 1749	2	57
Timothy, s. Sammuel, m. Rebecca **SPOONER**, d. Tho[ma]s, Jan. 2, 1763	3	23
Timothy, s. Timothy & Rebec[c]a, b. Sept. 23, 1763	3	23
Timothy F., of East Haddam, m. Sarah **RAYMOND**, of New London, Dec. 30, 1845, by Rev. Stephen A. Loper, of Hadlyme	4	129
William, s. Lydia, b. May 8, 1765	2	16
William, s. Timothy & Rebecca, b. Sept. 14, 1771	3	23
William Elliott, s. [William W. & Rebecca], b. Apr. 20, 1847	3	195
William Pool, s. [Samuel & Sally Field], b. Feb. 17, 1801	3	162
William [W.], b. [　　　　　], 1815; m. Rebecca **ELLIOTT**, Apr. 4, 1841, by Mr. Williams* *(Mr. Williams written in pencil)	3	195
GREENFIELD, James, s. Archibald, of Lyme, m. Elizabeth **RAYMOND**, d. Sands Raymond, of New London, Jan. 25, 1740/1	2	106
James, Capt. of New London, m. Eleonor **LESTER**, of East Lyme, Nov. 12, 1848, by Rev. L. G. Leonard	4	143
Janette C., m. Horace B. **BROCKWAY**, b. of Lyme, Nov. 21, 1847, by Rev. L. G. Leonard	4	138
Raymond, s. James & Elizabeth, b. Jan. 21, 1744/5	2	107
Sarah, d. James & Elizabeth, b. June 30, 1742	2	107
GREENLEAF, Hannah, d. of Rev. Daniel, of Boston, m. John **RICHARDS**, Jr., s. George, of New London, Oct. 30, 1738	2	51
GREETHURST, George, of England, m. Maria **COATS**, of [New London], Jan. 3, 1830, by Rev. Alvan Ackley	4	64
GREY, [see under **GRAY**]		
GRIFFING, GRIFFIN, Augustus S., of New York, m. Emeline **LESTER**, of [New London], Nov. 23, 1848, by Rev. Tryon Edwards	4	143
Betsey, d. [James & Hannah], b. Oct. 4, 1781	3	226
Betsey, m. Richard **SAVAGE**, June 14, 1800	3	132
Charlotte R., m. William **MONTGOMERY**, July 29, 1839, by James M. Macdonald	4	86
Christopher, m. Susan **DESHON**, d. Col. Richard Deshon, Apr. 25, 1795	3	178
Christopher, s. [John & Eliza], b. June 7, 1812	3	182
Ebenezer, m. Wid. Mary **HUBBLE**, Feb. 11, 1702/3	1	27
Eben[eze]r, s. John & Elizabeth, b. Mar. 19, 1732	2	78
Ebenezer, s. [John & Mary], b. Dec. 23, 1761; d. Jan. [　], 1761	3	11

	Vol.	Page

GRIFFING, GRIFFIN (cont.)

	Vol.	Page
Ebenezer, s. [John & Mary], b. Jan. 17, 1766	3	11
Ebenezer, s. [Joseph & Hannah], b. Feb. 18, 1794	3	115
Ebenezer, m. Mary Ann **HAYNES**, Oct. 12, 1828, by Rev. Daniel Wildman	4	35
Edward, m. Mary **BOYLE**, Sept. 23, 1849, by Rev. William Logan	4	150
Elizabeth, d. John & Elizabeth, b Sept. 10, 1729	2	78
Elisabeth, d. [John & Mary], b. June 17, 1753; d. Mar. [ ], 1755	3	11
Elisabeth, d. [John & Mary], b. Jan. 11, 1755	3	11
Elizabeth Starr, d. [John & Eliza], b. Mar. 15, 1807	3	182
Elizabeth Starr, m. Marcus Aurelius **STARR**, Aug. 24, 1829	3	267
Frances, [child of James & Hannah], b. Aug. 14, 1795	3	226
Frances M., b. Aug. 14, 1797; m. Joseph **MINER**, [s. Joseph], Sept. 7, 1817	3	215
Frederick William, s. [Christopher & Susan], b. Aug. 3, 1797	3	178
Hannah, d. [James & Hannah], b. July 7, 1783	3	226
Hannah, b. July 7, 1787; m. Jeremiah S[mith] **POTTS**, Jan. 1, 1803	3	215
Henry, of Branford, m. Esther **ROSE**, of New London, Apr. 4, 1830, by Rev. B. Judd	4	41
James, s. [John & Mary], b. July 31, 1751	3	11
Jeremiah, s. [John & Mary], b. Mar. 15, 1772; d. Aug. [ ], 1773	3	11
Jeremiah, s. James & Hannah, b. Oct. 30, 1773	3	226
John, s. Ebenezer & Mary, b. Nov. 14, 1703	1	29
John, m. Elizabeth **TRUEMAN**, June 8, 1725	2	30
John, s. Eben[eze]r, m. Elizabeth **TRUEMAN**, d. Joseph, b. of New London, June 8, 1725	2	78
John, s. John & Elizabeth, b. Nov. 8, 1726	2	30
John, s. John & Elizabeth, b. Nov. 8, 1726	2	78
John, m. Mary **ROGERS**, Aug. 22, 1750	3	11
John, [s. John & Mary], b. Nov. 2, 1759; d. Mar. [ ], 1780	3	11
John, s. [Peter & Nabby], b. May 14, 1802	3	125
John, m. Eliza **STARR**, d. Jonathan, Nov. 16, 1803	3	182
John, s. [John & Eliza], b. Oct. 28, 1804	3	182
Jonathan Starr, s. [John & Eliza], b. June 27, 1809	3	182
Joseph, s. John & Elizabeth, b. Sept. 12, 1740	2	79
Joseph, s. [John & Mary], b. Oct. 3, 1763	3	11
Joseph, s. [James & Hannah], b. June 23, 1786	3	226
Joseph, m. Hannah **CHELES**, Nov. 7, 1791	3	115
Joseph, d. Oct. 4, 1798	3	115
Leonard Beatty, s. [Peter & Nabby], b. Oct. 29, 1805	3	125
Lucretia, d. [John & Mary], b. Feb. 4, 1757	3	11
Lucretia, d. [James & Hannah], b. July 13, 1789	3	226
Lucretia, m. Joseph **MILLER**, July 1, 1806	3	170
Martha Howard, d. [Peter & Nabby], b. Feb. 4 ,1799	3	125

	Vol.	Page
GRIFFING, GRIFFIN (cont.)		
Mary, d. Ebenezer & Mary, b. Aug. 17, 1711	1	36
Mary, m. Nicholas **DARROW**, Dec. 9, 1731	2	14
Mary, d. John & Elizabeth, b. Apr. 29, 1735	2	78
Mary, d. [Christopher & Susan], b. Feb. 1, 1796; d.		
Sept. 18, 1796	3	178
Mary, d. [Peter & Nabby], b. Apr. 18, 1797	3	125
Nabby, d. [Peter & Nabby], b. June 9, 1794	3	125
Nabby, d. [Peter & Nabby], b. Oct. 29, 1807	3	125
Nancy, d. [Joseph & Hannah], b. June 3, 1797	3	115
Peter, s. Ebenezer & Mary, b. June 19, 1707	1	32
Peter, s. Ebenezer & Elizabeth*, d. Sept. 10, 1722		
*(Changed to "Mary" by L.B.B.)	1	59
Peter, s. [John & Mary], b. Aug. 5, 1769	3	11
Peter, s. John & Elizabeth, b. Mar. 27, 1738	2	78
Peter, m. Nabby **LEWIS**, Sept. 1, 1793	3	125
Peter, s. [Peter & Nabby], b. Dec. 15, 1803	3	125
Polly, m. Isaac **ROGERS**, Apr. 13, 1786	3	82
Polly, d. [Joseph & Hannah], b. Oct. 27, 1792	3	115
Samuel, s. Ebenezer & Mary, b. June 9, 1705	1	31
Samuel, m. Ann **AVERY**, Nov. 16, 1727	2	30
Samuel, s. Sam[ue]l & Ann, b. Sept. 27, 1728	2	30
Susan, d. [Christopher & Susan], b. Feb. 22, 1799	3	178
Susan, d. Christo[pher], m. Thomas P. **TROTT**, Dec.		
24, 1823	3	265
Susan, m. Thomas **TROTT**, b. of New London, Dec.		
24, 1823, by Rev. Abel McEwen	4	17
Thomas, s. Ebenezer & Mary, b. June 8, 1705	1	30
Thomas, s. Samuel & Ann, b. Nov. 27, 1730	2	30
William, s. John & Elizabeth, b. Dec. 12, 1743	2	79
GRIMES, Deborah, of Wethersfield, m. Thomas		
STUBBINS, of New London, May 2, 1727	2	9
Deborah, m. Thomas **STUBBENS**, May 2, 1727	2	104
GRISWOLD, Charles, of Lyme, m. Ellen E. **PERKINS**,		
of New London, Nov. 15, 1820, by Rev. Abel		
McEwen	4	3
Deborah, m. Robert **DENISON**, Oct. 19, 1721	2	12
Elizabeth, d. Mat[t]hew, of Lyme, m. John		
ROGERS, s. James, Oct. 17, [1670], by		
W[illia]m Griswold, Com.	1	7
Elizabeth, d. Deac. John, of Lyme, m. Jacob B.		
GURLEY, Mar. 28, 1802	3	207
Eunice, of Lyme, d. Rev. George, m. Ebenezer		
WEEKS, of New London, s. Eben[eze]r, of		
Pomfret, Feb. 2, 1764	3	29
Lucretia, d. Rev. George, of Lyme, m. Jonathan		
LAT[T]IMORE, Jr., s. Capt. Jona[than], of		
New London, Jan. 28, 1747/8	2	61
Martha, d. Andrew, of Lyme, m. Elisha **WATERUS**,		
Dec. 5, 1795	3	213

	Vol.	Page
GRISWOLD (cont.)		
Mary, of Lyme, m. Josiah **DOUGLASS**, of New London, Aug. 20, 1798, in Lyme, by Andrew Griswold, J.P.	2	124
Rhodilla, of Norwich, m. Libbeus **HORTON**, of New London, May 7, 1778, by Rev. Andrew Lee, of Norwich	3	62
GROSS, Asahel, m. Abby **TRIBBY**, d. Isaac, July 16, 1804	3	231
GROSVENOR, Samuel H., of Norwich, m. Ursula W. **NOYES**, of [New London], Mar. 9, 1848, by Rev. Abel McEwen	4	138
GUARD, Daniel, of Groton, m. Mary Ann **PACKER**, Jan. 4, 1829, by Rev. Samuel West	4	35
Mary E., m. Dewitt C. **REED**, b. of New London, Aug. 1, 1847, by Rev. Jabez S. Swan	4	133
GUARTER, Frank, m. Harriet **JOHNSON**, b. of New London, July 16, 1845, by Rev. Jabez S. Swan	4	120
GUILBERT, [see under **GILBERT**]		
GUION, Thomas Durfey, s. Thomas & Rebecca, b. May 18, 1787	3	115
GURLEY, Charles, s. [Jacob B. & Elizabeth], b. June 4, 1808	3	207
Charles A., m. Ellen **GURLEY**, d. Jacob B., Oct. 22, 1851	3	298
Charles A., of New York, m. Ellen **GURLEY**, of [New London], Oct. 22, 1851, by Rev. Abel McEwen	4	165
Elizabeth, d. [Jacob B. & Elizabeth], b. May 29, 1810	3	207
Ellen, d. Jacob B., m. Charles A. **GURLEY**, Oct. 22, 1851	3	298
Ellen, of [New London], m. Charles A. **GURLEY**, of New York, Oct. 22, 1851, by Rev. Abel McEwen	4	165
Hannah, d. Jacob B. & Elizabeth, b. Apr. 10, 1814	3	207
Jacob B., m Elizabeth **GRISWOLD**, d. Deac. John, of Lyme, Mar. 28, 1802	3	207
John Griswold, s. [Charles A. & Ellen], b. Feb. 20, 1853	3	298
Mary Brainard, d. [Jacob B. & Elizabeth], b. Sept. 11, 1806	3	207
Sally Griswold, d. [Jacob B. & Elizabeth], b. Nov. 28, 1804	3	207
Sarah G., of New London, m. Joseph **NOYES**, of Lyme, May 14, 1823, by Rev. Abel McEwen	4	13
Ursula Wolcott, d. [Jacob B. & Elizabeth], b. May 13, 1812	3	207
GURTUR (?), Maria, of New London, m. Robert **McDONALD**, of Scotland, June 6, 1844, by [Rev.] G. Thompson	4	112

	Vol.	Page
GUSTIN, Herman, of Pollard, Me., m. Louisa **LATHROP**, of [New London], July 29, 1846, by John Howson	4	130
GUY, Theresa, of Jamesborough, Ms., m. Joseph **DEE**, of Hartford, Nov. 18, 1847, by Rev. Jabez S. Swan	4	136
GUYER, Fred[eric]k W[illia]m, m. Mary S. **RICHARDS**, b. of New London, Apr. 25, 1824, by Rev. B. Judd	4	18
HACK, Elijah, s. William & Susannah, b. Dec. 20, 1731	2	38
John, s. William & Susannah, b. Mar. 19, 1729/30	2	38
Mary, d. William & Susannah, b. Mar. 13, 1733/4	2	40
William, s. William & Susannah, b. Apr. 1, 1728	2	37
HACKER, Henrietta, m. Samuel **MONDAY**, b. of N[ew] London, Mar. 19, 1834, by Rev. Abel McEwen	4	55
HACKLEY, Elizabeth, d. Peter & Elizabeth, b. Feb. 1, 1709	1	42
George, s. Peter & Elizabeth, b. Aug. 13, 1719	1	59
Johanna, d. Peter & Elizabeth, b. Apr. 3, 1703	1	29
Joan[n]ah, d. Peter & Elizabeth, b. Apr. 3, 1703	1	42
Joannah, m. Thomas **CROCKER**, Jr., June 22, 1721	2	7
Joanna, d. of Peter, m. Thomas **CROCKER**, Jr., s. Thomas, June 22, 1721	2	21
Marshall, s. Peter & Elizabeth, b. Oct. 21, 1715	1	46
Peter, m. Lydia **DARROW**, Aug. 3, 1708	1	33
Richard, s. Peter & Elizabeth, b. Apr. 14, 1711	1	42
Sarah, d. Peter, b. Sept. 2, 1713	1	42
HADLEY, James B., of New York, m. Lucy Ann **PHILIPS**, of New London, Nov. 27, 1844, by Rev. Jabez S. Swan	4	114
HADLOCK, Lydia, m. Job **DART**, Dec. 2, 1787	3	2
HAGAN, Henry, m. Mercy **PERRY**, b. of New London, Jan. 19, 1846, by Frederick M. Walker, J.P.	4	124
HAGERMAN, Charlotte C., of [New London], m. John **COMSTOCK**, of New York, July 26, 1849, by Rev. Jabez S. Swan	4	147
HAGGERMOND, John G., of Brooklin, N.Y., m. Charlotte O. **ROGERS**, of [New London], Nov. 22, 1840, by H. R. Knapp	4	93
HAINES, HAYNES, HAINS, Abigail, d. [James & Phebe], b. Apr. 3, 1772	3	37
Abigail, d. James, m. Samuel **BUNNELL**, Feb. [ ], 1754	3	14
Ann, d. Jonathan & Elizabeth, b. Dec. [ ], 1722	2	40
Betsey, d. Eliphalet, b. Feb. 1, 1780; m. John **HARRIS**, 3d, Apr. 1, 1798	3	96
Betsey Ingham, m. James Fitch **SHEPARD**, Jan. 6, 1833	3	147
Charles, s. Charles & Mary, b. Sept. 25, [1669]	1	6
Charles, s. Jonathan & Sarah, b. Apr. 10, 1705	1	51
Charles, s. Jonathan, m. Lydia **TABOR**, d. Philip, Apr. 3, 1728	2	16
Charles, m. Lydia **TABOR**, Apr. 3, 1728	2	37

	Vol.	Page
HAINES, HAYNES, HAINS (cont.)		
Charles, s. Charles & Lydia, b. Jan. 22, 1738/9	2	17
Charlotte E., m. James **STEBBINS**, b. of New		
London, Apr. 17, 1834, by Chester Tilden	4	56
Edmond, s. Jonathan & Sarah, b. May 20, 1719	1	51
Edmond, s. Jonathan & Sarah, b. May 24, 1719	2	40
Ele[a]nor, d. Jonathan & Sarah, b. Dec. 16, 1724	2	40
Eleanor, d. Jona[than], late of New London, decd., m.		
Pain **TURNER**, s. Jonathan, of New London,		
Nov. 3, 1745	3	10
Elizabeth, d. Jonathan & Sarah, b. Apr. 1, 1703	1	51
Elizabeth, d. Charles & Lydia, b. Dec. 18, 1731	2	16
Elizabeth, d. Charles, late of New London, decd., m.		
John **TURNER**, of New London, s. Jonathan,		
decd., Nov. 4, 1750	2	99
Ellen P., of Lyme, m. Charles C. **VAIL**, of River		
Head, L.I., N.Y., Sept. 16, 1847, by Rev. L. G.		
Leonard	4	138
Gurdon, s. [James & Phebe], b. Nov. 20, 1779	3	37
Henry W., m. Mary A. **DeWOLFE**, July 3, 1839, by		
James M. Macdonald	4	86
Hercules, s. Charles & Mary, b. Apr. 27, [1681]	1	15
James, s. Charles & Mary, b. Mar. 1, [1664]	1	4
James, s. Jonathan & Sarah, b. Nov. 5, 1707	1	51
James, of New London, s. James, decd., m. Phebe		
CHAPPLE, of New London, d. George, Nov.		
30, 1767	3	37
James, s. James & Phebe, b. Sept. 14, 1770	3	37
James, Sr., d. Aug. 9, 1780	3	37
James, of Lyme, m. Mary A. **KNIGHT**, of New		
London, Feb. 15, 1852, by Rev. J. M. Eaton	4	167
John, s. Charles & Mary, b. June 29, [1674]	1	9
John, s. [James & Phebe], b. Feb. 1, 1774	3	37
Jonathan, s. Jonathan & Sarah, b. Aug. 30, 1699	1	51
Jonathan, s. Charles & Lydia, b. Mar. 7, 1728/9	2	16
Jonathan, s. Charles & Lydia, b. Mar. 7, 1728/9	2	37
Jonathan, s. Charles & Lydia, b. Nov. 12, 1736	2	17
Jonathan, s. Charles & Lydia, d. [ ]	2	17
Luce, d. Jonathan & Sarah, b. Aug. 28, 1710	1	51
Lucy, d. Jonathan, of New London, m. Stephen		
POTTER, s. Benj[ami]n, of Providence, Feb.		
22, 1730/1	2	25
Lucy, m. W[illia]m **STATES**, b. of [New London],		
Nov. 29, 1826, by Rev. Newel S. Spaulding	4	27
Lydia, d. Charles & Lydia, b. Aug. 16, 1751	2	17
Margaret, d. James & Margaret, b. Feb. 2, 1692	1	35
Mary, d. Charles & Mary, b. June 29, [1676]	1	11
Mary, d. Charles & Mary, b. Oct. 28, [1678]	1	13
Mary, d. James & Margaret, b. Aug. 21, 1689	1	35
Mary, d. Jonathan & Sarah, b. Aug. 28, 1701	1	51
Mary, m. William **PENDALL**, Sept. 8, 1712	1	39
Mary, d. Jonathan & Sarah, b. Oct. 8, 1721	2	40

	Vol.	Page
HAINES, HAYNES, HAINS (cont.)		
Mary Ann, m. Ebenezer **GRIFFING**, Oct. 12, 1828,		
by Rev. Daniel Wildman	4	35
Peter, s. Charles & Mary, b. Oct. 22, [1668]	1	6
Peter, s. James & Margaret, b. Mar. 9, 1695	1	35
Phebe, d. James & Phebe, b. Oct. 5, 1768	3	37
Phillip, s. Charles & Lydia, b. Mar. 4, 1733/4	2	17
Sarah, d. Jonathan & Sarah, b. Aug. 8, 1708	1	51
Sarah, d. [James & Phebe], b. Aug. 17, 1777	3	37
William, s. Jonathan & Sarah, b. Apr. 8, 1713	1	51
HAKES, [see under **HAWKES**]		
HALE, Dennis, of Norwich, m. Ann **RILEY**, of New		
London, Oct. 31, 1843, by Rev. Lemuel Covell	4	109
Mary, m. Anthony **SMITH**, b. of New London, Mar.		
27, 1846, by Rev. L. Geo[rge] Leonard	4	125
HALEY, HALLEY, Andrew N., s. [Thomas & Hellen], b.		
Apr. 1, 1843	3	289
Anne, d. William & Mary, b. Sept. 1, [1689]	1	19
Mary Ann, [d. Thomas & Hellen], b. June 9, 1833.		
"Their oldest"	3	289
Savillion, m. Maria F. **BALDWIN**, Oct. 6, 1833, by		
Daniel Wildman	4	52
Thomas, m. Hellen **MAHAN**, Oct. 31, 1831	3	289
HALL, Archibald, m. Sophia **GOODING**, b. of New		
London, Apr. 12, 1835, by Rev. Hiram Walden	4	60
Benja[min], s. Joshua & Hannah, b. Sept. 18, 1766	3	35
Daniell, m. Elizabeth **MAYHEW**, Apr. 24, 1716	1	45
David, s. [John & Susanna], b. Dec. 8, 1771	3	38
Desire, d. John & Susanna, b. Mar. 16, 1767	3	38
Esther, d. John & Susanna, b. Apr. 5, 1761	3	38
Florence, d. John & Susanna, b. Jan. 5, 1759/60	2	45
Hannah, d. John & Susanna, b. June 10, 1765	3	38
Hannah, m. Seaberry **FISH**, Sept. 9, 1787	3	7
James, m. Olive **WARNER**, Dec. 15, 1802	3	139
James, of Portsmouth, R.I., m. Mary E. **SMITH**, of		
New London, July 28, 1844, by Rev. Jabez S.		
Swan	4	113
John, of New London, s. David, of New Castle upon		
Lyne, Northumberland, m. Susannah **HOBBS**,		
of New London, d. John, formerly of Boston,		
late of New London, decd., Dec. 1, 1751	2	44
John, s. John & Susanna, b. Oct. 5, 1752	2	45
John, s. [John & Susana], b. Apr. 25, 1769	3	38
Margaret, m. Barachrah **FAIRBANKS**, b. of [New		
London], Nov. 12, 1834, by Daniel Huntington	4	60
Martha Ann, m. William P. **BARKER**, b. of New		
London, Dec. 30, 1832, by Chester Tilden	4	49
Mary, d. John & Susanna, b. Sept. 2, 1754	2	45
Mary, m. Jesse B. **CRUMB**, b. of Charleston, R.I.,		
Jan. 11, 1835, by Rev. Alven Ackley	4	59
Mary E., m. John W. **COCHRAN**, b. of New		
London, Oct. 27, 1851, by Rev. Jabez S. Swan	4	173

	Vol.	Page
HALL (cont.)		
Sarah, d. John & Susanna, b. Aug. 8, 1756	2	45
William, s. John & Susanna, b. Apr. 25, 1763	3	38
HALLADAY, Aaron, m. Mary **POWERS**, d. Joshua, Dec.		
25, 1804	3	217
Aaron, s. [Aaron & Mary], b. Feb. 6, 1806	3	217
David Reed, s. David, b. Oct. 16, 1800	3	217
Edward, of New York, m. Harriet **SIRLES**, of New		
London, Oct. 10, 1831, by Rev. Abel McEwen	4	44
Joshua Powers, s. [Aaron & Mary], b. May 9, 1808	3	217
Mary P., of N[ew] London, m. W[illia]m L. **PAINE**,		
Jr., of Lyme, Jan. 26, 1834, by Rev. D.		
Wildman	4	54
Nancy, m. Junies **APHIN***, b. of [New London],		
May 13, 1850, by Aaron E. Stone, J.P.		
*(Perhaps "**UPHIN**")	4	153
HALLAM, Abby Christophers, d. [Orlando & Lucy], b.		
July 30, 1811	3	192
Abigail Hortence, d. [John & Elisabeth], b. Sept. 13,		
1791	3	65
Alexander, s. Nicholas & Sarah, b. Oct. 27, [1688]	1	18
Amos, s. Edward & Grace, b. Mar. 14, 1725/6	2	36
Amos, of Groton, m. Sarah **DART**, of Waterford,		
Sept. 23, 1837, by Rev. Abel McEwen	4	73
Ann Boradell, d. Nicholas & Elizabeth, b. Dec. 10,		
1763	2	33
Caroline Mary, d. [Edward & Sarah], b. June 10,		
1806	3	194
Edward, s. Nicholas & Sarah, b. Apr. 25, 1692	1	21
Edw[ar]d, m. Grace **DENISON**, July 30, 1713	2	36
Edw[ar]d, s. Edward & Grace, b. Sept. 1, 1721	1	58
Edw[ar]d, s. Edw[ar]d & Grace, b. Sept. 1, 1721; d.		
June 11, 1726	2	36
Edw[ar]d, s. Edw[ar]d & Grace, d. June 11, 1726	2	36
Edw[ar]d, s. Edward &Grace, b. Feb. 17, 1727/8; d.		
Oct. [ ], 1728	2	37
Edward, d. Oct. 16, 1736	2	41
Edward, s. Nich[ola]s & Eliza[beth], b. Aug. 26,		
1750	2	33
Edward, s. Nicholas & Elisabeth, of New London, m.		
Mary **SAGE**, d. Comfort & Sarah, of		
Middletown, Jan 8, 1775, by Rev. Enoch		
Huntington, of Middletown	3	59
Edward, s. [John & Mary], b. Aug. 27, 1778	3	65
Edward, m. Sarah **JOHNSTON**, d. Capt. Samuel, of		
Middletown, Oct. 20, 1803	3	194
Eliza, d. John & Mary, b. Oct. 29, 1740; christened		
Nov. 2, 1740	2	32
Eliza Ann, of New London, m. Edward **BULL**, of		
Lebanon, Nov. 3, 1825, by Rev. Abel McEwen	4	24

	Vol.	Page

HALLAM (cont.)

Elizabeth, d. Nicholas & Elizabeth, b. Feb. 22,
1701/2, in the Parish of St. John, near Wapping,
London   1   33

Elisabeth, d. Nicholas, m. Samuel **LATIMER**, s.
Robert, b. of New London, [   ]. 1722   3   81

Elizabeth, d. Edw[ar]d & Grace, b. Apr. 18, 1732   2   38

Elizabeth, w. Nicholas, d. Mar. 14, 1735/6   2   40

Elizabeth, d. Nicholas & Elizabeth, b. May 10, 1759   2   33

Elisabeth, d. Nicholas, m. Charles **BULKLEY**, s.
Charles, decd., Dec. 14, 1779   3   66

Elizabeth, relict, of John, m. George **CHAPMAN**,
June 23, 1807   3   175

Elisabeth Ann, d. [John & Elisabeth], b. July 6, 1794   3   65

George, s. Nicholas & Elizabeth, b. Dec. 4, 1761   2   33

George, s. Nicholas & Grace, m. Abigail **COIT**, d.
Dr. Thomas & Abigail, Nov. 3, 1784   3   59

Grace, d. Edward & Grace, b. May 5, 1714; d. June
11, 1714   2   36

Grace, d. Nich[ola]s & Eliza[beth], b. Dec. 19, 1748;
d. Nov 12, 1751   2   33

Grace, d. Nich[ola]s & Eliza, b. Oct. 14, 1754   2   33

Grace, m. Amasa **LEARNED**, Apr 1, 1773   3   90

John, s. Nicholas & Elizabeth, b. Aug. 3, 1708   1   33

John, s. Edw[ar]d & Grace, b. Sept. 6, 1715   2   36

John, s. Edward & Grace, b. Sept. 6, 1715   1   45

John, of New London, s. Nicholas, decd., m. Mary
JOHNSON, of Newport, d. Isaac, of Newport,
decd., Dec. 30, 1730   2   31

John, s. John & Mary, b. Nov. 11, 1731; christened
the 22d of the same month by Mr. Seabury   2   31

John, s. Edw[ar]d & Grace, d. Oct. 8, 1736   2   41

John, d. June 14, 1745   2   32

John, s. Nich[ola]s & Eliza[beth], b. Oct. 7, 1752; d.
May 8, 1800   1   33

John, m. Mary **HARRISS**, d. Peter, Jr., decd., Dec.
25, 1777   3   65

John, s. [John & Mary], b. Feb. [ ], 1780; d. the 3rd
day   3   65

John, s. [John & Mary], b. May 1, 1781   3   65

John, m. Elisabeth **PRENTIS**, Oct. 2, 1785   3   65

John, had slave Fame **CONE**, d. Phillis & Ceaser
Cone, b. Feb. 28, 1789   3   128

John, d. May 7, 1800   3   65

Lucretia, d. Nicholas & Elizabeth, b. Aug. 2, 1766   2   33

Mary, d. Nicholas & Elizabeth, b. Oct. 11, 1705   1   33

Mary, m. Nathaniel **HEMPSTEAD**, July 18, 1723   2   38

Mary, d. John & Mary, b. June 1, 1737; christened
the 19th of the same month by Mr. Seabury   2   32

Mary, d. [John & Mary], b. Apr. 8, 1783   3   65

Mary, w. John d. Mar. 4, 1785, ae 23 y. 4m. 6d.   3   65

	Vol.	Page
HALLAM (cont.)		
Nancy, of [New London], m. Joshua **COIT**, of New		
London, Jan. 2, 1785, by Timo[thy] Green, J.P.	3	81
Nicholas, m. Sarah **PYGAM**, July 8, [1686]	1	18
Nicholas, m. Elizabeth **MEADES**, nee **JULLIVER**,		
Jan. 2, 1700, in Bramly Church, London	1	33
Nicholas, d. Sept. [ ], 1714	2	40
Nicholas, s. Edw[ar]d & Grace, b. Apr. 6, 1718	2	36
Nicholas, s. Eddw[ar]d, decd., m. Elizabeth		
LATTIMORE, d. Capt. Jona[than], all of New		
London, Jan. 21, 1747/8	2	33
Nicholas, s. [John & Elisabeth], b. May 8, 1789; d.		
Sept. 29, 1790	3	65
Orlando, s. [Robert & Lydia], b. Nov. 16, 1780	3	59
Orlando, m. Lucy **CHRISTOPHERS**, d. Peter, June		
22, 1806	3	192
Orlando Adams, s. [Orlando & Lucy], b. Oct. 28,		
1809	3	192
Prudence, d. John & Mary, b. Feb. 23, 1743/4	2	32
Robert, s. Nicholas & Elizabeth, b. Jan. 14, 1757	2	33
Robert, m. Lydia **ADAMS**, Sept. 17, 1779	3	59
Robert Alexander, s. [Orlando & Lucy], b. Sept. 30,		
1807	3	192
Sarah, d. Nicholas & Sarah, b. Mar. 29, [1695]	1	22
Sarah, m. Jonathan **STARR**, Oct. 18, 1770	3	84
HALLET, Lucy G., m. Gurdon B. **SMITH**, b. of New		
London, Sept. 10, 1843, by Jabez S. Swan	4	111
HALPIN, Doritha Manly, twin with Ebenezer Boon, d.		
James Peter & Margaret, b. Oct. 23, 1790	3	58
Ebenezer Boon, twin with Doritha Manly, s. James		
Peter & Margaret, b. Oct. 23, 1790	3	58
HAMBLETON, HAMBLTON, Ann, d. Jonas & Eliza, b.		
Dec. 6, 1731	2	39
Basheba, d. Jonathan & Ann, b. Dec. 1 ,1732	2	39
Daniel, s. Jonas & Eliza, b. Aug. 3, 1729	2	39
Eliza, d. Jonas & Eliza[beth], b. Nov. 13, 1716	2	39
James, s. Jonas & Eliza, b. Mar. 10, 1720	2	39
Jonas, m. Elizabeth **WICKWARE**, Sept. 9, 1708	1	33
Jonas, m. Elizabeth **WICKWARE**, Sept. 9, 1708	2	39
Jonathan, s. Jonas & Eliza[beth], b. June 17, 1709	2	39
Jonathan, m. Ann **CAMP**, May 2, 1732	2	39
Lucretia, d. Jonas & Eliza, b. Aug. 3, 1724	2	39
Mary, d. Jonas & Eliza[beth], b. May 30, 1714	2	39
Solomon, s. Jonas & Eliza[beth], b. Aug. 10, 1711	2	39
HAMBLEY, Sarah Ann, m. William H. **CRANDALL**, b.		
of [New London], Oct. 28, 1834, by Rev.		
Ebenezer Blake	4	58
HAMILTON, HAMELTON, Ann, d. [William & Ann],		
b. May 2, 1822	3	247
Ann, m. Lester S. **PHILLIPS**, Feb. 17, 1841, by H.		
R. Knapp	4	94

	Vol.	Page
HAMILTON, HAMELTON (cont.)		
Ann, m. Lester S. **PHILLIPS**, Feb. 17, 1841, by H.		
R. Knapp {Entire entry crossed out)	4	97
Benjamin, m. Charlotte **DART**, b. of [New London],		
Nov. 6, 1823, by Rev. Thomas W. Tucker	4	16
Elisha Lyman, s. [Joshua & Mary Ann], b. Dec. 13,		
1828	3	267
Elizabeth, d. [Joshua & Mary Ann], b. Aug. 22, 1836	3	267
Ellen, of New London, m. Jonathan **LATHAM**, of		
Groton, Sept. 15, 1852, by Rev. Charles Willett	4	174
Jane R., m. William W. **SMITH**, b. of [New		
London], Aug. 5, 1846, by Rev. Tryon Edwards	4	127
John, s. [Joseph & Rebeckah], b. Sept. 4, 1791	3	139
John, s. [Joshua & Mary Ann], b. Feb. 4, 1831	3	267
Joseph, late of East Grinwich, Kent county, R.I., m.		
Rebeckah **HEMPSTE[A]D**, d. Joshua, Oct. 23,		
1783	3	139
Joseph, s. [Joseph & Rebekcah], b. Aug. 1, 1784	3	139
Joshua, s. [Joseph & Rebekcah], b. Oct. 7, 1798	3	139
Joshua, m. Mary Ann **LYMAN**, Jan. 1, 1828	3	267
Joshua, m. Mary Ann **LYMAN**, Jan. 1, 1828, by		
Rev. Henry Wightman	4	38
Louisa, d. [Joshua & Mary Ann], b. Jan. 30, 1839	3	267
Mary, d. [Richard & Mary], b. Apr. 13, 1823	3	156
Richard, s. [Joseph & Rebeckah], b. Apr. 2, 1789	3	139
Richard, of New London, m. Mary **WILLIAMS**, of		
Stonington, July 3, 1822, by Rev. John G.		
Wightman, of Stonington	3	156
William, m. Mary **BILLINGS**, Oct. 19, 1783	2	121
William, s. [Joseph & Rebeckah], b. Apr. 2, 1795	3	139
William, m. Ann **STARK**, Feb. 8, 1820, by		
Nehemiah Dodge	3	247
William, s. [Joshua & Mary Ann], b. May 28, 1834	3	267
HAMLEY, George W., m. Fanny **HILL**, Apr. 23, 1839,		
by Rev. Abraham Holway	4	85
Sally Ann, m. John **WINGROVE**, b. of New		
London, July 4, 1841, by Rev. R. W. Allen	4	98
HAMLIN, Nancy, of New London, m. Landon **REEVE**,		
of Bromfield, Mass., Feb. 15, 1827, by Rev. B.		
Judd	4	29
HAMMELL, HAMMEL, Catharine, m. W[illia]m T.		
CROCKER, Feb. 19, 1843, by H. R. Knapp	4	104
Henrietta, d. Jacob & Regina, m. Charles **BAKER**,		
all of [New London], Sept. 27, 1847, by Rev. T.		
Edwards	4	134
John, m. Ann E. **WINSLOW**, b. of [New London],		
Aug. 29, 1852, by Rev. T. Edwards	4	171
HAMMOND, Anne, d. Noah & Anne, b. Oct. 13, 1739	2	46
Anne, w. Noah, d. June 17, 1755	2	46
Daniel, s. Noah & Anne, b. Feb. 18, 1752	2	46
Elisha, s. Noah & Anne, b. Sept. 22, 1746	2	46
Eunice, d. Noah & Anne, b. Dec. 30, 1740	2	46

	Vol.	Page
HAMMOND (cont.)		
Joshua, s. Noah & Anne, b. Jan. 1 ,1749/50	2	46
Lois, d. Noah & Anne, b. June 6, 1755	2	46
Noah, of New London, s. Isaac, of New London, m. Ann **BAKER**, d. Joshua, of New London, Nov. 9, 1738	2	46
Noah, s. Noah & Anne, b. July 14, 1743	2	46
HAMPTON, Thomas, of North Carolina, m. Mary **GODFREY**, of Cape Cod, August [ ], 1774, in Nantucket	3	120
Thomas, s. [Thomas & Mary], b. Aug. 31, 1777	3	120
HANCOCK, Ann, d. W[illia]m, of New London, m. Richard **POTTER**, from Exminster, Devonshire County, Great Britain, Feb. 14, 1777	3	69
Nancy, d. [Thomas & Rebeckah], b. Feb. 13, 1783	3	228
Nancy, d. Thomas, m. James **STEBBINS**, Oct. 12, 1800	3	228
Polly, d. [Thomas & Rebeckah], b. Sept. 9, 1786; d. Apr. 9, 1788	3	228
Rebeckah, d. [Thomas & Rebeckah], b. May 30, 1776	3	228
Sarah, d. [Thomas & Rebeckah], b. Feb. 1, 1781	3	228
Susanna, d. [Thomas & Rebeckah], b. July 10, 1787	3	228
Thomas, m. Rebeckah **LESTER**, d. Eliphalet, Aug. 20, 1775	3	228
Thomas, s. [Thomas & Rebeckah], b. May 16, 1779	3	228
William, s. [Thomas & Rebeckah], b. Mar. 16, 1790; d. Sept. 22, 1791	3	228
William, s. [Thomas & Rebeckah], b. July 30, 1794	3	228
HANDY, Carolina, d. [William & Abby], b. Aug. 1, 1800	3	163
Elizabeth, d. [William & Abby], b. Jan. 16, 1803	3	163
William, m. Abby **SALTONSTALL**, d. Roswell Saltonstall, June 23, 1799	3	163
HANLAN, William, m. Ann **LAMB**, Oct. 13, [18]50, [by Peter J. Blenkinsop]. Witnesses: Martin Noonan, Cath Maxwell	3	306
HARDING, Amy, d. Stephen, of Warwick, m. William **ANGELL**, s. James, of Warwick, Aug. 31, 1732	2	97
Amie, [d. Thomas & Mary], b. May 28, 1764	3	61
Avis, d. [Thomas, Jr. & Bethiah], b. Nov. 20, 1778	3	108
Charles, s. [Jeremiah & Lydia], b. Mar. 11, 1787	3	10
Charles W., m. Harriet **LATHAM**, b. of New London, Sept. 29, 1834, by Rev. Ebenezer Blake	4	57
Daniel, s. [Thomas & Mary], b. July 14, 1768	3	61
Delight, d. [Thomas & Mary], b. Oct. 2, 1757	3	61
James, s. [Thomas & Mary], b. Mar. 11, 1762	3	61
James, s. [Thomas, Jr. & Bethiah], b. Oct. 20, 1780	3	108
Jemima, d. [Thomas & Mary], b. May 8, 1766	3	61
Jeremiah, s. [Thomas & Mary], b. Dec. 22, 1759	3	61

	Vol.	Page
HARDING (cont.)		
Jeremiah, s. [Thomas, Jr. & Bethiah], b. Dec. 12, 1782	3	108
Jeremiah, m. Lydia **CHAPMAN**, Aug. 30, 1787	3	10
Jeremiah, m. Ethelinda **REED**, Mar. 30, 1828, by Rev. Rob[er]t Bowzer	4	35
Jesse, twin with Mary, [s. Thomas, Jr. & Bethiah], b. Aug. 5, 1786	3	108
Mary, twin with Jesse, [d. Thomas, Jr. & Bethiah], b. Aug. 5, 1786	3	108
Patty, twin with Sally, [d. Thomas, Jr. & Bethiah], b. Sept. 13, 1773	3	108
Russell, m. Abby **DOWSITT**, b. of Lyme, Oct. 18, 1821, by Abel McEwen	4	6
Sally, twin with Patty, [d. Thomas, Jr. & Bethiah], b. Sept. 13, 1773	3	108
Thomas, m. Mary **RICHARDS**, Mar. 29, 1745	3	61
Thomas, Jr., s. Thomas & Mary, b. Nov. 20, 1747	3	61
Thomas, Jr., m. Bethiah **CHAPEL**, Mar. 16, 1769	3	108
HARGILL, Eliza, d. [William & Elizabeth], b. Mar. 8, 1800	3	179
Mary, d. [William & Elizabeth], b. Feb. 22, 1798	3	179
Nancy, d. [William & Elizabeth], b. Apr. 25, 1802	3	179
Thomas, s. [William & Elizabeth], b. Mar. 27, 1795; d. Apr. 17, 1800, run over by a colt	3	179
William, m. Elizabeth **BLACKLEY**, d. John, Apr. 5, 1794	3	179
HARKLY, Peter, m. Wid. Elizabeth **BAKER**, July 31, 1699	1	25
HARKNESS, Elizabeth, of [New London], m. John W. **SHELLEY**, of Waterford, Jan. 27, 1839, by Rev. Abel McEwen	4	80
HARRINGTON, Eliza, m. Oliver S. **BARNS**, Apr. 21, 1821, by Elijah Hedding	4	5
Elizabeth, of Thompson, Ct., m. Zalmon **PRICE**, of Norwich, Nov. 14, 1843, by Rev. Sanford Benton	4	110
Lydia, m. Charles **JEFFERY**, b. of New London, Mar. 15, 1837, by Rev. Squire B. Hascall	4	68
Mary, m. John **JEFFERY**, b. of New London, Aug. 4, 1831 ,by Rev. Abel McEwen	4	43
Thomas, of Boston, m. Julia Ann **KEENEY**, of New London, July 15, 1833, by Chester Tilden	4	52
HARRIS, Abigail, d. James & Joanna, b. Apr. 10, 1753	2	57
Abigail, d. Walter, m. Amos **LESTER**, s. Jonathan, Feb. 8, 1761	3	20
Abigail, wid. & mother of Timothy **LESTER**, d. Feb. 7, 1772	2	97
Abigail, m. William **WEAVER**, Nov. 10, 1775 (First written April)	3	97
Abraham, s. Gabriel & Barsheba, b. Mar. 11, 1733/4	2	40
Absalam, m. Eunice **CHAPMAN**, June 15, 1773	3	112

	Vol.	Page

HARRIS (cont.)

	Vol.	Page
Absalom, s. [Absalam & Eunice], b. July 26, 1779	3	112
Albert, s. [Giles & Rebecca], b. July 2, 1813	3	254
Albert R., m. Jane E. **COIT**, Jan. 16, 1838, by Rev. Nathan Wildman	4	85
Alfred, s. [Dyar & Lucinda], b. Mar. 4, 1807	3	143
Almira L., m. Thomas B. **CARROL**, Nov. 15, 1840, by H. R. Knapp	4	93
Alpheas, s. Jonathan & Rachel, b. Mar. 22, 1735/6	2	90
Alvira, of New London, m. James **HICKEY**, of Liverpool, Mar. 31, 1843, by R. A. George Thompson	4	105
An[n], d. John, Jr. & Elizabeth, b. Jan. 27, 1745/6	2	27
Ann Mercy, d. James, Jr., s. James & Mercy, b. July 14, 1746	2	69
Annah, d. Asa, m. Samuel **BEEBE**, May 14, 1739	2	19
Augustus L., m. Elizabeth W. **KEENEY**, Jan. 1, 1850, by Rev. Charles Willett	4	151
Austin, s. [Dyar & Lucinda], b. Mar. 8, 1800	3	143
Austin, m. Centhia **HARRIS**, b. of New London, Sept. 30, 1827, by Henry Wightman	4	32
Barsheba, d. Gabriel & Barsheba, b. Jan. 23, 1727/8; d. May 21, 1728	2	40
Bathsheba, d. [Absalam & Eunice], b. June 4, 1777	3	112
Benjamin, s. Gibson & Phebe, b. July 23, 1724	2	37
Benjamin, s. Peter & Mary, b. Feb. 3, 1734/5	2	41
Benj[amin], s. James & Joanna, b. July 8, 1748	2	57
Betsey, d. [Thomas & Elizabeth], b. Oct. 11, 1784	3	160
Betsey, d. [Henry & Betsey], b. Aug. 23, 1792	3	138
Betsey, d. [John, 3d & Betsey], b. Oct. 28, 1802	3	96
Betsey, w. John, 3d, d. Nov. 11, 1802	3	96
Betsey, m. Asa[h]el **PEMBER**, Jan. 8, 1815	3	211
Betsey, w. Henry, d. Feb. 13, 1817	3	138
Bradley, m. Lydia **DANIELS**, Dec. 29, 1827, by Rev. Robert Bowzer	4	32
Burtis, s. [Giles & Rebecca], b. June 13, 1816	3	254
Caleb, s. Eliphalet & Mary, b. June 20, 1769	3	42
Catherine, w. Nathaniel, d. June 7, 1802	3	244
Catherine, d. [Isaac & Lucretia], b. Sept. 15, 1821	3	191
Catharine, m. Eliphalet M. **CROCKER**, b. of New London, Feb. 14, 1848, by Rev. Jabez S. Swan	4	137
Catharine, m. George C. **HARRIS**, b. of N[ew] London, May 10, 1851, by Rev. Jabez S. Swan	4	163
Caty, d. [Nathaniel & Catherine], b. Nov. 8, 1793	3	244
Celinda Dunham, m. William **ANDERSON**, May 21, 1834	3	282
Charles, m. Charlotte **BROOKS**, b. of New London, Dec. 21, 1823, by Rev. Ebenezer Loomis	4	16
Charles O., m. Frances A. **AYERS**, Apr. 13, 1851, by Rev. Charles Willett	4	161

	Vol.	Page
HARRIS (cont.)		
Charlotte, of New London, m. Griswold W.		
LOOMIS, of Norwich, Nov. 15, 1846, by Rev.		
Jabez S. Swan	4	128
Charlotte, m. Christopher C. **FENGAR**, Sept. 21,		
1852, by Rev. Charles Willett	4	172
Christopher, s. John & Elizabeth, b. Mar. 26, 1749; d.		
Dec. 31, 1751	2	27
Christopher, of New London, m. Margaret **LYON**, of		
Montville, June 6, 1849, by Rev. Jabez S. Swan	4	146
Clarretta B., of New London, m. George B.		
DARROW, of Providence, R.I., Mar. 31, 1845,		
by Rev. Jabez S. Swan	4	118
Courtland*, [s. Giles & Rebecca] *(Written in		
pencil)	3	254
Cynthia, d. [Daniel & Phebe], b. Dec. 19, 1765	3	92
Cynthia, d. [John, 3d & Betsey], b. May 26, 1801	3	96
Centhia, m. Austin **HARRIS**, b. of New London,		
Sept. 30, 1827, by Henry Wightman	4	32
Daniell, s. Joseph & Mary, b. July 9, 1718	1	50
Daniel, s. Gibson & Phebe, b. May 27, 1726	2	37
Daniel, s. Henry, b. Apr. 24, 1736	3	92
Daniel, s. John & Elizabeth, b. Mar. 6, 1747/8	2	27
Daniel, m. Phebe **LESTER**, July [ ], 1758	3	92
Daniel, s. [Daniel & Phebe], b. Feb. 8, 1760	3	92
Daniel, s. John, 3d, & Hannah, b. July 2, 1770	3	43
Daniel, s. John, d. Oct. 6, 1771	2	52
Daniel, Jr., m. Elisabeth **HARRIS**, Mar. [ ], 1785	3	92
David, s. William & Bridgett, b. June 6, 1753	2	61
David, s. [William & Prudence], b. Feb. 25, 1779	3	31
Deborah, w. John, d. [ ]	2	52
Delight, d. James, m. Alpheus **ROGERS**, s. Daniel,		
Jan. 31, 1745	3	47
Dinah, d. Samuel & Dinah, b. Mar 18, 1733	2	40
Dinah, d. Samuel & Dinah, b. May 18, 1733	2	80
Douglass W., m. Mary Ann **ROGERS**, Nov. 1, 1833,		
by Rev. Alvan Ackley	4	63
Douglass Woodworth, s. [Dyar & Lucinda], b. Dec.		
22, 1802	3	143
Dyer, s. Thomas & Mary, b. Nov. 25, 1765	2	78
Dyar, m. Lucinda **STARR**, d. William, of Groton,		
Feb. 3, 1793	3	143
Dyar, d. Aug. 23, 1813	3	143
Ebenezer, s. Samuell & Elizabeth, b. July 6, 1703	1	19
Eben[eze]r, s. Sam[ue]ll, of New London, decd., m.		
Lydia **ALLIN**, dau. of Gideon, of Killingworth,		
Mar. 25, 1729	2	58
Ebenezer, s. [Dyar & Lucinda], b. Aug. 4, 1795	3	143
Edmon, s. [Elihpalet & Betsey], b. July 18, 1801	3	49
Edmund T., s. [John, Jr. & Polly], b. Nov. 10, 1821	3	253
Edw[ar]d, s. Sam[ue]l & Dinah, b. July 17, 1739	2	41
Edward, s. Samuel & Dinah, b. July 17, 1739	2	80

	Vol.	Page
HARRIS (cont.)		
Edward, s. [Absalam & Eunice], b. Dec. 1, 1774	3	112
Edward, s. [John, 3d, & Betcy], b. Aug. 3, 1805	3	228
Edward, m. Fanny R. **RAYMOND**, b. of New		
London, Apr. 8, 1833, by Chester Tilden	4	50
Elias, s. [Nathaniel & Cynthia], b. Nov. 21, 1809	3	244
Elijah Leach, s. [John, 3d, & Betcy], b. Jan. 17, 1797	3	228
Eliphalet, b. Aug. 15, 1743	3	42
Eliphalet, of New London, s. Henry, decd., m. Mary		
COMSTOCK, of New London, d. Caleb, Oct.		
31, 1765	3	42
Eliphalet, s. Eliphalet & Mary, b. Aug. 18, 1766	3	42
Eliphalet, Jr., m. Nancy **WHITING**, Feb. 14, 1790	3	164
Eliphalet, s. [Eliphalet, Jr. & Nancy], b. May 26,		
1795	3	164
Eliphalet, m. Betsey **BEEBE**, Mar. 10, 1797	3	42
Eliza, d. [Eliphalet & Betsey], b Apr. 20, 1798	3	49
Elizabeth, [d. Gabriell & Elizabeth], b. June 5, 165[ ]	1	67
Elizabeth, d. Samuell & Elizabeth, b. May 7, 1690	1	19
Elizabeth, d. Peter & Elizabeth, b. Aug. 10, 1693	1	22
Elizabeth, wid., d. Aug. 17, 1702	1	28
Elizabeth, m. William **ROGERS**, Aug. 28, 1713	1	54
Elizabeth, m. Richard **BURCH**, Oct. 16, 1713	1	41
Elizabeth, m. Richard **BURCH**, Oct. 18, 1713	1	42
Elizabeth, m. Samuel **TINKER**, Nov. 30, 1720	2	111
Elizabeth, d. William & Rebeckah, b. May 6, 1723	1	65
Elizabeth, m. Joseph **SMITH**, Apr. 5, 1726	2	104
Elizabeth, d. Peter & Mary, b. Mar. 29, 1727	2	39
Elizabeth, d. Joseph, Jr. & Phebe, b. Sept. 6, 1734	2	36
Elizabeth, d. John, Jr. & Elizabeth, b. Jan. 3, 1737/8	2	27
Elizabeth, d. W[illia]m & Bridgett, b. Apr. 23, 1740	2	61
Elizabeth, wid., of Daniel, of New London, & d. of		
John & Hannah **TINKER**, m. Peter **ROGERS**,		
s. William & Elizabeth, Feb. 9, 1744	2	11
Elizabeth, d. Lebbeus & Alice, b. Feb. 22, 1745/6	2	77
Elizabeth, m. Guy **RICHARDS**, Jan. 18, 1746/7	3	99
Elizabeth, d. Richard & Lucy, m. Pardon **TABOR**, s.		
Philip & Elizabeth, May 17, 1747	2	91
Elizabeth, w. John, d. June 11, 1749	2	52
Elisabeth, d. Capt. Joseph, m. John **SHAPLEY**, s.		
Daniel, b. of New London, Nov. 15, 1753	3	18
Elisabeth, of New London, m. Samuel **JACKSON**,		
of New London, Nov. 15, 1753	3	40
Elizabeth, d. Gabriell & Mary, b. June 5, [1756]*		
*(1656 written in pencil)	1	2
Elisabeth, m. Samuel **CHAMPLIN**, July 12, 1759	3	32
Elisabeth, d. John & Lydia, b. July 24, 1761	3	11
Elisabeth, d. [William & Prudence], b. Feb. 27 1768	3	31
Elisabeth, d. [John, 3d, & Hannah], b. Aug. 8, 1772	3	43
Elisabeth, m. Daniel **HARRIS**, Jr., Mar. [ ], 1785	3	92
Elisabeth, m. Josiah **TINKER**, June 3, 1790	3	123

	Vol.	Page

HARRIS (cont.)

Elizabeth, m. Silas **KEENEY**, b. of New London,
Nov. 8, 1829, by Rev. Abel McEwen — 4, 37

Elizabeth, m. Charles **FRENCH**, b. of [New
London], May 5, 1830, by Rev. Daniel
Wildman — 4, 39

Ellen, m. Christopher **CULVER**, b. of New London,
Sept. 25, 1845, by Rev. Jabez S. Swan — 4, 122

Emala, d. [Thomas & Elizabeth], b. Oct. 30, 1790 — 3, 160

Emelia, m. William **BUTLER**, Sept. 11, 1810 — 3, 173

Ephraim Terry, s. [Frances & Esther], b. Jan. 31,
1787 — 3, 135

Est[h]er, d. Thomas & Mary, b. July 29, 1755 — 2, 78

Esther, b. July 29, 1755; m. William **WESCOTE**,
Jan. 7, 1773 — 3, 16

Esther, d. Eliphalet & Mary, b. Apr. 17, 1791 — 3, 42

Eunice, d. [Absalam & Eunice], b. Apr. 13, 1784 — 3, 112

Eunice, m. Rowland B. **GARDINER**, Mar. 5, 1837,
by Rev. Alvan Ackley — 4, 67

Ezra, s. Thomas & Mary, b. Nov. [ ], 1749 — 2, 78

Ezra, m. Sarah **ROGERS**, Feb. 1, 1782 — 3, 83

Ezra, s. [Thomas & Elizabeth], b. Jan. 19, 1794 — 3, 160

Fanny, d. [Thomas & Elizabeth], b. Oct. 2, 1786 — 3, 160

Fanny R., of [New London], m. Samuel D.
STODDARD, of West Brookfield, Mass., July
3, 1845, by Abel McEwen — 4, 120

Frances, m. Esther **BAILEY**, Mar. 30, 1785 — 3, 135

Francis, s. Thomas & Mary, b. Oct. 26, 1751 — 2, 78

Franklin B., s. [Giles & Rebecca], b. Apr. 7, 1819 — 3, 254

Frederick, s. [Eliphalet, Jr. & Nancy], b. Nov. 19,
1790 — 3, 164

Gabriell, m. Wid. Abigail **LESTER**, Apr. 8, 1714 — 1, 41

Gabriel, m. Barsheba **ROGERS**, Apr. 29, 1725 — 2, 37

Gabriel, s. Gabriel & Barsheba, b. Mar. 25, 1725/6 — 2, 37

George, s. Gibson & Phebe, b. Aug. 21, 1720 — 1, 58

George, m. Frances M. **LEWIS**, Dec. 14, 1831, by
Rev. Chester Tilden — 4, 46

George, of New London, s. Gibson Harris, of
Norwich, m. Sarah **HUBBARD**, of Windsor, d.
of Isaac Hubbard, of Windsor, Aug. 15, 1749 — 2, 27

George C., m. Catharine **HARRIS**, b. of N[ew]
London, May 10, 1851, by Rev. Jabez S. Swan — 4, 163

Gibson, s. Samuell & Elizabeth, b. Apr. 20, 1694 — 1, 19

Gibson, m. Phebe **DENISON**, Jan. 12, 1720 — 1, 58

Gilbert, s. [John, Jr. & Polly], b. June 30, 1816; d.
Oct. 4, 1819 — 3, 253

Giles, s. [Nathaniel & Catherine], b. June 9, 1788 — 3, 244

Giles, m. Rebecca **ROGERS**, Nov. 5, 1810 — 3, 254

Grace, d. Joseph & Mary, b. Feb. 2, 1706/7 — 1, 32

Grace, d. Joseph, m. James **ROGERS**, s. John, Dec.
8, 1726 — 2, 20

Grace, d. John, Jr. & Elizabeth, b. Feb. 23, 1740/1 — 2, 27

	Vol.	Page

HARRIS (cont.)

	Vol.	Page
Grace, d. James & Joanna, b. Mar. 23, 1755	2	57
Grace, d. [Daniel & Phebe], b. June 29, 1761	3	92
Grace, d. [John, 3d, & Hannah], b. Apr. 20, 1782	3	43
Grace, d. John & Eliza, m. Robert **SMITH**, from Stewartstown, county of Tyrone, Ireland, July 14, 1782	3	68
Griswold, s. [Daniel & Phebe], b. Apr. 30, 1775	3	93
Griswold, m. Betsey **BEEBE**, Dec. 20, 1795	3	136
Hannah, d. Peter & Elizabeth, b. May 14, 1698	1	24
Hannah, d. William & Rebec[c]ah, b. Dec. 23, 1720	1	58
Hannah, m. John **PLUMBE**, June 25, 1721	1	57
Hannah, d. of William, of North Carolina, m. John **PRESTON**, s. John, of New London, June 23, 1743	2	85
Hannah, d. [John, 3d, & Hannah], b. Apr. 19, 1776	3	43
Hannah, d. John, m. Crancall **SPRAGUE**, Mar. 5, 1796	3	60
Hannah, d. [John, 3d, & Betcy], b. Oct. 24, 1798	3	228
Harriot, d. [Frances & Esther], b. Mar. 21, 1789	3	135
Harriot, d. Francis, m. Henry **DOWGLASS**, Dec. 6, 1807	3	235
Harriet, d. [Giles & Rebecca], b. July 28, 1821	3	254
Harriet, m. Antone **ENOS**, of New London, Apr. 10, 1848, by Rev. Tho[ma]s J. Greenwood	4	140
Henry, s. John & Lydia, b. Sept. 26, 1763	3	11
Henry, s. Eliphalet & Mary, b. Nov. 30, 1784	3	42
Henry, m. Betsey **ROGERS**, Oct. 29, 1786	3	138
Henry, s. [Henry & Betsey], b. Sept. 26, 1790	3	138
Henry, Deac., d. [ ], 1830* *(Written in pencil)	3	138
Isaac, s. [Nathaniel & Catherine], b. July 16, 1791	3	244
Isaac, s. [Eliphalet, Jr. & Nancy], b. June 28, 1793	3	164
Isaac, of New London, m. Lucretia **STEWART**, of Waterford, Dec. 10, 1812	3	191
James, s. Jonathan & Rachel, b. Dec. 13, 1740	2	90
James, s. Gabriel, of New London, m. Joanna **STARR**, d. Ben, of New London, Dec. 11, 1744	2	57
James, s. James & Joanna, b. Aug. 27, 1745; d. May 9, 1751	2	57
James, s. [Daniel, Jr. & Elisabeth], b. Aug. 23, 1786	3	92
James C., m. Elizabeth **LYON**, Apr. 25, 1838, by Rev. Francis Darrow	4	77
Jane, m. James R. **KENNY**, b. of New London, Jan. 30, 1825, by Ebenezer Loomis	4	20
Janett, d. [Dyar & Lucinda], b. Apr. 4, 1809	3	143
Janette, m. Francis William **HOLT**, b. of N[ew] London, Jan. 4, 1832, by Rev. B. Judd	4	48
Jeremiah, m. Lucretia **DeWOLF**, Mar. 10, 1850, by Rev. Charles Willet	4	152

	Vol.	Page
HARRIS (cont.)		
Jesse Miner, s. [Thomas & Elizabeth], b. Apr. 14,		
1796	3	160
Joanna, d. John, Jr. & Elizabeth, b. Mar. 2, 1738/9	2	27
Joanna, d. John, of New London, m. Ebenezer		
HOLT, s. William, Nov. 4, 1759	3	7
Job, s. Samuel & Dinah, b. Feb. 10, 1734/5	2	80
Job, s. Samuel & Dinah, b. [ ]	2	41
John, s. Gabrielle & Mary, b. June 12, [1663]	1	4
John, [s. Gabriell & Elizabeth], b. June 12, 1663	1	67
John, m. Mary STEPHENS, Dec. 1, 1696	1	23
John, s. Joseph & Mary, b. Apr. 18, 1715	1	44
John, s. Lieut. Joseph, of New London, m. Elizabeth		
CHAMPLAIN, d. of John, of Lyme, Mar. 31,		
1737	2	27
John, s. John, Jr. & Elizabeth, b. June 8, 1743	2	27
John, s. Lieut. Joseph, of New London, m. Deborah		
ROGERS, d. John, of New London, decd.,		
Mar. 10, 1754	2	52
John, s. Henry, late of New London, decd., m. Lydia		
WAY, d. Daniel, of New London, Jan. 16, 1755	3	11
John, s. John & Lydia, b. Sept. 2, 1757	3	11
John, 3d, of New London, s. John, m. Hannah		
ROGERS, of New London, d. Samuel, Feb. 25,		
1768	3	43
John, s. John, 3d & Hannah, b. Nov. 2, 1768	3	43
John, d. Mar. 19, 1779	2	52
John, 3d, m. Nancy ROGERS, June 9, 1782	3	96
John, s. [John, 3d, & Nancy], b. July 29, 1793	3	96
John, d. Feb. [ ], 1794	3	11
John, 3d, m. Betcy LEACH, d. Elijah, Feb. 5, 1795	3	228
John, 3d., m. Betsey HAINS, d. Eliphalet, Apr. 1,		
1798	3	96
John, Jr., m. Polly TINKER, Dec. 25, 1814	3	253
John Leach, s. [John, 3d, & Betcy], b. Dec. 1, 1800	3	228
Jonathan, m. Rachel OTIS, July 28, 1735	2	40
Jona[than], s. James, of New London, m. Rachel		
OTIS, d. Jos[eph] of New London, July 28,		
1735	2	90
Jonathan, s. Jonathan & Rachel, b. June 6, 1739	2	90
Jona[than], s. William & Bridgett, b. Feb. 6, 1751	2	61
Jonathan, s. [William & Prudence], b. Mar. 7, 1781	3	31
Joseph, s. Gabriell & Mary, b. Jan. 16, [1672]	1	8
Joseph, [s. Gabriell & Elizabeth], b. Jan. 16, 1672	1	67
Joseph, s. Joseph & Mary, b. Oct. 14, 1711	1	37
Joseph, s. Joseph & Mary, b. Oct. 14, 1711	1	38
Joseph, Jr., s. Lieut. Joseph, of New London, m.		
Phebe HOLT, d. of Nathaniell, of New		
London, Dec. 27, 1733	2	36
Joseph, Lieut., d. Aug. 26, 1737	2	41
Joseph, s. Joseph, Jr. & Phebe, b. Dec. 1, 1739	2	36
Joshua, s. Gibson & Phebe, b. July 29, 1722	2	37

	Vol.	Page
HARRIS (cont.)		
Joshua, s. George & Sarah, b. May 10, 1754	2	27
Josiah, s. [John, 3d, & Nancy], b. June 30, 1788	3	96
Lebbeus, s. James, of New London, m. Alice		
RANSOM, dau. of Rob[er]t, of Colchester,		
Nov. 20, 1738	2	77
Lebbeus, s. Lebbeus & Alice, b. Dec. 22, 1741	2	77
Lee Hallam, s. [Eliphalet & Betsey], b. Nov. 10, 1799	3	49
Leonard, m. Phebe **KEENEY**, b. of New London,		
Feb. 4, 1838, by Chester Tilden	4	54
Lois, d. Samuel & Dinah, b. Nov. 20, 1736	2	41
Lois, d. Samuel & Dinah, b. Nov. 20, 1736	2	80
Lucinda, d. [Dyar & Lucinda], b. Jan. 11, 1798; d.		
Sept. 1, 1801	3	143
Lucretia, d. [Richard & Mary], b. Mar. 31, 1763	3	54
Lucretia, d. [Richard & Mary], b. Mar. 31, 1763	3	79
Lucretia, d. [Daniel & Phebe], b. Dec. 15, 1767	3	92
Lucretia, d. [William & Prudence], b. Sept. 17, 1775;		
d. Aug. 23 1787	3	31
Lucretia, d. Richard & Mary, m. Isaac **TREBY**, s.		
Sam[ue]l & Elizabeth, of Newport, RI., Jan. 23,		
1783	3	83
Lucretia S., of New London, m. Ralph G. **ABEL**, of		
Norwich, Mar. 30, 1848, by Rev. Jabez S. Swan	4	138
Lucy, m. Peter **ROGERS**, Feb. 21, 1744	3	88
Lucy, d. George & Sarah, b. Dec. 18, 1752	2	27
Lucy, d. Thomas & Mary, b. Nov. 15, 1769	2	78
Lucy, d. [Thomas & Elizabeth], b. Mar. 2, 1798	3	160
Lucy, d. [Eliphalet, Jr. & Nancy], b. Feb. 23, 1801	3	164
Lucy Ann, of New London, m. Warren **GIFFORD**,		
of New York, Oct. 15, 1827, by Henry		
Wightman	4	32
Lydia, d. Samuell & Elizabeth, b. Aug. 2, 1706	1	19
Lydia, d. James & Joanna, b. June 23, 1750	2	57
Lydia, d. Joseph, Jr. & Phebe, b. Dec. 14, 1754	2	36
Lydia, d. John & Lydia, b. Aug. 29, 1770	3	11
Lydia, m. Rufus **GARDNER**, May 11, 1786	3	160
Lydia, d. [Daniel, Jr. & Elisabeth], b. Mar. 26, 1789	3	92
Lydia, m. Jonathan **BARKER**, b. of [New London],		
Apr. 24, 1831, by Rev. Daniel Wildman	4	41
Lydia, m. John **LEONARD**, Mar. 23, 1840, by John		
Lovejoy	4	89
Lyman, s. [Dyar & Lucinda], b. Aug. 25, 1804	3	143
Lyman, m. Nancy P. **BECKWITH**, b. of New		
London, Aug. 29, 1836, by Rev. Alvan Ackley	4	83
Margaret F., m. Eldredge **BECKWITH**, Dec. 11,		
1834, by Rev. Alvan Ackley	4	59
Martha, d. William, of Wethersfield, m. Joseph		
COITE, s. John & Martha, July 17, [1667]	1	5
Martha L., m. John L. **CHAMPLIN**, b. of New		
London, Jan. 5, 1851, by Rev. Abel McEwen	4	58
Marvin, s. [Henry & Betsey], b. Oct. 31, 1805	3	138

	Vol.	Page
HARRIS (cont.)		
Mary, w. Walter, d. Jan. 24, [1655]	1	2
Mary, d. Gabriell & Mary, b. May 12, [1667]	1	5
Mary, [d. Gabriell & Elizabeth], b. May 21, 1667	1	67
Mary, d. Thomas & Mary, b. Nov. 4, 1690	1	20
Mary, d. Joseph & Mary, b. Apr. 4, 1699	1	25
Mary, d. Peter & Elizabeth, b. Mar. 14, 1702	1	28
Mary, m. Ebenezer **WAY**, Nov. 9, 1714	1	44
Mary, d. William & Rebec[c]ah, b. Aug. 7, 1718	1	58
Mary, d. Peter & Mary, b. Sept. 8, 1732	2	39
Mary, d. Joseph, Jr. & Phebe, b. July 15, 1741	2	36
Mary, d. George & Sarah, b. July 30, 1755	2	27
Mary, d. James & Joanna, b. Jan. 6, 1757	2	57
Mary, d. [Richard & Mary], b. July 31, 1761; d. Oct. 7, 1765	3	54
Mary, d. [Richard & Mary], b. July 31, 1761; d. Oct. 7, 1765	3	79
Mary, d. Capt. John Prentice, m. Richard **DESHON**, Oct. 2, 1763	3	150
Mary, d. Thomas & Mary, b. Apr. 20, 1767	2	78
Mary, d. Peter, Jr., decd., m. John **HALLAM**, Dec. 25, 1777	3	65
Mary, w. Richard, d. May 19, 1793. She was the first buried in the new burying ground.	3	79
Mary, d. [Henry & Betsey], b. Feb. 23, 1798	3	138
Mary, m. Ira R. **STEWARD**, Jan. 12, 1819	3	206
Mary Ann, d. [Dyar & Lucinda], b. Dec. 29, 1813	3	143
Mary L., m. Frederick A. **CHAMPLIN**, b. of New London, May 29, 1842, by Rev. Lemuel Covell	4	99
Mercy, d. Peter & Elizabeth, b. Mar. 10, 1696	1	23
Meriah, d. [Eliphalet & Betsey], b. Sept. 5, 1802	3	49
Nancy, [d. Eliphalet, Jr. & Nancy], b. May 17, 1766	3	164
Nancy, d. [John, 3d, & Nancy], b. May 10, 1784	3	96
Nancy, d. [John, 3d, & Betsey], b. Oct. 18, 1795	3	228
Nancy, w. John, 3d., d. Jan. 23, 1797	3	96
Nancy, d. [Eliphalet, Jr. & Nancy], b. Sept. 10, 1798	3	164
Nancy, m. John **HOWARD**, Jr., Jan. 12, 1817	3	203
Nathan, s. [William & Prudence], b. Aug. 15, 1763	3	31
Nath[anie]l, s. Jonathan & Rachel, b. Apr. 2, 1743	2	90
Nathaniel, s. Joseph, Jr. & Phebe, b. Oct. 7, 1750; d. Oct. 30, 1751	2	36
Nathaniel, s. John & Lydia, b. Nov. 15, 1755	3	11
Nathaniel, b. Nov. 15, 1755; m. Catherine **ROGERS**, Nov. 27, 1777	3	244
Nathaniel, s. [Nathaniel & Catherine], b. Aug. 24, 1780	3	244
Nathaniel, m. Cynthia **WAY**, Dec. 28, 1802	3	244
Noah, s. John & Lydia, b. Nov. 29, 1767	3	11
Oliver, s. [William & Prudence], b. Mar. 28, 1766; d. May 18, 1776	3	31
Pamela, of N[ew] London, m. Charles **SMITH**, of Waterford, Feb. 2, 1854, by Chester Tilden	4	54

	Vol.	Page

HARRIS (cont.)

	Vol.	Page
Paul, s. Sam[ue]l & Dinah [sic], b. Mar. 20, 1724	1	63
Paul, s. Samuel & Dianh, b. Mar. 21, 1724	2	80
Peleg Ransom, s. Lebbeus & Alice, b. Jan. 9, 1743/4	2	77
Peter, s. Gabriel & Mary, b. Dec. 8, [1660]	1	3
Peter, [s. Gabriell & Elizabeth], b. Xbr. 8, 1660	1	67
Peter, m. Elizabeth **MANWARING**, July 7, 1686	1	18
Peter, s. Samuell & Elizabeth, b. May 9, 1699	1	19
Peter, s. Peter & Elizabeth, b. Apr. 6, 1700	1	26
Peter, s. William & Rebeckah, b. Jan. 18, 1724/5	1	65
Peter, m. Mary **TRUMAN**, July 3, 1726	2	39
Peter, s. Peter & Mary, b. May 11, 1729	2	39
Peter, s. John & Lydia, b. Nov. 15, 1765	3	11
Peter, s. [William & Prudence], b. Nov. 22, 1773	3	31
Peter, s. [Nathaniel & Catherine], b. Sept. 16, 1785	3	244
Phebe, b. Joseph & Mary, b. Jan. 24, 1700	1	26
Phebe, m. Stephen **PRENTICE**, Jr., May 1, 1723	1	63
Phebe, d. Joseph, Jr. & Phebe, b. July 29, 1736	2	36
Phebe, d. [Daniel & Phebe], b. June 10, 1763	3	92
Phebe, of Lyme, m. Joseph **LEWIS**, of New London, Dec. 26, 1784, by Elias Worthington, J.P., of Colchester	3	118
Phebe, d. Daniel, m. Benjamin **GARDINER**, Mar. 15, 1795	3	177
Phebe, d. [Nathaniel & Cynthia], b. Sept. 23, 1807; d. Oct. 14, 1808	3	244
Polly, d. [John, 3d, & Nancy], b. Mar. 22, 1791	3	96
Polly R., d. [John, Jr. & Polly], b. July 27, 1818; d. Jan. 30, 1820	3	253
Rachel, d. Jonathan & Rachel, b. Sept. 30, 1738	2	90
Rebeckah, d. Joseph, Jr. & Phebe, b. Feb. 3, 1746	2	36
Rebeckah, d. W[illia]m & Bridgett, b. Apr. 16, 1749	2	61
Rebecca, d. [John, 3d, & Hannah], b. Apr. 9, 1778	3	43
Rebeckah, d. [Daniel & Phebe], b. June 19, 1779	3	92
Rebecca, m. James **SPRINGER**, July 3, 1796	3	133
R[e]uben, s. Samuel & Dinah, b. Dec. 6, 1741	2	41
Reuben, s. Samuel & Dinah, b. Dec. 6, 1741	2	80
Richard, m. Mary **WHITTEMORE**, Nov. 2, 1760	3	54
Richard, m. Mary **WHITTEMORE**, Nov. 2, 1760	3	79
Richard, s. [Richard & Mary], b. Aug. 5, 1765; d. Nov. 12, 1767	3	54
Richard, s. [Richard & Mary], b. Aug. 5, 1765; d. Nov. 12, 1767	3	79
Richard, s. [Richard & Mary], b. Nov. 21, 1767	3	54
Richard, s. [Richard & Mary], b. Nov. 21, 1767	3	79
Richard, s. [Nathaniel & Catherine], b. July 7, 1798	3	244
Richard, m. Rebecca **STEWARD**, Dec. 21, 1819	3	171
Robert, s. John & Lydia, b. May 23, 1759	3	11
Robert, s. [Richard & Mary], b. Feb. 19, 1770	3	54
Robert, s. [Richard & Mary], b. Feb. 19 ,1770	3	79
Robert, s. [Nathaniel & Catherine], b. Mar. 24, 1796	3	244
Royal, s. William & Bridgett, b. May 30, 1755	2	61

	Vol.	Page
HARRIS (cont.)		
Ruth, d. Samuel & Dinah, b. Mar. 24, 1725/6	2	36
Ruth, d. Samuel & Dinah, b. Mar. 24, 1725/6	2	80
S., m. Joshua **BOLLES**, b. of harbour's mouth, New London, Jan. 12, 1839, by Rev. C. C. Williams	4	82
Sally, d. [Nathaniel & Catherine], b. Aug. 24, 1778; d. Dec. 22, 1779	3	244
Sally, d. [Thomas & Elizabeth], b. Oct. 27, 1788	3	160
Sally, d. [Dyar & Lucinda], b. Nov. 26, 1793	3	143
Sally, d. John, m. Richard **TINKER**, Dec. 14, 1798	3	104
Sally, d. [Henry & Betsey], b. Apr. 3, 1801	3	138
Sally, d. Benjamin, m. Pearce **DARROW**, Jan. 14, 1809	3	212
Sally, d. Deac. Henry, m. Daniel **ROGERS**, Jr., Dec. 26, 1819	3	246
Sally, m. Joshua **POTTER**, Jr., [ ]	3	30
Samuel, s. Gabrill, b. July 14, 1665	1	4
Samuel, s. Gabriell & Mary, b. July 14, [1666]* *(Error, see 1665)	1	5
Samuell, [s. Gabriell & Elizabeth], b. July 14, 1666	1	67
Samuel, s. John, of Charlestown, m. Agnes, d. George **WAY**, of Providence, May 14, [1679]; d. June 7, [1679]	1	14
Samuel, s. Gabriell & Elizabeth, b. July 14, 1685	1	19
Samuell, m. Elizabeth **GIPSON**, Aug. 5, 1687	1	19
Samuell, s. Peter & Elizabeth, b. Apr. 29, 1689	1	19
Samuell, s. Samuell & Elizabeth, b. Mar. 5, 1697	1	19
Samuel, 3rd, s. Samuel & Dinah, b. Sept. 26, 1722	1	59
Samuel, s. Samuel & Dinah, b. Sept. 26, 1722; d. July 24, 1726	2	80
Samuel, s. Samuel & Dinah, b. Dec. 18, 1727	2	80
Samuel, s. [John, 3d, & Hannah], b. Apr. 13, 1774	3	43
Samuel, s. [John, 3d, & Betsy], b. Apr. 5, 1803	3	228
Samuel, s. Samuel, of New London, m. Dinah **WILLCOCKS**, dau. of [ ], of Killingworth, [ ]	2	80
Sarah, d. Joseph & Mary, b. Jan. 1, 1704/5	1	30
Sarah, d. William & Rebec[c]ah, b. Jan. 19, 1715	1	58
Sarah, m. Samuel **JACKSON**, Sept. 16, 1730	2	49
Sarah, d. of William, late of New London, now of Carolina, m. Zacheaus **WHEELER**, s. Joshua, of New London, Sept. 23, 1736	2	58
Sarah, d. Lebbeus & Alice, b. Dec. 18, 1739	2	77
Sarah, d. Joseph, Jr. & Phebe, b. June 19, 1743	2	36
Sarah, d. William & Bridgett, b. Oct. 29, 1746	2	61
Sarah, d. Thomas & Mary, b. Aug. 5, 1747	2	78
Sarah, d. George & Sarah, b. Feb. 14, 1757	2	27
Sarah, d. [William & Prudence], b. Jan. 8, 1777; d. Mar. 18, 1778	3	31
Sarah, d. [John, 3d, & Hannah], b. Apr. 19, 1780	3	43
Sarah B., m. George W. **TOWN**, Apr. 29, 1835, by Rev. Alvan Ackley	4	166

	Vol.	Page

HARRIS (cont.)

	Vol.	Page
Sibel, relict of Col. Joseph, m. Douglass		
WOODWORTH, Sept. 11, 1799	3	37
Silas, s. Samuel & Dinah, b. Jan. 3, 1730/1	2	38
Silas, s. Samuel & Dinah, b. Jan. 3, 1730/1	2	80
Sylas, s. [Nathaniel & Cynthia], b. Sept. 21, 1805	3	244
Silas, m. Mary **STEWART**, Sept. 25, 1826, by Rev.		
Francis Darrow	4	28
Sophronia, d. [Nathaniel & Cynthia], b. Nov. 23,		
1803	3	244
Stephen, s. Jonathan & Rachel, b. Mar. 22, 1735/6	2	40
Sybil, see under Sibel		
Temperance, d. Ensign Joseph & Mary, b. May 24,		
1709; d. June 28, 1796	1	66
Temperance, m. Nathaniel **SHAW**, Nov. 5, 1730	2	104
Temperance, d. Joseph, Jr. & Phebe, b. Jan. 30, 1748	2	36
Thaddeus, s. Lebbeus & Alice, b. Feb. 29, 1747/8	2	77
Thomas, s. Gabriell & Mary, b. July 29, [1658]	1	3
Thomas, [s. Gabriell & Elizabeth], b. July 29, 1658	1	67
Thomas, s. Peter & Elizabeth, b. Aug. 31, 1691	1	20
Thomas, s. John & Hannah, drowned Oct. 21, 1719;		
bd. the day following	1	54
Thomas, s. Richard & Lucy, of New London, m.		
Mary **BECKET**, dau. of Thomas & Sarah, of		
Lyme, Dec. 5, 1744	2	78
Thomas, s. Thomas & Mary, b Aug. 16, 1757	2	78
Thomas, m. Elizabeth **MINER**, d. Turner, Oct. 28,		
1780	3	160
Thomas, s. [Thomas & Elizabeth], b. Jan. 10, 1782	3	160
Uriah, s. Gabriel & Bathshua, b. Oct. 8, 1729	2	38
Uriah, s. [Absalam & Eunice], b. May 30, 1781	3	112
Ursula, d. [Isaac & Lucretia], b. Aug. 27, 1813	3	191
Ursula, m. Christopher C. **COMSTOCK**, Aug. 11,		
1830, by Rev. Francis Darrow	4	39
Walter, f. of Gabryell, d. Nov. 6, [1654]	1	2
Walter, s. Gabriell & Mary, b. Nov. 24, [1654]; d. "in		
ye beginning of December"	1	2
Walter, m. Phebe **CHIPMAN**, b. of New London,		
Aug. 17, 1828, by Abel McEwen, Pastor	4	34
Wethy Ann, d. [Eliphalet, Jr. & Nancy], b. Sept. 12,		
1805	3	164
William, s. Samuell & Elizabeth, b. Feb. 29, 1692	1	19
William, m. Rebecca **RATHBONE**, Oct. 29, 1713	1	58
William, s. William & Rebec[c]ah, b. Oct. 17, 1716	1	58
William, of New London, s. W[illia]m, m. Bridgett		
TURNER, d. of Jonathan, of New London,		
July 15, 1739	2	61
William, s. William & Bridgett, b. Dec. 12, 1742	2	61
William, m. Prudence **BROOKS**, formerly Prudence		
CHAMPLAIN, Apr. 7, 1763	3	31
William, s. [William & Prudence], b. Aug. 22, 1770	3	31
William, s. [Nathaniel & Catherine], b. Oct. 28, 1782	3	244

	Vol.	Page
HARRIS (cont.)		
William, s. [John, 3d, & Betcy], b. Apr. 27, 1808	3	228
William, s. [Dyar & Lucinda], b. Dec. 29, 1810	3	143
William, m. Charlotte A. **TYLER**, Oct. 1, 1845, by Rev. Tryon Edwards	4	121
W[illia]m M., of Canterbury, m. Eunice A. **SNOW**, of [New London], Dec. 29, 1846, by Rev. T. Edwards	4	128
-----, d. Joseph & Mary, b. Jan. 12, 1697/8; d. Feb. 8, 1697/8	1	23
HARRISON, Aseneth, m Elias **BROWN**, b. of [New London], Nov. 12, 1843, at Mr. Crocker's house, by Rev. W[illia]m Palmer	4	108
George, m. Prudence **ARTHER**, b. of New London, June 12, 1837, by Daniel Huntington	4	70
John, of Southhold, N.Y., m. Jane Maria **CONDLON**, of Southhampton, N.Y., Sept. 16, 1840, by Rev. Abel McEwen	4	91
Mary, of East Haddam, m. Lawrence **VALENTINE**, of New York, June 8, 1845, by Rev. Jabez S. Swan	4	120
Mary Ann, m. James **McMORRAN**, b. of [New London], Sept. 8, 1839, by Ira R. Steward	4	87
HART, George, of St. Louis, Mo., m. Sarah S. **POTTER**, of [New London], Aug. 26, 1850, by Rev. T. Edwards	4	154
Hannah, m. Joseph **ENOS**, b. of [New London], Jan. 27, 1846, by Rev. John Howson	4	126
James, m. Lucy **JACKSON**, Oct. 8, 1794	3	138
John A., of Sagg Harbor, N.Y., m. Loisa **EDGERTON**, of [New London], June 17, 1839, by Rev. Abel McEwen	4	86
HARTSHORN, [see under **HEARTSHORNE**]		
HARVEY, George, s. William & Ruth, b. Sept. 26, 1758	3	36
George, s. [Thomas & Patty], b. Oct. 9, 1786	3	17
Ruth, d. William & Ruth, b. Aug. 30, 1760	3	36
Thankfull, d. William & Ruth, b. Mar. 19, 1766	3	36
Thomas, s. William & Ruth, b. Apr. 17, 1763	3	36
Thomas, m. Patty **FITCH**, Oct. 7, 1785	3	17
William, s. William & Ruth, b. Oct. 17, 1754	3	36
William, s. [Thomas & Patty], b. Sept. 5, 1791	3	17
HASTINGS, Sally, m. James **PATTERSON**, July 19, 1796	3	172
HATCH, Daniel, s. William & Susanna, b. Apr. 9, 1741	2	41
Dinah, m. Sam[ue]l **CHAPMAN**, Mar. 8, 1722	1	62
Dinah, d. William, m. Samuel **CHAPMAN**, Jr., s. Sam[ue]l, Mar. 8, 1722	2	16
Elizabeth d. William & Susannah, b. June 4, 1736	2	41
Heman, of Falmouth, Mass., m. Lucy **TINKER**, of New London, June 2, 1829, by Rev. Abel McEwen	4	36

	Vol.	Page

HATCH (cont.)

	Vol.	Page
Job, s. William & Susannah, b. June 27, 1744; d. July 26, 1744	2	42
Jos[eph], s. W[illia]m & Susannah, b. May 25, 1753	2	42
Joshua, s. William & Susanna, b. June 21, 1743	2	41
Peter, s. William & Susannah, b. June 26, 1745	2	42
Samuel, s. William & Susanna, b. Sept. 15, 1738	2	41
Ste[phe]n, s. William & Susannah, b. Jan. 10, 1750/1	2	42
Susannah, d. William & Susannah, b. May 10, 1748	2	42
Susannah, [w. William], d. Mar. 16, 1760	2	52
William, m. Susannah **BAKER**, Oct. 13, 1726	2	37
William, s. William, d. Dec. 25, 1746	2	42
William, d. July 24, 1754	2	52
HATCHET, John, s. John & Mary, b. Apr. 28, 1716	1	46
HAUGHTON, [see also **HOUGHTON**], Abigail, m. John **WICKWERE**, Dec. 27, 1705	2	58
Catharine, w. Richard, d. Aug. 9, [1670]	1	6
Charles, s. James & Philenah, b. Apr. 6, 1770; d. Nov. 26, 1773	2	46
Charles, s. [James & Philenah], b. Aug. 18, 1775	2	46
Deborah, w. James, d. Aug. 15, 1767	2	46
Elizabeth, d. James & Deborah, b. Feb. 12, 1761	2	45
George, s. James & Deborah, b. June 7, 1758	2	45
Jabens, s. James & Deborah, b. Aug. 14, 1752	2	45
[Jam]es, m. Ruth **ADGATE**, June 6, 1782	3	2
Jerusha, d. Sampson, of New London, m. Daniel **POLLY**, s. John, of Auburn, Mar. 24, 1725/6	2	63
Lucy, d. Sampson, m. Joseph **OTIS**, Jr., s. Joseph, all of New London, Feb. 4, 1761, by William, Hil[l]house, J.P.	3	16
Philena, d. [James & Philenah], b. Dec. 19, 1776	2	46
[ ]lena, w. James, [d.] Apr. 12 ,1781	3	2
William Whiting, s. James & Philenah, b. Feb. 28, 1769; d. Jan. 28, 1774	2	46
William Whiting, s. [James & Philenah], b. Jan. 12, 1774	2	46
HAULON, William, m. Ann **LAMB**, Oct. 13, 1850. Witnesses: Mastin Nooman, Catharine Maxwell	4	159
HAVENS, Eliza, m. Joseph **FRANCIS**, b. of New London, June 26, 1831, by Rev. Abel McEwen	4	43
Eliza E., m. Frank **KEENEY**, b. of New London, Nov. 28, 1849, by Rev. Geo[rge] M. Carpenter	4	153
Frances, m. Frank **ROGERS**, b. of New London, July 15, 1849, by Rev. Jabez S. Swan	4	146
Jane C., of New London, m. James C. **LANE**, of Groton, Mar. 27, 1837, by Rev. Erastus Denison	4	67
Lucy B., m. Elkanah **HEWITT**, Mar. 5, 1837, by Rev. Alvan Ackley	4	67
Matilda R., of Long Island, m. Elisha R. **LAMB**, of New London, Oct. 13, 1851, by Rev. Jabez S. Swan	4	173

	Vol.	Page
HAVENS (cont.)		
Urbane, m. Sarah **ROGERS**, b. of New London, June 4, 1843, by Rev. R. W. Allen	4	104
Urbane, m. Sarah **ROGERS**, b. of New London, June 4, 1843, by Rev. R. W. Allen	4	105
William H., of Lyme, m. Sophia **WHITTEMORE**, of N[ew] London, Mar. 5, 1837, by Rev. Squire B. Hascall	4	68
HAWKES, HAWKE, HAKE, Amy, d. John & Hannah, b. Apr. 13, 1701	1	27
James, s. John & Hannah, b. Aug. 16, 1703	1	29
Thomas, of Baltimore, Md., m. Mary E. **READ**, of Waterford, May 11, 1844, by Rev. Abel McEwen	4	111
HAWKINS, Benjamin, s. John & Deborah, b. Nov. 19, 1751	2	50
Deborah, d. John & Deborah, b. Apr. 15, 1753	2	50
John, s. Tho[ma]s, of New London, m. Deborah **MORGAN**, d. John, of New London, Sept. 1, 1748	2	50
John, of New York, m. Celia **PRIMAS**, of N[ew] L[ondon], colored people, Jan. 17, 1833, by Rev. J. W. Hallam	4	49
Mary, d. John & Deborah, b. Oct. 14, 1755	2	50
Sarah, d. John & Deborah, b. Mar. 15, 1749	2	50
Sarah, of New London, d. John, of New London, m. Darius **MORGAN**, of Norwich, s. Peter, Oct. 5, 1769, by Sam[ue]l Huntington, J.P.	3	45
HAYDEN, George W., of Essex, m. Louisa H. **MOORE**, of East Lyme, Apr. 16, 1848, by Rev. L. G. Leonard	4	138
Louisa, m. Royal M. **STRICKLAND**, b. of [New London], Sept. 3, 1839, by Rev. Robert A. Hallam	4	86
HAYES, HAYS, HAYSE, Bathsheba, m. Dennis **FANNING**, June 10, 1806	3	192
Edward, m. Mehetable **CHAPPEL**, [ ], 1783	3	90
Elizabeth, a colored woman, b. July 15, 1787	3	191
James, s. [Elizabeth], b. Nov. 18, 1812	3	191
John, s. [Edward & Mehetable], b. Apr. 28, 1784	3	90
John, m. Caroline A. **MORGAN**, of New London, Jan. 1, 1845, by Rev. G. Thompson	4	116
Nancy, d. [Edward & Mehetable], b. Mar. 2, 1788	3	90
Nancy, m. Thomas **DICKINSON**, June 17, 1805	3	95
HAYNES, [see under **HAINES**]		
HAYWOOD, Maria, m. Winslow L. **BOWKER**, Aug. 2, 1848, by Rev. Tho[ma]s J. Greenwood	4	141
HAZAN*, George S., m. Sarah J. **MERCER**, June 18, 1833, by Rev. J. W. Hallam *("**HAZARD**" written in pencil)	4	51
HAZARD, HAZZARD, Abigail, m. Jared **STARR**, Sept. 11, 1780	3	84

	Vol.	Page
HAZARD, HAZZARD (cont.)		
Abiga[i]l, d. [Charles & Ann], b. Oct. 3, 1804	3	211
Ann, d. [Charles & Ann], b. Oct. 8, 1809	3	211
Ann, w. Charles, d. Oct. 18, 1810	3	211
Charoline, d. [Charles & Ann], b. Nov. 3, 1806	3	211
Charles, m. Ann **BOURSE**, d. John, of Newport, Feb. 1, 1795	3	211
Charles, d. Nov. 16, 1810, at sea	3	211
Charles Cortland, s. [Charles & Ann], b. July 17, 1800	3	211
Charlotte, d. [Francis & Rebecah], b. Aug. 27, 1807	3	145
Elizabeth, d. [Francis & Rebecah], b Feb. 27, 1803	3	145
Francis, m. Rebecah **TRUMAN**, d. Capt. Henry Truman, July 2, 1798	3	145
G. C. of Newport, R.I., m. Eliza G. **COGGESHALL**, of [New London], Dec. 15, 1846, by Rev. Abel McEwen	4	128
Henry Truman, s. [Francis & Rebecah], b. Mar. 19, 1801	3	145
Jared Starr, s. [Charles & Ann], b. July 18, 1798	3	211
John Bours[e], s. [Charles & Ann], b. Sept. 6, 1802	3	211
Mary, d. [Francis & Rebecah], b. May 28, 1799	3	145
Robert Francis, s. [Francis & Rebecah], b. Oct. 1, 1805	3	145
HEARTSHORNE, Jonathan, of Norwich, m. Lucy **HEMPSTEAD**, of New London, Sept. 18, 1709	1	66
HEATH, Charlotte, of N[ew] London, m. John **MATOON**, of Wallingford, Oct. 27, 1837, by Rev. Alvan Ackley	4	66
Eunice, of [New London], m. Lyman **MATTOON**, of Wal[l]ingford, Sept. 29, 1834, by Rev. Ebenezer Blake	4	57
HEMPSTEAD, HEMPSTED, HEMPSTER, Abigail, d. Joshua & Abigail, b. Jan. 14, 1711/12	1	38
Abiga[i]l, w. Joshua, d. Aug. 6, 1716	2	37
Abigail, d. John & Hannah, b. Oct. 1, 1736; d. Sept. 19, 1736	2	42
Abigail, d. John & Hannah, b. Oct. 27, 1738	2	42
Abigail, m. James **SMITH**, Nov. 12, 1756	3	87
Alfred, m. Harriet **POTTER**, Nov. 13, 1833, by Daniel Wildman	4	53
Amanda, m. Cha[rle]s T. **DARROW**, b. of New London, Jan. 5, 1845, by Rev. T. Edwards	4	116
Ann E., d. [Daniel B. & Grace], b. May 21, 1817	3	194
Anna, d. [Nathaniel & Hannah], b. Sept. 6, 1750	3	101
Anna, d. Nathaniel, m. Joshua **HEMPSTE[A]D**, s. Joshua, May 23, 1769	3	39
Anna, d. [Nathaniel, Jr. & Elisabeth], b. May 2, 1784	3	102
Avery, m. Lucy **LEEDS**, d. William, Jan. 3, 1805	3	229
Benjamin, m. Elisabeth **COPP**, June 10, 1779	3	13
Benjamin, s. [Benjamin & Elisabeth], b. May 8, 1783	3	13

	Vol.	Page
HEMPSTEAD, HEMPSTED, HEMPSTER (cont.)		
Benjamin, d. Sept. 2, 1798	3	13
Benjamin Barber, s. [Henry & Nancy], b. Aug. 29, 1813	3	256
Benjamin F., of Groton, m. Mary **SPRAGUE**, of New London, Dec. 3, 1831, by Rev. Abel McEwen	4	44
Betsey, d. [Benjamin & Elisabeth], b. June 17, 1780	3	13
Caroline, d. [Daniel B. & Grace], b. Apr. 20, 1814	3	194
Caroline L., of New London, m. Henry O. **AMES**, of New Orleans, Oct. 3, 1837, by Rev. Abel McEwen	4	74
Charles, s. [Stephen & Mary], b. Sept. 10, 1794, in Hebron	3	77
Charles T., b. Sept. 18, 1785; m. Margaret **MILLER**, Nov. 8, 1809	3	205
Charles Turner, twin with Nancy, s. [Benjamin & Elisabeth], b. Sept. 18, 1785	3	13
Christopher, s. [Stephen & Mary], b. Mar. 24, 1785; d. Sept. 13, 1805	3	77
Christopher, s. [Nathaniel, Jr. & Elisabeth], b Apr. 17, 1787	3	102
Coit, s. [Henry & Nancy], b. Mar. 20, 1827	3	256
Cortland, s. [Avery & Lucy], b. Jan. 29, 1809	3	229
Daniel, s. [John, Jr. & Mary], b. July 22, 1781	3	88
Daniel B., m. Grace **LAMPHERE**, d. James, May 4, 1806	3	194
Daniel B., s. [Daniel B. & Grace], b. July 9, 1822	3	194
David, s. [John, Jr. & Mary], b. Mar. 9, 1787; d. Mar. 14, 1787	3	88
Denison, s. [Henry & Nancy], b. Oct. 3, 1817	3	256
Denison, of New London, m. Frances **CHAPELL**, July 18, 1844 by Rev. R. A. G. Thompson	4	113
Edward, s. [Joshua, Jr. & Lydia], b. July 5, 1745	2	43
Edward, s. [Stephen & Mary], b. June 3, 1790	3	77
Edward, s. [Joshua, 2d, & Mary], b. Nov. 2, 1807	3	107
Elias, s. [Henry & Nancy], b. Dec. 1, 1823	3	256
Elizabeth, d. Josh[u]a, b. Sept. 2, [1670]; d. Nov. [, 1670]	1	7
Elizabeth, d. Joshua, b. Dec. 24, [1672]	1	8
Elisabeth, m. John **PLUMBE**, Feb. 13, 1688/9	1	38
Elizabeth, d. Joshua & Abigail, b. Apr. [ ], 1714	2	37
Elizabeth, d. Joshua, m. Daniel **STARR**, s. Benjamin, b. of New London, Nov. 18, 1735	2	64
Elizabeth, m. Daniel **STARR**, Nov. 18, 1735	2	104
Elisabeth, d. Stephen & Sarah, b. Sept. 12, 1746	2	77
Elisabeth, m. William **HOLT**, 2d, Jan. 21, 1768, by Rev. Mather Boyles	3	12
Elisabeth, d. [Nathaniel, Jr. & Elisabeth], b. Nov. 7, 1778	3	102
Elizabeth, see Elizabeth **DODGE**	3	44
Elisabeth, m. Ezra **DODGE**, Sept. 26, 1790	3	119

	Vol.	Page
HEMPSTEAD, HEMPSTED, HEMPSTER (cont.)		
Elizabeth, of New London, m. Jeremiah		
MAHONEY, of Newburyport, Mass., Nov. 1,		
1831, by Rev. Abel McEwen	4	44
Elizabeth, of [New London], m. Samuel M.		
VALENTINE, of New York, May 13, 1843, by		
Rev. Abel McEwen	4	105
Elizabeth H., of New London, m. William S.		
HEMPSTEAD, of Norwich, May 11, 1846, by		
Rev. John Howson	4	126
Elizabeth Hannah, [d. Joshua, 2d, & Mary], b. Jan.		
10, 1817	3	167
Esther J., of [New London], m. Henry **GREEN**, of		
Nantucket, Mass., July 31, [1845], by Rev. John		
Howson	4	121
Frances H., of [New London], m. William A.		
RUMSEY, of Brockport, N.Y., June 23, 1836,		
by D. Huntington	4	97
Frances L., of [New London], m. Enoch **PROUT**, of		
Middletown, Ct., Oct. 23, 1848, by Rev. M. P.		
Alderman	4	144
Frederick William, s. [Avery & Lucy], b. Aug. 5,		
1807	3	229
George, s. [Joshua, 2d, & Mary], b. Nov. 10, 1819; d.		
Oct. 2, 1821	3	167
Giles G[e]orge, s. [Joshua, 2d, & Mary], b. Nov. 22,		
1826	3	167
Hallam, m. Polly **BARROW**, June 29, 1784, by		
Joseph Harris, J.P.	3	97
Hannah, d. Robert, m. Abell **MOORE**, s. Miles,		
Sept. 22, [1670]	1	7
Hannah, m. John **EDGECOMBE**, Feb. 28, [1699]	1	25
Hannah, d. John & Hannah, b. Oct. 19, 1734; d. about		
16 y. old	2	42
Hannah, w. John, d. June 8, 1765	3	88
Hannah, d. [John, Jr. & Mary], b. May 4, 1768	3	88
Hannah, d. Tho[ma]s & Mary, b. June 7, 1770	3	31
Hannah, d. [Nathaniel, Jr. & Elisabeth], b. Apr. 13,		
1792	3	102
Harriot, d. [Henry & Nancy], b. Jan. 19, 1820	3	256
Harriet, m. Daniel **LEE**, b. of New London, Feb. 29,		
1852, by Rev. Edwin R. Warren	4	166
Henry, m. Nancy **BARBER**, Aug. 7, 1808	3	256
Henry P., m. Lucy **KEENEY**, b. of New London,		
Sept. 4, 1845, by Rev. Jabez S. Swan	4	122
Henry Prentis, s. [Henry & Nancy], b. July 2, 1809	3	256
James, s. Thomas & Mary, b. Nov. 26, 1768	3	31
John, s. Joshua & Abigail, b. Dec. 26, 1709	1	66
John, of New London, m. Hannah **SALMON**, of		
South Hold, L.I., Nov. 17, 1731	2	42
John, s. John & Hannah, b. Aug. 18, 1733; d. Sept. 2,		
1733	2	42

	Vol.	Page
HEMPSTEAD, HEMPSTED, HEMPSTER (cont.)		
John, s. [John & Hannah], b. Oct. 27, 1741	2	42
John, Jr., m. Mary **BILL**, Nov. 1, 1767	3	88
John, s. [John, Jr. & Mary], b. Oct. 10, 1771	3	88
John, d. June 2, 1779	3	88
John P., m. Abby Ann **GREEN**, b. of [New London],		
June 19, 1844, by Rev. Abel McEwen	4	112
John Prentis, s. [Henry & Nancy], b. Oct. 21, 1815	3	256
Joseph, s. [Stephen & Mary], b. June 29, 1778	3	77
Joshua, s. Josh[ua] & Elizabeth, b. Sept. 1, [1678]	1	13
Joshua, s. Joshua & Abigail, b. July 20, 1699	1	25
Joshua, s. Nathaniel & Mary, b. June 14, 1724	2	38
Joshua, Jr., of New London, s. Nathaniel, decd., m		
Lydia **BURCH**, d. Richard, of New London,		
Nov. 3, 1743	2	43
Joshua, s. Joshua, Jr. & Lydia, b. June 10, 1744	2	43
Joshua, s. Joshua, m. Anna **HEMPSTE[A]D**, d.		
Nathaniel, May 23, 1769	3	39
Joshua, s. [Joshua & Anna], b. Apr. 12, 1775	3	39
Joshua, 2d, m. Mary **WIGHTMAN**, d. Zerobable, of		
Bozrah, Jan. 31, 1802	3	167
Joshua, s. [Joshua, 2d, & Mary], b. Sept. 16, 1802	3	167
Leonard, m. Sarah P. **DABOLL**, Sept. 14, 1835, by		
Rev. Alven Ackley	4	62
Lucretia, m. Ebenezer **COLFAX**, May 19, 1776	3	87
Lucretia Goddard, d. [Daniel B. & Grace], b. May 29,		
1808	3	194
Lucretia P., of New London, m. David **HUSTACE**,		
of New York, Apr. 22, 1827, by Rev. Abel		
McEwen	4	30
Lucy, of New London, m. Jonathan		
HEARTSHORNE, of Norwich, Sept. 18, 1709	1	66
Lucy, d. Stephen & Sarah, b. Oct. 6, 1751	2	77
Lydia, d. [Joshua, 2d, & Mary], b. Feb. 18, 1873	3	167
Maria, m. Henry **SCOTT**, b. of [New London], Oct.		
1, 1838, by Rev. Abel McEwen	4	79
Martha, d. [John, Jr. & Mary], b. Oct. 17, 1783	3	88
Martha, d. [Joshua, 2d, & Mary], b. Jan. 14, 1814	3	167
Mary, d. of Robert, m. Robert **DOUGLASS**, s. of		
William, Sept. 28, [1665]	1	4
Mary, d. Josh[u]a, b. Jan. 31, [1674]	1	10
Mary, m. Green **PLUMBE**, May 3, 1694	1	48
Mary, d. Joshua & Abiga[i]ll, b. July 31, 1716	2	37
Mary, d. Nathaniel & Mary, b. July 10, 1729	2	38
Mary, m. Joseph **TRUMAN**, Jr., Mar. 22, 1733	2	112
Mary, d. Joshua, of New London, m. Thomas		
PIERPOINT, s. James, of Roxbury, June 10,		
1736	2	49
Mary, m. Thomas **PIERPOINT**, June 10, 1736	2	82
Mary, d. Thomas & Mary, b. Mar. 6, 1766	3	31
Mary, d. [John, Jr. & Mary], b. Apr. 17, 1773; d.		
Sept. 20, 1773	3	88

	Vol.	Page
HEMPSTEAD, HEMPSTED, HEMPSTER (cont.)		
Mary, d. [John, Jr. & Mary], b. Mar. 4, 1775	3	88
Mary, d. [Stephen & Mary], b. Oct. 25, 1782	3	77
Mary, d. Stephen, m. John **KEENEY**, June 2, 1806	3	226
Mary, d. [Joshua, 2d, & Mary], b. Mar. 23, 1811	3	167
Mary, d. Joshua, m. John Rogers **BOLLES**, s.		
Hezekiah [& Anna], May 30, 1839	3	303
Nancy, twin with Charles Turner, d. [Benjamin &		
Elisabeth], b. Sept. 18, 1785	3	13
Nancy, d. Benjamin, m. Robert **HOLT**, Oct. 8, 1803	3	219
Nancy, d. [Joshua, 2d, & Mary], b. Feb. 7, 1805	3	167
Nancy, d. [Henry & Nancy], b. Aug. 3, 1811	3	256
Nancy, m. Henry **COIT**, b. of New London, May 16,		
1830, by Rev. Abel McEwen	4	38
Nathaniell, s. Joshua & Abigail, b. Jan. 6, 1700	1	26
Nathaniel, m. Mary **HALLAM**, July 18, 1723	2	38
Nathaniel, s. Nathaniel & Mary, b. Feb. 5, 1726/7	2	38
Nathaniel, s. Nathaniel & Mary, b. Feb. 5, 1726/7	3	101
Nathaniel, d. July 9, 1729	2	38
Nathaniel, m. Hannah **BOOTH**, of Southold, L.I.,		
Nov. 22, 1749	3	101
Nath[anie]l, s. [Nathaniel & Hannah], b. Feb. 7, 1753	3	101
Nathaniel, Jr., m. Elisabeth **MANWARING**, d.		
Christopher, Aug. 26, 1777	3	102
Nathaniel, s. [Nathaniel, Jr. & Elisabeth], b. Sept. 2,		
1780	3	102
Nathaniel, 3d, m. Susannah **CHAPMAN**, July 2,		
1783	3	86
Nathaniel, s. [Richard & Sophia], b. Aug. 16, 1807	3	189
Patience, d. Stephen & Sarah, b. May 31, 1744	2	77
Patty, d. [Joshua & Anna], b. July 17, 1772	3	39
Phebe, d. Josh[u]a & Eliza, b. June 7, [1676]	1	11
Rebeckah, d. Joshua, m. Joseph **HAMELTON**, late		
of East Grinwich, Kent County, R.I., Oct. 23,		
1783	3	139
Richard, s. [Nathaniel & Susannah], b. Jan. 29, 1786	3	86
Richard, m. Sophia **SMITH**, of Groton, d. Moses,		
June 1, 1806	3	189
Robert, s. Joshua & Abigail, b. Nov. 30, 1702	1	28
Robert, s. Joshua, Jr. & Lydia, b. Feb. 27, 1746/7	2	43
Sally, d. Stephen, m. Elijah **BEEBE**, Sept. 13, 1808	3	209
Samuel, s. Joshua, Jr. & Lydia, b. Dec. 8, 1748	2	43
Samuel Bill, s. [John, Jr. & Mary], b. Nov. 21, 1777	3	88
Sarah, d. Thomas & Mary, b. June 28, 1767	3	31
Sarah, d. [Stephen & Mary], b. Sept. 7, 1789	3	77
Stephen, s. Joshua & Abigail, b. Dec. 1, 1705	1	31
Stephen, of New London, s. Joshua, m. Sarah		
HOLT, d. William, of New London, Sept. 19,		
1737	2	43
Stephen, s. Joshua, m. Sarah **HOLT**, d. William, all		
of New London, Sept. 19, 1737	2	76
Stephen, s. Stephen & Sarah, b. June 12, 1742	2	43

	Vol.	Page
HEMPSTEAD, HEMPSTED, HEMPSTER (cont.)		
Stephen, s. Stephen & Sarah, b. June 12, 1742; d.		
July 24, 1749	2	76
Stephen, m. Mary **LEWIS**, Sept. 4, 1777	3	77
Stephen, s. [Stephen & Mary], b. May 3, 1787	3	77
Sukey, d. [Stephen & Mary], b. Feb. 20, 1797, in		
Hebron	3	77
Susannah, d. [Nathaniel & Susannah], b. Mar. 1,		
1784	3	86
Temperance, d. [John, Jr. & Mary], b. Sept. 1, 1779	3	88
Thomas, s. Joshua & Abigail, b. Apr. 14, 1708	1	35
Thomas, s. Stephen & Sarah, b. July 4, 1738; d. June		
17, 1739, ae 11 m. 13 d.	2	43
Thomas, s. Stephen & Sarah, b. July 4, 1738; d. June		
17, 1739	2	76
Thomas, s. Stephen & Sarah, b. Feb. 3, 1739/40	2	43
Thomas, s. Stephen & Sarah, b. Feb. 3, 1739/40	2	76
Thomas, of New London, s. Stephen, m. Mary		
CHAPMAN, d. James, all of New London,		
Oct. 28, 1764	3	31
Thomas, s. [Stephen & Mary], b. Nov. 13, 1791	3	77
William, s. Stephen & Sarah, b. Jan. 19, 1748/9	2	77
William, s. [Stephen & Mary], b. Dec. 23, 1800	3	77
William N., of Saybrook, m. Hannah **JEPSON**, of		
[New London], Nov. 18, 1838, by Rev. James		
M. Macdonald	4	80
William S., of Norwich, m. Elizabeth H.		
HEMPSTEAD, of New London, May 11,		
1846, by Rev. John Howson	4	126
HENDRICK, William, of New York, m. Fanny		
ASHCRAFT, of New London, Apr. 27, 1823,		
by Thomas W. Tucker, Elder	4	13
HENDERSON, HANDERSON, Abigail, d. Jno. &		
Susannah, b. May 30, 1738	2	62
Eliza, d. John & Susannah, b. Aug. 8, 1731	2	62
Elizabeth, d. John & Susannah, b. Aug. 8, 1731	2	39
Elizabeth, d. John & Susannah, b. May 24, 1734	2	40
James, s. Jno. & Susannah, b. Mar. 20, 1740	2	62
John, m. Susannah **MORGAN**, Feb. 10, 1728/9	2	39
Jno., m. Susannah **MORGAN**, Feb. 10, 1728/9	2	62
John, s. John & Susannah, b. Apr. 10, 1736	2	41
John, s. Jno. & Susannah, b. Apr. 10, 1736	2	62
Susannah, d. John & Susannah, b. May 25, 1734	2	41
Susannah, d. Jno. & Susannah, b. May 25, 1734	2	62
William, s. John & Susannah, b. Oct. 1, 1729	2	39
William, s. John & Susannah, b. Oct. 1, 1729	2	62
HENEY, [see under **KEENEY**]		
HENFIELD, George, m. Nancy H. **HOWARD**, of [New		
London], Dec. 31, 1837, by Rev. Daniel Webb	4	75
Joseph H., of Salem, m. Lydia **GODDARD**, Dec. 24,		
1809	3	239
Lydia Ann, d. [Joseph H. & Lydia], b. Sept. 14, 1810	3	239

	Vol.	Page
HENNESSY, Eliza, m. Robert **SISK**, Dec. 29, 1848, by		
Rev. William Logan	4	150
HENRIGHT, Bridget, m. Edward **DAVIS**, June 18, 1848,		
by Rev. John Brady	4	139
HENRY, Hugh, m. Betsey **GESTIN**, b. of New London,		
Nov. 12, 1796, by Andrew Griswold, J.P.	2	124
Lydia, d. [Sarah, negro], b. Nov. 14, 1786	3	6
Margaret, m. Francis **LANSON**, b. of New London,		
Apr. 18, 1824, by Rev. Abel McEwen	4	17
Samuel Nicholas, s. [Sarah, negro], b. June 6, 1792	3	6
Sarah, d. Sarah (negro), b. Aug. 31, 1784	3	6
HERN, Samuel, m. Elisabeth **POWERS**, Mar. 20, 1780	3	5
HERRINGTON, HERINGTON, Elizabeth, d. [Lyman &		
Polly], b. Dec. 15, 1800	3	92
Isaac, twin with John, s. [Lyman & Polly], b. Feb. 4,		
1807	3	92
Jeremiah, m. Hannah **BROWN**, d. Jeremiah, Jan. 17,		
1801	3	195
John, twin with Isaac, s. Lyman & Polly], b. Feb. 4,		
1807	3	92
Lucy Parmelee, d. [Jeremiah & Hannah], b. Apr. 19,		
1803	3	195
Lyman, m. Polly **MARTIN**, Dec. 1, 1799	3	92
Lyman, s. [Lyman & Polly], b. July 9, 1803	3	92
HERSKELL, Oscar, m. Jane **BROWN**, b. of New		
London, Apr. 4, 1830, by Abel McEwen	4	37
HEWITT, HEWETT, HEWIT, Anna, d. [Nathaniel &		
Sarah], b. July 21, 1792	3	42
Elkanah, m. Lucy B. **HAVENS**, Mar. 5, 1837, by		
Rev. Alvan Ackley	4	67
Emeline S., m. Josiah **KINNEY**, Dec. 25, 1831, by		
Chester Tilden	4	46
Henry, s. [Nathaniel & Sarah], b. Oct. 8, 1797	3	42
Joseph, s. [Nathaniel & Sarah], b. May 5, 1794	3	42
Mary, of New London, m. Robert **FRINK**, of North		
Stonington, Aug. 8, 1832, by Rev. Abel		
McEwen	4	47
Mary, m. George **CRAIG**, b. of [New London], Feb.		
4, 1836, by Rev. Abel McEwen	4	64
Nancy, d. Israel, of Stonington, m. George		
WILLIAMS, s. Geo[rge] & Eunice, Dec. 3,		
1778	3	73
Nathaniel, s. Nathaniel & Sarah, b. Aug. 28, 1788	3	42
Prudence, d. [Nathaniel & Sarah], b. May 16, 1800	3	43
Sarah, d. [Nathaniel & Sarah], b. Aug. 1, 1790	3	42
HEWITSON, Anne, d. John, of New London, m. Anthony		
WOLF, a high German, now resid. in New		
London, Oct. [ ], 1753, by Rev. Stephen		
Gorton	3	2
HEWLET, Cinderilla, m. John **DAY**, b. of New London,		
May 5, 1833, by Rev. Abel McEwen	4	51

	Vol.	Page

HEWLET (cont.)

Hannah M., of Groton, m. Augustus W. **ROATH**, of New London, May 4, 1833, by Rev. Abel McEwen — 4, 51

Patty, of New London, m. Stephen **RICHARDS**, of Salem, Mass., Apr. 28, 1823, by Thomas W. Tucker, Elder — 4, 13

HIBBERT, Joanna, d. Joseph, of Windham, m. Jonathan **STICKLAND**, s. Samuel, of New London, Oct. 31, 1754 — 2, 25

HICKEY, Catharine, m. Michael **IGO**, May 12, 1849, by Rev. William Logan — 4, 150

James, of Liverpool., m Alvira **HARRIS**, of New London, Mar. 31, 1843, by R. A. George Thompson — 4, 150

HICKOX, [see also **HISCOX**], James L., of Durham, m. Helen **CORNELL**, of [New London], June 21, 1852, by Rev. T. Edwards — 4, 168

HIDE, [see under **HYDE**]

HIGGINS, HIGGINGS, HIGGANS, Elizabeth, m. John **McATTER**, Dec. 5, 1849, by Rev. W[illia]m Logan — 4, 151

Mary, d. [William & Wealthy], b. Nov. 23, 1786 — 3, 68

Mary, d. William, m. Uzzed **MAGAW**, Oct. 6, 1803 — 3, 122

Richard, m. Ellen **DESMOND**, Dec. 8, [18]50, [by Peter J. Blenkinsop]. Witnesses: John Halpin, Mary Reordan — 3, 306

Richard, m. Ellen [   ], Dec. 8, 1850 — 4, 159

Thomas, s. [William & Wealthy], b. July 17, 1789 — 3, 68

William, from Webley, Herefordshire County, Great Britain, m. Wealthy **POWERS**, d. Capt. Sylvester & Sarah, b. of New London, Nov. 27, 1776, by John Hempste[a]d — 3, 68

William, s. [William & Wealthy], b. Feb. 2, 1784 — 3, 68

HILL, Abigail, d. Charles & Abigail, b. Feb. 24, 1708/9 — 1, 15

Abigail, d. Capt. Charles, formerly of New London, decd., m. Dea. Timothy **GREEN**, Mar. 26, 1749 — 2, 57

Ann Elizabeth, of Groton, m. Charles T. **SMITH**, of [New London], May 15, 1845, by Rev. Robert Hallam — 4, 119

Charles, s. George, of Darby in Darbishire, Old England, m. Ruth **PICKETT**, widow of John Pickett, July 16, [1668] — 1, 5

Charles, s. Charles & Ruth, b. Oct. 16, [1671] — 1, 7

Charles, of New London, m. Rachell, d. Maj. John **MASON**, Deputy Governor of ye colony, June 12, [1678] — 1, 12

Charles, m. Abigail **FOX**, Aug. 28, 1701 — 1, 26

Charles, s. Charles & Abigaill, b. Nov. 23, 1710 — 1, 36

Fanny, m. George W. **HAMLEY**, Apr. 23, 1839, by Rev. Abraham Holway — 4, 85

	Vol.	Page

HILL (cont.)

Hannah, d. Charles & Abigail, b. Mar. 8, 1704/5 — 1 — 35

Hannah, of New London, d. Charles, late of New
London, decd., m. Palmer **CAREW**, of
Norwich, June 1, 1730 — 3 — 20

Jane, d. Charles & Ruth, b. Dec. 9, [1669] — 1 — 6

Jane, m. Abraham **AVERY**, Mar. 14, 1727 — 2 — 1

Jonathan, s. Charles & Ruth, b. Dec. [,1674] — 1 — 9

Mary, of Fairfield, d. Thomas Hill, of Fairfield, m.
Merrett **SMITH**, of New London, s. William
Henry Smith, of Long Island, N.Y., Nov. 6,
1745 — 2 — 108

Rachel, w. Charles, d. Apr. 4, [1679] in childbirth. A
daughter born dead. — 1 — 13

Ruth, d. Charles & Ruth, b. & bd. in Oct. [1673] — 1 — 9

Ruth, w. Charles, d. Apr. 30, [1677] — 1 — 11

Stephen, m. Julia A. **TOSSETT**, b. of [New
London], May 21, 1847, by Rev. M. P.
Alderman — 4 — 132

-----, s. Ruth & Charles, b. Apr. 27, 1677; lived but
half an hour — 1 — 11

HILLHOUSE, HILHOUSE, James, Rev., s. John, decd.,
of Freehall, County of Londonderry, Ireland,
m. Mary **FICH**, Jan. 18, 1725/6 in New London — 2 — 38

James, Rev., d. Dec. 15, 1740, ae 53 y. He was
descended from a respectable family in Ireland
being the second son of John Hillhouse, of
Freehall — 3 — 28

James Abraham, s. Rev. James & Mary, b. May 12,
1730 — 2 — 38

John, s. Rev. James & Mary, b. Dec. 18, 1726 — 2 — 38

Mary, m. William **PRINCE**, May 6, 1775 — 3 — 63

Squire John, eldest s. Rev. James & Mary, d. Apr. 9,
1735, ae 9 y. — 3 — 28

William, s. Rev. James & Mary, b. Aug. 25, 1728 — 2 — 38

HINES, HYNES, John, m. Lucy **FARGO**, d. Zachariah,
Oct. 18, 1795 — 3 — 224

John, s. [John & Lucy], b. Dec. 7, 1801 — 3 — 224

Joseph, s. [John & Lucy], b. May 12, 1804 — 3 — 224

Lucy Frances, d. [John & Lucy], b. May 11, 1807 — 3 — 224

Mary Ann, d. [John & Lucy], b. Oct. 23, 1797 — 3 — 224

HINMAN, Catharine, d. [Noble & Catharine], b. Dec. 12,
176[ ] — 3 — 5

Catharine, m. James **EDGERTON**, May 29, 1788 — 3 — 124

Elisha, m. Abigail **DOLBEARE**, Mar. 24, 1777 — 3 — 76

Elisha, s. [Elisha & Abigail], b. Jan. 29, 1784 — 3 — 76

Elisabeth, formerly Elisabeth **CHRISTOPHERS**, m.
Joseph **HURLBUT**, Jan. 23, 1763 — 3 — 66

Elisabeth, d. [Noble & Catharine], b. Jan. 29, 1763 — 3 — 5

Elisabeth, m. Ebenezer **HOTCHKISS**, Oct. 31, 1785 — 3 — 93

Hannah, d. [Elisha & Abigail], b. Oct. 10, 1779 — 3 — 76

Hannah, d. Capt. Elisha, m. James **DAY**, [   ] — 3 — 253

	Vol.	Page
HINMAN, (cont.)		
Lydia, d. [Noble & Catharine], b. Mar. 26, 1775	3	5
Mary, d. [Noble & Catharine], b. Aug. 1, 1773	3	5
Molly Sherwood, d. [Elisha & Abigail], b. Jan. 6, 1778	3	76
Nancy, d. [Elisha & Abigail], b. July 24, 1786	3	76
Nathan, s. Capt. Nathan & Elisabeth*, b. July 17, 1761. *(Later the wife of Joseph **HURLBUT**)	3	66
Noble, m. Catharine **GREEN***, Oct. 16, 1760. *(Hinman first and crossed out)	3	5
Sally, d. Noble, m. George **PACKWOOD**, Dec. 1, 1799	3	174
Sarah, Jones, d. [Noble & Catharine], b. Oct. 14, 1779	3	5
HINSDALE, Catherine J., of Hartford, m. Christopher C. **MANWARING**, of New London, July 1, 1823, at Hartford	3	202
HISCOX, [see also **HICKOX**], Hannah, d. of Tho[ma]s, of Westerly, R.I., m. Jonathan **ROGERS**, s. Capt. Jno. & grdson of Jno. decd., of New London, Oct. 26, 1737, at Westerly, by John Maxson, Elder	2	32
HOBART, Mary, m. Peter **MASON**, July 8, 1703	2	66
HOBBS, HOBS, John, s. John & Susanna, of Boston, m. Mary **ROGERS**, d. of John, Sr., of New London, Jan. 22, 1729/30, by Christ[opher] Allyn, of S. Kingstown, R.I.	2	117
John, s. John & Mary, b. Aug. 9, 1732	2	117
Susanna, d. John & Mary, b. Feb. 2, 1730/1	2	117
Susannah, of New London, d. John, formerly of Boston, late of New London, m. John **HALL**, of New London, s. David, of New Castle upon Lyne, Northumberland, Dec. 1, 1751	2	44
William, s. John & Mary, b. May 15, 1734	2	118
HOBRON, HOBERN, Andrew A., m. Lucretia A. **HOBRON**, of [New London], July 14, 1844, by Rev. S. Benton	4	113
Andrew J., m. Laura P. **GOFF**, b. of New London, Sept. 5, 1852, by Rev. Jabez S. Swan	4	175
Andrew Jackson, s. [William & Fanny], b. Mar. 1, 1829	3	255
Charles, s. [George & Elizabeth], b. Mar. 3, 1799	3	162
Charles, m. Martha **STEBBINS**, Apr. 14, 1822, by V. R. Osborn	4	7
Daniel P., s. [Russell & Martha], b. Oct. 2, 1826	3	268
Edward, m. Nancy **HOWARD**, b. of New London, Apr. 24, 1829, by Rev. Abel McEwen	4	36
Edward Jones, s. [George & Elizabeth], b. June 7, 1807	3	162
Elizabeth, d. [George & Elizabeth], b. June 7, 1805	3	162
Elizabeth C., m. Benjamin F. **BOLLES**, Mar. 18, 1838, by Rev. James M. Macdonald	4	76

	Vol.	Page
HOBRON, HOBERN (cont.)		
Fanny, of [New London], m. John C. **BAYWOOD**, of New York City, June 23, 1837, by Rev. Abel McEwen	4	71
Frances, d. [William & Fanny], b. Apr. 26, 1820	3	255
George, m. Elizabeth **MASON**, d. Samuel, Feb. 6, 1792	3	162
George, s. [George & Elizabeth], b. Apr. 7 ,1801	3	162
George, m. Mary **HOWARD**, b. of New London, Apr. 28, 1822, by Rev. Abel McEwen	4	8
John Demster, m. Adeline **QUINLINE**, May 4, 1843, by Rev. R. A. G. Thompson	4	104
John H., s. [Russell & Martha], b. Jan. 5, 1825	3	268
John H., m. Adelia **ROGERS**, b. of New London, June 1, 1847, by Rev. Jabez S. Swan	4	132
Leonard, s. [William & Fanny], b. June 29, 1822	3	255
Lucretia, d. [William & Fanny], b. July 25, 1827	3	255
Lucretia A., of [New London], m. Andrew A. **HOBRON**, July 14, 1844, by Rev. S. Benton	4	113
Maria, d. Thomas, of [New London], m. John B. **COIT**, of Philadelphia, [June] 18, [1845], by Rev. Edwards	4	124
Mary, m. Thomas **PAYNE**, July 3, 1836, at Waterford, by Rev. Frances Darrow	4	84
Russell, s. [George & Elizabeth], b. Apr. 7, 1803	3	162
Russel[l], m. Martha **HOWARD**, b. of New London, Jan. 12, 1823, by Thomas W. Tucker, Elder	4	12
Russel[l], s. [Russell & Martha], b. May 1, 1823	3	268
Russell, m. Martha **HOWARD**, [ ]	3	268
Samuel, s. [George & Elizabeth], b. Oct. 16, 1794	3	162
Thomas, s. [George & Elizabeth], b. Oct. 19, 1796	3	162
William, s. [George & Elizabeth], b. Sept. 21, 1792	3	162
William, m. Fanny **BRANCH**, Dec. 3, 1814	3	255
William, s. [William & Fanny], b. Feb. 12, 1817	3	255
Wolcott, s. [Russell & Martha], b. Sept. 15, 1828	3	268
HODGE, Phebe, late of Stonington, m. Jasper **DANIELS**, of New London, Feb. 15, 1789, by Andrew Griswold, J.P.	2	123
HODGSON, William G., m. Jane S. **STEWART**, b. of [New London], Oct. 26, 1847, by Rev. Robert A. Hallam	4	135
HOFMAN, Peter, of Germany, m. Charlotte **OSBORN**, of New London, Sept. 22, 1822, by Thomas W. Tucker, Elder	4	10
HOLDEN, Hannah, of New London, m. Giles **LEEDS**, of Groton, July 11, 1824, by Lodowick Fosdick, J.P.	4	18
HOLDRIDGE, William Franklin, s. William & We[a]lthy, b. Oct. 8, 1801	3	121
HOLLAND, Elisabeth, d. Joseph, Jr. & Mary, b. May 3, 1762	3	25
Elisabeth, w. Joseph, d. Aug. 23, 1762	3	25

	Vol.	Page
HOLLAND (cont.)		
Francis, m. Lucy Bartlet[t] **HOLMES**, Apr. 19, 1807	3	231
Joseph, s. Joseph, Jr. & Mary, b. Sept. 12, 1760	3	25
Joseph, d. Nov. 18, 1762	3	25
Lucy Jane, d. [Francis & Lucy], b. Apr. 15, 1808	3	231
Sarah, d. Joseph, Jr. & Mary, b. Feb. 12, 1759	3	25
William, m. Martha **BEEBE**, of [New London], Aug. 14, 1843, by Rev. S. Benton	4	107
HOLLOWAY, Ann, m. John **FORD**, May 26, 1729	2	24
HOLLY, Mercey, m. David **TUCKER**, negroes, Jan. 12, 1809, by Elder Samuel West	3	106
HOLMAN, Lydia, m. Elisha **DOUGLASS**, b. of New London, Aug. 2, 1823, by Thomas W. Tucker, Elder	4	15
HOLMES, Catharine, m. Joseph **PEABODY**, Mar. 28, 1833, by James Porter	4	50
Elizabeth, d. James, m. Jacob **CHANEY**, Jan. 1, 1792	3	34
George, m. Adeline **COMSTOCK**, b. of New London, Jan. 26, 1845, by Rev. Jabez S. Swan	4	116
Jacob, m. Catherine **WISENBAKER**, b. of New London, Feb. 10, 1823, by Thomas W. Tucker, Elder	4	12
John, s. Thomas & Lucretia, b. Mar. 11, [1686]	1	18
John, m. Mary **WILLEY**, Feb. 11, 1706/7	1	32
John, s. John & Mary, b. Feb. 24, 1708/9	1	33
John, m. Charlot[te] **YENTON**, d. Ezekiel, of Preston, Mar. 10, 1809	3	225
Lucretia, d. John & Mary, b. July 11, 1711	1	37
Lucy Bartlet[t], m. Francis **HOLLAND**, Apr. 19, 1807	3	231
Mary, d. John & Mary, b. Feb. 7, 1712/13	1	39
Mary, m. John **DOUGLASS**, Aug. 12, 1791	3	139
Mary, m. Leonard **DART**, b. of New London, Aug. 28, 1836, by Rev. Squire B. Hascall	4	68
Sally, m. Jeremiah **SHEFFIELD**, July 22, 1823, by Christopher Griffing, J.P.	4	14
Thomas, s. John & Mary, b. Dec. 4, 1707	1	33
HOLT, HOULT, Abba, d. [Ebenezar, Jr. & Elisabeth], b. Jan. 23, 1800	3	161
Abby M., d. Robert, m. Henry G. **DENNIS**, Nov. 2, 1834	3	218
Abby M., m. Henry G. **DENNIS**, b. of [New London], Nov. 2, 1834, by Rev. Abel McEwen	4	58
Abby S., m. Enoch D. **AMES**, b. of New London, Feb. 5, 1832, by Rev. B. Judd	4	48
Abigail, d. William, Jr. & Sarah, b. Feb. 4, 1750/1	2	60
Abigail, d. [Joseph & Elisabeth], b. Dec. 25, 1775	3	32
Abigail Mercer, d. [Robert & Nancy], b. Mar. 3, 1814	3	219
Ann, d. Ebenezer & Joanna, b. Mar. 30, 1773	3	7
Asa, s. [William & Phebe], b. Dec. 13, 1758	3	86

	Vol.	Page

HOLT, HOULT (cont.)

	Vol.	Page
Asa, m. Mary **SMITH**, b. of New London, Apr. 7, 1785, by Andrew Griswold, J.P.	3	86
Asa, s. [Asa & Mary], b. Feb. 12, 1788	3	86
Benj[amin], s. William, Jr. & Sarah, b. Oct. 2, 1740; d. May 5, 1743	2	59
Benjamin, s. William, Jr. & Sarah, b. June 17, 1744	2	59
Benjamin, s. [Joseph & Elisabeth], b. Dec. 22, 1766	3	32
Betsey, d. Jonathan, m. Henry **DUNCKIN**, Dec. 22, 1805	3	174
Catharine, d. W[illia]m & Catherine, b. Dec. 8, 1715; d. Feb. 9, 1715/16	1	55
Catherine, of New London, m. William **CODNER**, of Middletown, July 3, 1774	3	58
Catherine, d. Ebenezer & Joanna, b. Dec. 25, 1774; d. Nov. 6, 1775	3	7
Charles, s. [William, 2d, & Elisabeth], b. Aug. 10, 1774	3	12
Charles, s. William & Elisabeth, b. Aug. 10, 1774	3	46
Charles, m. Mary **DOBBS**, of New York, Aug. 10, 1800, in New York, by Rev. John McKnight	3	46
Charlotte Harris, d. [Giles & Mary], b. Mar. 8, 1817	3	201
Christopher, s. Eben[eze]r & Joanna, b. Sept. 18, 1764	3	7
Christopher, s. [Ebenezer, Jr. & Elisabeth], b. June 10, 1790	3	161
Constant Freeman, s. [Joseph & Elisabeth], b. Jan. 24, 1784	3	32
Daniel, s. William, Jr. & Sarah, b. May 3, 1738	2	59
Daniel, of New London, s. William **HOLT**, 2d, of New London, m. Mary **PEIRPONT**, of Middletown, d. Thomas, of Middletown, Dec. 16, 1762	3	33
Daniel, s. Daniel & Mary, b. Feb. 6, 1764	3	33
David, s. William, Jr. & Sarah, b. Oct. 9, 1756	2	60
David, s. [William, 2d, & Elisabeth], b. May 30, 1779	3	12
Dolly, d. [Jonathan & Abiah], b. May 15, 1791	3	152
Dolly M., d. Jona[than], m. Thomas **WAY**, s. Eben, Nov. 26, 1812	3	226
Ebenezer, s. William, m. Joanna **HARRIS**, d. John, of New London, Nov. 4, 1759	3	7
Ebenezer, s. Ebenezer & Joanna, b. Aug. 15, 1760	3	7
Ebenezer, Jr., m. Elisabeth **CHRISTOPHERS**, June 12, 1786	3	161
Elisha, s. [Asa & Mary], b. Feb. 20, 1786	3	86
Elizabeth, d. Nathaniell & Phebe, b. Nov. 12 ,1707	1	39
Elizabeth, d. William, Jr. & Sarah, b Dec. 4, 1741; d. Sept. 23, 1742	2	59
Elizabeth, d. William, Jr. & Sarah, b. Mar. 14, 1743/4	2	59
Elisabeth, d. Ebenezer & Joanna, b. Sept. 12, 1761	3	7

	Vol.	Page
HOLT, HOULT (cont.)		
Elisabeth, d. [William & Phebe], b. May 9, 1762; d. Sept. 27, 1762	3	86
Elisabeth, d. [William & Phebe], b. Dec. 14, 1763	3	86
Elisabeth, d. William, 2d, m. John **CROCKER**, s. William, all of New London, Nov. 24, 1765	3	34
Elisabeth, d. [William, 2d, & Elisabeth], b. May 30, 1771; d. June 4, 1771	3	12
Elisabeth, d. [Joseph & Elisabeth], b. July 20, 1773	3	32
Elizabeth, d. James, m. Richard **BEEBE**, Jan. 31, 1796	3	171
Elizabeth, d. [Ebenezer, Jr. & Elisabeth], b. Feb. 6, 1796	3	161
Elizabeth, d. Ebenezer, m. Daniel **TINKER**, [ ]	3	166
Elizabeth Ann, d. [Robert & Nancy], b. Sept. 1, 1808	3	219
Elizabeth Ann, m. William P. **COLFAX**, Oct. 25, 1834	3	285
Elizabeth Ann, m. William P. **CO[L]FAX**, b. of New London, Oct. 25, 1834, by Rev. Abel McEwen	4	58
Ellen C., d. of the late Robert & Ann, of [New London], m. Chester R. **BISHOP**, of Danielsonville, s. Gurdon & Lucy, of Chesterfield, Sept. 6, 1847, by Rev. Tryon Edwards	4	134
Esther, m. Jefferson **AVERY**, of New London, Oct. 27, 1844, by Rev. G. Thompson	4	115
Eunice, d. [Joseph & Elisabeth], b. Mar. 1, 1777	3	32
Eunice, d. Joseph, m. Samuel **PITMAN**, Nov. 10, 1799	3	226
Everard, s. [Robert & Nancy], b. Sept. 9, 1810	3	219
Everard, m. Frances C. **COLFAX**, b. of [New London], Nov. 2, 1834, by Rev. Abel McEwen	4	58
Francis William, s. [Ebenezer, Jr. & Elisabeth], b. Jan. 6, 1802	3	161
Francis William, m. Janette **HARRIS**, b. of N[ew] London, Jan. 4, 1832, by Rev. B. Judd	4	48
Freeman, s. [Joseph & Elisabeth], b. July 30, 1771; d. Apr. 24, 1775	3	32
George, s. [William & Phebe], b. Apr. 6, 1757, in Lyme	3	86
George Potter, s. [Robert & Nancy], b. Mar. 6, 1821	3	219
Giles, s. [Daniel & Mary], b. Jan. 13, 1781, d. May 18, 1783	3	33
Giles, s. [Daniel & Mary], b .Aug. 30, 1784	3	33
Giles, m. Mary **ROGERS**, Dec. 25, 1804	3	201
Giles, s. [Giles & Mary], b. May 1, 1807	3	201
Hannah, d. Eben[eze]r & Joanna, b. June 5, 1766	3	7
Hannah, d. [Stephen & Hannah], b. Feb. 3, 1776	3	163
Hannah, m. Stephen **WATEROUS**, Mar. 9, 1788	3	34
Hannah, d. Stephen, m. Henry **JEPSON**, Jr., May 14, 1797	3	164
Harriet, d. [James & Jerusha], b. Sept. 14, 1806	3	218

	Vol.	Page
HOLT, HOULT (cont.)		
Harry, s. [Stephen & Hannah], b. July 23, 1780; d.		
Sept. 7, 1781	3	163
Harry, s. [Stephen & Hannah], b. Feb. 19, 1787	3	163
Henry William, s. [Robert & Nancy], b. June 10,		
1819	3	219
James, s. [Thomas & Patty], b. Apr. 22, 1772; d.		
[ ], 1773	3	93
James, s. [Thomas & Patty], b. Mar. 19, 1778	3	93
James, m. Jerusha **CAFFREY**, relict of John,		
[ ], 1797	3	218
Jesse, s. [Jonathan & Abiah], b. July 30, 1785	3	152
Joanna, w. Ebenezer, d. Jan. 12, 1775	3	7
Joanna, d. [Ebenezer, Jr. & Elisabeth], b. Jan. 21,		
1794	3	161
Joel, s. [Asa & Mary], b. July 30, 1790	3	86
John, s. W[illia]m & Catherine, b. Jan. 11, 1718/19	1	55
John, Jr., m. Martha **COIT**, Nov. 21, 1771	3	88
John, s. [John, Jr. & Martha], b. Sept. 5, 1774; d.		
Aug. 21, 1777	3	88
John, Jr., was slain Sept. 6, 1781, at Fort Griswold	3	88
John, s. [John, Jr. & Martha], b. June 28, 1778	3	88
John Christopher, s. [Ebenezer, Jr. & Elisabeth], b.		
May 2, 1787	3	161
John Rogers, s. [Giles & Mary], b. Feb. 10, 1814	3	201
Jonathan, s. John, b. Sept. 29, 1760	3	152
Jonathan, m. Abiah **DUNTON**, d. Ebenezar, Oct. 24,		
1784	3	152
Joseph, s. William, Jr. & Sarah, b. Aug. 14, 1739	2	59
Joseph, m. Elisabeth **CROCKER**, July 30, 1766	3	32
Joseph, s. [Joseph & Elisabeth], b. Sept. 7, 1769	3	32
Joseph, Sr., d. Mar. 28, 1785, ae 46 y.	3	32
Joshua, s. [Daniel & Mary], b. Mar. 3, 1778	3	33
Lucretia, d. Ebenezer & Joanna, b. Mar. 12, 1763	3	7
Lucretia, d. [Ebenezer, Jr. & Elisabeth], b. Jan. 3,		
1789	3	161
Lucretia Havens, d. [Stephen, Jr. & Jerusha], b. July		
7, 1801* *(Perhaps July 19, 1801)	3	163
Lucy, d. Daniel & Mary, b. Aug. 10, 1768	3	33
Lucy, d. [Jonathan & Abiah], b. June 29, 1793	3	152
Lucy, m. Joshua **KILB[O]URN**, of Wethersfield,		
May 28, 1800	3	227
Lucy Ann, m. George **MINER**, b. of New London,		
Jan. 1, 1832, by Rev. Abel McEwen	4	44
Lucy W., d. Jonathan, m. Gurdon **KIMBALL**, Nov.		
19, 1809	3	238
Martha Coit, d. [Jonathan & Abiah], b. July 26, 1800	3	152
Marthew Coit, d. [Robert & Nancy], b. July 10, 1804	3	219
Mary, d. Daniel & Mary, b. Oct. 29, 1765	3	33
Mary, b. Oct. 29, 1765; m. James **CHAPMAN**, Dec.		
25, 1784	3	245

	Vol.	Page
HOLT, HOULT (cont.)		
Mary, d. [Thomas & Patty], b. Oct. 16, 1776; d. Aug. 26, 1787	3	93
Mary, d. [Asa & Mary], b. Aug. 25, 1793	3	86
Mary, d. [Thomas, Jr. & Mary], b. Apr. 7, 1798	3	220
Mary, relict of Thomas Holt, m. Benjamin **RUMSEY**, Mar. 25, 1801	3	220
Mary, d. [Charles & Mary], b. Nov. 9, 1801	3	46
Mary Ann, d. [James & Jerusha], b. Nov. 6, 1808	3	218
Mary Ann, d. [Giles & Mary], b. July 5, 1809	3	201
Mary J., m. Samuel P. **BILL**, b. of M[as]s., Sept. 6, 1846, by Rev. Jabez S. Swan	4	127
Mary Mumford, d. [Ebenezer, Jr. & Elizabeth], b. Mar. 4, 1798	3	161
Nabby, d. Joseph, m. William **YOUNG**, May 10, 1794	3	217
Nancy, d. [Thomas, Jr. & Mary], b. Feb. 29, 1792	3	220
Nancy, d. [James & Jerusha], b. Aug. 19, 1798	3	218
Nathan, s. [William & Phebe], b. June 18, 1760; d. Feb. 22, 1761	3	86
Nathaniel, s. William, of New Haven, m. Rebecca, d. Thomas **BEEBE**, Apr. 5, [1680]	1	15
Nathaniel, s. Nath[anie]ll & Rebecca, b. July 18, [1683]	1	17
Nathaniell, m. Phebe **TOMLIN**, Dec. 20, 1706	1	39
Nathaniell, s. Nathaniell & Phebe, b. Feb. 28, 1716	1	46
Nathaniel, Jr., s. Nath[anie]l, m. Mary **STRICKLAND**, d. Thomas, July 29, 1735	2	18
Nathaniel, s. Nath[anie]l & Mary, b. June 19, 1736; d. June 29, 1736	2	18
Nath[anie]l, s. Nath[anie]l & Mary, b. Dec. 7, 1737	2	18
Nathaniel, d. Jan. 3 ,1738/9	2	41
Nathaniel, s. [Thomas & Patty], b. Apr. 29, 1774; d. Sept. 19, 1783	3	93
Nathaniel, s. [James & Jerusha], b. Apr. 3 ,1804	3	218
Phebe, d. Nathaniell & Phebe, b. June 21, 1713	1	40
Phebe, d. of Nathaniel, of New London, m. Joseph **HARRIS**, Jr., s. Lieut. Joseph, of New London, Dec. 27, 1733	2	36
Phebe, d. [Joseph & Elisabeth], b. May 22, 1779	3	32
Phebe, m. Christopher **COLVER**, Dec. 14, 1779	3	91
Pierpoint, d. Daniel & Mary, b. Sept. 15, 1773, d. Nov. 23, 1774	3	33
Pierpoint, s. [Daniel & Mary], b. Nov. 24, 1776	3	33
Polly, d. [Thomas & Patty], b. May 10, 1781; d. Aug. 29, 1781	3	93
Rebeckah, d. Eben[eze]r & Joanna, b. Feb. 4, 1768	3	7
Richard Coit, s. [John, Jr. & Martha], b. Aug. 25, 1772	3	88
Richard Coit, s. [Jonathan & Abiah], b. May 29, 1795	3	152
Richard Coit, s. [Robert & Nancy], b. Dec. 23, 1805	3	219
Robert, s. [John, Jr. & Martha], b. Jan. 28, 1782	3	88

	Vol.	Page
HOLT, HOULT (cont.)		
Robert, m. Nancy **HEMPSTE[A]D**, d. Benjamin, Oct. 8, 1803	3	219
Robert, s. [Robert & Nancy], b. July 21, 1816	3	219
Robert, m. Nancy **RENOUF**, b. of N[ew] London, Nov. 20, 1838, by James M. Macdonald	4	80
Royal, s. [Jonathan & Abiah], b. Aug. 7, 1785 [sic]* *(Date conflicts with that of Jesse Holt's birth)	3	152
Russell, s. [William, 2d, & Elisabeth], b. Jan. 25, 1782; d. Mar. 11, 1782	3	12
Samuel, s. William, Jr. & Sarah, b. Feb. 27, 1753/4	2	60
Sarah, d. W[illia]m & Catherine, b. Oct. 28, 1716	1	55
Sarah, d. William, of New London, m. Stephen **HEMPSTEAD**, of New London, s. Joshua, Sept. 19, 1737	2	43
Sarah, d. William, m. Stephen **HEMPSTEAD**, s. Joshua, all of New London, Sept. 19, 1737	2	76
Sarah, d. William, Jr. & Sarah, b. Jan. 28, 1745/6; d. Aug. 25, 1747	2	59
Sarah, d. William, Jr. & Sarah, b. Dec. 27, 1749	2	60
Sarah, d. Daniel & Mary, b. Nov. 11, 1770	3	33
Sarah, m. Richard **LATIMER**, Oct. 20, 1773	3	61
Sarah, d. [William, 2d, & Elisabeth], b. Nov. 5, 1776	3	12
Sarah S., m. Charles M. **GORHAM**, b. of [New London], Apr. 19, 1852, by Rev. Tryon Edwards	4	167
Simeon, s. [Daniel & Mary], b. Mar. 10, 1786	3	33
Sophia, d. [Stephen & Hannah], b. Oct. 30, 1783	3	163
Sophia, d. Stephen, m. Arnold **CLARKE**, Oct. 14, 1804; by Rev. H. Channing	3	158
Stephen, s. William, Jr. & Sarah, b. June 30, 1747	2	59
Stephen, m. Hannah **DOUGLASS**, d. Capt. Nathan, Sept. 17, 1775	3	163
Stephen, s. [Stephen & Hannah], b. Mar. 31, 1777	3	163
Stephen, Jr., m. Jerusha **HOWELL**, d. James, of Sag Harbour, L.I., Oct. 11, 1800, by Rev. Hall	3	163
Surviah Rogers, [d. Giles & Mary], b. Mar. 4, 1811	3	201
Thomas, m. Patty **MORGAN**, Sept. 24, 1769	3	93
Thomas, s. [Thomas & Patty], b. Mar. 19, 1770	3	93
Thomas, Jr., m. Mary **YOUNG**, d. William, Oct. 3, 1791	3	220
Thomas, s. [James & Jerusha], b. Jan. 29, 1802	3	218
Thomas Harris, s. [Giles & Mary], b. Oct. 2 ,1805; d. Oct. 22, 1806	3	201
William, s. Nathaniel & Rebecca, b. July 15, [1681]	1	16
William, s. Nathaniell & Phebe, b. Sept. 12, 1709	1	39
William, m. Catharine **BUTLER**, Jan. 7, 1713/14	1	55
William, Jr., s. Nathaniel, of New London, m. Sarah **WAY**, d. of Samuel, of New London, May 12, 1736	2	59
William, s. William, Jr. & Sarah, b. Jan. 29, 1736/7	2	59

	Vol.	Page
HOLY, HOULT (cont.)		
William, m. Phebe **LAY**, d. John Lay, of Lyme,		
Apr. 20, 1756	3	86
William, 2d, m. Elisabeth **HEMPSTEAD**, Jan. 21,		
1768, by Rev. Mather Boyles	3	12
William, s. [William, 2d, & Elisabeth], b. June 28,		
1769	3	12
William, s. Eben[eze]r & Joanna, b. Nov. 7, 1769; d.		
May 19, 1770	3	7
William, s. Eben[eze]r & Joanna, b. Sept. 8, 1771	3	7
William, s. [William, 2d, & Elisabeth], b. Apr. 20,		
1772	3	12
William, s [Thomas, Jr & Mary], b. Jan. 22, 1795	3	220
William, m. Ann **DANIELS**, b. of New London,		
Aug. 3, 1823, by Thomas W. Tucker, Elder	4	15
Zurviah, see under Surviah		
HOOD, Keysiah, m. Samuel **HOUGH**, of New London,		
Feb. 27, 1718/19	1	52
HOOESOE, George, of New London, m. Jane Miller, of		
Waterford, June 29, 1845, by Rev. T. Edwards	4	121
HOOKER, John W., m. Matilda **SCRUTON**, Nov. 16,		
1851, by Rev. James W. Dennis	4	165
Mehetable, of Hartford, dau. of Samuel, of		
Farmington, decd., m. Daniel **COIT**, Jan. 21,		
1741/2	2	74
Mehetable, of Hartford, wid. of Samuel, late of		
Farmington, d. Jan. 29, 1748/9, at Hartford, ae		
87 y.	2	75
HOPKINS, Jane, d. Benjamin, m. William **WOOD**, May		
8, 1805	3	228
Nathaniel, m. Emeline **CROSBY**, Jan. 1, 1832, by		
Rev. Nathan Wildman	4	45
Samuel S., of Providence, m. Elizabeth P. **BROOKS**,		
of New London, Sept. 30, 1824, by Rev. Abel		
McEwen	4	19
HORTON, Benony, m. Mary **TRUEMAN**, Apr. 15, 1700	1	25
Humphrey P., m. Sarah E. **BUTLER**, b. of [New		
London], May 4, 1847, by Rev. Abel McEwen	4	131
Libbeus, of New London, m. Rhodilla **GRISWOLD**,		
of Norwich, May 7, 1778, by Rev. Andrew Lee,		
of Norwich	3	62
Margaret, m. William **YOUNG**, Dec. 7, 1715	1	49
Sarah, d. Samson, m. William **LAMSON**, s. John, of		
Boston, [ ]	2	90
HOSKINS, HORSKINS, Dorcas, of Win[d]sor, m.		
William **CARDWELL**, formerly of the Parish		
of Zebulon County of Cornwall, now of New		
London, Jan. 19, 1738/9	2	22
James E., of Philadelphia, m. Nancy **VAN COTT**, of		
[New London], June 9 ,1840, by Rev. Abel		
McEwen	4	90

	Vol.	Page
HOSSACK, Alexander, m. Sarah **CARPENTER**, b. of		
New London, Nov. 13, 1842, by Eld. L. Covell	4	103
HOTCHKISS, Abigail Dolbe[a]re, d. [Ebenezer &		
Elisabeth], b. July 26, 1793	3	93
Ebenezer, m. Elisabeth **HINMAN**, Oct. 31, 1785	3	93
Elisabeth Hurlburt, d. [Ebenezer & Elisabeth], b.		
Dec. 30, 1786	3	93
Harriet W., d. [Ebenezer & Elisabeth], b. May 10,		
1791	3	93
HOUGH, Abiah, d. John & Sarah, b. Oct. 30, 1690	1	20
Abiah, of New London, m. Abiell **MARSHALL**, of		
Norwich, Nov. 18, 1708	1	34
Abigail, d. William & Sarah, b. Mar. 7, [1665]	1	4
Abigail, d. William, m. Hiram **DOUGLASS**, s.		
W[illia]m, Dec. 18, 1667	1	5
Ann, m. Thomas **WILLEY**, Dec. 16, 1708	1	34
Ann, m. Samuel **RICHARDS**, May 9, 1726	2	93
Anna, d. William & Anna, b. Dec. 23, [1683]	1	17
Anne, d. William & Sarah, b. Aug. 29, [1667]	1	5
David, s. John & Sarah, b. Oct. 23, 1699	1	25
David, s. John & Hannah, b. Jan. 27, 1723/4	1	64
Deborah, d. William & Sarah, b. Oct. 21, [1662]	1	3
George, s. John & Hannah, b. Feb. 4, 1732/3	2	40
Hannah, d. John & Sarah, b. Jan. 30, 1688	1	18
Hannah, m. Oliver **MANWARING**, Mar. 15, 1704/5	1	30
Hannah, m. Oliver **MANWARING**, Mar. 15, 1704/5	1	50
Hester, d. John & Sarah, b. Apr. 6, 1695	1	23
Hester, m. George **RICHARDS**, Nov. 13, 1716	1	47
Hester, m. George **RICHARDS**, Nov. 14, 1716	1	54
Jabez, s. John & Sarah, b. May 21, 1702	1	28
Jabez, m. Ann **DENISON**, Jan. 7, 1724/5	1	64
Jabez, d. Jan. 24, 1724/5	1	64
Jabez, s. John & Hannah, b. Nov. 16, 1728	2	37
John, s. William & Sarah, b. Oct. 17, [1655]	1	2
John, s. John & Sarah, b. Oct. 1, 1697	1	23
John, m. Hannah **BEEBE**, Jan. 16, 1698/9	1	24
John, Capt., d. Aug. 26, 1715	1	2
John, m. Hannah **DENISON**, Sept. 4, 1718	1	51
John, s. Jno. & Hannah, b. Aug. 14, 1719	1	54
John, s. John & Hannah, d. Mar. 6, 1719/20	1	64
John, s. John & Hannah, b. Dec. 17, 1730	2	38
Jonathan, s. William & Sarah, b. Feb. 7, [1659]	1	3
Samuell, s. William & Sarah, b. Mar. 9, [1653]	1	2
Samuel of New London, m. Keysiah **HOOD**, Feb.		
27, 1718/19	1	52
Samuell, s. William & Sarah, b. "in another place",		
[1756*] *("[1656]" written in pencil)	1	2
Sarah, d. of W[illia]m, m. John **BOURDEN**, July 11,		
[1661]	1	3
Sarah, d. John & Sarah, b. Apr. 23, [1683]	1	17
Sarah, d. John & Sarah, b. Apr. 23, [1684]	1	17
Sarah, m. Eben[eze]r **DENNISS**, Feb. 20, 1706/7	1	53

	Vol.	Page
HOUGH (cont.)		
Sarah, d. John & Hannah, b. Apr. 6, 1722	1	64
William, s. William & Sarah, b. Oct. 17, [1657]	1	2
William, Sr., d. Aug. 10, [1683]	1	17
William, m. Mehetable **PRATT**, of Saybrook, Nov. 2, 1706	1	34
William, s. William & Elizabeth, b. Mar. 24, 1732	2	40
HOUGHTON, [see also **HAUGHTON**], Abigail, d. Sampson & Sarah, b. Apr. 16, 1687	1	60
Christopher, s. Sampson & Sarah, b. Feb. 23, 1702/3. Recorded, Feb. 19, 1722/23	1	60
Ebenezer, s. Sampson & Sarah, b. July 28, 1699	1	60
Ebenezer, s. Ebenezer & Kasiah, b. Sept. 27, 1732	2	39
Elijah, s. Ebenezer & Kasiah, b. Mar. 7, 1734/5	2	40
Elizabeth, d. Sampson & Sarah, b. July 29, 1738	2	41
James, s. Sampson & Sarah, b. Apr. 29, 1719	1	61
James, of New London, s. Sampson, of New London, m Deborah **BA[I]LEY**, of Groton, d. John, Jan. 4, 1748/9	2	45
James, s. James & Deborah, b. Apr. 9, 1756	2	45
James, m. Philenah **WHITING**, d. Col. John, of New London, Apr. 28, 1768	2	46
Jerusha, d. Sampson & Sarah, b. Jan. 25, 1706/7	1	60
John, s. Sampson & Sarah, b. Apr. 27, 1744	2	41
Katharine, d. Sampson & Sarah, b. Mar. 19, 1711	1	60
Lebbeus, s. Sam[p]son & Sarah, b. Mar. 11, 1724	1	63
Lucy, d. Sampson & Sarah, b. July 12, 1741	2	41
Margaret, d. Sampson & Sarah, b. July 8, 1735	2	40
Mary, d. Sampson & Sarah, b. June 1, 1727	2	37
Mercy, d. Sampson & Sarah, b. July 23, 1704	1	60
Sampson, s. Sampson & Sarah, b. May 29, 1692	1	60
Sampson, Sr., d. Jan. 12, 1718	1	60
Sampson, m. Sarah **PEMBERTON**, July 23, 1719	1	61
Sampson, s. Sampson & Sarah, b. Oct. 8, 1731	2	38
Sampson, d. Feb. 26, 1756	2	45
Sampson, s. Sampson, [decd.], d. Feb. 24, 1761	2	45
Sarah, d. Sampson & Sarah, b. July 19, 1721	1	61
Sarah, w. Sampson, d. Dec. 14, 1749	2	42
Sarah, d. James & Deborah, b. Apr. 14, 1750	2	45
Stephen, s. Ebenezer & Kaziah, b. Apr. 12, 1730	2	38
HOUSE, Benjamin Hawkins, twin with Thomas Jefferson, s. [George & Mary], b. July 23, 1796	3	19
George, m. Mary **SHAPLEY**, Dec. 25, 1780	3	19
George, s. [George & Mary], b. Sept. 8, 1783	3	19
Polly, d. [George & Mary], b. July 7, 1785	3	19
Thomas Jeffferson, twin with Benjamin Hawkins, s. [George & Mary], b. July 23, 1796	3	19
HOVEY, Charles, m. Nancy **WORTHINGTON**, b. of New London, Apr. 1, 1832, by Rev. Abel McEwen	4	46
HOWARD, Abigail, d. Eben[eze]r & Elizabeth, b. July 7, 1736	2	85

	Vol.	Page

HOWARD (cont.)

Abigail, had son Ezekiel Lyons, b. May 2, 1756	3	78
Amia, d. [Daniel & Amia], b. Sept. 25, 1787	3	105
Amos, s. [Nathan & Sarah], b. May 8, 1772	3	108
Anna, [d. William & Martha], b. July 6, 1781	3	78
Anne, d. Nov. 24, 1765	3	78
Benjamin, s. Nathan & Lucy, b. May 20, 1761	3	18
Caleb, m. Frances B. **CROSBY**, Mar. 4, 1822, by V. R. Osborn	4	3
Charles, s. [John, Jr. & Nancy], b. Oct. 27, 1820; d. Sept. 12 ,1821	3	203
Daniel, s. Nathan & Lucy, b. Jan. 15, 1744	3	18
Daniel, m. Amia **BECKWITH**, Jan. 22, 1769	3	105
Daniel, s. [Daniel & Amia], b. Apr. 11, 1779	3	105
David, twin with Nathan, s. Nathan & Hannah, b. Jan. 29, 1720	2	6
David, s. Nathan & Lucy, b. Nov. 17, 1751	3	18
Ebenezer, of New London, s. Nathan, of New London, m. Elizabeth **MAYHEW**, of New London, dau. of John, late of New London, decd., Dec. 23, 1729	2	85
Ebenezer, s. Eben[eze]r & Elizabeth, b. Nov. 11, 1733	2	85
Ebenezer, s. [Nathan & Sarah], b. Oct. 22, 1766	3	108
Ebenezer, 1st, d. Nov. 3, 1766	3	78
Edmund, m. Ruth E. **SKINNER**, b. of New London, Oct. 23, 1843, by Rev. S. Benton	4	108
Elisha Smith, s. [Joshua & Mary], b. Oct. 31, 1801	3	119
Elizabeth, d. Eben[eze]r & Elizabeth, b. Sept. 30, 1730; d. Jan. 10, 1731/2	2	85
Elizabeth, d. Eben[eze]r & Elizabeth, b. Dec. 25, 1731	2	85
Elizabeth, of Wethersfield, m. Patrick **ROBERTSON**, of North Briton, Feb. 10, 1737/8, by J. Hempstead, J.P.	3	72
Elizabeth, of New London, d. Ebenezer, m. John **MONROW**, Jr., of New London, s. John, Dec. 4, 1748	2	44
Elisabeth, d. [Nathan & Sarah], b. Mar. 1, 1765	3	108
Elisabeth, d. [William & Martha], b. Mar. 30, 1773	3	78
Elisabeth, w. Ebenezer, d. Sept. 23, 1773	3	78
Elisabeth, d. [Daniel & Amia], b. Jan. 13, 1783	3	105
Elizabeth, d. [John, 2d, & Polly], b. Nov. 17, 1808	3	174
Elizabeth, of [New London], m. Thomas **PAYNE**, of Waymouth, Nov. 30, 1826, by Rev. N. S. Spaulding	4	27
Elizabeth C., m. Oliver **NASON**, Jr., b. of New London, Dec. 15, 1850, by Rev. Jabez S. Swan	4	158
Ellen, d. [John, Jr. & Nancy], b. July 1, 1819; d. Sept. 12, 1821	3	203
Emeline, d. [John, 2d, & Polly], b. Sept. 22, 1810	3	174
Eunice, d. [Nathan, Jr. & Eunice], b. Jan. 30, 1775	3	51

	Vol.	Page
HOWARD (cont.)		
Ezekiel, s. Nathan & Lucy, b. Nov. 9, 1748	3	18
Francis, of [New London], m. John **BUTTIN**, of		
Bona Vista, Sept. 28, 1850, by Rev. Abel		
McEwen	4	155
George B., m. Emely N. **ROGERS**, b. of [New		
London], Apr. 6, 1851, by Rev. Jabez S. Swan	4	163
Grace, d. Nathan & Lucy, b. Oct. 18, 1746	3	18
Hannah, d. Nathan & Lucy, b. Jan. 11, 1754	3	18
Harriet A., m. Edwin A. **DELANEY**, Nov. 1, 1850,		
by Rev. James W. Dennis	4	157
James, s. [Nathan & Sarah], b. July 3, 1774	3	108
James, s. [Joshua & Mary], b. Jan. 10, 1799	3	119
James M., m. Harriet **ROGERS**, b. of New London,		
May 11, 1843, by Rev. G. Thompson	4	104
James Monroe, s. [John, 2d, & Polly], b. June 25,		
1817	3	174
John, s. Eben[eze]r & Elizabeth, b. Oct. 3, 1740	2	85
John, m. Esther **BARROW[S]**, Sept. 10, 1774	3	78
John, s [Daniel & Amia], b. Dec. 1, 1774	3	105
John, [s. William & Martha], b. Jun. 30, 1777	3	78
John, 2d., m. Polly **NEWBUARY**, d. Daniel, May		
31, 1795	3	174
John, s. [John, 2d, & Polly], b. Aug. 30, 1795	3	174
John, Jr., m. Nancy **HARRIS**, Jan. 12, 1817	3	203
Jonathan, s. [Nathan & Sarah], b. Aug. 4, 1768	3	108
Joseph, s. Nathan & Lucy, b. Apr. 19, 1757	3	18
Joseph T., m. Frances A. **BARKER**, b. of New		
London, July 17, 1842, by Rev. R. W. Allen	4	100
Joshua, s. [Daniel & Amia], b. Feb. 22, 1771	3	105
Joshua, m. Mary **ELDERKIN**, d. James, of Norwich,		
Mar. 29, 1795	3	119
Joshua, s. [Joshua & Mary], b. Jan. 24, 1797	3	119
Lucretia, d. Nathan, [Jr.], & Eunice, b. Aug. 23, 1773	3	51
Lucy, d. Nathan & Lucy, b June 17, 1750	3	18
Lucy, w. Nathan, d. May 04, 1761	3	18
Lucy, d. [Daniel & Amia], b. Feb. 23, 1781	3	105
Lydia, of Wethersfield, m. John **MINOR**, of New		
London, May 8, 1729, by Stephen Hicks	2	67
Lydia, of Waterford, m. Francis **GILBERT**, of		
Meriden, Nov 8, 1846, by Rev. L. Geo[rge]		
Leonard	4	129
Lydia S., m. Daniel W. **THORP**, Apr. 24, 1851, by		
Rev. Charles Willett	4	161
Martha, d. [William & Martha], b. Aug. 27, 1769; d.		
Dec. 18, 1773	3	78
Martha, m. Russel[l] **HOBRON**, b. of New London,		
Jan. 12, 1823, by Thomas W. Tucker, Elder	4	12
Martha, m. Russell **HOBRON**, [ ]	3	268
Mary, d. Eben[eze]r & Elizabeth, b. Sept. 28, 1743	2	85
Mary, m. George **HOBRON**, b. of New London,		
Apr. 28, 1822, by Rev. Abel McEwen	4	8

	Vol.	Page

HOWARD (cont.)

Nancy, d. [John, 2d, & Polly], b. June 15, 1807	3	174
Nancy, d. [John, Jr. & Nancy]. b. Nov. 12, 1817	3	203
Nancy, m. Edward **HOBRON**, b. of New London, Apr. 24, 1829, by Rev. Abel McEwen	4	36
Nancy h., of [New London], m. George **HENFIELD**, Dec. 31, 1837, by Rev. Daniel Webb	4	75
Naomi, d. [Daniel & Amia], b. Oct. 30, 1769	3	105
Nathan, twin with David, s. Nathan & Hannah, b. Jan. 29, 1720	2	6
Nathan, s. Nathan, m. Lucy **MINOR**, d. Clement, b. of New London, Mar. 17, 1743	3	18
Nathan, s. Nathan & Lucy, b. Apr. 10, 1745	3	18
Nathan, m. Sarah **CHAPMAN**, May 30, 1762	3	108
Nathan, Jr., s. Nathan, m. Eunice **MINER**, d. Jesse, decd., all of New London, Sept. 26, 1771	3	51
Nathan, d. Mar. 2, 1777	3	108
Nathan, s. [Daniel & Amia], b. May 26, 1777	3	105
Nathan, s. [Nathan, Jr. & Eunice], b. Dec. 3, 1777	3	51
Patty, [d. William & Martha], b. May 30, 1779; d. Sept. 4, 1781	3	78
Patty, d. [John, 2d, & Polly], b. Sept. 24, 1803	3	174
Polly, d. [John, 2d, & Polly], b. Dec. 16, 1801	3	174
Ruth, d. [Nathan & Sarah], b. Aug. 10, 1770	3	108
Samuel, s. [Nathan & Sarah], b. Mar. 3, 1776	3	108
Sarah, d. Ebenezer & Elizabeth, b. Mar. 25, 1739	2	85
Sarah, d. [Nathan & Sarah], b. Mar. 17, 1763	3	108
Sarah, d. Ebenezer, d. May 9, 1769	3	78
Susan, of New London, m. William **PESTON** (?), of New York, Mar. 31, 1850, by Rev. Jabez S. Swan	4	152
Thedee, d. Nathan & Lucy, b. Mar. 31, 1759	3	18
Thomas, s. Nathan & Lucy, b. June 22, 1755	3	18
William, s. [Eben[eze]r & Elizabeth], b. Apr. 18, 1745	2	85
William, s. Eben[eze]r , m. Martha **CROCKER**, June 6, 1768	3	78
William, [s. William & Martha], b. Apr. 10, 1771; d. Dec. 10, 1773	3	78
William, s. [William & Martha], b. May 30, 1775	3	78
William, of New Bedford, Mass., m. Ann E. **PENNIMAN**, of [New London], Sept. 9, 1850, by Rev. Abel McEwen	4	155
HOWE, Nancy A., m. Francis D. **BECKWITH**, b. of New London, Nov. 4, 1832, by Chester Tilden	4	49
HOWELL, Jerusha, d. James, of Sag Harbour, L.I., m. Stephen **HOLT**, Jr., Oct. 11, 1800, by Rev. Hall	3	163
HOXIE, M. D., m. James B. **VANDERWATER**, Nov. 23, 1851, by Rev. James W. Dennis	4	165

	Vol..	Page
HOXIE (cont.)		
Orrin, of Norwich, m. Euretta **JEFFREY**, of New		
London, Feb. 10, 1846, by Rev. L. Geo[rge]		
Leonard	4	124
Thomas S., m. Rachel **DABOLL**, Nov. 15, 1835, by		
Rev. Squire B. Hascall	4	83
HOY, Cath[arine], m. John **KILLIAN**, Oct. 13, [18]50,		
[by Peter J. Blenkinsop]. Witnesses : James		
Gorman, Cath McCann	3	306
Catharine, m. John **KILLIAN**, Oct. 13, 1850.		
Witnesses: James Gorman, Cath[arin]e		
McCann	4	159
HUBART, Elizabeth, d. Sam[ue]l & Sarah, b. Sept. 6,		
1732	2	38
HUBBARD, Carolina, d. Willard & Lucy, b. Dec. 14,		
1772	3	54
Charles W., of Springfield, Mass., m. Sarah O.		
KIMBALL, of [New London], May 10, 1841,		
by Rev. A. Boies	4	95
Daniel, m. Martha **COIT**, Aug. 18, 1731	2	38
Daniel, s. Daniel & Martha, b. June 13, 1736	2	40
Hugh, of Dorsetshire, Old England, m. Jane		
LATHAM, d. Carey, Mar. [, 1672]	1	8
Joseph, s. Hugh & Jane, b. & d. in Nov. [1678]	1	13
Lucretia, d. Daniel & Martha, b. June 18, 1734	2	40
Lucretia, of New Haven, d. of the late Dr. Liveret		
Hubbard, m. Jirah **ISHAM**, Aug. 29, 1799	3	203
Lydia, d. Hugh & Jane, b. Feb. 7, [1675]	1	10
Margaret, d. Hugh & Jane, b. Apr. 14, [1681]	1	15
Martha, m. David **WRIGHT**, of New London, Mar.		
6, 1786, by Joshua Coit, J.P.	3	85
Mary, d. Hugh & Jane, b. Nov. 17, [1674]	1	10
Mary, d. Russel[l] & Mary, b. July 22, 1756	2	26
Mary, of New London, m. David L. **WHEELER**, of		
Stonington, Oct. 17, 1831, by Rev. Abel		
McEwen	4	44
Mary Ann, of New London, m. Lucius H. **CASEY**,		
of Norwich, Ct., Mar. 19, 1842, by Rev. R. W.		
Allen	4	99
Russell, s. Daniel & Martha, b. June 28, 1732	2	38
Russell, s. Daniel & Martha, m. Mary **GRAY**, d.		
Ebenezer & Mary Gray, of Newport, Jan. 30,		
1755	2	26
Sarah, of Windsor, d. of Isaac Hubbard, of Windsor,		
m. George **HARRIS**, of New London, s.		
Gibson Harris, of Norwich, Aug. 15, 1749	2	27
Simeon, s. Willard & Lucy, b. Jan. 30, 1771	3	54
Simeon Carew, s. Willard & Lucy, b. Sept. 10, 1769;		
d. Mar. 6, 1771	3	54
Thomas, s. Russel[l] & Mary, b. Feb. 24, 1758	2	26
Willard, s. Benjamin, of Pomfret, m. Lucy **STARR**,		
d. Samuel, of Norwich, July 20, 1767	3	54

	Vol.	Page
HUBBARD (cont.)		
William W., of Middletown, m. Mary **DANIELS**, of		
New London, Jan. 20, 1822, by Rev. B. Judd	4	7
William W., b. Sept. 13, 1827	3	282
HUBBEL[L], HUBBLE, Ebenezer, d. Apr. [ ], 1720	1	59
Elizabeth, m. Joshua **APPLETON**, Nov. 5, 1713	1	41
Mary, wid., m. Ebenezer **GRIFFIN**, Feb. 11, 1702/3	1	27
HUDSON, John, m. Alvira L. **DIBBLE**, Sept. 4, 1839, by		
Rev. James. M .Macdonald	4	89
Mary, of London, Eng., m. Dennis **SPRINGER**, of		
Ireland, Oct. [ ], 1667	1	5
HUGHES, HUSE, Catharine B., youngest d. Samuel &		
Catharine, of Maryland, m. Tryon **EDWARDS**,		
May 29, 1843, in Philadelphia, by Rev. H. A.		
Boardman	3	293
Elizabeth, m. Nathaniel **THORP**, Sept. [ ], 1786	3	86
Henry, m. Mercy Ann Beebe **AUSTIN**, Dec. 2, 1832,		
by Rev. Francis Darrow	4	49
HULL, Daniel, m. Elizabeth **CORNELL**, d. Job, Oct. 3,		
1784	3	146
Daniel, s. [Daniel & Elizabeth], b. Aug. 1, 1798	3	146
Elizabeth, d. [Daniel & Elizabeth], b. Aug.* 19, 1785		
*(First written "July")	3	146
Elsie, of [New London], m. George D. **BENJAMIN**,		
of St. Helana, Apr. 23, 1851, by Rev. T.		
Edwards	4	161
Esther, d. [Daniel & Elizabeth], b. July 29, 1793	3	146
Frederick, m. Lucretia **CARROL**, b. of [New		
London], Aug. 12, 1838, by Rev. Abel McEwen	4	78
James, s. [Daniel & Elizabeth], b. Mar. 13, 1809	3	146
John, m. Nancy **WHIPPEL**, d. Thomas, May 6, 1794	3	222
John, s. [Daniel & Elizabeth], b. June 24, 1804	3	146
Julia, d. [Daniel & Elizabeth], b. Oct. 31, 1806	3	146
Mary Ann, d. [Daniel & Elizabeth], b. Nov. 25, 1795	3	146
Nancy, d. [John & Nancy], b. June 12, 1795	3	222
Nancy, relict of John, m. John **DENNIS**, May 21,		
1797	3	222
Peter A., m. Martha P. **FREEMAN**, b. of [New		
London], Jan. 14, 1847, by Rev. Robert A.		
Hallam	4	129
Samuel, s. [Daniel & Elizabeth], b. May 24, 1801	3	146
Theodore F., of Marietta, Ohio, m. Evelyn **BUTLER**,		
of [New London], Sept. 9, 1850, by Rev. Abel		
McEwen	4	155
HUMPHREY, Elizabeth, of Hartford, m. Henry		
COTTON, of New London, June 1, 1845, by		
Rev. L. Geo[rge] Leonard	4	123
Sarah Ann, of Hartford, m. Charles H. **BEEBE**, of		
New London, Dec. 8, 1844, by Rev. Jabez S.		
Swan	4	115

	Vol.	Page
HUNT, Alonzo, of New Bedford, Mass., m. Emma W.		
SMELL (?), of [New London], Aug. 31, 1835,		
by Rev. Robert A. Hallam	4	61
Mary Ann, of [New London], m. Franklin **BROWN**,		
of Waterford, May 3, 1840, by John Lov[e]joy	4	90
HUNTER, Francis S., m. Lucy **DARROW**, b. of New		
London, June 26, 1844, by Rev. I. Blain	4	112
HUNTINGTON, Ann Channing, d. Genl. Jedediah, m.		
Peter **RICHARDS**, s. Guy, Nov. 27, 1800	3	141
Ann Elizabeth, d. [Thomas & Elizabeth], b. Dec. 19,		
1819	3	156
Ann Maria, of N[ew] London, m. Orren F.		
BABCOCK, of Lyme, Mar. 12, 1837, by Rev.		
Squire B. Hascall	4	68
Betsey M., of Norwich, m. Elam **CHESEBROUGH**,		
of Bozrah, Feb. 19, 1823, by Lodowick		
Fosdick, J.P.	4	12
Charles B., of New York, m. Caroline A. **BARRY**,		
of [New London], May 10, 1849, by Rev. T.		
Edwards	4	145
Daniel, of North Bridgewater, Mass., m. Sarah S.		
RAINEY, of [New London], Nov. 1, 1841, by		
Rev. Robert A. Hallam	4	116
Elizabeth, d. Capt. Samuel Champlin, m. Isaac		
TRACY, Sept. 23, 1796	3	155
Jedidiah had a slave Hagar, d. Negro Nelly, b. Apr. 1,		
1799	3	65
John, m. Eliza H. **SKINNER**, b. of [New London],		
Aug. 31, 1823, by Rev. Thomas W. Tucker	4	16
Mary Whiting, d. [Thomas & Elizabeth], b. July 2,		
1821	3	156
Ruth A., of N[ew] London, m. Erastus **SAUNDERS**,		
of Hebron, Aug. 12, 1833, by Rev. Abel		
McEwen	4	53
Thomas, s. Jedidiah & Ann, b. Dec. 4, 1793	3	65
Thomas, m. Elizabeth **COLFAX**, Oct. 21, 1818, in		
New York	3	156
HUNTLEY, HUNTLY, Edmund, of Norwich, m. Sarah		
A. **DAVENPORT**, of New London, Aug. 12,		
1849, by Rev. Edwin R. Warren	4	148
Elizabeth, of Lyme, m. John **LEWIS**, May 24,		
[1677]	1	11
James R., of Waterford, m. Harriet **MARTIN**, of		
New London, Oct. 17, 1824, by Rev. Abel		
McEwen	4	20
Jane E., m. Horace T. **COMSTOCK**, June 4, 1845,		
by Rev. Francis Darrow	4	122
Joseph, m. Ruth **WILLIAMS**, Jan. 7, 1728/9	2	37
Mehetable, of Lyme, m. James **ROBINSON**, of New		
London, Oct. 14, 1770	3	57
Nelson, of Colchester, m. Caroline **ATWELL**, of		
Lyme, Apr. 17, 1827, by Rev. Abel McEwen	4	29

	Vol.	Page
HUNTLEY, HUNTLY (cont.)		
Reaney, m. James **RYON**, Dec. 21, 1780	3	106
William, of Waterford, m. Francis E. **BOLLES**, of		
Livonia, N.Y., Oct. 5, 1846, by Rev. Abel		
McEwen	4	128
HURLBUT, HURLBURT, HURLBUTT, Daniel, s. Titus		
& Lydia, b. Sept. 9, 1739	2	44
Denison, s. [Samuel & Matilde], b. Sept. 3, 1801	3	156
Elisabeth, d. [Joseph & Elisabeth], b. Jan. 23, 1764	3	66
[Elisabeth, w. Joseph], d. Mar. 11, 1798	3	66
Elizabeth Christophers, d. [Samuel & Matilde], b.		
July 6, 1797	3	156
George, s. [William & Lowes], b. May 9, 1785, in		
Carlile, Pa.	3	184
George Bottolph, s. Titus & Lydia, b. Jan. 27, 1738	2	44
Hannah, d. [Joseph & Elisabeth], b. Dec. 12, 1769	3	66
John, s. [Samuel & Matilde], b. July 16, 1808	3	156
Joseph, Jr., s. Capt. Jos[eph], of New London, m.		
Mary **BOLLES**, d. Ebenezer, late of New		
London, decd., July [ ], 1762	3	46
Joseph, m. Elisabeth **HINMAN**, formerly Elisabeth		
CHRISTOPHERS, Jan. 23, 1763	3	66
Joseph, twin with Mary, d. [Joseph & Elisabeth], b.		
Mar. 2, 1773	3	66
Joseph, s. [Samuel & Matilde], Aug. 22, 1799	3	156
Joseph, Capt., had negro servant Romeo King, s.		
Lettice, b. Feb. 10, 1785	3	128
Joseph, of Boston, m. Sarah **FOX**, of New London,		
Apr. 15, 1823, by Rev. Abel McEwen	4	13
Keturah, m. Thomas **MANWARING**, Feb. 28, 1782	3	4
Lemon, m. Joshua **WEEKS**, b. of New London, May		
16, 1727	2	108
Lydia, d. Titus & Lydia, b. Dec. 17, 1741	2	44
Lydia, d. Daniel, b. Apr. 12, 1764; m. Ebenezer		
GODDARD, [s. Ebenezer], Sept. 18, 1782	3	154
Lydia, w. Titus, d. Apr. 20, 1769	2	44
Mary, d. Joseph, Jr. & Mary, b. Jan. 14, 1767	3	46
Mary, twin with Joseph, d. [Joseph & Elisabeth], b.		
Mar. 2, 1773	3	66
Mary, d. [William & Lowes], b. Sept. 5, 1790, in		
Kingstown, Suscahanna	3	184
Merriam, m. Joshua **BAKER**, Mar. 27, 1705	1	55
Nancey, d. [William & Lowes], b. June 9, 1788, in		
Kingstown, Suscahanna	3	184
Richard, s. [Joseph & Elisabeth], b. May 8, 1768	3	66
Richard, s. [Samuel & Matilde], b. July 24, 1803; d.		
Aug. 30, 1804	3	156
Samuel, s. [Joseph & Elisabeth], b. July 17, 1765	3	66
Samuel, m. Matilde **DENISON**, d. Elisha, of		
Stonington, June 2, 1796	3	156
Samuel, s. [Samuel & Matilde], b. Mar. 4, 1806	3	156

	Vol.	Page
HURLBUT, HURLBURT, HURLBUTT (cont.)		
Sarah, of East Lyme, m. Linus P. **LUTHER**, of		
Norwich, Sept. 27, 1846, by Rev. Jabez S.		
Swan	4	128
Tabor, s. [William & Lowes], b. June 5, 1793, in		
Kingston, Suscahanna	3	184
Titus, of New London, s. Stephen, decd., m. Lydia		
BOTTOLPH, d. George, of New London,		
Aug. 19, 1734	2	44
Titus, m. Wid. Mercy Wheeler, d. Col. John		
WILLIAMS, of Stonington, Feb. 7, 1770	2	44
William, m. Lowes **READ**, of Ashford, d. James,		
Sept. [ ], 1777	3	184
HURSY, William, s. William & Mary, b. July [ ], 1693	1	19
HUSTACE, HUSTICE, David, of New York, m. Lucretia		
P. **HEMPSTE[A]D**, of New London, Oct. 9,		
1837, by Rev. Abel McEwen	4	30
John, of New York, m. Caroline **LANPHERERE**, of		
New London, Oct. 9, 1837, by Rev Abel		
McEwen	4	74
HUTCHINS, Sarah W., m. William H. **CHAPMAN**, Sept.		
13, 1843	3	291
HYATT, Ebenezer, s. John & Abiga[i]ll, b. Jan. 16,		
1721/22	1	59
HYDE, Betsey, d. Ebenezer, of Lebanon, m. John		
FRENCH, July 22, 1804	3	149
Betsey, d. Ebenezer, of Lebanon, m. John **FRENCH**,		
July 22, 1804* *(First written 1808. Changed		
by L. B. B.)	3	208
Elizabeth, m. Benjamin **ROCKWELL**, Mar. 4, 1804	3	242
Thomas, s. Thomas & Rebecca **RICHARDS**, b.		
Sept. 23, 1719 (Illegitimate)	1	56
HYERS, Mary, m. Richard **MARTIN**, Sept. 19, 1785	3	89
HYNES, [see under **HINES**]		
IGO, Michael, m. Catharine **HICKEY**, May 12, 1849, by		
Rev. William Logan	4	150
IMLEY, William E., of Hartford, m. Lucretia W. **STARK**,		
of New London, Sept. 27, 1843, by Rev. Robert		
A. Hallam	4	106
IMMICH, Peter, m. Elizabeth **SLYDER**, b. of [New		
London], Mar. 30, 1851, by Rev. T. Edwards	4	161
INGHAM, Benony, s. Joseph & Mary, b. June 10, [1686]	1	18
ISBELL, Hannah, d. Eleazer & Eliza, b. Mar. 15, [1673]	1	9
Hannah, d. Robert, decd., m. Thomas **STEDMAN**,		
who had by his 2d wife a s. John, b. Dec. 25,		
1669, and a dau. Ann, b. June [ ], 1668.		
Testified to by Mrs. Elizabeth Trueman & Mrs.		
Susannah Fox., Mar. 4, 1708/9	1	19
Robert, sometime of New London, died leaving 2		
children, Eleazer & Hannah. Testified to by		
Mrs. Elizabeth Trueman & Mrs. Susannah Fox,		
Mar. 4, 1708/9	1	19

	Vol.	Page

ISHAM, George Jirah, s. [Jirah & Elizabeth C.], b. Mar.
 15, 1824 — 3 — 203

Harriet T., of [New London], m. George S.
 WEBSTER, of Island of Cuba, Nov. 19, 1850,
 by Rev. Robert A. Hallam — 4 — 160

Jirah, m. Lucretia HUBBARD, of New Haven, d. of
 the late Dr. Liveret Hubbard, Aug. 29, 1799 — 3 — 203

Jirah, m. Sarah STARR, d. Jona[than], Oct. 16, 1805 — 3 — 203

Jirah, m. Elizabeth C. TROTT, May 28, 1823 — 3 — 203

Jirah, Genl., m. Elizabeth C. TROTT, b. of New
 London, May 28, 1823, by Rev. B. Judd — 4 — 14

Julia H., m. Josiah B. TURNER, July 15, 1822, by
 Rev. B. Judd — 4 — 10

Julia Hubbard, d. [Jirah & Lucretia], b. Mar. 6, 1801 — 3 — 203

Louisa J., of [New London], m. Henry M.
 WOODWARD, of Boston, Dec. 10, 1849, by
 Rev. Robert A. Hallam — 4 — 151

Lucretia, [w. Jirah], d. Mar. 11, 1804 — 3 — 203

Lucretia, d. [Jirah & Sarah], b. July 24, 1806 — 3 — 203

Lucretia, of New London, m. Lewis D. ALLEN, of
 Buffalo, N.Y., July 25, 1837, by Rev. Robert A.
 Hallam — 4 — 72

Mary S., d. Jirah, m. John DICKINSON [   ] — 3 — 268

Mary Starr, d. [Jirah & Sarah], b. Apr. 7, 1808 — 3 — 203

Sarah, w. Jirah, d. Dec. 6, 1814 — 3 — 203

Sarah Elizabeth, d. [Jirah & Sarah], b. July 5, 1810;
 d. May 24, 1812 — 3 — 203

Sarah Elizabeth, d. [Jirah & Sarah], b. Aug. 25, 1812 — 3 — 203

Sarah Elizabeth, of New London, m. Edwin ROSE,
 of U. S. Army, Dec. 13, 1832, by Rev. J. W.
 Hallam — 4 — 49

ISHMAL, Sarah, m. Isaac ROGERS, Oct. 13, 1797, by
 Rev. Henry Channing — 3 — 56

ISOPH*, Christian, m. Ellen Maria AYRES, Apr. 7, 1850,
 by Rev. James W. Dennis   *(Perhaps
 "LSOPH") — 4 — 152

JACKLIN, Freeman, s. Robert & Hagar, b. Nov. 25, 1716 — 1 — 47

Mary, d. Robert & Mary, b. Apr. 24, 1713 — 1 — 47

Robert, a negro, owned for 20 y. by Dr. Peter
 Tappin and sons, was granted freedom Oct 15,
 1711, and permission to go unmolested to New
 Jersey and Newbury — 1 — 48

Robert, m. Mary WRIGHT, Oct. 9, 1712 — 1 — 47

Robert, m. Hager, [   ] Oct. 13, 1713 — 1 — 47

Robert, s. Robert & Hager, b. Mar. "the last day",
 1715 — 1 — 47

JACKSON, Anna, d. [Nathan & Elizabeth], b. Mar. 9,
 1808 — 3 — 196

Antony F., m. Francess MEGARY, b. of [New
 London], Sept. 20, 1840, by Rev. Abel
 McEwen — 4 — 92

	Vol.	Page
JACKSON (cont.)		
Antone F., of [New London], m. Elizabeth **CHURCH**, of Waterford, July 23, 1845, by Rev. John Howson	4	121
Caleb Strong, s. [Nathan & Elizabeth], b. Nov. 13, 1806	3	196
Elisabeth, d. Sam[ue]l & Elisabeth, b. Apr. 23, 1757	3	40
Frederick, s. Samuel & Elisabeth, b. Aug. 25, 1762	3	40
Grace, d. Sam[ue]l & Elisabeth, b. Apr. 8, 1766	3	40
[H]arriot, d. [John & Martha], b. Sept. 23, 1786	3	73
Harriet, m. Daniel **TINKER**, b. of New London, June 26, 1849, by Rev. Edwin R. Warren	4	148
James, s. [Nathan & Elizabeth], b. July 24, 1803, in Boston	3	196
John, m. Martha **BLOYD**, Nov. 14, 1784	3	73
Joseph, s. [John & Martha], b. May 16, 1785	3	73
Lucretia, d. Sam[ue]l & Elisabeth, b. Nov. 12, 1760	3	40
Lucy, m. James **HART**, Oct. 8, 1794	3	138
Martha, of N[ew] London, m. David T. **LISCOMB**, of Providence, R.I., Jan. 1, 1847, by Rev. L Geo[rge] Leonard	4	129
Nathan, s. Giles, of Tyringham, Mass., b. Mar. 13, 1780, m. Elizabeth **THAYER**, of Lynconvill Districk, Me., Sept. 5, 1802	3	196
Nathan, s. [Nathan & Elizabeth], b. Dec. 8, 1804	3	196
Robert B., m. Phebe Ann **COMSTOCK**, b. of New London, Sept. 23, 1849, by Rev. Edwin R. Warren	4	149
Rose, d. Peter & Hagar, b. Mar. 18, 1732/3. Recorded Apr. 14, 1741	2	50
Salisbury, of Wilmington, Del., m. Mary Ann **DUNTON**, of [New London], Nov. 11, 1842, by Rev. Abel McEwen	4	103
Samuel, m. Sarah **HARRIS**, Sept. 16, 1730	2	49
Samuel, s Samuel, & Sarah, b. Sept. 14, 1732	2	49
Samuel, of New London, m. Elisabeth **HARRIS**, of New London, Nov. 15, 1753	3	40
Samuel, s. Samuel & Elisabeth, b. Nov. 22, 1755	3	40
Sarah, d. Samuel & Sarah, b. July 5, 1731	2	49
Sarah, d. Samuel & Elisabeth, b. Feb. 28, 1754	3	40
Silas, s. Samuel & Elisabeth, b. Nov. 30, 1768	3	40
William, s. Sam[ue]l & Elisabeth, b. Feb. 7, 1759	3	40
Zadock, s. Samuel & Elisabeth, b. Oct. 16, 1764	3	40
JACOBS, Henry E., m. Hannah **BILLINGS**, b. of [New London], Feb. 4, 1849, by Rev. Abel McEwen	4	145
JAGGAR, John E., of New York, m. Mary E. **TOOKER**, of [New London], [Mar. , 1851], by Rev. Abel McEwen	4	161
JAMES, Elisabeth, m. John **BARR**, Sept. 6, 1778	3	100
Elizabeth, m. John **ALLENDER**, [ ], at Arston Church, Birmingham, Warwickshire, England	3	290

	Vol.	Page
JARED, Agnes, d. [Richard, alias Richard Parkin, &		
Violet], b. Mar. 16, 1790	3	67
Mary, d. Richard, alias Richard Parkin, & Violet, b.		
Dec. [ ], 1787	3	67
Nancy, d. [Richard, alias Richard Parkin, & Violet],		
b. Sept. 19, 1798	3	67
Richard, d. Sept. 19, 1798	3	67
Violet, d. [Richard, alias Richard Parkin, & Violet],		
b. July 24, 1792	3	67
JARMAN, John, of New Orleans, m. Jane **DOHERTY**, of		
[New London], Nov. 30, 1846, by Rev. Abel		
McEwen	4	128
JEFFERY, JEFFRAY, Abigail, d. [Charles, Jr. &		
Elisabeth], b. Oct. 13, 1777	3	113
Ann, d. [Moses & Lucy], b. Mar. 15, 1780	3	123
Anna, d. [Charles, Jr. & Thankfull], b. Jan. 9, 1767	3	113
Cat[h]erine, d. [Moses & Lucy], b. Feb. 1, 1773	3	123
Catharine, m. Thomas **WHIPPLE**, Sept. 13, 1773	3	123
Catharine, d. [Charles, Jr. & Elisabeth], b. Nov. 5,		
1782	3	113
Catherine, d. Moses, m. Isaac **THORP**, Mar. 25,		
1798	3	172
Charles, Jr., m. Thankfull **BOVEL**, May 14, 1759	3	113
Charles, s. [Charles, Jr. & Thankfull], b. Oct. 10,		
1759	3	113
Charles, Jr., m. Elisabeth **WHALIN**, May 16, 1772	3	113
Charles, 3d, m. Lydia **LEECH**, July 21, 1782	3	113
Charles, m. Lydia **LEACH**, d. Samuel, July 21, 1782	3	223
Charles, s. [Charles, 3d, & Lydia], b. Oct. 17, 1784	3	113
Charles, s. [Charles & Lydia], b. Oct. 17, 1784	3	223
Charles, m. Abiga[i]l **WATSON**, Nov. 24, 1790	3	223
Charles, m. Lydia **HARRINGTON**, b. of New		
London, Mar. 15, 1837, by Rev. Squire B.		
Hascall	4	68
Elizabeth, of Groton, dau. of Capt. Jonathan **STARR**,		
decd., m. Daniel **COIT**, Dec. 16, 1764	2	75
Eunis, d. [Charles & Abiga[i]l, b. Jan. 21, 1797	3	223
Eunice, m. Robert **GOODWIN**, of Dresden, Maine,		
July 23, 1815	3	196
Euretta, of New London, m. Orrin **HOXIE**, of		
Norwich, Feb. 10, 1846, by Rev. L. Geo[rge]		
Leonard	4	124
Euretta, see also Uretta		
Frances M., m. Oliver W. **DART**, b. of [New		
London], Sept. 21, 1851, by Rev. Tryon		
Edwards	4	165
Francis, [child of Moses & Lucy], b. Feb. 24, 1783	3	123
George, s, [Charles & Abiga[i]l, b. June 29, 1808	3	223
Grace, d. [Moses & Lucy], b. Sept. [ ], 1777	3	123
Grace, d. [Charles, Jr. & Elisabeth], b. Mar. 5, 1790	3	113
Gurdon, s. [Charles & Abiga[i]l], b. Nov. 9, 1798	3	223
Henry, s. [Charles & Abiga[i]l], b. May 7, 1792	3	223

	Vol.	Page
JEFFERY, JEFFRAY (cont.)		
James, s. [Charles, Jr. & Thankfull], b. Apr. 16, 1761	3	113
James, m. Sarah **BEEBE**, d. Joab, May 11, 1795	3	190
James, s. [Charles & Abiga[I]l], b. Jan. 28, 1802	3	223
James, s. [James & Sarah], b. June 20, 1805	3	190
James, of N[ew] London, m. Phebe **PARKS**, of		
Groton, Mar. 2, 1834, by Rev. Ebenezer Blake	4	54
Joab B., m. Betsey **JOHNSON**, b. of New London,		
Oct. 3, 1824, by Rev. Abel McEwen	4	19
Joab Beebe, s. [James & Sarah], b. June 2, 1801	3	190
John, s. [Charles, Jr. & Thankfull], b. Oct. 7, 1764	3	113
John, s. [Charles & Abiga[i]l], b. Dec. 19, 1805	3	223
John, of New London, m Eliza Ann		
WATERHOUSE, of Waterford, Feb. 23, 1825,		
by Rev. Abel McEwen	4	21
John, m. Mary **HARRINGTON**, b. of New London,		
Aug. 4, 1831, by Rev. Abel McEwen	4	43
Lucretia, d. [Charles & Abiga[i]l], b. Sept. 21, 1795;		
d. Mar. 20, 1805	3	223
Lucretia, d. [Charles & Abiga[i]l], b. Aug. 29, 1806	3	223
Lucretia, of New London, m. Jonas **WILLIAMS**, of		
Norwich, Jan. 31, 1825, by Rev. Abel McEwen	4	21
Lucy, d. [Moses & Lucy], b. Apr. 27, 1768	3	123
Lydia, [w. Charles], d. [ ], 1787	3	223
Lydia, d. [Charles, Jr. & Elisabeth], b. Sept. 5, 1788	3	113
Martha, d. [Charles, Jr. & Elisabeth], b. Apr. 10,		
1786	3	113
Mary, d. [Moses & Lucy], b. Aug. 9, 1775	3	123
Mary, d. [Charles, Jr. & Elisabeth], b. Nov. 8, 1780	3	113
Matilde, d. [James & Sarah], b. Jan. 8, 1808	3	190
Moses, m. Lucy **OTIS**, Mar. 5, 1768	3	123
Moses, s. [Moses & Lucy], b. Apr. 23, 1771	3	123
Richard, s. [Moses & Lucy], b. Aug. 25, 1789	3	123
Robert, s. [Charles & Abiga[I]l], b. Jan. 10, 1794	3	223
Russel[l], s. [Moses & Lucy], b. June 22, 1786	3	123
Samuel, s. [Charles, 3d, & Lydia], b. Aug. 1, 1786	3	113
Samuel, s. [Charles & Lydia], b. Aug. 1, 1786	3	223
Samuel, m. Harriet **ROGERS**, b. of New London,		
June 25, 1837, by Rev. Nathan Wildman	4	71
Sarah Miner, d. [James & Sarah], b. Aug. 2, 1797	3	190
Thankfull, d. [Charles, Jr. & Thankfull], b. Mar. 27,		
1768	3	113
Thankfull, w. Charles, [Jr.], d. Mar. [ ], 1768	3	113
Thankfull, d. Charles, m. John **LEMMEY**, May 7,		
1798	3	120
Thomas, s. [Charles, Jr. & Thankfull], b. July 27,		
1762	3	113
Thomas, s. [Charles & Abiga[i]l], b. Aug. 21, 1800	3	223
Uretta F., m. Homer **WHEELER**, b. of New		
London, July 31, 1842, by Rev. R. W. Allen	4	100
Uretta, see also Euretta		

	Vol.	Page

JEFFERY, JEFFRAY (cont.)

William, s. [Charles, Jr. & Elisabeth], b. Sept. 30,
1772 — 3 — 113

William, s. [Charles & Abiga[i]l], b. Apr. [ ], 1804 — 3 — 223

-----, d. Charles & Ann, [b.] Oct. [ ], 1737 — 2 — 120

-----, d. Charles & Ann, [b.] [ ] 1, 1738 — 2 — 120

JENISON, Samuel, m. Rebecca **DOUGLASS**, Nov. 20,
1791 — 3 — 122

JENKINS, JENKENS, Anna, d. John, late of Warwick,
R.I., m. James **ANGELL**, s. William, of New
London, Feb. 23, (21?), 1760, by Rev. Joshua
Mors[e] — 3 — 12

Archabald, of Norwalk, Va., m. Emela **NEWTON**,
of Norwich, Ct., Sept. 12, 1842, at Mrs. King's
house on Potter St., by Henry Douglass, J.P. — 4 — 101

JENNINGS, JINNINGS, JENNINS, Ann, wid., d.
SamuelCHAMPLIN, m. Richard
DOUGLAS[S], Nov. 9, 1777 — 3 — 189

Anne, m. Richard **DOUGLASS**, Nov. 9, 1777 — 3 — 65

Christina Ann, m. Jabez **BROOKS**, b. of [New
London], June 21, 1848, by Rev. Robert A.
Hallam — 4 — 141

Eleonor, m. Richard **MANWARING**, May 25, 1710 — 1 — 19

Richard, m. Elizabeth **REYNOLDS**, b. of Barbadoes,
June [ ], [1678] — 1 — 12

Richard, m. Elizabeth **REYNOLDS**, of Barbadoes,
the beginning of June, 1678 — 1 — 67

Richard, s. Rich[ar]d & Elizabeth, b. Mar. 11, [1680] — 1 — 14

Richard, s. [Richard & Elizabeth], b. Mar. 11, [ ] — 1 — 68

Samuel, s. Richard & Elizabeth, b. Mar. 8, [1679] — 1 — 14

Samuell, s. [Richard & Elizabeth], b. Mar. 11, 1679 — 1 — 68

JEPSON, Adeline, m. Charles M. **WILLOUGHBY**, of
Wintonburg, Mar. 30, 1831, by Rev. Leonard
B. Griffing — 4 — 40

Ann, d. [Henry & Hannah], b. Nov. 17, 1771 — 3 — 41

Charles Henry, s. [Henry, Jr. & Hannah], b. July 15,
1803 — 3 — 164

Daniel, s. [Henry & Hannah], b. Jan. 8, 1775 — 3 — 41

Eliza, of New London, m. Allyn H. **TOOKER**, of
Saybrook, Oct. 17, 1824, by Rev. Abel
McEwen — 4 — 19

Eliza Holt, d. [Henry & Hannah], b. Feb. 12, 1798 — 3 — 164

Esther, d. [Henry & Hannah], b. Sept. 17, 1779 — 3 — 41

Hannah, d. [Henry & Hannah], b. Sept. 7, 1769 — 3 — 41

Hannah, of [New London], m. William N.
HEMPSTE[A]D, of Saybrook, Nov. 18, 1838,
by Rev. James M. Macdonald — 4 — 80

Henry, m. Hannah **DENISON**, Jan. [ ], 1769 — 3 — 41

Henry, s. [Henry & Hannah], b. May 6, 1773 — 3 — 41

Henry, Jr., m. Hannah **HOLT**, d. Stephen, May 14,
1797 — 3 — 164

John, s. [Henry & Hannah], b. Apr. 13, 1783 — 3 — 41

	Vol.	Page
JEPSON (cont.)		
Julia, m. George **THATCHER**, b. of New London,		
Apr. 11, 1826, by Rev. Isaac Stoddard	4	25
Julia Aann, d. [Henry, Jr. & Hannah], b. Aug. 29,		
1799	3	164
Margaret, d. [Henry & Hannah], b. Dec. 12, 1776	3	41
Margaret, d. [Henry, Jr. & Hannah], b. May 26, 1808	3	164
Martha, of New London, m. Elbert **LATHAM**, of		
Sag Harbor, N.Y., Apr. 17, 1825, by Rev.		
Daniel Dorchester	4	22
Mary, d. [Henry, Jr. & Hannah], b. July 7, 1805	3	164
Mary C., of New London, m. Joseph **JOHNSON**, of		
New York, Sept. 17, 1833, by Chester Tilden	4	52
Patty Douglass, d. [Henry, Jr. & Hannah], b. Feb. 28,		
1801	3	164
JEROME, JEROM, Abba, m. Riley **SWEET**, Apr. 25,		
1839, by Rev. Abraham Holway	4	85
Abigail, d. [Benjamin & Desire], b. Apr. 7, 1785	3	155
Antonio, of New London, m. Harriet **BROWN**, of		
Waterford, June 13, 1830, by Rev. Abel		
McEwen	4	38
Benjaman, m. Desire **BROWN**, d. Benjaman, Dec.		
22, 1773	3	155
Benjaman, s. [Benjaman & Desire], b. Oct. 12, 1775;		
d. Oct. 5, 1796	3	155
Benjamin, d. Dec. 30, 1824	3	155
Frances, d. [Benjaman & Desire], b. Jan. 25, 1782	3	155
Hannah, d. [Benjaman & Desire], b. July 22, 1774	3	155
Harriet A., of [New London], m. Stephen **BEENEY**,		
of Sag Harbor, N.Y., Aug. 3, 1851, by Rev. J.		
M. Eaton	4	164
Jesse, s. [Benjaman & Desire], b. Oct. 11, 1780	3	155
John, s. [Benjaman & Desire], b. Aug. 31, 1783	3	155
Lucinda, m. John **GORMAS**, b. of [New London],		
Feb. 9, 1849, by Rev. Abel McEwen	4	145
Mary Ann, m. John P. **KING**, Sept. 21, 1829, by		
Rev. Francis Darrow	4	36
Richard, s. [Benjaman & Desire], b. Oct. 22, 1778	3	155
William, s. [Benjaman & Desire], b. Feb. 8, 1777;		
lost at sea Sept. [ ], 1796	3	155
JEWETT, Lucy, of Lyme, d. Capt. Nathaniel Jewett, of		
Lyme, m. Joshua **RAYMOND**, Jr., of New		
London, s. Joshua, of New London, Oct. 4,		
1750, by Rev. Geo[rge] Beckwith	2	113
Lucy, m. Samuel **CHAPPELL**, Jr., Dec. 15, 1803	3	255
JIGGLES, Thomas, of Boston, m. Mary **FOSDICK**, of		
N[ew] London, Nov. 17, 1708 (Arnold copy		
gives the name "**JOGGLES**". See Caulkins'		
History for correction)	1	34
JILLET, [see also **GILLETT**], Joyce, of Hebron, m.		
John **LEWIS**, of New London, Sept. 4, 1794	3	130

	Vol.	Page
JINISSAN, Patrick, m. Catharine **TOOPY**, July 20, 1847, by Rev. John Brady	4	132
JOHN, Joseph F., m. Mary Ann **CONE**, b. of New London, July 7, 1844, by Rev. Robert A. Hallam	4	112
JOHNSON, JOHNSTON, JOHNSTONE, Amasa, of Manchester, Ct., m. Ellen **MANIERRA**, of New London, May 3, 1848, by John Grace, J.P.	4	139
Betsey, m. Joab B. **JEFFREY**, b. of New London, Oct. 3, 1824, by Rev. Abel McEwen	4	19
Bettey, d.* Dan[ie]l & Kezia, b. Oct. 25, 1743 *(Copy says "son")	2	49
David, s. Dan[ie]l & Kezia, b. Mar. 26, 1741/2	2	49
David, m. Nancy **ROGERS**, d. Peter, July 16, 1797	3	173
David, s. [David & Nancy], b. July [ ], 1808	3	173
Francis, m. Sarah **DUNBAR**, b. of New London, May 14, 1846, by Rev. L. Geo[rge] Leonard	4	129
Franklin, m. Miranda **STANLEY**, b. of New London, Mar. 21, 1832, by Rev. Abel McEwen	4	46
Hannah, d. [David & Nancy], b. May 27, 1798	3	173
Harriet, m. Frank **GUARTER**, b. of New London, July 16, 1845, by Rev. Jabez S. Swan	4	120
Harry D., of New York, m. Susan **O'HARA**, Jan. 20, 1837, by Rev. Robert A. Hallam	4	84
John, s. Dan[ie]l & Keziah, b. Sept. 17, 1745	2	49
John, m. Sally **BEEBE**, d. James, Nov. 16, 1798	3	40
John, s. [John & Sally], b. May 24, 1804	3	40
Joseph, of New York, m. Mary C. **JEPSON**, of New London, Sept. 17, 1833, by Chester Tilden	4	52
Lucretia, d. [David & Nancy], b. Nov. 28, 1804	3	173
Lydia, of New London, m. Isaac **WEEDEN**, of Newport, July 16, 1785	3	44
Mary, of Newport, d. Isaac, of Newport, decd., m. John **HALLAM**, of New London, s. Nicholas, decd., Dec. 30, 1730	2	31
Mary Ann, m. James **CLARK**, b. of N[ew] London, July 28, 1851, by Rev. J. M. Eaton	4	164
Nancy, d. [David & Nancy], b. Mar. 4, 1802	3	173
Nancy, [d. William & Nancy], b. May 30, 1804	3	131
Nicholas, s. [William & Nancy], b. Feb. 6, 1803	3	131
Robert, s. [William & Nancy], b. July 1, 1801	3	131
Samuel, s. [John & Sally], b. Jan. 16, 1799; d. July 28, 1815, ae 15 y. on board the sloop "Mary" on her passage from Orracock, N. Carolina. Buried on Powder Island	3	40
Sarah, d. Capt. Samuel, of Middletown, m. Edward **HALLAM**, Oct. 20, 1803	3	194
Thomas Hicks, s. [William & Nancy], b. July 30, 1807	3	131
William, m. Nancy **LEACH**, d. John, of Montville, June 26, 1799	3	131
William G., s. [William & Nancy], b. Apr. 3, 1800	3	131

	Vol.	Page

JOHNSON, JOHNSTON, JOHNSTONE (cont.)

William H., of Portsmouth, Va., m. Mary Ann
BEEBE, of New London ,Oct. 27, 1831, by
Rev. Abel McEwen ... 4 ... 44

JONES, JOANES, Abby, of [New London], m. Peter
MILLER, of Gurnsey, Europe, July 28, 1843,
by R. A. G. Thompson ... 4 ... 106

Alexander, m. Hannah Maria **POTTS**, Aug. 21, 1831 ... 3 ... 299

Alexander, of Lyme, m. Hannah Maria **POTTS**, of
New London, Aug. 21, 1831, by Rev. Abel
McEwen ... 4 ... 43

Alexander, s [Alexander & Hannah Maria], d. Feb.
14, 1833 ... 3 ... 299

Alexander, s. [Alexander & Hannah Maria], b. Sept.
16, 1833 ... 3 ... 299

Alexander, s. [Alexander & Hannah Maria], b. July
7, 1848 ... 3 ... 299

Bartholomew, m. Ann **DONOVAN**, Sept. 9, 1849,
by Rev. William Logan ... 4 ... 150

Catherine, d. Tho[ma]s & Katharine, b. Dec. 20,
[1679] ... 1 ... 14

Catharine, d. [Thomas & Katharine], b. 8ber 20, [   ] ... 1 ... 67

David, of Utica, N.Y., m. Jane A. **TILLOTSON**, of
[New London], Dec. 10, 1848, by Rev. M. P.
Alderman ... 4 ... 144

Dyer, s. Henry & Mary, b. Apr. 11, 1755 ... 3 ... 4

Edward, m. Bathsheba **FANNING**, b. of New
London, June 9, 1822, by Rev. Abel McEwen ... 4 ... 9

Elisha C., of Hartland, m. Julia **CHAPPEL[L]**, of
[New London], Sept. 7, 1835, by Rev. Abel
McEwen ... 4 ... 62

Eliza, of East Haddam, m. Stiles **FRINK**, of
Stonington, Jan. 18, 1835, by Rev. Alven
Ackley ... 4 ... 59

Ellen M., d. [Alexander & Hannah Maria], b Sept. 1,
1840 ... 3 ... 299

Erastus, of East Haddam, m. Elizabeth **MAYNARD**,
May 2, 1831, by Rev. Daniel Wildman ... 4 ... 42

Erastus, m. Sarah W. **MALLORY**, b. of [New
London], Apr. 5, 1835, by Rev. Ebenezer Blake ... 4 ... 60

Eunice, of Waterford, m. Samuel H. **SHIPLY**, of
Rochdell, England, July 6, 1823, by Thomas
W. Tucker, Elder ... 4 ... 15

Eunice L., m. Samuel N. **STRICKLAND**, b. of New
London, Nov. 21, 1842, by Eld[er] L. Covell ... 4 ... 103

George, m. Frances E. **FOSDICK**, b. of [New
London], Oct. 5, 1834, by Rev. Abel McEwen ... 4 ... 58

George, of Boston, m. Ann Saltonstall
CHRISTOPHERS, of New London, [   ],
by Rev. B. Judd ... 4 ... 42

	Vol.	Page
JONES, JOANES (cont.)		
Henry, of New London, s. George, of Ireland, m.		
Mary **BEEBE**, d. William Beebe, late of New		
London, decd., Nov. [ ], 1754	3	4
Henry, s. Henry & Mary, b. Nov. 13, 1757	3	4
Henry, of Hamburg, France, m. Pavilla		
CROSSMAN, of New London, May 8, 1832,		
by Chester Tilden	4	46
Henry F., of Salem, m. Ann E. **CHAP[P]EL[L]**, of		
Waterford, Nov. 8, 1848, by Rev. Abel		
McEwen	4	143
James, of Stratford, m. Esther **WEEKS**, of New		
London, June 9, 1799	3	21
Jane, d. Tho[mas] & Catharine, b. Feb. 26, [1677]	1	12
Jane, d. [Thomas & Katharine], b. Feb. 26, 1677	1	67
Joel, m. Lucretia **LEWIS**, Dec. 1, 1830, by Rev.		
Daniel Wildman	4	39
John, s. John, of Boston, dec., m. Abigail **ROGERS**,		
d. Adam, of New London, Mar. 8, 1736/7	2	19
John, m. Mary **TOOKER**, b. of New London, Apr.		
9, 1843	4	102
Katharine, m. Adam **ROGERS**, Sept. 1, 1702	1	28
Louisa A., d. [Alexander & Hannah Maria], b. Dec.		
10, 1842	3	299
Lucretia, d. [Thomas & Rebecca], b. Nov. 29, 1789	3	139
Mary, d. [Alexander & Hannah Maria], b. Mar. 27,		
1845; d. Dec. 26, 1850	3	299
Mary, d. Capt. Jonas, m. Timothy **LESTER**, of New		
London, s. Timo[thy], decd., June 13, 1751	2	97
Patty, m. Marvin **WAIT**, b. of New London, Apr. 25,		
1779	3	42
Pri[s]cilla, d. [Alexander & Hannah Maria], b. May		
14, 1851	3	299
Rebekah, d. [Thomas & Rebecca], b. Jan. 23, 1778	3	139
Sarah, d. Rytie, of Boston, m. John **PRENTICE**, s.		
John, Nov. 23, [1675]	1	10
Sarah C., of [New London], m. Guy D. **MORGAN**,		
of Waterford, Nov. 15, 1841, by Rev. Abel		
McEwen	4	96
Susan, d. [Alexander & Hannah Maria], b. Feb. 26,		
1838	3	299
Thomas, m. Catherine, d. Thomas **GAM[M]ON**,		
June 25, [1677]	1	11
Thomas, m. Katharine **GAMON**, d. Thomas, of New		
Foundland, June 25, 1677	1	67
Thomas, Jr., m. Mary **POLLY**, Dec. 30, 1703	1	29
Thomas, s. Thomas, Jr. & Mary, b. June 22, 1704	1	30
Thomas, m. Rebecca **CHURCH**, Dec. 25, 1776	3	139
Thomas, d. Sept. 2, 1798	3	139
Thomas C., s. [Alexander & Hannah Maria], b. June		
10, 1836	3	299

	Vol.	Page

JONES, JOANES (cont.)

William A., s. [Alexander & Hannah Maria], b. June
    23, 1834 — 3 — 299

JORDON, JORDAN, Edward, m. Ellen **ANTHONY**, b.
    of [New London], Aug. 20, 1851, by Rev.
    Samuel Fox — 4 — 164

Martha M., m. Samuel **WHITE**, b. of New London,
    June 9, 1844, by Rev. Jabez S. Swan — 4 — 112

Mary, d. Jeffrey, of Ireland, m. James **ROGERS**, s.
    [ ], Sr., of New London, Nov. 5, [1674] — 1 — 9

JOSEPH, Emanuel, m. Sophia **EMANUEL**, July 1, 1850,
    by Rev. James W. Dennis — 4 — 155

Mary, m. Charles **FRANCESCO**, b. of New London,
    July 7, 1850, by Rev. George M. Carpenter — 4 — 155

JOY, Mary Ann, of Norwich, m. Daniel R. **DARBY**, Nov.
    14, 1843, by Rev. Sanford Benton — 4 — 110

JOYCE, William, m. Mary B. **BECKWITH**, Feb. 19,
    1823, by Lodowick Fosdick, J.P. — 4 — 12

JUDD, Ann Maria Chandler, of New London, m. George
    FETTERMAN, of U. S. Army, [ ],
    by Rev. B. Judd — 4 — 42

James, of Glastenbury, m. Eliza T. **SNELL**, of [New
    London], Aug. 1, 1830, by Daniel Wildman — 4 — 39

JULLIVER, [see under **ELIZABETH MEADES**]

KEABLES, John L., of Stonington, m Caroline **BEEBE**,
    of New London, Apr. 19, 1836, by Rev. Squire
    B. Hascall — 4 — 83

KEENEY, KEENY, KEYNEY, Abby A., of [New
    London], m. Joel **SEYMOUR**, of New York,
    [ ] 7, [1832?], by Rev. Abel McEwen
    (Perhaps Abby A. **HENEY**) — 4 — 57

Abby Jane, of New London, m. Joseph A.
    SHIPMAN, Jan. 9, 1848, by Rev. L. G.
    Leonard — 4 — 137

Alvira, d. [John, Jr & Lucretia], b. July 20, 1797 — 3 — 226

Amos, m. Anna **ROGERS**, d. John, Dec. 31, 1775 — 3 — 177

Amos, s. [Amos & Anna], b. Aug. 12, 1787 — 3 — 177

Anna, d. [Amos & Anna], b. May 16, 1775 — 3 — 177

Bets[e]y, d. John, m. John **MASON**, Nov. 22, 1795 — 3 — 202

Betsey, d. [Nathaniel & Betsey], b. Jan.* 29, 1799
    *(First written "Sepr") — 3 — 229

Betty, d. [William & Betty], b. Sept. 19, 1787 — 3 — 106

Caroline, m. Samuel **LESTER**, Dec. 31, 1840, by H.
    R. Knapp — 4 — 93

Charlot[te], d. [John, Jr. & Lucretia], b. Sept. 28,
    1799 — 3 — 226

Christopher Hempste[a]d, s. [John & Mary], b. Mar.
    12, 1807 — 3 — 226

Danforth Wales, s. [Jeremiah & Susan], b. Oct. 11,
    1803 — 3 — 177

Daniel, 3rd, s. John & Abigail, b. Oct. 26, 1781; m.
    Gennet **GORDON**, d. John, Jan. 1, 1804 — 3 — 188

	Vol.	Page

KEENEY, KEENY, KEYNEY (cont.)

	Vol.	Page
Daniel G., m. Elizabeth B. **BECKWITH**, b. of New London, July 31, 1844, by Rev. Jabez S. Swan	4	113
Daniel S., m. Martha T. **CHAMPLIN**, b. of New London, Oct. 9, 1849, by Rev. Edwin R. Warren	4	149
David, s. [Amos & Anna], b. Apr. 13, 1800	3	177
Elizabeth, d. John & Elizabeth, b. Oct. 27, 1690	1	20
Elizabeth W., m. Augustus L. **HARRIS**, Jan. 1, 1850, by Rev. Charles Willett	4	151
Emeline, m. Isaac **WHIPPLE**, b. of New London, Mar. 9, 1851, by Rev. Jabez S. Swan	4	163
Erastus, m. Lucretia Ann **MASON**, b. of New London, June 11, 1843, by Rev. Lemuel Covell	4	109
Ezra, s. [William & Betty], b. May 24, 1784	3	106
Fanny, m. James **DANIELS**, b. of New London, Oct. 7, 1827, by Rev. Robert Bowzer	4	32
Fanny Everline, d. [Nathaniel & Betsey], b. Sept. 16, 1800	3	229
Frank, m. Eliza E. **HAVENS**, b. of New London, Nov. 28, 1849, by Rev. Geo[rge] M. Carpenter	4	153
Goodwife, w. W[illia]m, d. Aug. 4, [1689]	1	69
Hannah, d. John & Elizabeth, b. Nov. 30, 1698	1	24
Hannah, d. Samuel, m. Joseph **DANIELS**, Aug. [ ], 1791	3	229
James, s. [Daniel, 3d, & Gennet], b. Dec. 6, 1807	3	188
James, m. Ellen **LEWIS**, b. of New London, Jan. 6, 1839, by Rev. C. C. Williams	4	82
Jane, d. [Daniel, 3rd, & Gennet], b. Nov. 14, 1804	3	188
Jane, of New London, m. Nathaniel **GARDNER**, of New Bedford, July 29, 1824, by Rev. Abel McEwen	4	19
Jeremiah, s. [Amos & Anna], b. Feb. 27, 1780	3	177
Jeremiah, m. Susan **WALES**, d. Shub[a]el, Oct. 21, 1802	3	177
Jerome, m. Julia Ann **ROSE**, Apr. 26, 1840, by J. Lovejoy	4	89
John, s. John & Elizabeth, b. Feb. 13, 1700	1	26
John, s. [William & Betty], b. Nov. 16, 1778; d. Mar. 1, [ ]	3	106
John, s. [William & Betty], b. Feb. 18, 1782	3	106
John, Jr., m. Lucretia **MANWARING**, Dec. 25, 1792	3	226
John, s. [John, Jr. & Lucretia], b. Sept. 11, 1793; d. Oct. 31, 1800	3	226
John, m. Mary **HEMPSTE[A]D**, d. Stephen, June 2, 1806	3	226
John M., m. Louisa **YOUNG**, b. of N[ew] London, Jan. 20, 1854, by Rev. Abel McEwen	4	54
Joseph, s. [William & Betty], b. Feb. 13, 1780	3	106
Josiah, m. Sally B. **MAYNARD**, b. of New London, July 15, 1832, by Chester Tilden	4	47

	Vol.	Page
KEENEY, KEENY, KEYNEY (cont.)		
Julia Ann, of New London, m. Thomas		
HARRINGTON, of Boston, July 15, 1833, by		
Chester Tilden	4	52
Lucretia, d. [Amos & Anna], b. Oct. 16, 1785; d.		
Aug. [ ], 1785	3	177
Lucretia, d. [Amos & Anna], b. Oct. 16, 1791	3	177
Lucretia, w. John, d. Aug. 28, 1805	3	226
Lucy, d. [Amos & Anna], b. Dec. 20, 1783	3	177
Lucy, m. Henry P. **HEMPSTEAD**, b. of New		
London, Sept. 4, 1845, by Rev. Jabez S. Swan	4	122
Lydia, d. John & Elizabeth, b. Mar. 17, 1696	1	22
Lydia, m. Richard **KEENEY**, July 18(?)*, 1820, by		
Rev. Nehemiah Dodge *(Perhaps 12)	4	2
M. Jerome, of New London, m. Caroline M.		
STANTON, of Norwich, Jan. 26, 1845, by		
Rev. S. Benton	4	116
Margaret, m. Francis **FOX**, b. of New London, Apr.		
5, 1846, by Rev. Jabez S. Swan	4	127
Maria, m. Hezekiah B. **SMITH**, May 19, 1822	3	248
Maria, of New London, m Hezekiah G. **SMITH**, of		
East Haddam, May 19, 1822, by Rev. Abel		
McEwen	4	8
Mariah, d. [Nathaniel & Betsey], b. Feb. 13, 1805	3	229
Martha, of Groton, m. Gilbert **BEEBE**, of [New		
London], Mar. 30, 1851, by Rev. Abel McEwen	4	161
Mary, d. John & Elizabeth, b. Jan. 20, 1694	1	22
Mary, m. Jonathan **PEMBER**, Apr. 3, 1751	3	102
Mary, m. Richard **SQUIRES**, b. of Lyme, Apr. 18,		
1838, by Rev. James M. Macdonald	4	76
Nathaniel, m. Betsey **ROBERTS**, d. Samuel, Apr.		
19, 1797	3	229
Pamela, of New London, m. Isaiah **BEEBE**, of		
Waterford, June 28, 1821, by Tho[ma]s Shaw		
Perkins, J.P.	4	6
Permelia, d. [Amos & Anna], b. Oct. 29, 1802	3	177
Phebe, m. Leonard **HARRIS**, b. of New London,		
Feb. 4, 1834, by Chester Tilden	4	54
Polly, d. [Amos & Anna], b. Sept. [ ], 1782; d. Sept.		
[ ], 1782	3	177
Rebecca, m. Daniel **NEWBURY**, Oct. 21, 1821, by		
V. R. Osborn, V.D.M.	4	6
Richard, m. Lydia **KEENEY**, July 18 (?)*, by Rev.		
Nehemiah Dodge *(Perhaps 12)	4	2
Sally, d. [Amos & Anna], b. Apr. 13, 1796	3	177
Samuel, m. Chloe **WHITAKE**, Dec. 25, 1835, by		
Rev. Alvan Ackley	4	66
Samuel C., of New London, m. Mahala **BROOKS**,		
of Waterford, Aug. 6, 1832, by Rev. Abel		
McEwen	4	48
Samuel Roberts, s. [Nathaniel & Betsey], b. Oct. 8,		
1802	3	229

	Vol.	Page
KEENEY, KEENY, KEYNEY (cont.)		
Sanford, of New York, m. Lucretia **CHAPPELL**, of New London, Sept. 4, 1829, by Rev. Abel McEwen	4	36
Sarah, d. John & Elizabeth, b. May 27, 1692	1	21
Sarah, of New London, m. Jonathan **LANE**, Dec. 24, 1826, by Rev. George Spratt	4	28
Silas, s. [John, Jr. & Lucretia], b. Dec. 16, 1802; d. Jan. 8, 1807	3	226
Silas, m. Elizabeth **HARRIS**, b. of New London, Nov. 8, 1829, by Rev. Abel McEwen	4	37
Silvester, s. [Nathaniel & Betsey], b. Jan. 12 ,1807	3	229
Susanna, d. John & Sarah, b. Sept. 6, [1662]	1	3
Susannah, m. Ezekiel **TURNER**, Dec. 26, 1678	1	14
Susannah, d. Jno., m. Ezekiel **TURNER**, s. John, of Sittuate, Dec. 26, 1678	1	68
Tasey I., m. Charles **LEWIS**, Mar. 13, 1842, by H. R. Knapp	4	101
William, m. Betty **MORE**, July 14, 1775	3	106
William, s. [William & Betty], b. Feb. 9, 1776	3	106
William, m. Lydia **LANE**, b. of New London, Oct. 3, 1830, by Rev. Abel McEwen	4	39
KEHR, George Bernard, m. Eliza **BRONNER**, b. of Norwich, Aug. 18, 1839, by Rev. Robert A. Hallam	4	86
KEITH, [see under **KIETH**]		
KELLEY, KELLY, Alice, m. John **SHUGRIE**, Apr. 12, 1850, by Rev. James W. Dennis	4	153
Betsey, m. Jonathan **CROCKER**, Jr., Dec. 18, 1792	3	26
Betsey, of N[ew] London, m. John H. **MINSON**, of Sweden, Apr. 17, 1837, by Rev. Squire B. Hascall	4	69
Catharine B., m. John M. **ROCKWELL**, b. of New London, Jan. 26, 1851, by Rev. Edward E. R. Warren	4	159
Elizabeth Ann, b. Feb. 5, 1816; m. John Henry **MINSON**, Apr. 16, 1838	3	233
Emeline, d. [William & Demarias], b. Dec. 7, 1806	3	178
John, of [New London], m. Mary A. **CHAPMAN**, of East Lyme, Oct. 20, 1850, by Rev. Abel McEwen	4	156
Loruamah, d. William & Hannah, b. Jan. 16, 1728. Recorded at the desire of the mother July 15, 1735	2	52
Mary, m. Frank **BURNS**, b. of New London, July 30, 1839, by Rev. Daniel Webb	4	73
Mary Ann, d. [William & Demarias], b. Nov. 20, 1804	3	178
Rebecca, m. Robert **ANDERSON**, b. of [New London], May 4, 1843, by Rev. Robert A. Hallam	4	117
Richard, s. [William & Demarias], b. Oct. 4, 1803	3	178

	Vol.	Page

KELLEY, KELLY (cont.)

Robert, m. Caroline **NASON**, b. of New London,
Nov. 27, 1842, by Eld[er] L. Covell — 4 — 103

William, of New London, m. Damaris **PERKINS**, of
Lyme, Feb. 19, 1803, by Andrew Griswold,
J.P., in Lyme — 2 — 124

William, m. Demarias **PERKINS**, d. Youngs
Perkins, Feb. 19, 1803 — 3 — 178

KELLOGG, Ebenezer, of Williamstown, Mass., m. Susan
COIT, of New London, June 2, 1826, by Rev.
Abel McEwen — 4 — 26

KENNARD, Sarah, of New London, m. Phillip M. **BOSS**,
of Newport, R.I., June 21, 1835, by Rev. Daniel
Huntington — 3 — 282

Sarah, of [New London], m. Philip M. **BOSS**, of
Newport, R.I., June 21, 1835, by Daniel
Huntington — 4 — 61

KENNEDY, Marcella, m. John **CARRINGTON**, Sept. 9,
1849, by Rev. William Logan — 4 — 150

Mary, m. John **MORIARTY**, Apr. 11, 1852, by Rev.
J. Stokes. Witnesses. Cornelius Kennedy,
Mary G. Kennedy — 4 — 170

KENNEY, KEENY, KENNENY, [see also **KINNEY**],
Elizabeth, m. David **CULVER**, Oct. 7, 1708 — 1 — 34

James R., m. Jane **HARRIS**, b. of New London, Jan.
30, 1825, by Ebenezer Loomis — 4 — 20

John, s. William, m. Sarah, d. William **DOUGLASS**,
"in ye month of October", [1661] — 1 — 3

Patrick, m. Elizabeth **COLLINS**, Apr. 16, 1852, by
Rev. J. Stokes. Witnesses: Timothy Lynch,
Mary Forrest — 4 — 170

Susanna, d. John, of New London, m. Ezekiel
TURNER, s. John, of Cittuate, [Mass.], Dec.
26, [1678] — 1 — 13

KENSTRY, Thomas M., m. Lucretia **LEWIS**, May 3,
1829, by Rev. Daniel Wildman (See also
M'KENSTRY) — 4 — 36

KENYON, KINYON, Hannah, d. James **CHAPMAN**, of
New London, m. Ephraim **LEACH**, Feb. 8,
1761 — 2 — 106

Reuben, of Richmond, R.I., m. Sally **MOTT**, of
Groton, Ct., Aug. 5, 1827, by Rev. Nehemiah
Dodge — 4 — 31

KERSON, Jemima E., m. Charles **STROH**, b. of [New
London], Sept. 11, 1851, by Rev. J. M. Eaton — 4 — 165

KETTLE, Elizabeth, m. John **SIMMONS**, Jan. [ ], 1810 — 3 — 277

KIBBLINS, Fisher, of Vermont, m. Phebe A.
MANCHESTER (?), of Groton, Apr. 11, 1845,
by Rev. Tho[ma]s J. Greenwood — 4 — 119

KIBBY, Epaphras, Lieut., of U. S. Army, m. Susan H.
BURBECK, of New London, June 9, 1835, by
Rev. Robert A Hallam — 4 — 61

	Vol.	Page

KIDDER, Edward, m. Ann **POTTER**, b. of Wilmington,
    N.C., Aug. 11, 1836, by Rev. Abel McEwen   4   83
KIETH, Henry S., of Bridgewater, Mass., m. Sarah H.
    MANLY, of [New London], Dec. 9, 1847, by
    Rev. M. P. Alderman   4   136
KILBOURN, KILBURN, Ann, d. Freeman, of Hartford,
    m. John H. **FRINK**, Dec. 17, 1806   3   206
    Jonathan, s. [Joshua & Lucy], b. Nov. 11, 1807; d.
    Nov. 30, 1807   3   227
    Joshua, of Wethersfield, m. Lucy **HOLT**, May 28,
    1800   3   227
    Joshua Peirpoint, s. [Joshua & Lucy], b. June 29,
    1801; d. Jan. 11, 1806   3   227
KILDOFF, James, m. Margaret **FERGUSON**, Oct. 14,
    1849, by Rev. William Logan   4   150
KILLIAN, John, m. Cath **HOY**, Oct. 13, [18]50, [by Peter
    J. Blenkinsop]. Witnesses: James Gorman,
    Cath McCann   3   306
    John, m. Catharine **HOY**, Oct. 13, 1850. Witnesses:
    James Gorman, Cath[arin]e McCann   4   159
KIMBALL, Abigail, m. James B. **LYMAN**, b. of New
    London, Sept. 15, 1822, by Rev. Abel McEwen   4   10
    Abiga[i]ll Holt, d. [Chester & Lucy], b. Mar. 8, 1803   3   51
    Abigail Holt, m. James B. **LYMAN**, Sept. 15, 1822   3   266
    Charlotte E., m. James B. **LYMAN**, b. of [New
    London], May 2, 1836, by Rev. Robert A.
    Hallam   4   65
    Chester, m. Lucy **FOX**, d. John Fox, of Chatham,
    Nov. 8, 1786   3   51
    Chester, s. [Chester & Lucy], b. Jan. 31, 1790   3   51
    Chester, s. Chester & Lucy, b. Jan. 31, 1790 (Entry
    crossed out)   3   51
    Edwin, s. [Chester & Lucy], b. Nov. 4, 1808   3   51
    Gurdon, s. [Chester & Lucy], b. Jan. 29, 1788   3   51
    Gurdon, m. Lucy W. **HOLT**, d. Jonathan, Nov. 19,
    1809   3   238
    Gurdon, s. [Gurdon & Lucy W.], b. Feb. 6, 1814   3   238
    Harriot, d. Chester & Lucy], b. July 31, 1805   3   51
    Harriet, m. Gurdon T. **BISHOP**, b. of New London,
    Aug. 27, 1829, by Rev. Abel McEwen   4   36
    John, s. [Chester & Lucy], b. Mar. 23, 1792; d. Sept.
    5, 1793   3   51
    John, s. [Chester & Lucy], b. Nov. 4, 1800   3   51
    John, s. [Gurdon & Lucy W.], b. Oct. 25, 1819   3   238
    John, m. Maria S. **LEWIS**, b. of New London, June
    1, 1843, by Rev. Lemuel Covell   4   109
    Lovell, of Catskill, N.Y., m. Lucy Ann **PRATT**, of
    Montville, July 5, 1839, by Rev. Robert A.
    Hallam   4   88
    Lucy, d. [Chester & Lucy], b. Mar. 17, 1796   3   51
    Lucy, d. [Gurdon & Lucy W.], b. Mar. 16, 1816   3   238

	Vol.	Page

KIMBALL (cont.)

Mary, m. Zebadiah C. **BAKER**, b. of New London, May 14, 1823, by Rev. Abel McEwen	4	15
Mary Ann, d. [Gurdon & Lucy W.], b. Aug. 23, 1810	3	238
Mary Ann, of N[ew] London, m. Benjamin T. **LATIMER**, of N[ew] York, Apr. 20, 1834, by Rev. Ebenezer Blake	4	56
Mary Waterman, d. [Chester & Lucy], b. Oct. 15, 1798	3	51
Richard, s. [Chester & Lucy], b. Jan. 30, 1794	3	51
Royal James, s. [Gurdon & Lucy W.], b. May 26, 1822	3	238
Sarah O., of [New London], m. Charles W. **HUBBARD**, of Springfield, Mass., May 10, 1841, by Rev. A. Boies	4	95
Sarah Owen, d. [Gurdon & Lucy W.], b. Nov. 19, 1817	3	238

KIMBERLY, George R., m. Margaret H. **TINKER**, b. of New London, Nov. 17, 1850, by Rev. Jabez S. Swan | 4 | 157 |

KING, Bathshua, m. George **SHEFFIELD**, Dec. 16, 1742, at Southold, by Eben[eze]r Gould, Clerk | 2 | 60 |

Christopher, s. [Rufus & Pegg], b. Aug. 18, 1789	3	96
Eliza, m. Michael **BENNET**, May 2, 1852, by Rev. J. Stokes. Witnesses: Peter McCaffery, Catharine King	4	170
Elizabeth, d. William & Elizabeth, b. Apr. 29, 1739	2	60
Elizabeth, m. Isaac **CHAPEL**, 2d, Nov. [ ], 1783	3	238
Elizabeth, d. [Rufus & Pegg], b. Apr. 16, 1797	3	96
John, s. [Rufus & Pegg], b. Oct. 4, 1793	3	96
John P., m. Mary Ann **JEROME**, Sept. 21, 1829, by Rev. Francis Darrow	4	36
Jonathan, m. Abba **TILL**, b. of New London, June 1, 1851, by Rev. J. M. Eaton	4	162
Jonathan R., of Waterford, m. Mary Ann **NICHOLS**, of Groton, Aug. 15, 1830, by Rev. Abel McEwen	4	39
Josephine, of Stonington, m. Edward **MEAD**, of [New London], Feb. 27, 1848, by Rev. Abel McEwen	4	137
Lucretia, d. [Rufus & Pegg], b. Mar. 7, 1788	3	96
Mark D., m. Mary E. **FURZE**, [**FARGO**?], b. of New London, Apr. 7, 1833, by Abel McEwen, Pastor	4	50
Mary, m. Paul **SMITH**, Oct. [ ], 1746	3	111
Nancey, d. [Rufus & Pegg], b. Sept. 4, 1791	3	96
Rufus, m. Pegg **WOLF**, Jan. 3, 1785	3	96
William, s. William, of Oyster Pond, Southold, L.I., m. Elizabeth **BEEBE**, d. Samuel, of Plumb Island, July 26, 1738	2	60
William, s. [Rufus & Pegg], b. Apr. 3, 1795	3	96

	Vol.	Page
KINGSLEY, Abby Ann, m. Charles **GIFFORD**, b. of New London, Feb. 26, 1843, by L. Covell	4	101
W[illia]m W., m. Phebe Ann **BRIGGS**, b. of New London, June 12, 1845, by Rev. Tho[ma]s J. Greenwood	4	124
KINNEY, [see also **KENNEY**], Josiah, m. Emeline S. **HEWITT**, Dec. 25, 1831, by Chester Tilden	4	46
KINYON, [see under **KENYON**]		
KIRKWOOD, James P., of Edinburgh, Scotland, m. Mary Harper **ADAMS**, of [New London], Nov. 9, 1835, by Rev. Abel McEwen	4	63
KIRTLAND, Frederick, m. Betsey Sewell **CROSS**, b. of [New London], Jan. 5, 1843, by Rev. Abel McEwen	4	104
Frederick W., m. Eliza C. **CL[E]AVELAND**, b. of [New London], May 25, 1837, by Rev. Abel McEwen	4	70
Jerusha, d. Nath[anie]l of Saybrook, decd., m. Daniel **WAY**, Jr., s. Daniel, of New London, May 20, 1763	3	26
KNAPP, Mary had s. Elisha **DOUGLASS**, b. Nov. 2, 1800	3	40
Mary, m. John **WALKER**, Dec. 9, 1807	3	40
KNIGHT, Albert, m. Sarah **SHELLY**, Aug. 19, 1840, by H. R. Knapp	4	91
Ann, m. Joseph **FRANCIS**, b. of [New London], Sept. 30, 1846, by Rev. T. Edwards	4	128
Daniel, m. Tacy Berry **SKINNER**, b. of New London, Aug. 1, 1824, by Rev. Abel McEwen	4	19
Daniel B., of Waterford, m. Harriet **MALLORY**, of N[ew] London, Jan. 6, 1836, by Jirah Isham, J. P., (Daniel B. was a minor)	4	64
Leander, of New London, m. Jane Palmer **BINDLOSS**, of Liverpool, England, Apr. 9, 1843, by Rev. Lemuel Covel	3	295
Leander, of New London, m. Jane Palmer **BINDLOSS**, of Liverpool, England, Apr. 9, 1843, by L. Covell	4	101
Leander Thompson, s. [Leander & Jane Palmer], b. Mar. 13, 1845	3	295
Leonard, m. Emma **DANIELS**, b. of Waterford, Mar. 27, 1839, by Rev. Abel McEwen	4	82
Louisa, of [New London], m. Zimri **ELLIOTT**, of Cleaveland, Ohio, Feb. 21, 1843, by Rev. Abel McEwen	4	102
Mary A., of New London, m. James **HAYNES**, of Lyme, Feb. 15, 1852, by Rev. J. M. Eaton	4	167
Palmer Knight, s. [Leander & Jane Palmer], b. Feb. 14, 1848; d. Feb. 16, 1851	3	295
Sarah, d. Sept. 25, 1727	2	52

	Vol.	Page

KNIGHT (cont.)

Tacy, of [New London], m. Daniel S. **AYRE**, of Lyme, Feb. 27, 1831, by Rev. Leonard B. Griffing — 4 — 40

KNOWLAND, [see under **NOWLAND**]

KNOWLES, Henry, m. Mary **ROOCAT**, b. of [New London] & late of Germany Nov. 1, 1848, by rEv. M. P. Alderman — 4 — 144

Sophronia, m. Perry J. **MOORE**, b. of [New London], Apr. 25, 1852, by Rev. Edwin R. Warren — 4 — 168

LAMASNEY, Timothy, m. Ellen **MAHER**, June 22, 1847, by Rev. John Brady — 4 — 132

LAMB, Albert B., m. Julia **ROCKWELL**, b. of New London, Mar. 12, 1845, by Rev. J. Blain — 4 — 118

Ann, m. William **HANLAN**, Oct. 13, [18]50, [by Peter J. Blenkinsop]. Witnesses: Martin Noonan, Cath Maxwell — 3 — 306

Ann, m. William **HAULON**, Oct. 13, 1850. Witnesses: Mastin Nooman, Catharine Maxwell — 4 — 159

Anne, m. Maurice **COLBERT**, Jan. 6, 1852, by Rev. J. Stokes. Witnesses: Bartholomew Lynch, Bridget Donahue — 4 — 169

Avery, m. Charlotte C. **CHAP[P]EL[L]**, b. of New London, May 27, 1832, by Chester Tilden — 4 — 47

Elisha R., of New London, m. Matilda R. **HAVENS**, of Long Island, Oct. 13, 1851, by Rev. Jabez S. Swan — 4 — 173

Hannah, d. Abiah, m. Charles **LATHAM**, June 18, 1793 — 3 — 232

James C., of Groton, m. Jane C. **HAVENS**, of New London, Mar. 27, 1837, by Rev. Erastus Denison — 4 — 67

John C., m. Ann J. **GARDNER**, b. of New London, July 13, 1851, by Rev. Jabez S. Swan — 4 — 171

Lydia, m. John **LEWIS**, b. of New London, Apr. 2, 1843, by Rev. R. W. Allen — 4 — 102

Mary C., of New London, m. Denison S. **PACKER**, of Ledyard, Apr. 16, 1843, by L. Covell — 4 — 101

Nancy, of Groton, m. James **SLIP**, of New London, Nov. 11, 1833, by Rev. Abel McEwen — 4 — 53

Reuben R., m. Sarah E. **CHAPMAN**, Dec. 16, 1851, by Rev. Jabez S. Swan — 4 — 172

LAMPHERE, LANPHERE, LANPHERERE, LANPHEAR, LANPHEER, LAMPHIRE, LANPHER,

Albert, m. Lucretia **WOODARD**, b. of New London, Feb. 9, 1843, by Rev. R. W. Allen — 4 — 104

Andrew Arcalorius, s. [James & Caroline], b. Mar. 18, 1826 — 3 — 155

Caroline, d. [James & Caroline], b. Feb. 25, 1815 — 3 — 155

	Vol.	Page

LAMPHERE, LANPHERE, LANPHERERE, LANPHEAR, LANPHEER, LAMPHIRE, LANPER (cont.)

	Vol.	Page
Caroline, of New London, m. John **HUSTICE**, of New York, Oct. 9, 1837, by Rev. Abel McEwen	4	74
Daniel, s. [James & Grace], b. Feb. 17, 1799; d. Mar. 23, 1800	3	155
Elizabeth, d. [James & Grace], b. Feb. 16, 1793	3	155
Elizabeth, of New London, m. Thaddeus **BROOKS**, Jr., of New London, Jan. 1, 1823, by Rev. Abel McEwen	4	11
Emily, of [New London], m. Nathan **TINKER**, of Lyme, Ct., Aug. 17, 1848, by Rev. M. P. Alderman	4	142
Grace, d. [James & Grace], b. June 19, 1784	3	155
Grace, d. James, m. Daniel B. **HEMPSTE[A]D**, May 4, 1806	3	194
Hannah, m. Moses **FARGO**, [ ], 1763	3	128
Henry, s. [James & Grace], b. Jan. 22, 1791; d. Oct. 13 ,1796	3	155
Henry M., s. [James & Caroline], b. May 4, 1817	3	155
James, m. Grace **DESHON**, d. Henery, May 27, 1776	3	155
James, s. [James & Grace], b. Sept. 14, 1788	3	155
James, m. Caroline **MASON**, June 5, 1814	3	155
James R., s. [James & Caroline], b. Oct. 31, 1819	3	155
Jemima, m. Thomas **BUTLER**, Mar. 22, 1770	3	70
John Mahew, s. [James & Grace], b. Sept. 9, 1796	3	155
Lucinda, of Westerly, R.I., m. Arnold **CRUMYER**, of North Stonington, Jan. 3, 1826, by Christopher Griffing, J.P.	4	25
Lucretia, d. [James & Grace], b. Oct. 4, 1781	3	155
Lucretia, m. Nathaniel **SALTONSTALL**, Jr., May 22, 1800, by Rev. Henry Channing	4	146
Lucretia, m. John B. **GRAY**, May 6, 1847, by Rev. Charles Willett	4	146
Mary, d. [James & Grace], b. Apr. 8, 1777	3	155
Mary, d. James, m. Hezekiah **PAIN[E]**, Dec. 22, 1798	3	214
Mary M., d. [James & Caroline], b. Dec. 5, 1821	3	155
Sally, d. Capt. James, m. Joseph B. **MANNING**, Mar. 22, 1798	3	171
Sarah, d. [James & Grace], b. Apr. 19, 1779	3	155
Sophia M., d. [James & Caroline], b. [ ]	3	155
LAMSON, John, s. William & Sarah, b. Nov. 29, 1743	2	90
Sarah, d. William & Sarah, b. Feb. 9, 1740/1	2	90
William, s. John, of Boston, m. Sarah **HORTON**, d. of Samson, [ ]	2	90
LANE, Charles, m. Harriet E. **PARMELEE**, b. of Killingworth, Ct., Oct. 6, 1847, by Rev. M. P. Alderman	4	134

	Vol.	Page

LANE (cont.)

Charlotte, m. George **MINARD**, b. of [New
London], June 30, 1844, by Rev. Abel McEwen | 4 | 112

Francis W., m. Ann E. **SMITH**, b. of [New London],
June 13, 1846, by John Howson | 4 | 130

Jonathan, m. Sarah **KEENEY**, of New London, Dec.
24, 1846, by Rev. George Spratt | 4 | 28

Lucy Ann, m. William H. **DUNTON**, b. of New
London, June 21, 1849, by Rev. Abel McEwen | 4 | 146

Lydia, m. William **KEENEY**, b. of New London,
Oct. 3, 1830, by Rev. Abel McEwen | 4 | 39

Susan E., of [New London], m. Joel
WORTHINGTON, of Norwich, Apr. 7, 1846,
by Rev. L. Geo[rge] Leonard | 4 | 125

LANGDON, Abby Eliza, d. [Reuben & Patience], b. May
20, 1807 | 3 | 199

Reuben, m. Patience **GILBERT**, d. Sylvester, of
Hebron, Sept. 18, 1803 | 3 | 199

Sylvester Gilbert, s. [Reuben & Patience], b. July 2,
1804 | 3 | 199

LANSON, Francis, m Margaret **HENRY**, b, of New
London, Apr. 18, 1824, by Rev. Abel McEwen | 4 | 17

LARKIN, Jennet, d. Benajah & Bashebah, b. May 7, 1762.
Recorded June 24, 1769, at the desire of Avery
[   ] | 2 | 53

LAR[R]ABEE, LARABY, Jerusha, m. John **CROCKER**,
May. 20, 1733/4 | 2 | 8

Rachel, m. Alexander **ROGERS**, May 7, 1777 | 3 | 92

Sarah, d. Grenfield, m. John **FOX**, of Concord, June
28, [1678] (First written Sarah **CAVERLY**.
Corrected, by L. B. B.) | 1 | 12

LASSALL, Seraphine, m. Frances T. **EVANS**, b. of New
London, Apr. 15, 1847, by Rev. Jabez S. Swan | 4 | 131

LATHAM, Abigail, d. Capt. Edward, of Groton, m,
William **GOOD**, June 24, 1787 | 3 | 133

Betsey, m. James **FITCH**, Jr., b. of [New London],
May 31, 1848, by Rev. L. G. Leonard | 4 | 139

Betsey M., d. Giles, m .Lodowick **LEEDS**, Aug. 26,
1802 | 3 | 196

Carey, s. Joseph & Mary, b. July 14, [1668], in New
Foundland | 1 | 6

Carey, m. Susannah **FOSTER**, Dec. 26, 1688 | 1 | 18

Carey, s. Carey & Susannah, b. Sept. 3, 1690 | 1 | 20

Cary, of Groton, m. Dorothy **McCLAVIN**, Jan. 30,
1734/5, by James Hillhouse, Clerk | 2 | 12

Charles, m. Hannah **LAMB**, d. Abiah, June 18, 1793 | 3 | 232

Charles Lasly, s. [Charles & Hannah], b. Dec. 26,
1794; d. Feb. 18, 1796 | 3 | 232

Charles Lasley, s. [Charles & Hannah], b. Mar. 9,
1797 | 3 | 232

Daniel D., m. Mary Ann **STRICKLAND**, May 30,
1849, by Rev. Charles Willett | 4 | 146

	Vol.	Page
LATHAM (cont.)		
Delia A., m. Archabald T. **DOUGLASS**, Dec. 25, 1850, by Rev. Charles Willett	4	158
Elbert, of Sag Harbor, N.Y., m. Martha **JEPSON**, of New London, Apr. 17, 1825, by Rev. Daniel Dorchester	4	22
Elizabeth, d. Joseph & Mary, b. Sept. 21, [1673]	1	9
Elizabeth, d. Carey, of New London, m. John **LEEDS**, of Staplehews, Old England, June 25, [1678]	1	12
Hannah, d. [Charles & Hannah], b. Sept. 2, 1807	3	232
Harriet, m. Charles W. **HARDING**, b. of New London, Sept. 29, 1834, by Rev. Ebenezer Blake	4	57
Ire, s. [Charles & Hannah], b. Apr. 30, 1799	3	232
Jane, m. John **LUTZ**, b. of [New London], Dec. 21, 1845, by Rev. John Howson	4	122
Jasper, s. Joseph* & Mary, b. Sept. 29, [1682] *(First written "Jasper". Corrected by L. B. B.)	1	16
John, s. Joseph & Mary, b. May 12, [1677]	1	12
Jonathan, of Groton, m. Ellen **HAMILTON**, of New London, Sept. 15, 1852, by Rev. Charles Willett	4	174
Lydia, m. Benjamin **STARR**, May 20, 1702	1	15
Lydia, m. Benjamin **STARR**, May 20, 1702	1	28
Lydia, m. John **DAY**, b. of New London, Apr. 4, 1837, by Daniel Huntington	4	70
Mary, d. Joseph & Mary, b. Apr. 22, [1676]	1	11
Mary, widow of Tho[ma]s, m. John **PACKER**, Jr., June 24, [1678]	1	13
Mary, d. Joseph & Mary, b. Sept. 5, [1679]	1	14
Mary, d. Cary & Dorothy, b. Nov. 26, 1735	2	12
Prentis Nelson, s. [Charles & Hannah], b. Oct. 22, 1805; d. Sept. 1 1806	3	232
Rebecca, d. Thomas & Rebecca, b. June 15, [1679]	1	14
Samuel, s. Tho[mas] & Rebecca, b. Dec. 14, [1676]	1	11
Samuel S., of Lyme, m. Jane M. **NEWTON**, of New London, Aug. 5, 1844, by Rev. S. Benton	4	113
Sarah, d. Tho[ma]s & Rebecca, b. Oct. 30, [1674]	1	10
Sarah, m. John **MAYHEW**, May 26, 1704	1	30
Sarah, m. John **MAYHEW**, May 26, 1704	1	34
Thomas, s. Cary, m. Rebecca, d. Hugh **WILLEY**, of Wethersfield, Oct. 15, [1673]	1	9
Thomas, s. Carey, d. Dec. 14, [1677]	1	12
Thomas, m. Anne **FOSDICK**, Mar. 13, 1715/16	1	45
William, s. Joseph & Mary, b. July 9, [1670]	1	7
LATHROP, [see also **LOTHROP**], Eliza Ann, m. Anthony **BAILEY**, May 19, 1830, by Rev. B. Judd	4	41
Freeman, m. Eliza **WILLIAMS**, b. of New London, June 9, 1830, by Rev. B. Judd	4	41
Harriet, m. William **GLASS**, Apr. 7 ,1839, by Rev. Abraham Holway	4	85

	Vol.	Page
LATHROP (cont.)		
Louisa, of [New London], m. Herman **GUSTIN**, of		
Pollard, Me., July 29, 1846, by John Howson	4	130
Rodman, of New London, m. Clarissa **CONGDON**,		
of Franklin, Apr. 17, 1830, by Abel McEwen	4	37
Rodman, of Groton, m. Elizabeth **SHAW**, of		
Charleston, R.I., Oct. 3, 1845, by Rev. Robert		
A. Hallam	4	124
Samuel, of Walingsford, was 1st child of John &		
Ruth who first lived in N. London, where		
Samuel was born, then removed to Walingsford		
(Wallingford). Test by Israel Lathrop, ae 69 y.		
& Joseph Lathrop & 67 y., b. of Norwich &		
brothers of John, Nov. 5, 1728	2	53
Sarah G., m. Charles **CHAMPLIN**, b. of [New		
London], May 6, 1845, by Rev. S. Benton	4	119
William, s. Rodman & Sarah, b. Sept. 30, 1817	3	241
LATIMER, LATIMORE, LATTERMORE,		
LATTIMORE, Amos, s. [Samuel &		
Elisabeth], b. Jan. 28, 1737	3	81
Ann, d. [Samuel & Elisabeth], b. Aug. 28, 1759	3	81
Ann had son John **GORDON**, b. Apr. 28, 1759	3	81
Anna, d. Jonathan & Barradell, b. [ ]	1	59
Benjamin T., of N[ew] York, m. Mary Ann		
KIMBALL, of N[ew] London, Apr. 20, 1834,		
by Rev. Ebenezer Blake	4	56
Boradell, d. Jonathan & Boradell, b. Nov. 26, 1743	2	52
Boradill, d. Jona[than], Jr. & Lucretia, b. Dec. 13,		
1750; d. Sept. 17, 1752	2	61
Boradill, d. Jona[than], Jr. & Lucretia, b. Apr. 12,		
1755	2	61
Cha[rle]s, s. Jona[than], Jr. & Lucretia, b. Jan. 30,		
1759	2	61
Clarissa, d. Jona[than] & Elisa[beth], b. July 26,		
1776	3	60
Courtland L., of Norwalk, Ohio, m. Charlotte		
McEWEN, of N[ew] London, July 7, 1834, by		
Rev. Abel McEwen	4	56
Daniel, s. Jonathan & Boradell, b. Aug. 16, 1739	2	56
Daniel, s. Jona[than], Jr. & Lucretia, b. May 4, 1771	2	62
David, s. [Samuel, Jr. & Elisabeth], b. June 7, 1776;		
d. Aug. 17, 1776	3	82
Elizabeth, d. Robert & Ann, b. Nov. 14, [1667]	1	5
Elizabeth, d. Jonathan & Boradell, b. Sept. 6, 1726	2	53
Elisabeth, d. [Samuel & Elisabeth], b. Aug. 28, 1728;		
d. May 23, 1797	3	81
Elizabeth, d. Capt. Jona[than], m. Nicholas		
HALLAM, s. Edw[ar]d, decd., all of New		
London, Jan. 21, 1747/8	2	33
Elisabeth, d. [Richard & Sarah], b. June 3, 1774	3	61

	Vol.	Page

LATIMER, LATIMORE, LATTERMORE, LATTIMORE (cont.)

	Vol.	Page
Elisabeth, d. [Samuel, Jr. & Elisabeth], b. Mar. 18, 1775; d. Sept. 26, 1773 (sic)* *(So in the original. Probably 1775)	3	82
Elisabeth, the elder [w. Samuel], d. Sept. 1, 1777	3	81
Elizabeth Lucas, d. [Picket & Eunice], b. Feb. 14, 1798	3	120
Eunice, d. [Picket & Eunice], b. July 9, 1792	3	120
George, s. Jonathan & Boradell, b. July 26, 1734; d. Aug. 27, 1728 [sic]	2	54
George, s. Jona[than], Jr. & Lucretia, b. July 22, 1749	2	61
George Griggs, s. [Samuel, Jr. & Elisabeth], b. Dec. 4, 1768	3	82
Griswold, s. Jonathan, Jr. & Lucretia, b. Sept. 8, 1764	2	61
Hannah, d. Peter & Hannah, b. Aug. 29, 1735	2	48
Hannah, d. Jonathan, Jr. & Lucretia, b. Sept. 19, 1748	2	61
Hannah Picket, d. [Picket & Eunice], b. Mar. 12, 1794	3	120
Hannah Pickett, m. Ephraim **CHESEBROUGH**, July 20, 1815	3	207
Henry A., m. Mary A. **STODDARD**, b. of [New London], Jan. 2, 1844, by Rev. Abel McEwen	4	110
John, s. Peter & Hannah, b. Nov. 9, 1737; d. June 9, 1738	2	48
John, s. Jonathan & Boradell, b. Dec. 21, 1741; d. Dec. 31, 1741	2	56
John, s. [Samuel, Jr. & Elisabeth], b. Nov. 11, 1764; d. Nov. 29, 1764	3	82
John, s. [Samuel, Jr. & Elisabeth], b. Nov. 25, 1765	3	82
Jonathan, m. Barradill **DENISON**, Apr. 6, 1721	1	57
Jonathan, s. Jonathan & Barradell, b. May 27, 1724	1	63
Jonathan, Jr., s. Capt. Jona[than], of New London, m. Lucretia **GRISWOLD**, d. Rev. George, of Lyme, Jan. 28, 1747/8	2	61
Jonathan, s. Jona[than], Jr. & Lucretia, b. Apr. 12, 1753	2	61
Jonathan, Jr., formerly 3rd, s. Jonathan, m. Elisabeth **CHAPELL**, d. Jonathan, all of New London, Aug. 3, 1775	3	60
Joseph, s. Jona[than], Jr. & Lucretia, b. June 8 1766	2	61
Lewis, s. [Charles & Hannah], b. May 8, 1803	3	232
Lucretia, d. Peter, m. Nathaniel **SALTONSTALL**, Dec. 21, 1768	3	161
Lucretia, d. [Picket & Eunice], b. July 9, 1802	3	120
Lucy, d. [Samuel & Elisabeth], b. Feb. 18, 1745; d. May 10, 1751	3	81
Lynds, s. [Jonathan & Elisabeth], b. Feb. 28, 1778	3	60
Mary, d. Jonathan & Boradell, b. Apr. 16, 1729	2	54
Mary, d. [Samuel & Elisabeth], b. Nov. 5, 1742	3	81
Mary had d. Mary **MILLER**, b. Apr. 11, 1767	3	81

	Vol.	Page
LATIMER, LATIMORE, LATTERMORE,		
LATTIMORE (cont.)		
Mary, m. Thomas **EDGAR**, of Newcastle upon		
"Tine", Great Britian, Nov. 9, 1777	3	55
Mary, m. Nathaniel **LATTIMORE**, b. of New		
London, Oct. 8, 1786, by Andrew Griswold,		
J.P.	2	123
Nathan, s. [Samuel & Elisabeth], b. Mar. 15, 1730	3	81
Nathaniel, s. Jona[than], Jr. & Lucretia, b. Feb. 25,		
1768	2	62
Nathaniel, m. Mary **LATTIMORE**, b. of New		
London, Oct. 8, 1786, by Andrew Griswold,		
J.P.	2	123
Nicholas, s. Jona[than], Jr. & Lucretia, b. Jan. 8, 1763	2	61
Peter, s. Capt. Richard, m. Hannah **PICKETT**, d.		
John, b. of New London, Apr. 23, 1732	2	48
Peter, s. Peter & Hannah, b. Sept. 12, 1733	2	48
Peter, s. [Picket & Eunice], b. Mar. 30, 1800	3	120
Picket, m. Eunice **DOUGLASS**, Jan. 13, 1791	3	120
Picket, s. [Picket & Eunice], b. Jan. 20, 1796*		
*(Perhaps Jan. 28, 1796)	3	120
Richard, s. [Samuel & Elisabeth], b. Mar. 27, 1749	3	81
Richard, m. Sarah **HOLT**, Oct. 20, 1773	3	61
Robert, s. Robert & Ann, b. Feb. 5, [1663]	1	4
Robert, Capt., d. Nov. 29, 1728	2	54
Robert, s. Jonathan & Boradell, b. Feb. 26, 1731/2	2	54
Robert, s. Jona[than], Jr. & Lucretia, b. Nov. 2, 1760	2	61
Samuel, s. Robert, m. Elisabeth **HALLAM**, d.		
Nicholas, b. of New London, [ ], 1722	3	81
Samuel, s. Samuel & Elisabeth], b. Feb. 11, 1733	3	81
Samuel, Jr., m. Elisabeth **PRENTIS**, d. Capt. Jno.,		
June 1, 1761	3	82
Samuel, s. [Samuel, Jr. & Elisabeth], b. Dec. 25,		
1761; drowned June 8, 1770, ae 8 y. 5 m. 14 d.	3	82
Samuel, s. [Samuel, Jr. &Elisabeth], b. Jan. 5, 1771;		
d. Oct. 2, 1771	3	82
Samuel, the elder, d. Apr. 1, 1774	3	81
Samuel, s. [Richard & Sarah], b. July 11, 1775	3	61
Samuel, m. Lydia **GREEN**, Nov. 9, 1793	3	82
Samuel, d. [ ] 7, 1808	3	82
Sarah, d. [Richard & Sarah], b. July 4, 1780	3	61
Wetherell, s. Jona[than], Jr. & Lucretia, b. Mar. 18,		
1757	2	61
LAVEE, Arabella, m. Alonzo F. **MANWARING**, b. of		
Lyme, CT., Dec. 9, 1850, by Rev. George M.		
Carpenter	4	157
LAW, Ann, d. Richard & Ann, b. July 22, 1768	3	25
Ann P., of [New London], m. Asa B. **BEMENT**, of		
Evansville, Ind., Oct. 26, 1847, by Rev. Abel		
McEwen	4	135
Ann Prentice, d. [Lyman & Elizabeth], b. Nov. 10,		
1818	3	211

	Vol.	Page
LAW (cont.)		
Benjamin, s. Richard & Ann, b. Jan. 26, 1767	3	25
Edward, of New London, m. Janette **MAIN**, Sept. 24, 1844, by Rev. G. Thompson	4	115
Edward Ellenborough, s. [Lyman & Elizabeth], b. Mar. 11, 1801	3	211
Elizabeth Learned, d. [Lyman & Elizabeth], b. Oct. 18, 1798	3	211
Eunice Ann, d. [Richard, Jr. & Lucretia], b. Aug. 6, 1800	3	168
Grace Hallam, d. [Lyman & Elizabeth], b. Mar. 31, 1806	3	211
Jane*, [d. Lyman & Elizabeth, b.]		
*(Written in pencil)	3	211
John, s. Richard & Ann, b. Apr. 21, 1761	3	25
John, s. [Lyman & Elizabeth], b. Oct. 28, 1796	3	211
Jonathan, s. Richard & Ann, b. Mar. 11, 1765	3	25
Lucretia, d. [Richard, Jr. & Lucretia], b. June 3, 1797	3	168
Lyman, m. Elizabeth **LEARNED**, d. Amasa, Oct. 12, 1794	3	211
Lyman Richard, s. [Lyman & Elizabeth], b. Mar. [ ], 1819	3	211
Mary C., m. Coleby **CHEW**, b. of New London, Oct. 11, 1832, by Rev. Abel McEwen	4	48
Mary Cecilia, d. [Richard, Jr. & Lucretia], b. Feb. 17, 1802	3	168
Richard, s. Jonathan, of Milford, m. Ann **PRENTISS**, d. Capt. John Prentiss, of New London, Sept. 21, 1760	3	25
Richard, s. Richard & Ann, b. Mar. 6, 1763	3	25
Richard, Jr., m. Lucretia **WOLCOTT**, d. Dr. Simon Wolcott, Oct. 28, 1793	3	168
Richard, s. [Richard, Jr. & Lucretia], b. Apr. 2, 1795; d. the same day	3	168
Richard, s. [Richard, Jr. & Lucretia], b. Oct. 10, 1798	3	168
William Henry, s. [Lyman & Elizabeth], b. Sept. 11, 1803	3	211
-----, d. [Lyman & Elizabeth], b. Aug. 12, 1795; d. Aug. 30, 1795	3	211
LAWRENCE, LAWRANCE, Andrew, m. Mary **FRENCH**, Oct. 13, 1836, by Rev. Alvin Ackley	4	84
Francis Watson, s. [Joseph & Nancy W.], b. Nov. 21, 1821	3	157
Henry, s. [John Abraham & Sally], b. Apr. 8, 1805	3	168
John, s. [John Abraham & Sally], b. Jan. 12, 1803	3	168
John, m. Elizabeth **CATON**, b. of New London, Apr. 10, 1823, by Rev. Abel McEwen	4	21
John Abraham, m. Sarah **PRENTIS**, Mar. 11, 1792	3	129
John Abraham, b. in Elworth Farm-house, township of Abbotsbury, Dorsetshire, England	3	168

	Vol.	Page
LAWRENCE, LAWRANCE (cont.)		
John Abraham, m. Sally **PRENTICE**, d. Capt.		
Stephen, Mar. 11, 1792	3	168
Joseph, m. Nancy W. **BROWN**, July 19, 1817, in		
Waterford	3	157
Joseph Jeremiah, s. [Joseph & Nancy W.], b. May 27,		
1820	3	157
Sebastian D., s. [Joseph & Nancy W.], b. Dec. 20,		
1823	3	157
LAWZON (?), James, m. Lucinda **CHAPPEL[L]**, Nov.		
29, 1842, by Henry R. Knapp	4	103
LAX, Dudley Bailey, s. [William & Fanny], b. Mar. 3,		
1813	3	249
Elijah Bailey, s. [William & Fanny], b. Feb. 12, 1815	3	249
Eliza, d. [William & Fanny], b. May 23, 1804	3	133
Eliza, d. [William & Fanny], b. May 23, 1804; d.		
Mar. 30, 1806	3	249
Emmy, d. [William & Fanny], b. Apr. 14, 1802	3	249
Enomy Bailey, d. [William & Fanny], b. Apr. 14,		
1802	3	133
John, s. [William & Fanny], b. Oct. 22, 1809	3	249
Leverett, s. [William & Fanny], b. May 11, 1811	3	249
Leverett G., m. Elizabeth **TINKER**, May 13, 1838,		
by Rev. James M. Macdonald	4	77
Louisa M., m. John **McGINLEY**, b. of New London,		
May 31, 1843, by Rev. Lemuel Covell	4	109
Robert, s. [William & Fanny], b. Nov. 19, 1818	3	249
Rodman, s. [William & Fanny], b. Oct. 22, 1814	3	249
William, b. Feb. 24, 1780; m. Fanny **ROGERS**, June		
24, 1801	3	249
William, m. Fanny **ROGERS**, d. George, June 24,		
1805	3	133
William, s [William &Fanny], b. Mar. 23, 1806	3	133
William, s. [William & Fanny], b. Mar. 23, 1806	3	249
Winthrop Earl, s. [William & Fanny], b. Sept. 30,		
1816	3	249
LAY, Carlos W., m. Abby Jane **ROGERS**, b. of New		
London, May 9, 1847, by Rev. Jabez S. Swan	4	131
Phebe, d. John, of Lyme, m. William **HOLT**, Apr.		
20, 1756	3	86
LEACH, LEECH, Abigail, d. Tho[ma]s & Mercy, b. July		
16, 1719	1	53
Abiga[i]ll, m. Joseph **COOMBS**, Aug. 22, 179[ ]	3	171
Abraham, s. Joseph & Mary, b. Feb. 17, 1749/50	2	69
Amos, s. Joseph & Mary, b. Feb. 17, 1745/6	2	69
Betcy, d. Elijah, m. John **HARRIS**, 3d, Feb. 5, 1795	3	228
Clement, m. Elizabeth **CULVER**, Oct. 25, 1725	2	53
Daniel, s. Joseph & Mary, b. Apr. 30, 1742	2	68
Daniel, m. Ruth **CHAPEL**, Sept. 6, 1787	3	105
David, s. Jonathan & Priscilla, b. Mar. 6, 1739/40	2	62
David, s. Lucy **CROCKER**, b. Jan. 26, 1787.		
Recorded at desire of Daniel Shaw	3	6

	Vol.	Page

LEACH, LEECH (cont.)

David, m. Eliza Ann **CLEFFORD**, d. Silvester

Clefford, Feb. 29, 1807	3	48
Elizabeth, d. Ephriam & Elizabeth, b. Nov. 8, 1754	2	106
Elizabeth, w. Ephraim, d. Apr. 9, 1759	2	106
Ephraim, twin with Manassah, s. Clement & Elizabeth, b. Aug. 13, 1726	2	53
Ephraim, s. Ephraim & Elizabeth, b. Aug. 24, 1751	2	106
Ephraim, m. Hannah **KENYON**, d. James **CHAPMAN**, of New London, Feb. 8, 1761	2	106
Esther, d. Clement & Elizabeth, b. Mar. 18, 1728/9	2	54
Esther, d. Clement, m. John **DOUGLASS**, s. Thomas, decd., b. of New London, May 11, 1746	2	99
Esther, d. Joseph & Mary, b. Apr. 20, 1752; d. [ ]	2	69
Esther, d. Joseph & Mary, b. July 23, 1760	2	69
Esther, m. Seth **BECKWITH**, Nov. 14, 1781	3	109
Eunice, m. Jonathan **CHAPEL**, Aug. [ ], 1750	3	103
Hannah, d. Ephraim & Elizabeth, b. Apr. 23, 1756	2	106
Hannah, twin with James, d. Ephraim & Hannah, b. Oct. 30, 1762	2	106
Hannah, d. [Daniel & Ruth], b. Apr. 24, 1788	3	105
Isaac, s. Joseph & Mary, b. Jan. 27, 1755	2	69
James, s. Joseph & Mary, b. Jan. 24, 1742/3	2	68
James, twin with Hannah, d. Ephraim & Hannah, b. Oct. 30, 1762	2	106
Jedediah, s. Ephraim & Elizabeth, b. July 22, 1748	2	106
Jonathan, s. Tho[mas] & Mercy, b. Nov. 18, 1716	1	53
Jonathan, s. Tho[ma]s, of New London, m. Presilla **ROGERS**, d. James, s. of Jos[eph], decd., b. of New London, June 10, 1739	2	62
Jonathan, s. Jonathan & Prescilla, b. Apr. 5, 1744	2	62
Joseph, s. Thomas & Mercy, b. Feb. 12, 1708/9	1	53
Joseph, s. Tho[ma]s, decd., m. Mary **ROGERS**, d. James, s. Jos[eph], decd., b. of New London, Apr. 22, 1739	2	68
Joseph, s. Joseph & Mary, b. Aug. 13, 1740	2	68
Joseph, m. Mary Ann **VANAPS**, b. of New London, Mar. 20, 1843, by L. Covell	4	101
Joshua, s. Jonathan & Prescilla, b. Oct. 2, 1749	2	63
Lydia, m. Charles **JEFFERY**, 3d, July 21, 1782	3	113
Lydia, d. Samuel, m. Charles **JEFFERY**, July 21, 1782	3	223
Manassah, twin with Ephraim, s. Clement & Elizabeth, b. Aug. 13, 1726	2	53
Mary, m. Stephen **BEEBE**, Nov. 16, 1716	2	4
Mary, had illeg. son John **DART**, b. July 5, 1731. Father John Dart	2	54
Mary, d. Joseph & Mary, b. Feb. 1, 1747/8	2	69
Mercy, s. Tho[ma]s & Mercy, b. Apr. 1, 1713	1	53

	Vol.	Page
LEACH, LEECH (cont.)		
Nancy, d. John, of Montville, m. William		
JOHNSON, June 26, 1799	3	131
Rich[ar]d, s. Thomas & Mercy, b. Feb. 2, 1710/11	1	53
Samuel, s. Thomas & Mercy, b. Feb. 21, 1706/7	1	53
Sarah, d. Thomas & Abigail, b. July 7, 1684	2	7
Sarah, d. Thomas & Abigail, b. July 7, 1684	2	54
Sarah, d. Thomas & Abigail, b. July 9, [1684]	1	17
Sarah, m. Andrew **CROCKER**, Sept. 10, 1706	1	31
Sarah, d. Jonathan & Prescilla, b. Mar. 19, 1741/2	2	62
Sarah, m. Zadock **BEEBE**, Dec. 11, 1764	3	30
Stephen, s. Jonathan & Prescilla, b. May 22, 1752	2	63
Thomas, m. Mary **CROCKER**, Dec. 4, 1706	1	32
Thomas, m. Mercy **CROCKER**, Dec. 24, 1706/9		
[sic]	1	53
Thomas, s. Jonathan & Precella, b. Jan. 13, 1746/7	2	63
LEARNED, [see also **LEONARD**], A., had negro servant		
Jack, s. Sylvia, b. Dec. 24, 1784	3	104
A., had negro servant Mira, d. Sylvia, b. July 10,		
1789 and Amy, d. Sylvia, b. June 26, 1792	3	104
Amasa, m. Grace **HALLAM**, Apr. 1, 1773	3	90
Ann, d. [Amasa & Grace], b. June 16, 1784	3	90
Betsey Peck, m. Robert **McEWEN**, b. of New		
London, May 31, 1833, by Rev. Abel McEwen	4	51
Coleby Chew, s. [Edward & Nancy], b. Nov. 24,		
1821; d. Sept. 20, 1825	3	179
Ebenezer, s. [Amasa & Grace], b. Mar. 27, 1780, at		
Killingly	3	90
Ebenezer, m. Charlotte **PECK**, d. Bela Peck, of		
Norwich, Oct. 10, 1808	3	233
Edward, s. [Amasa & Grace], b. Apr. 2, 1786	3	90
Edward, m. Nancy **COIT**, Nov. 24, 1814	3	179
Edward, d. Dec. 6, 1849 [Volume and page numbers		
not shown]		
Edward II., m. Sarah **EDGERTON**, b. of [New		
London], Jan. 12, 1837, by Rev. Abel McEwen	4	67
Edward Hallam, s. [Edward & Nancy], b. Oct. 14,		
1815	3	179
Elisabeth, d. [Amasa & Grace], b. Jan. 31, 1774, at		
Killingly	3	90
Elizabeth, d. Amasa, m. Lyman **LAW**, Oct. 12, 1794	3	211
Frances, d. [Amasa & Grace], b. Jan. 25, 1776, at		
Killingly	3	90
Frances, d. Amasa, m. Colby **CHEW**, Nov. 17, 1796	3	45
Francis Chew, s. [Edward & Nancy], b. July 8, 1828	3	179
Grace, d. [Amasa & Grace], b. Feb. 15, 1778, at		
Killingly	3	90
Grace, w. Amasa, d. Nov. 20, 1787	3	90
Joshua Coit, s. [Edward & Nancy], b. Aug. 9, 1819	3	179
Leonard Coit, s. [Edward & Nancy], b. Nov. 7, 1830	3	179
Nicholas, s. [Amasa & Grace], b. Mar. 10, 1783; d.		
Sept. 11, 1799	3	90

	Vol.	Page
LEARNED (cont.)		
Robert Coit, s. [Edward & Nancy], b. Aug. 31, 1817	3	179
Susan Kellogg, d. [Edward & Nancy], b. June 6, 1826; d. Sept. 28, 1828	3	179
LEARY, Mary, m. Jeremiah **SHEA**, Apr. 11, 1852, by Rev. J. Stokes. Witnesses: Patrick Shea, Julia Leary	4	170
LEAVITT, George, of New York, m. Jane **STEWART**, of New London, Apr. 6, 1847, by Rev. Jabez S. Swan	4	130
LEDYARD, Ebenezer Carlton, s. [Nathaniel & Elizabeth], b. Sept. 20, 1802	3	151
Edward Denison, twin with Elisha Denison, s. [Nathaniel & Elizabeth], b Sept. 11, 1805	3	151
Elisha Denison, twin with Edward Dension, s. Nathaniel & Elizabeth], b. Sept 11, 1805; d. Oct. 4, 1805	3	151
Elisha Denison, s. [Nathaniel & Elizabeth], b. Mar. 27, 1813	3	151
Elizabeth Denison, d. [Nathaniel & Elizabeth], b. Jan. 10, 1796	3	151
Frances P., d. [Nathaniel & Elizabeth], b. Aug. 11, 1799; d. Oct. 3, 1799	3	151
Frances P., d. [Nathaniel & Elizabeth], b Feb. 10, 1801	3	151
George Washington, s. [Nathaniel & Elizabeth], b. Oct. 5, 1809	3	151
Mary Latham, d. [Nathaniel & Elizabeth], b. Oct. 24, 1797	3	151
Nathaniel, m. Elizabeth **DENISON**, d. Elisha, of Stonington, Feb. 20, 1795	3	151
Nathaniel, s. [Nathaniel & Elizabeth], b. Sept. 30, 1804; d. Oct. 12 ,1804	3	151
Nath[anie]l had negro Amos, s. Rose, b. Aug. 7, 1811; d. June 11, 1812	3	151
Nathaniel Austin, s. [Nathaniel & Elizabeth], b. Oct. 30, 1807	3	151
William Stewart, s. [Nathaniel & Elizabeth], b. July 26, 1811	3	151
LEE, Abigail, d. [Edgecombe & Rachel], b. May 16, 1786	3	88
Betsey, d. Seth, m. James **FORSYTH**, June 12, 1800	3	232
Daniel, m. Mary **MILLIN**, Feb. 14, 1795	3	115
Daniel, Capt., lost at sea, Mar. [ ], 1799	3	115
Daniel, s. [Daniel & Mary], b. Sept. 2, 1799	3	115
Daniel, m. Harriet **HEMPSTEAD**, b. of New London, Feb. 29, 1852, by Rev. Edwin R. Warren	4	166
Edgecombe, s. Frederick & Margaret, b. Dec. 21, 1756	2	86
Edgecombe, m. Rachel **THOMPSON**, Dec. 7, 1780	3	68
Edgecombe, m. Rachel **THOMPSON**, Dec. 7, 1780	3	88
Elizabeth, d. Samuel & Jane, b. Feb. 15, 1735/6	2	26

	Vol.	Page
LEE (cont.)		
Elizabeth, of Lyme, m. Joseph **CHESTER**, Jr., of New London, Sept. 22, 1785, by Andrew Griswold, J.P.	2	123
Elizabeth, d. Levi, m. Hugh **MINER**, s. Hugh, May 3, 1789	3	239
Elizabeth, d. Abner, of Lyme, m. Nathan **BINGHAM**, July 29, 1801	3	203
Elizabeth, Chapman, d. [Samuel H. P. & Elizabeth], b. Feb. 18, 1799	3	145
Enoch Lord, s. [Dr. James & Hiphzebath], b. Nov. 1, 1795	3	171
Eunice, d. Sam[ue]l & Jane, b. Mar. 15, 1739/40	2	26
George William, s. [Dr. James & Hiphzebath], b. Nov. 8 ,1801	3	171
Harriet d. [Edgecombe & Rachel], b. Oct. 11, 1792	3	88
Harriet, d. [Dr. James & Hiphzebath], b. Feb. 9, 1797	3	171
Harriet, m. Orlando **CHIPMAN**, b. of New London, May 27, 1824, by Ebenezer Loomis	4	18
Hester, d. Joseph, of Lyme, m. Zadock **DARROW**, s. Eben[eze]r, Apr. 1, 1755	2	1
James, Dr., m. Hiphzebath **LORD**, d. Enoch Lord, of Lyme, Sept. 30, 1793	3	171
Jane, d. Samuel & Jane, b. Mar. 22, 1734	2	26
Jane, d. Samuel & Jane, b. Mar. 22, 1734	2	54
Janett, d. [Edgecombe & Rachel], b. Oct. 23 ,1788	3	88
Jennette, m. John **MANIER[R]E**, May 18, 1816, by Elder Reuben Palmer, of Montville	3	210
John, s. Stephen & Mary, b. Oct. 6, 1746, old style	2	87
John, s. Joseph & Sarah, b. May 11, 1756	2	52
John Sullivan, [s. Samuel H. P. & Elizabeth], b. Sept. 8, 1795	3	145
John Sullivan, [s. Samuel H. P. & Elizabeth], d. Nov. 19, 1819	3	145
Joseph, formerly of Hoston, now of New London, m. Sarah **POTTER**, d. Stephen & Lucy, Sept. 20, 1753	2	52
Joseph, s. Joseph & Sarah, b. July 7, 1754	2	52
Joshua Sumner, of Ithica, N.Y., m. Eliza S. **WOODWARD**, of New London, June 18, 1823, by Ebenezer Learned, J.P.	4	14
Margarett, wid., d. of Isaiah & Lydia **BOLLES**, m. Green **PLUMBE**, s. Peter & Hannah, Mar. 15, 1758	3	4
Maria Louisa, d. [Samuel H. P. & Elizabeth], b. July 26, 1810	3	145
Mary, d. [Edgecombe & Rachel], b. Feb. 9, 1785	3	68
Mary, d. [Edgecombe & Rachel], b. Feb. 9 ,1785	3	88
Mary Sullivan, d. [Samuel H. P. & Elizabeth], b. Oct. 31, 1804	3	145
Nancy, d. [Edgecombe & Rachel], b. June 28, 1790	3	88

	Vol.	Page

LEE (cont.)

Nancy, d. Edgecombe Lee, [of] Montville, m. John
    MANIERRE, Sept. 6, 1807 — 3 — 210

Rachel, m. William **CHAPPLE**, b. of New London,
    Oct. 3, 1793, by Andrew Griswold, J.P. — 2 — 124

Rhoda, m. John **STEBBINS**, of N[ew] London, Apr.
    6, 1788, in Lyme, by Andrew Griswold, J.P. — 2 — 123

Samuel, s. Thomas, of Lyme, m. Jane **TRUEMAN**,
    d. of Joseph, of New London, June 20, 1733 — 2 — 26

Samuel, m. Jane **TRUEMAN**, June 20, 1733 — 2 — 54

Sam[ue]ll, d. Dec. 13, 1742 — 2 — 26

Samuel, s. Sam[ue]ll, decd. & Jane, b. Apr. 16, 1743 — 2 — 26

Samuel H. P., m. Elizabeth **SULLIVAN**, Mar. 31,
    1794 — 3 — 145

Samuel Henery, s. [Samuel H. P. & Elizabeth], b.
    May 2, 1797 — 3 — 145

Samuel Holden Parsons, s. [Samuel H. P. &
    Elizabeth], b. Dec. 7, 1802 — 3 — 145

Sarah Taber, d. [Samuel H. P. & Elizabeth], b. Jan.
    23, 1801 — 3 — 145

Sarah Tully, [d. Samuel H. P. & Elizabeth], d. Oct.
    15, 1816 — 3 — 145

Thomas, s. Samuel & Jane, b. Jan. 3, 1737/8 — 2 — 26

Thomas Edgar, s. [Daniel & Mary], b. Nov. 12 ,1797 — 3 — 115

Thomas Ezra, s. [Samuel H. P. & Elizabeth], b. Sept.
    30, 1808; d. [   ], 1809 — 3 — 145

William Richard, s. [Samuel H. P. & Elizabeth], b.
    July 10, 1806 — 3 — 145

LEEDS, LEEDES, Abby, of New London, m. Franklin
    GARDINER, of New York, June 12, 1831, by
    Rev. Abel McEwen — 4 — 42

Amos, m. Abby **BROOKS**, d. Thaddeus, Apr. 23,
    1797 — 3 — 175

Amos, s. [Amos & Abby], b. Aug. 5, 1803 — 3 — 175

Carey, m. Mary **MILLET**, Jan. 31, 1828, by Rev.
    Robert Bowzer — 4 — 33

Clarine, d. [Lodowick & Betsey M.], b. June 10,
    1803 — 3 — 196

Cynthia A., m. Charles W. **COREY**, Oct. 13, 1850,
    by Rev. James W. Dennis — 4 — 156

Elizabeth Mary, d. [Lodowick & Betsey M.], b.
    Aug. 23, 1805 — 3 — 196

Fanny, d. [Amos & Abby], b. July 10, 1798 — 3 — 175

Frederick William, s. [Amos & Abby], b. June 6,
    1799 — 3 — 175

Giles, of Groton, m. Hannah **HOLDEN**, of New
    London, July 11, 1824, by Lodowick Fosdick,
    J.P. — 4 — 18

Henry Hubbel, s. [Amos & Abby], b. Jan. 27, 1802 — 3 — 175

Jane, of New London, m. William **BAIL[E]Y**, of
    Groton, Mar. 3, 1836, by Rev. John G.
    Wightman — 4 — 65

	Vol.	Page
LEEDS, LEEDES (cont.)		
John, of Staplehews, Old England, m. Elizabeth, d.		
Carey **LATHAM**, of New London, June 25,		
[1678]	1	12
Lodowick, m. Betsey M. **LATHAM**, d. Giles, Aug.		
26, 1802	3	196
Lodowick Coleman, s. [Lodowick & Betsey M.], b.		
Feb. 27, 1808	3	196
Lucy, d. William, m. Avery **HEMPSTE[A]D**, Jan. 3,		
1805	3	229
Mary Ann, d. [William & Lucy], b. Sept. 12, 1798	3	193
Mary Elizabeth, m. William **MINER**, b. of New		
London, Nov. 30, 1848, by Rev. Tryon		
Edwards	4	143
William, s. Jno. & Elizabeth, b. Mar. 3, [1682]	1	16
William, m. Lucy **DESHON**, d. Col. Richard		
Deshon, Oct. 20, 1797	3	193
William, d. Jan. 24, 1806, at Demerara	3	193
William Richard, s [William & Lucy], b. Apr. 19,		
1800	3	193
LEET, Caroline E., of Chester, Ct., m. Charles C.		
YOUNG, of [New London], Sept. 19, 1842, by		
A. Boise	4	101
LEFFINGWELL, Elizabeth, d. Daniel, of Norwich, m.		
Samuel **COPP**, s. Dea. Jonathan, of New		
London, Mar. 7, 1745	2	107
William, of Norwich, m. Frances **LEWIS**, of New		
London, Sept. 23, 1821, by Rev. B. Judd	4	6
LEMERLE, Augustus C., m. Eunice **LYMAN**, b. of New		
London, Jan. 2, 1823, by T. W. Tucker, Elder	4	11
LEMMEY, John, m. Thankfull **JEFFERY**, d. Charles,		
May 7, 1798	3	120
Mary, d. [John & Thankfull], b. Nov. 26, 1799	3	120
LEMMING, M., m. William **WELCH**, b. of [New		
London], Nov. 9, 1834, by Rev. Ebenezer Blake	4	58
LeMURLE, Henrietta, of [New England], m. Augustus C.		
SEAMAN, of [New London], Nov. 30, 1843,		
by Rev. R. A. G. Thompson	4	109
LEONARD, [see also **LEARNED**], John, m. Lydia		
HARRIS, Mar. 23, 1840, by John Lovejoy	4	89
John, of New London, m. Esther **DANIELS**, Dec.		
31, 1845, by G. Thompson	4	122
John Carson, s. Rev. L. G. & M. A., b. May 11, 1848	3	273
LEOPARD, Ellen, m. William G. **CARROLL**, b. of New		
London, Nov. 13, 1842, by Eld[er] L. Covell	4	103
Esther, m. Asahel **PEMBER**, Sept. 23, 1835, by Rev.		
Alvan Ackley	4	62
LESCETER, [see under **LESTER**]		
LESHURE, Ann, m. John **OVINGTON**, b. of N[ew]		
London, Apr. 24, 1836, by Rev. Squire B.		
Hascall	4	83

	Vol.	Page

LESHURE (cont.)
  Esther E., of [New London], m. Arthur B. **WELCH**,
    of Canterbury, May 9, 1841, by Rev. Abel
    McEwen — 4 — 95
LESTER, LESCETER, Abigail, wid., m. Gabriell
    HARRIS, Apr. 8, 1714 — 1 — 41
  Allyn, b. Aug. 8, 1775; m. Lydia **MINER**, Apr. 17,
    1803 — 3 — 205
  Amos, s. Jonathan & Patience, b. Dec. 5, 1731 — 2 — 54
  Amos, s. Jonathan, m. Abigail **HARRIS**, d. Walter,
    Feb. 8, 1761 — 3 — 20
  Amos, s. Amos & Abigail, b. Jan. 22, 1767 — 3 — 20
  Amy, d. Benj[amin] & Hannah, b. Mar. 20, 1739/40 — 2 — 56
  Andrew, s. Benjamin & Anne, b. Nov. 2, 1691 — 1 — 20
  Andrew, s. Benjamin, d. Mar. 1, 1712/13, ae 21 y, 3
    m. — 1 — 40
  Ann, d. Dan[ie]l & Hanna[h], b. Aug. 30, [1670] — 1 — 6
  Ann, d. Benjamin & Ann, b. Dec. 28, 1698 — 1 — 24
  Ann, w. Benjamin, d. Jan. 27, 1711/12, ae 43 y.,
    having been married 22 y. 2 m. "and some odd
    days" and left 9 sons and 2 daughters — 1 — 37
  Ann, m. Samuel **BEEBE**, s. Samuel, Jan. 1, 1717/18 — 2 — 5
  Ann, d. Daniel & Sarah, b. Jan. 30, 1720/1 — 2 — 55
  Ann, d. Timothy & Abigail, b. Sept. 11, 1724 — 1 — 64
  Ann, d. Jona[than] & Patience, b. Nov. 11, 1745 — 2 — 53
  Anna, d. Joseph & Katharine, b. July 2, [1693] — 1 — 21
  Anna, d. Joseph & Katharine, b. July 5, [1693] — 1 — 21
  Anne, d. Thomas & Lucretia, b. Jan. 2, 1759 — 3 — 12
  Austin Miner, s. [Allyn & Lydia], b. Feb. 2, 1804, in
    Groton — 3 — 205
  Barbara, w. Andrew, d. Feb. 2, [1653] — 1 — 2
  Benjamin, s. Benjamin & Ann, b. Sept. 15, 1700 — 1 — 26
  Benjamin, m. Ann **STEDMAN**, d. Thomas, by his
    2d w. Testified to by Mrs. Elizabeth Trueman &
    Mrs. Susannah Fox, Mar. 4, 1708/9 — 1 — 19
  Benjamin, m. Elizabeth **PLUMLEY**, wid., June 10,
    1713 — 1 — 40
  Benjamin, m. Hannah **LESTER**, Nov. 17, 1726 — 2 — 54
  Christian, d. Daniel & Abigail, b. Dec. 8, 1745 — 2 — 49
  Danyell, s. Andrew, m. Hannah, d. Thomas **FOX**,
    Aug. 11, [1669] — 1 — 6
  Danyel, s. Danyel & Hanna[h], b. Apr. 15, [1676] — 1 — 11
  Daniel, s. Daniel & Hannah, b. Apr. 15, 1676 — 2 — 55
  Daniell, m. Mary **WELLS**, Oct. 20, 1702 — 1 — 27
  Dan[ie]ll, s. Benj[amin], decd., m. Elizabeth
    DARROW, d. Christ[ophe]r, b. of New
    London, Sept. 25, 1739 — 2 — 65
  Daniel, s. Daniel, of New London, decd., m. Abigail
    SCERRETT, d. Richard, of Branford, decd.,
    Feb. 19, 1739/40 — 2 — 49
  Daniel, s. Daniel & Abigail, b. July 4, 1741 — 2 — 49
  Daniel, s. Daniel & Eliza[beth], b. June 28, 1748 — 2 — 65

	Vol.	Page
LESTER, LESCETER (cont.)		
Daniel, m. Sarah **BROWN**, Feb. 2, [ ]	2	55
David, s. John & Hannah, b. May 13 ,1706	1	34
David, m. Rachel **FOX**, Feb. 19, 1734/5	2	11
David, s. Benjamin, m. Hannah **FOX**, d. Samuell, 2d,		
Apr. 13, 1737	2	11
David, s. David & Hannah, b. Apr. 14, 1744	2	11
Ebenezer, s. Eliphalet, of New London, & Sarah, m.		
Ann **COLFAX**, d. George, of New London, &		
Lucy, July 5, 1778	3	71
Edward, s. Jonathan & Patience, b. May 15, 1748	2	53
Edw[ar]d, d. [sic.] Benj[amin] & Hannah, b. June 2,		
1748	2	53
Eleonor, of East Lyme, m. Capt. James		
GREENFIELD, of New London, Nov. 12,		
1848, by Rev. L. G. Leonard	4	143
Eliphalet, s. Daniel & Sarah, b. May 4, 1729	2	55
Elizabeth, d. Dan[ie]l & Hannah, b. Feb. 25, [1672]	1	8
Elizabeth, d. Joseph & Katharine, b. Aug. 4, [1697]	1	23
Elizabeth, d. David & Hannah, b. June 3, 1742; d.		
Dec. 9, 17[ ]	2	11
Elizabeth, d. Daniel & Eliza[beth], b. Nov. 10, 1745	2	65
Elizabeth, d. David & Hannah, b. Sept. 27, 1746	2	11
Elisabeth, m. Morris **FOWLER**, b. of New London,		
Sept. 10, 1754	3	14
Emeline, d. [Allyn & Lydia], b. Jan. 21, 1806, in		
New London	3	205
Emeline, of [New London], m. Augustus S.		
GRIFFING, of New York, Nov. 23, 1848, by		
Rev. Tryon Edwards	4	143
Esther, d. Daniel & Sarah, b. Apr. 11, 1732	2	55
Esther, d. Daniel & Eliza[beth], b. Oct. 29, 1743	2	65
Esther, d. Thomas & Lucretia, b. Jan. 6, 1766	3	12
Esther, m. Samuel **FOX**, Nov. 30, 1788	3	104
Frances S., of Sag Harbor, m. Charles W.		
STRICKLAND, of [New London], Sept. 26,		
1847, by Rev. T. Edwards	4	134
Frederick m. Nancy D. **WEBB**, b. of Norwich, Sept.		
22, 1840, by Rev. Robert A. Hallam	4	91
Geneveria, d. Benjamin & Hannah, b. Nov. 13, 1733	2	54
Grace, d. Daniel & Sarah, b. June 3, 1725	2	55
Grace, d, of Daniel of New London, decd., m David		
ROGERS, of New London, s. Capt. Jno., Jan.		
27, 1743/4	2	86
Grace, d. Amos & Abigail, b. May 9, 1762	3	20
Grace, m. George **COBB**, Oct. 14, 1821, by V. R.		
Osborn, V. D. M.	4	6
Hannah, d. Dan[ie]l & Hanna[h], b. Mar. 11, [1671]	1	8
Hannah, d. John & Hannah, b. Jan. 8, 1707	1	34
Hannah, w. John, d. Nov. 28, 1708	1	34
Hannah, d. Daniel & Sarah, b. May 3, 1723	2	55
Hannah, m. Benjamin **LESTER**, Nov. 17, 1726	2	54

	Vol.	Page
LESTER, LESCETER (cont.)		
Hannah, m. Nathaniel **NEWBURY**, Jr., Apr. 4, 1728	2	76
Hannah, d. Benjamin & Hannah, b. Aug. 28, 1730	2	54
Hannah, d. Jona[than] & Patience, b. Apr. 30, 1743	2	52
Hannah, d. Daniel & Abigail, b. Sept. 18, 1743	2	49
Hannah, d. Jonathan, m. William **BEEBE**, Jr., s. William all of New London, May 7, 1761	3	19
Hannah, d. Tho[ma]s & Lucretia, b. Sept. 4, 1762	3	12
Hannah, d. Timo[thy] & Zerviah, b. Dec. 28, 1767; d. Nov. 7, 1770	2	97
Harris, s. Amos & Abigail, b. Aug. 9, 1764	3	20
Harris, m. Sarah G. **FOWLER**, Oct. 5, 1851, by Rev. Charles Willett	4	165
Hulday, d. Andrew, m. Elisha **MILLER**, Apr. 1, 1800	3	229
Isaac, s. Benjamin & Ann, b. May 17, 1702	1	28
James, s. John & Lucretia, b. Sept. 12, 1803	3	233
James, m. Abby **FOWLER**, Mar. 20, 1831, by Nathan Wildman	4	40
Jason, s. Daniel & Eliza[beth], b. Dec. 27, 1741	2	65
Jeremiah, s. Benjamin & Hannah, b. July 13, 1745	2	53
John, s. Dan[ie]l & Hannah, b. Oct. 15, [1679]	1	14
John, s. Benjamin & Ann, b. Jan. 3 ,1696	1	23
John, m. Hannah **CARPENTER**, Apr. 8, 1702	1	27
John, m. Hannah **CARPENTER**, Apr. 8, 1702	1	34
John, s. John & Hannah, b. Feb. 23, 1702/3	1	34
John, s. Jonathan & Patience, b. Dec. 9 ,1740	2	56
John, m. Julia A. **ROCKWELL**, Jan. 5, 1851, by Rev. Charles Willett	4	158
John H., m. Frances E. **STRICKLAND**, b. of [New London], Sept. 3, 1840, by Rev. Abel McEwen	4	91
John Henry, m. Louisa H. **SMITH**, b. of [New London], Feb. 20, 1844, by Rev. Robert A. Hallam	4	110
Jonathan, s. Benjamin & Ann, b. July 28, 1706	1	31
Jonathan, m. Patience **TINKER**, May 15, 1729	2	54
Jonathan, s. Jonathan & Patience, b. Oct. 31, 1738	2	55
Joseph, s. Andrew & Ann, b. June 15, [1664]	1	4
Joseph, s. Joseph & Katharine, b. May 24, 1695	1	22
Joseph, s. Joseph & Katharine, b. June 12, 1707	1	32
Joseph H., of Norwich, m. Eliza **PRATT**, of N[ew] London, Oct. 31, 1833, by Rev. Isaac W. Hallam	4	52
Katharine, d. Joseph & Katharine, b. Dec. 23, [1702]	1	28
Levi, s. Timo[thy] & Zerviah, b. Aug. 10, 1757	2	97
Lucretia, d. Ben & Hannah, d. Apr. 19, 1735	2	55
Lucretia, d. Thomas & Lucretia, b. Feb. 26, 1757	3	12
Lucretia, of New London, m. James **POTTER**, of Groton, Dec. 7, 1828, by Rev. Samuel West	4	35
Lucy, d. Jonathan & Patience, b. Jan. 18, 1733/4	2	54

	Vol.	Page
LESTER, LESCETER (cont.)		
Lucy, w. Eliphalet & dau. of W[illia]m		
MANWARING, d. Sept. 10, 1779, at		
Saybrook, ae 41 y.	2	51
Lucy, d. [Ebenezer & Ann], b. Jan. 21, 1781	3	71
Lydia, d. Jona[than] & Patience, b. Mar. 11, 1754	2	53
Lydia, m. Samuel **AMES**, b. of New London, Sept.		
4, 1831, by Rev. Daniel Wildman	4	43
Mary, d. Daniel, Jr., m. Samuel **FOX**, s. Tho[ma]s,		
Mar. 31, [1675]	1	10
Mary, d. Joseph & Katharine, b. May 6, 1705	1	30
Mary, m. Robert **MORRIS**, Mar. 8, 1725	2	67
Mary, d. Thomas & Elizabeth, b. May 3, 1742	2	53
Mary, d. Timothy & Mary, b. May 20, 1755	2	97
Mary, w. Timo[thy], d. June 15, 1755	2	97
Mary, d. Timothy & Mary, d. Nov. 24, 1755	2	97
Mary, d. Timo[thy] & Zerviah, b. Sept. 3, 1763	2	97
Mary, of Lyme, m. Joseph **STEBBINS**, of New		
London, June 2, 1790, by Andrew Griswold,		
J.P.	2	123
Mary, of Lyme, m. Jeremiah **TINKER**, of New		
London, July 4, 1790, in Lyme, by Andrew		
Griswold, J.P.	2	123
Mary, of Norwich, m. Jonathan **WHALEY**, of		
Montville, July 15, 1831, by Th[omas] S.		
Perkins, J.P.	4	43
Mary Ann, of [New London], m. John M. **PARKS**,		
of Groton, June 15, 1835, by Rev. Alvan		
Ackley	4	66
Nancy, d. [Ebenezer & Ann], b. Apr. 3, 1779	3	71
Nancy, m. Parker H. **SMITH**, b. of [New London],		
Sept. 8, 1839, by J. Lovejoy	4	87
Nathan, s. David & Hannah, b. May 25, 1749	2	11
Nehemiah, s. Timothy & Abigail., b. Dec. 3, 1728	2	54
Palmer, m. Margaret F. **THOMPSON**, b. of New		
London, Nov. 25, 1841, by Rev. A. Bois	4	102
Pamelia, of New London, m. Charles **GRACE**, May		
20, 1823, by Thomas W. Tucker, Elder	4	14
Patience, d. Jonathan & Patience, b. Feb. 25, 1729/30	2	54
Phebe, d. Jonathan & Patience, b. June 25, 1736	2	55
Phebe, m. Daniel **HARRIS**, July [ ], 1758	3	92
Phebe, of East Hampton, L.I., m. William **PADDY**,		
of New London, May 5, 1824, by Rev. Thomas		
W. Tucker	4	18
Polly, m. Jeremiah **TINKER**, July 3, 1790	3	131
Rachel, d. David & Rachel, b. Aug. 25, 1736	2	11
Rachel, w. David, d. Aug. 30, 1736	2	11
Rachel, d. David & Hannah, b. Jan. 26, 1737/8	2	11
Rebeckah, d. Eliphalet, m. Thomas **HANCOCK**,		
Aug. 20, 1775	3	228
Rebekah Ann, d. [Allyn & Lydia], b. Nov. 6, 1808	3	205
Sally, m. Abel **BEEBE**, Jan. 12, 1794	3	129

	Vol.	Page

LESTER, LESCETER (cont.)

Samuel, m. Caroline **KEENEY**, Dec. 31, 1840, by H.
R. Knapp — 4 — 93

Sarah, d. Joseph & Katharine, b. "about the
beginning of Sept.", 1699 — 1 — 25

Sarah, widow of Daniel, of New London, m. Nathan
PLACE, formerly of Providence, May 27, 1736 — 2 — 34

Susan Caroline, of New London, m. John
PINKERTON, July 11, 1847, by Rev. L. G.
Leonard — 4 — 138

Sylvester, s. Daniel & Eliza[beth], b. May 8, 1740 — 2 — 65

Tacy, d. David & Hannah, b. May 13, 1751 — 2 — 11

Thomas, s. Benjamin & Anna, b. Nov. 26, [1693] — 1 — 21

Thomas, s. Benjamin, d. Apr. 8, 1713 — 1 — 40

Thomas, s. Timothy & Abigaill, b. May 24, 1720 — 1 — 57

Thomas, s. Daniel & Hannah, b. June 25, 1734 — 2 — 55

Thomas, of New London, s. Daniel, late of New
London, decd., m. Lucretia **BEEBE**, d. Samuel
Beebe, of Plumbe Island, May 30, 1756 — 3 — 12

Timothy, s. Andrew & Anne, b. July 4, [1662] — 1 — 3

Timothy, s. Benjamin & Ann, b. June 22, 1695 — 1 — 22

Timothy, m. Abigaile **WILLOU[GH]BY**, Aug. 31,
1719 — 1 — 51

Timothy, s. Timothy & Abigail, b. June 18, 1726.
Recorded Aug. 26, 1740 — 2 — 56

Timothy, of New London, s. Tinmo[thy], decd., m.
Mary **JONES**, d. Capt. Jones, all of New
London, June 13, 1751 — 2 — 97

Timothy, m. Zerviah **LESTER**, d. Benjamin Lester,
late of New London, decd., Nov. 9, 1755 — 2 — 97

Timothy, s. Timo[thy] & Zerviah, b. Aug. 7, 1759
(twin with Zerviah) — 2 — 97

Timothy had mother wid. Abigail **HARRIS**, who d.
Feb. 7, 1772 — 2 — 97

William, s. Timothy & Abigaill, b. June 18, 1722 — 1 — 60

William, s. Timothy & Mary, b. Apr. 16, 1752 — 2 — 97

William, m. Harriet **TINKER**, of N[ew] London,
July 28, 1842, by L. Covel — 4 — 103

Zurviah, d. Benjamin & Hannah, b. Sept. 28, 1729 — 2 — 54

Zerviah, d. Benjamin Lester, late of New London,
decd., m. Timothy **LESTER**, Nov. 9, 1755 — 2 — 97

Zerviah, twin with Timothy, d. Timo[thy] & Zerviah,
b. Aug. 7, 1759 — 2 — 97

LEVEE, Clarissa, m. Daniel **BROWN**, b. of Waterford,
May 7, 1844, by Jabez S. Swan — 4 — 111

LEWEY, John, m. Hager **MILLER**, people of color,
[   ], 1801 — 3 — 24

Lawry, d. [John & Hager, people of color], b. July 4,
1802 — 3 — 24

Sipp, s. [John & Hager, people of color], b. July 4,
1805 — 3 — 24

	Vol.	Page
LEWEY (cont.)		
Sip, m. Nancy H. **CORNWELL**, Sept. 25, 1832, by		
James Porter	4	48
LEWIS, [see also **LOUIS**], Alonzo, m. Abby A. **WARD**,		
b. of New London, Oct. 9, 1842	4	103
Ann Maria, m. Daniel **WATROUS**, b. of New		
London, Mar. 3, 1842, by Rev. R. W. Allen	4	97
Ann R., of [New London], m. Oliver R. **CRANE**, of		
East Windsor, Mar. 15, 1840, by John Lovejoy	4	89
Anne, b. Feb. 1, 1761; m. Joseph **SMITH**, 2d, May		
7, 1786	3	125
Betsey, m. Jonathan W. **SMITH**, Oct. 10, 1823, by		
Asa Dutton, J.P.	4	16
Betsey Crocker, d. [Edward & Fanny], b. Nov. 14,		
1798	3	116
Caroline, m. Elisha **DOUGLASS**, b. of [New		
London], Mar. 31, 1852, by Rev. Jabez S. Swan	4	172
Charles, s. [James & Harriet], b. July 2, 1807	3	207
Charles, s. [Pardon & Sally], b. May 25, 1816	3	204
Charles, m. Tasey I. **KEENEY**, Mar. 13, 1842, by		
H. R. Knapp	4	101
Edward, s. Joseph & Mary, b. June 15, 1765	3	24
Edward, of New London, s. Joseph, decd., m. Fanny		
ROSS, of Westerly, d. Isaac, decd., Apr. 29,		
1790, by Isaiah Willcox, Eld[e]r	3	116
Edward, s. [Edward & Fanny], b. July 23, 1793	3	116
Edward, drowned, Mar. 29, 1808	3	116
Elias, s. [Joseph & Mary], b. July 10, 1775	3	24
Elias F., m. Mary L. **FAGE**, b. of New London, Mar.		
24, 1833, by Chester Tilden	4	50
Elias Frederick, s. [Pardon & Sally], b. Dec. 31, 1808	3	204
Eliza Mary, m. Charles A. **BUSH**, b. of [New		
London], Oct. 23, 1848, by Rev. L. G. Leonard	4	142
Elizabeth, d. Jno. & Elizabeth, b. Sept. 27, [1678]	1	13
Elizabeth, d. John & Elizabeth, b. Sept. 27, 1678	1	13
Elizabeth, m. John **PLUMLY**, Aug. 2, 1702	1	27
Ellen, m. James **KEENEY**, b. of New London, Jan.		
6, 1839, by Rev. C. C. Williams	4	82
Emily, m. William H. **GARDNER**, b. of New		
London, Sept. 14, 1826, by Rev. N. S.		
Spaulding	4	27
Fanny, d. [Edward & Fanny], b. Feb. 13, 1802	3	116
Frances, of New London, m. William		
LEFFINGWELL, of Norwich, Sept. 23, 1821,		
by Rev. B. Judd	4	6
Frances M., m. George **HARRIS**, Dec. 14, 1831, by		
Rev. Chester Tilden	4	46
Freelove, m. Joseph **MILLER**, Sept. 20, 1782	3	69
George Richards, s. [James & Harriet], b. May 25,		
1809	3	207
Han[n]ah, d. John & Elizabeth, b. Oct. 24, 1692	1	20
Hannah, d. John & Elizabeth, b. Oct. 24, [1693]	1	21

	Vol.	Page

LEWIS (cont.)

Harriet, d. [Pardon & Sally], b. Dec. 7, 1814; d. June
    29, 1815   3   204

Harriet A., m. Thomas P. **BADET**, b. of [New
    London], Oct. 26, 1848, by Rev. Abel McEwen   4   142

Harriet Ann, d. [Pardon & Sally], b. June 13, 1822   3   204

Henry, s. [Pardon & Sally], b. Nov. 14 ,1810   3   204

Henry, s. [Pardon & Sarah], b. Nov. 14, 1810*
    *(Entire entry crossed out)   3   206

James, m. Harriet **RICHARDS**, d. Guy Richards,
    Aug. 28, 1806   3   207

James, m. Mary **MANIERRE**, b. of [New London],
    July 23, 1848, by Rev. M. P. Alderman   4   141

Jared, of Manchester, m. Mary **CROSBY**, of N[ew]
    London, Oct. 15, 1831, by Rev. Daniel
    Wildman   4   44

John, Sr., d. Dec. 8, [1676]   1   11

John, m. Elizabeth **HUNTLEY**, of Lyme, May 24,
    [1677]   1   11

John, s. John & Elizabeth, b. Aug. 16, 1685   1   17

John, s. [Joseph & Mary], b. June 21, 1767   3   24

John, of New London, m. Joyce **JILLET**, of Hebron,
    Sept. 4, 1794   3   130

John, m. Lydia **LAMB**, b. of New London, Apr. 2,
    1843, by Rev. R. W. Allen   4   102

John Leland, s. [John & Joyce], b. Mar. 14, 1796   3   130

Joseph, of New London, m. Phebe **HARRIS**, of
    Lyme, Dec. 26, 1784, by Elias Worthington,
    J.P., of Colchester   3   118

Joseph, d. [   ], with the small pox   3   24

Laura, of [New London], m. Orry **DOUGLASS**, of
    Norwich, Dec. [ ], 1835, by Rev. Abel
    McEwen   4   64

Lucretia, d. [Pardon & Sally], b. Dec. 15, 1806   3   204

Lucretia, m. Thomas **McKINSTREY**, May 3, 1829   3   204

Lucretia, m. Thomas **M'KENSTRY**, May 3, 1829,
    by Rev. Daniel Wildman   4   36

Lucretia, m. Joel **JONES**, Dec. 1, 1830, by Rev.
    Daniel Wildman   4   39

Lydia, d. [John & Joyce], b. Sept. 16, 1795   3   130

Maria S., m. John **KIMBALL**, b. of New London,
    June 1, 1843, by Rev. Lemuel Covell   4   109

Mary, d. Jno. & Elizabeth, b. Apr. 12, [1679]   1   13

Mary, d. John & Elizabeth, b. Apr. 12, 1679   1   14

Mary, m. Stephen **HEMPSTE[A]D**, Sept. 4, 1777   3   77

Mary, d. [Pardon & Sally], b. Mar. 12, 1824   3   204

Mary Ann, of New Haven, m. Albert **MAJOR**, of
    New London, June 29, 1827, by Rev. Abel
    McEwen   4   33

Mary Elizabeth, m. Edmond **AUSTIN**, b. of [New
    London], Sept. 17, 1838, by Rev. C. C.
    Williams   4   79

	Vol.	Page
LEWIS (cont.)		
Moses, m. Rachal **MORTIMORE**, Sept. 17, 1718	1	56
Moses, s. Moses & Rachel, stillborn, Apr. 18, 1719	1	56
Nabby, d. [Joseph & Mary], b. May 10, 1772	3	24
Nabby, m. Peter **GRIFFING**, Sept. 1, 1793	3	125
Nancy, d. [Edward & Fanny], b. Jan. 7, 1796	3	116
Pardon, b. Nov. 9, 1782, in Hopkinton, R.I.; m. Sally		
BECKWITH, [d. Frederick], Jan. 20 ,1805	3	204
Pardon, d. Oct. 14, 1824	3	204
Pardon, m. Sarah [ ]* *(Entry crossed out)	3	206
Samuell, s. John & Elizabeth, b. June 3, 1687	1	18
Sarah, d. John & Elizabeth, b. Aug. 18, 1683	1	17
Sarah, m. Thomas **ATWELL**, July 24, 1704	1	30
Sarah, m. John **CHEAFELL***, Aug. 26, 1708		
*(Probably "**CHAPPELL**")	1	33
Sarah, d. [Joseph & Mary], b. Apr. 26, 1770	3	24
Sarah, d. [Pardon & Sally], b. Aug. 31, 1812	3	204
Sarah, d. [Pardon & Sarah], b. Aug. 31 ,1812*		
*(Entire entry crossed out)	3	206
Sarah, d. Moses, m. Thomas **BUTLER***, Jr., s		
Thomas all of New London, [ ]		
*(Written "**BULLER**")	3	8
Silvia, m. Samuel **COIT**, Jr., Nov. 28, 1782	3	20
Thomas Pardon, s. [Pardon & Sally], b. Aug. 17,		
1807	3	204
William, s. John & Elizabeth, b. Oct. 22, [1690]	1	20
William, m. Rachel **BEEBE**, b. of N[ew] London,		
Aug. 10, 1832, by Chester Tilden	4	49
William, m. Elizabeth **FOSTER**, b. of New London,		
Aug. 7, 1843, by Rev. J. Benton	4	107
William H., of New London, m. Emeline A.		
TRIMBLE, of Newark, N.J., Jan. 10, 1847, by		
Rev. Frederick Wightman	4	128
William H., m. Ann E. **CASE**, b. of [New London],		
Oct. 18, 1849, by Rev. Abel McEwen	4	147
William P., s. [Pardon & Sally], b. Nov. 11, 1818; d.		
Dec. 15, 1820	3	204
Winslow, of Boston, Mass., m. Emmeline		
RICHARDS, of New London, Feb. 22, 1828,		
by Rev. B. Judd	4	34
L'HOMMEDIEU, Phebe, m. Richard **FOSDICK**, Oct.		
20, [1796], by Aaron Woolworth, V.D.M., of		
Sag Harbor	3	135
LIBBEE, John, of [New London], m. Ann **WILLIAMS**,		
of Norwich, Aug. 4, 1845, by Rev. Abel		
McEwen	4	120
LILLEY, LILLY, Alex, s. Gilbert & Mary, b. May 13,		
1736	2	56
Christian, d. Gilbert & Mary, b. July 24, 1740	2	56
Mary, d. Gilbert & Mary, b. Apr. 23, 1738	2	56
Sarah, d. Gilbert & Mary, b. Dec. 13, 1734	2	54

	Vol.	Page
LINCKHOME, Lydia, m. William **CHAPMAN**, Aug. 11, 1702	1	27
LINCOLN, Cornelius, s. Colins & Thankfull, b. Nov. 11, 1819	3	36
Frederick Sistare, s. [George B. & Mary A. M.], b. Dec. 1, 1845	3	295
George, s. [Colins & Thankfull], b. May 3, 1806	3	36
George B., m. Mary A. M. **BANISTER**, Dec. 28, 1841, at Brookfield, Mass.	3	295
George Banister, s. [George B. & Mary A. M.], b. Apr. 23, 1843	3	295
Ruth, d. [Colins & Thankfull], b. Jan. 19, 1802	3	36
LINDSEY, Martha Newton, of New London, m. George W. **CORPREW**, of U. S. Army, Oct. 22, 1830, by Rev. B. Judd	4	41
LINDSLEY, Ebenezer F., of Hudson, N.Y., m. Frances L. **MIDDLETON**, of [New London], June 28, 1841, by Rev. A. Boies	4	115
LINIHAN, Patrick, m. Bridget **MAHERTON**, Dec. 1, 1849, by Rev. W[illia]m Logan	4	151
LIREM, Peter, m. Caroline **WORTHINGTON**, b. of New London, Oct. 4, 1823, by Rev. Abel McEwen	4	16
LISCOMB, LISCUMB, David T., of Providence, R.I., m. Martha **JACKSON**, of N[ew] London, Jan. 1, 1847, by Rev. L. Geo[rge] Leonard	4	129
Eliza J., m. Nathan T. **MAXON**, Feb. 14, 1836, by Rev. Squire B. Hascall	4	83
LITTLE, LITLE, Elizabeth, d. David, of Scituate, m. Joseph **OTIS**, Jr., of New London, s. Joseph, June 6, 1738, by Shearjoshub Bourne, Clerk	2	118
Harriet, m. William **ROYCE**, May 7, 1822, by Rev. Francis Darrow	4	8
Robert, s. Mary **SADLER**, of New London, b. May 26, 1708	1	39
Remelia, d. [Samuel & Elizabeth], b. Apr. 6, 1800	3	166
Romelia, m. Nehemiah C. **POTTER**, b. of New London, June 8, 1823, by Rev. John Sterry, of Norwich	3	263
Samuel, m. Elizabeth **TINKER**, d. Daniel, June 24, 1799	3	166
William, m. Mary Ann **UNCAS**, b. of New London, June 5, 1831, by Rev. Abel McEwen	4	42
LIVERING, John, d. Oct. 19, [1689]	1	69
LIVINGSTONE, Elizabeth, d. Mar. 17, 1735/6, ae 48 y.	2	55
LOMBARD, Orlenzo, of Lebanon, CT., m. Hannah **BAILEY**, of New London, May 6, 1832, by Chester Tilden	4	46
LONG, Thomas, Capt. m. Caroline Elizabeth **CHESTER**, b. of [New London], Aug. 14, 1845, by Rev. John Howson	4	121

	Vol.	Page
LOOK, Henry, m. Margaret TREBY, b. of [New London], Sept. 10, 1838, by Rev. C. C. Williams	4	79
LOOMER, Mary, m. Caleb ABELL, of Norwich, June 25, 1701	1	26
LOOMIS, Griswold W., of Norwich, m. Charlotte HARRIS, of New London, Nov. 15, 1846, by Rev. Jabez S. Swan	4	128
Harriet L., m. Gideon BAKER, b. of New London, Jan. 1 ,1843, by L. Covell	4	101
Peleg T., of Coventry, m. Ma[r]tha B. TROOP, of New London, Oct. 19, 1826, by Rev. Abel McEwen	4	27
LOPER, Antonia, m. Lavina DAVIS, [May] 13, [1847], by Rev. Robert A. Hallam	4	131
Henry G., of Charleston, S.C., m. Julia FRINK, of [New London], Sept. 17, 1847, by Rev. Abel McEwen	4	134
LOPES, Antone, m. Mary CRAGUE, of New London, Aug. 23, 1843, by Rev. S. Benton	4	107
LORD, Abel S., of Boston, m. Sarah F. CHAPMAN, of New London, June 27, 1848, by Rev. L. G. Leonard	4	140
Harriet, of Norwich, m. Isaac ROGERS, of New London, Jan. 12, 1826, by Rev. David N. Bentley, of Norwich	4	25
Hiphzebath, d. Enoch, of Lyme, m. Dr. James LEE, Sept. 30, 1793	3	171
LOTHROP, [see also LATHROP], Asa, s. Nath[anie]ll & Ann, b. Feb. 13, 1717/18	1	54
Asa, s. Nath[anie]ll & Ann, b. Feb. 13, 1717/18	1	54
Azariah, s. Nathaniel & Ann, b. Feb. 5, 1728/9	2	55
Elizabeth, d. Nathaniel & Ann, b. Apr. 5, 1724	2	55
Lucy, d. Nathaniel & Ann, b. Jan. 3, 1730/1	2	55
Lydia, d. Tho[ma]s & Lydia, of Norwich, m. Joseph COIT, s. John & Mehetable, Jan. 9, 1739/40	2	72
Mary, d. Nathaniel & Ann, b. June 17, 1733	2	55
Mary, of Norwich, d. Nathaniel, m. William WAY, of New London, s. Ebenezer, May 3, 1765	3	44
Nathaniel, s. Nathaniel & Ann, b. Jan. 2, 1721/2	2	55
Zebediah, s. Nathaniel & Ann, b. July 20, 1726	2	55
LOUIS, [see also LEWIS], Scipio, m. Rachel B. CUFFEE, b. of [New London], May 29, 1834, by Rev. Abel McEwen	4	57
LOVELAND, Electa, b. July 16, 1768	3	185
Electa, of Darby, New Boston, m. Daniel AP[P]ELTON, Aug. 22, 1784	3	185
LOVERAGE, Emma, of East Lyme, m. John COMSTOCK, of Montville, Nov. 16, 1845, by Rev. Sandford Benton	4	133
LOVETT, Eleanor, d. Oct. 27, 1773	3	22
Eleanor, d. [Josephus & Elisabeth], b. May 9, 1786	3	22

	Vol.	Page
LOVETT (cont.)		
Eliphaz, s. [Joseph & Eleanor], b. Mar. 19, 1761; d		
Nov. 3, 1783	3	22
Eliphaz, s. [Josephus & Elisabeth], b. Mar. 14, 1792	3	22
Elisha, s. Josephus & Elisabeth, b. Oct. 11, 1777	3	22
Elisabeth, d. [Josephus & Elisabeth], b. May 19, 1783	3	22
Elizabeth Ann, m. Thomas **SANDINO**, Oct. 1, 1820,		
by B. Judd	4	1
Elizabeth Ann, m. Nathaniel C. **PIKE**, Apr. 21, 1833,		
by Chester Tilden	4	50
Grace, d. [Josephus & Elisabeth], b. Apr. 19, 1780; d.		
Feb. 7, 1790	3	22
John, s. [Joseph & Eleanor], b. June 21, 1757	3	22
Joseph, d. Apr. 22, 1786	3	22
Joseph, s. [Josephus & Elisabeth], b. Feb. 26, 1789	3	22
Josephus, m. Elisabeth **WAY**, Jan. 12, 1772	3	22
Samuel, s. Joseph & Ele[a]nor, b. Nov. 14, 1753	2	53
Samuel, s. Joseph & Eleanor, b. Nov. 17, 1753	3	22
LOWDEN, George, m. Jenney **BIRCH**, Aug. 6, 1803		
(free negroes)	3	18
LOYD, Charles, m. Sally Ann **CULVER**, of New London,		
Apr. 25, 1833, by Chester Tilden	4	50
Sally, of [New London], m. Franklin **DART**, of		
Waterford, Mar. 28, 1841, by John Lovejoy	4	94
Samuel, m. Sarah E. **GALE**, b. of New London, Aug.		
15, 1833, by Rev. Isaac Stoddard	4	52
LSOPH*, Christian, m. Ellen Maria **AYRES**, Apr. 7,		
1850, by Rev. James W. Dennis *(Perhaps		
"ISOPH")	4	152
LUCAS, Elisabeth, m. George **DOUGLAS**, Feb. 3, 1765	3	67
Mary, d. Jerry & Mary, m. William **DOUGLASS**, s.		
William & Sarah, of New London, May 31,		
1752	2	87
LUKE, Oliver, of Tiverton, R.I., m. Maria **COTTRELL**,		
of [New London], Feb. 22, 1838, by James M.		
Macdonald	4	75
LUTHER, Linus P., of Norwich, m. Sarah **HURLBUT**, of		
East Lyme, Sept. 27, 1846, by Rev. Jabez S.		
Swan	4	128
LUTZ, John, m. Jane **LATHAM**, b. of [New London],		
Dec. 21, 1845, by Rev. John Howson	4	122
LYER, Bridget, m. Antona **CHRISTANY**, b. of [New		
London], June 13, 1847, by Rev. M. P.		
Alderman	4	132
LYMAN, Abby, d. Elisha, of New London, m. Alexander		
CRAIG, Oct. 22, 1815	3	283
Abby Kimball, d. [James B. & Abigail Holt], b. Feb.		
25, 1826	3	266
Abby R., m. William H. **ROBBINS**, Nov. 10, 1847,		
by Rev. Tho[ma]s Greenwood	4	137
Abigail, d. [Elisha & Abigail], b. May 28, 1792	3	260
Abigail, 1st, d. [Elisha & Abigail], d. Dec. 20, 1796	3	260

	Vol.	Page
LYMAN (cont.)		
Abigail., 2d, d. [Elisha & Abigail], b. Jan. 19, 1798	3	260
Caroline S., m. Henry S. **COMSTOCK**, b. of [New London], July 14, 1847, by Rev. M. P. Alderman	4	133
Edwin Kimball, s. [James & Abigail Holt], b. Apr. 8, 1828	3	266
Elisha, m. Abigail **BLOYD**, Mar. 10, 1789	3	260
Elisha, s. [Elisha & Abigail], b. May 22, 1790	3	260
Elisha, m. Abiga[i]l **DEWEY**, Oct. 1, 1835, by Rev. Alvan Ackley	4	63
Esther Rowland, d. [Elisha & Abigail], b. Mar. 21, 1796	3	260
Eunice, d. [Elisha & Abigail], b. Dec. 21, 1793; d. Dec. 29, 1796	3	260
Eunice, 2d, d. [Elisha & Abigail], b. Aug. 3, 1803	3	260
Eunice, m. Augustus C. **LEMERLE**, b. of New London, Jan. 2, 1823, by T. W. Tucker, Elder	4	11
Harriet Dayton, d. [Elisha & Abigail], b. Dec. 6, 1807; d. Dec. 31, 1808	3	260
James B., m. Abigail Holt **KIMBALL**, Sept. 15, 1822	3	266
James B., m. Abigail **KIMBALL**, b. of New London, Sept. 15, 1822, by Rev. Abel McEwen	4	10
James B., m. Charlotte E. **KIMBALL**, b. of [New London], May 2, 1836, by Rev. Robert A. Hallam	4	65
James B., Jr., of New London, m. Jane **BATES**, Sept. 24, 1848, by Rev. Tho[ma]s J. Greenwood	4	142
James Bloyd, s. [Elisha & Abigail], b. Nov. 30, 1799	3	260
James Bloyd, s. [James B. & Abigail Holt], b. May 4, 1824	3	266
Leonard, s. [Elisha & Abigail], b. Sept. 29, 1791	3	260
Leonard, s. [Elisha & Abigail], d. Dec. 19, 1796	3	260
Martha, m. Timothy **SIZER**, Jr., b. of New London, Nov. 25, 1824, by Rev. Abel McEwen	4	20
Martha Jackson, d. [Elisha & Abigail], b. July 31, 1805	3	260
Mary Ann, d. [Elisha & Abigail], b. Nov. 30, 1801	3	260
Mary Ann, m. Joshua **HAMILTON**, Jan. 1, 1828	3	267
Mary Ann, m. Joshua **HAMILTON**, Jan. 1, 1828, by Rev. Henry Wightman	4	38
LYNCH, Nancy E., m. Henry N. **COMSTOCK**, b. of New London, Apr. 23, 1848, by Rev. Jabez S. Swan	4	138
LYNDE Sarah, m. Joshua **RAYMOND**, Nov. 23, 1730	2	94
LYNN, Aaron, m. Mary **CHEILDS**, d. Joseph, June 8, 1806, by Guy Richards	3	186
LYON, LYONS, Aaron, s. Amariah & Lydia, b. Apr. 5, 1753	2	47

	Vol.	Page

LYON, LYONS (cont.)

Daniel, m. Mary **FITCHGERALD**, Feb. 10, 1852,
by Rev. J. Stokes. Witnesses: John Begley,
Mary Kennedy — 4 — 169

Electia R., m. Giles P. **CHAPMAN**, b. of
Waterford, May 16, 1842, by H. R. Knapp — 4 — 100

Elizabeth, m. James C. **HARRIS**, Apr. 25, 1838,
Rev. Francis Darrow — 4 — 77

Ezekiel, s. Abigail Howard, b. May 2, 1756 — 3 — 78

Hannah, d. Amariah & Lydia, m. Sept. 3, 1746 — 2 — 47

John, s. Amariah, & Lydia, b. Jan. 12, 1747/8 — 2 — 47

Margaret, of Montville, m. Christopher **HARRIS**, of
New London, June 6, 1849, by Rev. Jabez S.
Swan — 4 — 146

Martin, m. Eliza **STARR**, b. of [New London], June
24, 1847, by Rev. M. P. Alderman — 4 — 132

Mary, m. James M. **GREEN**, b. of [New London],
June 8, 1847, by Rev. Abel McEwen — 4 — 132

Thomas, s. Amariah & Lydia, b. May 7, 1751 — 2 — 47

William, m. Ellen M. **DOUGLASS**, b. of [New
London], May 12, 1844, by Rev. Abel McEwen — 4 — 111

MAGAW, Silvester Powers, s. [Uzzed & Mary], b. Nov.
10, 1807 — 3 — 122

Uzzed, m. Mary **HIGGINGS**, d. William, Oct. 6,
1803 — 3 — 122

William Glendman, s. [Uzzed & Mary], b. May 25,
1806 — 3 — 122

MAGEE, Patrick, s. Gerrett & Eleanor, b. Nov. 24, 1754.
Recorded at his mother's desire, Aug. 20, 1765 — 2 — 119

MAGINLEY, John, Jr., s. John & Louisa, b. Mar. 8, 1844 — 3 — 296

MAGINNESS, Bridget, m. Thomas **COUGHY**, Sept. 9,
1849, by Rev. William Logan — 4 — 150

MAGO, Rebekah Dart, d. Thomas & Sarah, b. Aug. 11,
1791 — 3 — 124

MAHAN, Hellen, m. Thomas **HALEY**, Oct. 31, 1831 — 3 — 289

MAHER, Andrew, m. Catharine **CURTIN**, July 16, 1848,
by Rev. John Brady — 4 — 141

Ellen, m. Timothy **LAMASNEY**, June 22, 1847, by
Rev. John Brady — 4 — 132

James, m. Ellen **DOYLE**, Sept. 9, 1849, by Rev.
William Logan — 4 — 150

MAHERTON, Bridget, m. Patrick **LINIHAN**, Dec. 1,
1849, by Rev. W[illia]m Logan — 4 — 151

MAHONEY, Elizabeth, m. Capt. William **SISSON**, Oct.
3, 1842, by H. R. Knapp — 4 — 103

Jeremiah, of Newburyport, Mass., m. Elizabeth
HEMPSTEAD, of New London, Nov. 1, 1831,
by Rev. Abel McEwen — 4 — 44

Mary, m. Thomas **CARROLL**, Oct. 28, 1849, by
Rev. William Logan — 4 — 150

Thomas, m. Bridget **PINE**, Jan. 16, 1848, by Rev.
John Brady — 4 — 139

	Vol.	Page
MAID, Mary, m. William **BRICKLEY**, May 21, 1846, by Rev. John Brady	4	126
MAIN, David O., m. Patience M. **SWAIN**, Mar. 15, 1840, by Caleb I. Allen, J.P.	4	89
Janette, m. Edward **LAW**, of New London, Sept. 24, 1844, by Rev. G. Thompson	4	115
MAJOR, Albert, of New London, m. Mary Ann **LEWIS**, of New Haven, June 29, 1827, by Rev. Abel McEwen	4	33
MALADA, MALLADE, John F., of Montville, m. Rebecca **WATERMAN**, of New London, May 15, 1831, by Rev. Daniel Wildman	4	43
Rebecca, m. John **SIMMONS**, Apr. 7, 1839, by Rev. Abraham Holway	4	85
MALAY, John, m. Ann **BRENNAN**, Oct. 28, 1849, by Rev. William Logan	4	150
MALLORY, MALARY, Abby, m. Charles H. **FELLOWS**, b. of [New London], Jan. 24, 1841, by John Lovejoy	4	93
Amos, m. Pemela **MANWARRING**, b. of New London, Jan. 18, 1827, by Rev. Abel McEwen	4	29
David, m. Amey **CROCKER**, Feb. 23, 1778	3	8
David, s. [David & Amey], b. Feb. 15, 1785	3	8
Emmeline, m. Alford**SMITH**, b. of [New London], b. Aug. 26, 1827, by Henry Wightman	4	32
Frances, d. [David & Amey], b. Nov. 22, 1778	3	8
Haarriet, of N[ew] London, m. Daniel B. **KNIGHT**, of Waterford, a minor, Jan. 6 ,1836, by Jirah Isham, J.P.	4	64
Lucretia, m. Lyman **PECK**, Dec. 30, 1838, by Rev. Abraham Holway	4	85
Nathan, m. Sally **STOCKMAN**, b. of New London, Dec. [ ], 1827, by Rev. Robert Bowzer	4	32
Rebeckah, d. [David & Amey], b. Mar. 17, 1787	3	8
Richard, s [David & Amey], b. Oct. 9, 1789	3	8
Richard, m. Fanny **DANIELS**, b. of New London, Apr. 3, 1845, by Rev. S. Benton	4	118
Sally, d. [David & Amey], b. Apr. 20, 1783	3	8
Sally, d. David, m. Nathan **BEEBE**, Aug. 12, 1807	3	162
Sarah J., m. George E. **STARR**, b. of New London, Feb. 3, 1851, by Rev. Jabez S. Swan	4	162
Sarah W., m. Erastus **JONES**, b. of [New London], Apr. 5, 1835, by Rev. Ebenezer Blake	4	60
MALLYAR, Philip, m. Lydia **MYNOR**, June 29, 1704	1	29
MALONA, Hannah, d. William, m. William **CONGDON**, Feb. 16 ,1805	3	111
MALONEY, MALONY, Mary, m. Michael **CARROL[L]**, Oct. 27, 1850. Witnesses: John Power, Ellen Pheloir	4	159
Nancy, m. Tucker **SHERMAN**, b. of New London, May 13, 1846, by Frederick M. Walker, J.P.	4	126

	Vol.	Page
MALROONY, Mary, m. Michael **CARROLL**, Oct. 27, [18]50, by Peter J. Blenkinsop]. Witnesses: John Power, Ellen Phelan	3	306
MALSAR, Richard, s. Philip & Lydia, b. Dec. 6, 1720	2	68
MANCHESTER, Lydia, d. [Thomas & Phebe], b. July 6, 1781	3	95
Phebe A., of Groton, m. Fisher **KIBBLINS**, of Vermont, Apr. 11, 1845, by Rev. Tho[ma]s J. Greenwood	4	119
Thomas, m. Phebe **PRENTIS**, Mar. 28, 1780	3	95
MANGAN, Cath, m. John **SMITH**, Oct. 27, [18]50, [by Peter J. Blenkinsop]. Witnesses: Timothy Robasney, Ellen Robasney	3	306
MANIERRE, MANEIRRE, MANIERE, Benjamin, s. [Louis & Rebecca], b. May 10, 1790	3	193
Edward, s. [John & Nancy], b. June 22, 1812	3	210
Ellen, of New London, m. Amasa **JOHNSON**, of Manchester, Ct., May 3, 1848, by John Grace, J.P.	4	139
Emeline, s. [John & Nancy], b. Apr. 28, 1814	3	210
George, s. [John & Jennette], b. July 15, 1817	3	210
John, s. [Louis & Rebecca], b. Sept. 25, 1782	3	193
John, m. Nancy **LEE**, d. Edgecome Lee, [of] Montville, Sept. 6, 1807	3	210
John, m. Jennette **LEE**, May 18, 1816, by Elder Reuben Palmer, of Montville	3	210
John Thompson, s. [John & Nancy], b. Aug. 25, 1808	3	210
Joseph, s. [Louis & Rebecca], b. Mar. 11, 1786	3	193
Louis, m. Rebecca **MINER**, Dec. 26, 1779	3	193
Louis, s. [Louis & Rebecca], b. Oct. 30, 1780	3	193
Lydia, d. [Louis & Rebecca], b. May 11, 1784	3	193
Lydia, d. [Louis & Rebecca], b. July 30, 1792	3	193
Mary, m. James **LEWIS**, b. of [New London], July 23, 1848, by Rev. M. P. Alderman	4	141
Nancy, [w. John], d. Sept. 2, 1815	3	210
Rebecca, d. [Louis & Rebecca], b. Feb. 13, 1787	3	193
Rebecca, m. Jacob **PREST**, b. of New London, Aug. 18, 1851, by Rev. Jabez S. Swan	4	173
MANLY, Sarah H., of [New London], m. Henry S. **KIETH**, of Bridgewater, Mass., Dec. 9, 1847, by Rev. M. P. Alderman	4	136
MAN[N], Elisabeth, of Groton, d. Timo[thy], m. John **WATERHOUSE**, Dec. 2, 1770	3	51
MANNING, Ann Maria, d. [Joseph B. & Sally], b. Feb. 1, 1802	3	171
Edward, s. [Joseph B. & Sally], b. June 7, 1804	3	171
Grace, d. [Joseph B. & Sally], b. Nov. 12, 1805	3	171
Henry, m. Clarissa **MILLER**, b. of [New London], Apr. 26, 1835, by Rev. Ebenezer Blake	4	60
Joseph, s. [Joseph B. & Sally], b. Dec. 28, 1798	3	171
Joseph B., m. Sally **LAMPHERE**, d. Capt. James, Mar. 22, 1798	3	171

	Vol.	Page
MANNING (cont.)		
Sally, d. [Joseph B. & Sally], b. Mar. 15, 1808	3	171
MANWARING, Alonzo F., m. Arabella **LAVEE**, b. of		
Lyme, Ct., Dec. 9, 1850, by Rev. George M.		
Carpenter	4	157
Ann, d. Oliver & Hannah, b. Nov. 25, 1723	1	65
Anna, d. [Thomas & Lydia], b. Nov. 8, 1755	3	102
Anne, d. [Christopher & Deborah], b. Sept. 11, 1752	3	80
Asa, s. [Christopher & Deborah], b. Nov. 28, 1756	3	80
Asa, d. Mar. 20, 1779. Recorded at request of Roger		
Gibson, Adms.	3	66
Betty, d. Oliver, Jr. & Mary, b. Jan. 19, 1748/9	2	35
Christopher, s. Richard, of New London, m. Deborah		
DENISON, d. Capt. Robert, of New London,		
Jan. 31, 1745	3	80
Christopher, s. [Robert & Elizabeth], b. Dec. 13,		
1774	3	55
Christopher, m. Sally **BRADLEY**, d. Joshua, Nov. 5,		
1797	3	144
Christopher, s. [Christopher & Sally], b. Dec. 14,		
1799	3	144
Christopher, m. Mary **WOLCOTT**, d. Dr. Simon		
Wolcott, Jan. 21, 1807	3	144
Christopher C., of New London, m. Catherine J.		
Hinsdale, of Hartford, July 1, 1823, at Hartford	3	202
David, s. William & Rebeccah, b. Feb. 8, 1740/1	2	51
David, s. Will[ia]m, m. Martha **SALTONSTALL**, d.		
Hon, Gurdon, Jan. 15, 1767	3	83
David, s. [David &Martha], b. May 13, 1772	3	83
David, m. Lucy **STARR**, relict of Joshua Starr, &		
dau. of George Colfax, July 28, 1802	3	86
Deborah, d. [Christopher &Deborah], b. Sept. 3, 1747	3	80
Deborah, d. Robert & Elizabeth, b. July 10, 1773	3	55
Ele[a]nor, d. [Christopher & Deborah], b. Sept. 12,		
1751; d. Nov. 10, 1751	3	80
Ele[a]nor, d. [Robert & Elizabeth], b. Dec. 22, 1780;		
d. Sept. 30, 1782	3	55
Elizabeth, m. Peter **HARRIS**, July 7, 1686	1	18
Elizabeth, d. Peter & Mary, b. Apr. 17, 1702	1	27
Elizabeth, d. Peter &Mary, b. Apr. 21, 1702	1	28
Elizabeth, d. Thomas &Est[h]er, b. Apr. 6, 1723	1	61
Elizabeth, d. Oliver & Hannah, b. July 11, 1727	2	66
Elisabeth, d. [Christopher & Deborah], b. Sept. 26,		
1754	3	80
Elisabeth, d. [Thomas &Lydia], b. Feb. 5, 1765	3	102
Elisabeth, d. [Jabez &Mercy], b. Apr. 23, 1765	3	71
Elisabeth, d. Christopher, m. Nathaniel		
HEMPSTE[A]D, Jr., Aug. 26, 1777	3	102
Elisabeth, d. [Robert & Elizabeth], b. June 22, 1778	3	55
Elizabeth, twin with Lydia, d. [Thomas & Keturah],		
b. July 20, 1788	3	4
Esther, d. [Thomas & Lydia], b. Nov. 27, 1753	3	102

	Vol.	Page
MANWARING (cont.)		
Fanny, d. [Robert & Elizabeth], b. Nov. 6, 1776	3	55
Fanny, d. [William & Surviah], b. Dec. 31, 1801	3	221
Gurdon, s. [David &Martha], b. Nov. 10, 1776	3	83
Hannah, d. Oliver &Hannah, b. Feb. 27, 1715	1	60
Hannah, d. Oliver & Hannah, b. Feb. 27, 1715/16	1	51
Hannah, d. Oliver, Jr. & Mary, b. Aug. 14, 1746	2	35
Hannah, d. [Christopher & Deborah], b. Oct.3, 1749	3	80
Hannah, m. Jedidiah **CALKINS**, Aug. 21, 1768	3	29
Hannah, d. [David & Martha], b. Nov. 29, 1770, d. July 19, 1771	3	83
Hannah, d. [Jabez & Mercy], b. July 20, 1771	3	71
Isaac, s. [Thomas & Lydia], b. Mar. 14, 1763	3	102
Jabez, s. Oliver & Hannah, b. Jan. 1, 1729/30	2	67
Jabez, b. Jan. 12, 1731; m. Mercy **MINER**, June 25, 1761	3	71
Jabez, s. [Jabez & Mercy], b. Oct. 21, 1775	3	71
John, s. Oliver & Hannah, b. June 28, 1721	1	51
John, s. John & Elisabeth, b. July 25, 1766	3	103
John, s. [Christopher & Deborah], b. Mar. 21, 1765	3	80
John, m. Sarah **MANWARING**, Apr. 20, 1788	3	103
Jerusha, d. [Thomas & Keturah], b. Jan. 13, 1786	3	4
Keturah, d. [Thomas & Keturah], b. June 17, 1784	3	4
Leonard, s. [William & Surviah], b. Sept. 20, 1807	3	221
Lois, d. [Christopher & Deborah], b. Aug. 16, 1767	3	80
Love, d. Peter & Mary, b. Aug. 2, 1710	1	35
Love, d. Richard, of New London, & Ele[a]nor, m. Roger **GIBSON**, s. William, of Edinburgh, North Britain, Notary Public, & Margaret, Feb. [ ], 1754	3	10
Lucretia, d. Oliver, Jr. & Mary, b. Sept. 16, 1751	2	35
Lucretia, d. [Robert & Elizabeth], b. Oct. 28, 1783	3	55
Lucretia, m. John **KEENEY**, Jr., Dec. 25, 1792	3	226
Lucretia, d. [Christopher & Sally], b. Oct. 16, 1803	3	144
Lucretia, d. [William & Surviah], b. Oct. 27, 1804; d. June 10, 1806	3	221
Lucretia, m. Thomas L. **AVERY**, Jan. 31, 1819	3	276
Lucretia, m. Nathan **CULVER**, b. of N[ew] London, Mar. 23, 1834, by Rev. Ebenezer Blake	4	55
Lucretia, of Waterford, m. John G. **BUTLER**, of Saybrook, Sept. 13, 1835, by Rev. Robert A. Hallam	4	62
Lucy, d. William & Rebecca, b. Nov. 11, 1738	2	51
Lucy, d. [David & Martha], b. Dec. 19, 1778	3	83
Lucy, of New London, m. Frederick **PEABODY**, of New London, Apr. 13, 1829, in New York, by Rev. R. McCarter. Witnesses: Samuel Slater, Mary L. Young	3	276
Lydia, d. [Thomas & Lydia], b. Sept. 28, 1759	3	102
Lydia, twin with Elizabeth, d. [Thomas & Keturah], b. July 20, 1788	3	4

	Vol.	Page

MANWARING (cont.)

	Vol.	Page
Marcy, d. [Jabez & Mercy], b. Nov. 23, 17[ ]*		
*(Entry crossed out)	3	71
Maria, m. Thomas L. **AVERY**, Nov. 27, 1834	3	276
Martha, d. [David & Martha], b. May 15, 1774	3	83
Mary, d. Peter & Mary, b. Feb. 16, 1713/14	1	42
Mary, d. Peter & Mary, b. Feb. [ ], 1714* *(First written 1614)	1	45
Mary, d. Oliver, Jr. & Mary, b. Aug. 31, 1744	2	35
Mary, d. Oliver of New London, m. John **GORTON**, s. William, late of New London, decd., Feb. 2, 1764	3	29
Mary W., of N[ew] London, m. Edwin **COLVER**, of Groton, Mar. 6, 1836, by Rev. Squire B. Hascall	4	83
Mary Wolcott, d. [Christopher & Mary], b. Dec. 4, 1807	3	144
Mercy, d. Aug. 24, 1784	3	71
Nancy, d. [William & Surviah], b. Apr. 2, 1799	3	221
Oliver, m. Hannah **HOUGH**, Mar. 15, 1704/5	1	30
Oliver, m. Hannah **HOUGH**, Mar. 15, 1704/5	1	50
Oliver, s. Oliver & Hannah, b. Jan. 24, 1710/11	1	50
Oliver, Jr., s. Oliver, of New London, m .Mary **SMITH**, d. Nehemiah, of Lyme, Nov. 10, 1743	2	35
Oliver, s. Oliver & Mary, b. Aug. 3, 1755	2	35
Pemela, m. Amos **MALLORY**, b. of New London, Jan. 18, 1827, by Rev. Abel McEwen	4	29
Peter, s. Thomas & Esther, b. June 7, 1730	2	67
Phebe, d. [Robert & Elizabeth], b. Mar. 18, 1786	3	55
Rebeckah, d. William & Rebeckah, b. Nov. 7, 1746	2	51
Rebecca, d. [David & Martha], b. Dec. 27, 1768	3	83
Rebecca, m. Thomas **DURFEY**, Oct. 23, 1776	3	59
Rebecca, w. William, d. Jan. 8, 1779, ae 79 y.	2	51
Richard, s. Oliver & Hannah, b. Jan. 10, 1706/7	1	50
Richard, m. Eleanor **JENNINGS**, May 25, 1710	1	19
Robert, s. [Christopher & Deborah], b. Dec. 16, 1745	3	80
Robert, s. Christopher, m. Elizabeth **ROGERS**, d. James, of Hogneck, now decd., [all of New London], Oct. 8, 1772	3	55
Robert Alexander, s. [Christopher & Mary], b. Aug. 2, 1811	3	144
Roger, s. [Christopher & Deborah], b. Aug. 27, 1758	3	80
Sally, d. [Christopher & Sally], b. Oct. 25, 1798; d. Nov.* 22, 1798 *(October?)	3	144
Sally, w. Christopher, d. Oct. 31, 1805	3	144
Samuel, s. Oliver & Hannah, b. Aug. 25, 1713	1	51
Sarah, d. Oliver & Hannah, b. Aug. 9, 1718	1	51
Sarah, d. William & Rebeckah, b. Nov. 16, 1743	2	51
Sarah, d. [Thomas & Lydia], b. Aug. 8, 1752	3	102
Sarah, d. [Christopher & Deborah], b. Apr. 1, 1762	3	80
Sarah, d. [Jabez & Mercy], b. Nov. 23, 1767*		
*(First written Aug. 11, 1767)	3	71

	Vol.	Page

MANWARING (cont.)

	Vol.	Page
Sarah, m. John **MANWARING**, Apr. 20, 1788	3	103
Sarah Delia, m. Ch. S. **SMALL**, June 27, 1857	3	202
Sibbil, d. [Christopher & Deborah], b. June 14, 1760	3	80
Silas, m. Frances **SMITH**, Dec. 5, 1831, by Rev.		
Francis Darrow	4	44
Simon Wolcott, s. [Christopher & Mary], b. Sept. 30,		
1809	3	144
Susannah, d. [David & Martha], b. Sept. 23, 1783	3	83
Sybil, see under Sibbil		
Thomas, m. Est[h]er **CHRISTOPHER**, Feb. 14,		
1721/22	1	61
Thomas, m. Lydia **WATERHOUSE**, Apr. 14, 1748	3	102
Thomas, s. [Thomas & Lydia], b. June 20, 1757	3	102
Thomas, m. Keturah **HURLBUT**, Feb. 28, 1782	3	4
Thomas, s. [Thomas & Keturah], b. May [ ], 1792	3	4
William, s. Oliver & Hannah, b. Sept. 17, 1708	1	50
William, s. Oliver, of New London, m. Rebecca		
GAGER, d. of Sam[ue]l, of Norwich, Nov. 5,		
1735	2	51
William, s. [David & Martha], b. Nov. 12, 1767; d.		
May 2, 1768	3	83
W[illia]m, d. Nov. 13, 1779, ae 72 y.	2	51
William, m. Surviah **GIFFORD**, d. Justice Gifford,		
Sept. 9, 1798	3	221
William, s. [William & Surviah], b. Feb. 4, 1803; d.		
Jan. 7, 1804	3	221
William Gager, s. [David & Lucy], b. Sept. 22, 1808	3	86
William H. Crawford, s. [Christopher C. & Catherine		
J.], b. May 11, 1824	3	202
William Hurlbut, s. [Thomas & Keturah], b. Aug. 20,		
1797	3	4
MAPLES, Andrew, s. John & Sarah, b. July 23, 1764	2	65
Anna, d. John & Sarah, b. May 14, 1760	2	65
David, s. John & Sarah, b. Feb. 3, 1755	2	65
[E]unice, of New London, wid. of St.* **MAPLES**, Jr.,		
& d. of Thomas **WAY**, of Lyme, m. Samuel		
WITTER, Feb. 9, 1758 *(Perhaps meant for		
"Stephen")	2	18
John, s. Ste[phe]n, of New London, m. Sarah		
BAKER, d. Joshua, of New London, decd.,		
May 12, 1743	2	65
John, s. Jno. & Sarah, b. June 5, 1744	2	65
Joshua, s. John & Sarah, b. Jan. 15, 1753, new style	2	65
Josiah, s. John & Sarah, b. May 15, 1762	2	65
Sarah, d. John & Sarah, b. Dec. 19, 1757	2	65
Stephen, s. John & Sarah, b. Jan. 3, 1749	2	65
Susannah, d. John & Sarah, b. Jan. 2, 1751	2	65
MARBURY, Serena, m. Enoch **FISHER**, b. of N[ew]		
London, July 20, 1833, by Rev. Abel McEwen	4	53

	Vol.	Page
MARCY, Plympton, m. Caroline **YOUNG**, b. of Providence, R.I., Feb. 25, 1844, by Rev. S. Benton	4	110
MARDELAINE, Clarrisa, m. Joseph **CASE**, Jan. 1, 1829, by Rev. Samuel West	4	35
MARIETT, James, s. Micah Clothier, b. in Bow, Stradford, near London, in Great Britain, m. Catharine **ROGERS**, d. Adam, of New London, Oct. 20, 1737	2	19
MARKS, Anthony, m. Abby **ELLIS**, June 14, 1842, in Providence, by J. Dowling, of Providence, R.I.	3	197
Anthony, m. Abby **ELLIS**, June 14, 1842, at Providence, R.I., by I. Dowling, of Providence	4	175
Melissa, d. Anthony & Abby Ellis, b. Mar. 21, 1843	3	197
MARRAT, Elizabeth, m. Ezra **DODGE**, Oct. 5, 1820, at New York	3	171
MARSHALL, Abiell, of Norwich, m. Abiah **HOUGH**, of New London, Nov. 18, 1708	1	34
Amelia J., of East Haddam, m. Martin S. **COATS**, of [New London], Mar. 19, 1846, by Rev. John Howson	4	126
Elizabeth, of Hartford, m. George **DAR[R]OW**, of N[ew] London, Aug. 10, 1702	1	27
Harriet L., of East Haddam, Ct., m. Samuel H. **EDWARDS**, of Portland, Ct., Sept. 13, 1849, by Rev. James W. Dennis	4	152
MARSTON, Samuel, m. Jennet H. **PARKS**, b. of New London, Oct. 12, 1834, by Rev. Abel McEwen	4	58
MARTIN, MARTINS, Harriet, d. Lucey, b. Sept. 29, 1802	3	36
Harriet, of New London, m. James R. **HUNTLY**, of Waterford, Oct. 17, 1824, by Rev. Abel McEwen	4	20
Henry, m. Fanny **COFFMAN**, b. of [New London], Feb. 9, 1840, by Rev. Abel McEwen	4	89
Joseph, of Inland of Martinico, m. Harriet **FREEMAN**, of [New London], Apr. 21, 1841, by Rev. Abel McEwen	4	94
Nancy, d. [Richard & Mary], b. July 3, 1787	3	89
Polly, m. Lyman **HER[R]INGTON**, Dec. 1, 1799	3	92
Richard, m. Mary **HYERS**, Sept. 19, 1785	3	89
Rufus, m. Sally **OGDEN**, May 17, 1830, by Rev. Daniel Wildman	4	38
MASON, Abby Jane, of New London, m. Orrin **DARROW**, of Waterford, Sept. 2, 1833, by Chester Tilden	4	52
Abigail, d. Peter & Mary, b. Sept. 3, 1715	2	67
Allathiah, d. Peter & Mary, b. Dec. 9, 1720	2	67
Amos, m. Naomi **THOMPSON**, Feb. 24, 1771	3	117
Amos, died at sea, Aug. 4 ,1773	3	117
Andrew, m. Mary **COLLINS**, d. Joseph, Jan. 1, 1801	3	169
Andrew, s. [Andrew & Mary], b. May 15, 1804	3	169

	Vol.	Page

MASON (cont.)

	Vol.	Page
Betsey, d. Japhet, m. Lyman **PECK**, Nov. 20, 1803	3	219
Bets[e]y, d. [John & Bets[e]y], b. July 20, 1804	3	202
Caroline, d. [Andrew & Mary], b. Oct. 15, 1801	3	169
Caroline, m. James **LANPHEER**, June 5, 1814	3	155
Caroline L., of [New London], m. Richard H. **COIT**, of Norwich, Mar. 17, 1846, by Rev. Abel McEwen	4	125
Charlotty, d. [John & Bets[e]y], b. June 27, 1806	3	202
Cornelius, of Waterford, m. Harriet E. **CHAP[P]EL[L]**, of New London, Sept. 6, 1846, by Rev. L. Geo[rge] Leonard	4	129
Daniel, s. Peter & Mary, b. Sept. 13, 1705; d. June 25, 1706	2	66
Daniel, s. Peter & Mary, b. Mar. 28, 1707	2	66
Edward H., m. Catharine **BEEBE**, b. of New London, Nov. 21, 1847, by Rev. L. G. Leonard	4	138
Eliphalet, s. [Amos & Naomi], b. Dec. 2, 1773	3	117
Eliphalet, s. [Samuel, Jr. & Patty], b. Dec. 19, 1797	3	36
Elizabeth, d. [Samuel & Elizabeth], b. Feb. 7, 1775	3	35
Elizabeth, d. Samuel, m. George **HOBERN**, Feb. 6, 1792	3	162
Elizabeth, d. [Thomas & Elizabeth], b. June 10, 1817	3	219
Ellen, m. Jared **WADE**, Nov. 7, 1847, by Rev. M. P. Alderman	4	135
Esther, m. Prentice A. **WAIT**, b. of New London, July 15, 1833, by Chester Tilden	4	52
[E]unice, d. Japhet & Mary, b. July 27, 1736	2	68
Gurdon, m. Fanny B. **WHEAT**, b. of New London, Sept. 22, 1822, by Rev. Abel McEwen	4	10
Japheth, s. Peter & Mary, b. Dec. 28, 1709	2	66
Japheth, s. Peter & Mary, b. July 11, 1711	2	66
Japheth, s. Peter & Mary, b. Sept. 30, 1713	2	66
John, m. Bets[e]y **KEENEY**, d. John, Nov. 22, 1795	3	202
John, 2d, m. Pauline **GODDARD**, b. of New London, June 28, 1824, by Rev. Abel McEwen	4	19
John Hempste[a]d, s. [John & Bets[e]y], b. Feb. 3, 1798	3	202
Joseph, m. Fanny **FENGARR**, Oct. 30, 1841, by Abel T. Sizer	4	96
Lucretia, d. [Samuel & Elizabeth], b. Apr. 22, 1788	3	85
Lucretia, d. Samuel, m. Moses **CROCKER**, Aug. 18, 1805	3	85
Lucretia Ann, m. Erastus **KEENEY**, b. of New London, June 11, 1843, by Rev. Lemuel Covell	4	109
Mary, d. Peter & Mary, b. May 31, 1711	2	66
Mary, d. [Samuel, Jr. & Patty], b. Nov. 14, 1795	3	36
Mary L., m. Peter C. **TURNER**, b. of New London, Dec. 6, 1826, by Rev. Bethel Judd	4	28
Nancy, d. [Peter & Mary], b. May 21, 1806	3	68
Nancy, m. William **DENISON**, b. of [New London], June 3, 1824, by Rev. Thomas W. Tucker	4	19

	Vol.	Page
MASON (cont.)		
Naomy, d. Japhet, m. Amos **THORP**, Dec. 16, 1782	3	182
Patty, d. [Samuel, Jr. & Patty], b. Apr. 12, 1800	3	36
Patty, m. Robert **WILLEY**, b. of New London, Feb. 11, 1821, by Rev. Nehemiah Dodge	4	4
Peter, m. Mary **HOBART**, July 8, 1703	2	66
Peter, s. Peter & Mary, b. Dec. 28, 1717	2	67
Peter, s. [Samuel & Elizabeth], b. Apr. 28, 1785	3	35
Peter, m. Mary **WELCH**, June 27, 1805	3	68
Rachell, d. Maj. John, Deputy Governor of ye Colony, m. Charles **HILL**, of New London, June 12, [1678]	1	12
Sally, d. Noah, m. Joseph **COIT**, Dec. 6, 1807	3	200
Sally, d. [Andrew & Mary], b. Nov. 4, 1808	3	169
Samuel, m. Elizabeth **ROGERS**, June 10, 1774	3	35
Samuel, s. [Samuel & Elizabeth], b. Mar. 23, 1778	3	35
Samuel, s. [Samuel, Jr. & Patty], b. May 1, 1802	3	36
Samuel, Jr., m. Patty **STONE**, [ ]	3	36
Sarah, d. Noah & Lucretia, b. May 3, 1788	3	8
Sarah, m. Richard **BEEBE**, Nov. 7, 1847, by Rev. M. P. Alderman	4	135
Silas Keeney, s. [John & Bets[e]y], b. Mar. 8 ,1800	3	202
Thomas, m. Elizabeth **POTTER**, Apr. 7, 1816	3	219
Thomas, d. Nov. 14, 1816, at sea	3	219
William F., m. Louisa Jane **DAYTON**, b. of [New London], Mar. 22, 1847, by Rev. L. G. Leonard	4	129
Willson Lee, s. [Samuel & Elizabeth], b. Mar. 18, 1795	3	35
-----, s. Peter & Mary, b. Aug. 25, 1704; d. Sept. 9, 1704	2	66
MATHER, MATHERS, Andrew, Capt., m. Mary **WETMORE**, of Middletown, July 7, 1810	3	156
Catharine, d. [James & Ann], b. Dec. 25, 1779	3	23
Henry, m. Sarah T. P. **WHITTEMORE**, b. of New London, Jan. 1, 1851, by Rev. George M. Carpenter	4	158
James, of New York, m. Ann **STARK**, of New London, Nov. 3, 1776	3	23
James, s. [James & Ann], b. May 9, 1783	3	23
Jane, d. [James & Ann], b. Jan. 29, [1782]; d. July 3, 1782	3	23
John, s. [James & Ann], b. July 26, 1790	3	23
John P. C., s. [Capt. Andrew & Mary], b. Sept. 23, 1816	3	156
Nancy, d. [James & Ann], b. Dec. 28, 1777	3	23
MATSON, John, m. Mary **CARROLL**, May 26, [18]50, by Peter J. Blenkinsop. Witnesses: John Fahy, Mary Guinness	3	306
John, m. Mary **CARROL[L]**, May 26, 1850. Witnesses: John Failey, Mary Guinness	4	159
MAT[T]HEW, Wayti, s. Jno. & Johanna, b. Oct. 4, [1680]	1	14

	Vol.	Page

MATTOON, MATOON, John, of Wallingford, m.
Charlotte **HEATH**, of N[ew] London, Oct. 27,
1837, by Rev. Alvan Akley | 4 | 66
Lyman, of Wal[l]ingford, m. Eunice **HEATH**, of
[New London], Sept. 29, 1834, by Rev.
Ebenezer Blake | 4 | 57
MAUGAN, Catharine, m. John **SMITH**, Oct. 27, 1850.
Witnesses: Timothy Robasney, Ellen Robasney | 4 | 159
MAXSON, Content, d. John & Tacy, b. Aug. 14, 1741 | 2 | 48
Eliza Jane, m. Lorenzo D. **GALLOP**, b. at
Glastonbury, July 12, 1843, by R. A. G.
Thompson | 4 | 106
Nathan, s. John & Tacy, b. Aug. 2, 1745 | 2 | 48
Nathan T., m. Eliza J. **LISCUMB**, Feb. 14, 1836, by
Rev. Squire B. Hascall | 4 | 83
MAY, Abby, m. James **BURGESS**, Feb. 11, 1849, by
Rev. William Logan | 4 | 150
Bridget, m. John **BROWN**, Nov. 27, 1851, by Rev. J.
Stokes. Witnesses: James Brown, Johanna
Cullin | 4 | 169
George A., of New London, m. Ellen **DANIELS**, of
Groton, [   ], by Rev. R. W. Allen | 4 | 98
Hanna[h], m. William **MELLERICH**, Feb. 22, 1852,
by Rev. J. Stokes. Witnesses: Stephen Hays,
T. Quird | 4 | 169
MAYHEW, MAHEW, Elizabeth, d. Jno. & Johanna, b.
Feb. 7, [1683] | 1 | 17
Elizabeth, d. John & Sarah, b. Oct. 26, 1709 | 1 | 42
Elizabeth, d. John & Sarah, b. Oct. 26, 1709 | 1 | 66
Elizabeth, m. Daniell **HALL**, Apr. 24, 1716 | 1 | 45
Elizabeth, of New London, dau. of John, late of New
London, decd., m. Ebenezer **HOWARD**, of
New London, s. Nathan, of New London, Dec.
23, 1729 | 2 | 85
Johannah, twin with Sarah, d. John & Sarah, b. June
8, 1705; d. June 16, 1705 | 1 | 42
Johana, d. John & Sarah, b. Jan. 28, 1710 | 1 | 42
John, of Devonshire, Old England, m. Johanna, d.
Geofry **CHRISTOPHERS**, Dec. 25, [1676] | 1 | 11
John, s. John & Johanna, b. Dec. 17, [1677] | 1 | 12
John, m. Sarah **LATHAM**, May 26, 1704 | 1 | 30
John, m. Sarah **LATHAM**, May 26, 1704 | 1 | 34
Sarah, twin with Johanna, d. John & Sarah, b. June 7,
1705; d. June 15, 1705 | 1 | 42
Sarah, d. John & Sarah, b. Nov. 15, 1713 | 1 | 42
Sarah testified Apr. 14, 1741, at the desire of Peter
Jackson, that Eunice, d. of Hagar, a woman in
the service of Madam Eliza Winthrop &
reputed wife of Peter **JACKSON**, was b. Feb.
[ ], 1729/30. Sarah, ae about 65 y. | 2 | 50
Waite, s. John & Sarah, b. Mar. 6, 1708 | 1 | 34
-----, w. Jno., d. Aug. 25, [1690] | 1 | 69

	Vol.	Page
MAYNARD, Abby Shepard, d. [Lucius P. & Mary], b.		
Apr. 14 ,1830	3	279
Asahel, s. [Stephen & Sarah], b. Oct. 21, 1766	3	107
Betty, d. [Stephen & Sarah], b. July 23, 1782	3	107
Cynthia, m. William **DANIELS**, b. of Waterford,		
Mar. 11, 1832, by Rev. Abel McEwen	4	45
Eliza, m. Alfred **BROWN**, Apr. 4, 1832, by Rev.		
Francis Darrow	4	46
Elizabeth, m. Erastus **JONES**, of East Haddam, May		
2, 1831, by Rev. Daniel Wildman	4	42
Eunice, d. [Stephen & Sarah], b. Apr. 25, 1775	3	107
Jehiel, s. [Stephen & Sarah], b. Nov. 27, 1772	3	107
Jerusha, d. [Stephen & Sarah], b. Aug. 24, 1768	3	107
Lucius P., m. Mary **EDWARDS**, Apr. 14, 1828	3	279
Lucius P., of Waterford, m. Mary **EDWARDS**, of		
New London, Apr. 2, 1828, by Rev. Abel		
McEwen	4	34
Lydia, d. [Stephen & Sarah], b. Jan. 7, 1765	3	107
Lydia, d. Andrew, m. John **DENNIS**, Aug. 24, 1788	3	155
Mary A., m. Charles **CHAPPEL[L]**, Oct. 20, 1834,		
by Rev. Francis Darrow	4	58
Richards, s. [Lucius P. & Mary], b. Apr. 27, 1833	3	279
Sally, d. [Stephen & Sarah], b. Oct. 1, 1777	3	107
Sally B., m. Josiah **KEENEY**, b. of New London,		
July 15, 1832, by Chester Tilden	4	47
Stephen, s. David & Rebekah, b. Oct. 9 1741; m.		
Sarah **FITCH**, d. Gideon, Jan. 11, 1764	3	107
Stephen, s. [Stephen & Sarah], b. Mar. 20, 1780	3	107
Stephen, of New London, m. Susan **THOMAS**, of		
Waterford, July 29, 1832, by Chester Tilden	4	47
Susan, m. William A. **DAVIS**, b. of New London,		
Apr. 4, 1832, by Rev. Abel McEwen	4	46
Woodbridge, s. [Stephen & Sarah], b. Sept. 12, 1770	3	107
McATTER, John, m. Elizabeth **HIGGINS**, Dec. 5, 1849,		
by Rev. W[illia]m Logan	4	151
McBURNAY, Martha, m. Patrick **ADAMS**, b. of New		
London, Oct. 11, 1849, by Rev. Jared R. Avery	4	147
McCARTEY, McCARTY, Abiga[i]l, twin with		
Rebec[c]a, d. [John & Rebecca], b. Apr. 19,		
1795	3	167
Celia, d. [John & Rebecca], b. Apr. 17, 1791	3	167
John, b. Jan. 21, 1756; m. Rebecca **WILLIAMS**,		
Nov. 15, 1781	3	167
John, s. [John & Rebecca], b. Aug. 28, 1797	3	167
Mary, d. [John & Rebecca], b. Aug. 17, 1782	3	167
Rebec[c]a, twin with Abiga[i]l, d. [John & Rebecca],		
b. Apr. 19, 1795	3	167
Robert, s. [John & Rebecca], b. Feb. 19, 1784; d.		
Nov. 8, 1801	3	167
Sally, d. [John & Rebecca], b. Feb. 1 ,1789	3	167
William, m. Jane **WEEKS**, Dec. 23, 1787	3	20
William, s. [William & Jane], b. Dec. 14, 1788	3	20

	Vol.	Page
McCLAVIN, Dorothy, d. Patrick & Dorothy, b. Sept. 25, 1728	2	12
Dorothy, m. Cary **LATHAM**, of Groton, Jan. 30, 1734/5, by James Hillhouse, Clerk	2	12
Patrick, late of Edinburgh, Scotland, now of New London, m. Dorothy **OTIS**, d. Jd. Otis, of New London, Nov. 8, 1727, by James Hillhouse, Clerk	2	12
McCLINTOCK, Samuel, of New York, m. Ellen E. **BOLLES**, of New London, Mar. 1, 1829, by Rev. Abel McEwen	4	35
Samuel, of Portsmouth, N.H., m. Mary Ann **BABCOCK**, of N[ew] London, Dec. 13, 1833, by Rev. Abel McEwen	4	54
McCOY, John, s. John & Lucy, b. Dec. 9, 1791	3	138
McCRIB, Bridget, of Groton, m. Edward **EMERSON**, July 9, 1851, by Rev. Jabez S. Swan	4	172
McCURDY, Sally, of Lyme, m. Henry **CHANNING**, of New London, s. John & Mary of Newport, R.I., Sept. 25, 1787	3	136
McDERMOTT, James, of Rochester, N.Y, m. Sarah **DAVIS**, of [New London], Nov. 12, 1845, by Rev. L. Geo[rge] Leonard	4	123
McDONALD, John, m. Temperance **WILSON**, b. of New London, June 21, 1823, by Christopher Griffing, J.P.	4	14
Mary, m. John **CAHILL**, June 23, [18]50, [by Peter J. Blenkinsop]. Witnesses: Patrick Ryan, Mary Hickey	3	306
Mary, m. John **CAHILL**, June 23, 1850. Witnesses: Patrick Ryon, Mary Hickey	4	159
Robert, of Scotland, m. Maria **GURTUR** (?), of New London, June 6, 1844, by [Rev.] G. Thompson	4	112
McDOWELL, Andrew, m. Hannah Smith **BROWN**, b. of New London, Jan. 20, 1823, by Rev. B. Judd	4	11
McENERY, John, m. Elizabeth **REODEN**, Nov. 10, [18]50, [by Peter J. Blenkinsop]. Witnesses: Thomas McEnery, Cath Foley	3	306
McEVERY, John, m. Elizabeth **REODEN**, Nov. 10, 1850. Witnesses: Thomas McEvery, Catharine Fooley	4	159
McEWEN, Abel, Rev., m. Sally B. **BATTELL**, d. William, of Torrington, Jan. 21, 1807	3	227
Ann Buckingham, d. [Rev. Abel & Sally B.], b. Jan. 15, 1817	3	227
Charlotte, d. [Rev. Abel & Sally B.], b. Feb. 9, 1810	3	227
Charlotte, of N[ew] London, m. Courtland L. **LATIMER**, of Norwalk, Ohio, July 7, 1834, by Rev. Abel McEwen	4	56
Harriet, d. [Rev. Abel & Sally B.], b. Sept. 15, 1818	3	227
John Battell, s. [Rev. Abel & Sally B.], b. Apr. 19, 1821	3	227

	Vol.	Page

McEWEN (cont.)

Robert, s. [Rev. Abel & Sally B.], b. June 22, 1808 — 3 — 227

Robert, m. Betsey Peck **LEARNED**, b. of New
London, May 31, 1833, by Rev. Abel McEwen — 4 — 51

Sarah, d. [Rev. Abel & Sally B.], b. May 25, 1812 — 3 — 227

Sarah, m. Henry **GARRETT**, b. of [New London],
June 5, 1838, by Rev. Abel McEwen — 4 — 77

William B., of Norwalk, Ohio, m. Abby
CLEAVELAND, of N[ew] London, July 5,
1838, by Rev. Abel McEwen — 4 — 78

William Battell, s. [Rev. Abel & Sally B.], b. May
29, 1814 — 3 — 227

McGARRY, McGAREY, [see also **McGAWREY**],
James, m. Ellen **MILLER**, Apr. 5, 1846, by
Rev. Sandford Benton — 4 — 125

Patrick, m. Anna **CULLINS**, Feb. 23, 1852, by Rev.
J. Stokes. Witnesses: Walter Brown, Mary
McGarry — 4 — 169

McGAWREY, [see also **McGARRY**], Hannah Wheeler,
m. Daniel **BEEBE**, b. of New London, Apr. 5,
1835, by Rev. Alven Ackley — 4 — 60

McGINLEY, Abby Ann, d. [John & Wealthy Ann], b.
Mar. 14, 1809 — 3 — 242

Betsey, d. [John & Wealthy Ann], b. Dec. 1, 1803 — 3 — 242

Eleanor, d. [John & Wealthy Ann], b. Mar. 10, 1812 — 3 — 242

John, m. Wealthy Ann **BROWN**, Apr. 25, 1800 — 3 — 242

John, s. [John & Wealthy Ann], b. Dec. 2, 1805 — 3 — 242

John, m. Louisa M. **LAX**, b. of New London, May
31, 1843, by Rev. Lemuel Covell — 4 — 109

Laura, d. [John & Wealthy Ann], b. Dec. 12, 1807 — 3 — 242

Laura, m. Newel S. **SPAULDING**, [   ], 1826,
by Robert Bowzer — 4 — 27

Mary Ann, d. [John & Wealthy Ann], b. Aug. 2, 1801 — 3 — 242

Nancy, d. [John & Wealthy Ann], b. Aug. 10, 1814 — 3 — 242

McGOWAN, Mary, m. Oliver **FINGERS**, July 23, 1849,
by Rev. William Logan — 4 — 150

McGRATH, James, m. Eliza **MURRAY**, Nov. 26, 1848,
by Rev. William Logan — 4 — 150

Rodger, m. Johanna **COLLIN[S]**, Sept. 22, [18]50,
[by Peter J. Blenkinsop]. Witnesses: John
McNerny, Elizabeth Collins — 3 — 306

Rodger, m. Johanna **COLLINS**, Sept. 22, 1850.
Witnesses: John McNerny, Elizabeth Collins — 4 — 159

McHUGO, Isabella, m. George **FINE**, Mar. 10, 1852, by
Rev. Robert A. Hallam — 4 — 166

McKANINNAY, Alice, m. Alexander **ROBINSON**, b. of
[New London], Nov. 5, 1843, by Rev. Abel
McEwen — 4 — 108

McKEAN, Margarett, m. Patrick **RAFFATY**, May 2,
1852, by Rev. J. Stokes. Witnesses: Martin
Cullin, Catharine Cullin — 4 — 170

	Vol.	Page
McKENNE, Francis, m. Ann BOURLLE, Nov. 9, 1851, by Rev. J. Stokes. Witnesses: Tarnes Kine, Ann Carlin	4	169
McKINSTREY, M'KENSTRY, Lucretia Lewis, d. [Thomas & Lucretia], b. Jan. 25, 1830	3	204
Thomas, m. Lucretia LEWIS, May 3, 1829	3	204
Thomas, m. Lucretia LEWIS, May 3, 1829, by Rev. Daniel Wildman (See also KENSTRY)	4	36
Thomas, of Hartford, m. Cornelia C. DOUGLASS, of [New London], Mar. 18, 1836, by Rev. Abel McEwen	4	65
McLAUGHLIN, McGHOUGHLIN, Mary, m. Thomas FARRELL, Aug. 22, 1847, by Rev. John Brady	4	133
Timothy, m. Ellen GOUGH, Aug. 12, 1849, by Rev. William Logan	4	150
McLEAN, Albert, m. Mary E. BEACH, b. of N[ew] London, Mar. 5, 1833, by Abel McEwen, Pastor	4	51
Frances, m. Josiah CHESTER, b. of [New London], Oct. 8, 1851, by Rev. Samuel Fox	4	167
Hannah E., m. Chauncey E. BEACH, b. of [New London], July 9, 1846, by Rev. Tryon Edwards	4	127
James W., of Andover, Mass., m. Ann H. RICHARDS, of New London, Dec. 2, 1833, by Rev. Abel McEwen	4	53
William, m. Frances BOWSER, b. of New London, June 27, 1842, by Rev. R. W. Allen	4	99
McLELLAN, John, m. Harriet BACKUS, Aug. 25, 1833, by Rev. Abel McEwen	4	53
McMORIN (?), John, m. Emma CHAPIN, Dec. 9, 1838, by Rev. Abraham Holway	4	85
McMORRAN, James, m. Mary Ann HARRISON, b. of [New London], Sept. 8, 1839, by Ira R. Steward	4	87
McPHERSON, John, m. Margaret CHECKEROUGH*, b. of New London, June 30, 1850, by Rev. George M. Carpenter *(Perhaps "CHESBEROUGH")	4	153
MEAD[E], MEADES, Edward, of [New London], m. Josephine KING, of Stonington, Feb. 27, 1848, by Rev. Abel McEwen	4	137
Edward S., of [New London], m. Mary P. BRAITON, of Norwich, Sept. 14, 1835, by Rev. Abel McEwen	4	62
Elizabeth, maiden name, JULLIVER, m. Nicholas HALLAM, Jan. 2, 1700, in Bramly Church, London	1	33
George, of [New London], m. Prudence MORRIS, of Groton, Nov. 5, 1835, by Rev. Abel McEwen	4	63
MEADY, Hannah, d. William & Rebecca, b. Aug. 27, [1655]	1	2

	Vol.	Page
MEDCALF, Dexter, m. Mary BISHOP, b. of Cumberland, R.I., Nov. 26, 1821, by V. R. Osborn	4	7
James E., m. Lois BEEBE, b. of New London, Feb. 22, 1846, by Rev. L. Geo[rge] Leonard	4	124
MEECH (?), Frederick Lennig, of Philadelphia, m. Ellen Douglass THOMPSON, d. Dr. J. Thompson, of N[ew] London, Apr. 17, 1833, by Rev. J. W. Hallam	4	51
MEGARY, Francess, m. Antony F. JACKSON, b. of [New London], Sept. 20, 1840, by Rev. Abel McEwen	4	92
MELLERICH, William, m. Hanna[h] MAY, Feb. 22, 1852, by Rev. J. Stokes. Witnesses: Stephen Hays, T. Quird	4	169
MELONE, Alese, d. [William & Ann], b. Nov. 6, 1768	3	64
Anna, d. [William & Ann], b. July 29, 1771	3	64
Elisabeth, d. [William & Ann], b. July 6, 1776	3	64
Hannah, d. [William & Ann], b. Mar. 31, 1788	3	64
Sarah, d. [William & Ann], b. Sept. 11, 1766	3	64
William, m. Ann WEEKS, Oct. 6, 1764	3	64
William, s. [William & Ann], b. Apr. 23, 1779	3	64
MELOY, Catharine, d. [William & Aliss], b. Apr. 21, 1782	3	53
William, m. Aliss BROOKS, Aug. 1, 1779	3	53
William, s. [William & Aliss], b. July 7, 1780	3	53
MELSUR, Philip, m. Lydia MINOR, June 29, [1704]	1	30
MENOID, Andrew, s. David & Rebeckah b. Dec. 12, 1724	2	65
David, s. David & Rebeckah, b. Nov. 30, 1722	2	65
James, s. David & Rebeckah, b. Dec. 2, 1729	2	67
Sarah, d. David & Rebeckah, b. Jan. 6, 1727	2	67
MERCER, Abby Starr, d. [Peter S. & Rebecca], b. Sept. 23, 1818	3	256
Charlotte Frelinghuysen, m. James MORGAN, June 27, 1831, by Rev. Bethel Judd	3	271
Margarett Nesbitt, d. [Peter S. & Rebecca], b. July 21, 1820; d. Oct. 28, 1821	3	256
Peter Augustus, s. [Peter S. & Rebecca], b. Feb. 12, 1817	3	256
Peter S., m. Rebecca STARR, d. Jonathan & Elizabeth, Nov. 24, 1815	3	256
Sarah J., m. George S. HAZAN, June 18, 1833, by Rev. J. W. Hallam	4	51
MERRELL, MERRIL, MERRELS, Alexander, m. Lovina POTTER, Jan. 1, 1828, by Rev. Robert Bowzer	4	33
Edward, m. Mary DARROW, b. of [New London], Nov. 16, 1823, by Rev. Thomas W. Tucker	4	17
John, m. Polly SAVAGE, Feb. 28, 1827, by R[ober]t Bowzer	4	29
Sarah, d. Joseph & Sarah, b. Feb. 13, 1729/30	2	67

	Vol.	Page
MERRITT, Emeline, m. Warren ANDREWS, b. of New London, Apr. 16, 1833, by Chester Tilden	4	50
Maribah, m. Giles BAILEY, June 27, 1824, in Groton	3	299
MIDDLETON, Eliza J., of [New London], m. George W. CLAXTON, of Philadelphia, Pa., June 24, 1846, by John Howson	4	130
Frances L., of [New London], m. Ebenezer F. LINDSLEY, of Hudson, N.Y., June 28, 1841, by Rev. A. Boies	4	115
Harriet, of N[ew] London, m. Horace S. GILBERT, of Lyme, Sept. 8, 1833, by Rev. Ebenezer Blake	4	53
Nathaniel, m. Abby C. CROCKER, b. of New London, Apr. 5, 1830, by Rev. Abel McEwen	4	37
Sally, of New London, m. Dennison BURROWS, of Groton, July 16, 1822, by Rev. Abel McEwen	4	9
MILLER, Abigail, d. Capt. John, m. Peter CHRISTOPHERS, Feb. 9, 1777	3	232
Abby A., of Waterford, m. John CUTTER, of New London, Mar. 11, 1850, by Rev. Jabez S. Swan	4	152
Albert, m. Susan WATROUS, b. of N[ew] London, May 18, 1837, by Rev. Squire B. Hascall	4	69
Albert, of Wallingford, m. Mary Ann SMITH, of Norwich, Oct. 5, 1844, by Rev. Jabez S. Swan	4	114
Amasa, m. Eliphel SWADDLE, d. Samuel, May 17, 1795	3	236
Amasy, s. [Amasa & Eliphel], b. Sept. 28, 1799, in Lyme	3	236
Amasa, Jr., m. Fanny T. BROWN, d. Jed[edia]h, May 9, 1816	3	258
Axey, [s. Amasa & Eliphel], b. Nov. 30, 1805, in Waterford	3	236
Bernard, m. Julia TYE, b. of New London, July 14, 1850, by T. Edwards	4	154
Betsey, d. [James & Nancy], b. July 31, 1816	3	270
Charles, m. Nancy CROSBY, b. of New London, May 13, 1822, by William Stockman, J.P.	4	8
Charles Pinckney, s. [Elisha & Hulday], b. Apr. 3, 1803	3	229
Charles S., m. Abby Jane ARTHUR, b. of [New London], Mar. 3, 1845, by Rev. S. Benton	4	117
Clarissa, m. Henry MANNING, b. of New London], Apr. 26, 1835, by Rev. Ebenezer Blake	4	60
Desire, m. John WHIPPLE, Dec. 31, 1789	3	63
Edmond, s. [Amasa & Eliphel], b. Sept. 20, 1802, in Lyme	3	236
Elisha, m. Hulday LESTER, d. Andrew, Apr. 1, 1800	3	229
Eliza, m. Charles BRIGGS, May 7, 1822, by Rev. Francis Darrow	4	8

	Vol.	Page
MILLER (cont.)		
Elizabeth, d. Jeremiah, m. James **TILLEY**, Jan. 15,		
1797	3	225
Ellen, m. James **McGAREY**, Apr. 5, 1846, by Rev.		
Sandford Benton	4	125
Erastus, s. [Elisha & Hulday], b. Oct. 21, 1808	3	229
Fanny Elizabeth Church, d. [Amasa, Jr. & Fanny T.],		
b. Sept. 25, 1819	3	258
Gurdon, s. Jeremiah & Mary, b. Apr. 12, 1725	1	65
Gurdon, s. Jeremiah & Mary, b. Apr. 12, 1725	2	20
Hager, m. John **LEWEY**, people of color, [ ],		
1801	3	24
Harriet Ann, m. James T. **SKINNER**, b. of [New		
London], Feb. 7, 1835, by Ebenezer Blake	4	59
Harriet B., m. Henry **WATROUS**, b. of New		
London, May 12, 1833, by Rev. Edw[ar]d Bull	4	51
Harry, m. Hannah **COLVER**, Feb. 29, 1787	3	119
Harry, s. [Amasa & Eliphcl], b. Nov. 12, 1800, in		
Lyme	3	236
James, s. [James & Nancy], b. July 31, 1819	3	270
Jane, of Waterford, m. George **HOOESOE**, of New		
London, June 29, 1845, by Rev. T. Edwards	4	121
Jason, s. Jeremiah & Mary, b. Oct. 24, 1729; d. Nov.		
24, [1729]	2	20
Jason, 2d, s. Jeremiah & Mary, b. July 6, 1732	2	20
Jeremiah, m. Mary **SALTONSTALL**, Mar. 2,		
1717/18	1	49
Jeremiah, m. Mary **SALTONSTALL**, Mar. 2,		
1717/18	2	20
Jeremiah, s. Jeremiah & Mary, b. Aug. 19, 1719	1	65
Jeremiah, s. Jeremiah & Mary, b. Aug. 19, 1719	2	20
John, of Wethersfield, s. Joseph, decd., m. Lucy		
STARR, d. Benjamin, of New London, Sept.		
27, 1750	2	64
John, of Waterford, m. Ann **COIT**, of New London,		
Dec. 19, 1824, by Geo[rge] W. Fairbank	4	20
John Rice, s. [James & Nancy], b. Jan. 29, 1823	3	270
Joseph, s. Jeremiah & Mary, b. Feb. 18, 1734/5; d.		
Apr. 10, following. (Twin with Roland)	2	20
Joseph, m. Freelove **LEWIS**, Sept. 20, 1782	3	69
Joseph, m. Lydia **GRAY**, [ ], 1803	3	170
Joseph, m. Lucretia **GRIFFING**, July 1, 1806	3	170
Joseph Lewis, s. [Joseph & Freelove], b. Apr. 23,		
1784	3	69
Julia Ann, m. Christopher **CRISBY**, b. of New		
London, Apr. 19, 1832, by Chester Tilden	4	46
Lucindy, d. [Amasa & Eliphel], b. Dec. 18, 1797, in		
Lyme	3	236
Lucretia G., m. George M. **GRACE**, b. of New		
London, June 24, 1830, by Rev. Abel McEwen	4	38
Lucretia Griffing, d. [Joseph & Lucretia], b. Oct. 24,		
1808	3	170

	Vol.	Page

MILLER (cont.)

	Vol.	Page
Lucy Smith, d. [Elisha & Hulday], b. Apr. 25, 1806	3	229
Lydia, [w. Joseph], d. Jan. [ ], 1805	3	170
Lyman Lester, s. [Elisha & Hulday], b. Mar. 23, 1801; d. May 16, 1802	3	229
Margaret, b. June 23, 1788; m. Charles T. HEMPSTE[A]D, Nov. 8, 1809	3	205
Mariah, d. [Amasa & Eliphel], b. Sept. 12, 1807, in New London	3	236
Mary, d. Jeremiah & Mary, b. Apr. 6, 1722	2	20
Mary, d. Jeremiah & Mary, b. Apr. 7, 1722	1	65
Mary, d. Mary LATIMER, b. Apr. 11, 1767	3	81
Mary, d. Jeremiah, m. James TILLEY, Sept. [ ], 1771	3	225
Nancy, d. [James & Nancy], b. Apr. 11, 1821	3	270
Peter, s. [Joseph & Lydia], b. July 9, 1804	3	170
Peter, of Gurnsey, Europe, m. Abby JONES, of [New London], July 28, 1843, by R. A. G. Thompson	4	106
Rebekah, d. [Harry & Hannah], b. July 12, 1788	3	119
Roland, s. Jeremiah & Mary, b. Feb. 18, 1734/5; d. Apr. 5, following. (Twin with Joseph)	2	20
Thomas Shaw Perkins, s. [Amasa, Jr. & Fanny T.], b. June 22, 1817	3	258
William, m. Ann Elizabeth DEVRO, Nov. 8, 1826	3	202
William H., m. Elizabeth H. DENISON, b. of New London, Jan. 13, 1851, by Rev. George M. Carpenter	4	158
William Henry, s. [William & Ann Elizabeth], b. Oct. 16, 1827	3	202
-----, d. Rob, d. Aug. 2, [1689], ae 4 y.	1	69
MILLET, Mary, m. Carey LEEDS, Jan. 31, 1828, by Rev. Robert Bowzer	4	3
MILLIN, Mary, m. Daniel LEE, Feb. 14, 1795	3	115
MILLS, Isaiah, s. [James & Jerusha], b. Apr. 22, 1793	3	129
James, m. Jerusha BEEBE, Feb. 17, 1791	3	129
MINARD, MYNARD, George, m. Charlotte LANE, b. of [New London], June 30, 1844, by Rev. Abel McEwen	4	112
William, m. Lydia, d. John RICHARDS, Nov. 15, [1678] (First written William MYNER)	1	13
William, of New London, m. Sarah PARKE, of Preston, Feb. 10, 1747/8, by Rev. Solman Treat	2	12
MINER, MINOR, MYNOR, Abby S., m. John F. FRENCH, b. of New London, Nov. 20, 1849, by Rev. Robert A. Hallam	4	147
Abiga[i]ll, d. Clement, Jr. & Abiga[i]ll, b. Nov. 29, 1726	2	9
Abigail, d. Clement, Jr. & Abigail, b. Nov. 29, 1726	2	66
Abigail, d. Eben[eze]r & Bettey, b. Dec. 1, 1756	2	45
Amos, s. Jesse & Jane, b. Aug. 6, 1755	2	34

	Vol.	Page
MINER, MINOR, MYNOR (cont.)		
Ann, d. Thomas & Grace, b. Apr. 28, 1649; d. Aug.		
13, 1652	1	1
Ann, d. Clem[en]t & Francis, b. Nov. 30, [1672]	1	8
Bettey, d. Ebenezer & Bettey, b. May 25, 1751	2	45
Charles, m. Elizabeth **POWERS**, b. of Waterford,		
[, 1835], by Daniel Huntington	4	63
Charles, m. Emily Jane **WARRIER**, b. of New		
London, Sept. 29. 1846, by Rev. Jabez S. Swan	4	128
Charles H., s. [Joseph & Frances M.], b. Sept. 1,		
1827	3	215
Christopher, m. Rebecca **BROOKS**, May 7, 1790	3	119
Clement, s. Clem[en]t & Frances, b. Oct. 6, [1668]	1	6
Clement, m. Martha **MOULD**, Aug. 4, 1698	1	24
Clement, Deac., d. Oct. [ ], 1700	1	52
Clement, s. Clement & Martha, b. Dec. 14, 1700	1	26
Clement, m. Abiga[I]ll **TURNER**, Jan. 9, 1721/2	1	58
Clement, Jr., m. Abiga[I]l **TURNER**, Jan. 9, 1721/2	2	9
Clement, s. Clement, Jr. & Abigaill, b. Apr. 13, 1735	2	10
Darius, s. Thomas & Martha, b. Mar. 31, 1729	2	67
David, m. Naomi **THOMAS**, b. of New London,		
June 28, 1821, by Rev. Abel McEwen	4	4
Dezier, d. Ephra[I]m, m. David **FRINK**, June 2,		
1773	3	157
Ebenezer, s. Clement, Jr. & Abiga[i]ll, b. Jan. 5,		
1730/1	2	10
Ebenezer, of New London, s. Clement, m. Betty		
BOWLEES [BOLLES], Aug. 23, 1750	2	45
Edw[ar]d, s. Clement & Abigail, b. Jan. 5, 1730/1	2	67
Elisha, m. Eunice **CAPRON**, Feb. 12, 1792	3	126
Elisha, s. [Elisha & Eunice], b. Mar. 8, 1793	3	126
Elizabeth, w. Joseph, d. May 3, 1692	1	39
Elizabeth, d. Joseph & Elizabeth, b. Oct. 29, 1693*		
*("1693" is crossed out with "1691" written in		
pencil)	1	38
Elizabeth, d. Joseph, Jr. & Grace, b. July 23, 1719	1	51
Elizabeth, d. Jesse & Jane, b. July 23, 1740	2	33
Elisabeth, m. Ebenezer **DART**, May 14, 1759	3	6
Elisabeth, d. Turner & Rebeckah, b. Apr. 1, 1760	3	17
Elizabeth, d. Turner, m. Thomas **HARRIS**, Oct. 28,		
1780	3	160
Elizabeth, of New London, m. Russel H. **AVERY**, of		
Norwich, Aug. 31, 1825, by Christopher		
Griffing, J.P.	4	31
Elizabeth, m. John **BEAUMIS**, b. of New London,		
May 2, 1851, by Rev. Jabez Swan	4	163
Ellen, d. [Joseph & Frances M.], b. Aug. 22, 1822	3	215
Ellen, m. Nathaniel **RICHARDS**, b. of New London,		
Mar. 26, 1843, by L. Covell	4	101
Elnathan, s. Manassah & Lydia, b. Oct. 5, [1671]	1	7

	Vol.	Page

MINER, MINOR, MYNOR (cont.)

	Vol.	Page
Emeline, of [New London], m. Isaac A. **AVERY**, of Groton, Dec. 1, 1830, by Rev. Leonard B. Griffing	4	40
Ephra[i]m, d. Nov. 13, 1802 (See also Ephraim Minor Frink)	3	157
Erastus, s. [Elisha & Eunice], b. Apr. 11, 1795	3	126
Esther, d. [Hugh & Elizabeth], b. July 11, 1790	3	239
Eunice, d. Jesse & Jane, b. May 27, 1753	2	34
Eunice, d. Jesse, decd., m. Nathan **HOWARD**, Jr., s. Nathan, all of New London, Sept. 26, 1771	3	51
Ezekiel, s. Joseph & Grace, b. Aug. 20, 1723	1	63
Francis, w. Clement, d. Jan. 6, 1673	1	8
Frances, d. [Joseph & Frances M.], b. Aug. 11, 1818	3	215
Frances Ann, m. Joseph **SHELLY**, b. of Waterford, Sept. 2, 1848, by Rev. Jabez S. Swan	4	141
Frederick, s. Simeon & Mary, b. Sept. 28, 1768, in Stonington	3	213
Frederick, m. Hannah **WOOD**, d. John, Jan. 18, 1795	3	213
Frederick Alford*, s. [Frederick & Hannah], b. June 25, 1799 *(Alfred written in pencil)	3	213
George, m. Lucy Ann **HOLT**, b. of New London, Jan. 1, 1832, by Rev. Abel McEwen	4	44
George Merrill, s. [Joseph & Frances M.], b. [ ]	3	215
Grace, d. Clement & Martha, b. May 1, 1718	1	50
Grace, s. Joseph & Grace, b. Apr. 22, 1732	2	67
Grace, d. Clement & Martha, m. Tho[ma]s **FOSDICK**, s. Samuel & Mercy, Sept. 2, 1755	2	24
Hannah, d. Thomas & Grace, b. Sept. 15, [1655]	1	2
Hanna[h], d. Manassa & Lydia, b. Dec. 1, [1676]	1	11
Hanna[h], d. Thomas, of Stonington, m. Thomas **AVERY**, s. Capt. James, Oct. 22, [1677]	1	12
Hannah, d. Joseph & Grace, b. Aug. 29, 1721	1	59
Hannah, b. Dec. 29, 1793; m. Samuel **CULVER**, [s. Samuel], June 20, 1813	3	278
Hannah, d. [Frederick & Hannah], b. Dec. 12, 1796	3	213
Hannah, of New London, m. Charles **THOMPSON**, of Stratford, June 30, 1825, by Rev. Abel McEwen	4	23
Henry, s. [Turner & Rebeckah], b. June 23, 1779	3	17
Hugh, s. Clement & Martha, b. Apr. 12, 1710	1	36
Hugh, s. Hugh, m. Elizabeth **LEE**, d. Levi, May 3, 1789	3	239
Hugh, s. [Hugh & Elizabeth], b. Dec. 9, 1792; d. Apr. 4, 1801	3	239
Hugh, d. Nov. 29, 1807	3	239
Isaac, s. Jesse & Jane, b. Dec. 15, 1750	2	34
Israel, of New York, m. Charlotte L. **CRANNELL**, of New London, June 4, 1837, by Rev. Robert A. Hallam	4	70
Jane, d. Jesse & Jane, b. May 28, 1742	2	33

	Vol.	Page
MINER, MINOR, MYNOR (cont.)		
Jane, m. Jonathan **CROCKER**, Mar. 1, 1762	3	31
Jane, d. Sept. 20, 1787	3	31
Jedediah, s. Joseph & Grace, b. Oct. 10, 1728	2	66
Jeremiah, s. [Hugh & Elizabeth], b. Mar. 1, 1794	3	239
Jeremiah, m. Fanny **DOUGLAS[S]**, d. Richard, Mar.		
1, 1801	3	189
Jerusha, d. Thomas & Martha, b. Dec. 5, 1731; d.		
Dec. 28, 1732	2	67
Jesse, s. Joseph & Grace, b. Aug. 13, 1716	1	48
Jesse, s. Joseph, m. Jane **WATROUS**, d. Isaac, of		
Lyme, Nov. 3, 1737	2	33
Jesse, s. Turner & Rebeckah, b. Feb. 4, 1770	3	17
Jesse Gove, s. [Nathan & Sarah], b. June 10, 1793	3	181
Johanna, w. Deac. Clement, d. Oct. [ ], 1700	1	52
John, s. Clement & Martha, b. Sept. 16, 1706; d.		
Aug. 9, 1790	1	32
John, of New London, m. Lydia **HOWARD**, of		
Wethersfield, May 8, 1729, by Stephen Hicks	2	67
John, d. Aug. 9, 1790	3	36
John, s. [Hugh & Elizabeth], b. Oct. 14, 1800	3	239
Jonathan, s. Clement, Jr. & Abigail, b. Feb. 10,		
1728/9	2	9
Jonathan, s. Clement & Abigail, b. Feb. 10, 1728/9	2	67
Jonathan, [s. Clement, Jr. & Abigail], d. Jan. 30,		
1734/5	2	10
Jonathan, s. Ebenezer & Bettey, b. May 19, 1754	2	45
Joseph, s. Clement & Frances, b. Aug. 6, [1666]	1	5
Joseph, m. Elizabeth **COMSTOCK**, Mar. 12, 1689	1	38
Joseph, s. Joseph & Elizabeth, b. Mar. 3, 1690	1	38
Joseph, s. Clement & Martha, b. Dec. 29, 1704	1	30
Joseph, m. Wid. Susanna **TURNER**, Aug. 20, 1706	1	52
Joseph, Jr., m. Grace **TURNER**, Feb. 26, 1712/13	1	39
Joseph, d. Apr. 26, 1752, ae 86 y.	2	68
Joseph, s. Clement & Martha, d. Dec. 5, 1755	2	10
Joseph, s. Joseph, b. July 4, 1793; m. Frances M.		
GRIFFING, Sept. 7, 1817	3	215
Lucretia, d. Jesse & Jane, b. Feb. 14, 1743/4	2	33
Lucretia, [d. Jesse & Jane], d. Feb. 20, 1753	2	34
Lucretia, d. Turner & Rebeckah, b. Feb. 1, 1768	3	17
Lucretia, d. [Nathan & Sarah], b. Feb. 10, 1789	3	181
Lucy, d. Clement, Jr. & Abigail, b. Mar. 8, 1723	1	62
Lucy, d. Clement, Jr. & Abigail, b. Mar. 8, 1723	2	9
Lucy, d. Clement, m. Nathan **HOWARD**, s. Nathan,		
b. of New London, Mar. 17, 1743	3	18
Lucy, d. Jesse & Jane, b. Jan. 14, 1745/6	2	33
Lucy, d. Ebenezer & Bettey, b. July 24, 1752	2	45
Lucy, d. Turner & Rebeckah, b. July 23, 1771; d.		
July 31, 1771	3	17
Lucy, d. [Turner & Rebeckah], b. July 1, 1774	3	17
Lydia, d. W[illia]m & Lydia, b. Nov. 16, [1680]	1	15
Lydia, m. Philip **MALLYAR**, June 29, 1704	1	29

	Vol.	Page
MINER, MINOR, MYNOR (cont.)		
Lydia, m. Philip **MELSUR**, June 29, [1704]	1	30
Lydia, m. Daniell **STUB[B]ENS**, Dec. 9, 1716	1	47
Lydia, d. Clement, Jr. & Abigail, b. Oct. 23, 1724	2	9
Lydia, d. Clement, Jr. & Abigail, b. Oct. 23, 1724	2	66
Lydia, b. Feb. 25, 1782; m. Allyn **LESTER**, Apr. 17, 1803	3	205
Lydia, d. W[illia]m & Lidia, b. 8br. 16, [ ]	1	67
Manassa[h], s. Thomas & Grace, b. Apr. 28, 1647	1	1
Martha, w. Clement, d. July 5, [1681]	1	15
Martha, d. Clement & Martha, b. June 20, 1699	1	25
Martha, d. Clement, Jr. & Abigaill, b. Mar. 7, 1732/3; d. Feb. 11, 1734/5	2	10
Martha, d. [Turner & Rebeckah], b. Jan. 10, 1776	3	17
Mary, d. Thomas & Grace, b. May 5, 1651	1	1
Mary, d. Clement & Francis, b. Jan. 29, [1664]	1	4
Mary, d. Clement & Martha, b. Sept. 5, 1708	1	65
Mary, d. [Nathan & Sarah], b. July 28, 1787	3	181
Mary, of Waterford, m. Henry **GARDNER**, of New London, May 16, 1824, by Ebenezer Loomis	4	18
Matthew, s. [Turner & Rebeckah], b. Aug. 28, 1778	3	17
Mercy, b. Nov. 23, 1738; m. Jabez **MANWARING**, June 25, 1761	3	71
Nathan, m. Sarah **GOVE**, May 22, 1786	3	181
Norman B., Capt. of New London, m. Eunice **WOODWARD**, of Hingham, Mass., Oct. 29, 1849, by Rev. Edwin R. Warren	4	149
Olive P., m. Richard B. **FENGAR**, b. of New London, Nov. 18, 1849, by Rev. Edwin R. Warren	4	149
Olive Prentiss, d. [Joseph & Frances M.], b. [ ]	3	215
Phebe, m. John **STEB[B]INS**, June 17, 1697	1	23
Phebe, d. Clem[ent] & Frances,* b. Apr. 13, [1679] *("Frances" is crossed out and "Martha" is written in)	1	13
Phebe, d. Thomas & Martha, b. Aug. 17, 1727	2	67
Rebeckah, d. Turner & Rebeckah, b. June 28, 1766	3	17
Rebecca, m. Louis **MANEIRRE**, Dec. 26, 1779	3	193
Rebecca, d. [Nathan & Sarah], b. Feb. 15, 1791	3	181
Richard, s. Jesse & Jane, b. Oct. 24, 1760	2	34
Richard, s. [Turner & Rebeckah], b. May 9, 1784	3	17
Rufus, s. Jesse & Jane, b. Aug. 8, 1757	2	34
Samuel, s. Thomas & Grace, b. Mar. 4, 1652	1	1
Samuel, s. Manassa & Lydia, b. Sept. 20, [1675]	1	10
Sarah, d. David & Rebeckah, b. Jan. 6, 1726/7	2	66
Sarah, d. of William, of Lyme, decd., m. Clement **STUBBINS**, s. John, of New London, decd., Nov. 25, 1727	2	29
Sarah, d. Joseph, of Lyme, m. John **STUBBINS**, s. Clement, of New London, July 18, 1754	2	28
Sarah, w. Nathan, d. Feb. 21, 1802	3	181

	Vol.	Page
MINER, MINOR, MYNOR (cont.)		
Sidney, s. [Frederick & Hannah], b. Dec. 16, 1806*		
*(1805 written in pencil)	3	213
Sollomon, s. Lieut. Clement & Martha, b. Oct. 31,		
1713	1	42
Stephen, m. Mary **CROCKER**, Mar. 3, 1790	3	77
Susan Augusta, m. Homer **WHEELER**, b. of [New		
London], May 13, 1849, by Rev. Abel McEwen	4	145
Susanna, d. Jesse & Jane, b. Mar. 27, 1748; d. Feb. 5,		
1762	2	33
Susanna, d. Turner & Rebeckah, b. Apr. 6, 1763	3	17
Susannah, m John **CHAPMAN**, Jr., Jan. 4, 1784	3	22
Theody, d. Joseph & Grace, b. Apr. 27, 1726	2	66
Theoday, d. Joseph, of Lyme, m. Nath[anie]l		
ROGERS, s. William, late of New London,		
decd., Sept. 13, 1747	2	34
Theoda, d. Turner & Rebeckah, b. July 21, 1772	3	17
Thomas, s. Clement & Martha, b. Feb. 3, 1712	1	39
Thomas, m. Martha **STUBBENS**, Nov. 21, 1726	2	67
Tu[r]ner(?), s. Jesse & Jane, b. Nov. 12, 1738	2	33
Turner, s. Jesse, m. Rebeckah **MOOR**[E], d. Joshua,		
Jr., b. of New London, Jan. 23, 1760	3	17
Turner, s. Turner & Rebekcah, b. Dec. 2, 1764	3	17
Turner* Mather, s. Turner & Rebeckah, b. Oct. 28,		
1761; d. Apr. 24, 1762 *(First written		
"Jesse")	3	17
William, s. Clement & Francis, b. Nov. 6, [1670]	1	7
William, m. Lydia, d. John **RICHARDS**, Nov. 15,		
[1678] (William **MINARD** in margin)	1	13
W[illia]m, m. Lidia, d. John **RICHARDS**, 8br. 15,		
1678	1	67
William, s. Clement & Martha, b. Mar. 11, 1703	1	29
William, of Lyme, m Elizabeth **TINKER**, of [New		
London], Dec. 18, 1843, by Rev. R. A. G.		
Thompson	4	109
William, of Buffalo, N.Y., m. Ellen **ALLEN**, of		
[New London], Sept. 13, 1847, by Rev. Robert		
A. Hallam (Perhaps William Weever)	4	135
William, of Buffalo, N.Y., m. Ellen **ALLEN**, of New		
London], Sept. 13, 1847, by Rev. Robert A.		
Hallam	4	135
William, m. Mary Elizabeth **LEEDS**, b. of New		
London, Nov. 30, 1848, by Rev. Tryon		
Edwards	4	143
William C., m. Betsey Ann **PERKINS**, b. of New		
London, Sept. 13, 1846, by Rev. L. Geo[rge]		
Leonard	4	129
William N., s. [Joseph & Frances M.], b. Sept. 10,		
1824	3	215
William Wood, s. [Frederick & Hannah], b. Feb. 26,		
1803	3	213

	Vol.	Page

MINER, MINOR, MYNOR (cont.)

Zebadiah, of Norwich, m. Desire **COMSTOCK**, of
Montville, May 13, 1827, by C. Griffing, J.P. — 4 — 30

-----, w. Clement, d. [   ] — 1 — 67

MINOR, [see under **MINER**]

MINSON, Catharine Elizabeth, d. [John Henry &
Elizabeth Ann], b. Apr. 24, 1840 — 3 — 233

Charles Henry, s. [John Henry & Elizabeth Ann], b.
Apr. 8, 1843 — 3 — 233

Edward, s. [John Henry & Elizabeth Ann], b. Oct. 6,
1846 — 3 — 233

Elizabeth Ann, d. [John Henry & Elizabeth Ann], b.
Nov. 8, 1844 — 3 — 233

Frederick, s. [John Henry & Elizabeth Ann], b. Feb.
2, 1842 — 3 — 233

George Williams, s. [John Henry & Elizabeth Ann],
b. Jan. 12, 1848 — 3 — 233

John H., of Sweden, m. Betsey **KELLY**, of N[ew]
London, Apr. 17, 1837, by Rev. Squire B
.Hascall — 4 — 69

John H., of New London, m. Sophia **ROEDIL**, of
New York, Jan. 20, 1865, by J. Dowling, D.D. — 3 — 241

John Henry, b. Mar. 21, 1814, in Parish of
Aldenburg; m. Elizabeth Ann **KELLEY**, Apr.
16, 1838 — 3 — 233

John Henry, s. [John Henry & Elizabeth Ann], b.
Nov. 3, 1841 — 3 — 233

MINTER, Hanna[h], widow of Trustram , m. Joshua
BAKER, s. Alexander, of Boston, Sept. 13,
[1674] — 1 — 9

Rebecca, widow of Tobias **MINTER**, m. John
DYMOND, June 17, [1674] — 1 — 9

Tobias, s. Ezra, of New Foundland, m. Rebeckah
BEAMIS, d. James, Apr. 3, [1672] — 1 — 8

Tobias, s. Tobias & Rebecca, b. Apr. 26, [1673] — 1 — 9

MIRICK, Sarah, m. Peter **COMSTOCK**, May 12, 1774 — 3 — 75

MITCHEL, MITCHELL, James, m. Filema **ANTONY**,
(negroes), Aug. 1, 1808 — 3 — 14

Maria, m. Thomas S. **SIZER**, Sept. 29, 1844, by Rev.
Tho[ma]s J. Greenwood — 4 — 116

Sarah, m. Jerry **CUFFEE**, b. of New London, Jan. 8,
1832, by Rev. B. Judd — 4 — 48

MIXLEY, Elizabeth, m. William **RYLEY**, b. of [New
London], Dec. 27, 1849, by Rev. Tryon
Edwards — 4 — 151

MOFFATT, Amy*, d. [Anthony & Lilly], b. Feb. 29,
1775   *(First written Susan) — 3 — 104

Anthony, s. Anthony & Lilly, b. July [ ], 1773 — 3 — 104

Nancy, d. [Anthony & Lilly], b. Mar. 12, 1778 — 3 — 104

MOISER, Daniel, s. James & Katharine, b. Oct. 13, 1705 — 1 — 45

James, s. James & Katharine, b. May 9, 1711 — 1 — 45

Mary, d. James & Katharine, b. May 11, 1708 — 1 — 45

	Vol.	Page
MOLD, [see under MOULD]		
MONDAY, Samuel, m. Henrietta HACKER, b. of N[ew]		
London, Mar. 19, 1834, by Rev. Abel McEwen	4	55
MONROE, Elizabeth, d. John & Lydia, b. Aug. 29, 1734	2	68
Hannah A., m. Henry A. PERKINS, b. of Norwich,		
July 9, 1850, by Rev. Geo[rge] M. Carpenter	4	154
John, s. John & Lydia, b. Feb. 11, 1725/6	2	66
John, m. Lydia PLUMBE, Apr. 18, 1725	2	66
John, Jr., of New London, s. John, m. Elizabeth		
HOWARD, of New London, d. Ebenezer, Dec.		
4, 1748	2	44
Joshua, s. John & Lydia, b. Apr. 5, 1728	2	66
MONTGOMERY, William, m. Charlotte R. GRIFFING,		
July 19, 1839, by James M. Macdonald	4	86
MOORE, MOOR, Abba, m. Henry W. BURDICK, Apr.		
9, 1837	3	159
Abell, s. Miles, m. Hannah, d. Robert		
HEMPSTEAD, Sept. 22, [1670]	1	7
Abell, s. Abell & Hanna[h], b. July 14, [1674]	1	9
Abell, d. July 9, [1689] on the road coming from		
Boston and was buried at Dedham July 10,		
[1689]	1	69
Caleb, of New London, s. Joseph, of South Hampton,		
m. Esther DANIELS, of New London, d. John,		
Jr., of New London, Mar. 2, 1734/5	2	109
Daniel, s. [Jesse & Polly], b. Sept. 13, 1797	3	184
Daniel, s. [Jesse & Polly], b. Oct. 8, 1798	3	184
David, s. Caleb & Esther, b. July 24, 1741	2	109
Eliza, m. David CULVER, Nov. 17, 1833, by Rev.		
Daniel Wildman	4	84
Eliza, m. John DEARBORN, b. of [New London],		
Mar. 28, 1841, by John Lovejoy	4	94
Elisabeth, d. Miles & Grace, b. Jan. 14, 1746	3	26
Hannah, d. Joshua, m. Enoch BOLLES, s. John, b. of		
New London, Nov. 2, 1738	2	47
Hannah, d. [Jesse & Polly], b. Feb. 17, 1800	3	184
Hannah, m. Sabin K. SMITH, Feb. 3, 1832, by Rev.		
Francis Darrow	4	45
James, s. [William, 2d, & Sarah], b. Jan. 16, 1779	3	75
Jesse, b. July 29, 1771	3	184
Jesse, m. Polly BECKWITH, d. Nathan, of Lyme,		
Mar. 19, 1795	3	184
John, s. Caleb & Esther, b. Aug. 24, 1737	2	109
Jonathan, s. Caleb & Esther, b. Oct. 13, 1743	2	109
Joseph, s. Caleb & Esther, b. Jan. 6, 1735/6	2	109
Louisa H., of East Lyme, m. George W. HAYDEN,		
of Essex, Apr. 16, 1848, by Rev. L. G. Leonard	4	138
Lydia, m. William CROCKER, Feb. 17, 1792	3	169
Margaret, m. Samuel BOLLES, Dec. 18, 1766	3	98
Martin, S. T. J., m. Sarah L. SHONE, b. of New		
London, Sept. 12, 1844, by Rev. J. Blain	4	117

	Vol.	Page

MOORE, MOOR (cont.)

Mehitabel, d. [William, 2d, & Sarah], b. Oct. [ ],
1776 — 3 — 75

Merriam, d. Myles, of New London, m. John
WILLY, s. Isa[a]ack, [ ] 8. [1670] — 1 — 7

Miles, s. Abel & Hannah, b. Oct. 24, [1671] — 1 — 7

Miles, m. Sarah **DANNIELLS**, Dec. 28, 1698 — 1 — 24

Miles, s. Miles & Grace, b. Oct. 9, 1757 — 3 — 26

Nathan, s. [Jesse & Polly], b. Feb. 11, 1796 — 3 — 184

Parnold, d. Miles & Grace, b. July 8, 1752 — 3 — 26

Patience, d. Miles & Grace, b. June 11, 1748 — 3 — 26

Perry J., m. Sophronia **KNOWLES**, b. of [New
London], Apr. 25, 1852, by Rev. Edwin R.
Warren — 4 — 168

Rebeckah, d. Joshua, Jr., m. Turner **MINER**, s. Jesse,
b. of New London, Jan. 23, 1760 — 3 — 17

Ruth, d. Joshua, of New London, m. John **DART**, s.
Eben[eze]r, late of New London, decd., [ ] — 2 — 64

Sarah, d. [William, 2d, & Sarah], b. July 4, 1783 — 3 — 75

Shubael, s. [Jesse & Polly], b. June 11, 1802, in
Hartford — 3 — 184

Turbannee, d. Miles & Grace, b. July 8, 1750 — 3 — 26

William, s. Miles & Grace, b. Aug. 15, 1755 — 3 — 26

William, 2d, m. Sarah **ROGERS**, Jan. 4, 1776 — 3 — 75

William, s. [William, 2d, & Sarah], b. Apr. 19, 1781;
d. Jan. 17, 1783 — 3 — 75

MORAN, Daniel, m. Margaret **NEVIN**, Apr. 25, 1852, by
Rev. J. Stokes. Witnesses: Patrick Neilan,
Bridget Nevin — 4 — 170

MORE, Betty, m. William **KEENEY**, July 14, 1775 — 3 — 106

Lydia, m. Wetherell **DENISON**, Nov. 9, 1726 — 2 — 13

MORELAND, Alfred, m. Ellen **EGARD**, b. of New
London, Nov. 3, 1831, by Rev. Abel McEwen — 4 — 44

MORGAN, Abigail, m. John **EMS**, Feb. 1, 1698/9 — 1 — 24

Alexander, b. Oct. 3, 1771; m. Sally **CLAY**, [d. Capt.
Stephen], Sept. 21, 1794 — 3 — 173

Alexander, s. [Alexander & Sally], b. Dec. 29, 1797 — 3 — 173

Allyn Clay, s. [Alexander &Sally], b. Jan. 7, 1803 — 3 — 173

Ann, d. Joseph & Dorothy, b. Nov. 10, [1678] — 1 — 13

Anna, m. Jonathan **STARR**, Jr., b. of New London,
May 30, 1822, by Rev. B. Judd — 4 — 9

Anna, of [New London], m. James T. **MORGAN**, of
Horndean, England, Sept. 14, 1852, by Rev.
Robert C. Hallam — 4 — 173

Anne, d. John & Anne, b. Dec. 9, 1703 — 1 — 46

Anne, m. Thomas **ATWELL**, Sept. 7, 1714 — 1 — 42

Archibald Mercer, s. James & Charlotte [F.], b. Apr.
5, 1844 — 3 — 271

Benjamin, s. Benjamin & Christian, b. Nov. 3, 1696 — 1 — 43

Bethea, d. John & Anne, b. Apr. 2, 1700 — 1 — 46

Caroline A., of New London, m. John **HAYS**, Jan. 1,
1845, by Rev. G. Thompson — 4 — 116

	Vol.	Page

MORGAN (cont.)

	Vol.	Page
Charles W., of Poughkeepsie, N.Y., m. Phoebe M. **GOFF**, of New London, May 6, 1843, by Rev. R. W. Allen	4	117
Darius, of Norwich, s. Peter, m. Sarah **HAWKINS**, of New London, d. John, of New London, Oct. 5, 1769, by Sam[ue]l Huntington, J.P.	3	45
Deborah, d. John, of New London, m. John **HAWKINS**, s. Tho[ma]s, of New London, Sept. 1, 1748	2	50
Dorothy, d. Joseph & Dorothy, b. Feb. 25, 1675	1	9
Dorothy, d. Joseph & Dorothy, b. Feb. 25, [1675]	1	10
Dorothy, d. Joseph & Dorothy, b. Nov. 18, [1678]	1	13
Edmund Pellet, s. [William & Orra], b. Aug. 23, 1807	3	209
Elijah, s. William & Eliza[beth], b. May 19, 1741	2	109
Eliza, m. Lorenzo D. **THOMPKINS**, b. of [New London], Sept. 28, 1847, by Rev. Jabez S. Swan	4	134
Elizabeth, d. James & Mary, b. Sept. 9, [1678]	1	13
Elizabeth, m. Jonathan **STARR**, Jan. 12, [1698]	1	24
Elizabeth, d. John & Anne, b. Mar. 16, 1705	1	46
Elizabeth, d. William & Eliza[beth], b. Nov. 8, 1736	2	109
Elizabeth, d. William, of New London, m. Nathaniel **WATERHOUSE**, s. Joseph, of New London, Nov. 22, 1756	2	98
Elisabeth, d. Darius & Sarah, b. Nov. 1, 1770	3	45
Elizabeth, of New London, m. George W. **GARDNER**, of Bristol, R.I., May 12, 1822, by Rev. B. Judd	4	4
Emelar Fitch, d. [Alexander & Sally], b. Aug. 7, 1804	3	173
Emmaly, d. [William & Orra], b. June 24, 1803	3	209
Esther, d. William & Eliza[beth], b. June 20, 1734	2	109
Experience, d. John, Jr. & Ruth, b. Mar. 24, 1704	1	30
Frances Jane, m. Alva A. **BROWN**, b. of Waterford, July 9, 1849, by Rev. Alva McEwen	4	146
Grace, m. Caleb **DOUGLASS**, Feb. 20, 1787	3	38
Guy D., of Waterford, m. Sarah C. **JONES**, of [New London], Nov. 15, 1841, by Rev. Abel McEwen	4	96
Hannah, d. James, m. Nehemyah **ROYCE**, s. Robert, Nov. 20, [1660]	1	3
Hanna[h], d. James & Mary, b. June 8, [1674]	1	9
Hannah, d. Joseph & Dorothy, b. Dec. 3, [1683]	1	17
Hannah, d. John & Anne, b. Apr. 18, 1714	1	46
Hannah, m. Peter **PLUMBE**, Nov. 13, 1729	2	81
Harriet, d. [Alexander & Sally], b. May 4, 1800	3	173
Isa[a]ck, s. Jno. & Rachel, b. Oct. 24, [1671]	1	7
James, s. James & Mary, b. Feb. 6, [1667]	1	5
James*, s. James, Sr., m. Dorothy, d. Thomas **PARK[E]**, "sometime in April", [1670] *(Changed to Joseph by L. B. B.)	1	6
James, s. Benjamin & Christian, b. Apr. 21, 1700	1	43
James, m. Susannah **ROGERS**, Oct. 3, 1725	2	66
James, s. James & Susannah, b. June 1, 1726	2	66

	Vol.	Page

MORGAN (cont.)

	Vol.	Page
James, of Groton, m. Ab[b]y H. **BROWN**, of New London, Aug. 5, 1826, by Rev. John G. Wightman	4	26
James, m. Charlotte Frelinghuysen **MERCER**, June 27, 1831, by Rev. Bethel Judd	3	271
James, s. James, m. Mary **VINE**, of Old England, "sometime in the month of November", [1666]	1	5
James T., of Horndean, England, m. Anna **MORGAN**, of [New London], Sept. 14, 1852, by Rev. Robert C. Hallam	4	173
Jerusha, d. Benjamin & Christian, b. Oct. 12, 1705	1	44
John, s. James, m. Rachell **DYMAN**, Nov. 16, [1665]	1	4
John, s. John & Rachel, b. June 10, [1667]	1	5
John, m. Anne **DARTT**, [ ], 1699	1	46
John, s. John, Jr. & Ruth, b. Jan. 4 ,1700	1	26
John, s. Benjamin & Christian, b. Mar. 7, 1702	1	44
John, s. John & Anne, b. May 30, 1708	1	46
John, d. Apr. 24, 1754	2	68
John S., of Waterford, m. Jane E. **BECKWITH**, of East Lyme, Feb. 17, 1850, by Rev. Abel McEwen	4	152
Johnathan, s. Benjamin & Christian, b. Sept. 12 ,1707	1	44
Jonathan, s. William & Eliza[beth], b. Apr. 13, 1739	2	109
Joseph*, s. James, Sr., m. Dorothy, d. Thomas **PARK[E]**, "sometime in April", [1670] *(First written "James". Changed by L. B. B.)	1	6
Joseph, s. James, m. Dorytha, d. Thomas **PARKER**, b. of New London, Apr. [, 1670]	1	7
Joseph, s. Joseph & Dorothy, b. Nov. 6, [1671]	1	8
Joseph, s. Joseph & Dorothy, b. Nov. 6, [1672]	1	8
Joseph, s. Benjamin & Christian, b. Feb. 15, 1695	1	43
Katharine, d. William & Eliza[beth], b. Mar. 28, 1743	2	109
Lucy A., m. John H. **CROCKER**, Mar. 20, 1843, by H. R. Knapp	4	104
Martha, d. Joseph & Dorothy, b. Mar. 20, [1681]	1	15
Mary, d. James & Mary, b. Mar. 20, [1670]	1	7
Mary, d. John, Jr. & Ruth, b. Dec. 18, 1698	1	24
Mary, d. Benjamin & Christian, b. July 8, 1698	1	43
Mary, d. James & Charlotte F., b. Oct. 9, 1834	3	271
Michael, m. Bridget **DONOVAN**, Nov. 26, 1848, by Rev. William Logan	4	150
Patty, m. Thomas **HOLT**, Sept. 24, 1769	3	93
Peter, s. John & Anne, b. Jan. 10, 1711/12	1	46
Philip, s. William & Eliza[beth], b. May 31, 1745	2	109
Rebecca, m. Amos **WEEKS**, Oct. 19, 1768	3	89
Richard, s. John & Anne, b. Sept. 23 ,1701	1	46
Richard R., of Waterford, m. Elizabeth **CHAPEL**, of New London, Dec. 29, 1826, by Rev. Abel McEwen	4	28
Ruth, d. John, Jr. & Ruth, b. Aug. 29, 1697	1	23

	Vol.	Page
MORGAN (cont.)		
Samuel, s. John & Rachel, b. Sept. 9, [1669]	1	6
Sandford, of Groton, m. Lavina AVERY, of New		
London, Oct. 2, 1821, by Abel McEwen	4	6
Sarah, d. Jno. & Rachell, b. Apr. 13, [1678]	1	12
Sarah, d. John, Jr. & Ruth, b. Feb. 24, 1702	1	28
Sarah, d. Benjamin & Christian, b. July 1, 1709	1	44
Sarah C., of New London, m. Richard DOUGLASS,		
of Waterford, Oct. 1, 1846, by Rev. Robert A.		
Hallam	4	128
Solomon, m. Belinda BUDDINGTON, b. of New		
London, [ ], by Christopher		
Griffing, J.P.	4	25
Susannah, m. John HANDERSON, Feb. 10, 1728/9	2	39
Susannah, m. Jno. HENDERSON, Feb. 10, 1728/9	2	62
William, s. James & Mary, b. Mar. 4, [1669]	1	6
William, s. Benjamin & Christian, b. Sept. 5, 1711	1	44
William, s. Benjamin, of New London, decd., m.		
Elizabeth CROCKER, d. William, of New		
London, decd., Jan. 13, 1732	2	108
William, s. William & Elizabeth, b. Feb. 16, 1732	2	109
William, m. Naomi DANIELS, b. of New London,		
May 7, 1789, by Andrew Griswold, J.P.	2	123
William, [m.] Orra PELLET, d. David, of		
Canterbury, Mar. 11, 1802	3	209
William, m. Joanna CRANNELL, b. of [New		
London], May 18, 1840, by Rev. William		
Warland, of Say Brook, Ct.	4	90
William, Griswold, [s. William & Orra], b. Feb. 8,		
1805	3	209
-----, w. Ensign, d. Aug. 6, [1689]	1	69
MORIARTY, John, m. Mary KENNEDY, Apr. 11, 1852,		
by Rev. J. Stokes. Witnesses: Cornelius		
Kennedy, Mary G. Kennedy	4	170
MORRIS, Abby, of [New London], m. Perry WALES, of		
New York, (colored), Aug. 12, 1845, by Rev.		
O. Geo[rge] Leonard	4	123
Henry, m. Emma ROGERS, b. of New London, Apr.		
20, 1834, by Rev. Abel McEwen	4	55
James, m. Sally CROCKER, b. of New London,		
Dec. 25, 1827, by Rev. Abel McEwen	4	33
Mary, d. Robert & Mary, b. Apr. 15, 1779	2	67
Nancy, of Groton, m. George FREEMAN, of New		
London, Aug. 25, 1839, by J. Lovejoy	4	87
Nancy, m. Horace BARBER, b. of [New London],		
Mar. 16, 1845, by Rev. Abel McEwen	4	118
Prudence, of Groton, m. George MEAD[E], of [New		
London], Nov. 5, 1835, by Rev. Abel McEwen	4	63
Robert, m. Mary LESTER, Mar. 8, 1725	2	67
MORTIMORE, Rachal, m. Moses LEWIS, Sept. 17,		
1718	1	56

	Vol.	Page
MORTON, Clara, of Schenectady, N.Y., m. George **ANTONE**, of Cape de Verds, May 18, 1847, by Rev. Jabez S. Swan	4	131
John, m. Betsey **WELCH**, b. of New London, June 8, 1831, by Rev. Abel McEwen	4	42
MOSHER, Lydia, m. Frederick **BECKWITH**, Apr. 3, 1783	3	49
MOSIER, [see also **MOISER**], Sarah, m. John **PRENTIS**, Oct. 15, 1771	3	68
MOTT, Sally, of Groton, Ct., m. Reuben **KINYON**, of Richmond, R.I., Aug. 5, 1827, by Rev. Nehemiah Dodge	4	31
MOULD, MOLD, Christian, d. Hugh & Mary, b. May 8, [1670]	1	7
Hester, d. Hugh & Martha, b. Aug. 27, [1681]	1	15
Hugh, of Barnstable, m. Martha, d. Jno. **COIT**, June 11, [1662]	1	3
Hugh, s. Hugh & Mary, b. Oct. [ ], [1667]	1	5
Jane, d. Hugh & Martha, b. Feb. 7, [1676]	1	11
Martha, d. Hugh & Martha, b. Dec. 25, [1674]	1	10
Martha, m. Clement **MYNOR**, Aug. 4, 1698	1	24
Mary, d. Hugh & Martha, b. July 26, [1665]	1	4
Susanna, d. Hugh & Martha, b. Apr. 2, [1663]	1	4
MOWER, Joseph A., m. Betsey [ ], June 6, 1852, by Rev. Jabez S. Swan	4	173
MOXLEY, Eliza, m. James **ADAMS**, Nov. 11, 1847, by Rev. M. P. Alderman	4	135
John S., m. Fanny **NOYES**, b. of [New London], Mar. 15, 1846, by Rev. L. Geo[rge] Leonard	4	124
MUDGE, Oliver A., m. Elizabeth S. **BEACH**, b. of [New London], Oct. 18, 1841, by Rev. Abel McEwen	4	97
MULCAHY, Honora, m. John **QUIRK**, Nov. 20, 1847, by Rev. John Brady	4	136
MULHALL, Elizabeth, m. John **CORCORAN**, May 16, 1852, by Rev. J. Stokes, Witnesses: Francis Keefe, Anne Drumm	4	170
MULLENS, MULLIN, MULLEIN, Abigail, d. Allen & Abigail, b. May 11, 1735; d. June 7, 1735	2	88
Alexander, s. Allen & Abigail, b. Nov. 27, 1732	2	88
Allen, s. Dr. Alexander, of Galway, Ireland, m. Abigail **BUTLER**, d. John, of New London, Apr, 8, 1725	2	87
Ann, m. Daniel **BEEBE**, b. of New London, July 18, 1768, by David Sprague, Elder	3	38
Anna, d. Allen & Abigail, b. June 21, 1727; d. Apr. 13, 1728	3	87
Anna, d. Allen & Abigail, b. July 13, 1739	2	88
Catharine, d. Allen & Abigail, b. Aug. 16, 1729	2	87
Mary, m. Abraham **CLARK**, Mar. 1, 1698/9	1	24
Mary, d. Allen & Abigail, b. Nov. 11, 173[7?]; d. Feb. 5, [1738?]	2	88

	Vol.	Page

MULLENS, MULLIN, MULLEIN (cont.)

-----, first born of Allen &Abigail, b. & d. Apr. 28, 1726 — 2 — 87

MULLFORD, Elizabeth, d. Capt. of Long Island, m. John **CHRISTOPHERS**, July 28, 1696 — 1 — 22

MULROONEY, MULRONY, Margaret, m. John **POWERS**, Nov. 11, 1849, by Rev. William Logan — 4 — 151

Margaret, m. John **POWERS**, Nov. 11, 1849, by Rev. W[illia]m Logan — 4 — 151

MUMFORD, Catharine, d. John, of Lyme, m. Dr. Isaac **THOMPSON**, Jan. 5, 1800 — 3 — 97

Daniel Coit, s. Robinson & Sarah, b. Dec. 5, 1762; d. Aug. 10, 1763 — 3 — 16

Elizabeth, d. Robinson & Sarah, b. Nov. 8, 1769 — 3 — 16

James, s. Robinson & Sarah, b. May 17, 1767 — 3 — 16

Lucretia, d. John, m. Anthony **THATCHER**, July 24, 1806* *(The words "Should be February" are written in pencil) — 3 — 233

Mary, d. John, m. Elias **PERKINS**, Feb. 11, 1805 — 3 — 118

Mehetable, d. Robinson & Sarah, b. Oct. 13, 1771 — 3 — 16

Robinson, s. James, m. Sarah **COIT**, d. Daniel, Feb. 1, 1761 — 3 — 16

Robinson, s. Robinson & Sarah, b. July 7, 1761 — 3 — 16

Sarah, d. Robinson & Sarah, b. Sept. 14, 1765 — 3 — 16

MUNSELL, Timothy, s. John, m. Eleshiba **SMITH**, d. Hezekiah **SMITH**, all of Lyme, Feb. 11, 1768 — 3 — 45

William Wescote, s. Timothy & Eleshiba, b. Jan. 24, 1770 — 3 — 45

MURDOCK, John James, of New York City, m. Ann **OBINGTON**, of Middletown, Ct., Aug. 8, 1842, by Henry Douglass, J.P. — 4 — 100

MURPHY, Catharine, m. Richard **DENEEFE**, Oct. 14, 1849, by Rev. William Logan — 4 — 150

Richard, m. Rosanna **DOUGHERTY**, Apr. 8, 1849, by Rev. William Logan — 4 — 150

MURRAY, MURRY, Eliza, m. James **McGRATH**, Nov. 26, 1848, by Rev. William Logan — 4 — 150

John, s. Silva **PEMBELTON** (Negro), Dec. 19, 1801 — 3 — 10

Michael, m. Jane **WARD**, June 22, 1846, by Rev. John Brady — 4 — 127

William, m. Margaret **WARD**, b. of New London, July 25, 1830, by Rev. Abel McEwen — 4 — 39

MUSSEY, Abby E., m. George W. **BROWN**, b. of [New London], [, 1838], by Rev. James M. Macdonald — 4 — 76

Abby Eldredge, d. [Thomas & Mary Ann], b. May 4, 1818 — 3 — 230

Elizabeth F., of New London, m. Charles **RAMSDELL**, of Buffalo, N.Y., Apr. 22, 1844, by Rev. Tho[ma]s J. Greenwood — 4 — 111

	Vol.	Page

MUSSEY (cont.)

Elizabeth Fosdick, d. [Thomas & Mary Ann], b. Dec.
8, 1819 — 3 — 230

Martha P., d. Thomas, of [New London], m. Horace
T. **ASH**, of Springfield, Ill., Sept. 4, 1850, by
Rev. T. Edwards — 4 — 155

Thomas, m. Mary Ann **FOSDICK**, d. Capt. Nicoll
Fosdick, May 16, 1817 — 3 — 230

MYERS, Frederick H., m. Jane **ROY**, b. of New London,
May 12, 1852, by Jabez S. Swan — 4 — 172

NAIL, Nancy, d. [Peras & Hannah], b. Jan. 12, 1800 — 3 — 190

Peras, m. Hannah **WILLIAMS**, d. Jonathan, Sept.
[ ], 1793 — 3 — 190

Sophia, d. [Peras & Hannah], b. Oct. 29, 1801 — 3 — 190

Sophia, m. Clifton **GREEN**, b. of New London, May
14, 1837, by Rev. Nathan Wildman — 4 — 69

Stephen, s. [Peras & Hannah], b. Apr. 4, 1794 — 3 — 190

NASON, Abby S., of [New London], m. George D.
TINKER, of New York, Nov. 30, 1851, by
Rev. Jabez S. Swan — 4 — 172

Caroline, m. Robert **KELLEY**, b. of New London,
Nov. 27, 1842, by Eld[er] L. Covell — 4 — 103

Oliver, Jr., m. Elizabeth C. **HOWARD**, b. of New
London, Dec. 15, 1850, by Rev. Jabez S. Swan — 4 — 158

NEVINS, NEVIN, David H., of New York, m. Cornelia L.
PERKINS, of [New London], May 25, [1847],
by Rev. Tryon Edwards — 4 — 131

Margaret, m. Daniel **MORAN**, Apr. 25, 1852, by
Rev. J. Stokes. Witnesses: Patrick Neilan,
Bridget Nevin — 4 — 170

NEWBURY, NEWBUARY, Adelia, of N[ew] London,
m. Edward R. **PLATT**, of Philadelphia, July 9,
1851, by Rev. Jabez S. Swan — 4 — 171

Albert B., m. Sarah E. **DUNBAR**, b. of New London,
May 23, 1852, by Rev. Jabez S. Swan — 4 — 173

Ann, d. Nathaniel & Hannah, b. Mar. 10, 1736/7 — 2 — 76

Daniel, s. Nath[anie]l & Hannah, b. May 23, 1749 — 2 — 76

Daniel, m. Rebecca **KEENEY**, Oct. 21, 1821, by V.
R. Osborn, V.D.M. — 4 — 6

Elizabeth, d. Nathaniel & Elizabeth, b. Dec. 9, 1709 — 1 — 66

Esther, d. [Stedman & Hannah], b. Sept. 14, 1782 — 3 — 103

Eunice, d. Nathaniel & Elizabeth, b. Oct. 9, 1726 — 2 — 75

Eunice, d. Nathaniel, of New London, m. Jabez
BEEBE, s. William, Jr., of New London ,Oct.
11, 1747 — 2 — 62

George, s. [Stedman & Hannah], b. Nov. 29 ,1779 — 3 — 103

Hannah, d. Nathaniel & Elizabeth, b. Nov. 10, 1717 — 1 — 49

Hannah, d. Nathaniel & Hannah, b. July 8, 1734 — 2 — 55

Hannah, d. Nathaniel & Hannah, b. July 8, 1735 — 2 — 76

Hannah, d. [Stedman & Hannah], b. Sept. 17, 1786 — 3 — 103

Isaac, s. [Stedman & Hannah], b. Mar. 29, 1789 — 3 — 103

Jeremiah, s. Nath[anie]l & Hannah, b. Aug. 22, 1743 — 2 — 76

	Vol.	Page
NEWBURY, NEWBUARY (cont.)		
Lester, s. [Stedman & Hannah], b. Aug. 23, 1784	3	103
Love, d. [Stedman & Hannah], b. June 3, 1773	3	103
Lucy, d. [Stedman & Hannah], b. Dec. 3, 1777	3	103
Mary, d. Nathaniel & Elizabeth, b. Sept. 4, 1715	1	45
Mary, d. Nath[anie]l & Hannah, b. May 27, 1739	2	76
Mary, d. Nath[anie]l, 2d, m. Asa **BEEBE**, s. Hezekiah, b. of New London, Mar. 20, 1758	3	5
Mehetable, d. Nath[anie]l & Elizabeth, b. Mar. 2, 1724	2	75
Mehitable, d. Nathaniel, of New London, m. James **ROGERS**, 3d of New London, s. James, decd., & grdson of Ja[me]s, decd., Jan. 24, 1847, by Rev. Stephen Gorton	2	23
Nathan, s. Nathaniel & Elizabeth, b. Dec. 23, 1721	1	60
Nathan, s. Nathaniel & Hannah, b. Oct. 19, 1732	2	76
Nathan, m. Laura **BEEBE**, b. of New London, Jan. 12, 1851, by Rev. Jabez S. Swan	4	162
Nathaniel, s. Nathaniel & Elizabeth, b. May 5, 1707	1	66
Nathaniel, Jr., m. Hannah **LESTER**, Apr. 4, 1728	2	76
Nathaniel, s. Nathaniel & Hannah, b. Jan. 16, 1728/9	2	76
Patience, d. Nathaniel & Elizabeth, b. Jan. 29, 1719/20	1	57
Polly, d. Daniel, m. John **HOWARD**, 2d, May 31, 1795	3	174
Richard, s. Nathaniel & Hannah, b. Apr. 12, 1731	2	76
Samuell, s. Nathaniell & Elizabeth, b. July 9, 1712	1	39
Samuel, s. Nath[anie]l & Hannah, b. Oct. 25, 1746	2	76
Sarah, d. Nathaniel & Elizabeth, b. Oct. 15, 1728	2	75
Sarah, d. of Nath[anie]l, m. Jona[than] **ROGERS**, s. Capt. Jona[tha]n, Nov. 17, 1751	2	32
Stedman, s. Nathaniel & Hannah, b. May 16, 1752	2	76
Stedman, m. Hannah **CHAPPEL**, Dec. 21, 1772	3	103
Stedman, s. [Stedman & Hannah], b. Mar. 13, 1775	3	103
NEWBY, Aaron, of Philadelphia, m. Frances **RICH**, of New London, Apr. 30, 1830, by Rev. Abel McEwen	4	37
NEWCOMBE, NEWCOMB, Elizabeth, d. [George & Tathyer], b. Sept. 16, 1807	3	52
George, m. Tathyer **BEEBE**, d. Samuel, Mar. 1, 1799	3	52
George, s. [George & Tathyer], b. Feb. 12, 1803	3	52
James, m. Caroline M. **NOYES**, b. of New London, Nov. 6, 1844, by Rev. Jabez Swan	4	115
James, m. Sarah A. **WEAVER**, b. of [New London], Sept. 7, 1847, by Rev. Jabez S. Swan	4	134
John, s. [George & Tathyer], b. Apr. 24, 1805	3	52
William, s. [George & Tathyer], b. Sept. 1, 1800	3	52
NEWDEGATE, Patty, m. Benjaman **SULLAVAN**, Apr. 3, 1800	3	80
NEWMAN, William, m. Esther W. **CHAPMAN**, Aug. 29, 1841, by Peter D. Irish, J.P.	4	96

	Vol.	Page
NEWSON, Bridget, d. Robert, m. Josiah **CLARK**, Mar.		
[ ], 1794	3	189
Mary, d. Robert, m. John **TURNER**, Oct. 2, 1798	3	205
NEWTON, Emela, of Norwich, Ct., m. Archabald		
JENKINS, of Norwalk, Va., Sept. 12, 1842, at		
Mrs. King's house on Potter St., by Henry		
Douglass, J.P.	4	101
Jane M., of New London, m. Samuel S. **LATHAM**,		
of Lyme, Aug. 5, 1844, by Rev. S. Benton	4	113
NICHOLAS, Caroline N., of New London, m. Henry S.		
WOOD, of Unadilla, N.Y., June 15, 1843, by		
R. A. G. Thompson	4	105
NICHOLS, NICOLLS, Abba, of Groton, m. Levy		
TEFFT, of New London, Mar. 27, 1836, by		
Rev. Squire B. Hascall	4	83
Ann Eliza, m. John **BREWSTER**, b. of Norwich,		
Oct. 5, 1844, by Rev. Jabez S. Swan	4	114
Christopher M., of Gloucester, Mass., m. Mary		
WILSON, of [New London], June 19, 1838, by		
Rev. Abel McEwen	4	78
Harvey, of New London, m. Lydia **BUNNELL**, of		
Groton, Aug. 15, 1830, by Rev. Abel McEwen	4	39
James, m. Fanny C. **SMITH**, b. of New London, Oct.		
5, 1845, by Rev. Jabez S. Swan	4	122
Mary Ann, of Groton, m. Jonathan R. **KING**, of		
Waterford, Aug. 15, 1830, by Rev. Abel		
McEwen	4	39
William, d. Sept. 4, [1673]	1	9
-----, wid., d. Sept. 15, [1689]	1	69
NILES, Esther, m. Jared **STARR**, Mar. 5, 1805	3	84
NOBLES, James, s. John & Mercy, b. Oct. 3, 1721	1	65
Jedediah, s. John & Marcy, b. Nov. 11, 1729, (twin		
with Zebediah)	2	76
John, s. John & Mercy, b. Mar. 7, 1719	1	65
Jonathan, s. John & Mercy, b. Aug. 25, 1723	1	65
Marcy, d. John & Marcy, b. Apr. 5, 1726	2	76
Mary, d. John & Mercy, b. Jan. 24, 1714/5	1	65
Sarah, d. John & Mercy, b. Nov. 19, 1717	1	65
Zebediah, s. John & Marcy, b. Nov. 11, 1729 (twin		
with Jedediah)	2	76
NORCUTT, John, m. Alice **BROOKS**, Aug. 8, 1782	3	136
John, twin with Mary, [s. John & Alice], b. July 23,		
1784; d. ae 24 hr	3	136
John, s. [John & Alice], b. Aug. 4, 1787	3	136
[John], Capt., lost at sea, [ ], 1796	3	136
Mary, twin with John, [d. John & Alice], b. July 23,		
1784	3	136
Nancy, d. [John & Alice], b. Dec. 18, 1785	3	136
Robert, s. [John & Alice], b. Aug. 9, 1789	3	136
William, s. [John & Alice], b. Oct. 14, 1791	3	136
NORRIS, Betsey, d. [Henry, Jr. & Desire], b. June 15,		
1788	3	165

	Vol.	Page
NORRIS (cont.)		
Desire, d. [Henry, Jr. & Desire], b. Aug. 12, 1790	3	165
Elizabeth, d. Henry, m. Martin **BEEBE**, Feb. 9, 1806	3	202
Fanny, m. Henry **SMITH**, Feb. 16, 1788	3	60
Fanney, d. [Henry, Jr. & Desire], b. Jan. 28, 1792	3	165
Henry, b. Nov. 5, 1765	3	165
Henry, Jr., m. Desire **GARDINER**, d. Christopher, Oct. 14, 1786	3	165
Henry, s. [Henry, Jr. & Desire], b. Oct. 17, 1793	3	165
James, s. [Henry, Jr. & Desire], b. Nov. 1, 1796	3	165
James, m. Mary **GILSON**, b. of New London, Oct. 3, 1836, by Rev. Squire B. Hascall	4	68
Lucretia, d. [Henry, Jr. & Desire], b. Apr. 2, 1795; d. Aug. 28, 1798	3	163
Lucy, d. [Henry, Jr. & Desire], b. Mar. 25, 1798	3	165
Nancy, d. [Henry, Jr. & Desire], b. Nov. 18, 1801	3	165
William, s. [Henry, Jr. & Desire], b. Jan. 30, 1800	3	165
NORTH, Ann H., of [New London], m. Jackson **BOLTON**, of New York City, Oct. 5, 1841, by Rev. Abel McEwen	4	96
NORTHROP, NORTHUP, Benjamin C., of Norwich, m. Rosetta J. **GARDINER**, of New London, Jan. 24, 1848, by Rev. L. G. Leonard	4	137
Eunice, d. Nicholass, of North Kingston, R.I., & Freelove, m. Ichabod **POWERS**, Jr., s. Ichabod, of New London, & Meribah, Nov. 20, 1759	3	71
NORTON, Elisabeth, widow, formerly Elisabeth **SKINNER**, m. Owen **WILLIAMS**, July [ ], 1785	3	128
John, s. William, b. Dec. 16, 1721	1	61
Sarah, d. William, b. Aug. 26, 1724	1	64
Thomas, s. William, b. Dec. 13, 1718	1	61
NOTT, Bridget, m. John **FLOOD**, Aug. 11, [18]50, [by Peter J. Blenkinsop]. Witnesses: Pat Meillen, Sarah Campbell	3	306
Bridget, m. John **FLOOD**, Aug. 11, 1850. Witnesses: Pat Meiller, Sarah Campbell	4	159
Henry, m. Ann Elizabeth **CORNELL**, of New London, June 2, 1842, by H. R. Knapp	4	100
NOWLAND, Ann Stephenson, d. [Asa & Nancy], b. Oct. 4, 1808	3	235
Asa, m. Nancy **DOWGLASS**, d. Jonathan, Jan. 31, 1808	3	235
NOYES, Caroline M., m. James **NEWCOMB**, b. of New London, Nov. 6, 1844, by Rev. Jabez Swan	4	115
Catharine E., of [New London], m. Jairus **DICKERMAN**, of Troy, N.Y., May 9, 1841, by Rev. Abel McEwen	4	95
Enoch, of Lyme, m. Clarissa **DUTTON**, of New London, June 28, 1820, by Rev. Abel McEwen	4	1

	Vol.	Page

NOYES (cont.)

Fanny, m. John S. **MOXLEY**, b. of [New London],
Mar. 15, 1846, by Rev. L. Geo[rge] Leonard — 4 — 124

Henry D., of Mass., m. Esther **TILLEY**, of New
London, Mar. 30, 1837, by Rev. Squire B.
Hascall — 4 — 68

Joseph, of Lyme, m. Sarah G. **GURLEY**, of New
London, May 14, 1823, by Rev. Abel McEwen — 4 — 13

Joseph, of Lyme, m. Catherine **EDGERTON**, of
[New London], Oct. 15, 1835, by Rev. Abel
McEwen — 4 — 63

Mary E., m. Allen **BROWN**, b. of New London,
Aug. 6, 1848, by Rev. Jabez S. Swan — 4 — 141

Mary G., of [New London], m. Henry K W.
BOARDMAN, of Northford, Mar. 18, 1846, by
Rev. Abel McEwen — 4 — 125

Nancy, m. Jonathan P. **STEWARD**, b. of [New
London], May 24, 1835, by Rev. Alvan Ackley — 4 — 66

Sarah, m. Joseph **BISHOP**, Nov. 5, 1837, by Rev.
Alvan Ackley — 4 — 74

Ursula W., of [New London], m. Samuel H.
GROSVENOR, of Norwich, Mar. 9, 1848, by
Rev. Abel McEwen — 4 — 138

OBINGTON, Ann, of Middletown, Ct., m. John James
MURDOCK, of New York City, Aug. 8, 1842,
by Henry Douglass, J.P. — 4 — 100

O'BRIEN, O'BRION, James, m. Rose **FARLEY**, Nov. 8,
1851, by Rev. J. Stokes. Witnesses: Owen
Clifford, Ann Farley — 4 — 169

Patrick, m. Winifred **REILLY**, Sept. 22, [18]50, [by
Peter J. Blenkinsop]. Witnesses: Timothy
Maxwell, Maria Maxwell — 3 — 306

Patrick, m. Winifred **REILLY**, Sept. 22, 1850.
Witnesses: Timothy Maxwell, Maria Maxwell — 4 — 159

William, m. Elizabeth F. **COLWELL**, b. of New
London, Apr. 4, 1852, by Rev. Seth Chapin — 4 — 166

O'CENISBURY, Stephen, s. Jacob & Phebe, b. Dec. 28,
1739 — 2 — 79

OCREY, Fanny, of Lyme, m. William **SCOTT**, of New
London, July 22, 1838, by Rev. Chester Colton — 4 — 66

O'DONOVAN, Jeremiah, m. Johanna **CONKLIN**, Sept.
22, [18]50, [by Peter J. Blenkinsop].
Witnesses: James Young, Julia O'Donovan — 3 — 306

Jeremiah, m. Johanna **CULLIN**, Sept. 22, 1850.
Witnesses: James Young, Julian O'Donovan — 4 — 159

OGDEN, Peirce H., m. Rebecca L. **COOK**, b. of [New
London], Mar. 23, 1845, by Rev. Abel McEwen — 4 — 118

Sally, m. Rufus **MARTIN**, May 17, 1830, by Rev.
Daniel Wildman — 4 — 38

O'HARA, Susan, m. Harry D. **JOHNSON**, Jan. 20, 1837,
by Rev. Robert A. Hallam — 4 — 84

	Vol.	Page
O'HARE, John, m. Mary GRAHAM, Nov. 16, 1845, by		
Rev. John Brady	4	122
OLCOTT, Lucy, m. Gilbert AVERY, July 21, 1799	3	137
ONLEY, Benjamin, of Lyme, m. Margarette WYYOUGS,		
of Mohegan, Dec. 14, 1851, by Rev. Jabez S.		
Swan	4	172
ORAM, Emeline L., of Bristol, Me., m. Thomas W.		
ROGERS, of New London, May 13, 1849, by		
Rev. Edwin R. Warren	4	148
OSBORN, Almira, m. David WALKER, Aug. 25, 1833,		
by Rev. Abel McEwen	4	53
Charlotte, of New London, m. Peter HOFMAN, of		
Germany, Sept. 22, 1822, by Thomas W.		
Tucker, Elder	4	10
Edwin, m. Malvina DAY, b. of New London, May		
14, 1830, by Rev. Abel McEwen	4	38
Henry, m. Betsey BEEBE, b. of New London, May		
9, 1824, by Rev. B. Judd	4	18
Nancy, of [New London], m. John WINSLOW, of		
Wiscassett, Maine, Apr. 23, 1826, by Rev.		
Isaac Stoddard	4	26
OTIS, Barnabus Little, s. Joseph & Elizabeth, b. Jan. 14,		
1759	2	118
David, s. Joseph, Jr. & Elizabeth, b. June 3, 1743	2	118
Dorothy, d. Jd., of New London, m. Patrick		
McCLAVIN, late of Edinburgh, Scotland, now		
of New London, Nov. 8, 1727, by James		
Hillhouse, Clerk	2	12
Dorothy, d. Joseph & Elizabeth, b. Feb. 24, 1755	2	118
Elizabeth, d. Joseph, Jr. & Elizabeth, b. Oct. 11, 1740	2	118
James, s. Joseph, Jr. & Elizabeth, b. June 26, 1751	2	118
Jonathan, s. Joseph & Elizabeth, b. Mar. 1, 1753	2	118
Joseph, Jr., of New London, s. Joseph, m. Elizabeth		
LITTLE, d. David, of Scituate, June 6, 1738,		
by Shearjoshub Bourne, Clerk	2	118
Joseph, s. Joseph, Jr. & Elizabeth, b. Aug. 11, 1739	2	118
Joseph, Jr., s. Joseph, m. Lucy HAUGHTON, d.		
Sampson, all of New London, Feb. 4, 1761, by		
William Hilhouse, J.P.	3	16
Lucy, m. Moses JEFFERY, Mar. 5, 1768	3	123
Mabel, d. Joseph, Jr. & Elizabeth, b. Aug. 31, 1745	2	118
Marcy, d. Joseph, Jr. & Elizabeth, b. June 5, 1747	2	118
Mary, d. Joseph, of New London, m. John		
TOMSON, of New London, Nov. 5, 1724	2	110
Nath[anie]l, s. Joseph, Jr. & Elizabeth, b. Mar. 26,		
1742	2	118
Olive, d. Joseph & Elizabeth, b. Jan. 14, 1757	2	118
Rachel, m. Jonathan HARRIS, July 28, 1735	2	40
Rachel, d. Jos[eph], of New London, m. Jona[than]		
HARRIS, s. James, of New London, July 28,		
1735	2	90
Shuball, s. Joseph & Elizabeth, b. Dec. 6, 1760	2	118

	Vol.	Page
OVINGTON, John, m. Ann **LESHURE**, b. of N[ew] London, Apr. 24, 1836, by Rev. Squire B. Hascall	4	83
OWEN, Anna, d. [John & Mary], b. Dec. 13, 1774	3	41
Charles Harris, s. [John & Elisabeth], b. Dec. 27, 1789	3	41
Charlotte, d. [John & Mary], b. Apr. 22, 1786; d. June 2, 1786	3	41
Charlotte, d. [John & Elisabeth], b. Oct. 10, 1791	3	41
Charlotte, d. John, m. Peter **ROGERS**, Feb. 5, 1808	3	222
Edmund Burke, [s. John & Mary], b. Oct. 26, 1783	3	41
Hannah, d. [John & Susannah], b. Apr. 2, 1773	3	68
Harriott, d. [John & Elisabeth], b. Nov. 25, 1793	3	41
Harriet, m. Edmond **ROGERS**, b. of [New London], Oct. 15, 1840, by Rev. Abel McEwen	4	92
John, of New London, s. Rev. John **OWEN**, of Groton, decd., m. Mary **DOWGLASS**, d. Caleb, of New London, decd., June 21, 1767	3	41
John, s. [John & Susannah], b. Apr. 14, 1769	3	68
John, [s. John & Mary], b. Feb. 10, 1771; d. Apr. 12, 1772	3	41
John, s. [John & Mary], b. Dec. 19, 1772	3	41
John, m. Elisabeth **ROGERS**, Jan. 15, 1789	3	41
Joseph, s. William, of Boston, m. Susannah **WILLIAMS**, widow, d. of [ ] **PENNIMAN**, of Braintree, Sept,. [ ], 1768	3	68
Lucy, d. [John & Elisabeth], b. June 5, 1795	3	41
Margarett, [d. John & Mary], b. Feb. 18, 1778; d. Sept. 28, [1778]	3	41
Mary, d. John & Mary, b. Apr. 1, 1768	3	41
Mary, [w. John], d. July 18, 1787, ae 42 y.	3	41
Mehitable, d. [John & Mary], b. Oct. 5, 1769	3	41
Mehetable, d. John, m. John A. **FULTON**, formerly of Boston, Jan. 9, 1789	3	147
Nancy, d. John, m. Enoch **BOLLES**, June 16, 1802	3	201
Sally, d. John, m. Chauncey **ARNOLD**, Sept. 24, 1803	3	218
Sarah, d. [John & Susannah], b. Nov. 11, 1770	3	68
Sarah, d. [John & Mary], b. Aug. 4 ,1779	3	41
Thomas, twin with [ ], s. [John & Mary], b. Mar. 11, 1782; d. July 27, 1782	3	41
Thomas Williams, s. [John & Elisabeth], b. Apr. 21, 1800	3	41
-----, s. [John & Mary], stillborn, Feb. [ ], 1777	3	41
-----, twin with Thomas, [s. John & Mary], b. Mar. 11, 1782; d. ae 5 days	3	41
-----, d. [John & Mary], stillborn June 20, 1787	3	41
PACHEY, Mary E., m. William C. **BEEBE**, b. of Waterford, Aug. 8, 1850, by Rev. T. Edwards	4	154
PACKER, [see also **PARKER**], Denison S., of Ledyard, m. Mary C. **LAMB**, of New London, Apr. 16, 1843, by L. Covell	4	101

	Vol.	Page
PACKER (cont.)		
Elizabeth, d. Tho[mas] & Lydia, b. Mar. 25, [1679]	1	14
Elizabeth, m. Christopher **DARROW**, June 27, 1701	1	26
Esther P., of New London, m. Henry H. **BEEBE**, of South Hold, N.Y., Aug. 31, 1823, by Ebenezer Loomis	4	16
John, Jr., m. Mary, widow of Tho[ma]s **LATHAM**, June 24, [1678]	1	13
Lydia, d. John & Mary*, b. Jan. 10, [1681] *(First written "Lydia". Corrected by L. B. B.)	1	15
Lydia, d. John & Mary*, b. Jan. 10, 1681 *(First written "Lydia". Corrected by L. B. B.)	1	16
Mary Ann, m. Daniel **GUARD**, Jan. 4, 1829, by Rev. Samuel West	4	35
Thomas, s. Thomas, of New London, m. [ ], Jan. 4, [1671]	1	8
William, m. Mary Ann **COBB**, b. of [New London], Mar. 12, 1846, by Rev. L. Geo[rge] Leonard	4	124
PACKSON, Charles A., m. Esther P. **DABOLL**, b. of [New London], Oct. 7, 1851, by Rev. Samuel Fox	4	167
PACKWOOD, Abigail, d. |William & Abigail|, b. Mar. 4, 1781	3	7
Addeline, d. [George & Sally], b. Aug. 24, 1802	3	174
Eliza Hern, d. [Samuel & Eliza], b. June 10, 1802	3	170
Emily, d. [Samuel & Eliza], b. Sept. 13, 1797	3	170
Frances, d. [William & Abigail], b. July 4, 1762	3	7
George, s. [William & Abigail], b. Mar. 24, 1773	3	7
George, m. Sally **HINMAN**, d. Noble, Dec. 1, 1799	3	174
George, A[u]gustus, s. [George & Sally], b. Sept. 11, 1800	3	174
Mary Ann, d. [William & Abigail], b. Mar. 10, 1764	3	7
Mary Ann, d. William & Abigail, m. Daniel **DESHON**, s. Henry & Bathsheba, Dec. 9, 1784	3	135
Richard D., s. [William & Abigail], b. Feb. 25, 1766	3	7
Sally, d. [George & Sally], b. Aug. 24, 1805	3	174
Samuel, s. [William & Abigail], b. Feb. 15, 1775	3	7
Samuel, m. Eliza **WOODWARD**, d. Abisha, May 1, 1795	3	170
Samuel, s. [Samuel & Eliza], b. July 30, 1795	3	170
Sarah, d. [William & Abigail], b. Apr. 16, 1768	3	7
Thomas, s. [William & Abigail], b. Jan. 16, 1783	3	7
William, m. Abigail **POWERS**, Sept. 4 ,1761	3	7
William, s. [William & Abigail], b. Dec. 5, 1770	3	7
PADDY, William, of New London, m. Phebe **LESTER**, of East Hampton, L.I., May 5, 1824, by Rev. Thomas W. Tucker	4	18
PAGE, Arletta, m. Samuel **ALLY**, May 8, 1836, by Daniel Huntington	4	97
John F., m. Harriet **BEEBE**, of N[ew] London, Apr. 14, 1834, by Rev. Ebenezer Blake	4	55

	Vol.	Page

PAINE, PAIN, PAYNE, PAYN, Abel G., of Waterford,
m. Almyra L. **CARROLL**, of [New London],
May 21, 1848, by Rev. L. G. Leonard — 4 — 138

Asa H., m. Frances **WHIPPLE**, Aug. 16, 1835, by
Rev. Alven Ackley — 4 — 61

Barekiah, m. Mary **LAMPHERE**, d. James, Dec. 22,
1798 — 3 — 214

Clarrissa, d. [Nathaniel & Abby], b. Aug. 5, 1797 — 3 — 134

Lucretia, d. [Barekiah & Mary], b. Mar. 22, 1803 — 3 — 214

Lucretia, of New London, m. Dudley
WOODWORTH, of Norwich, Mar. 22, 1823,
by Rev. Abel McEwen — 4 — 13

Lucy, d. [Nathaniel & Abby], b. Jan. 9 ,1794 — 3 — 134

Margaret, m. John **AGENS**, b. of New London, Mar.
4, 1832, by Rev. Abel McEwen — 4 — 45

Mary Ann, d. [Barekiah & Mary], b. June 23, 1801 — 3 — 214

Mary Ann, m. Nehemiah **DODGE**, Jr., Nov. 16,
1820 — 3 — 251

MaryAnn, m. Nehemiah **DODGE**, Jr., b. of New
London, Nov. 16, 1820, by Rev. Nehemiah
Dodge — 4 — 3

Nathaniel, m. Abby **RICHARDS**, Mar. 24, 1793 — 3 — 134

Phebe, d. [Nathaniel & Abby], b. May 14, 1799 — 3 — 134

Sally, d. [Barekiah & Mary], b. Sept. 28, 1805 — 3 — 214

Thomas, of Waymouth, m. Elizabeth **HOWARD**, of
[New London], Nov. 30, 1826, by Rev. N. S.
Spaulding — 4 — 27

Thomas, m. Mary **HOBRON**, July 3, 1836, at
Waterford, by Rev. Frances Darrow — 4 — 84

Thomas Barekiah, s. [Barekiah & Mary], b. Jan. 21,
1808 — 3 — 214

W[illia]m L., Jr., of Lyme, m. Mary P.
HALLADAY, of N[ew] London, Jan. 26, 1834,
by Rev. D. Wildman — 4 — 54

PAINTER, Lyman, of New York, m. Ann E. **SHEPARD**,
of [New London], June 16, 1852, by Rev. Abel
McEwen — 4 — 168

PALMER, Andrew, s. Guy & Lucy, b. Apr. 9, 1737 — 2 — 45

Edward, of New London, s. Andrew, of New
London, m. Lucretia **CHRISTOPHERS**, of
New London, d. of Christopher, late of New
London, decd., Oct. 19, 1740 — 2 — 71

Edward, s. Edward & Lucretia, b. Apr. 7, 1744 — 2 — 71

Franklin A., of Stonington, m. Arabella
STODDARD, of [New London], June 22,
1848, by Rev. Abel McEwen — 4 — 140

Guy, of New London, s. Andrew, decd., m. Lucy
DOUGLASS, wid. of Jno. Douglass, late of
New London, decd., Mar. 6, 1736/7 — 2 — 45

Lucretia, d. Edward & Lucretia, b. Aug. 18, 1741 — 2 — 71

	Vol.	Page
PALMER (cont.)		
Lucy, m. Samuel **GRAY**, of Boston, Apr. 2, 1707	*	*
*(No reference was made to volume or page		
number in the Barbour Collection.)		
Sarah, m. Richard **DURPHY**, Feb. 25, 1738/9	2	48
Sarah, d. Edward & Lucretia, b. Aug. 8, 1742	2	71
Theresa, m. Daniel **WAY**, Oct. 25, 1801	3	292
PALMES, PALMS, Darkis, m. John **CATO**, negroes,		
Apr. 16, 1783	3	47
Hannah, m. Peter **BADET**, June 6, 1784, by Rev.		
Samuel Buel. Witnesses: Tho[ma]s Shaw,		
Lucy Prentis	3	16
Lucy, relict, of Samuel & dau. of John **WAY**, m.		
Richard **DOUGLASS**, 2d, Sept. 2, 1804	3	212
PARKER, [see also **PACKER**], Dorytha, d. Thomas		
Parker, m. Joseph **MORGAN**, s. James, b. of		
New London, Apr. [, 1670]	1	7
Hannah, m. John **BROMEFIELD**, Jan. 16, 1698/9	1	24
Harriet E., of New York, m. Charles H. **SEARLS**,		
of New London, May 14, 1848, by Rev. L. G.		
Leonard	4	139
John C., of New York, m. Harriet Ann **PRINCE**, of		
N[ew] London, Apr. 9, 1837, by Rev. Squire B.		
Hascall	4	68
John Rowe, of Boston, m. Jane **PARKIN**, of New		
London, Feb. 8, 1813, by Rev. Charles Seabury	3	235
Josephine, of New London, m. John J. **FLORENCE**,		
of Floras Western Islands, Oct. 10, 1850, by		
Rev. Geo[rge] M. Carpenter	4	156
Ralph, s. Ralph & Susanna, b. Aug. 29, [1670]	1	6
Sally, m. Peter **DAY**, June 20, 1802	3	21
Susanna, d. Ralph, m. Thomas **FOSTER**, s. John J.,		
of Kingsware, Mar. 27, [1665]	1	4
Thomas, s. Thomas, m. Mary **ALLYN**, d. Robert,		
Jan. 4, [1672]	1	8
PARKES, PARK, PARKE, PARKS, Deborah, d.		
Tho[ms]a & Mary, b. Dec. [, 1680]	1	15
Dorothy, d. Thomas, m. Joseph* **MORGAN**, s.		
James, Sr., "sometime in April", [1670]		
*(First written "James". Corrected by L. B. B.)	1	6
Jennet H., m. Samuel **MARSTON**, b. of New		
London, Oct. 12, 1834, by Rev. Abel McEwen	4	58
John M., of Groton, m. Mary Ann **LESTER**, of		
[New London], June 15, 1835, by Rev. Alvan		
Ackley	4	66
Jonathan, s. Thomas & Mary, b. Apr. 6, [1679]	1	13
Jonathan, [s.] Tho[ma]s & Mary, b. Apr. 6, [1679]	1	14
Mary, d. Tho[mas] & Mary, b. Jan. 28, [1677]	1	12
Phebe, of Groton, m. James **JEFFERY**, of N[ew]		
London, Mar. 2, 1834, by Rev. Ebenezer Blake	4	54
Samuel, s. Tho[ma]s & Mary, b. Nov. 26, [1673]	1	9

	Vol.	Page

PARKES, PARK, PARKE, PARKS (cont.)
Sarah, of Preston, m. William **MYNARD**, of New
London, Feb. 10, 1747/8, by Rev. Solman Treat — 2, 12

Thomas, s. Tho[mas] & Mary, b. Jan. 28, [1675] — 1, 10

PARKIN, Jane, d. [Richard W. & Mary], b. Aug. 15, 1793 — 3, 87

Jane, of New London, m. John Rowe **PARKER**, of
Boston, Feb. 8, 1813, by Rev. Charles Seabury — 3, 235

John Stil Wintrhop, s. [Richard W. & Mary], b. Mar.
25, 1792 — 3, 87

Margarett Ann, d. [Richard W. & Mary], b. Dec. 30,
1798 — 3, 87

Margarett Ann, of New London, m. William Henry
WINTHROP, of New York, June 7, 1818, by
Rev. Solomon Blakesley, of East Haddam — 3, 248

Mary, d. [Richard W. & Mary], b. Jan. 15, 1797 — 3, 87

Richard W., m. Mary **WINTHROP**, July 9, 1786 — 3, 87

Richard W., d. Sept. 10, 1798 — 3, 87

Thomas, s. [Richard W. & Mary], b. Nov. 8, 1794 — 3, 87

William, s. [Richard W. & Mary], b. Mar. 2, 1788 — 3, 87

PARMELEE, Harriet E., m. Charles **LANE**, of
Killingworth, Ct., Oct. 6, 1847, by Rev. M. P.
Alderman — 4, 134

PARSONS, [see also **PERSON**, and **PURSON**], Anne, m.
Benjamin **BEACH**, May 14, 1828, by Rev.
Rob[er]t Bowzer — 4, 35

Israel F., of New Bedford, m. Emma O. **SIMMONS**,
May 18, 1845, by Tho[ma]s J. Greenwood — 4, 119

Thomas, of New York, m. Frances C. **CHAPPELL**,
of New London, Mar. 18, 1822, by Rev. Abel
McEwen — 4, 3

PARTELOW, John, s. William & Anne, b. Nov. 3, 1735.
Recorded July 10, 1756 — 2, 83

PATTERSON, PATTISON, Caroline, d. [James &
Sally], b. Oct. 6, 1801 — 3, 172

Charles H., m. Sophia **TILLITSON**, b. of New
London, Oct. 21, 1849, by Rev. Edwin R.
Warren — 4, 149

James, m. Sally **HASTINGS**, July 19, 1796 — 3, 172

James, d. Jan. 21, 1803 — 3, 172

Mary, d. [James & Sally], b. Nov. 7, 1799 — 3, 172

Sally, m. John **FARGO**, July 9, 1803 — 3, 172

PAULK, Ephraim, m. Sally **STARR**, Feb. 1, 1816 — 3, 242

Ephraim, s. [Ephraim & Sally], b. Dec. 16, 1816 — 3, 242

PAYNE, [see under **PAINE**]

PEABODY, Caroline, m. Franklin **STRICKLIN**, Mar. 27,
1842, by H. R. Knapp — 4, 101

Franklin S., s. [Frederick & Lucy], b. Feb. 6, 1833 — 3, 276

Frederick, of New London, m. Lucy
MANWARING, of New London, Apr 13,
1829, in New York, by Rev. R. McCarter.
Witnesses: Samuel Slater, Mary L. Young — 3, 276

John F., s. [Frederick & Lucy], b. Feb. 20, 1831 — 3, 276

	Vol.	Page
PEABODY (cont.)		
Joseph, m. Catharine **HOLMES**, Mar. 28, 1833, by		
James Porter	4	50
Lucy M., d. [Frederick & Lucy], b. Feb. 26, 1839	3	276
PEARSALL, Lewis, m. Rosana **GARVIN**, of New		
London, June 3, 1847, by Rev. Thomas J.		
Greenwood	4	132
PEASE, Anna, of [New London], m .Anson **GILLETT**,		
of Hebron, Nov. 18, 1849, by Rev. Abel		
McEwen	4	151
Elbridge G., of Edgartown, Mass., m. Eliza **CLARK**,		
of New London, June 27, 1825, by Rev. B. Judd	4	23
William, of [New London], m. Louisa **ROE**, of New		
York, May 7, 1851, by Rev. Robert A. Hallam	4	162
PECK, PECKE, Betsey, d. [Lyman & Betsey], b. June 20,		
1804	3	219
Charles, of New York, m. Hannah **DAVIS**, of New		
London, Sept. 6, 1826, by Rev. Newel S.		
Spaulding	4	27
Charlotte, d. Bela Peck, of Norwich, m. Ebenezer		
LEARNED, Oct. 10, 1808	3	233
Elias, m. Ellen P. **ROGERS**, [d. Daniel, Jr. & Sally],		
[ ], in New York	3	246
Elias, m. Ellen P. **ROGERS**, May 15, 1850, by Rev.		
Charles Willett	4	153
Lydia B., m. Daniel H. **POTTER**, Dec. 22, 1833	3	171
Lydia B., m. Daniel H. **POTTER**, b. of N[ew]		
London, Dec. 22, 1833, by Rev. Abel McEwen	4	53
Lyman, m. Betsey **MASON**, d. Japhet, Nov. 20, 1803	3	219
Lyman, m. Lucretia **MALLARY**, Dec. 30, 1838, by		
Rev. Abraham Holway	4	85
Mary, d. [Nathaniel & Mary], b. Sept. 24, 1787	3	111
Mary, d. [Lyman & Betsey], b. Mar. 10, 1810	3	219
Nancy, d. [Lyman & Betsey], b. Mar. 22, 1806	3	219
Nathaniel, m. Mary **WEEKS**, Nov. 23, 1786	3	111
Palmer, m. Clarrissa **DOUGLAS[S]**, d. Richard, May		
26, 1802	3	189
Sally, d. [Lyman & Betsey], b. Dec. 3, 1807	3	219
Sally, of New London, m. George **CHURCHILL**, of		
Chatham, June 1, 1830, by Rev. Abel McEwen	4	38
Sarah, d. William, of New London, m. Abraham		
DAYNES, of North Yarmouth, Dec. 27, [1671]	1	7
Stephen, m. Ann W. **GREEN**, d. Deac. Timothy,		
May 13, 1806	3	191
PECKHAM, John, of Philadelphia, m. Frances **SMITH**,		
of New London, May 2, 1823, by T. W. Tucker,		
Elder	4	14
Philo, m. Sylvia **BABCOCK**, b. of Lyme, Dec. 5,		
1822, by Rev. Abel McEwen	4	11
William, of Norwich, m. Fanny M.		
WOODWORTH, of Montville, Jan. 3, 1848,		
by Rev. Jabez S. Swan	4	136

	Vol.	Page
PEGASH, Edmund, m. Mary **DUNN**, b. of New London,		
July 10, 1850, by Rev. Geo[rge] M. Carpenter	4	154
PELHAM, Uriah W., of Norwich, m. Mary **ANDERSON**,		
of New London, Oct. 24, 1844, by Rev. S.		
Benton	4	114
PELL, Alice, m. Daniel **COLLINS**, Feb. 22, 1730/1	2	7
PELLET, Orra, d. David, of Canterbury, m. William		
MORGAN, Mar. 11, 1802	3	209
PELLEY, George, m. Almor **CORNELL**, Apr. 9, 1827,		
by C. Griffing, J.P.	4	30
PELTON, Elizabeth, b. Sept. 15, 1756; m. Jonathan		
SIZER, Nov. 29, 1778	3	169
PEMBER, Alred, s. [Thomas & Esther], b. Sept. 23, 1793	3	112
Ann, m. Jonathan **CALKINS**, Dec. 8, 1719	1	61
Asahel, s. [Jonathan & Polly], b. Feb. 22, 1792	3	97
Asa[h]el, m. Betsey **HARRIS**, Jan. 8, 1815	3	211
Asahel, s. [Asahel & Betsey], b. Nov. 21, 1824	3	211
Asahel, m. Esther **LEOPARD**, Sept. 23, 1835, by		
Rev. Alvan Ackley	4	62
Calvin, s. [Asahel & Betsey], b. Sept. 13, 1822	3	211
Calvin, m. Angeline **BECKWITH**, Aug. 22, 1852,		
by Rev. C. Willett	4	171
Frances, of New London, m. George W. **BROWN**,		
May 7, 1837, by Rev. Nathan Wildman	4	69
Hannah, d. [Thomas & Hannah], b. Apr. 7, 1714	1	54
Hannah, d. [Jonathan & Mary], b. Jan. 7, 1752	3	102
Jonathan, m. Mary **KEENEY**, Apr. 3, 1751	3	102
Jonathan, s. [Jonathan & Mary], b Dec. 22, 1758	3	102
Jonathan, m. Polly **STEWARD**, Apr. 17, 1788	3	97
Mary, [d. Thomas & Hannah], b. Oct. 7, 1718	1	54
Mary Elizabeth, m. John **DARROW**, Jr., Oct. 25,		
1835, by Rev. Alvan Ackley	4	63
Mary Elizabeth Harris, d. Asahel & Betsey, b. Mar.		
5, 1816	4	211
Mercy, m. [John] **WADE**, of Lyme, Jan. 8, 1707	1	33
Nancy, d. [Jonathan & Polly], b. July 28, 1788	3	97
Sally, d. [Jonathan & Polly], b. July 27, 1794	3	97
Thomas, m. Hannah **TURNER**, Mar. 18, 1712	1	54
Thomas, s. [Jonathan & Mary], b. Mar. 2 ,1753	3	102
Thomas, m. Esther **DANIELS**, Apr. 8, 1789	3	112
Thomas, s. [Thomas & Esther], b. Feb. 28, 1790	3	112
William, s. [Jonathan & Mary], b. Jan. 12, 1757	3	102
William, s. [Jonathan & Polly], b. Jan. 25, 1790	3	97
PEMBERTON, Elizabeth, m. Jonathan **ROGERS**, s.		
Samuel, [ ]	1	56
Joseph, d. Oct. 14, 1702	1	27
Mary, m. Alexander **BAKER**, Apr. 27, 1707	1	32
Mary, wid., of Joseph, d. Dec. 4, 1717	1	49
Silva, m. Robert **FREEMAN** (negroes), Nov. 6,		
1806	3	10
PENDALL, John, m. Elizabeth **CARPENTER**, June 19,		
1704	1	29

	Vol.	Page
PENDALL (cont.)	1	39
William, m. Mary **HAIMES**, Sept. 8, 1712	1	39
William, s. William & Mary, b. Nov. 10, 1713	1	44
PENDLETON, Eliza, of New London, m. W[illia]m		
CHAPMAN, of Norwich, Sept. 2, 1834, by		
Daniel Huntington	4	57
Gilbert, m. Frances **CHAMPLIN**, Mar. 3, 1839, by		
Rev. Abraham Holway	4	85
Harris, of Stonington, m. Sarah A. **CHESTER**, of		
New London, Apr. 3, 1844, by Rev. S. Benton	4	111
PENHALLAM, Rebecca, m. William C. **CHAMPLIN**, of		
Colchester, Sept. [ ], 1842, by Rev. B. W.		
Allen	4	94
PENHALLOW, Thomas Isaac Benjamin, m. Emma Ann		
CROCKER, b. of [New London], May 22,		
1847, by Rev. L. Geo[rge] Leonard	4	131
PENHARLOW, Miranda, m. Abijah R. **SNOW**, b. of		
New London, Oct. 31, 1828, by Nehemiah		
Dodge	4	35
Thomas I. O., of New London, m. Lucretia		
STRICKLAND, of Montville, Apr. 10, 1842,		
by Rev. Lemuel Covell	4	99
PENNIMAN, Ann E., of [New London], m. William		
HOWARD, of New Bedford, Mass., Sept. 9,		
1850, by Rev. Abel McEwen	4	155
Benjamin, s. [James & Elizabeth], b. Jan. 15, 1775; d.		
Sept. 14, 1798	3	39
Benjamin, s. [John & Mary], b. Mar. 29, 1800; d.		
June 24, 1800	3	156
Daniel, s. [James & Elizabeth], b. Apr 11, 1773	3	39
Elisabeth, d. [James & Elizabeth], b. Jan. 16, 1781	3	39
James, m. Elizabeth **STARR**, Sept. 17, 1763	3	39
James, s. [James & Elizabeth], b. Aug. 27, 1765	3	39
James, s. [John & Mary], b. Sept. 17, 1795	3	156
John, s. [James & Elizabeth], b. Mar. 28, 1769	3	39
John, m. Mary **STARR**, d. Joshua, Nov. 29, 1792	3	156
Joshua, s. [James & Elizabeth], b. Oct. 1, 1776	3	39
Joshua, s. [John & Mary], b. Nov. 21, 1798	3	156
Louisa, d. [John & Mary], b. Apr. 24, 1801	3	156
Lucy, of New London, m. Ezekiel **CHAP[P]EL[L]**,		
of Waterford, Jan. 13, 1827, by Rev. Abel		
McEwen	4	28
Mary, d. [John & Mary], b. May 29, 1793	3	156
William, s. [James & Elizabeth], b. Jan. 31, 1771	3	39
PERKINS, Benjamin R., s. [Nathaniel Shaw & Ellen], b.		
Nov. 1, 1820; d. July 13, 1821	3	170
Benjamin Richards, s. [Nathaniel Shaw & Ellen], b.		
Aug. 2, 1832	3	170
Betsey Ann, m. William C. **MINER**, b. of New		
London, Sept. 13, 1846, by Rev. L. Geo[rge]		
Leonard	4	129

	Vol.	Page

PERKINS (cont.)

Cornelia L., of [New London], m. David H.
NEVINS, of New York, May 25, [1847], by
Rev. Tryon Edwards | 4 | 131

Damaris, of Lyme, m. William **KELLEY**, of New
London, Feb. 19, 1803, in Lyme, by Andrew
Griswold, J.P. | 2 | 124

Demaris, d. Youngs Perkins, m. William **KELLEY**,
Feb. 19, 1803 | 3 | 178

Elias, m. Lucretia Shaw **WOODBRIDGE**, b. of New
London, Mar. 14, 1790 | 3 | 118

Elias, m. Mary **MUMFORD**, d. John, Feb. 11, 1805 | 3 | 118

Elias, s. [Elias & Mary], b. July 28, 1808 | 3 | 118

Elias, s. [Nathaniel Shaw & Ellen], b. Feb. 6, 1819 | 3 | 170

Ellathear, d. [William & Tabitha], b. Nov. 2, 1769 | 3 | 10

Ellen, d. [Nathaniel Shaw & Ellen], b. Apr. 15, 1827;
d. Sept. 9, 1827 | 3 | 170

Ellen, d. [Nathaniel Shaw & Ellen], b. Feb. 24, 1837;
d. Dec. 11, 1839 | 3 | 170

Ellen E., of New London, m. Charles **GRISWOLD**,
of Lyme, Nov. 15, 1820, by Rev. Abel McEwen | 4 | 3

Ellen Elizabeth, [d. Elias & Lucretia Shaw], b. May
23, 1799 | 3 | 118

Fanny S., of [New London], m. Jacob A. **CAMP**, of
Sandusky, Ohio, Oct. 22, 1850, by Rev. T.
Edwards | 4 | 156

Francis Allyn, [s. Nathaniel Shaw & Ellen], b. Mar.
18, 1839 | 3 | 170

Henry A., m. Hannah A. **MONROE**, b. of Norwich,
July 9, 1850, by Rev. Geo[rge] M. Carpenter | 4 | 154

Henry L., m. Frances G. **CHESTER**, b. of [New
London], Apr. 4, 1847, by John Howson | 4 | 130

James M., m. Eunice **GOODWIN**, b. of New
London, June 2, 1851, by Rev. Jabez S. Swan | 4 | 164

Joanna, m. Pember **CALKINS**, Jan. 6, 1780 | 3 | 42

Jonathan Coit, s. [Nathaniel Shaw & Ellen], b. Apr.
15, 182[ ]; d. Dec. [   ] | 3 | 170

Joseph, s. [Elias & Lucretia Shaw], b. Sept. 25,
1794; d. in 3 weeks | 3 | 118

Lucretia Shaw, [w. Elias], d. Mar. 6, 1802 | 3 | 118

Lucretia W., d. Elias & Lucretia, m. Thomas W.
WILLIAMS, May 15, 1817 | 3 | 257

Lucretia Woodbridge, d. [Elias & Lucretia Shaw], b.
Feb. 23, 1797 | 3 | 118

Mary, d. [William & Tabitha], b. July 12, 1766 | 3 | 10

Mary B., of Groton, m. James H. **BEEBE**, of New
London, Feb. 13, 1825, by Rev. Abel McEwen | 4 | 21

Mary H., d. Ebenezer, m. Alexander B.
ANDERSON, Feb. 21, 1805, by Rev. Charles
Seabuary | 3 | 199

Mary Richards, d. [Nathaniel Shaw & Ellen], b. July
6, 1828 | 3 | 170

	Vol.	Page

PERKINS (cont.)

Mary W., of [New London], m. Levi II.
GODDARD, of Mariet[t]a, Ohio, May 12,
1835, by Rev. Abel McEwen | 4 | 61

Nathaniel Shaw, s. [Elias & Lucretia **SHAW**], b. Feb.
11, 1792 | 3 | 118

Nathaniel Shaw, m. Ellen **RICHARDS**, May 10,
1818 | 3 | 170

Nathaniel Shaw, s. [Nathaniel Shaw & Ellen], b. Apr.
19, 1822 | 3 | 170

Oliver Elsworth, s. [Elias & Lucretia Shaw], b. Aug.
16, 1801; d. Nov. 25, 1801 | 3 | 118

Oliver Ensworth, s. [Elias & Mary], b. Jan. 26, 1806 | 3 | 118

Peter, s. William & Mary, b. Oct. 14, 1745 | 2 | 115

Peter, s. Peter & Lucy, b. Mar. 7, 1767 | 3 | 34

Sarah, d. John & Sarah, b. Sept. 7, 1751 | 2 | 85

Thomas Shaw, s. [Elias & Lucretia Shaw], b. Aug.
11, 1793 | 3 | 118

Thomas Williams, s. [Nathaniel Shaw & Ellen], b.
Aug. 15, 1830 | 3 | 170

William, s. William & Mary, b. Apr. 13, 1743 | 2 | 115

William, m. Tabitha **COLVER**, July 18, 1765 | 3 | 10

William Williams, [s Nathaniel Shaw &Ellen], b.
Apr. 7, 1841 | 3 | 170

Winslow Lewis, s. [Nathaniel Shaw & Ellen], b. Dec.
8, 1834 | 3 | 170

-----, d. [Elias & Lucretia Shaw], b. & lived 12 hrs.,
Oct. 2, 1795 | 3 | 118

PERREMAN, Elizabeth, d. John & Elizabeth, b. May 3,
1745 | 2 | 83

John, m. Elizabeth **CAULKINS**, Apr. 22, 1731 | 2 | 82

John, s. John & Elizabeth, b. May 10, 1732 | 2 | 82

John, d. Dec. 6, 1744 | 2 | 83

Sarah, d. John & Elizabeth, b. May 14, 1734 | 2 | 82

PERRY, David, m. Polly **CALVIN**, d. Gabriel, Dec. 1,
1802 | 3 | 111

David, s. [David & Polly], b. Mar. 3, 1808 | 3 | 112

James, of Troy, N.Y., m. Lydia **WARD**, of [New
London], Aug. 6, 1843, by Rev. R. A. G.
Thompson | 4 | 106

Mercy, m. Henry **HAGAN**, b. of New London, Jan.
19, 1846, by Frederick M. Walker, J. P. | 4 | 124

Nancy, d. [David & Polly], b. Dec. 3, 1806 | 3 | 112

Nathaniel H., of U. S. Navy, m. Lucretia M.
THATCHER, b. of New London, Jan. 27,
1828, by Rev. B. Judd | 4 | 34

Thomas, s. [David & Polly], b. Dec. 27, 1803 | 3 | 112

Thomas F., m. Ellen S. **DAYTON**, Aug. 22, 1852, by
Rev. Jabez S. Swan | 4 | 174

PERSON, [see also **PARSON** and **PURSON**], Abiga[i]ll,
of Killingworth, m. Daniel **SHAPELY**, of New
London, Nov. 11, 1714 | 2 | 10

	Vol.	Page
PESTON (?), [see also **PRESTON**], William, of New York, m. Susan **HOWARD**, of New London, Mar. 31, 1850, by Rev. Jabez S. Swan	4	152
PETERS, Ziba, m. Hose **WORTHINGTON**, free negroes, Oct. 18, 1805	3	29
PETTRIE, Elisabeth, d. [James & Jane], b. Feb. 16, 1788	3	121
James, m. Jane **COLVERT**, Sept. 2, 1782	3	121
James, s. [James & Jane], b. Mar. 19, 1791	3	121
PETTY, Martha E., m. James M. **WILLIAMS**, b. of New London, May 12, 1846, by Rev. John Howson	4	126
PHELPS, Elsworth C., of Stonington, m. Ann H. **SWAN**, of New London, Sept. 21, 1851, by Rev. Jabez S. Swan	4	174
Marion E., of Hebron, Ct., m. Frederick P. **ROOT**, of Sweden, Monroe Co., N.Y., Oct. 15, 1839, by J. Lovejoy	4	87
PHILLIPS, PHILIPS, Ann, d Michael, m. John **WALKER**, Dec. 24, 1786	3	223
Elisha, m. Ann **BEEBE**, b. of New London, July 4, 1845, by Rev. Jabez S. Swan	4	120
Hannah, of Lyme, m. Jerome **STICKLAND**, of New London, Nov. 18, 1792, in Lyme, by Andrew Griswold, J.P.	2	124
Hannah, m. William **BENTLY**, Dec. 21, 1823, by Rev. Thomas W. Tucker	4	17
Hannah, of Plainfield, m. John **ANDREWS**, of [New London], July 12, 1847, by Rev. M. P. Alderman	4	133
John C., of South Kingston, R.I., m. Esther **CALDWELL**, of New London, June 10, 1821, by Abel McEwen	4	5
Joseph, m. Mercy **SMITH**, Dec. 7, 1778	3	12
Lester S., m. Ann **HAMILTON**, Feb. 17, 1841, by H. R. Knapp	4	94
Lester S., m. Ann **HAMILTON**, Feb. 17, 1841, by H. R. Knapp (Entire entry crossed out)	4	97
Lucy Ann, of New London, m. James B. **HADLEY**, of New York, Nov. 27, 1844, by Rev. Jabez S. Swan	4	114
Olive A., m. Abel M. **ROGERS**, Jan. 3, 1836	3	280
PICKETT, PICKET, Adam, s. John & Ruth, b. Nov. 15, [1658]	1	3
Adam, of New London, m. Hanna[h], d. Danyell **WETHERELL**, of New London, May 26, [1680]	1	14
Adam, s. Adam & Hannah, b. Sept. 7, [1681]	1	15
Adam, b. –ber 7, 1681	1	68
Adam, m. Susannah **TURNER**, Nov. 26, 1702	1	27
Adam, s. John & Elizabeth, b. May 26, 1708	1	34
Elizabeth, d. John & Mary, b. Nov. 17, 1739	2	52
Han[n]ah, d. Adam & Han[n]ah, b. June 6, [1689]	1	19
Han[n]ah, w. Adam, d. Sept. 16, [1689]	1	19

	Vol.	Page

PICKETT, PICKET (cont.)

Hannah, w. Adam, d. Sept. 16, [1689]; ae 29 y. 5 m.
16 d. — 1 — 69

Hannah, d. John & Elizabeth, b. Sept. 9, 1712 — 1 — 39

Hannah, d. John, m. Peter LAT[T]IMORE, s. Capt.
Richard, b. of New London, Apr. 23, 1732 — 2 — 48

John, s. Adam & Han[n]ah, b. July 28, [1685] — 1 — 17

John, m. Elizabeth CHRISTOPHERS, Oct. 21, 1706 — 1 — 32

John, s. John & Elizabeth, b. Dec. 5, 1710 — 1 — 35

John, d. Dec. 9, 1738 — 2 — 83

John, s. John, of New London, m. Mary
COGSWELL, d. [ ], of East Hampton, N.Y.,
Jan. 3, 1738/9 — 2 — 52

John, s. John & Ruth, b. July 25, [1756*] *([1656]
written in pencil) — 1 — 2

Marcy, d. John & Ruth, b. Jan. 16, 16[60?] — 1 — 3

Mary, d. John, of New London, m. Benj[ami]n
SHAPLEY, s. Nicholas, of Charlestown, Apr.
10, [1672] — 1 — 8

Mary, d. John & Ruth, m. Samuel FOSDICK, s.
John, of Charlestown, New England, Nov. 1,
[1682] — 1 — 16

Mary, d. John & Elizabeth, b. Aug. 24, 1714 — 1 — 43

Mary, d. John, m. Richard CHRISTOPHERS, Jr., s.
Richard, [ ], 1734 — 2 — 47

Ruth, widow of John, m. Charles HILL, s. George,
of Barby in Darbishire, Old England, July 16,
[1668] — 1 — 5

PIERCE, PEARCE, Abigail, of Providence, R. I., d. of
Nathan, of Providence, R.I., m. Jonathan
TRUMAN, of New London, Dec. 7, 1751, in
Providence, by Christopher Harris, J. P. — 2 — 119

Elizabeth, d. Eben[eze]r & Lydia, b. Nov. 27, 1728 — 2 — 81

Joanna, m. Edwin ROBINSON, b. of New London,
colored people, Apr. 13, 1843, by L. Covell — 4 — 101

John, m. Hester BEEBE, Apr. 20, 1839, by Rev.
Abraham Holway — 4 — 85

John, m. Julia E. BECKWITH, b. of Waterford,
Sept. 6, 1846, by John Howson — 4 — 130

Mary, d. Robert & Ann, m. John COIT, s. John &
Grace, June 13, 1742 — 2 — 59

Mary, d. William of S. Kingston, decd., m. John
FOX, s. Benjamin, of New London, decd., Mar.
19, 1745/6 — 2 — 52

Samuel, s. Ebenezer & Lydia, b. Apr. 7, 1727 — 2 — 81

William, s. Ebenezer & Lydia, b. Apr. 12, 1724 — 1 — 63

PIERPOINT, PEIRPONT, Abigail, d. Tho[ma]s & Mary,
b. Dec. 17, 1740 — 2 — 49

Jonathan, s. Tho[ma]s & Mary, b. Oct. 28, 1738 — 2 — 49

Mary, of Middletown, d. Thomas, of Middletown, m.
Daniel HOLT, of New London, s. William
Holt, 2d, of New London, Dec. 16, 1762 — 3 — 33

	Vol.	Page

PIERPOINT, PEIRPONT (cont.)

Sally, m. Ebenezer **BISHOP**, May 9, 1776 — 3 — 113

Thomas, s. James, of Roxbury, m. Mary
HEMPSTEAD, d. of Joshua, of New London,
June 10, 1736 — 2 — 49

Thomas, m. Mary **HEMPSTEAD**, June 10, 1736 — 2 — 82

Tho[ma]s. s. Tho[ma]s & Mary, b. July 13, 1737 — 2 — 49

PIKE, John, s. John & Mary, b. Nov. 4, 1690 — 1 — 47

John, m. Hannah **SPENCER**, May 12, 1712 — 1 — 47

Mary, d. John & Hannah, b. Sept. 15, 1715 — 1 — 46

Nathaniel C., m. Elizabeth Ann **LOVETT**, Apr. 21,
1833, by Chester Tilden — 4 — 50

Samuell, s. John & Hannah, b. July 19, 1713 — 1 — 46

PILGRIM, Israel, s. [Thomas & Lydia], b. Sept. 7, 1783;
d. 13 months old — 3 — 96

Israel, s. [Thomas & Lydia], b. Aug. 13, 1788 — 3 — 96

James, s. [Thomas & Lydia], b. May 12, 1785 — 3 — 96

John, s. [Thomas & Lydia], b. Oct. 15, 1787; d. ae 9
days — 3 — 96

Thomas, b. Feb. 10, 1753, in Rumford, Exeter
County, Old England; m. Lydia **RICHARDS**,
Nov. 7, 1780 — 3 — 96

Thomas, s. [Thomas & Lydia], b. Aug. 8, 1781
(First written Israel) — 3 — 96

PIMER, Susan J., m. Carlos S. **BECKWITH**, b. of New
London, Nov. 6, 1851, by Rev. Robert A.
Hallam — 4 — 165

PINE, Bridget, m. Thomas **MAHONEY**, Jan. 16, 1848, by
Rev. John Brady — 4 — 139

Ellen, m. Martin **RIORDEN**, July 16, 1848, by Rev.
John Brady — 4 — 141

Joanna, m. Edmund **WELCH**, Oct. 28, 1849, by Rev.
William Logan — 4 — 151

PINER, Abigail, d. [John & Anstrias], b. Sept. 16, 1774 — 3 — 71

John, of London, m. Anstriss **POWERS**, d. Ichabod
& Meribah, Sept. 14, 1763 — 3 — 71

John, of [New London], m. Sarah A. **CUFFEE**, of
Groton, Mar. 14, 1850, by Rev. Abel McEwen — 4 — 152

Lydia, d. [John & Anstriss], b. May 15, 1764 — 3 — 71

PINKERTON, John, m. Susan Caroline **LESTER**, of
New London, July 11, 1847, by Rev. L. G.
Leonard — 4 — 138

PITMAN, Abigail, d. [James & Abigail], b. June 14, 1758 — 3 — 70

Abigaill Green, d. [Samuel & Eunice], b. Aug. 11,
1806 — 3 — 226

Anne, d. [James & Abigail], b. May 26, 1759 — 3 — 70

Benjamin, [s. James & Abigail], b. Sept. 16, 1768 — 3 — 70

Eliza Holt, d. [Samuel & Eunice], b. June 1, 1803 — 3 — 226

Elizabeth, d. [James & Abigail], b. Jan. 9, 1761 — 3 — 70

Gilbert, s. [James & Abigail], b. Feb. 5, 1763 — 3 — 70

	Vol.	Page
PITMAN (cont.)		
James, formerly of Rhode Island, m. Abigail		
GREEN, d. Samuel, of New London, Feb. 22,		
1757	3	70
James, [s. James & Abigail], b. Mar. 30, 1776	3	70
Lucy, [d. James & Abigail], b. Jan. 17, 1765	3	70
Samuel, [s. James & Abigail], b. Mar. 1, 1778	3	70
Samuel, m. Eunice **HOLT**, d. Joseph, Nov. 10, 1799	3	226
Samuel Gilbert, s. [Samuel & Eunice], b. Sept. 19,		
1800	3	226
William, s. [Samuel & Eunice], b. Sept. 2, 1808	3	226
PLACE, Esther, d. Nathan & Sarah, b. June 29, 1740	2	34
Nathan, formerly of Providence, m. Sarah **LESTER**,		
widow of Daniel, of New London, May 27,		
1736	2	34
Sarah, d. Nathan & Sarah, b. Dec. 4, 1737	2	34
PLATT, Edward R., of Philadelphia, m. Adelia		
NEWBURY, of N[ew] London, July 9, 1851,		
by Rev. Jabez S. Swan	4	171
PLUMBE, PLUMB, Abigaill, m. Samuel **ROGERS**, Jan.		
16, 1694	1	23
Abigaill, [d. John & Elizabeth], b. Jan. 1, 1694/5	1	38
Abraham, s. Joshua & Amy, b. Oct. 8, 1731	2	73
Amy, d. Joshua & Amy, b. Sept. 24, 1733	2	73
Daniell, [s. John & Elizabeth], b. June 12, 1708; d.		
Sept. 28, following	1	38
Daniel, s. [Green & Margarett], b. Sept. 8, 1760	3	4
Elisha, [s. John & Elizabeth], b. Mar. 10, 1710/11	1	38
Elisha, s. Peter & Hannah, b. Oct. 29, 1742; d. Oct.		
24, 1744	2	83
Elizabeth, [d. John & Elizabeth], b. Feb. 27, 1688/9	1	38
Elizabeth, d. Joshua & Amy, b. Sept. 4, 1725; d. July		
[ ], 1727	2	73
Elizabeth, [d.] Joshua & Amy, b. Sept. 4, 1725; d.		
July [ ], 1727	2	81
Elizabeth, d. John & Hannah, b. Jan. 22, 1725/6	2	81
Elisabeth, d. [Green & Margarett], b. Aug. 21, 1780	3	4
George, s. [Green & Margarett], b. Aug. 7, 1762	3	4
Green, m. Mary **HEM[P]STEAD**, May 3, 1694	1	48
Green, s. Peter & Hannah, b. Mar. 29, 1735	2	82
Green, s. Peter & Hannah, m. Wid. Margarett **LEE**,		
dau. of Isaiah & Lydia **BOLLES**, Mar. 15,		
1758	3	4
Hannah, [d. John & Elizabeth], b. July 15, 1705	1	38
Hannah, d. John & Hannah, b. Dec. 8, 1723	1	63
Isaiah, s. [Green & Margarett], b. Sept. 26, 1767	3	4
John, m. Elizabeth **HEM[P]STEAD**, Feb. 13, 1688/9	1	38
John, [s. John & Elizabeth], b. Nov. 21, 1692	1	38
John, m. Hannah **HARRIS**, June 25, 1721	1	57
John, s. John & Hannah, b. Apr. 18, 1722	1	59
John, s. John & Hannah, d. Mar. 8, 1724/5	2	81

	Vol.	Page

PLUMBE, PLUMB (cont.)

	Vol.	Page
John, s. John & Hannah*, b. May 6, 1727 *(First written "Elizabeth". Corrected by L. B. B.)	2	81
John, s. Nathaniel & Esther, b. Jan. 11, 1761	3	40
Joseph, s. [Green & Margarett], b. Feb. 3, 1759	3	4
Joshua, [s. John & Elizabeth], b. Aug. 3, 1697	1	38
Joshua, s. John, of New London, m. May SKELINKS, of East Hampton, d. Abraham, decd., Nov. 11, 1723	2	73
Joshua, m. Amy SKELINKS, Nov. 11, 1723	2	81
Joshua, s. Joshua & Amy, b. June 14, 1729	2	73
Lucretia, d. Peter & Hannah, b. July 27, 1740	2	83
Lydia, [d. John & Elizabeth], b. Apr. 24, 1703	1	38
Lydia, m. John MONROE, Apr. 18, 1725	2	66
Lydia, d. Peter & Hannah, b. June 21, 1737	2	82
Lydia, d. [Green & Margarett], b. Feb. 21, 1778	3	4
Margarett, d. [Green & Margarett], b. Mar. 11, 1776	3	4
Mary, d. Green & Mary, b. Mar. 29 ,1695	1	48
Mary, m. Thomas TAYLOR, June 25, 1724	2	111
Mary, d. Jno. & Hannah, b. June 13, 1741	2	83
Mercy, d. Green & Mary, b. Nov. 13, 1701	1	48
Nathaniel, s. John & Hannah, b. July 29, 1731	2	82
Patience, [d. John & Elizabeth], b. Mar. 4, 1609/10 [1709/10]; d. Mar. 22, 1710/11	1	38
Patience, d. Peter & Hannah, b. Oct. 30, 1732; d. July 7, 1747	2	82
Peter, [s. John & Elizabeth], b. Dec. 26, 1700	1	38
Peter, m. Hannah MORGAN, Nov. 13, 1729	2	81
Peter, s. Peter & Hannah, b. Aug. 16, 1730	2	81
Rachall, d. Joshua & Amy, b. Aug. 24, 1739	2	74
Sally, d. [Samuel & Sally], b. Oct. 13, 1786	3	23
Samuel, s. Green & Mary, b. July 7, 1697	1	48
Samuel, s. [Green & Margarett], b. July 3, 1764	3	4
Samuel, m. Sally AMES, Aug. 27, 1785	3	23
Sarah, [d. John & Elizabeth], b. Dec. 22, 1699; d. Feb. 15 following	1	38
William, s. Joshua & Amy, b. Aug. 16, 1737; d Aug. 23, 1737	2	73

PLUMLEY, PLUMBLEY, PLUMLY, Elizabeth, wid.,

	Vol.	Page
m. Benjamin LESTER, June 10, 1713	1	40
Jane, d. John & Elizabeth, b. Jan. 4, 1702	1	45
John, m. Elizabeth LEWIS, Aug. 2, 1702	1	27

POLLOCK, David A., m. Mary E. SIZER, b. of [New

	Vol.	Page
London], June 29, 1852, by Rev. Abel McEwen	4	168
Margaret, m. John CLARK, b. of New London, July 19, 1848, by Rev. Jabez S. Swan	4	141

POLLY, Daniel, s. John, of Auburn, m. Jerusha

	Vol.	Page
HAUGHTON, d. Sampson, of New London, Mar. 24, 1725/6	2	63
Daniel, s. Daniel & Jerusha, b. June 5, 1741	2	64
Desire, d. Daniel & Jerusha, b. May 9, 1738	2	63
Desire, d. Daniel & Jerusha, b. May 9, 1738	2	83

	Vol.	Page
POTTER (cont.)		
Daniel H., m. Lydia B. **PECK**, Dec. 22, 1833	3	171
Daniel H., m. Lydia B. **PECK**, b. of N[ew] London, Dec. 22, 1833, by Rev. Abel McEwen	4	53
Delia L., m. Henry L. **SLIDER**, b. of New London, June 19, 1849, by Rev. Geo[rge] M. Carpenter	4	146
Edward, s. [John & Elisabeth], b. June 13, 1791	3	14
Eleanor, d. Stephen & Lucy, b. Jan. 15, 1741/2	2	26
Ele[a]nor, d. William, m. Thomas **RICE**, July 8, 1783	3	169
Elisabeth, d. [John & Elisabeth], b. Aug. 18, 1782	3	14
Elizabeth, d. [George & Elizabeth], b. Aug. 20, 1794	3	147
Elizabeth, m. Thomas **MASON**, Apr. 7, 1816	3	219
Emma S., m. David A. **REDFIELD**, b. of [New London], Sept. 18, 1838, by Rev. C. C. Williams	4	79
Emmela W., d. [Daniel H. & Lydia B.], b. Jan. 23, 1838	3	171
Fanny, d. [Joshua, Jr. & Sally], b. Aug. 21, 1811	3	30
Frances, m. James **CLARK**, Mar. 19, 1834	3	179
Frances, d. Joshua, m. James J. **CLARK**, b. of New London, Mar. 19, 1834	3	292
Frances, m. James **CLARKE**, b. of N[ew] London, Mar. 19, 1834, by Rev. Abel McEwen	4	55
George, m. Elizabeth **CALKINS**, d. Capt. Jonathan, Nov. 10, 1791	3	147
George, s. [George & Elizabeth], b. Aug. 16, 1792	3	147
George, Jr., m. Mary **STARKS**, b. of New London, Nov. 24, 1824, by Rev. John W. Case	4	20
George A., of Norwich, m. Martha J. **SIZER**, of New London, Oct. 28, 1848, by Rev. Tho[ma]s J. Greenwood	4	142
Gilbert, m. Susan F. **FOX**, Oct. 26, 1817	3	196
Gilbert, of Wilmington, N. C., m. Susan **SMITH**, of [New London], Nov. 9, 1840, by Rev. Abel McEwen	4	92
Hannah, wid. of Thomas, of Newport, & dau. of Henry **GARDINER**, of N. Kingstown, m. John **COIT**, s. John & Mehetable, June 20, 1748	2	57
Hannah, d. [Joshua & Lydia], b. Nov. 24, 1782	3	15
Hannah, d. [John & Elisabeth], b. July 5, 1793; d. Oct. 9 ,1798	3	14
Hannah, m. Charles **BUTLER**, Apr. 26, 1808	3	261
Harriet, d. [Joshua, Jr. & Sally], b. Dec. 4, 181[ ]	3	30
Harriet, m. Alfred **HEMPSTEAD**, Nov. 13, 1833, by Daniel Wildman	4	53
Harriet, m. Edmund **ROGERS**, [ ]	3	227
James, of Groton, m. Lucretia **LESTER**, of New London, Dec. 7, 1828, by Rev. Samuel West	4	35
John, s. William & Phebe, b. Apr. 23, 1775	3	208
John, s. William of England, & Phebe, b. Apr. 23, 1775	3	208

	Vol.	Page
POTTER (cont.)		
John, m. Elisabeth **WITTER**, Oct. 24, 1776, in Preston	3	14
John, s. [John & Elisabeth], b. Sept. 6, 1777, in Preston	3	14
Joseph, s. [John & Elisabeth], b. June 19, 1785	3	14
Joshua, m. Lydia **COIT**, May 4, 1780	3	15
Joshua, s. [Joshua & Lydia], b. Aug. 12, 1784	3	15
Joshua, m. Susan **BECKWITH**, b. of [New London], Jan. 7, 1827, by Rev. B. Judd	4	29
Joshua, Jr., m. Sally **HARRIS**, [ ]	3	30
Lavina, d. [George & Elizabeth], b. Feb. 8, 1809	3	147
Lovina, m. Alexander **MERRELL**, Jan. 1, 1828, by Rev. Robert Bowzer	4	**33**
Lucretia, d. [Joshua & Lydia], b. Mar. 14, 1788	3	15
Lucy, d. Stephen & Lucy, b. May 28, 1734	2	25
Lucy, d. Stephen & Lucy, of New London, m. Ephraim **GOFF**, of Wethersfield, Sept. 25, 1757	2	30
Lucy, d. [John & Elisabeth], b. May 25, 1800	3	14
Lydia, d. [Joshua & Lydia], b. Mar. 12, 1781	3	15
Lydia, d. Joshua, m. Ebenezer **COLFAX**, Sept. 25, 1803	3	114
Lydia, d. [George & Elizabeth], b. Jan. 8, 1804	3	147
Lydia C., m. Isaac S. **SIZER**, b. of New London, June 2, 1822, by William Stockman, J.P.	4	8
Mary, d. Stephen & Lucy, b. Aug. 12, 1739	2	25
Mary, d. [George & Elizabeth], b. July 13, 1801	3	147
Mary Ann, d. [Richard & Ann], b. Sept. 9 ,1786	3	69
Mary Ann, m. Ephraim H. **BABCOCK**, Jan. 13, 1811	3	258
Mary T., m. William **STOCKMAN**, Dec. 24, 1820, by Rev. Elijah Hedding	4	1
Nehemiah C., s. [George & Elizabeth], b. May 14, 1799	3	147
Nehemiah C., m. Romelia **LITTLE**, b. of New London, June 8, 1823, by Rev .John Sterry, of Norwich	3	263
Richard, from Exminster, Devonshire County, Great Britain, m. Ann **HANCOCK**, d. W[illia]m, of New London, Feb. 14, 1777	3	69
Richard Humphrey, s. [Richard & Ann], b. June 27, 1784	3	69
Romelia, d. [Nehemiah C. & Romelia], b. Sept. 27, 1825	3	263
Romelia, m. Peregrine **TURNER**, of New London, Apr. 8, 1844, by Rev. G. Thompson	4	111
Samuel, s. [John & Elisabeth], b. Dec. 29, 1779, in Preston	3	14
Sarah, d. Stephen & Lucy, b. Dec. 1, 1732	2	25
Sarah, d. Stephen & Lucy, m. Joseph **LEE**, formerly of Boston, now of New London, Sept. 20, 1753	2	52

	Vol.	Page
POTTER (cont.)		
Sarah, d. [John & Elisabeth], b. Feb. 6, 1796	3	14
Sarah, d. [Richard & Ann], b. Dec. 3, 1781	3	69
Sarah, m. Mat[t]hew **WHITE**, of North Shields,		
Eng., Sept. 1, 1816	3	219
Sarah S., of [New London], m. George **HART**, of St.		
Louis, Mo., Aug. 26, 1850, by Rev. T. Edwards	4	154
Stephen, s. Benj[ami]n, of Providence, m. Lucy		
HAYNES, d. of Jonathan, of New London,		
Feb. 22, 1730/1	2	25
Susan, m. Capt. William H. **CLARK**, Feb. 3, 1822,		
by V. R. Osborn, V.D.M.	4	7
Susan C., m. Sabin **SMITH**, b. of [New London],		
Sept. 18, 1844, by Rev. Abel McEwen	4	113
Susan Childs, d. [Gilbert & Susan F.], b. June 30,		
1821	3	196
Susan[n]ah, d. [George & Elizabeth], b. Dec. 29,		
1797	3	147
Virginia, b. Apr. 5, 1822, at Norfolk, Va.	3	304
Virginia, m. William **TATE**, Oct. 17, 1842, by Rev.		
Boss. Copied from Family Bible Apr. 23, 1896	3	304
William, 2d, s. William, of England, & Abigail		
(**DURFEE**), b. Aug. 5, 1748	3	208
William, 2d, s. William, of England, & Abigail		
(**DURFEE**), b. Aug. 5, 1749	3	208
William, of England, d. Oct. 12, 1763, ae 42 y.	3	208
William, 2d, s. William, of England, & Abigail		
(**DURFEE**) Potter, m. Phebe **WOODWARD**,		
Aug. 20, 1771, by Rev. Matthew Graves	3	207
William, Jr., s. William & Phebe, b. Sept. 10, 1772	3	208
William, Jr., s. William & Phebe, b. Sept. 10, 1772	3	208
William, s. [John & Elisabeth], b. May 10, 1788	3	14
William, s. [George & Elizabeth], b. Mar. 17, 1806	3	147
William Hancock, s. [Richard & Ann], b. Feb. 9,		
1778	3	69
POTTS, Christopher A., of New London, m. Susan A.		
BANKS, of Groton, Aug. 1, 1830, by Rev.		
Abel McEwen	4	38
Christopher Armar, s. [Jeremiah S. & Hannah], b.		
Jan. 10, 1804	3	215
Frances, m. Frederick **CHAPMAN**, Mar. 31, 1831,		
by Rev. Leonard B. Griffing	4	41
Frances Ann, d. [Jeremiah S. & Hannah], b. July 23,		
1811	3	215
Hannah Maria, d. [Jeremiah S. & Hannah], b. Apr.		
23, 1809	3	215
Hannah Maria, m. Alexander **JONES**, Aug. 21, 1831	3	299
Hannah Maria, of New London, m. Alexander		
JONES, of Lyme, Aug. 21, 1831, by Rev. Abel		
McEwen	4	43
Jane Smith, d. [Jeremiah S. & Hannah], b. Mar. 26,		
1807	3	215

	Vol.	Page
POTTS (cont.)		
Jeremiah Smith, b. Dec. 10, 1779; m. Hannah **GRIFFING**, Jan. 1, 1803	3	215
Johanna, d. William & Rebecca, b. May 10, [1679]	1	13
Joseph, s. [Jeremiah S. & Hannah], b. June 1, 1805; d. Sept. 16, 1806	3	215
Mary, m. Jona[than] **DANIELS**, Jan. 1, 1717/18	1	56
Mary Susannah, d. [Jeremiah S. & Hannah], b. June 26, 1818	3	215
William, of Newcastle, Old England, m. Rebecca, d. Capt. James **AVERY**, of New London, Aug. 5, [1678]	1	13
William, s. William & Rebecca, b. Mar. 13, [1680]	1	14
William, s. W[illia]m & Rebecca, b. Mar. 13, 1680	1	68
POWERS, Abigail, m. William **PACKWOOD**, Sept. 4, 1761	3	7
Abigail, m. Stephens **ROGERS**, Apr. 11, 1786	3	82
Anne, m. John **BYRNE**, Nov. 16, 1784	3	3
Anstriss, d. Ichabod & Meribah, m. John **PINER**, of London, Sept. 14, 1763	3	71
Elisabeth, m. Samuel **HERN**, Mar. 20, 1780	3	5
Elisabeth, d. [Sylvester & Elisabeth], b. Nov. 19, 1785	3	103
Elizabeth, m. Charles **MINER**, b. of Waterford, [, 1835], by Daniel Huntington	4	63
Elizabeth Ann, of Lebanon, m. George **BEEBE**, of New London, Oct. 5, 1834, by Rev. Ebenezer Blake	4	57
Enoch, m. Wealthy A. **CHAPMAN**, b. of New London, May 19, 1844, by Rev. Tho[ma]s J. Greenwood	4	111
Esther, d. Samuel & Zerviah, b. Jan. 15, 1747	2	60
Eunice, twin with Lucy, d. [Ichabod, Jr. & Eunice], b. May 22, 1773; d. June 12, 1773	3	71
Eunice, wid., m. Benjamin **FOSTER**, Jan. 22, 1785	3	91
Hannah, d. [Hazzard & Hannah], b. Apr. 15, 1794	3	40
Hazzard, m. Hannah **ROGERS**, Mar. 30, 1788	3	40
Ichabod, Jr., s. Ichabod, of New London, & Meribah, m. Eunice **NORTH[R]UP**, d. Nicholass, of North Kingston, R.I., & Freelove, Nov. 20, 1759	3	71
Ichabod, s. [Ichabod, Jr. & Eunice], b. Aug. 4, 1776	3	71
Ichabod, s. [Hazzard & Hannah], b. Nov. 27, 1790	3	40
Jerusha, d. Samuel & Zerviah, b. Mar. 11, 1742/3	2	60
John, m. Margaret **MULROONEY**, Nov. 11, 1849, by Rev. W[illia]m Logan	4	151
John, m. Margaret **MULRONY**, Nov. 11, 1849, by Rev. William **LOGAN**	4	151
Jos[eph], had negro servant Frank, m. Jemima, Nov. [ ], 1737, by Rev. Samuel Seabury	2	119
Joseph, s. Samuel & Zerviah, b. Dec. 28, 1748	2	60
Joseph, s. [Hazzard & Hannah], b. June 1, 1789	3	40

	Vol.	Page

POWERS (cont.)

Lucy, twin with Eunice, d. [Ichabod, Jr. & Eunice], b. May 22, 1773	3	71
Lucy, m. Charles H. **SISSON**, Mar. 24, 1839, by James M. Macdonald	4	86
Lydia, d. of Joseph, m. Isaiah **BOLLES**, s. John, all of New London, [ ], 1735	2	86
Mary, d. Samuel & Zerviah, b. Sept. 9 ,1741	2	60
Mary, m. Oliver **CROCKER**, Jan. 13, 1793	3	134
Mary, d. [Sylvester & Elisabeth], b. Oct. 2, 1795	3	103
Mary, d. Joshua, m. Aaron **HALLADAY**, Dec. 25, 1804	3	217
Mary, m. John A. **FULTON**, b. of [New London], Mar. 15, 1837, by Rev. Robert A. Hallam	4	67
Nicholas, s. [Ichabod, Jr. & Eunice], b. July 26, 1766	3	71
Richard, [s. Ichabod, Jr. & Eunice], b. Aug. 18, 1770	3	71
Rosamond, m. James **COTTERELL**, July 2, 1786	3	84
Samuel, s. Joseph, of New London, m. Zerviah **ROGERS**, d. of James, Joseph's son, of New London, Mar. 22, 1738/9	2	60
Samuel, d. Feb. 7, 1791	2	60
Samuel, s. [Hazzard & Hannah], b. July 17, 1792	3	40
Sarah, m. Thomas **POOL**, June 1, 1769	3	89
Sarah, d. [Hazzard & Hannah], b. Dec. 31, 1797	3	40
Sophia H., m. Nathan S. **ANGELL**, July 8, 1814, at New Haven	3	247
Sylvester, m. Elisabeth **SMITH**, Nov. 11, 1784	3	103
Sylvester, s. [Sylvester & Elisabeth], b. Jan. 30, 1789	3	103
Wealthy, d. Capt. Sylvester & Sarah, b. of New London, m. William **HIGGINS**, from Webley, Herefordshire County, Great Britain, Nov. 27, 1776, by John Hempste[a]d	3	68
William Howland, s. [Ichabod, Jr. & Eunice], b. July 6, 1768	3	71
PRATT, Dean, s. [Edward & Elizabeth], b. [ ]	3	180
Edward, m. Elizabeth **PRENTIS**, Oct. 2, 1806	3	180
Edward, s. [Edward & Elizabeth], b. Mar. 22, 1815	3	180
Eliza, of N[ew] London, m. Joseph H. **LESTER**, of Norwich, Oct. 31, 1833, by Rev. Isaac W. Hallam	4	52
Elizabeth, d. [Edward & Elizabeth], b. Apr. 10, 1813	3	180
Francis, s. [Edward & Elizabeth], b. Sept. 4, 1810	3	180
Francis, late of England, d. Apr. 21, 1824	3	180
Lucy Ann, of Montville, m. Lovell **KIMBALL**, of Catskill, N.Y., July 5, 1839, by Rev. Robert A. Hallam	1	88
	4	
Mehetable, m. William **HOUGH**, of Saybrook, Nov. 2, 1706	1	34
William Dean, s. [Edward & Elizabeth], b. Oct. 2, 1807	3	180

	Vol.	Page
PRENTICE, PRENTIS, PRENTISE, PRENTISS, Adam		
Frink, s. [John & Eunice], b. May 23, 1809	3	250
Andrew Jackson, s. [John & Eunice], b. Apr. 27,		
1815	3	250
Ann, d. John & Sarah, b. Jan. 8, [1678]	1	13
Ann, d. Joseph & Marcy, b. May 4, 1730	2	81
Ann, d. Capt. John **PRENTISS**, of New London, m.		
Richard **LAW**, s. Jonathan, of Milford, Sept.		
21, 1760	3	25
Anna, m. John **RICHARDS**, Dec. 16, 1725	3	108
Anna, d. [Stephen, Jr. & Anna], b. Jan. 21, 1759	2	119
Anne, d. Jonathan & Elizabeth, b. Feb. 18, 1700	1	26
Benjamin, s. Stephen & Elizabeth, b. Dec. 3, 1707	1	33
Benj[amin], s. Joseph & Mercy, b. Sept. 16, 1738	2	83
Benjamin, s. [Joseph & Margarett], b. Nov. 29, 1778	3	112
Bethiah, of New London, m. Zebadiah		
COMSTOCK, of New London, July 11, 1743	2	100
Betsey, d. [Ebenezer & Elisabeth], b. Aug. 12, 1785	3	89
Bridget, m. Benjamin **BARBER**, Sept. 5, 1786	3	96
Caroline B., m. John **DANFORTH**, b. of New		
London, Sept. 7, 1823, by Rev. Abel McEwen	4	15
Caroline Bulkeley, d. [John & Eunice], b. June 24,		
1805	3	250
Charles, s. [John & Eunice], b. May* 3, 1811		
*("March 3d Error" written in pencil)	3	250
Daniel, s. [Joseph & Margarett], b. Dec. 17, 1772	3	112
Daniel, s. [Stephen & Abigail], b. May 27, 1798	3	138
David, s. [Stephen, Jr. & Anna], b. Nov. 12, 1765	2	119
David F., s. [John & Eunice], d. Nov. 13, 1816, of		
yellow fever at St. Pierre Martinique	3	250
David Frink, s. [John & Eunice], b. Sept. 23, 1799	3	250
Dolly, d. John, m. Charles **SOLES**, Nov. 12, 1792	3	208
Ebenezer, m. Elisabeth **SHAPLEY**, July 6, 1783	3	89
Ebenezer, s. [Ebenezer & Elisabeth], b. Jan. 29, 1788	3	89
Edward, s. [John & Eunice], b. May 10, 1813	3	250
Elizabeth, twin with Thomas, s. Tho[mas]* &		
Hester, b. Nov. 6, [1675]; d. Dec. 13, 1770		
*(Corrected to "John", by L. B. B.)	1	10
Elizabeth, d. Jonathan & Elizabeth, b. June 19, 1692	1	21
Elizabeth, d. Stephen & Elizabeth, b. Sept. 7, 1703	1	29
Elizabeth, m. Samuel **EDGECOMBE**, Nov. 24,		
1720	1	57
Elizabeth, d. [Stephen, Jr. & Anna], b. June 9, 1756	2	119
Elisabeth, m. John **HALLAM**, Oct. 2, 1785	3	65
Elisabeth, d. Capt. Jno., m. Samuel **LATIMER**, Jr.,		
June 1, 1761	3	82
Elizabeth, m. Edward **PRATT**, Oct. 2, 1806	3	180
Esther, d. Joseph & Marcy, b. May 7, 1728	2	81
Frances, d. [John & Eunice], b. May 7, 1803	3	250
Hannah, d. Jno. & Hester, b. June [ ], [1672]	1	8
Hannah, d. Stephen & Elizabeth, b. Jan. 5, 1697	1	23
Hannah, d. [Stephen, Jr. & Anna], b. Jan. 21, 1754	2	119

	Vol.	Page
PRENTICE, PRENTIS, PRENTISE, PRENTISS (cont.)		
Harriot, d. [Stephen & Abigail], b. Oct. 3, 1789	3	138
Heaster, d. John & Heaster, b. July 20, [1660]	1	3
Irene, m. Naboth **GRAVES**, May 13, 1725	2	30
Jared, s. [Joseph & Margarett]l, b. Sept. 12, 1769	3	112
John, s. John & Hester, b. Aug. 6, 1652	1	1
John, s. John, m. Sarah, d. Rytie **JOANES**, of Boston, Nov. 23, [1675]	1	10
John, s. Stephen & Elizabeth, b. Dec. 11, [1693]	1	21
John, s. Joseph & Mercy, b. Sept. 9, 1736	2	82
John, m. Sarah **MOSIER**, Oct. 15, 1771	3	68
John, d. Mar. 17, 1773	3	68
John, m. Eunice **FRINK**, Nov. 1, 1795	3	250
John Adam, s. [John & Eunice], b. June 16, 1796	3	250
Jonathan, s. John & Hester, b. July 15, [1657]	1	2
Jonathan, s. Jonathan & Elizabeth, b. Feb. 26, 1696	1	22
Jonathan, d. July 28, 1727	2	83
Jona[than], s. Joseph & Mercy, b. July 1, 1750	2	83
Joseph, s. John & Hester, b. Apr. 2, [1655]	1	2
Joseph, s. Tho[mas]* & Hester, d. June [, 1676] *(Corrected to "John", by L. B. B.)	1	11
Joseph, s. Stephen & Elizabeth, b. May 27, 1701	1	26
Joseph, m. Marcy **GUILBERT**, May 2, 1727	2	81
Joseph, s. Joseph & Marcy, b Feb. 13, 1733/4	2	82
Joseph, m. Margarett **COMSTOCK**, Mar. [ ], 1759	3	112
Joseph, s. [Joseph & Margarett], b. Aug. 24, 1762	3	112
Joseph, s. [Stephen & Abigail], b. Feb. 17, 1796	3	138
Lodowick, s. [Stephen & Abigail], b. Nov. 7, 1787	3	138
Lucy, d. Stephen, Jr. & Anna, b. Apr. 16, 1751	2	119
Lucy, d. [Stephen & Abigail], b. Dec. 25, 1793	3	138
Martha, d. [Joseph & Margarett], b. July 29, 1775	3	112
Mary, see Mary **HARRISS**	3	150
Mary, w. Thomas, d. Dec. 31 ,1720	1	57
Mary, m. Thomas **COIT**, Nov. 5, 1723	1	63
Mary, d. Stephen & Phebe, b. May 24, 1726	2	81
Mary, d. Stephen, Jr. ,decd., m. William **CALKINS**, s. Joseph, all of New London, May 20, 1746, old style	3	22
Mary, d. [Stephen, Jr. & Anna], b. July 15, 1769	2	119
Mary ,of New London, m. Constant F. **DANIELS**, of Chatham, Dec. 30, 1821, by Rev. B. Judd	4	7
Mary Avery, d. [John & Eunice], b Sept. 5, 1797	3	250
Mercy, d. Stephen & Elizabeth, b. Dec. 6, 1710	1	36
Mercy, d. Joseph & Mercy, b. Oct. 18, 1740	2	83
Nathaniel, s. [Joseph & Margarett], b. Dec. 24, 1766	3	112
Peter, s. John & Hester, b. July 31, [1663]	1	4
Peter, s. Jno., d. Aug. 14, [1670]	1	6
Peter, s. [John & Sarah], b. Feb. 23, 1773	3	68
Phebe, d. [Stephen, Jr. & Anna], b. July1, 1761	2	119
Phebe, m. Thomas **MANCHESTER**, Mar. 28, 1780	3	95
Rebeckah, d. [Stephen & Abigail], b. Apr. 25, 1784	3	138

	Vol.	Page
PRENTICE, PRENTIS, PRENTISE, PRENTISS (cont.)		
Sally, d. Capt. Stephen, m. John Abraham		
LAWRANCE, Mar. 11, 1792	3	168
Sally Ann, d. [John & Eunice], b. Aug. 21, 1801	3	250
Samuel, s. [Joseph & Margarett], b. Aug. 26, 1764	3	112
Samuel, s. [Stephen, Jr. & Anna], b. May 26, 1768; d.		
Aug. [ ], 1768	2	119
Samuel, s. [Stephen & Abigail], b. Apr. 25, 1784	3	138
Sarah, d. Capt. John, dec., m. William **COIT**, s.		
Daniel, all of New London, [, 1763]	3	28
Sarah, d. [Stephen, Jr. & Anna], b. Mar. 2, 1774	2	119
Sarah, m. John Abraham **LAWRENCE**, Mar. 11,		
1792	3	129
Sarah A., m. William F. **BRAINARD**, b. of New		
London, Mar. 13, 1832, by Rev. Abel McEwen	4	45
Stephen, s. Jno. & Hester, b. Dec. 26, [1666]	1	5
Stephen, s. Stephen & Elizabeth, b. Mar. 23, 1698/9	1	24
Stephen, Jr., m. Phebe **HARRIS**, May 1, 1723	1	63
Stephen, s. Stephen & Phebe, b. Oct. 28, 1728	2	81
Stephen, Jr., d. Dec. 7, 1728	2	81
Stephen, s. Joseph & Mercy, b. Aug. 1, 1743	2	83
Stephen, of New London, s. Stephen, decd., m. Anna		
STARR, of Norwich, d. Samuel, May 31, 1750,		
by Benj[amin] Lord, Clerk	2	119
Stephen, s. [Stephen, Jr. & Anna], b. Oct. 16, 1763	2	119
Stephen, m. Abigail **SLATER**, Apr. 8, 1783	3	138
Thomas, twin with Elizabeth, s. Tho[mas]* & Hester,		
b. Nov. 6, [1675] *(Corrected to "John", by L.		
B. B.)	1	10
Thomas, m. Mary **ROGERS**, Jan. 30, 1704/5	1	30
Thomas, s. Joseph & Marcy, b. Mar. 6, 1731/2	2	82
Thomas, s. [Joseph & Margarett], b. Jan. 19, 1760	3	112
Thomas, s. [Stephen & Abigail], b. Dec. 7, 1791	3	138
William, s. [John & Eunice], b. Apr. 14, 1807	3	250
-----, m. Daniel **COMSTOCK**, May 23, 1700	1	14
PRESCOTT, Mary Elizabeth Shannon, m. Felix		
ANSART, Jan. 13, 1834, in Portsmouth, N.H.	3	164
PREST, Jacob, m. Rebecca **MANIEERE**, b. of New		
London, Aug. 18, 1851, by Rev. Jabez S. Swan	4	173
Nancy, of [New London], m. George **BOOTH**, Jr., of		
Newark, N.J., Jan 2, 1849, by Rev. M. P.		
Alderman	4	144
PRESTON, [see also **PESTON**], John, s. John & Hannah,		
b. June 11, 1709	1	52
John, m. Hannah **CHAPMAN**, Sept. 9, 1718	1	50
John, s. John, of New London, m. Hannah **HARRIS**,		
d. of William, of North Carolina, June 23, 1743	2	85
John, m. Zerviah **FRENCH**, [ ]	2	85
Lydia, d. [John & Zerviah], b. Sept. 21, 1765	2	85
Prudence, m. William **BOLTON**, b. of New London,		
Jan. 12, 1823, by Rev. B. Judd	4	11
Stephen, s. [John & Zerviah], b. Apr. 14, 1767	2	85

	Vol.	Page
PRESTON (cont.)		
William, s. John & Hannah, b. Feb. 2, 1723	2	81
William, s. [John & Zerviah], b. Jan. 29, 1769	2	85
PRICE, John, of New York, m. Harriet L.		
TILLOTTSON, of New London, June 25, 1849, by Rev. Edwin R. Warren	4	148
Zalmon, of Norwich, m. Elizabeth **HARRINGTON**, of Thompson, Ct., Nov. 14, 1843, by Rev. Sanford Benton	4	110
PRIM (?), Ann, m. William **WATROUS**, b. of New London, May 9, 1833, by James Porter	4	51
PRIMAS, Celia, of N[ew] L[ondon], m. John **HAWKINS**, of New York, colored people, Jan. 17, 1833, by Rev. J. W. Hallam	4	49
PRIME, Christopher, s. [Kimbell & Lucretia], b. Dec. 22, 1799	3	87
Edward Burch Hempste[a]d, s. [Kimbell & Lucretia], b. May 22, 1793	3	87
Elizabeth Burnet, d. [William & Elizabeth], b. Apr. 4, 1802	3	35
Frederick, s. [Kimbell & Lucretia], b. Mar. 17, 1795	3	87
James, s. [Kimbell & Lucretia], b. Apr. 9, 1789; d. Sept. 8, 1790	3	87
John, s. [Kimbell & Lucretia], b. July 5, 1787	3	87
Kimbell, m. Wid. Lucretia **COLFAX**, Feb. 19, 1784	3	87
Kimbell, s. [Kimbell & Lucretia], b. Oct. 17, 1784	3	87
Thomas, s. [Kimbell & Lucretia], b. Feb. 2, 1786; d. Sept. 24, 1787	3	87
William, m. Elizabeth **STIL[L]MAN**, d. Robert, of Norwich, Apr. 26, 1801	3	35
William Hempste[a]d, s. [Kimbell & Lucretia], b. Feb. 2, 1791	3	87
PRINCE, Christopher, m. Lucy **COLFAX**, Jan. 11, 1778	3	59
Elisabeth, d. William & Mary, b. Sept. 11, 1760	3	19
Frances, m. T. Clifford **BUSH**, b. of New London, Dec. 31, 1851, by Rev. Samuel Fox	4	167
Harriet Ann, of N[ew] London, m. John C. **PARKER**, of New York, Apr. 9, 1837, by Rev. Squire B. Hascall	4	68
John, m. Esther **THOMAS**, Apr. 4, 1811	3	259
John Alexander, adopted s. John & Esther, b. Dec. 1, 1820	3	259
Martha, d. William & Mary, b. Jan. 25, 1763	3	19
Mary, d. William & Mary, b. Apr. 21, 1758	3	19
William, m. Mary **HIL[L]HOUSE**, May 6, 1775	3	63
William, s. William & Mary, b. May 6, 1776	3	63
PRIST, Thomas, m. Ann **REED**, b. of [New London], Jan. 30, 1848, by Rev. M. P. Alderman	4	137
PROCTOR, PROCTER, PROCKTER, Abel, m. Wid. Elisabeth **CLARK**, Oct. 5, 1788	3	79
John, of Boston, m. Lydia **RICHARDS**, of New London, Jan. 31, 1724/5, by Eliphalet Adams	2	82

	Vol.	Page
PROCTOR, PROCTER, PROCKTER (cont.)		
Leonard, s. [Abel & Elisabeth], b. Feb. 12, 1790	3	79
Love, m. Samuel **RICHARDS**, Jr., Oct. 13, 1763, in		
Boston	3	5
PROUT, Enoch, of Middletown, Ct., m. Frances L.		
HEMPSTEAD, of [New London], Oct. 23,		
1848, by Rev. M. P. Alderman	4	144
Sarah, m. Christopher **CHRISTOPHERS**, at New		
Haven, Jan. 22, 1711/12	1	43
PURSON, [see also **PERSON**], Abigail, m. Daniel		
SHAPLEY, Nov. 11, 1714	1	55
PYGAN, PIGAN, Alexander, of Norwich, Old England,		
m. Judeth, d. of William **REDFIN**, of New		
London, June 17, [1667]	1	5
Jane, d. Alexander & Judeth, b. Feb. 23, [1670]	1	7
Jane, m. Jonas* **GREEN**, Mar. 29, [1694] *(First		
written "James". Corrected by L. B. B.)	1	22
Judith, w. Alexander, d. Apr. 30, [1678]	1	13
Sarah, d. Alexander & Judeth, b. Feb. 23, [1669]	1	6
Sarah, m. Nicholas **HALLAM**, July 8, [1686]	1	18
QUINLINE, Adeline, m. John Domster **HOBRON**, May		
4, 1843, by Rev. R. A. G. Thompson	4	104
QUIRK, John, m. Honora **MULCAHY**, Nov. 20, 1847, by		
Rev. John Brady	4	136
RAFFATY, Patrick, m. Margaret **McKEAN**, May 2,		
1852, by Rev. J. Stokes. Witnesses: Martin		
Cullin, Catharine Cullin	4	170
RAINEY, Sarah S., of [New London], m. Daniel		
HUNTINGTON, of North Bridgewater, Mass.,		
Nov. 1, 1841, by Rev. Robert A. Hallam	4	116
RAMSDELL, Charles, of Buffalo, N.Y., m. Elizabeth F.		
MUSSEY, of New London, Apr. 22, 1844, by		
Rev. Tho[ma]s J. Greenwood	4	111
RAMSEY, Eliza, m. Simeon **FRANCIS**, b. of New		
London, Dec. 5, 1820, by Rev. Abel McEwen	4	4
RANSFORD, Elizabeth, d. Jonathan, decd., sometime of		
Boston, m. Samuel **AVERY**, of Saybrook, June		
23, 1702	1	27
RANSOM, Alice, d. of Rob[er]t, of Colchester, m.		
Lebbeus **HARRIS**, s. James, of New London,		
Nov. 20, 1738	2	77
Alpheas, s. Joshua & Sarah, b. May 14, 1742	2	95
Elizabeth, d. Joshua & Sarah, b. July 11, 1747	2	95
Joshua, s. Joshua & Sarah, b. Oct. 21, 1744	2	95
Sarah, d. Joshua & Sarah, b. Apr. 18, 1750	2	95
RASBOURN, Thomas, m. Mary **WELSH**, Oct. 5, 1829,		
by Rev. Francis Darrow	4	37
[RATHBURN], RATHBUN, RATHBONE, Frances A.,		
of Lyme, Ct., m. Dr. Linas B. **SMITH**, of New		
York, Sept. 16, 1851, by Rev. T.Edwards	4	164
George, of Salem, m. Olive **CHAPMAN**, of [New		
London], Oct. 25, 1835, by Daniel Huntington	4	63

	Vol.	Page
[RATHBURN], RATHBUN, RATHBONE (cont.)		
Rebecca, m. William **HARRIS**, Oct. 29, 1713	1	58
RAWSON, Edward, of Akron, Ohio, m. Helen P.		
BASSETT, of [New London], Nov. 8, 1848, by		
Rev. Tryon Edwards	4	143
Emma, d. [Thomas H. & Milinda], b. Jan. 22, 1795	3	149
Mary, d. [Thomas H. & Milinda], b. Feb. 4 ,1799	3	149
Milinda, d. [Thomas H. & Milinda], b. Mar. 4,		
1793	3	149
Thomas H., m. Milinda **BINGHAM**, d. Elijah, Feb.		
19, 1792	3	149
RAY, Mary, of New London, m. William **WILLIAMS**, of		
Duanesburgh, N.Y., Apr. 24, 1825, by Rev.		
Abel McEwen	4	22
RAYMOND, RAYMON, Ann, d. Joshua & Eliza, b. May		
12, [1664]	1	4
Caleb, s. [Edward & Sarah], b. Jan. 21, 1759	3	28
Christopher, s. Joshua & Eliza, b. July 17, 1729	2	94
Edmund A., m. Lucy **CROCKER**, b. of New		
London, July 3, 1831, by Rev. Abel McEwen	4	43
Edmund Augustus, [s. Nathan & Hannah], b. July 22,		
1811	3	243
Edward, s. Joshua & Eliza, b. Feb. 15, 1727/8	2	94
Edward, m. Sarah **DOUGLAS**, Feb. 14, 1758, by		
Rev. Mather Boyles	3	28
Edward, d. Sept. 14, 1788	3	28
Elizabeth, d. Joshua & Elizabeth, b. May 24, [1662]	1	3
Elizabeth, wid., of Joshua, m. George **DENNIS**, of		
Long Island, Jan. 26, [1681]	1	16
Elizabeth, m. David **RICHARDS**, Dec. 14, [1698]	1	24
Elizabeth, d. Joshua & Elizabeth, b. Apr. 24, 1720	1	57
Elizabeth, d. Joshua & Elizabeth, b. Apr. 24, 1720	2	93
Elizabeth, w. Joshua, d. May 11, 1730	2	94
Elizabeth, d. Sands Raymond, of New London,		
m. James **GREENFIELD**, s. Archibald, of		
Lyme, Jan. 25, 1740/1	2	106
Elizabeth, d. [Edward & Sarah], b .Nov. 25, 1761	3	28
Experience, d. Joshua & Elizabeth, b. Jan. 20, [1673]	1	9
Experience, d. June 26, 1689, ae 16 y.	1	69
Fanny, [d. Nathan & Hannah], b. June 19, 1815	3	243
Fanny R., m. Edward **HARRIS**, b. of New London,		
Apr. 8, 1833, by Chester Tilden	4	50
Gabriel Sistare, s. [Nathan & Hannah], b. Feb. 5,		
1818	3	243
Hannah, d. Joshua & Eliza, b. Aug. 8, [1668]	1	5
Hannah, d. [Edward & Sarah], b. June 13, 1774	3	28
John, s .Joshua & Eliza, b. Jan. 18, 1725/6	2	94
Joshuah, s. Richard, of Salem, m. Elizabeth, d.		
Nehemyah **SMITH**, Dec. 10, [1659]	1	3
Joshua, s. Joshua & Elizabeth, b. Sept. 18, [1660]	1	3
Joshua, d. Apr. [ ], 1675	1	10
Joshua, d. Apr. 24, [1676]	1	11

	Vol.	Page
RAYMOND, RAYMON (cont.)		
Joshua, s. Joshua, of New London, m. Mercy		
SANDS, d. James, of Block Island, Apr. 29,		
[1683]	1	17
Joshua, m. Elizabeth **CHRISTOPHERS**, Aug. 31,		
1719	1	51
Joshua, s. Joshua & Eliza, b. Dec. 22, 1723	2	94
Joshua, m. Sarah **LYNDE**, Nov. 23, 1730	2	94
Joshua, Jr., of New London, s. Joshua, of New		
London, m. Lucy **JEWETT**, of Lyme, d. Capt.		
Nathaniel Jewett, of Lyme, Oct. 4, 1750, by		
Rev. Geo[rge] Beckwith	2	113
Joshua, s. [Edward & Sarah], b. Jan. 2 ,1766; d. Nov.		
13, 1789	3	28
Marcy, d. Joshua & Elizabeth, b. Dec. 24, 1721	2	93
Mary, d. John & Elizabeth, b. Mar. 12, [1671]	1	8
Mayhetable, d. Joseph & Elizabeth, b. Dec. 19,		
[1675]	1	10
Mayhitable, d. Joseph & Mehitable, d. Aug. 15,		
[1677]	1	12
Mehetabel, d. [Edward & Sarah], b. Mar. 18, 1763	3	28
Mercy, m. Richard **ROGERS**, of New London,		
[ ], 1710 in Westerly, by William		
Champlain, Justice	1	37
Richard, s. Joshua & Elizabeth, b. Apr. 7, [1670]	1	6
Richard, s. Joshua & Elizabeth, d. Sept. 1, [1670]	1	7
Sarah, of New London, m. Rev. As[a]h[el]		
STRONG, of Windham, June 13, 1701/2	1	26
Sarah, d. [Edward & Sarah], b. Mar. 11, 1777	3	28
Sarah, of New London, m. Timothy F. **GREEN**, of		
East Haddam, Dec. 30, 1845, by Rev. Stephen		
A. Loper, of Hadlyme	4	129
Susan, of New London, m. John **BURDICK**, of		
Portugal, Mar. 13, 1831, by Rev. B. Judd	4	42
Ursula, of Pine, Mass., m. John M. **CHADWICK**, of		
Lyme, Sept. 29, 1828, by Rev. Abel McEwen	4	34
READ, [see under **REED**]		
REDDIN, Michael, m. Margaret **McANERNY**, Aug. 12,		
1849, by Rev. William Logan	4	150
REDFIELD, Charles, m. Eliza E. **DENNIS**, b. of [New		
London], Sept. 28, 1846, by Rev. Abel		
McEwen	4	127
David A., m. Emma S. **POTTER**, b. of [New		
London], Sept. 18, 1838, by Rev. C. C.		
Williams	4	79
REDFIN, Judeth, d. of William, of New London, m.		
Alexander **PYGAN**, of Norwich, Old England,		
June 17, [1667]	1	5
Lydda, d. James, m. Thomas **BAYLEY**, Jan. 20,		
[1655]	1	2
Rebecca, m. Thomas **ROACH**, Dec. 12, [1661]	1	3

	Vol.	Page

REED, READ, REID, Ann, m. Thomas **PRIST**, b. of
[New London], Jan. 30, 1848, by Rev. M. P.
Alderman — 4 — 137

Charles, m. Hannah **REED**, b. of New London, July
16, 1776, by Joshua Clarke, Elder — 3 — 77

Dewitt C., m. Mary E. **GUARD**, b. of New London,
Aug. 1, 1847, by Rev. Jabez S. Swan — 4 — 133

Elizabeth, d. [Charles & Hannah], b. Jan. 17, 1779 — 3 — 77

Ethelinda, m. Jeremiah **HARDING**, Mar. 30, 1828,
by Rev. Rob[er]t Bowzer — 4 — 35

Grace, m. Paul **BEEBEE**, Jr., b. of Waterford, Mar.
23, 1828, by Rev. Abel McEwen — 4 — 34

Hannah, m. Charles **REED**, b. of New London, July
16, 1776, by Joshua Clarke, Elder — 3 — 77

Hannah, d. [Charles & Hannah], b. Mar. 26, 1781 — 3 — 77

James, s. [Charles & Hannah], b. Nov. 9, 1782 — 3 — 77

James, of [New London], m. Eliza **WILLIAMS**, of
Waterford, June 11, 1848, by Rev. Abel
McEwen — 4 — 139

John Frink, s. [Bely & Betsey], b. Mar. 16, 1806 — 3 — 76

Lowes, of Ashford, d. James, m. William
HURLBUTT, Sept. [ ], 1777 — 3 — 184

Lucy, d. Charles & Hannah, b. Jan. 13, 1777 — 3 — 77

Mary E., of Waterford, m. Thomas **HAWKES**, of
Baltimore, Md., May 11, 1844, by Rev. Abel
McEwen — 4 — 111

Sarah, m. David B. **SEXTON**, Nov. 3, 1850, by Rev.
Charles Willett — 4 — 156

REEVES, REEVE, Joseph, m. Abba **BARNES**, b. of
[New London], Oct. 27, 1839, by J. Lovejoy — 4 — 87

Landon, of Bromfield, Mass., m. Nancy **HAMLIN**,
of New London, Feb. 15, 1827, by Rev. B. Judd — 4 — 29

REGAN, John, m. Catharine **WARD**, May 12, 1849, by
Rev. William Logan — 4 — 150

REID, [see under **READ**]

RENOUF, Charlotte, d. [Peter & Charlotte], b. Apr. 10,
1817 — 3 — 288

Ellen, d. [Peter & Charlotte], b. Feb. 12, 1822 — 3 — 288

Hester, d. [Peter & Charlotte], b. May 8, 1823 — 3 — 288

Nancy, d. [Peter & Charlotte], b. Sept. 22, 1819 — 3 — 288

Nancy, m. Robert **HOLT**, of N[ew] London, Nov.
20, 1838, by James M. Macdonald — 4 — 80

Peter, m. Charlotte **SOULES**, June 30, 1816, by Rev.
Nehemiah Dodge — 3 — 288

Sarah, d. [Peter & Charlotte], b. Sept. 30, 1827 — 3 — 288

Susan, d. [Peter & Charlotte], b. June 15, 1825 — 3 — 288

REODEN [see under **RIORDEN**]

REXFORD, Elijah, m. Mary **DART**, b. of New London,
Oct. 25, 1823, by Rev. Abel McEwen — 4 — 16

REYNOLDS, Elizabeth, m. Richard **JENNINGS**, b. of
Barbadoes, June [ ], [1678] — 1 — 12

	Vol.	Page
REYNOLDS (cont.)		
Elizabeth, of Barbadoes, m. Richard **JENNINGS**, the		
beginning of June, 1678	1	67
Maria, m. James **SAUL**, Apr. 25, 1852, by Rev. J.		
Stokes. Witnesses: Patrick Tarrell, Bridget		
Saul	4	170
Nancy, of [New London], m. Joshua Van **COTT**, of		
Long Island, Dec. 16, 1838, by Rev. J. M.		
Macdonald	4	80
Sarah E., m. Richard **WHITE**, Jan. 9, 1850, by Rev.		
Jabez S. Swan	4	152
RICE, Abisha, s. Gershom & Elizabeth, b. Oct. 16, 1701	1	27
Caleb H., m. Eliza J. **BAILEY**, b. of [New London],		
Apr. 10, 1851, by Rev. Abel McEwen	4	161
Charlot[te], d. [Thomas & Elenor], b. Aug. 30, 1796	3	169
Charlotte, m. Benjamin **STARK**, July 5, 1825	3	273
Charlotte, of New London, m. Benjamin **STARK**, of		
New London, July 5, 1825, by Rev. Abel		
McEwen	4	23
John, s. [Thomas & Elenor], b. May 10, 1798	3	169
John, m. Hannah B. **SMITH**, b. of New London, July		
8, 1820, by Rev. Abel McEwen	4	1
Nancey, d. [Thomas & Elenor], b. Oct. 8, 1786	3	169
Nancy, d. Thomas, m. Joseph **BOLLES**, Aug. 10,		
1804	3	214
Thomas, m. Ele[a]nor **POTTER**, d. William, July 8,		
1783	3	169
Thomas, s. [Thomas & Elenor], b. July 8, 1793	3	169
William, s. [Thomas & Elenor], b. Feb. 3, 1802	3	169
RICH, Charles F., of Chatham, m. Eliza **SIMMONS**, of		
New London, Apr. 11, 1824, by Rev. Abel		
McEwen	4	17
Frances, of New London, m. Aaron **NEWBY**, of		
Philadelphia, Apr. 30, 1830, by Rev. Abel		
McEwen	4	37
Jesse, m. Martha F. **BUCKINGHAM**, Oct. 11, 1847,		
by Rev. Tho[ma]s Greenwood	4	136
RICHARDS, Abby, m. Nathaniel **PAYN[E]**, Mar. 24,		
1793	3	134
Abby, m. W[illia]m P. **CLEAVELAND**, Jan. 15,		
1806	3	50
Abigail, d. [John & Anna], b. Oct. 2, 1733; d. Aug		
19, 1761, wife of Dr. Thomas Coit	3	108
Abigail. d. John, m. Thomas **COIT**, May 23, 1756	3	98
Abigail, d. [Edward & Sarah]b, Nov. 2, 1773	3	110
Abigail Dolbeare, d. [Guy & Hannah], b. Dec. 15,		
1775	3	74
Adelaide D., m. Jonathan T. **TURNER**, b. of New		
London, Nov. 5, 1833, by Rev. Abel McEwen	4	53
Alexander, s. [Guy & Elizabeth], b. Jan. 23, 1767	3	99

	Vol.	Page

RICHARDS (cont.)

Alexander, of New London, m. Mary **COLFAX**, of
New London, May 15, 1788, by Rev. Henry
Channing   3   100

Allen, m. Ann Eliza **BOLLES**, b. of [New London],
June 11, 1848, by Rev. M. P. Alderman   4   139

Ann, d. Israel, of New London, m. John **WIRE**, s.
John, of Glasgow, Scotland, Oct. 23, 1734   2   88

Ann, d. [Jabez & Hannah], b. Mar. 28, 1783   3   57

Ann, w. Sam[ue]l, [Sr.], d. Aug. 1, 1787   3   5

Ann H., of New London, m. James W. **McLEAN**, of
Andover, Mass., Dec. 2, 1833, by Rev. Abel
McEwen   4   53

Ann Huntington, d. [Peter & Ann Channing], b. Sept.
1, 1807   3   141

Anna, d. [John & Anna], b. Sept. 18, 1726   3   108

Anna, w. [John], d. June 16, 1763   3   108

Anna, d. [Samuel, Jr. & Love], b. Aug. 7, 1766; d.
Mar. 4, 1781   3   5

Anne, d. John & Anne, b. Sept. 18, 1728   3   74

Anne, m. Pygan **ADAMS**, June 7, 1744   3   74

Benjamin, s. [Guy & Elizabeth], b. Jan. 24, 1765   3   99

Benjamin, m. Mary **COIT**, d. Dr. Thomas Coit, Dec.
18, 1795   3   182

Caroline, d. [Samuel, Jr. & Love], b. June 2, 1782   3   5

Catharine, d. [Capt. William & [E]unice], b. Feb. 13,
1783   3   83

Catharine, d. William, m. Zabadiah **ROGERS**, Oct.
12, 1800   3   157

Channing, s. [Peter & Ann Channing], b. May 2,
1805   3   141

Charles, s. [Guy & Hannah], b. May 12, 1777; d.
Apr. 26, 1781   3   74

Charles s. [Guy & Hannah], b. June 3, 1784   3   74

Daniel, s. Samuel & Ann, b. Aug. 23, 1737   2   94

David, m. Elizabeth **RAYMOND**, Dec. 14, [1698]   1   24

David, s. David & Elizabeth, b. Dec. 28, 1703   1   29

David, Jr., s. David, m. Elizabeth **EDGECOMB**, d.
John & Hannah, Apr. 3, 1733   2   118

Edward, m. Sarah **BISHOP**, Jan. 24, 1773   3   110

Eleazer Gaylord, s. [Jabez & Hannah], b. Feb. 22,
1781   3   57

Elijah, s. Samuel & Ann, b. June [ ], 1734   2   94

Elijah, s. [Samuel, Sr.], d. Sept. 20, 1781   3   5

Eliza, d. [Guy & Hannah], b. Apr. 9, 1795   3   74

Eliza, d. [Peter & Ann Channing], b. Oct. 18, 1809   3   141

Elizabeth, d. David & Elizabeth, b. Apr. 28, 1700   1   26

Elisabeth, d. [John & Anna], b. Jan. 19, 1730; d.
Sept. 17, 1734   3   108

Elizabeth, d. David & Elizabeth, b. Feb. 9, 1733; m.
Samuel **COIT**, Feb. 18, 1753   2   83

Elizabeth, d. David & Elizabeth, b. Feb. 9, 1733/4   2   118

	Vol.	Page
RICHARDS (cont.)		
Elizabeth, d. [Guy & Elizabeth], b. Apr. 1, 1763	3	99
Elisabeth, d. [Edward & Sarah], b. Feb. 26, 1781; d.		
July 27, 1782	3	110
Elisabeth, d. [Edward & Sarah], b. July 19, 1788	3	110
Elisabeth, d. [Capt. William & [E]unice], b. Apr. 14,		
1791	3	83
Elisabeth Harris, d. [Alexander & Mary], b. Dec. 21,		
1788	3	100
Ellen, d. [Benjamin & Mary], b. Jan. 28, 1801	3	182
Ellen, m. Nathaniel Shaw **PERKINS**, May 10, 1818	3	170
Emeline, d. [Benjamin & Mary], b. Oct. 18, 1804	3	182
Emmeline, of New London, m. Winslow **LEWIS**, of		
Boston, Mass., Feb. 22, 1828, by Rev. B. Judd	4	34
Esther, d. David & Elizabeth, b. Nov. 10, 1735	2	118
Esther, d. George, Jr. & Katharine, b. Sept. 5, 1749;		
d. [ ]	2	102
Esther, d. [Guy & Elizabeth], b. Nov. 14, 1751	3	99
Esther, of New London, m. Capt. John **GIBBONS**, of		
Island of St. Croix, Jan. 31, 1781, by Timo[thy]		
Green, J.P.	3	80
Etherlinda, d. Elijah & Mary, b. Nov. 28, 1766; m.		
Henry **GARDINER**, Aug. 25, 1789	3	137
Fanny, d. [Guy & Hannah], b. May 28, 1791	3	74
Fanny, m. Erastus **SMITH**, b. of New London, Oct.		
5, 1820, by Rev. Abel McEwen	4	1
Frances, d. Elijah, m. John **WINANTS**, Jan. [ ],		
1789	3	137
Francis, or Frank, s. [Nathaniel & Elisabeth], b. Mar.		
[ ], 1787, the day the meeting-house steeple		
was raised	3	85
Francis, m. Mary S. **STANTON**, Nov. 5, 1809, by		
Rev. Abel McEwen	3	241
Frederick, s. [Capt. William & [E]unice], b. Mar. 11,		
1794	3	83
George, s. John & Love, b. Mar. 26, [1695]	1	22
George, m. Hester **HOUGH**, Nov. 13, 1716	1	47
George, m. Hester **HOUGH**, Nov. 14, 1716	1	54
George, Jr., s. Capt. Geo[rge], m. Katharine		
FOSDICK, d. Dec. Thomas, b. of New		
London, Dec. 21, 1747	2	102
George, s. George, Jr. & Katharine, b. July 20, 1748;		
d. [ ]	2	102
George, s. [Guy & Hannah], b. June 1, 1774	3	74
George, s. [Peter & Ann Channing], b. Nov. 2, 1816	3	141
George Henry, s. [Nathaniel & Elisabeth], b. May 9,		
1791	3	85
Guy, m. Elizabeth **HARRIS**, Jan. 18, 1746/7	3	99
Guy, s. Guy & Elizabeth, b. Aug. 11, 1747	3	74
Guy, s. [Guy & Elizabeth], b. Aug. 11, 1747	3	99
Guy, m. Hannah **DOLBEARE**, June 17, 1773	3	74
Guy, s. [Guy & Hannah], b. Jan. 8, 1788	3	74

	Vol.	Page

RICHARDS (cont.)

	Vol.	Page
Hannah, d. [Guy & Elizabeth], b. Dec. 3, 1769	3	99
Hannah, twin with Lydia, d. [Jabez & Hannah], b. Apr. 6, 1792	3	57
Hannah Dolbeare, d. [Peter & Ann Channing], b. Aug. 10, 1814	3	141
Harriott, d. [Guy & Hannah], b. Jan. 20, 1783	3	74
Harriet, d. Guy, m. James **LEWIS**, Aug. 28, 1806	3	207
Henrietta, d. [Capt. William & [E]unice], b. Oct. 22, 1788	3	83
Henry Augustus, s. [Peter & Ann Channing], b. Nov. 13, 1801	3	141
Jabez, s. Samuel & Ann, b. Aug. 5, 1739	2	95
Jabez, m. Hannah **DANN[I]ELS**, Oct. 15, 1777	3	57
James, s. [Samuel, Jr. & Love], b. Nov. 21, 1776	3	5
Jedidiah, s. [Jabez & Hannah], b. Oct. 16, 1785	3	57
Jerusha, d. Samuel & Ann, b. Feb. 22, 1735/6	2	94
Jerusha, d. [Samuel, Sr. & Ann], b. Apr. 3, 1786	3	5
Jerusha, d. [Jabez & Hannah], b. Dec. 3, 1787	3	57
John, s. John & Love, b. Jan. 1, [1691]	1	20
Jno., s. George & Hester, b. Nov. 23, 1717	1	54
John, m. Anna **PRENTIS**, Dec. 16, 1725	3	108
John, s. [John & Anna], b. Jan. 9, 1736/7	3	108
John, Jr., s. George, of New London, m. Hannah **GREENLEAF**, d. of Rev. Daniel, of Boston, Oct. 30, 1738	2	51
John, d. May 31, 1765	3	108
John, s. John & Anna, m. Susannah **GRAY**, July 7, 1765	3	108
John, m. Catharine **SALTONSTALL**, June 16, 1768	3	108
John, s. [Jabez & Hannah], b. Mar. 28, 1783	3	57
John, m. Mary A. **DARROW**, b. of New London, Dec. 20, 1842, by Eld[er] L. Covell	4	103
John Procter, s. [Samuel, Jr. & Love], b. Feb. 8, 1773; d. May 23, 1774	3	5
Joseph, s. David & Elizabeth, b. Jan. 3, 1709	1	39
Joseph, d. Jan. [ ], 1800, ae 93 y.	3	69
Katharine, d. George, Jr. & Katharine, b. Apr. 27, 1751	2	102
Leonard D., m. Harriot **WAIT**, Nov. 5, 1809, by Rev. Abel McEwen	3	241
Leonard Deminsville, s. [Nathaniel & Elisabeth], b. Oct. 22, 1784	3	85
Love, d. John & Love, b. Oct. 20, [1701]	1	27
Love, d. [John & Anna], b. Aug. 5, 1738; d Nov. 26, 1738	3	108
Love, d. Samuel & Ann, b. May 2, 1741	2	95
Love, d. Capt. George, of New London, m. Lemuel **ROGERS**, Oct. 6, 1745	2	96
Love, d. [Jabez & Hannah], b. Apr. 11, 1778	3	57
Lucy, d. Samuel & Ann, b. June 11, 1728	2	93
Lucy, d. [Jabez & Hannah], b. June 25, 1779	3	57

	Vol.	Page
RICHARDS (cont.)		
Lydia, d. John, m. William **MINARD***, Nov. 15,		
[1678] *(First written "**MYNER**")	1	13
Lidia, d. John, m. W[illia]m **MINOR**, 8br. 15, 1678	1	67
Lydia, of New London, m. John **PROCKTER**, of		
Boston, Jan. 31, 1724/5, by Eliphalet Adams	2	82
Lydia, d. Samuel & Ann, b. June 24 ,1730	2	93
Lydia, d. Samuel & Ann, d. Sept. 3, 1734	2	94
Lydia, b. Nov. 24, 1751, in New London; m. Thomas		
PILGRIM, Nov. 7, 1780	3	96
Lydia, d. [Samuel, Jr. & Love], b. Oct. 17, 1764	3	5
Lydia, twin with Hannah, d. [Jabez & Hannah], b.		
Apr. 6, 1792	3	57
Maria, d. [Benjamin & Mary], b. Oct. 10, 1798	3	182
Martha, d. David & Elizabeth, b. Mar. 28, 1716	1	47
Mary, m. Thomas **HARDING**, Mar. 29, 1745	3	61
Mary, d. [Guy & Elizabeth], b. Dec. 3, 1758	3	99
Mary, d. [Samuel, Jr. & Love], b. Oct. 24, 1774	3	5
Mary, m. Lodowick **CHAMPLIN**, June 19, 1778	3	99
Mary Ann, d. [Capt. William & [E]unice], b. Dec. 28,		
1784	3	83
Mary S., m. Fred[eric]k W[illia]m **GUYER**, b. of		
New London, Apr. 25, 1824, by Rev. B. Judd	4	18
Nathaniel, s. [Guy & Elizabeth], b. May 25, 1756	3	99
Nathaniel, s. [Guy & Hannah], b. Feb. 26, 1780	3	74
Nathaniel, m. Elisabeth **COIT**, Jan. 22, 1784	3	85
Nathaniel, s. [Nathaniel & Elisabeth], b. Apr. 1, 1798	3	85
Nathaniel, Jr., m. Elizabeth **GALE**, b. of New		
London, May 12, 1825, by Rev. Abel McEwen	4	22
Nathaniel, m. Ellen **MINER**, b. of New London,		
Mar. 26, 1843, by L. Covell	4	101
Peter, s. [Guy & Elizabeth], b. Feb. 11, 1754	3	99
Peter, s. [Guy & Hannah], b. July 11, 1778	3	74
Peter, s. Guy, m. Ann Channing **HUNTINGTON**, d.		
Gen. Jedediah, Nov. 27, 1800	3	141
Peter, s. [Peter & Ann Channing], b. Oct. 28, 1811	3	141
Phebe, d. [Jabez & Hannah], b. Oct. 15, 1789	3	57
Rebecca, had s. Thomas **HIDE**, b. Sept. 23, 1719.		
Father was Thomas Hide	1	56
Robert, s. [Edward & Sarah], b. Aug. 25, 1777	3	110
Ruth, d. David & Elizabeth, b. Aug. 5, 1712	1	39
Sally, d. [Guy & Hannah], b. May 23, 1786	3	74
Samuell, s. John & Love, b. July 6, [1699]	1	25
Samuel, m. Ann **HOUGH**, May 9, 1726	2	93
Samuel, s. Sam[ue]l & Ann, b. Apr. 20, 1732	2	93
Samuel, Jr., m. Love **PROCTOR**, Oct. 13, 1763, in		
Boston	3	5
Samuel, s. [Samuel, Jr. & Love], b. Aug. 7, 1768	3	5
Samuel, Sr., d. Jan. 8, 1781	3	5
Sarah, d. David & Elizabeth, b. Aug. 27, [1707]	1	33
Sarah, d. [Edward & Sarah], b. Mar. 19, 1779	3	110

	Vol.	Page
RICHARDS (cont.)		
Sarah A., m. Henry L. **BUTTS**, Dec. 3, 1849, by		
Rev. Charles Willett	4	151
Sophia, d. [Guy & Hannah], b. Oct. 6, 1781	3	74
Stephen, of Salem, Mass., m. Patty **HEWLET**, of		
New London, Apr. 28, 1823, by Thomas W.		
Tucker, Elder	4	13
Susannah, [w. John], d. Feb. 20, 1768	3	108
Susannah Procter, d. [Samuel, Jr. & Love], b. Jan. 5,		
1771	3	5
William, s. Sam[ue]l & Ann, b. Oct. 1, 1743	2	95
William, Capt., m. [E]unice **WELLS**, Apr. 21, 1782,		
by Abraham Ketletos (?)	3	83
William Sam[ue]l, s. [Capt. William & [E]unice], b.		
Jan. 1, 1787	3	83
William Wallace, s. [Leonard D. & Harriet], b.		
[ ]	3	241
Wolcott, s. [Peter & Ann Channing], b. June 15, 1803	3	141
-----, first born of Sam[ue]l & Ann, b. Apr. 7, 1727;		
d. the same day	2	93
RICHARDSON, Benjamin, of Providence, R.I., m.		
Hannah H. **DAVIS**, of New Bedford, Mass.,		
Aug. 8, 1844, by John Grace, J.P.	4	116
RIDGEWAY, Abigail D., m. Valentine **WILLETTS**,		
May 16, 1852, by Rev. Edwin R. Warren	4	168
RILEY, RYLEY, RYLY, REILLY, Ann, of New		
London, m. Dennis **HALE**, of Norwich, Oct.		
31, 1843, by Rev Lemuel Covell	4	109
Edward C., of New York, m. Eliza W. **CHAMPLIN**,		
of New London, Sept. 10, 1826, by Rev. B.		
Judd	4	30
George, s. [Thomas & Esther], b. Sept. 9, 1819	3	218
James, s. [Thomas & Esther], b. Jan. 12, 1823	3	218
John Covington, s. [Thomas & Esther], b. July 24,		
1834	3	218
Mary, d. John & Sarah, b. Aug. 17, 1732	2	94
Mathias, m. Sarah **BENNET[T]**, July 8, 1731	2	94
Sarah Godfrey, d. [Thomas & Esther], b. Feb. 2, 1825	3	218
Thomas, m. Esther **ROGERS**, d. Ichabod, Mar. 4,		
1816	3	218
Thomas, m. Esther **ROGERS**, Mar. 4, 1816	3	270
Thomas, s. [Thomas & Esther], b. Sept. 8, 1817	3	218
William, s. [Thomas & Esther], b. Feb. 17, 1827	3	218
William, m. Elizabeth **MIXLEY**, b. of [New		
London], Dec. 27, 1849, by Rev. Tryon		
Edwards	4	151
Winifred, m. Patrick **O'BRIEN**, Sept. 22, [18]50, [by		
Peter J. Blenkinsop]. Witnesses: Timothy		
Maxwell, Maria Maxwell	3	306
Winifred, m. Patrick **O'BRION**, Sept. 22, 1850.		
Witnesses: Timothy Maxwell, Maria Maxwell	4	159

	Vol.	Page
RIORDEN, REODEN, Elizabeth, m. John **McENERY**, Nov. 10, [18]50, [by Peter J. Blenkinsop]. Witnesses: Thomas McEnery, Cath Foley	3	306
Elizabeth, m. John **McEVERY**, Nov. 10, 1850. Witnesses: Thomas McEvery, Catharine Fooley	4	159
Martin, m. Ellen **PINE**, July 16, 1848, by Rev. John Brady	4	141
RIXFORD, [see also **REXFORD**], Harriet N., m. Charles A. **BENTLEY**, b. of New London, July 8, 1846, by Rev. Tryon Edwards	4	127
ROACH, Rebeckah, w. Thomas, d. Aug. 16, [1670]	1	6
Thomas, m. Rebecca **REDFIN**, Dec. 12, [1661]	1	3
ROATH, Ann, m. Sidney L. **SMITH**, b. of [New London], May 8, 1838, by Rev. Abel McEwen	4	77
Augustus W., of New London, m. Hannah M. **HOWLET**, of Groton, May 4, 1833, by Rev. Abel McEwen	4	51
Fredcrick, of Wurtemburg, Germany, m. Ann **BOILING**, of Ireland, Feb. 4, 1849, by Rev. Edwin R. Warren	4	148
Harriet, of [New London], m. Stillman H. **FICKETT**, of Portland, Me., June 21, 1842, by Rev. Abel McEwen	4	99
James, Gen., of Norwich, m. Cynthia **BOWEN**, of Thompson, Ct., Aug. 13, 1845, by Rev. L. Geo[rge] Leonard	4	123
ROBBINS, ROBINS, Edwin, of Groton, m. Caroline **WILLIAMS**, of [New London], July 10, 1839, by Rev. Abel McEwen	4	85
George S., of New York, m. Frances C. **WOLCOTT**, of New London, Feb. 19, 1827, by Rev. Abel McEwen	4	29
Lucy, of Wethersfield, m. John **GORDON**, of New London, Apr. 4, 1782	3	72
Mary, of Wethersfield, m. George **COLFAX**, of New London, Oct. 2, 1777	3	62
Rebekah, d. Appleton Robins, m. Nathan **DWIGHT**, June 24, 1798, by Rev. John Marsh, at Wethersfield	3	188
William H, m. Abby R. **LYMAN**, Nov. 10, 1847, by Rev. Tho[ma]s Greenwood	4	137
ROBERTS, ROBARTS, Betsey, d. Samuel, m. Nathaniel **KEENEY**, Apr. 19, 1797	3	229
David, m. Jane **FOX**, Nov. 20, 1776	3	67
David, s. [David & Jane], b. July 6, 1779	3	67
Emelia, d. [Frederick & Dolly], b. Apr. 13, 1807	3	208
Frederick, m. Dolly **SOLES**, relict, of Charles, June 29, 1806	3	208
Mary, d. Hugh & Mary, b. Dec. 9, 1652	1	1
Mary, d. [David & Jane], b. Aug. 24, 1781	3	67
Mary Ann, d. [Frederick & Dolly], b. Feb. 8, 1809	3	208

	Vol.	Page
ROBERTS, ROBARTS (cont.)		
Mary Ann, of New London, m. Homer H.		
WHEELER, of Stonington, Mar. 26, 1832, by		
Rev. Abel McEwen	4	46
Mehetable, d. Hugh & Mary, b. Apr. 15, [1658]	1	3
Rebecca A., of New London, m. Pitt **WHEELER**, of		
Stonington, May 7, 1830, by Rev. Abel		
McEwen	4	38
Samuel, s. Hugh & Mary, b. Apr. 25, [1756]*		
*("1656" written in pencil)	1	2
ROBERTSON, Agnes, d. [Patrick & Elizabeth], b. Jan.		
25, 1749/50	3	72
Anne, d. [Archabold & Synthia], b. Mar. 29, 1780	3	72
Archabold, s. [Patrick & Elizabeth], b. Feb. 4,		
1747/8	3	72
Archabold, s. Patrick & Elisabeth, m. Synthia		
ALLEN, Feb. 23, 1775	3	72
Arthur, s. [Patrick & Elizabeth], b. Sept. 22, 1755	3	72
David, s. [Patrick, & Elizabeth], b. June 3, 1753; d.		
Aug. 3, 1753	3	72
Elizabeth, d. [Patrick & Elizabeth], b. Mar. 14, 1739;		
d. Sept. 9, 1751	3	72
Elizabeth, [d. Patrick & Elizabeth], b. Jan. 7, 1762	3	72
Elizabeth, w. Patrick, d. July 4, 1768	3	72
Elizabeth, d. [Archabold & Synthia], b. Feb. 15,		
1778; d. Apr. 5, 1778	3	72
John, first s. [Patrick & Elizabeth], b. Feb. 3, 1742/3;		
d. Feb. 24, 1753	3	72
John, s. [Patrick & Elizabeth], b. Nov. 2, 1759	3	72
John, m. Sarah **TILLEY**, d. John, Nov. 23, 1806	3	187
Mary, d. [Patrick & Margaret], b. Jan. 3, 1773	3	72
Patrick, of North Briton, m. Elizabeth **HOWARD**, of		
Wethersfield, Feb. 10, 1737/8, by J. Hempstead,		
J.P.	3	72
Patrick, s. Patrick & Elizabeth, b. Aug. 17, 1751	3	72
Patrick, m. Margaret **CHURCH**, Nov. 14, 1769	3	72
Patrick, d. Dec. 12, 1775	3	72
Samuel, s. [Patrick & Margaret], b. Aug. 18, 1775	3	72
Thomas, s. [Archabold & Synthia], b. Aug. 13, 1775	3	72
William, s. [Patrick & Margaret], b. Aug. 22 ,1770	3	72
ROBINSON, Alexander, m. Alice **McKANINNAY**, b. of		
[New London], Nov. 5, 1843, by Rev. Abel		
McEwen	4	108
Ann, d. Edw[ar]d & Mary, b. Feb. 8, 1726/7	2	93
Betty, d. [James & Mehetable], b. July 25, 1777	3	57
Edw[ar]d, s. Geo[rge] & Mary, m. Mary **WILLSON**,		
Nov. 8, 1721	1	59
Edward, s. Edw[ar]d & Mary, b. Dec. 2, 1732	2	93
Edwin, m. Joanna **PEARCE**, b. of New London,		
colored people, Apr. 13, 1843, by L. Covell	4	101
Elizabeth, d. Edw[ar]d & Mary, b. Aug. 28, 1730	2	93

	Vol.	Page
ROBINSON (cont.)		
James, of New London, m. Mehetable **HUNTLEY**,		
of Lyme, Oct. 14, 1770	3	57
James, s. [James & Mehetable], b. Dec. 24, 1773	3	57
John, s. Edward & Mary, b. July 13, 1722	1	59
John, s. Edw[ar]d & Mary, b. July 13, 1722	2	93
John, m. Margaret **CURTIS**, b. of [New London],		
Aug. 4, 1845, by Rev. Abel McEwen	4	120
Mary, d. Edw[ar]d* & Mary, b. Jan. 7, 1724/5		
*(First written "Eba", Corrected by L. B. B.)	1	64
Mary, d. Edw[ar]d & Mary, b. Jan. 7, 1724/5	2	93
Polly, d. [James & Mehetable], b. Jan. 21, 1771	3	57
Sally, m. Daniel **DESHON**, Jun. 31, 1799	3	135
Sarah, d. Edw[ar]d & Mary, b. May 10 ,1729	2	93
Willson, s. Edw[ar]d & Mary, b. Apr. 16, 1723	1	61
Wilson, s. Edw[ar]d & Mary, b Apr. 16, 1723	2	93
-----, two sons & two daus. [James & Mehetable], b.		
Dec. [ ], 1775. Two stillborn and two died		
soon after	3	57
ROCKWELL, Anjanora Jane, [d. Merrit & Phebe], b.		
Dec. 31, 1826	3	141
Benjamin, s. [Merrit & Deborah], b. Nov. 27, 1783	3	138
Benjamin, m. Elizabeth **HYDE**, Mar. 4, 1804	3	242
Benjamin, 2d, s. [Benjamin & Elizabeth], b. Dec. 10,		
1812	3	242
Benjamin, [s. Merrit & Phebe], b. July 3, 1846	3	141
Benjamin Dennis, twin with Elizabeth Hyde, [s.		
Benjamin & Elizabeth], b. Aug. 23, 1808; d.		
Sept. 19, 1809	3	242
Charles Ross, [s. Merrit & Phebe], b. Oct. 19, 1839	3	141
Courtland Butler, [s. Merrit & Phebe], b. Nov. 10,		
1841	3	141
Daniel, s. [Merrit & Deborah], b. Apr. 9, 1797	3	138
Ebenezer, s. [Merrit & Deborah], b. June 9, 1791	3	138
Elias Dliss, s. [Benjamin & Elizabeth], b. Apr. 5,		
1815	3	242
Elizabeth, d. [Merrit & Deborah], b. Mar. 4, 1795	3	138
Elizabeth Hyde, twin with Benjamin Dennis, [d.		
Benjamin & Elizabeth], b. Aug. 23, 1808	3	242
Emily Hyde, d. [Benjamin & Elizabeth], b. Feb. 25,		
1810	3	242
Eva Loomis, [d. Merrit & Phebe], b. June 19, 1848	3	141
Everlne, d. [Merrit & Phebe], b. Mar. 2, 1825	3	141
George Rufus, [s. Merrit & Phebe], b. Oct. 25, 1829	3	141
Gurdon, s. [Merrit & Deborah], b. Sept. 15, 1797	3	138
John M., m. Catharine B. **KELLEY**, b. of New		
London, Jan. 26, 1851, by Rev. Edward E. R.		
Warren	4	159
John Mason, s. [Benjamin & Elizabeth], b. Aug. 11,		
1823	3	242
Julia, m. Albert B. **LAMB**, b. of New London, Mar.		
12, 1845, by Rev. J. Blain	4	118

	Vol.	Page
ROCKWELL (cont.)		
Julia A., m. John **LESTER**, Jan. 5, 1851, by Rev.		
Charles Willett	4	158
Juliann, d. [Benjamin & Elizabeth], b. [ ],		
1816	3	242
Mary Ann, [d. Merrit & Phebe], b. Feb. 14, 1844	3	141
Merrit, m. Deborah **DENNIS**, Aug. 10, 1782	3	138
Merrit, s. [Merrit & Deborah], b. Sept. 23, 1787	3	138
Merret, d. May, [ ], 1800	3	138
Merrit, s. [Benjamin & Elizabeth], b. Feb. 8, 1805	3	242
Meritt, m. Phebe **BURDICK**, May 2, 1824, by Rev.		
Thomas W. Tucker	4	18
Mer[r]it, m. Phebe **BURDICK**, May 31, 1824	3	141
Nancy, d. [Merrit & Deborah], b. Mar. 9, 1789	3	138
Nathaniel Harris, [s. Merrit & Phebe], b. Oct. 16,		
1837	3	141
Sarah Matilda, [d. Merrit & Phebe], b. Feb. 9, 1831	3	141
Simeon, s. [Merrit & Deborah], b. Apr. 2, 1793	3	138
William R. H., m. Eliza **WAY**, of [New London],		
Mar. 27, 1831, by Rev. Leonard B. Griffing	4	40
William Rufus Hyde, s. [Benjamin & Elizabeth], b.		
[ ] 11, 1806	3	242
ROE, [see under **ROWE**]		
ROEDIL, Sophia, of New York, m. John H. **MINSON**, of		
New London, Jan. 20, 1865*, by J. Dowling,		
D.D. *(This is the date given in text.)	3	241
ROFFE, ROFF, Daniell, s. Jonathan & Ann, b. Aug. 9,		
1712	1	39
Daniell, s. Jonathan & Anne, b. Aug. 9, 1713	1	44
John, s. Jonathan & Anne, b. Dec. 9, 1714	1	44
Jonathan, m. Anne **AVERY**, wid., Nov. 21, 1712	1	44
Mary, d. Jonathan & Ann, b. May 10, 1718	1	49
ROGERS, Aaron, s. James & Freelove, b. Apr. 9 ,1726	2	92
Aaron, s. [Jeremiah & Hannah], b. Feb. 27, 1799	3	140
Ab[b]y, d. James & Sarah, b. Mar. 28, 1708	1	50
Abby Ann, m. Francis E. **BAKER**, b. of [New		
London], Nov. 13, 1848, by Rev. L. G. Leonard	4	143
Abby Jane, m. Carlos W. **LAY**, b. of New London,		
May 9, 1847, by Rev. Jabez S. Swan	4	131
Abel M., m. Olive A. **PHILLIPS**, Jan. 3, 1836	3	280
Abigail, d. Adam, a mulatto & Katharine, b. Oct. 14,		
1706	1	31
Abigail, d. Adam, of New London, m. John **JONES**,		
s. John, of Boston, decd., Mar. 8, 1736/7	2	19
Abigail, d. Ich[abo]d & Mary, b. Mar. 8, 1763	3	53
Abigail, d. [Stephens & Abigail], b. Sept. 24, 1792	3	82
Adam, m. Katharine **JONES**, Sept. 1, 1702	1	28
Adam, s. Adam, the mulatto, & Katharine, b. Nov.		
18, 1710	1	35
Adelia, m. John H. **HOBRON**, b. of New London,		
June 1, 1847, by Rev. Jabez S. Swan	4	132
Adonijah, s. Thomas & Sarah, b. Nov. 18, 1754	3	48

	Vol.	Page
ROGERS (cont.)		
Albert LeRoy, s. [Abel M. & Olive A.], b. Jan. 1,		
1843	3	280
Albert LeRoy, s. Abel M., b. Jan. 1, 1843	3	291
Alexander, s. John, s. John & Elizabeth, b. Jan. 3,		
1728/9	2	92
Alexander, s. [John & Delight], b. Mar. 26, 1775	2	96
Alexander, m. Rachel **LARABEE**, May 7, 1777	3	92
Alexander, [twin with Desire], s. [Alexander &		
Rachel], b. July 20, 1780	3	92
Almy, d. John & Delight, b. Sept. 7, 1757	2	95
Alpheus, s. Daniel, m. Delight **HARRIS**, d. James,		
Jan 31, 1745	3	47
Alpheus, s. Alpheus & Delight, b. Oct. 12, 1750	3	47
Amos, s. Nathan & Martha, b. June 16, 1743	3	1
Amos, s. Ebenezer & Neomi, b. Nov. 22, 1755	3	7
Amy, d. Jona[than], & Hannah, b. Oct. 31, 1738	2	32
Amy, d. Joseph & Martha, b. Jan. 19, 1755	3	35
Andrew, s. Thomas & Sarah, b. July 24, 1759	3	48
Ann, d Sam[ue]l & Mary, b. May 8, [1673]	1	9
Ann, d. Samuell, d. July 26, [1689], ae 16 y. odd		
months	1	69
Ann, d. James & Sarah, b. Nov. 27, 1701	1	50
Ann, m. Jonathan **WICKS**, Aug. 24, 1732	2	116
Ann, d. John & Ann, b. July 24, 1749	2	100
Ann, d. John & Ann, d. Jan. 1, 1755	2	100
Ann, d. John & Ann, b. Aug. 11, 1757	2	100
Ann, d. [Nathan & Catherine], b. May 2, 1792, in		
Montville	3	159
Ann M., of New London, m. Nelson **WOODWARD**,		
of Lester, Mass., Mar. 2, 1851, by Rev. Edwin		
R. Warren	4	160
Anna, d. John & Delight, b. June 13, 1766	2	96
Anna, d. John, m. Amos **KEENEY**, Dec. 31, 1775	3	177
Anna, d. [Peter, Jr. & Hannah], b. Apr. 23, 1779	3	90
Anna, d. John Rogers & Delight **GREENE**, m.		
Hezekiah **BOLLES**, s. Joshua Bolles & Joanna		
WILLIAMS, Feb. 1, 1791	3	303
Anne, d. Samuell & Abigaill, b. Apr. 24, 1698	1	23
Anne, d. James & Susannah, b. Sept. 10, 1754	3	39
Anne, d. Will[ia]m & Anne, b. Feb. 5, 1773	3	57
Anne, d. [Jason & Fanny], b. Feb. 12, 1792	3	130
Asa, s. Alpheus & Delight, b. Feb. 19, 1756	3	47
Aviss, d. Jonathan & Hannah, b. Aug. 22, 1749	2	32
Azel, s. Thomas & Sarah, b. Jan. 27, 1765	3	48
Barsheba, w. John, 2d, d. Nov. 13, 1721	1	59
Barsheba, m. Gabriel **HARRIS**, Apr. 29, 1725	2	37
Barsheba, d. Samuel, [s. Jno.] & Hannah, b. Mar. 20,		
1748	2	105
Bathsheba, d. John, Jr. & Bathsheba, b. Mar. 1, 1708	1	34
Bathsua, d. James & Grace, b. May 14, 1734	2	20

	Vol.	Page
ROGERS (cont.)		
Benjamin, twin with Joseph, s. [Lester & Mary], b. Sept. 25, 1796	3	134
Benjaman F., s. [Jason & Fanny], b. Aug. 24, 1800; d. Nov. 24, 1801	3	130
Benjamin Green, s. John & Delight, b. May 17, 1769	2	96
Bethiah, d. Jonathan & Judeth, b. Apr. 1, 1725	1	65
Betsey, d. [George & Desire], b. Mar. 1, 1781	3	85
Betsey, m. Henry **HARRIS**, Oct. 29, 1786	3	138
Betsey, d. [Zebulon & Sarah], b. Jan. 27, 1788	3	93
Betsey, d. Benjamin, m. John **FRENCH**, 2d, Oct. 13, 1807	3	208
Betsey, d. [Daniel, Jr. & Sally], b. Sept. 29, 1821; d. Oct. 17, 1831	3	246
Betty, d. Thomas & Sarah, b. June 25, 1751, old style	3	48
Caroline, d. [Jason & Fanny], b. May 4, 1805	3	130
Cary, s. Nathan & Martha, b. May 9, 1745	3	1
Catharine, d. Adam, a mulatto & Catharine, b. May 15, 1712	1	40
Catharine, d. Adam, of New London, m. James **MARIETT**, s. Micah, clothier, b. in Bow Stradford, near London, in Great Britain, Oct. 20, 1737	2	19
Catherine, b. Nov. 27, 1755; m. Nathaniel **HARRIS**, Nov. 27, 1777	3	244
Catharine, d. [Zabadiah & Catharine], b. Nov. 25, 1804	3	157
Charles Williams, s. [Abel M. & Olive A.], b. July 21, 1847	3	280
Charlotte O., of [New London], m. John G. **HAGGERMOND**, of Brooklin, N.Y., Nov. 22, 1840, by H. R. Knapp	4	93
Clark, s. Jonathan & Hannah, b. Jan. 15, 1744/5	2	32
Clark, m. Hannah **ROGERS**, Sept. 11, 1788	3	115
Daniell, m. Grace **WILLIAMS**, Sept. 24, [1702]	1	27
Daniel, s. John & Elizabeth, b. Sept. 7, 1739	2	95
Daniel, s. Peter & Lucy, b. Feb. 20, 1745	2	11
Daniel, s. [Peter & Lucy], b. Feb. 22, 1745; in his fifteenth year	3	88
Daniel, s. [Peter, Jr. & Hannah], b. May 29, 1774	3	90
Daniel, s. Ebenezer, m. Rebecca **CROCKER**, Jan. 28, 1790	3	132
Daniel, s. [Daniel & Rebecca], b. Sept. 5, 1795	3	132
Daniel, Jr., m. Sally **HARRIS**, d. Deac. Henry **HARRIS**, Dec. 26, 1819	3	246
David, s. Jonathan & Judeth, b. Mar. 8, 1719/20	1	60
David, of New London, s. Capt. Jno., m. Grace **LESTER**, d. of Daniel, of New London, decd., Jan. 27, 1743/4	2	86
David, s. Lemuel & Love, b. Feb. 23, 1748/9	2	96
David, s. David & Grace, b. Oct. 15, 1750; d. Feb. 12, 1771	2	86

	Vol.	Page
ROGERS (cont.)		
David, s. Joseph & Martha, b. June 22, 1765	3	35
David, m. Judeth **GREEN**, of Hopkinton, Sept. 12, 1771	2	86
David, s. [John & Elisabeth], b. Aug. 31, 1776	3	64
David, s. [Zebulon & Sarah], b. Jan. 24, 1786	3	93
David, s. [Isaac & Polly], b. Oct. 7, 1789	3	82
David, s. [Isaac & Sarah], b. Nov. 30, 1802	3	56
David Allen, s. [Jason & Fanny], b. Feb. 24, 1784	3	130
Davis, s. Nathan & Martha, b. Sept. 1, 1754	3	1
Deborah, d. Jno., Jr. & Bathsheba, b. Dec. 6, 1716	1	47
Deborah, d. John, s. Joseph & Deborah, b. Jan. 6, 1723	2	92
Deborah, d. Samuel, s. [Jno.] & Hannah, b. Mar. 21, 1736	2	105
Deborah, of New London, d. of John, decd., & grdau. of Joseph Rogers, formerly of New London, decd., m. Moses **STARK**, of Scarborough, Yorkshire, Old England, Dec. 7, 1646	2	25
Deborah, d. of Samuel, of New London, m. Joseph **BOLLES**, Jr., s. Joseph, of New London, Dec. 30, 1753	2	107
Deborah, d. John, of New London, decd., m. John **HARRIS**, s. Lieut. Joseph, of New London, Mar. 10, 1754	2	52
Deborah, m. Seth **SEARS**, May 12, 1776	3	91
Delight, d. John & Delight, b. Mar. 16, 1764	2	96
Desiah, d. Richard & Mary, b. Dec. 25, 1717	1	56
Desire, d. Nathaniel & Ziporah, b. Oct. 28, 1765	3	13
Desire, [twin with Alexander], d. [Alexander & Rachel], b. July 20, 1780	3	92
Dorothy, d. Jona[than], & Elizabeth, b. Sept. 8, 1709	1	56
Drusilla, m. Nathan **STEWARD**, Dec. 8, 1793	3	126
Ebenezer, s. Adam, a mulatto, & Katharine, b. Feb. 6, 1713/14; d. Dec. 20, 1738	1	40
Ebenezer, s. William, decd., m. Neomi **BEEBE**, d. Sam[ue]ll **FOX**, of Great Neck, decd., all of New London, Oct. 18, 1754	3	7
Ebenezer, s. Ebenezer & Neomi, b. Sept. 5, 1758	3	7
Edmond, m. Harriet **OWEN**, b. of [New London], Oct. 15, 1840, by Rev. Abel McEwen	4	92
Edmund, m. Harriet **POTTER**, [ ]	3	227
Edward, s. James, Jr. & Elizabeth, b. May 14, 1702	1	28
Edward, s. Ichabod & Mary, b. Oct. 28, 1752	3	53
Edward Coit, s. [Edmund & Harriet], b. Feb. 2, 1816	3	227
Elihu White, s. [Jonathan & Lucretia], b. Oct. 9, 1836	3	287
Eliza, 2d, d. James & Grace, b. June 9, 1742	2	20
Eliza, d. [John & Hannah], b. Jan. 24, 1797	3	114
Elizabeth, d. Jno. & Elizabeth, b. Nov. 8, [1671]	1	7
Elizabeth, d. James & Mary, b. Aug. 29, [1680]	1	15
Elizabeth, d. James, Sr., m. Samuel **BEEBE**, s. Samuel, of New London, Feb. 9, 1681/2	1	16

	Vol.	Page
ROGERS (cont.)		
Elizabeth, m. Theophilus **STANTON**, Jan. 5, [1698]	1	24
Elizabeth, m. James **SMITH**, b. of New Haven, Jan. 8, 1701/2	1	26
Elizabeth, d. James, m. Samuel **ROGERS**, Mar. 24, 1702/3	1	28
Elizabeth, w. Samuell, d. June 29, 1703	1	29
Elizabeth, d. James, Jr. & Elizabeth, b. June 14, 1706	1	31
Elizabeth, d. John, Jr. & Bathsheba, b. June 14, 1706	1	34
Elizabeth, d. Jona[than] & Elizabeth, b. Oct. 1, 1711	1	56
Elizabeth, d. John, s. John & Elizabeth, b. May 22, 1734	2	94
Elizabeth, d. James & Grace, b. Nov. 18, 1738	2	20
Elezabeth, d. Nathan & Martha, b. June 3, 1747	3	1
Elizabeth, d. Nathaniel & Theoday, b. Apr. 12, 1748	2	34
Elizabeth, d. James & Mehetable, b. Nov. 12, 1749	2	23
Elizabeth, d. John & Martha, b. Dec. 27, 1750; d. Sept. 16, 1751	2	110
Elisabeth, d. Joseph & Martha, b. Mar. 23, 1756	3	35
Elizabeth, d. John & Delight, b. Sept. 2, 1759	2	96
Elisabeth, d. James & Susannah, b. Mar. 27, 1760	3	39
Elisabeth, d. Nathaniel & Ziporah, b. Nov. 14, 1762	3	13
Elizabeth, d. James, of Hogneck, now decd., m. Robert **MANWARING**, s. Christopher, [all of New London], Oct. 8, 1772	3	55
Elizabeth, m. Samuel **MASON**, June 10, 1774	3	35
Elisabeth, d. [William & Anne], b. Apr. 16, 1776	3	57
Elisabeth, d. [John & Elisabeth], b. Oct. 20, 1780	3	64
Elisabeth, d. [William & Elisabeth], b. Mar. 27, 1784	3	91
Elisabeth, m. John **OWEN**, Jan. 15, 1789	3	41
Elizabeth, m. William **TATE**, Aug. 27, 1797	3	175
Elizabeth, of New London, m. James **THELFEL**, of New York, Apr. 15, 1832, by Rev. B. Judd	4	48
Elizabeth, of New London, m. Charles A. **CLARK**, of N[ew] York, Apr. 14, 1837, by Rev. Squire B. Hascall	4	68
Elizabeth, d. John & Martha, b. Apr. 24, [　]	2	110
Elizabeth R., of [New London], m. Richard H. **SMITH**, of the U.S.A., Nov. 6, 1850, by Rev. Robert A. Hallam	4	160
Elizabeth, Reynolds, d. George W. & Anna M., b. Nov. 28, 1828	3	221
Ellen P., d. [Daniel, Jr. & Sally], b. Nov. 14, 1830; m. Elias **PECK**, [　　　　], in New York	3	246
Ellen P., m. Elias **PECK**, May 15, 1850, by Rev. Charles Willett	4	153
Emely N., m. George B. **HOWARD**, b. of [New London], Apr. 6, 1851, by Rev. Jabez S. Swan	4	163
Emma, m. Henry **MORRIS**, b. of New London, Apr. 20, 1834, by Rev. Abel McEwen	4	55
Ephraim, s. Jonathan & Hannah, b. May 16, 1747	2	32

	Vol.	Page

ROGERS (cont.)

	Vol.	Page
Ephraim, Jr., m. Hannah **ROGERS**, d. Ezekiel, decd., Dec. 5, 1799	3	80
Erastus, s. [Jason & Fanny], b. Nov. 6, 1802	3	130
Esther, d. James & Grace, b. Oct. 27, 1736	2	20
Est[h]er, d. John & Martha, b. Apr. 9, 1744	2	110
Esther, d. David & Grace, b. July 30 ,1746	2	86
Esther, d. [George & Desire], b. Jan. 13, 1777	3	85
Esther, d. [Zebulon & Sarah], b. Apr. 12, 1784	3	93
Esther, d. [Jason & Fanny], b. May 30, 1798; d. Nov. 16, 1801	3	130
Esther, d. Ichabod, m. Thomas **RYLEY**, Mar. 4, 1816	3	218
Esther, m. Thomas **RYLEY**, Mar. 4, 1816	3	270
Ethan, s. Nathan & Hannah, b. Dec. [ ]	3	1
Eunice, d. James & Susannah, b. Apr. 24, 1762	3	39
Eunice, [d. John & Elisabeth], b. Feb. 23, 1785	3	64
Ezekiel, s. David & Grace, b. Dec. 7, 1744	2	86
Ezekiel, s. [Jonathan & Milla], b. July 14, 1786	3	93
Fanny, d. [John & Elisabeth], b. June 20, 1769	3	64
Fanny, d. [James & Mary], b. Mar. 20, 1778	3	63
Fanny, d. [George & Desire], b. Jan. 4, 1779	3	85
Fanny, b. Jan. 4, 1779; m. William **LAX**, June 24, 1801	3	249
Fanny, d. [Jason & Fanny], b. Mar. 19, 1788	3	130
Fanny, d. [Nathan & Catherine], b. Sept. 3, 1788, in Lyme	3	159
Fanny, d. [Isaac & Polly], b. Nov. 22, 1791	3	82
Fanny, m. Daniel **DESHON**, Aug. 22, 1798* *(Incorrect date?)	3	135
Fanny, d. George, m. William **LAX**, June 24, 1805	3	133
Fanny, d. Nathan, m. George **DESTIN**, Feb. 19, 1807	3	221
Fanny, the elder, [w. Jason], d. Sept. 22, 1808	3	130
Frances, d. Nath[aniel] & Ziporah, b. Nov. 21, 1768	3	13
Francis Alexander, s. [Jonathan & Sarah], b. Oct. 22, 1802	3	209
Francis Alexander, s. [Jonathan & Sarah], d. Feb. 15, 1827, at St. Jago de Cuba	3	209
Francis Alexander, s. [Jonathan & Lucretia], b. Mar. 14, 1835	3	287
Frank, m. Frances **HAVENS**, b. of New London, July 15, 1849, by Rev. Jabez S. Swan	4	146
Frederick, s. Thomas & Sarah, b. Apr. 11, 1767	3	48
Gammon, s. Adam & Catharine, b. Apr. 28, 1720	1	57
George, s. Samuell & Abigail, b. May 21, 1710	1	33
George, s. Samuell & Abigaill, b. May 21, 1710	1	35
George, s. John & Martha, b. Apr. 19, 1739; d. Sept. 7, 1751	2	110
George, s. Lemuel & Love, b. Aug. 11, 1746	2	96
George, s. John & Martha, b. Feb. 14, 1755	2	110
George, m. Desire **SPRINGER**, Oct. 7, 1770	3	85
George, s. [George & Desire], b. Sept. 27, 1774	3	85

	Vol.	Page
ROGERS (cont.)		
George, m. Wid., Mary **WHEELER**, d. Edward		
TINKER, June 15, 1779	3	157
George, s. [George & Mary], b. Feb. 20, 1781	3	157
George, d. Oct. 8, 1800, "an honest shoemaker"	3	85
George, m. Susan **EWEN**, b. of N[ew] London, Oct.		
17, 1838, by Rev. C. C. Williams	4	81
George Courtland, s. [Abel M. & Olive A.], b. Sept.		
5, 1839	3	280
George Courtland, s. Abel M., b. Sept. 5, 1839	3	291
Giles, s. Samuel & Elizabeth, b. May 22, 1792.		
Entered at the request of his mother now		
Elizabeth **TATE**	3	175
Grace, d. James & Grace, b. June 24, 1730	2	20
Grace, d. James, a cooper, m. Peter **ROGERS**, s.		
James, mariner, Nov. 5, 1749	2	69
Grace, d. Alpheus & Delight, b. Jan. 28, 1754	3	47
Grace, d. David & Grace, b. Mar. 25, 1760	2	86
Grace, w. David, d. Nov. 16, 1770	2	86
Grace, d. [Jason & Fanny], b. Mar. 25, 1790	3	130
Green, s. [Jonathan & Milla], b. Nov. 27, 1788	3	93
Green, of Waterford, m. Sarah **BEEBE**, of New		
London, Aug. 30, 1845, by Rev. Jabez S. Swan	4	121
Gurdon, s. [Jeremiah & Hannah], b. Mar. 16, 1795	3	140
Guy, s. [George & Desire], b. July 21, 1790	3	85
Hailey, s. Ichabod & Mary, b. June 21, 1761	3	53
Hannah, d. James & Sarah, b. Aug. 3, 1710	1	50
Hannah, s. Jonathan, s. Jonathan & Judeth, b. Dec.		
25, 1727	2	92
Hannah, m. Ezekiel **BEEBE**, Nov. 13, 1729	2	4
Hannah, d. Samuel, [s. Jno.] & Hannah, b. Apr. 8,		
1740	2	105
Hannah, d. Jona[than], & Hannah, b. Apr. 13, 1743	2	32
Hannah, w. Jona[than], d. Oct. 7, 1750	2	32
Hannah, d. John & Ann, b. Aug. 7, 1751	2	100
Hannah, d. James & Mehetable, b. July 11, 1756	2	23
Hannah, d. Nathaniel & Theoday, b. July 15, 1756	2	34
Hannah, of New London, d. Samuel, m. John		
HARRIS, 3d, of New London, s. John, Feb.		
25, 1768	3	43
Hannah, m. Peter **ROGERS**, Jr., Sept. 4, 1773	3	90
Hannah, d. [John & Hannah], b. Oct. 15, 1785	3	114
Hannah, d. [Peter, Jr. & Hannah], b. Jan. 18, 1786	3	90
Hannah, m. Hazzard **POWERS**, Mar. 30, 1788	3	40
Hannah, m. Clark **ROGERS**, Sept. 11, 1788	3	115
Hannah, d. Ezekiel, decd., m. Ephraim **ROGERS**,		
Jr., Dec. 5, 1799	3	80
Hannah, d. John, m. Benjamin **BROWN**, Nov. 11,		
1804	3	204
Harriot, d. [Zabadiah & Catharine], b. Jan. 18, 1808	3	157
Harriet, m. Samuel **JEFFERY**, b. of New London,		
June 25, 1837, by Rev. Nathan Wildman	4	71

	Vol.	Page

ROGERS (cont.)

	Vol.	Page
Harriet, m. James M. **HOWARD**, b. of New London, May 11, 1843, by Rev. G. Thompson	4	104
Harris, s. Peter & Lucy, b. Jan. 13, 1755	2	12
Harris, s. [Peter & Lucy], b. Feb. 12, 1755; lost at sea May, 1785	3	88
Henry, s. [William & Elisabeth], b. Aug. 6, 1786	3	91
Henry, d. [John & Hannah], b. Mar. 19, 1795	3	114
Henry A., s. [Abel M. & Olive A.], b. Nov. 17, 1836	3	280
Ichabod, s. John, Jr. & Bethsheba, b. Oct. 20, 1709	1	47
Ichabod, s. John, of New London, m. Mary **SAVEL**, d. John, of New London, Feb. 3, 1744	3	53
Ichabod, d. May 30, 1771	3	53
Ichabod, s. [William & Anne], b. Apr. 24, 1777	3	57
Isaac, s. Samuel, [s. Jno.], & Hannah, b. May 7, 1744	2	105
Isaac, s. James & Mehetable, b. June 30, 1762	2	23
Isaac, m. Polly **GRIFFING**, Apr. 13, 1786	3	82
Isaac, s. [Isaac & Polly], b. Nov. 3, 1793	3	82
Isaac, m. Sarah **ISHMAL**, Oct. 13, 1797, by Rev. Henry Channing	3	56
Isaac, s. [Isaac & Sarah], b. Dec. 22, 1805	3	56
Isaac, of New London, m. Harriet **LORD**, of Norwich, Jan. 12, 1826, by Rev. David N. Bentley, of Norwich	4	25
Isreal, s. John & Ann, b. Sept. 4, 1761	2	101
James, s. James & Mary, b. Feb. 2, [1674]	1	9
James, s. [ ], Sr., of New London, m. Mary **JORDAN**, d. Jeffrey, of Ireland, Nov. 5, [1674]	1	9
James, s. Joseph, m. Sarah **STEVENS**, Mar. 27, 1699	1	50
James, s. John, Jr. & Bathsheba, b. Dec. 7, 1701	1	34
James, s. James, Jr. & Elizabeth, b. Aug. 20, 1704	1	30
James, s. Jonathan & Elizabeth, b. Jan. 20, 1713/14	1	56
James, s. James & Sarah, b. July 6, 1717	1	50
James, d. July 20, 1721	1	58
James, s. John, m. Grace **HARRIS**, d. Joseph, Dec. 8, 1726	2	20
James, s. James & Grace, b. Apr. 14, 1740	2	20
James, 3d, of New London, s. James, decd. & grdson of Ja[me]s decd., m. Mehitablel **NEWBURY**, d. Nathaniel, of New London, Jan. 24, 1747, by Rev. Stephen Gorton	2	23
James, s. Jona[than], of New London, North Parish, m. Susanna **CONGDON**, d. Jeremiah, of New London, Mar. 12, 1751	3	39
James, s. James & Mehetable, b. Oct. 6, 1751	2	23
James, s. Alpheus & Delight, b. July 7, 1759	3	47
James, of Mamacock, m. Mary **COMSTOCK**, July 22, 1764	3	63
James, s. James & Susannah, b. Aug. 8, 1764	3	39
James, s. [James & Mary], b. Oct. 30, 1765	3	63

	Vol.	Page
ROGERS (cont.)		
James, 3d, s. James, of G. Neck, m. Sarah **FISK**, d.		
Capt. Ebenezer & Sarah, of Southington, Dec.		
9, 1783	3	84
James, s. [Isaac & Polly], b. Jan. 10, 1787	3	82
James, d. Apr. 20, 1790, ae 73 y.	2	23
James, s. [Nathan & Catherine], b. Feb. 2 ,1801	3	159
James, of Montville, Ct., m. Harriet **SMITH**, of New		
London, May 19, 1846, by Rev. John Howson	4	126
Jason, s. Ich[abo]d & Mary, b. Nov. 28, 1757	3	53
Jason, m. Fanny **ALLYN**, May 29, 1783	3	130
Jason, s. [Jason & Fanny], b. June 1, 1786	3	130
Jehiel Harris, s. Alpheus & Delight, b. Jan. 3, 1747	3	47
Gemima, d. Jno., Jr. & Bathsheba, b. Nov. 23, 1714	1	47
Jemima, d. Adam & Katharine, b. Jan. 27, 1718	1	49
Jemima, d. Adam, of New London, m. John **FOX**, of		
Willington, Feb. 24, 1742/3, by Rev. Eliphalet		
Adams	2	19
Jeremiah, s. James & Elizabeth, b. Sept. 10, 1712	2	92
Jeremiah, s. W[illia]m & Elizabeth, b. Sept. 30, 1716	1	54
Jeremiah, s. Nathan & Martha, b. July 2, 1749	3	1
Jeremiah, s. Nathaniel & Theoday, b. Mar. 1,		
1749/50	2	34
Jeremiah, s. James & Susannah, b. Sept. 3, 1752	3	39
Jeremiah, s. [John & Elisabeth], b. June 10, 1766	3	64
Jeremiah, m. Hannah **BOLLES**, Dec. 11, 1791	3	140
Jerusha, d. James & Sarah, b. Jan. 15, 1705/6	1	50
Jerusha, m. William **BEEBE**, Jr., June 9, 1720	2	3
Jesse, s. Nathan & Hannah, b. Jan. 16, 1767	3	1
John, s. James, m. Elizabeth, d. Mat[t]hew		
GRISWOLD, of Lyme, Oct. 17, [1670], by		
W[illia]m Griswold, Com.	1	7
John, s. John & Elizabeth, b. Mar. 20, [1674]	1	9
John, s. Joseph & Sarah, b. Mar. 30, 1675/6	1	10
John, Jr., m. Bathsheba **SMITH**, Jan. 2, 1700	1	34
John, s. John, Jr. & Bathsheba, b. Nov. 1, 1700	1	34
John, s. Adam, a mulatto, & Katharine, b. Oct. 13,		
1704	1	30
Jno., s. Jno. & Elizabeth, b. Aug. 14, 1716	1	56
John, s. Joseph, m. Deborah **DEIGHTON**, Feb. 1,		
1718/19	1	56
John, Sr., d. Oct. 17, 1721	1	59
John, 3d, d. Nov. 6, 1721	1	59
John, s. John & Deborah, b. Aug. 6, 1722	1	62
John, s .John, m. Elizabeth **DODGE**, Jan. 28, 1722/3,		
by Ephraim Woodbridge	1	60
John, s. John & Elizabeth, b. Apr. 14, 1724	1	63
John, s. James & Grace, b. May 9, 1732	2	20
John, s. Adam, m. Mary **TOMKIN**, d. William, of		
St. Ann, in Cornhill, Gt. Britain, Dec. 13, 1733	2	94
John, s. Samuel, s. Jno. & Hannah, b. July 21, 1734	2	105
John, s. John, s. Adam & Ann, b. Oct. 14, 1734	2	94

	Vol.	Page

ROGERS (cont.)

John, m. Martha **COLVER**, d. Daniel & Elizabeth,
    May 15, 1738 — 2, 110

John had negro servants James & Dinah married
    Apr. 17, 1741, by J. Hempstead, J.P. — 2, 119

John, s. Ichabod & Mary, b. July 1, 1744. Recorded
    in 1791 at desire of John Rogers — 3, 115

John, s. Ichabod & Mary, b. Dec. 13, 1744 — 3, 53

John, 2d, s. Ichabod & Mary, b. July 1, 1748 — 3, 53

John, s. John, late of New London, decd., m. Ann
    TINKER, d. John, of New London, Nov. 17,
    1748 — 2, 100

John, of New London, s. John, decd., late of New
    London, who lived in Mamecock, m. Delight
    GREEN, d. of Capt. Benjamin, of New
    London, Jan. 2, 1755 — 2, 95

John, s. Samuel, m. Ann **GREEN**, d. Benjamin, all of
    New London, Oct. 17, 1759 — 3, 8

John, s. John & Ann, b. Dec. 2, 1759 — 2, 101

John, s. John & Martha, b. Jan. 4, 1760 — 2, 110

John, m. Abagail **SALMON**, d. William, of
    Southold, L.I., July 27, 1760 — 3, 15

John, s. John & Delight, b. Oct. 14, 1761 — 2, 96

John, s. Sam[ue]l, m. Elisabeth **BOLLES**, Apr. 24,
    1763, by Pygan Adams, Esq. — 3, 64

John, s. [John & Elisabeth], b. Nov. 26, 1765 — 3, 64

John, s. [James & Mary], b. Oct. 16, 1771 — 3, 63

John, m. Hannah **SMITH**, Oct. 8, 1782 — 3, 114

John, s. [John & Hannah], b. Oct. 10, 1783 — 3, 114

John, of New London, m. Molly **VAN DEUSEN**, of
    [Great Barrington], Sept. 24, 1792, by Rev.
    Gideon Bostwick, of Great Barrington — 3, 77

John, the elder, lost at sea, Aug. [ ], 1796 — 3, 114

John, s. James, m. Sally **SEARS**, Nov. 23, 1800 — 3, 118

John Frederick, s. George W. & Anna M., b. Jan. 13,
    1830 — 3, 221

John Van [Deusen?], d. [John & Molly], b. June 30,
    1795 — 3, 77

Jonathan, s. James & Mary, b. Apr. 13, [1687] — 1, 18

Jonathan, s. Adam, a mulatto, & Katharine, b. Mar.
    29, 1708; d. Mar. 4, 1709/10 — 1, 34

Jonathan, s. John, Jr. & Bathsheba, b. June 25, 1711 — 1, 47

Jonathan, s. Jonathan & Judeth, b. Nov. 24, 1714 — 1, 44

Jonathan, s. John & Elizabeth, b. Mar. 9, 1735 — 2, 95

Jonathan, s. John & Elizabeth, b. Mar. 8, 1736 — 2, 82

Jonathan, s. Capt. Jno. & gds. of Jno. decd., of New
    London, m. Hannah **HISCOX**, d. of Tho[ma]s,
    of Westerly, R.I., Oct. 26, 1737, at Westerly, by
    John Maxson, Elder — 2, 32

Jonathan, s. James & Grace, b. Mar. 26, 1745 — 2, 20

Jonathan, s. Samuel, [s. Jno.] & Hannah, b. May 12,
    1745 — 2, 105

	Vol.	Page

ROGERS (cont.)

Jona[than], s. Capt. Jona[tha]n, m. Sarah
NEWBURY, d. of Nath[anie]l, Nov. 17, 1751 — 2 — 32

Jona[than], s. Nathan & Hannah, b. Nov. 6, 1760 — 3 — 1

Jonathan, s. James & Susannah, b. Apr. 2, 1767 — 3 — 39

Jonathan, s. [James & Mary], b. Oct. 18, 1767 — 3 — 63

Jonathan, m. Milla **GREEN**, Oct. [ ], 1781 — 3 — 93

Jonathan, s. [Jonathan & Milla], b. July 8, 1783 — 3 — 93

Jonathan, s. [Jason & Fanny], b. Dec. 29, 1794 — 3 — 130

Jonathan, s. James & Mary, m. Sarah **ROGERS**, d.
John & Delight, Jan. 14, 1798 — 3 — 209

Jonathan, s. [Jonathan & Sarah], b. Aug. 10, 1800 — 3 — 209

Jonathan, Jr., s. Jonathan & Sarah, b. Aug. 10, 1800;
m. Lucretia **WHITE**, [d. Elihu & Lucretia],
Aug. 14, 1831 — 3 — 287

Jonathan, Jr., m. Lucretia **WHITE**, b. of [New
London], Aug. 14, 1831, by Rev. Asa Bronson — 4 — 43

Jonathan, s. [Jonathan & Lucretia], b. May 29, 1832 — 3 — 287

Jonathan, s. Samuel, m. Elizabeth **PEMBERTON**,
[ ] — 1 — 56

Jordon, s. W[illia]m & Elizabeth, b. May 8, 1715 — 1 — 54

Jordon, s. [Peter & Lucy], b. Feb. [ ], 1753; d. Oct.
27, 1770 — 3 — 88

Jordon, s. Peter & Lucy, b. Dec. 12, 1754 — 2 — 12

Jordon, s. [John & Elisabeth], b. July 1, 1771 — 3 — 64

Jordon, s. [William & Elisabeth], b. July 2, 1775 — 3 — 91

Jordon, s. [Peter & Charlotte], b. Mar. 27, 1809 — 3 — 222

Joseph, d. Feb. 14, 1703/4 — 1 — 63

Joseph, s. John & Deborah, b. Sept. 16, 1720 — 1 — 62

Joseph, s. Ann, b. Nov. 5, 1730 — 2 — 94

Joseph, s. Jona[than], of New London, North Parish,
m. Martha **CONGDON**, d. Jeremiah, of New
London, Jan. 23, 1754 — 3 — 35

Joseph, s. Joseph & Martha, b. Aug. 10, 1761 — 3 — 35

Joseph, twin with Benjamin, s. [Lester & Mary], b.
Sept. 25, 1796; d. Oct. 2, 1796 — 3 — 134

Joseph Griffing, s. [Isaac & Polly], b. July 25, 1796 — 3 — 82

Joseph Sanford, s. [Lester & Mary], b. Oct. 17, 1799 — 3 — 134

Joshua, s. Roland & Mary, b. Sept. 10, 1711 — 2 — 93

Joshua Whe[e]lor, s. [John & Elisabeth], b. May 28,
1788 — 3 — 64

Josiah, s. [George & Mary], b. Aug. 28, 1789 — 3 — 157

Josiah, m. Harriet **EWEN**, b. of [New London], Jan.
7, 1835, by Rev. Alvin Ackley — 4 — 59

Josiah, m. Betsey **GALLOP**, b. of [New London],
Sept. 20, 1838, by Rev. C. C. Williams — 4 — 81

Judith, d. Jonathan & Judeth, b. Nov. 30, 1712 — 1 — 41

Judith, d. Nathan & H[annah], b. Sept. 3, 1758 — 3 — 1

Julia Ann, d. [Jonathan & Sarah], b. June 11, 1808 — 3 — 209

Katharine, d. Adam, a mulatto, & Katharine, b. May
15, 1712 — 1 — 39

	Vol.	Page
ROGERS (cont.)		
Katharine, m. William **BROOKFIELD**, Apr. 10, 1720	1	60
Katharine, d. Jonathan, of New London, m. William **BROOKFIELD**, s. William, of Elizabethtown, in the Province of Jerseys, Apr. 15, 1720	2	29
Katharine, d. John & Deborah, b. Dec. 6, 1728	2	93
Katharine, d. John, s. Adam & Mary [sic]*, b. Dec. 22, 1736 *(Perhaps Ann?)	2	94
Katharine, d. John & Ann, b. Nov. 27, 1755	2	100
Katharine, see also Catherine		
Lemuel, s. Capt. James, of New London, & Mary, b. Dec. 10, 1723	2	96
Lemuel, m. Love **RICHARDS**, d. Capt. George, of New London, Oct. 6, 1745	2	96
Lemuel, s. [George & Desire], b. Aug. 13, 1771; d. in about 3 weeks	3	85
Lester, s. David & Grace, b. Dec. 11, 1762	2	86
Lester, m. Mary **TUTHILL**, Jan. 22, 1795	3	134
Lester, m. Susannah **TRUMAN**, of Southold, L.I., Apr. 14, 1795	3	45
Lester Tuthill, s. [Lester & Mary], b. Sept. 24, 1797	3	134
Love, d. [George & Desire], b. Nov. 29, 1772	3	85
Love, d. George, m. James **BURTWELL**, Jan. 20, 1793	3	158
Lucinda, d. Nathaniel & Theoday, b. Apr. 16, 1761	2	34
Lucretia, d. Nath[anie]l & Ziporah, b. Mar. 18, 1771	3	13
Lucretia, m. William **STEWARD**, Jr., Nov. 7, 1782	3	17
Lucretia, d. [William & Elisabeth], b. Apr. 5, 1782; d. July 15, 1797	3	91
Lucretia, d. [Jonathan & Lucretia], b. Oct. 3, 1833	3	287
Lucretia Van Deuson, d. John & Molly, b. Jan. 7, 1794	3	77
Lucy, d. John, s. Jos[eph], dec'd. & Deborah, b. Jan. 8, 1737/8	2	93
Lucy, d. [Peter & Lucy], b. July [ ], 1751	3	88
Lucy, d. Peter & Lucy, b. July 25, 1752	2	11
Lucy, d. John & Ann, b. Oct. 25, 1763	2	101
Lucy, d. [Peter, Jr. & Hannah], b. Aug. 1, 1776	3	90
Lucy, m. Henry P. **GREEN**, Sept. 10, 1823, by Rev. Thomas W. Tucker	4	19
Lydia, d. Jona[than] & Hannah, b. Nov. 14, 1740	2	32
Lydia, d. John & Martha, b. Mar. 30, 1741; d. Aug. 11, 1751	2	110
Lydia, d. Nathaniel & Theoday, b. Aug. 8, 1751	2	34
Lydia, d. John & Martha, b. Oct. 27, 1752	2	110
Lydia, d. James & Susannah, b. May 23, 1756	3	39
Lydia, m. Elijah **SMITH**, Apr. 10, 1788	3	126
Lydia, d. [Stephens & Abigail], b. Jan. 2, 1791	3	82
Lyman, s. [Daniel & Rebecca], b. Mar. 11, 1798	3	132
Martha, d. John & Martha, b. Mar. 12, 1746	2	110
Martha, d. Nathan & Martha, b. Feb. 9, 1751/2	3	1

	Vol.	Page
ROGERS (cont.)		
Martha, w. Nathan, d. Apr. [ ], 1756	3	1
Martha, d. Joseph & Martha, b. Feb. 16, 1758	3	35
Martha, w. John, d. Feb. 17, 1760	2	110
Martha, d. [James & Mary], b. Apr. 7, 1776	3	63
Martha, d. [Zabadiah & Catharine], b. Feb. 2, 1802	3	157
Martin C., s. [Daniel, Jr. & Sally], b. Mar. 17, 1833	3	246
Marvin H., s. [Daniel, Jr. & Sally], b. Oct. 4, 1825; d. July 31, 1856	3	246
Mary, d. Samuel & Mary, b Apr. 17, [1667]	1	5
Mary, d. James & Mary, b. May 1, [1678]	1	12
Mary, d. James, Jr. & Elizabeth, b. Jan. 12 ,1699	1	25
Mary, d. Samuel & Abigail, b. Dec. 17, 1704	1	23
Mary, m. Thomas **PRENTISS**, Jan. 30, 1704/5	1	30
Mary, d. Jonathan & Elizabeth, b. July 18, 1718	1	56
Mary, d. James & Sarah, b. May 15, 1719	1	58
Mary, d. James & Sarah, b. May 18 ,1719	2	92
Mary, d. John, s. John & Elizabeth, b. Jan. 8, 1725/6	2	92
Mary, d. Daniel, m. Thomas **BOLLES**, s. John, all of New London, May 2, 1728	2	68
Mary, d. John, Sr., of New London, m. John **HOB[B]S**, s. John & Susanna, of Boston, Jan. 22, 1729/30, by Christ[opher] Allyn, of S. Kingstown, R.I.	2	117
Mary, d. Jonathan, s. Jonathan & Judeth, b. May 26, 1731	2	93
Mary, d. James, s. Jos[eph], decd., b. of New London, m. Joseph **LEACH**, s. Tho[ma]s, decd., Apr. 22, 1739	2	68
Mary, d. John, of New London, m. Ebenezer **BOLLES**, s. John, of New London, Nov. 29, 1744	2	114
Mary, d. James & Grace, b. July 30, 1747	2	21
Mary, m. John **GRIFFING**, Aug. 22, 1750	3	11
Mary, d. John & Delight, b. Jan. 25, 1756	2	95
Mary, d. James & Mehitable, b. Jan. 21, 1760	2	23
Mary, d. [John & Elisabeth], b. Oct. 3, 1764	3	64
Mary, d. [James & Mary], b. Jan. 23, 1774	3	63
Mary, d. Will[ia]m & Anne, b. Sept. 1, 1774	3	57
Mary, m. Nathan **COMSTOCK**, Jr., Feb. 14, 1782	3	73
Mary, m. Paul **BEEBE**, May 6, 1782	3	123
Mary, d. [Savell & Sarah], b. July 27, 1785	3	80
Mary, d. [Nathan & Catherine], b. Mar. 7, 1787, in Montville	3	159
Mary, d. [John & Hannah], b. Feb. 10, 1790	3	114
Mary, d. [Jeremiah & Hannah], b. Aug. 3, 1792	3	140
Mary, d. [Jason & Fanny], b. Aug. 20, 1796	3	130
Mary, d. [Jonathan & Sarah], b. Oct. 15, 1804	3	209
Mary, m. Giles **HOLT**, Dec. 25, 1804	3	201
Mary, m. William **WIESEMAN**, Jan. 26, 1806	3	190
Mary, d. [Isaac & Sarah], b. Dec. 23, 1807	3	56

	Vol.	Page
ROGERS (cont.)		
Mary, d. Jonathan & Sarah, m. John **TORRELL**,		
Aug. 11, 1825	3	209
Mary Ann, m. Douglass W. **HARRIS**, Nov. 1, 1835,		
by Rev. Alvan Ackley	4	63
Mary Ann, m. David **COIT**, 2d, b. of [New London],		
Sept. 17, 1838, by Rev. C. C. Williams	4	79
Mary E., of Montville, m. Richard D. **SPENCER**, of		
East Haddam, May 4, 1845, by Rev. Jabez S.		
Swan	4	119
Matthew, s. [Jonathan & Milla], b. Mar. 13, 1794	3	93
Maxson, s. [Jonathan & Milla], b. Mar. 17, 1791	3	93
Mehetable, d. James & Mehetable, b. June 16, 1746	2	23
Mehetable, d. Ichabod & Mary, b. July 23, 1751	3	53
Mehetabel, 2d, d. Ichabod & Mary, b. July 1, 1756	3	53
Mehetable, d. James, of Great Neck, m. John		
TINKER, 3d, June 4, 1767	3	190
Mehetable, w. James, d. Dec. 8, 1787	2	23
Mercy, d. Samuell, Jr. & Abigaill, b. July 11, 1712	1	40
Mility, d. [Jonathan & Milla], b. July 13, 1796	3	93
Molly, d. [George & Desire], b. Jan. 19, 1783	3	85
Moses, s. James & Freelove, b. Apr. 22, 1724	2	92
Nancy, m. John **HARRIS**, 3d, June 9, 1782	3	96
Nancy, d. [George & Desire], b. Oct. 12, 1786	3	85
Nancy, d. Ephraim & Tasse, b. Sept. 14, 1788	3	51
Nancy, d. Peter, m. David **JOHNSON**, July 16, 1797	3	173
Naomie, m. Benjamin **FOX**, Feb. 25, 1707/8	1	33
Nathan, s. Capt. Jona[than], b. of New London, m.		
Martha **DAVIS**, d. John, b. of Stonington, Dec.		
17, 1740	3	1
Nathan, s. Nathan & Martha, b. Nov. 1, 1741	3	1
Nathan, of New London, m. Hannah **CRANDALL**,		
of Hopkinton, Sept. 1, 1757, in Westerly, by		
Rev. John Maxon, of Newport, R.I	3	1
Nathan, m. Catherine **RYON**, June 23, 1785	3	139
Nathaniel, s. John & Elizabeth, b. May 2, 1732	2	93
Nath[anie]l, s. William, late of New London, decd.,		
m. Theoday **MINOR**, d. Joseph, of Lyme, Sept.		
13, 1747	2	34
Nathaniel, s. Lemuel & Love, b. Apr. 6, 1750	2	96
Nathaniel, s. Nath[anie]l & Theoday, b. Nov. 11,		
1754	2	34
Nathaniel, of New London, s. John, late of New		
London, decd., m. Ziporah **WILLIAMS**, of		
Norwich, Dec. 6, 1759	3	13
Nathaniel, s. [George & Desire], b. Oct. 9, 1784	3	85
Nehemiah, s. James & Freelove, b. May 7, 1719	2	92
Othaniel, s. Richard & Mary, b. Dec. 13, 1720	1	56
Pace, d. Jonathan, s. of Jonathan & Judeth, b. Aug.		
30, 1716	1	47
Parthenia, d. Tho[ma]s & Sarah, b. Nov. 8, 1752	3	48
Patty, d. [John & Hannah], b. Apr. 27, 1788	3	114

	Vol.	Page
ROGERS (cont.)		
Patty, d. [George & Desire], b. Apr. 24, 1789	3	85
Paul, s. David & Grace, b. Aug. 27, 1766	2	86
Paul, m. Polly **BARTER**, Oct. 4, 1787	3	107
Paul, s. [Paul & Polly], b. May 1, 1790	3	107
Peter, s. James, a mariner, & Mary, b. Oct. 3, 1725	2	69
Peter, s. William & Elizabeth, m. Lucy, d. John & Hannah **TINKER**, & wid., of Daniel **HARRIS**, of New London, Feb. 9, 1744	2	11
Peter, m. Lucy **HARRIS**, Feb. 21, 1744	3	88
Peter, s. [Peter & Lucy], b. May 16, 1749; lost at sea May, 1785	3	88
Peter, s. James, a mariner, m. Grace **ROGERS**, d. James, a cooper, all of New London, Nov. 5, 1749	2	69
Peter, s. Peter & Lucy, b. May 5, 1750	2	11
Peter, Jr., m. Hannah **ROGERS**, Sept. 4, 1773	3	90
Peter, s. [Peter, Jr. & Hannah], b. Dec. 15, 1782	3	90
Peter, d. Dec. 19, 1793	3	88
Peter, m. Charlotte **OWEN**, d. John, Feb. 5, 1808	3	222
Phinehas, s. Nathan & Hannah, b. Mar. 1, 1764	3	1
Pre[s]cilla, d. James & Sarah, b. Feb. 8, 1715	1	50
Presilla, d. James, s. of Jos[eph], decd., b. of New London, m. Jonathan **LEACH**, s. Tho[ma]s, of New London, June 10, 1739	2	62
Rachel, d. [Alexander & Rachel], b. Feb. 9, 1787	3	92
Ralph, s. Adam & Katharine, b. May 29, 1715	1	49
Rebecca, d. [Daniel & Rebecca], b. Nov. 4, 1790	3	132
Rebecca, d. [Jeremiah & Hannah], b. Dec. 19, 1793	3	140
Rebecca, m. Giles **HARRIS**, Nov. 5, 1810	3	254
Richard, s. James & Mary, b. Oct. 13, [1689]	1	19
Richard, of New London, m. Mercy **RAYMOND**, [ ], 1710, in Westerly, by William Champlain, Justice	1	37
Richard, s. [Isaac & Sarah], b. Apr. 26, 1799	3	56
Rosanna Lucretia, d. [Jonathan & Lucretia], b. June 7, 1838	3	287
Rowland, s. John, s. Joseph & Deobrah, b. Apr. 26, 1733* *(Corrected to Apr. 23, 1732, by Roland Rogers.)	2	95
Russel[l], s. [John & Elisabeth], b. Sept. 8, 1777	3	64
Russsell, s. [Jeremiah & Hannah], b. May 7, 1797	3	140
Ruth, d. Adam & Katharine, b. May 26, 1703	1	29
Ruth, d. Jonathan, s. Jonathan, & Judith, b. Oct. 4, 1722	1	60
Ruth, d. Adam, m. John **BROWN**, Aug. 8, 1734	2	5
Ruth, d. David & Grace, b. Aug. 18, 1748	2	86
Sally, d. [George & Desire], b. Apr. 6, 1792	3	85
Sally, d. [Isaac & Sarah], b. Dec. 10, 1801	3	56
Samuell, s. James, m. Mary, d. Thomas **STANTON**, Nov. 17, [1662]	1	3
Samuell, s. Sam[ue]l & Mary, b. Dec. 22, [1669]	1	6

	Vol.	Page
ROGERS (cont.)		
Samuell, s. James & Mary, b. Mar. 23, [1685]	1	17
Samuel, m. Abigaill **PLUMB**, Jan. 16, 1694	1	23
Samuell, s. Samuell & Abigail, b. May 10, 1702	1	23
Samuell, m. Elizabeth, d. James **ROGERS**, Mar. 24, 1702/3	1	28
Samuel, s. John, Jr. & Bathsheba, b. June 1, 1703; d. Aug. 16, 1704	1	34
Samuel, s. John, Jr. & Bathsheba, b. Oct. 8, 1704; d. Jan. 27, 1708	1	34
Samuel, s. John, Jr. & Bathsheba, b. Apr. 17, 1713	1	47
Samuel, s. Samuel, [s. Jno.] & Hannah,b . Apr. 16, 1738	2	105
Sarah, d. Sam[ue]l & Mary, b. Aug. 9, [1676]	1	11
Sarah, d. James & Mary, b. Nov. 23, [1682]	1	16
Sarah, d. James & Sarah, b. May 13, 1700	1	50
Sarah, d. John, s. John & Elizabeth, b. July 17, 1727; d. Nov. 30, 1727	2	92
Sarah, d. John, s. John & Elizabeth, b. Nov. 4, 1730	2	92
Sarah, d. Alpheus & Delight, b. Oct. 27, 1745	3	47
Sarah, d. James & Mehetable, b. Aug. 9, 1748	2	23
Sarah, d. Jonathan & Sarah, b. Dec. 28, 1752	2	32
Sarah, d. John & Ann, b. Sept. 4, 1753	2	100
Sarah, twin with Thomas, s. Thomas & Sarah, b. Apr. 10, 1757	3	48
Sarah, d. Nathaniel & Theoday, b. June 15, 1758	2	34
Sarah, d. Ich[abo]d & Mary, b. Aug. 20, 1759	3	53
Sarah, d. Nathaniel & Ziporah, b. Aug. 20, 1760	3	13
Sarah, d. John & Delight, b. May 18 1772	2	96
Sarah, m. Nicholas **DARROW**, Nov. 12, 1773	3	70
Sarah, m. William **MOORE**, 2d, Jan. 4, 1776	3	75
Sarah, m. Ezra **HARRIS**, Feb. 1, 1782	3	83
Sarah, d. [Alexander & Rachel], b. Apr. 26, 1783	3	92
Sarah, d. [Stephens & Abigail], b. Mar. 6, 1787	3	82
Sarah, d. [Nathan & Catherine], b. Apr. 29, 1794; in New London	3	159
Sarah, d. John & Delight, m. Jonathan **ROGERS**, s. James & Mary, Jan. 14, 1798	3	209
Sarah, d. [Jonathan & Sarah], b. Jan. 26, 1818	3	209
Sarah, d. [Jonathan & Lucretia], b. Oct. 30, 1839	3	287
Sarah, m. Urbane **HAVENS**, b. of New London, June 4, 1843, by Rev. R. W. Allen	4	104
Sarah, m. Urbane **HAVENS**, b. of New London, June 4, 1843, by Rev. R. W. Allen	4	105
Sarah E., d. [Daniel, Jr. & Sally], b. May 28, 1836	3	246
Sarah F., m. Edwin **CHURCH**, b. of Montville, Oct. 15, 1850, by Rev. Geo[rge] M. Carpenter	4	156
Savell, s. Ichabod & Mary, b. Aug. 18, 1754	3	53
Savell, s. Ichabod, m. Sarah **BOLLES**, d. Joshua, Mar. 7, 1784	3	80
Serviah, d. James & Sarah, b. Sept. 11, 1712	1	50
Serviah, see also Zerviah		

	Vol.	Page
ROGERS (cont.)		
Seth Sears, s. [John & Sally], b. Oct. 25, 1801	3	118
Silas, s. [Paul & Polly], b. Sept. 15, 1788	3	107
Solomon, s. James & Mehetable, b. June 9, 1754	2	23
Sophia, m. Jason (?) L. **RYON**, b. of New London, July 11, 1832, by Chester Tilden	4	51
Sophia, m. Henry C. **VERGUSON**, b. of [New London], Mar. 29, 1846, by Rev. L. Geo[rge] Leonard	4	125
Stephen, s. James & Freelove, b. Feb. 28, 1721/2	2	92
Stephens, m. Abigail **POWERS**, Apr. 11, 1786	3	82
Stevens, s. James & Mehetable, b. Mar. 19, 1758	2	23
Stevens, s. [Stephens & Abigail], b. Feb. 13, 1789	3	82
Susannah, m. James **MORGAN**, Oct. 3, 1725	2	66
Susannah, d. Nathaniel & Theoday, b. May 20, 1763	2	34
Susannah, d. Jesse & Hannah, b. Mar. 22, 1794	3	127
Thomas, s. Samuell & Abigaill, b. July 30, 1707	1	33
Thomas, s. Adam & Catharine, b. Aug. 11, 1721	1	58
Thomas, s. Adam & Katharine, d. June 18, 1725	1	65
Thomas, s. Daniel, m. Sarah **FITCH**, d. Capt. Adonijah, of New London, Apr. 7, 1751, by Rev. Jewett	3	48
Thomas, s. David & Grace, b. Dec. 20, 1752	2	86
Thomas, twin with Sarah, s. Thomas & Sarah, b Apr. 10, 1757	3	48
Thomas W., of New London, m. Emeline L. **ORAM**, of Bristol, Me., May 13, 1849, by Rev. Edwin R. Warren	4	148
Theoday, d. Nathaniel & Theoday, b. Mar. 19, 1753	2	34
Theodore, s. Lemuel & Love, b. Dec. 9, 1747	2	96
Uriah, s. James & Elizabeth, b. Oct. 10, 1710	2	92
Uriah F., s. [Daniel, Jr. & Sally], b. July 14, 1828	3	246
William, s. James & Mary, b. May 10, [1693]	1	22
William, m. Elizabeth **HARRIS**, Aug. 28, 1713	1	54
William, s. Ichabod & Mary, b. Aug. 5, 1746	3	53
William, s. Peter & Lucy, b. Aug. 22, 1747	2	11
William, s. [Peter & Lucy], b Aug. 3, 1747	3	88
William, of New London, s. Ichabod, m. Anne **WHIPPLE**, d. Daniel, of Groton, Aug. 20, 1769	3	57
William, s. William & Anne, b. June 5, 1770	3	57
William, m. Elisabeth **TINKER**, Nov. 20, 1774	3	91
William, s. [William & Elisabeth], b. Apr. 17, 1778	3	91
William, s. [George & Mary], b. June 16, 1792	3	157
William Salmon, s. John & Abigail, b. May 30, 1763	3	15
William Salmon, s. [John & Hannah], b. Oct. 17, 1793	3	114
Zebediah, s. [James & Mary], b. Dec. 15, 1769	3	63
Zabadiah, m. Catharine **RICHARDS**, d. William, Oct. 12, 1800	3	157
Zabadiah, s. [Zabadiah & Catharine], b. Feb. 21, 1806	3	157

	Vol.	Page
ROGERS (cont.)		
Zebulon, s. David & Grace, b. July 3, 1757	2	86
Zebulon, m. Sarah **GREEN**, Jan. 9, 1783	3	93
Zebulon, s. [Zebulon & Sarah], b. Aug. 25, 1790	3	93
Zerviah, d. Richard & Mary, b. Jan. 18, 1722/23	1	60
Zerviah, d. James, Joseph's son, of New London, m. Samuel **POWERS**, s. Joseph, of New London, Mar. 22, 1738/9	2	60
Zerviah, see also Serviah		
ROOCAT, Mary, m. Henry **KNOWLES**, b. of [New London], & late of Germany, Nov. 1, 1848, by Rev. M. P. Alderman	4	144
ROOT, C[h]loe S , of Wilkesbarre, Pa., m. Albert D. **CULVER**, of New London, Sept. 5, 1852, by Rev. Jabez S. Swan	4	175
Eliakim, of Hartford, m. Rua **DART**, of New London, Apr. 11, 1825, by Rev. Abel McEwen	4	22
Frederick P., of Sweeden, Monroe Co, N. Y., m. Marion E. **PHELPS**, of Hebron, CT., Oct. 15, 1839, by J. Lovejoy	4	87
ROSE, Edwin, of U. S. Army, m. Sarah Elizabeth **ISHAM**, of New London, Dec. 13, 1832, by Rev. J. W. Hallam	4	49
Esther, of New London, m. Henry **GRIFFING**, of Branford, Apr. 4, 1830, by Rev. B. Judd	4	41
Julia Ann, m. Jerome **KEENEY**, Apr. 26 ,1840, by J. Lovejoy	4	89
Samuel S., of Norwich, m. Sally A. **WHIPPLE**, of New London, Jan. 31, 1831, by Rev. Abel McEwen	4	40
ROSS, Fanny, of Westerly, d. Isaac, decd., m. Edward **LEWIS**, of New London, s. Joseph, decd., Apr. 29, 1790, by Isaiah Willcox, Eld[e]r	3	116
ROSSIE, John, m. Margaret **THOMPSON**, b. of New London, May 31, 1846, by Rev. John Howson	4	126
ROUSE, Grace B., of New London, m. Thomas **BAXTER**, of St. Hellana, May 31, 1842, by Rev. R. W. Allen	4	98
ROWE, ROE, Catharine, m. Robert **ROBIN**, Dec. 25, 1849, by Rev. W[illia]m Logan	4	151
Louisa, of New York, m. William **PEASE**, of [New London], May 7, 1851, by Rev Robert A. Hallam	4	162
Thomas, m. Johanna **DOOLEY**, Nov. 23, 1851, by Rev. J. Stokes. Witnesses: Patrick Rowe, Ellen Tuohy	4	169
ROWLEY, ROWLEE, Nam(?), m. Samuell **FULLER**, of Malshamesdas (?), June 11, 1703	1	28
Wealthy, m. John **STYMEL**, Jan. 28, 1784	3	124
ROY, Jane, m. Frederick H. **MYERS**, b. of New London, May 12, 1852, by Rev. Jabez S. Swan	4	172

	Vol.	Page

ROY (cont.)

Mary, m. John **WEBBER**, Jan. 10, 1852, by Rev. J.
Stokes. Witnesses: Patrick Ward, Elizabeth
Roy ... 4 ... 169

ROYCE, Josia[h], s. Samuel & Han[n]a[h], b. Feb. 14,
[1670 ... 1 ... 7

Nehemyah, s. Robert, m. Hannah, d. James
MORGAN, Nov. 20, [1660] ... 1 ... 3

Robert, s. Sam[ue]l & Hannah, b. Jan. 29, [1669] ... 1 ... 6

Samuel, s. Robert, m. Hannah, d. Josiah[h]
CHURCHWOOD, of Wethersfield, Jan. 9,
[1666] ... 1 ... 5

Samuel, s. Sam[ue]l & Hannah, b. Apr. 17, [1673] ... 1 ... 9

William, m. Harriet **LITTLE**, May 7, 1822, by Rev.
Francis Darrow ... 4 ... 8

RU[ ], Ichabod, m. Mary **CORNWELL**, b. of New
London, Dec. 30, 1827, by Rev. B. Judd ... 4 ... 33

RUDD, Daniel, of Norwich, m. Abigail **ALLEN**, of New
London, Dec. 7, 1780, by David Jewit[t] ... 3 ... 151

RUFF, Jane, d. Jonathan & Ann, b. Aug. 2, 1722 ... 1 ... 62

RUMSEY, Benjamin, m. Mary **HOLT**, relict of Thomas
Holt, Mar. 25, 1801 ... 3 ... 220

Eliza, d. [Benjamin & Mary], b. Sept. 29, 1802 ... 3 ... 220

Eliza, d. Benjamin & Mary, m. Simeon **FRANCIS**,
Dec. 6, 1820 ... 3 ... 220

Harriet, d. [Benjamin & Mary], b. Mar. 23, 1803 ... 3 ... 220

Harriet, m. Robert N. **TATE**, b. of New London,
Mar. 21, 1824, by Rev. Abel McEwen ... 4 ... 17

William A., of Brockport, N.Y., m. Frances H.
HEMPSTE[A]D, of [New London], June 23,
1836, by D. Huntington ... 4 ... 97

RUSSELL, Danyell, m. Margaret **SPRINGER**, Jan. 20,
[1675] ... 1 ... 10

Daniel, s. Dan[ie]l & Margaret, b. Oct. 6, [1677] ... 1 ... 12

William, s. Dan[ie]l & Margaret, b. Jan. 26, [1679] ... 1 ... 14

RYON, RYAN, Abigail, d. [Samuel & Grace], b. Jan. 4,
1788 ... 3 ... 89

Bethiah, d. [William & Rebeckah], b. May 30, 1781 ... 3 ... 70

Catherine, m. Nathan **ROGERS**, June 23, 1785 ... 3 ... 159

Eliner, d. James, m. John **CAREL**, Apr. 5, 1786 ... 3 ... 159

James, m. Reaney **HUNTLEY**, Dec. 21, 1780 ... 3 ... 106

Jason (?) L., m. Sophia **RODGERS**, b. of New
London, July 11, 1832, by Chester Tilden ... 4 ... 51

Joseph, s. [James & Reaney], b. Oct. 29, 1784 ... 3 ... 106

Lucretia, d. [James & Reaney], b. May 9, 1787 ... 3 ... 106

Martha, d. [Samuel & Grace], b. June 2, 1786 ... 3 ... 89

Mary, d. James, m. Benjamin **BENTLEY**, Mar. 28,
1798 ... 3 ... 187

Mary, m. William **WELCH**, Feb. 11, 1849, by Rev.
William Logan ... 4 ... 150

Polly, d. [James & Reaney], b. Nov. 13, 1781; d.
Aug. 20, 1787 ... 3 ... 106

	Vol.	Page
RYON, RYAN (cont.)		
Rebekah, d. [William & Rebeckah], b. July 25, 1779	3	70
Samuel, m. Grace **BEEBE**, July 28, 1785	3	89
William, s. James & Bashuba, m. Rebekcah **DART**,		
d. Capt. John & Ruth, Oct. 3, 1778	3	70
SADLER, Mary of New London, had s. Robert **LITTLE**,		
b. May 26, 1708	1	39
Mary, m. George **WRIGHT**, Jan. 10, 1716/17	1	47
SAFLES, Elizabeth, d. John & Sarah, b. Oct. 24, 1724	1	64
SAGE, Hannah, m. James **ANGELL**, Nov. 11, 1771	3	2
Hannah, d. Gen. Comfort, of Middletown, m. Gurdon		
SALTONSTALL, Apr. 3, 1790	3	69
Mary, d. Comfort & Sarah, of Middlletown, m.		
Edward **HALLAM**, s. Nicholas & Elisabeth, of		
New London, Jan. 8, 1775, by Rev. Enoch		
Huntington, of Middletown	3	59
ST. JOHN, Joseph H., of New York City, m. Eliza		
SPENCER, of New London, Sept. 10, 1843, by		
Rev. Lemuel Covell	4	109
Mortimer Fred[eric]k, b. Apr. 19, 1817	3	249
SALES, Sarah, m. Thomas **BOHAM**, Dec. 1, 1719	1	58
SALMON, Abagail, d. William, of Southold, L.I., m. John		
ROGERS, July 27, 1760	3	15
Hannah, of South Hold, L.I., m. John		
HEMPSTEAD, of New London, Nov. 17,		
1731	2	42
SALTONSTALL, Abby, d. Roswell, m. William		
HANDY, June 23, 1799	3	163
Ann, d. Gurdon & Rebeckah, b. Feb. 29, 1739/40	2	89
Ann, d. Roswell, m. Rev. Charles **SEABUARY**, s.		
Bishop Seabuary, June 13, 1799	3	142
Ann, twin with Mary, [d. Nathaniel, Jr. & Lucretia],		
b. Oct. 6, 1817	3	158
Ann Dudley, [d. Winthrop & Ann], b. Jan. 8, 1770	3	69
Augusta, d. [Nathaniel, Jr. & Lucretia], b. Mar. 18,		
1804	3	158
Betsey, d. [Nathaniel & Lucretia], b. Apr. 1, 1784; d.		
Nov. 23, 1786	3	161
Catharine, m. John **RICHARDS**, June 16, 1768	3	108
Dudley, s. Gurdon & Rebeckah, b. Sept. 8, 1738	2	89
Eliza L., d. [Nathaniel, Jr. & Lucretia], b. June 8,		
1802	3	158
Elizabeth, d. Gurdon, Esq. & Jerusha, b. May 11,		
1690	1	36
Elizabeth, m. Richard **CHRISTOPHERS**, Aug. 14,		
1710	1	39
Elizabeth, w. Gurdon, Esq., d. Sept. 4, 1710	1	36
Elizabeth, d. Gurdon & Rebeckah, b. Jan. 12, 1742/3	2	89
Ellen, d. [Nathaniel, Jr. & Lucretia], b. Dec. 13, 1820	3	158
Frances, d. [Nathaniel, Jr. & Lucretia], b. Nov. 13,		
1809	3	158
Gilbert, s. Gurdon & Rebeckah, b. Feb. 27, 1751/2	2	89

	Vol.	Page

SALTONSTALL (cont.)

	Vol.	Page
Gurdon, s. Gurdon, Esq. & Jerusha, b. July 17, 1696; d. July 27, 1696	1	36
Gurdon, s. Gurdon, Esq. & Elizabeth, b. Dec. 22, 1708	1	36
Gurdon, s. Gurdon, the Gov., of Conn, m. Rebeckah **WINTRHOP**, d. John, of New London, Mar. 15, 1732/3	2	89
Gurdon, s. Gurdon & Rebeckah, b. Dec. 15, 1733; d. July 18, 1762, at Jamaica	2	89
Gurdon, [s. Winthrop & Ann], b. July 3, 1765	3	69
Gurdon, Hon., d. Sept. 19, 1785, at Norwich	2	89
Gurdon, m. Hannah **SAGE**, d. Gen. Comfort Sage, of Middletown, Apr. 3, 1790	3	69
Gurdon, d. June 9, 1795, at Cape Nichols Male (?) (Mass.?)	3	69
Gurdon Flower, s. [Nathaniel & Rebakah], b. May 18, 1760	3	161
Gurdon Winthrop, s. [William W. & Mary], b. June 3, 1827	3	267
Har[r]iet, m. Marvin **WAIT**, Apr. 22, 1805	3	42
Henrietta, d. Gurdon & Rebeckah, b. Mar. 19, 1749/50	2	89
Jane, d. [Nathaniel, Jr. & Lucretia], b. July 8, 1823	3	158
Jerusha, d. Gurdon, Esq., & Jerusha, b. July 5, 1695; d. Sept. 12, 1695	1	36
John, s. [Nathaniel & Lucretia], b. Jan. 26, 1781	3	161
John, s. [Nathaniel, Jr. & Lucretia], b. July 18, 1812	3	158
Joseph Leander, s. [Nathaniel & Rebakah], b. June 8, 1763	3	161
Katharine, d. Gurdon, Esq., & Elizabeth, b. June 19, 1704	1	36
Katharine, d. Gurdon & Rebeckah, b. Feb. 17, 1735/6	2	89
Lucretia, d. [Nathaniel & Lucretia], b. Aug. 1, 1770	3	161
Maria, d. [Nathaniel, Jr. & Lucretia], b. May 4, 1815	3	158
Maria, of New London, m. Peter R. **BENNET**, of New York City, Aug. 17, 1835, by Rev. Robert A. Hallam	4	61
Martha, d. Gurdon & Rebeckah, b. Oct. 8, 1748	2	89
Martha, d. Hon. Gurdon, m. David **MANWARING**, s. Will[ia]m, Jan. 15, 1767	3	83
Mary, d. Gurdon, Esq. & Jerusha, b. Feb. 15, 1691/2	1	36
Mary, m. Jeremiah **MILLER**, Mar. 2, 1717/18	2	20
Mary, d. Gurdon & Rebeckah, b. Mar. 28, 1744	2	89
Mary, twin with Ann, [d. Nathaniel, Jr. & Lucretia], b. Oct. 6, 1817	3	158
Mary, of New London, m. Harry **AUSTIN**, of New York, Oct. 10, 1838, by Rev. Robert Hallam	4	80
Mary Hallam, d. [Gurdon & Hannah], b. Apr. 13, 1791	3	69
Mary Wanton, [d. Winthrop & Ann], b. Mar. 14, 1767, N.S.	3	69

	Vol.	Page
SALTONSTALL (cont.)		
Mary Wanton, m. Thomas **COIT**, Jr., Nov. 29, 1789*		
*(Conflicts with date of birth of dau. Ann		
Wanton Coit)	3	176
Nancy, d. [Nathaniel & Lucretia], b. July 6, 1774	3	161
Nathaniel, s. Gurdon, Esq. & Elizabeth, b. July 1,		
1707	1	36
Nathaniel, m. Rebakah **YOUNG**, of Wethersfield,		
Sept. 16, 1755	3	161
Nathaniel, m. Lucretia **LATIMER**, d. Peter, Dec. 21,		
1768	3	161
Nathaniel, s. [Nathaniel & Lucretia], b. Dec. 18, 1776	3	161
Nathaniel, Jr., m. Lucretia **LAMPHIRE**, May 22,		
1800, by Rev. Henry Channing	3	158
Nathaniel, s. [Nathaniel, Jr. & Lucretia], b. Apr. 30,		
1807	3	158
Polly, d. [Nathaniel & Lucretia], b. Aug. 18, 1772	3	161
Rebeckah, d. Gurdon & Rebeckah, b. Dec. 31, 1734	2	89
Rebecca, [d. Winthrop & Ann], b. Mar. 4, 1764	3	69
Rebakah, w. Nathaniel, d. Oct. 8, 1766	3	161
Rebecca, d. Winthrop, m. Peter **CHRISTOPHERS**,		
Apr. 2, 1792	3	232
Rebekah Gardiner, d. [Nathaniel & Rebakah], b. July		
7, 1756	3	161
Richard, s. Gurdon, Esq. & Elizabeth, b. Sept. 1,		
1710	1	36
Richard, s. Gurdon, Esq. & Elizabeth, d. Sept. 12,		
1710	1	36
Richard, s. Gurdon & Rebeckah, b. Jan. 1, 1746/7	2	89
Roswell, s. Gurdon, Esq. & Elizabeth, b. Jan. 19,		
1701/2	1	36
Rosewell, s. Gurdon & Rebeckah, b. Aug. 29, 1741	2	89
Sally Crafts, d. [Nathaniel & Rebakah], b. Aug. 17,		
1758	3	161
Sarah, d. Gurdon, Esq. & Jerusha, b. Apr. 8, 1694	1	36
Sarah, m. John **GARDINER**, May 6, 1716	1	46
Sarah, d. Gurdon & Rebeckah, b. June 17, 1754, new		
style	2	89
William W., m. Mary **WINTRHOP**, [ ]	3	267
William Wanton, s. [Gurdon & Hannah], b. Jan. 10,		
1793	3	69
Winthrop, s Gurdon & Rebeckah, b. June 10, 1737	2	89
Winthrop, eldest surviving s. Gurdon & Rebecca, b.		
June 10, 1737, O.S.; m. Ann, eldest d. Hon.		
Joseph **WANTON** & Mary Wanton, Apr. 17,		
1763, N.S.	3	69
Winthrop, [s. Winthrop & Ann], b. Feb. 20, 1775	3	69
Winthrop had negro servant Hetty, b. Dec. 22, 1777	3	176
Winthrop had Scip[i]o, s. Juno, servants, b. July 22,		
1788	3	104
-----, d. [Gurdon & Rebeckah], b. Jan. 24, 1745/6; d.		
in half an hour	2	89

	Vol.	Page
SANDIFORTH, Daniel Wetherell, s. Ruport & Esther, b. June 22, 1759	3	21
Ruport, s. John, m. Esther **DENISON**, d. Wetherill Denison, Mar. 27, 1758	3	21
SANDINO, Thomas, m. Elizabeth Ann **LOVETT**, Oct. 1, 1820, by B. Judd	4	1
SANDS, Mercy, d. James, of Block Island, m. Joshua **RAYMOND**, s. Joshua, of New London, Apr. 29, [1683]	1	17
SASEQUENUT, Robert, s. of Old Indian Boss, b. July 22, 1700	1	38
SAT[T]ERLEE, Julia, m. Joseph **WILLIAMS**, b. of New London, Aug. 9, 1849, by Rev. Edwin R. Warren	4	148
SAUL, James, m. Maria **REYNOLDS**, Apr. 25, 1852, by Rev. J. Stokes. Witnesses: Patrick Tarrell, Bridget Saul	4	170
SAUNDERS, Erastus, of Hebron, m. Ruth A. **HUNTINGTON**, of N[ew] London, Aug. 12, 1833, by Rev. Abel McEwen	4	53
SAVAGE, John Dart, s. [Richard & Betsey], b. Feb. 21, 1813	3	132
Lucretia, d. [Richard & Betsey], b. Sept. 1, 1802	3	132
Polly, m. John **MERRIL[L]**, Feb. 28, 1827, by R[ober]t Bowzer	4	29
Richard, m. Betsey **GRIFFING**, June 14, 1800	3	132
Richard, s. [Richard & Betsey], b. Aug. 20, 1807	3	132
Thomas, s. [Richard & Betsey], b. Mar. 23, 1805	3	132
SAVELL, SAVIL, SAVEL, SAVALL, Bathyah, d. John & Sarah, b. Aug. 7, 1722	1	60
Elizabeth, d. John & Sarah, b. May 12, 1727	2	104
Hannah, twin with Mary, d. John & Sarah, b. June 27, 1720	1	57
Hannah, of New London, d. of John, of New London, m. James **TILLEY**, of New London, s. John, of Edford County, of Devonshire, Great Britian, May 27, 1742	2	84
John, s. John & Sarah, b. [ ]	2	105
Mary, twin with Hannah, d. John & Sarah, b. June 27, 1720	1	57
Mary, d. John, of New London, m. Ichabod **ROGERS**, s. John, of New London, Feb. 3, 1744	3	53
Mehetable, d. John & Sarah, b. Oct. 15, 1729	2	104
Sarah, d. John & Sarah, b. June 30, 1717	1	49
Sarah, d. John, m. Tho[ma]s **WAY**, s. Dan[ie]l, b. of New London, Dec. 29, 1737	2	69
SCANLON, Mary, m. John **SHEA**, Jan. 25, 1852, by Rev. J. Stokes. Witnesses: Owen Connors, Eliza Boyle	4	169
SCARIT, [see also **SCERRETT**], Thomas, s. Richard & Penelope, b. Aug. 20, 1696	1	21

	Vol.	Page

SCERRETT, [see also **SCARIT**], Abigail, d. Richard, of
    Branford, decd., m. Daniel **LESTER**, s. Daniel,
    of New London, decd., Feb. 19, 1739/40   2   49

SCHUYLER, SCHYLER, Jane, m. John **WILSON**, b. of
    [New London], June 19, 1838, by Rev. Abel
    McEwen   4   78

    Mary Ann, m. Benjamin **BROWN**, b. of [New
    London], June 14, 1848, by Rev. Abel McEwen   4   139

SCOFIELD, John, s. John & Sarah, b. June 11, 1756   2   103

SCOTT, Henry, m. Maria **HEMPSTEAD**, b. of [New
    London], Oct. 1, 1838, by Rev. Abel McEwen   4   79

    Jane M., of Hampton, m. William **TAYLOR**, of
    Brooklyn, July 26, 1847, by Frederick M.
    Walker, J.P.   4   133

    William, of New London, m. Fanny **OCREY**, of
    Lyme, July 22, 1838, by Rev. Chester Colton   4   66

SCOVEL[L], Rachel, d. Arthur, of Colchester, m. John
    BAKER, s. Joshua, late of New London, decd.,
    Mar. 14, 1754   3   4

    Rachel, m. Edward **COLBY**, b. of [New London],
    May 14, 1845, by Rev. Abel McEwen   4   119

SCRANTON, Anna, d. George Scranton & Lucy **FOX**, b.
    July 30, 1782   3   38

    Sarah, d. Stutely & Bethiah, b. Mar. 22, 1742   2   30

    Stutely, of Newport, R.I., s. John, of Warwick, decd.,
    m. Bethiah **CHAP[P]EL**, d. of Joseph, of New
    London, Jan. 3, 1735   2   30

    Stutely, s. Stutely & Bethah, b. Nov. 10, 1738   2   30

    Thomas, s. Stutely & Bethiah, b. June 19, 1745   2   30

    William, s. Stutely & Bethiah, b. Mar. 28, 1737   2   30

SCROGGIE, Joseph, m. Mary **BINDLOSS**, b. of [New
    London], Dec. 6, 1849, by Rev. Robert A.
    Hallam   4   151

SCRUTON, Almira Jane, m. Asa **BOND**, b. of [New
    London], Dec. 24, 1849, by Rev. James W. Dennis   4   151

    Matilda, m. John W. **HOOKER**, Nov. 16, 1851, by
    Rev. James W. Dennis   4   165

SEABURY, SEABUARY, Bishop had negro child Rose,
    d. Nelly born in his family June 20, 1787.
    Recorded Dec. 1, 1792   3   124

    Charles, Rev., s. Bishop Seabuary, m. Ann
    SALTONSTALL, d. Roswell Saltonstall, June
    13, 1799   3   142

    Charles Saltonstall, s. [Rev. Charles & Ann], b. Dec.
    10, 1802   3   142

    Edward, s. [Rev. Charles & Ann], b. May 14, 1807   3   142

    Esther, d. of James **ROGERS**, late of New London,
    then of Norwalk, decd., m. Jonathan **COP**, s.
    Jonathan, of Stonington, May 30, 1747   2   35

    John, s. Caleb & Esther, b. Apr. 7, 1763   3   24

    Richard Francis, s. [Rev. Charles & Ann], b. July 21,
    1809   3   142

	Vol.	Page

SEABURY, SEABUARY (cont.)

Samuel, Rt., Rev., Bishop of Conn. & R.I., d. Feb.
  28, 1796, ae 68 y. — 3 — 140

Samuel, s. [Rev. Charles & Ann], b. June 9, 1801 — 3 — 142

William, s. [Rev. Charles & Ann], b. Mar. 31, 1805 — 3 — 142

SEAMAN, Augustus G., of [New London], m. Henrietta
  LE MURLE, of [New London], Nov. 30, 1843,
  by Rev. R. A. G. Thompson — 4 — 109

SEARLS, SIRLES, SIRLS, Charles H., of New London,
  m. Harriet E. **PARKER**, of New York, May 14,
  1848, by Rev. L. G. Leonard — 4 — 139

Elizabeth, m. Charles **WILNEY**, b. of New London,
  June 12, 1831, by Rev. Abel McEwen — 4 — 42

Harriet, of New London, m. Edward **HALLADAY**,
  of New York, Oct. 10, 1831, by Rev. Abel
  McEwen — 4 — 44

SEARS, James, s. [Seth & Deborah], b. July 16, 1779 — 3 — 91

John, s. [Seth & Deborah], b. May 31, 1777 — 3 — 91

Mary, of Greenwich, m. Hiram **BUNDY**, of Hartford,
  May 22, 1825, by Lodowick Fosdick, J.P. — 4 — 22

Rowland, of Whitesborough, N.Y., m. Mary A.
  SMITH, of [New London], Nov. 12, 1837, by
  Rev. Abel McEwen — 4 — 74

Sally, d. [Seth & Deborah], b. July 10, 1782 — 3 — 91

Sally, m. John **ROGERS**, s. James, Nov. 23, 1800 — 3 — 118

Seth, m. Deobrah **ROGERS**, May 12, 1776 — 3 — 91

Seth, d. Apr. 13, 1783 — 3 — 91

SEBOR, Eliza, d. [Jacob & Elizabeth, Jr.], b. July 20, 1787 — 3 — 80

Jacob, m. Elizabeth **WINTHROP**, Jr., Apr. 27, 1786 — 3 — 80

Margaret Yates, d. [Jacob & Elizabeth, Jr.], b. Aug.
  15, 1790 — 3 — 80

SEECOMBE, -----, d. of Mr., d. Aug. 23, [1690] — 1 — 69

SEELEY, William, Jr., of New York, m. Hannah E.
  TRUE, of New London, Oct. 19, 1845, by Rev.
  Tho[ma]s J. Greenwood — 4 — 122

SEGUR, William C., of N[ew] London, m. Lucy M.
  BINGHAM, of East Haddam, July 12, 1846,
  by Rev. L. Geo[rge] Leonard — 4 — 129

SEWALL, Stephen, J.P., affidavit dated Feb. 4, 1716/7, in
  Salem, Mass., that Robert [Jacklin], negro, was
  a servant of his nephew Samuel Gerish, of
  Newbury — 1 — 48

SEXTINE, Cath[arine], m. William **DUNN**, Oct. 13,
  [18]50, [by Peter J. Blenkinsop]. Witnesses:
  John Curran, Maria Caldwell — 3 — 306

Catharine, m. William **DUNN**, Oct. 13, 1850.
  Witnesses: John Curran, Maria Caldwell — 4 — 159

SEXTON, David B., m. Sarah **REID**, Nov. 3, 1850, by
  Rev. Charles Willett — 4 — 156

SEYMOUR, Henrietta, of Norwich, m. Charles **FASSET**,
  of New London, July 14, 1851, by Rev. Abel
  McEwen — 4 — 164

	Vol.	Page
SEYMOUR (cont.)		
Joel, of New York, m. Abby A. **KEENEY***, of [New London], [ ] 7, [1832?], by Rev. Abel McEwen *(Perhaps "**HENEY**")	4	57
SHACKETT, Ann, m. Jams **BARRY**, Oct. 28, 1849, by Rev. William Logan	4	151
SHACKLEFORD, Elizabeth, m. William **STEENE**, b. of New London, Oct. 1, 1829, by Rev. Abel McEwen	4	37
SHACKMAPLE, John, m. Elizabeth **CHRISTOPHERS**, Aug. 31, 1732	2	104
John, d. Jan. 3, 1742/3	2	104
Sarah, d. John & Elizabeth, b. July 4, 1733	2	104
SHANNON, Mary H., of New London, m. Robert S. **DAVIS**, of Boston, Sept. 4, 1837, by Rev. Robert A. Hallam	4	73
SHAPLEY, [see also **SHIPLY**], Abga[i]ll, d. Daniel & Abiga[i]ll, b. Mar. 17, 1725	2	10
Adam, s. Daniel & Abiga[i]ll, b. May 23, 1738	2	11
Ann, m. Thomas **AVERY**, July 12, 1704	1	30
Anne, d. Benjamin & Mary, b. Aug. 31, 1685	1	18
Benj[ami]n, s. Nicholas, of Charlestown, m. Mary **PICKETT**, d. John, of New London, Apr. 10, [1672]	1	8
Benjamin, s. Benj[amin] & Mary, b. Mar. 20, [1675]	1	10
Benjamin, m. Ruth **DYMOND**, Feb. 29, 1699/1700	1	25
Benjamin, s. Benjamin, Jr. & Ruth, b. Sept. 9, 1702	1	28
Benjamin, s. Daniel & Abigaill, b. Oct. 11, 1716	1	47
Benjamin, s. Daniel & Abiga[i]ll, b. Oct. 11, 1716	2	10
Benjamin, s. Daniell & Abigail, b. Oct. 11, [1716?]	1	48
Benj[amin], s. Dan[ie]l [& Abigail], d. Jan. 24, 1728/9	2	10
Benjamin, s. Daniel & Abiga[i]ll, b. Feb. 1, 1731/2; d. Mar. 11, 1731/2	2	10
Benjamin, s. Daniel & Abiga[i]ll, b. Sept. 19, 1735	2	11
Danniell, s. Benjamin & Mary, b. Feb. 14, 1689	1	19
Daniel, m. Abigail **PURSON**, Nov. 11, 1714	1	55
Daniel, of New London, m. Abiga[i]ll **PERSON**, of Killingworth, Nov. 11, 1714	2	10
Daniel, s. Dan[ie]l & Abigail, b. Mar. 2, 1719; d. Mar. 29, 1719	1	55
Daniel, s. Daniel & Abiga[I]ll, b. Mar. 2, 1719; d. [ ]	2	10
Daniel, s. Daniel & Abigail, b. June 9, 1727	2	10
Elisabeth, d. John & Elisabeth, b. Sept. 19, 1755	3	18
Elisabeth, m. Ebenezer **PRENTIS**, July 6, 1783	3	89
Jane, m. Joshua **APPLETON**, Feb. 5, 1716	1	50
John, s. Daniel & Abigail, b. Aug. 29, 1722	2	10
John, s. Daniel, m. Elisabeth **HARRIS**, d. Capt. Joseph, b. of New London, Nov. 15, 1753	3	18
John, s. John & Elisabeth, b. Nov. 19, 1756	3	18
Joseph, s. Benj[amin] & Mary, b. Aug. 15, [1681]	1	16

	Vol.	Page

SHAPLEY (cont.)

Joseph, s. Benjamin, Jr.* & Ruth, b. Apr. 28, 1705

*(First written "Sr." Corrected by L. B. B.) — 1 — 31

Joseph, s. Benjamin, Jr. late decd., & Ruth, b. May 1, 1705 — 1 — 30

Joseph, s. Daniel & Abigail, b. Mar. 14, 1733 — 2 — 11

Mary, d. Benj[amin] & Mary, b. Mar. 26, [1677] — 1 — 12

Mary, m. Joseph **TRUMAN**, Dec. 5, 1701 — 1 — 27

Mary, d. Daniell & Abigail, b. Apr. 2, 1720 — 1 — 58

Mary, d. Daniel & Abiga[I]ll, b. Apr. 5, 1720 — 2 — 10

Mary, m. George **HOUSE**, Dec. 25, 1780 — 3 — 19

Ruth, d. Benj[amin] & Mary, b. Dec. 21, [1672] — 1 — 8

Ruth, d. Daniel & Abigaill, b. Oct. 30, 1729 — 2 — 10

SHARKEY, SHARKY, James, m. Rose **GAFFY**, July 22, 1849, by Rev. William Logan — 4 — 150

Sarah, m. Abraham George **WORKMAN**, Apr. 3, 1853, by Rev. Thomas Ryan — 4 — 174

SHARON, Maria L., of New London, m. Thomas **GILDERSLEEVE**, of Coldspring, N.Y., Mar. 3, 1846, by Rev. S. Benton — 4 — 125

SHARP, Elias, of Lyme, m. Fanny **GARDINER**, of New London, May 24, 1820, by Elder Lester Rogers — 4 — 3

Elias Benjamin, twin with Fanny Phebe Ann, b. Feb. 7 ,1821 — 3 — 212

Fanny Phebe Ann, twin with Elias Benjamin, b. Feb. 7, 1821 — 3 — 212

SHATTERLY, Benedict, s. W[illia]m, of Devonshire, near the City Exon (?), Old England, m. Rebecca, wid. ,of Jno. **DYMOND**, Aug. 2, [1682] — 1 — 16

Benedict, s. W[illia]m, of Devonshire, Old England, near Exon (?), m. Rebecca, wid., of Jno. **DYMOND**, Aug. 2, 1682 — 1 — 68

SHAW, Betsey, m. John R. **WILLIAMS**, b. of New London, Dec. 30, 1827, by Rev. B. Judd — 4 — 33

Ce[a]sar, m. Eader **DESHON** (negroes), May [ ], 1779 — 3 — 16

Ce[a]sar, s. [Ce[a]sar & Eader], b. Oct. 5, 1788 (Negroes) — 3 — 16

Ce[a]sar, m. Jane **FREEMAN**, Oct. 8, 1809 (Negroes) — 3 — 16

Christopher, m. Lucy Ann **WEEDON**, b. of [New London], July 13, 1843, by Rev. Abel McEwen — 4 — 106

Christopher A., [s. Ceasar, negro], b. July 5, 1809 — 3 — 222

Daniel, s. Nath[anie]l & Temperance, b. June 27, 1742 — 2 — 108

Eader, w. Ce[a]ser, d. Mar. 15, 1809 (Negroes) — 3 — 16

Eder, m. Thomas **DINON**, b. of New London, July 11, 1830, by Rev. B. Judd — 4 — 41

Eder Ann, of New London, m. James **CARTER**, of Hartford, July 7, 1840, by Rev. Robert A. Hallam — 4 — 90

	Vol.	Page

SHAW (cont.)

	Vol.	Page
Eader Prince Ann, [d. Ceasar, negro], b. Nov. 30, 1813	3	222
Edward, [s. Ceasar, negro], b. Oct. 5, 1810	3	222
Edward, m. Mary **BROWN**, b. of N[ew] London, July 31, 1834, by Rev. Ebenezer Blake	4	56
Elizabeth, of Charleston, R.I., m. Rodman **LATHROP**, of Groton, Oct. 3, 1845, by Rev. Robert A. Hallam	4	124
Ichabod, s. [Cesar & Eader], b. Mar. 11, 1786 (Negroes)	3	16
Jane Lo[u]isa, [d. Ceasar, negro], b. Dec. 25, 1818	3	222
Jeremiah, m. Mary Ann **BROCKWAY**, b. of New London, Dec. 28, 1845, by Rev. L. Geo[rge] Leonard	4	123
John, s. Nath[anie]l & Temperance, b. Feb. 10, 1745	2	108
Joseph, s. Nath[anie]l & Temperance, b. Sept. 27, 1737	2	108
Mary, d. Nath[anie]l & Temperance, b. Sept. 6, 1751	2	108
Nathaniel, m. Temperance **HARRIS**, Nov. 5, 1730	2	104
Nathaniel, s. Nath[anie]l & Temperance, b. Dec. 5, 1735	2	108
Prince, s. [Ce[a]sar & Eader], (Negroes), b. Nov. 5, 1782	3	16
Sarah, d. Nath[anie]l & Temperance **HARRIS**, b. Mar. 29, 1734	2	108
Seela, m. Jack **AMY**, a negro, Feb. 22, 1800	3	47
Thomas, s. Nath[anie]l & Temperance, b. Mar. 16, 1739	2	108
William, s. Nath[anie]l & Temperance, b. Sept. 22, 1746	2	108
SHEA, Jeremiah, m. Mary **LEARY**, Apr. 11, 1852, by Rev. J. Stokes. Witnesses: Patrick Shea, Julia Leary	4	170
John, m. Mary **SCANLON**, Jan. 25, 1852, by Rev. J. Stokes. Witnesses: Owen Connors, Eliza Boyle	4	169
Julia, m. Michael **SULLIVAN**, May 13, 1852, by Rev. J. Stokes. Witnesses: Arthur Hurley, Bridget Casey	4	170
Mary, m. Patrick **CALLANAN**, June 27, 1852, by Rev. J. Stokes. Witnesses: Daniel Shea, Julia Shea	4	171
SHEEHAN, John, m. Ellen **SULLIVAN**, June 20, 1852, by Rev. J. Stokes. Witnesses: John Sullivan, Mary Shea	4	171
SHEFFIELD, Bridget, d. [William & Bridget], b. Nov. 30, 1779	3	64
George, m. Bathshua **KING**, Dec. 16, 1742, at Southold, by Eben[eze]r Gould, Clerk	2	60
George, s. George & Bathshua, b. Jan. 8, 1743/4, at South Kingstown	2	60

	Vol.	Page

SHEFFIELD (cont.)

George, s. George, decd., m. Betsey **WOODWARD**,
d. Abishai, decd., Dec. 26, 1813, at Brooklin,
by Rev. J. Whiting — 3 — 240

George Woodward, d. [George & Betsey], b. Dec.
26, 1814 — 3 — 240

James, s. George & Bathsua, b. May 18, 1745, at
Southold, L.I. — 2 — 60

Jeremiah, m. Sally **HOLMES**, July 22, 1823, by
Christopher Griffing, J.P. — 4 — 14

Joseph, s. George & Bathsua, b. Mar. 12, 1746/7, at
New London — 2 — 60

Joseph, s. [William & Bridget], b. June 19, 1781 — 3 — 64

Samuel, s. George & Bathshua, b. Aug. 2, 1750 — 2 — 60

Washington W., of N. Stonington, m. Harriet Brown
TRACEY, of New London, Nov. 28, 1849, by
Rev. E. R. Warren — 4 — 153

William, s. George & Bathshua, b. Apr. 23, 1754 — 2 — 60

William, m. Bridget **WILLIAMS**, Dec. 10, 1778 — 3 — 64

SHELLY, SHELLEY, James, m. Tacy **CROCKER**, b. of
Waterford, Dec. 31, 1843, by Rev. Abel
McEwen — 4 — 110

John W., of Waterford, m. Elizabeth **HARKNESS**,
of [New London], Jan. 27, 1839, by Rev. Abel
McEwen — 4 — 80

Joseph, m. Frances Ann **MINOR**, b. of Waterford,
Sept. 2, 1848, by Rev. Jabez S. Swan — 4 — 141

Sarah, m. Albert **KNIGHT**, Aug. 19, 1840, by H. R.
Knapp — 4 — 91

SHEPARD, SHEPHERD, SHEPPARD, Ann E., of [New
London], m. Lyman **PAINTER**, of New York,
June 16, 1852, by Rev. Abel McEwen — 4 — 168

Charlot[te], d. [John & Pheby], b. Aug. 18, 1795 — 3 — 97

Frederick, s. [John], b. Oct. 15, 1779 — 3 — 117

Frederick, s. [John & Pheby], b. Oct. 5, 1800 — 3 — 97

Frederick, m. Abigail **CHAPPELL**, Mar. 13, 1825,
by Ebenezer Loomis — 4 — 21

George, m. Ann E. **BEEBE**, b. of New London, Apr.
22, 1827, by Rev. Abel McEwen — 4 — 30

Isaac, m. Abby S. **THATCHER**, Aug. 2, 1820 — 3 — 152

James Fitch, m. Betsey Ingham **HAYNES**, Jan. 6,
1833 — 3 — 147

John, s. [John], b. Aug. 16, 1775 — 3 — 117

John, m. Hannah **WHITE**, Aug. 2, 1789, by Jason
Lee, Elder, of Lyme — 3 — 117

John, m. Pheby **BEEBE**, d. Thaddeus, July 14, 1794 — 3 — 97

John, s. [John & Pheby], b. Mar. [ ], 1798; drowned
June 1, 1801 — 3 — 97

John Dwyer, s. [James Fitch & Betsey Ingham], b
Jan. 20, 1834 — 3 — 147

Julius Thatcher, s. [Isaac & Abby S.], b. Aug. 5, 1821 — 3 — 152

Lucy, d. [John], b. Feb. 4, 1782 — 3 — 117

	Vol.	Page
SHEPARD, SHEPHERD, SHEPPARD (cont.)		
Margarett, d. p[John], b. Nov. 20, 1773	3	117
Phebe, m. Jacob **SMITH**, b. of [New London], May		
11, 1834, by Rev. Ebenezer Blake	4	56
Sally, d. John, m. John **CHEENEY**, Sept. 3, 1804	3	146
Sarah, d. [John], b. Oct. 18, 1777	3	117
William, s. [John], b. Sept. 10, 1785	3	117
SHERMAN, Lucretia, m. Daniel **ADAMS**, Jr., b. of [New		
London], Jan. 8, 1849, by Rev. M. P. Alderman	4	144
Mary, of Waterford, m. Frances **BARROS**, of Rio		
Hache, May 8, 1831, by Rev. Daniel Wildman	4	41
Tucker, m. Nancy **MALONY**, b. of New London,		
May 13, 1846, by Frederick M. Walker, J.P.	4	126
SHIPLY, [see also **SHAPLEY**], Samuel H., of Rochdell,		
England, m. Eunice **JONES**, of Waterford, July		
6, 1823, by Thomas W. Tucker, Elder	4	15
SHIPMAN, Joseph A., m. Abby Jane **KEENEY**, of New		
London, Jan. 9, 1848, by Rev. L. G. Leonard	4	137
SHONE, Sarah L., m. Martin S. T. J. **MOORE**, b. of		
New London, Sept. 12, 1844, by Rev. J. Blain	4	117
SHORT, SHORTT, Charles, s. Thomas & Elizabeth, b		
Dec. 26, 1711	1	20
Charles, s. Thomas & Elizabeth, b. Dec. 26, 1711	1	37
Katharine, d Thomas & Elizabeth, b. Aug. 10, 1709	1	66
Thomas, d. Sept. 27, [ ]	1	20
SHUGRIE, John, m. Alice **KELLY**, Apr. 12, 1850, by		
Rev. James W. Dennis	4	153
SIMBRY, Jane, d. Bennett **THOMAS**, b. June 22, 1780		
(See also Jane Simbry Thomas)	3	6
SIMMONS, SIMONS, Abba, d. [John & Elizabeth], b.		
Oct. 20, 1818	3	277
Carroline, d. [John & Elizabeth], b. Jan. 16, 1820	3	277
Caroline Louisa, m. Francis **BURNS**, b. of [New		
London], Feb. 28, 1836, by Rev. Abel McEwen	4	64
Chapman, m. Elizabeth **FORSYTH**, May 13, 1780	3	281
Charles, s. [Chapman & Elizabeth], b. Aug. 21, 1782	3	281
Ebenezer, s. Robert, late of Ipswich, County of		
Essex, Mass., then of Wenham, Mass., m.		
Rebecca **CHAPMAN**, d. of Samuel, of New		
London, Mar. 7, 1733/4	2	35
Ebenezer, s. Eben[eze]r & Rebecca, b. Mar. 17,		
1744/5	2	35
Eliza, of New London, m. Charles F. **RICH**, of		
Chatham, Apr. 11, 1824, by Rev. Abel McEwen	4	17
Elizabeth, d. [John & Elizabeth], b. Feb. 28, 1829	3	277
Ellen, d. [John & Elizabeth], b. July 5, 1832	3	277
Emma O., m. Israel F. **PARSONS**, of New Bedford,		
May 18, 1845, by Tho[ma]s J. Greenwood	4	119
Harriet, d. [John & Elizabeth], b. Jan. 28, 1823	3	277
Jane Maria, d. [John & Elizabeth], b Feb. 16, 1825	3	277
John, m. Elizabeth **KETTLE**, Jan. [ ], 1810	3	277

	Vol.	Page

SIMMONS, SIMONS (cont.)

	Vol.	Page
John, m. Rebecca **MALADA**, Apr. 7, 1839, by Rev. Abraham Holway	4	85
Leonard, s. [John & Elizabeth], b. Jan. 15, 1811	3	277
Lucinda, d. [Chapman & Elizabeth], b. Apr. 1, 1788	3	281
Maria, d. [Chapman & Elizabeth], b. Feb. 11, 1799	3	281
Mary Ann, d. [John & Elizabeth], b. Sept. 5, 1814	3	277
Mary Ann, m. Franklin **CLIFFORD**, Feb. 6, 1835, by Abel T. Sizer, J.P.	4	59
Nancy d. [Chapman & Elizabeth], b Nov. 26, 1785	3	281
Nancy, d. [John & Elizabeth], b. Feb. 20, 1827	3	277
Patty, d. [Chapman & Elizabeth], b. Apr. 30, 1791	3	281
Ruhama, d. Eb[eneze]r & Rebecca, b. July 22, 1736	2	35
Ruamini, of New London, d. Eben[eze]r, of New London, m. William **WALDEN**, of Bristol, Gt. Britain, Aug. 5, 1754	2	71
Sally, d. [John & Elizabeth], b. Jan. 15, 1816	3	277
Samuel, b. in London, now of New London, m. Sarah **CHAPMAN**, d. Ezekiel, of New London, Feb. 24, 1756	2	33
Sarah, d. Samuel & Sarah, b. Nov. 6, 1757	2	33
Sarah, d. [Chapman & Elizabeth], b. Jan. 29, 1781	3	281
William, s. [Chapman & Elizabeth], b. June 6, 1795	3	281
William Picket, s. [Chapman & Elizabeth], b. May 27, 1803	3	281

SIMMS, John, of Canterbury, m. Julia **TREBY**, of New London, Oct. 30, 1822, by Thomas W Tucker, Elder · 4 · 10

SIMONS, [see under **SIMMONS**]

SIMPSON, Laura Ann, m. James **WILLIAMS**, b. of [New London], Mar. 29, 1846, by Rev. Abel McEwen · 4 · 125

SIRLES, [see under **SEARLS**]

SISK, Robert, m. Eliza **HENNESSY**, Dec. 29 ,1848, by Rev. William Logan · 4 · 150

SISSON, Abiga[i]ll, d. [Joseph & Elizabeth], b. May 22, 1791 · 3 · 98

	Vol.	Page
Charles H., m. Lucy **POWERS**, Mar. 24, 1839, by James M. Macdonald	4	86
Charles Hempste[a]d, [s. Joseph & Elizabeth], b. July 15, 1795	3	98
Elizabeth, d. [Joseph & Elizabeth], b. Jan. 4, 1800	3	98
Frances, d. [Joseph & Elizabeth], b. Feb. 15, 1806	3	98
Harriet, d. [Joseph & Elizabeth], b. Aug. 17, 1803	3	98
Harriet, of New London, m. Charles **FLAGG**, of Boston, Sept. 23, 1828, by Rev. Abel McEwen	4	34
Harriet F., m. Jason **BECKWITH**, Jr., b. of New London, Apr. 12, 1849, by Rev. Edwin R. Warren	4	148
Joseph, m. Elizabeth **SMITH**, Apr. 27, 1788	3	98
Joseph Francis, [s. Joseph & Elizabeth], b. Apr. 26, 1793	3	98

	Vol.	Page
SISSON (cont.)		
Oliver, s. [Joseph & Elizabeth], b. Sept. 20, 1797	3	98
Polly Park, d. [Joseph & Elizabeth], b. May 22, 1789	3	98
Sabra, d. [Joseph & Elizabeth], b. Oct. 30, 1801	3	98
William, s. [Joseph & Elizabeth], b. July 22, 1808	3	98
William, Capt. m. Elizabeth **MAHONEY**, Oct. 3, 1842, by H. R. Knapp	4	103
SISTARE, Burr, s. [Francis & Sally], b. Apr. 10, 1810	3	231
Burr, m. Abby D. **CHAP[P]EL[L]**, of New London, May 29, 1831, by Rev. Abel McEwen	4	42
Catherine, d. [Joseph & Nancy], b. Nov. 26, 1804	3	150
Delia A.*, [d. Joseph & Nancy] *(Written in pencil with no other data given)	3	150
Don Carloas, s. [Gabriel & Fanny], b. Aug. 5, 1797	3	156
Evando, s. [Joseph & Nancy], b. Apr. 2, 1803	3	150
Frances, d. [Gabriel & Fanny], b. Nov. 10, 1801	3	156
Frances E.*, [child of Joseph &Nancy] *(Written in pencil with no other data given)	3	150
Francis, m. Sally **BURR**, d. George, of Hartford, July 30, 1809	2	231
Gabriel, m. Fanny **CHEW**, d. Joseph, Aug. 3, 1786	3	156
Gabriel, s. [Gabriel & Fanny], b. May 2, 1788	3	156
George King, s. [Joseph & Nancy], b. July 12, 1809	3	150
Horace, s. [Joseph & Nancy], b. Nov. 4, 1807	3	150
John Way, s. [Joseph & Nancy], b. Apr. 5, 1796	3	150
Joseph, m. Nancy **WAY**, d. Capt. John Way, Feb. 1, 1795, by Rev. Henry Channing	3	150
Joseph C., m. Mary **CHRISTOPHERS**, May 2, 1824	3	147
Joseph Chew, s. [Gabriel & Fanny], b. Sept. 22, 1790	3	156
Joseph S., m. Mary **CHRISTOPHERS**, b. of New London, May 2, 1824, by Rev. B. Judd	4	18
Leonard Vallum, s. [Joseph & Nancy], b. Mar. 29, 1798	3	150
Lucy Way, d. [Joseph & Nancy], b. Nov. 28, 1800	3	150
Marer Hpa. Molas, d. [Gabriel & Fanny], b. Oct. 6, 1798	3	156
Sarah L.*, [d. Joseph & Nancy] *(Written in pencil with no other data given)	3	150
William Molas, s. [Gabriel & Fanny], b. July 2, 1794	3	156
SIZER, Abel T., s. [Jonathan & Mary], b. July 2, 1799	3	169
Abel T., m. Hannah **TREAT**, Apr. 25, 1822	3	168
Asahel T., s. [Samuel & Mary], b. July 5, 1804	3	200
Betsey, d. [Jonathan & Elizabeth], b. Apr. 20, 1781	3	169
Charles Olmste[a]d, s. [Abel T. & Hannah], b. [ ]	3	168
Daniel Goddard, s. [Jonathan & Mary], b. May 22, 1798; d. Mar. 22, 1799	3	169
Elizabeth, w. Jonathan, d. Sept. 25, 1795	3	169
Elizabeth Ellen, d. [Abel T. & Hannah], b. [ ]	3	168
Harriet Ann, d. [Abel T. & Hannah], b. [ ]	3	168

	Vol.	Page

SIZER (cont.)

Isaac S., m. Lydia C. **POTTER**, b. of New London,
June 2, 1822, by William Stockman, J.P. — 4 — 8

Isaac Sheffield, s. [Samuel & Mary], b. Oct. 16, 1801 — 3 — 200

Jane Maria, d. [Abel T. & Hannah], b. Feb. 19, 1823 — 3 — 168

Jane Maria, of New London, m. William E. **COIT**, of
Norwich, June 13, 1842, by Rev. A. Boies — 4 — 100

John Goddard Thompson, s. [Samuel & Mary]., b.
Oct. 22, 1806 — 3 — 200

Jonathan, b. Sept. 17, 1758; m. Elizabeth **PELTON**,
Nov. 29, 1778 — 3 — 169

Jonathan, s. [Jonathan & Elizabeth], b. June 8,
1785; d. Nov. 25, 1786 — 3 — 169

Jonathan, m. Mary **THOMPSON**, Dec. 3, 1795 — 3 — 169

Jonathan, s. [Samuel & Mary], b. Feb. 14, 1800 — 3 — 200

Jonathan, 2d, m. Sarah **WAY**, b. of New London,
June 24, 1826, by Rev. Abel McEwen — 4 — 26

Lydia C., m. Robert **BOWSER**, May 11, 1834, by
Th[omas] S. Perkins, J.P. — 4 — 56

Martha J., of New London, m. George A. **POTTER**,
of Norwich, Oct. 28, 1848, by Rev. Tho[ma]s J.
Greenwood — 4 — 142

Mary, d. [Jonathan & Mary], b. Dec. 27, 1796; d.
Oct. 14, 1797 — 3 — 169

Mary, m. John **DOUGLASS**, Dec. 9, 1826, by
Robert Bowzer — 4 — 27

Mary Augusta, d. [Abel T. & Hannah], b. Sept. 28,
1824 — 3 — 168

Mary E., m. David A. **POLLOCK**, b. of [New
London], June 29, 1852, by Rev. Abel McEwen — 4 — 168

Olive, of New London, m. William **CULVER**, of
Hebron, June 1, 1823, by Thomas W. Tucker,
Elder — 4 — 14

Samuel, s. [Jonathan & Elzabeth], b. Sept. 2, 1779 — 3 — 169

Samuel, b, Sept. [ ], 1779; m. Mary **TREBY**, May
26, 1799 — 3 — 200

Thomas S., m. Maria **MITCHELL**, Sept. 29, 1844,
by Rev. Tho[ma]s J. Greenwood — 4 — 116

Timothy, Jr., m. Martha **LYMAN**, b. of New
London, Nov. 25, 1824, by Rev. Abel McEwen — 4 — 20

SKELINKS, Amy, of East Hampton, d. Abraham, decd.,
m. Joshua **PLUMBE**, s. John, of New London,
Nov. 11, 1723 — 2 — 73

Amy, m. Joshua **PLUMBE**, Nov. 11, 1723 — 2 — 81

SKINNER, Benjamin F., m. Julia Ann **COMSTOCK**, b.
of New London, Apr. 2, 1843, by Rev. R. W.
Allen — 4 — 102

Eliza Ann, twin with Sarah Jane, d. [John & Anna],
b. July 25, 1801 — 3 — 199

Eliza H., m. John **HUNTINGTON**, b. of [New
London], Aug. 31, 1823, by Rev. Thomas W.
Tucker — 4 — 16

	Vol.	Page

SKINNER (cont.)

Eunice, of New London, m. Nelson P. **DOUGLASS**, of Norwich, June 30, 1844, by Rev. Thomas J. Greenwood | 4 | 116

James T., m. Harriet Ann **MILLER**, b. of [New London], Feb. 7, 1835, by Ebenezer Blake | 4 | 59

Jane, d. [Joseph & Jane], b. Mar. 15, 1794 | 3 | 101

John, s. Elisabeth, b. Apr. 13, 1782 | 3 | 128

John, s. Elizabeth, m. Anna **BROOKS**, Feb. 3, 1800 | 3 | 199

John M., m. Sarah **CHIPMAN**, b. of [New London], Dec. 5, 1847, by Rev. M. P. Alderman | 4 | 136

Joseph, m. Jane **STARK**, July 23, 1787 | 3 | 101

Joseph, s. [Joseph & Jane], b. July 26, 1788 | 3 | 101

Laura A., m. Lafayette **BURDICK**, Oct. 11, 1847, by Rev. Tho[ma]s Greenwood | 4 | 136

Margaret P., of [New London], m. James **SWEET**, of Providence, R.I., Oct. 27, 1833, by Rev. Ebenezer Blake | 4 | 52

Mary, m. Christopher **BILL**, b. of [New London], Feb. 6, 1827, by Rob[er]t Bowzer | 4 | 29

Mary Elizabeth, d. [John & Anna], b. Mar. 6, 1804 | 3 | 199

Rebecca, of [New London], m. William **SWEET**, of Providence, R.I., July 24, 1831, by Rev. Alpheus Hayden | 4 | 43

Ruth E., m. Edmund **HOWARD**, b. of New London, Oct. 23, 1843, by Rev. S. Benton | 4 | 108

Sarah Ellen, d. J. M. & Sarah, b. Oct. 3, 1851 | 3 | 285

Sarah Jane, twin with Eliza Ann, d. [John & Anna], b. July 25, 1801 | 3 | 199

Tacy Berry, d. [John & Anna], b. Dec. 14, 1806 | 3 | 199

Tacy Berry, m. Daniel **KNIGHT**, b. of New London, Aug. 1, 1824, by Rev. Abel McEwen | 4 | 19

SLATE, George R., of Lyme, m. Elizabeth C. **COLLINS**, of N[ew] London, Apr. 25, 1837, by Rev. Squire D. Hascall | 4 | 69

Jeremiah, m. Sophia R. **STEPHENS**, May 14, 1837, by Rev. Robert A. Hallam | 4 | 69

SLATER, Abigail, m. Stephen **PRENTIS**, Apr. 8, 1783 | 3 | 138

Amey, d. Zorobabel, m. Samuel **BECKWITH**, Nov. 20, 1800 | 3 | 166

SLIDER, **SLYDER**, Elizabeth, m. Peter **IMMICH**, b. of [New London], Mar. 30, 1851, by Rev. T. Edwards | 4 | 161

Henry L., m. Delia L. **POTTER**, b. of New London, June 19, 1849, by Rev. Geo[rge] M. Carpenter | 4 | 146

SLIP, James, of New London, m. Nancy **LAM**(?), of Groton, Nov. 11, 1833, by Rev. Abel McEwen | 4 | 53

SLYDER, [see under **SLIDER**]

SMALL, Ch. S., m. Sarah Delia **MANWARING**, June 27, 1857 | 3 | 202

Fanny Manwaring, d. [Ch. S. & Sarah Delia], b. May 2, [1858]; d. May 8, 1858 | 3 | 202

	Vol.	Page
SMELL, Emma W., of [New London], m. Alonzo **HUNT**, of New Bedford, Mass., Aug. 31, 1835, by Rev. Robert A. Hallam	4	61
SMITH, Abby Ann, m. Thomas **FITCH**, 2d, b. of [New London], Oct. 15, 1836, by Rev. Abel McEwen	4	76
Abby Ann, of Montville, m. Daniel Smith **AYRES**, of New London, Feb. 3, 1842, by Rev. R. W. Allen	4	97
Abel, s. [Joseph & Zerviah], b. Apr. 1, 1785	3	49
Abigail, d. [James & Abigail], b. June 28, 1757	3	87
Abigail, m. Thaddeus **BROOKS**, Mar. 10, 1776	3	73
Acros Sheffield, s. [Hezekiah B. & Maria], b. Mar. 10, 1823	3	248
Alford, m. Emmeline **MALLORY**, b. of [New London], Aug. 26, 1827, by Henry Wightman	4	32
Amy, d. Joseph & Zerviah, b. Mar. 12, 1769	3	49
Ann, d. Edward & Elizabeth, b. Oct. 25, [1665]	1	4
Ann E., m. Francis W. **LANE**, b. of [New London], June 13, 1846, by John Howson	4	130
Ana, m. Jonathan **CALKINS**, Dec. 29, 1791	3	111
Anson, m. Amy **DARROW***, May 4, 1817 *("**BECKWITH**" written in pencil)	3	245
Anthony, m. Mary **HALE**, b. of New London, Mar. 27, 1846, by Rev. L. Geo[rge] Leonard	4	125
Asena, d. Jonathan & Sarah, b. Octt. 14, 1766	3	39
Augusta C., m. Phineas C. **WILCOX**, Sept. 2, 1845, by Rev. Francis Darrow	4	121
Avery, s. [Daniel, Jr. & Hannah], b. June 20, 1794	3	122
Azubah, d. Josiah Smith, of Lyme, m. Joseph **BEEBE**, of New London, Dec. 27, 1789, in Lyme, by Andrew Griswold, J.P.	2	123
Bathsheba, m. John **ROGERS**, Jr., Jan. 2, 1700	1	34
Betsey, d. [Joseph & Lydia], b. Mar. 16, 1786	3	140
Betsey, d. [James, Jr. & Betsey], b. May 10, 1795	3	179
Betsey, m. Richard **COMSTOCK**, b. of New London, Dec. 6, 1838, by Rev. C. C. Williams	4	81
Betty, d. Joseph & Zerviah, b. Oct. 16, 1771	3	49
Bill, s. Daton & Marcy, b. Feb. 15, 1753	2	109
Catharine, d. [James & Abigail], b. Jan. 1, 1776	3	87
Catharine, m. Elihu **CROCKER**, Nov. 16, 1799	3	82
Catherine, d. [Ebenezer & Nancy], b. Dec. 3, 1806	3	222
Chandler, of New York, m. Mary E. **BURBECK**, of New London, Apr. 22, 1851, by Rev. Robert A. Hallam	4	161
Charles, s. [Joseph, 2d, & Anne], b. Oct. 18, 1791; d. Dec. 31, 1792	3	125
Charles, s. [David & Lucretia], b. June 10, 1813	3	163
Charles, m. Ellen **GOODRICH**, Apr. 7, 1849, by Rev. Charles Willett	4	145
Charles, of Waterford, m. Pamela **HARRIS**, of N[ew] London, Feb. 2, 1854, by Chester Tilden	4	54

	Vol.	Page
SMITH (cont.)		
Charles H., of Stonington, m. Ann S. **FRENCH**, of New London, Oct. 3, 1844, by Rev Tho[ma]s J. Greenwood	4	116
Charles T., of [New London], m. Ann Elizabeth **HILL**, of Groton, May 15, 1845, by Rev. Robert Hallam	4	119
Charlotte, d. Nathan, m. Simeon **SMITH**, May 13, 1784, at Groton	3	151
Charlotte, d. [Simeon & Charlotte], b. Feb. 24, 1785, at Groton	3	151
Charlotte, w. Simeon, d. Jan. 26, 1791	3	151
Charlotte, d. [Simeon], d. July 14, 1800	3	151
Clarine, d. Capt. Stephen, m. Clement **FOSDICK**, Oct. 22, 1786	3	105
Clarranda, d. [Simeon & Charlotte], b. Dec. 3, 1786, at Groton	3	151
Danyell, s. Nehemiah & Lidia, b. 8ber 28, 16[ ]	1	67
Danyell, s. Nehemiah & Lydia, b. Nov. 29, [1680]	1	14
Daniel, Jr., m. Hannah **WHITMAN**, Aug. 31, 1786	3	122
Daniel, s. [Daniel, Jr. & Hannah], b. Feb. 4, 1788	3	122
Daton, m. Marcy, d. Samuel & Hannah **BILL**, May 11, 1746	2	109
David, s. Jonathan & Sarah, b. May 7, 1735	2	105
David, had negro servant Necho, s. Nancy, b. May 10, 1786	3	104
David, m. Lucretia **CAULKINS**, Sept. 19, 1799	3	163
David, s. [David & Lucretia], b. Dec. 16, 1810	3	163
Ebenezer, m. Nancy **DENNIS**, relict of John Dennis, July 22, 1803	3	222
Edward, of New London, m. Elizabeth, d. Thomas **BLISS**, of Norridge, June 7, [1663]	1	4
Edward, d. July 14, 1689, 4 days after his wife	1	69
Edwine, s. [Simeon & Mary], b. June 25, 1796; d. Feb. 12 ,1798	3	151
Edwin H., of Essex, m. Philena **WHITTEMORE**, July 30, 1845, by Rev. G. Thompson	4	121
Eleshiba, d. Hezekiah Smith, m. Timothy **MUNSELL**, s. John, all of Lyme, Feb. 11, 1768	3	45
Elijah, m. Lydia **ROGERS**, Apr. 10, 1788	3	126
Eliza, d. [Simeon & Mary], b. Nov. 1, 1798; d. Feb. 2, 1799	3	151
Elizabeth, d. Nehemyah, m. Joshuah **RAYMOND**, s. Richard, of Salem, Dec. 10, [1659]	1	3
Elizabeth, d. Edward & Eliza, b. Aug. 16, [1664]	1	4
Elizabeth, d. James & Susannah, b. May 6, 1733	2	104
Elizabeth, d. Jonathan & Sarah, b. Jan. 11, 1736/7	2	105
Elizabeth, d. Josiah & Abigail, b. Nov. 3, 1754	2	120
Elizabeth, d. Jona[than], b. of New London, m. Mather **TURNER**, Feb. 14, 1760	2	101
Elisabeth, d. [James & Abigail], b. Oct. 21, 1765	3	87

	Vol.	Page
SMITH (cont.)		
Elisabeth, m. Sylvester **POWERS**, Nov. 11, 1784	3	103
Elizabeth, m. Joseph **SISSON**, Apr. 27, 1788	3	98
Elizabeth, d. Luther, of Plainfield, m. Ebenezer Pemberton **CADY**, Mar. 18, 1806	3	191
Elizabeth Turner, m. Lodowick **FOSDICK**, May 12, 1811, by Rev. Charles Seabury	3	241
Ephraim, m. Mary **WEEKS**, Aug. 13, 1786	3	18
Ephraim, s. [Ephraim & Mary], b. Nov. 26, 1788	3	18
Erastus, m. Fanny **RICHARDS**, b. of New London, Oct. 5, 1820, by Rev. Abel McEwen	4	1
Eunice, d. [Daniel & Hannah], b. May 1, 1765	3	110
Eunice, d. [Stephen & Jemima], b. July 11, 1782	3	107
Eunice, m. Isaac **DELONG**, b. of New London, Dec. 25, 1830, by Rev. Abel McEwen	4	40
Ezra, s. Joseph & Zerviah, b. Mar. 6, 1775	3	49
Ezra Chappell, s. [Henry & Fanny L.], b. Aug. 19, 1828	3	267
Fanny, m. William **BRIGGS**, Feb. 14, 1782	3	76
Fanny, d. [Stephen & Jemima], b. July 1, 1788	3	107
Fanny, m. John **BEETZ**, b. of New London, Dec. 3, 1826, by Rev. Bethel Judd	4	28
Fanny C., m. James **NICHOLS**, b. of New London, Oct. 5, 1845, by Rev. Jabez S. Swan	4	122
Frances, of New London, m. John **PECKHAM**, of Philadelphia, May 2, 1823, by T. W. Tucker, Elder	4	14
Frances, m. Silas **MANWARING**, Dec. 4, 1831, by Rev. Francis Darrow	4	44
Frances Frankling, d. [James, J. & Betsey], b. May 10, 1803	3	179
Frances Mary, d. [Jesse D. & Frances T.], b. July 30, 1816	3	252
Francis W., of [New London], m. William C. **BOLLES**, of Boston, Mass., Nov. 22, 1841, by Rev. Robert A. Hallam	4	116
Franklin F., m. Mary C. **CHAP[P]EL[L]**, b. of New London, May 23, 1830, by Rev. Abel McEwen	4	38
Gad, of East Haddam, m. Nancy **CONE**, of [New London], Jan. 31, 1838, by Rev. James M. Macdonald	4	75
Gardner, s. Jonathan, Jr. & Sarah, b. July 24, 1774	3	39
Genney, d. Benjaman & Genney, b. June 9, 1799	3	105
Genny, m. Scipio **ANDERSON**, Jan. 1, 1803	3	104
George, eldest, s. of George & Rachall, b. Mar. 15, 1696	1	24
George, m. Thankfull **TOMBLING**, June 5, 1720	1	63
George, Jr., of New London, m. Anna **CHAPMAN**, of Lyme, Mar. 3, 1793, by Andrew Griswold, J.P., in Lyme	2	124
George Nelson, s. [David & Lucretia], b. Aug. 2, 1818	3	163

	Vol.	Page
SMITH (cont.)		
George Washington, s. Joseph & Zerviah, b Aug. 15, 1780	3	49
Giles L., of Essex, m. Mary **CLARK**, d. John, of New London, Aug. 2, [1847], by Rev. Tryon Edwards	4	133
Gurdon, s. John & Mary, b. June 12, 1770	3	52
Gurdon B., m. Lucy G. **HALLET**, b. of New London, Sept. 10, 1843, by Jabez S. Swan	4	111
Gustavus W., of U. S. Corps of Engineers, m. Lucretia S. **BASSETT**, of New London ,Oct. 3, 1844, by Rev. Abel McEwen	4	114
Hamilton Lanphear, s. [Anson & Amy], b. Nov. 5, 1818	3	245
Hanna[h], d. Edw[ar]d & Elizabeth, b. Oct. 5, [1678]	1	13
Hannah, d. [James & Abigail], b. Mar. 24, 1761	3	87
Hannah, d. Daniel & Hannah, b. Sept. 18, 1762	3	110
Hannah, d. Joseph & Zerviah, b. Feb. 9, 1778	3	49
Hannah, m. John **ROGERS**, Oct. 8, 1782	3	114
Hannah, d. [Daniel, Jr & Hannah], b. May 8, 1790	3	122
Hannah, d. [James, Jr. & Betsey], b. Sept. 6, 1796	3	179
Hannah B., m. John **RICE**, b. of New London, July 8, 1820, by Rev. Abel McEwen	4	1
Harriet, of New London, m. James **ROGERS**, of Montville, Ct., May 19, 1846, by Rev. John Howson	4	126
Henry, m. Fanny **NORRIS**, Feb. 16, 1788	3	60
Henry, s. [Henry & Fanny], b. Oct. 13, 1788	3	60
Henry, s. [Simeon & Charlotte], b. May [ ], 1789	3	151
Henry, m. Fanny L. **ARNOLD**, Dec. 16, 1825	3	267
Henry, m. Fanny D. **ARNOLD**, b. of New London, Dec. 16, 1825, by Rev. Abel McEwen	4	25
Henry, m. Sarah A. **BROWN**, b. of [New London], Oct. 23, 1847, by Rev. Abel McEwen	4	135
Henry Arnold, s. [Henry & Fanny L.], b. Mar. 71, 1830	3	267
Hezekiah, s. [Paul & Mary], b. July 24, 1765	3	111
Hezekiah B., m. Maria **KEEN[E]Y**, May 19, 1822	3	248
Hezekiah G., of East Haddam, m. Maria **KEEN[E]Y**, of New London, May 19, 1822, by Rev. Abel McEwen	4	8
Jacob, m Phebe **SHEPARD**, b. of [New London], May 11, 1834, by Rev. Ebenezer Blake	4	56
James, m. Elizabeth **ROGERS**, b. of New Haven, Jan. 8, 1701/2	1	26
James, s. James & Elizabeth, b. Mar. 23 ,1703	1	29
James, m. Abigail **HEMPSTE[A]D**, Nov. 12, 1756	3	87
James, s. [James & Abigail], b. Apr. 24, 1768	3	87
James, s. Jona[than], Jr. & Sarah, b. Mar. 13, 1769	3	39
James, Jr., m. Betsey **BROWN**, d. Whe[e]lor Brown, May 10, 1791	3	179
James, s. [James, Jr. & Betsey], b. Mar. 21, 1800	3	179

	Vol.	Page

SMITH (cont.)

James, s. [David & Lucretia], b. Nov. 4, 1808; d.
Nov. 25, 1809 — 3 — 163

James D., m. Sarah M. **WILLIAMS**, b. of New
London, Oct. 18, 1848, by H. Brownson,
V.D.M. — 4 — 144

James Daniels, s. [Hezekaih B. & Maria], b. June 22,
1827 — 3 — 248

Jane, m. Alanson **STEWART**, b. of New London,
Sept. 20, 1846, by Rev. Jabez S. Swan — 4 — 127

Jemima, d. [Stephen & Jemima], b. Aug. 6, 1784 — 3 — 107

Jennie, see under Genney

Jeremiah, m. Sarah **SMITH**, July 9, 1850, by Rev.
Charles Willett — 4 — 154

Jesse D., m. Frances T. **ALLEN**, July 26, 1815 — 3 — 252

Job, s. [Stephen & Jemima], b. Apr. 1, 1786 — 3 — 107

John, s. Edward & Elizabeth, b. Dec. 28, [1674] — 1 — 9

John, s. Edward, d. July 8, [1689], ae 15 y. — 1 — 69

John, s. John & Deliverance, b. Nov. 15, 1728 — 2 — 3

John, s. Daton & Marcy, b. Mar. 7, 1747 — 2 — 109

John, s. John, of Lyme, decd., m. Mary **WAY**, of
New London, d. Daniel, Feb. 21, 1762 — 3 — 52

John, s. John & Mary, b. July 3, 1767 — 3 — 52

John, m. Cath[arine] **MANGAN**, Oct. 27, [18]50,
[by Peter J. Blenkinsop]. Witnesses: Timothy
Robasney, Ellen Robasney — 3 — 306

John, m. Catharine **MANGAN**, Oct. 27, 1850.
Witnesses: Timothy Robasney, Ellen Robasney — 4 — 159

John A., m. Mary A. **BOND**, Nov. 10, 1850, by Rev.
Charles Willett — 4 — 157

John Hempste[a]d, s. [James, Jr. & Betsey], b. Feb.
26, 1792 — 3 — 179

John R., s. [Anson & Amy], b. Nov. 24, 1820 — 3 — 245

John S., m. Mary **GILBERT**, Nov. 14, 1838, by Rev.
Abraham Holway — 4 — 85

John W., of Durham, m. Elizabeth J. **BATES**, of
Glastonbury, July 4, 1848, by Rev. Giles H.
Deshon, of Glastonbury — 4 — 140

Jonathan, m. Sarah **GARDINER**, of South Kingston,
Aug. 24, 1732 — 2 — 104

Jonathan, m. Sarah **GARDINER**, of South Kingston,
Aug. 24, 1732 — 2 — 105

Jonathan, s. Jonathan & Sarah, b. Nov. 5, 1733 — 2 — 105

Jonathan, Jr., s. Jonathan, m. Sarah **COMSTOCK**, d.
Nath[anie]ll, b. of New London, Nov. 13, 1755 — 3 — 39

Jonathan, s. Jonathan & Sarah, b. Feb. 21, 1759 — 3 — 39

Jonathan W., m. Betsey **LEWIS**, Oct. 10, 1823, by
Asa Dutton, J.P. — 4 — 16

Joseph, m. Elizabeth **HARRIS**, Apr. 5, 1726 — 2 — 104

Joseph, 2d, b. Oct. 3, 1762; m. Anne **LEWIS**, May 7,
1786 — 3 — 125

Joseph, s. Joseph & Zerviah, b. July 6, 1766 — 3 — 49

	Vol.	Page

SMITH (cont.)

Joseph, m. Mercy **FERGO**, Nov. 2, 1775	3	106
Joseph, m. Lydia **TURNER**, Feb. 20, 1785	3	140
Joseph, d. Sept. 19, 1787	3	106
Joseph, 2d, d. Feb. 7, 1793	3	125
Joseph, s. [Joseph & Lydia], b. June 30, 1800	3	140
Joseph, m. Eliza **STANTON**, b. of [New London], Mar. 16, 1849, by Rev. M. P. Alderman	4	145
Joseph, s. Nehemiah, d. Aug. 19, [1689], ae 4 y.	1	69
Josiah, s. John, m. Abigail **BEEBE**, d. Joseph, all of New London, Sept. [ ], 175[ ]	2	120
King, s. [Paul & Mary], b. Oct. 1, 1760	3	111
Linas B., Dr., of New York, m. Frances A **RATHBUN**, of Lyme, Ct., Sept. 16, 1851, by Rev. T. Edwards	4	164
Lorenzo K., of Waterford, m. Sally Ann **SMITH**, of New London, Feb. 6, 1833, by Chester Tilden	4	50
Louisa H., m. John Henry **LESTER**, b. of [New London], Feb. 20, 1844, by Rev. Robert A. Hallam	4	110
Lucy, d. [James & Abigail], b. Nov. 27, 1770	3	87
Lucy, d. [Joseph & Mercy], b. Oct. 22, 1778	3	106
Lucy, d. James, m. John **COIT**, Dec. 3, 1789	3	156
Lucy, m. Nehemiah **DODGE**, June 15, 1794	3	127
Lucey, d. Josiah, m. James **DAVISON**, May 22, 1808	3	204
Lydia, d. Nehemia[h] & Lydia, b. Oct. 29, [1670]	1	7
Lydia, d. [Paul & Mary], b. Nov. 23, 1762	3	111
Lydia, d. Nehemiah, of New London, m. Jonathan **CALKINS**, s. Thomas, decd., Apr. 24, 1764	3	37
Lydia, d. [Stephen & Abiga[I]ll, b. Sept. 22, 1800	3	171
Lydia Ann, d. [David & Lucretia], b. May 6, 1801	3	163
Margaret, d. George & Thankfull, b. Sept. 15, 1722	1	63
Mark Stoddard, s. [Daniel, Jr & Hannah], b. June 27, 1792	3	122
Mark W., m. Elizabeth **GETCHEL**, Sept. 10, 1835, by Rev. Alven Ackley	4	62
Martha, d. Nehemiah & Lydia, b. Oct. 15, [1678]	1	13
Mary, d. Edward & Elizabeth, b. Nov. 28, [1672]	1	8
Mary, d. Nehemiah, of Lyme, m. Oliver **MANWARING**, Jr., s. Oliver, of New London, Nov. 10, 1743	2	35
Mary, d. Daton & Marcy, b. Mar. 23, 1751/2	2	109
Mary, d. Jethro Smith, of New London, m. Lancaster **COMSTOCK**, s. Gideon, decd., May 2, 1754	3	5
Mary, d. [James & Abigail], b. May 30, 1763	3	87
Mary, m. Asa **HOLT**, b. of New London, Apr. 7, 1785, by Andrew Griswold, J.P.	3	86
Mary, m. William **WHEAT**, Mar. 15, 1789	3	112
Mary, d. Joseph & Anna, b. Oct. 14, 1789	3	25
Mary, d. [Simeon & Mary], b. Oct. 15, 1794	3	151
Mary, w. [Simeon], d. Mar. 17, 1799	3	151

	Vol.	Page
SMITH (cont.)		
Mary, m. Eley **BEEBE**, Oct. 18, 1807	3	153
Mary, m .Henry **CANELL**, b. of New London, May 7, 1830, by Rev. Abel McEwen	4	38
Mary, m. Henry **BISHOP**, b. of New London, Feb. 21, 1842, by Rev. Lemuel Covell	4	99
Mary A., of [New London], m. Rowland **SEARS**, of Whitesborough, N.Y., Nov. 12, 1837, by Rev. Abel McEwen	4	74
Mary A., m. William R. **BROWN**, Feb. 7, 1834	3	294
Mary A., m. William R. **BROWN**, b. of New London, Feb. 7, 1834, by Rev. Abel McEwen	4	54
Mary Ann, d. [David & Lucretia], b. May 19, 1806	3	163
Mary Ann, of [New London], m. Asahel **BURROWS**, of Groton, Jan. 1, 1824, by Tho[ma]s W. Tucker, Minister	4	17
Mary Ann, of Norwich, m. Albert **MILLER**, of Wallingford, Oct. 5, 1844, by Rev. Jabez S. Swan	4	114
Mary D., m. Lewis **ALLEN**, Sept. 18, 1805, at Groton	3	252
Mary E., of New London, m. James **HALL**, of Portsmouth, R.I., July 28, 1844, by Rev. Jabez S. Swan	4	113
Mat[t]hew, s. George & Rachall, b. Nov. 27, 1698	1	24
Mercy, m. Joseph **PHILLIPS**, Dec. 7, 1778	3	12
Mercy, m. Thomas **FERGO**, Mar. 25, 1779	3	106
Merrett, of New London, s. William Henry Smith, of Long Island, N.Y., m. Mary **HILL**, of Fairfield, d. of Thomas Hill, of Fairfield, Nov. 6, 1745	2	108
Molly, d. [Paul & Mary], b. Sept. 24, 1748	3	111
Nancy, d. [Joseph, 2d, & Anne], b. Jan. 27, 1787; d. Aug. 19, 1788	3	125
Nathaniel, s. Jonathan & Sarah, b. Mar. 9, 1764	3	39
Nehemyall, s. Nehemia[h], m. Lidia, d. Alexander **WINCHESTER**, of Roxbury, Oct. 24, [1669]	1	6
Nehemiah, s. Nehe[mia]h & Lydia, b. Nov. 14, [1673]	1	9
Nicholas L., of New London, m. Harriet A. **BECKWITH**, of East Lyme, Jan. 3, 1847, by Rev. Jabez S. Swan	4	129
Noah, s. [John & Mary], b. Dec. 24, 1775	3	52
Obadia[h], s. Edward & Elizabeth, b. Feb. 5, [1676]	1	11
Parker, s. James & Susannah, b. Aug. 2, 1730	2	104
Parker, s. [James, Jr. & Betsey], b. May 1, 1798	3	179
Parker H., m. Mary **STOCKMAN**, b. of New London, June 24, 1827, by Robert Bowzer, Pastor	4	31
Parker H., m. Nancy **LESTER**, b. of [New London], Sept. 8, 1839, by J. Lovejoy	4	87
Patty, d. [James, Jr. & Betsey], b. Sept. 25, 1801	3	179
Paul, m. Mary **KING**, Oct. [ ], 1746	3	111

	Vol.	Page

SMITH (cont.)

Peregreene, s. Jonathan & Sarah, b. Dec. 1, 1746; d.
    Aug. 26, 1751 — 2, 105

Peregreen, s. Jonathan & Sarah, b. Aug. 15, 1761; d.
    Feb. 6, 1772 — 3, 39

Polly, d. [Ephraim & Mary], b. Dec. 3, 1786 — 3, 18

Polly, d. [Joseph, 2d, & Anne], b. Oct. 14, 1788 — 3, 125

Priscilla A., of New London, m. William P.
    FERGUSON, of New York, Dec. 20, 1846, by
    Rev. Jabez S. Swan — 4, 128

Rachel, d. Ma[t]thew, of Lyme, m. William **BEEBE**,
    3d, s. William, 2d, of New London, Apr. 16,
    1749 — 2, 72

Rebecca, d. Edward & Mary*, b. Aug. 5, [1668]
    *(Changed to Elizabeth by L. B. B.) — 1, 6

Richard, of New London, s. John, m. Barsheba
    TRIPP, of North Kingston, d. of Job, June 6,
    1741 — 2, 99

Richard, s. Richard & Bathshua*, b. Oct. 24, 1743
    *(Barsheba) — 2, 99

Richard H., of the U.S. A., m. Elizabeth R.
    RODGERS, of [New London], Nov. 6, 1850,
    by Rev. Robert A. Hallam — 4, 160

Robert, s. Daton & Marcy, b. Mar. 10, 1757 — 2, 109

Robert, from Stewartstown, County of Tyrone,
    Ireland, m. Grace **HARRIS**, d. John & Eliza,
    July 14, 1782 — 3, 68

Robert, of Philadelphia, m. Sally Ann **WADE**, of
    [New London], June 6, 1842, by Rev. J. W.
    True — 4, 102

Robert Brown, s. [James, Jr. & Betsey], b. Sept. 20,
    1793 — 3, 179

Robert N., of Portland, Maine, m. Emeline **BOLLES**,
    of New London, Mar. 11, 1832, by Rev. Abel
    McEwen — 4, 15

Ruama, d. [Daniel & Hannah], b. Feb. 3, 1769 — 3, 110

Sabin, m. Susan C. **POTTER**, b. of [New London],
    Sept. 18, 1844, by Rev. Abel McEwen — 4, 113

Sabin K., m. Hannah **MOORE**, Feb. 3, 1832, by
    Rev. Francis Darrow — 4, 45

Sally, d. [Paul & Mary], b. [   ], 1758 — 3, 111

Sally, d. [Ephraim & Mary], b. Dec. 14, 1790 — 3, 18

Sally, d. [Joseph & Lydia], b. May 12, 1793 — 3, 140

Sally, m. Isaac **CLARK**, of Waterford, Mar. 24,
    1831, by Rev. Leonard B. Griffing — 4, 40

Sally Ann, of New London, m. Lorenzo K. **SMITH**,
    of Waterford, Feb. 6, 1833, by Chester Tilden — 4, 50

Samuel, s. Jeremiah* & Lydia, b. June 2, [1676]
    *(Corrected to "Nehemiah" by L. B. B.) — 1, 11

Samuel, s. Daton & Marcy, b. Feb. 7, 1749/50 — 2, 109

Samuel, s. [David & Lucretia], b. Apr. 19, 1804 — 3, 163

	Vol.	Page

SMITH (cont.)

	Vol.	Page
Sanford B., of Ledyard, m. Ann R. **WALKER**, of New London, Nov. 14, 1840, by Rev. Jared B. Avery	4	93
Sarah, d. Edw[ar]d & Elizabeth, b. Sept. 6, [1670]	1	7
Sarah, d. Daton & Marcy, b. Feb. 27, 1755	2	109
Sarah, d. Jonathan & Sarah, b. Jan. 24, 1757	3	39
Sarah, d. John & Mary, b. Dec. 11, 1762	3	52
Sarah, w. Jonathan, d. May 29, 1774	2	105
Sarah, d. [David & Lucretia], b. Aug. 30, 1802	3	163
Sarah, m. William **DAVIS**, b. of New London, Apr. 28, 1845, by Rev. L. Geo[rge] Leonard	4	123
Sarah, m. Jeremiah **SMITH**, July 9, 1850, by Rev. Charles Willett	4	154
Sarah D., [w. Ch. S.], d. July 10, 1858, at Newark, N.J.	3	202
Sarah E., m. Oliver **STEWART**, b. of New London, Nov. 3, 1845, by Rev. Jabez S. Swan	4	122
Sarah R., m. Thomas J. **AVERY**, June 1, 1836, by Rev. Francis Darrow	4	84
Sidney L., m. Ann **ROATH**, b. of [New London], May 8, 1838, by Rev. Abel McEwen	4	77
Simeon, m. Charlotte **SMITH**, d. Nathan, May 13, 1748, at Groton	3	151
Simeon, m. Mary **AVERY**, Sept. 11, 1792	3	151
Simeon, s. [Henry & Fanny L.], b. Mar. 19, 1827	3	267
Simon, s. [Daniel & Hannah], b. Mar. 7, 1767	3	110
Sophia, [of Groton, d. Moses], b. Oct. 25, 1787	3	189
Sophia, of Groton, d. Moses, m. Richard **HEMPSTE[A]D**, June 1, 1806	3	189
Stephen, s. Jonathan, Jr. & Sarah, b. May 2, 1772	3	39
Stephen, m. Jemima **COOLEDGE**, Feb. 4, 1781	3	107
Stephen, m. Abiga[I]ll **COOMBS**, Jan. 2, 1798	3	171
Suk[e]y, d. [Joseph & Lydia], b. Mar. 24, 1795	3	140
Susan, of [New London], m. Gilbert **POTTER**, of Wilmington, N. C., Nov. 9, 1840, by Rev. Abel McEwen	4	92
Susannah A., of New London, m. Germond **CRANDELL**, of White Plains, N.Y., Dec. 26, 1848, by Rev. Tryon Edwards	4	143
Thomas Merrett, s. Merrett & Mary, b. Dec. [ ], 1746	2	108
Timothy, s. [Daniel, Jr. & Hannah], b. Sept. 18, 1796	3	122
William, s. [David & Lucretia]., b. Nov. 30, 1816	3	163
William, of England, m. Lucy Ann **WILLIS**, of New London, May 14, 1846, by Rev. L. Geo[rge] Leonard	4	129
William B., m. Ellen **COLLINS**, Aug. 1, 1850, by Rev. Charles Willett	4	154
William Henry, s. [Hezekiah B. & Maria], b. Dec.* 31, 1824; d. Oct. 27, 1825 *(First written "April")	3	248

	Vol.	Page
SMITH (cont.)		
William Henry, s. [Hezekiah B. & Maria], b. Apr.		
11, 1826	3	248
William W., m. Jane R. **HAMILTON**, b. of [New		
London], Aug. 5, 1846, by Rev. Tryon Edwards	4	127
Zerviah, m. Benajah **DAVIS**, b. of [New London],		
Sept. 15, 1785, by Jason Lee, Elder, of Lyme	3	80
Zerviah, m. John Valentine **CORNEL**, Mar. 19,		
1796	3	137
-----, w. Edward, d. July 10, [1689]	1	69
-----, d. [Ebenezer & Nancy], b. July 27. 1809	3	222
SNELL, Eliza T., of [New London], m. James **JUDD**, of		
Glastenbury, Aug. 1, 1830, by Daniel Wildman	4	39
SNOW, Abijah R. m. Miranda **PENHARLOW**, b. of New		
London, Oct. 31, 1828, by Nehemiah Dodge	4	35
Eunice A., of [New London], m. W[illia]m M.		
HARRIS, of Canterbury, Dec. 29, 1846, by		
Rev. T. Edwards	4	128
James, s. Dudley & Mary, b. July 1, 1828	3	182
SOLES, SOULES, Charles, m. Dolly **PRENTICE**, d.		
John, Nov. 12, 1792	3	208
Charles, d. Sept. 17, 1798	3	208
Charlotte, d. [Charles & Dolly], b. Sept. 8, 1793	3	208
Charlotte, m. Peter **RENOUF**, June 30, 1816, by		
Rev. Nehemiah Dodge	3	288
Dolly, relict of Charles, m. Frederick **ROBERTS**,		
June 29, 1806	3	208
Elizabeth, d. [Charles & Dolly], b. Sept. 15, 1795	3	208
Susannah, d. [Charles & Dolly], b. Jan. 4, 1798	3	208
SPARROW, Hannah, relict of Timothy & dau. of Sperry		
DOUGLASS, m. Abraham **BROWER**, [s.		
Garrot, of Fredericksburg, N.Y.] June 1, 1806	3	216
SPAULDING, Newel S., m. Laura **McGINLEY**, [ ],		
1826, by Robert Bowzer	4	27
SPENCER, Asa, m. Elizabeth **IMMICE**, d. Nathaniel		
HEMPSTER, Nov. 1, 1801	3	44
Asa, of Philadelphia, m. Caroline **STARR**, of New		
London, Dec. 6, 1824, by Rev. Abel McEwen	4	21
Benjamin, s. [John & Abigail], b. Feb. 23, 1783; d.		
[ ]	2	121
Carroline, m. Emmanuel **BARTHOLOMEW**, b. of		
[New London], June 20, 1838, by Rev. Abel		
McEwen	4	77
Charlott[e], d. [Asa & Elizabeth], b. July 17, 1803	3	44
Charlotte, m. Edward **STANTON**, b. of New		
London, Oct. 16, 1825, by Rev. Abel McEwen	4	24
Eliza, of New London, m. Joseph H. **ST. JOHN**, of		
New York City, Sept. 10, 1843, by Rev.		
Lemuel Covell	4	109
Emily, m. Rogers **CLARK**, b. of New London, Oct.		
2, 1832, by Rev. Daniel Wildman	4	43
Fanny, d. [John & Abigail], b. [ ]; d.	2	121

	Vol.	Page

SPENCER (cont.)

Hannah, m. Thomas **DOUGLASS**, Nov. 25, 1703
(Written Hannah **SPERRY**. Questioned by L.
B. B.) — 1 — 52

Hannah, m. David **CAULKINS**, Jan. 29, 1708 — 2 — 6

Hannah, m. John **PIKE**, May 12, 1712 — 1 — 47

James, s. Houghton & Amelia Sarah, b. July 11, 1814 — 3 — 241

John, of Island of Bermudas, m. Abigail **BILLINGS**,
d. Capt. Benj[amin] & Abigail, Sept. 8, 1779 — 2 — 121

John, s. [John & Abigail], b. Aug. 15, 1780 — 2 — 121

John, Sr., d. Aug. 14, 1784 — 2 — 121

Lydia Ann, m. Nicholas **ANTHONY**, June 30, 1830,
by Rev. B. Judd — 4 — 41

Mary, m. Elisha **CROSBY**, b. of [New London],
May 13, 1834, by Rev. Abel McEwen — 4 — 56

Philena A., m. Hezekiah S. **WATROUS**, b. of
Westchester, Ct., Sept. 28, 1847, by Rev. Jabez
S. Swan — 4 — 134

Richard D., of East Haddam, m. Mary E. **ROGERS**,
of Montville, May 4, 1845, by Rev. Jabez S.
Swan — 4 — 119

SPERRY, Hannah, m. Thomas **DOUGLASS**, Nov. 25,
1703 (Perhaps Hannah **SPENCER**? L. B. B.) — 1 — 52

SPOONER, Alden, s. [Judah P. & Deborah], b. Jan. 23,
1783 — 3 — 25

Deborah, d. [Judah P. & Deborah], b. Feb. 8, 1777 — 3 — 25

Hannah, d. [Judah P. & Deborah], b. Feb. 24, 1775 — 3 — 25

Jacob, m. Catharine C. **DOUGLAS**, b. of New
London, Nov. 9, 1845, by Rev. Jabez Swan — 4 — 124

Judah P., m. Deborah **DOUGLASS**, Sept. 10, 1770 — 3 — 25

Nancy, d. [Judah P. & Deborah], b. July 21, 1771 — 3 — 25

Rebecca, d. Tho[ma]s, m. Timothy **GREEN**, s.
Sammuel, Jan. 2, 1763 — 3 — 23

Rebecca, d. [Judah P. & Deborah], b. May 10, 1773 — 3 — 25

Susannah, of Newport, m. Jacob **STOCKMAN**, of
Newport, July 16, 1786 — 3 — 146

SPRAGUE, Benjamin, s. [Crandall & Hannah], b. Dec.
17, 1799 — 3 — 60

Crandall, m. Hannah **HARRIS**, d. John, Mar. 5, 1796 — 3 — 60

David, s. [Crandall & Hannah], b. Jan. 22, 1798 — 3 — 60

Hannah, d. [Crandall & Hannah], b. Oct. 22, 1801 — 3 — 60

Lucretia H., of New London, m. Nelson B.
BECKWITH, of New York, Apr. 3, 1836, by
Rev. Alvan Ackley — 4 — 65

Lucy, m. Albert **BECKWITH**, Jan. 14, 1830, by
Daniel Wildman — 4 — 37

Mary, of New London, m. Benjamin F.
HEMPSTEAD, of Groton, Dec. 3, 1831, by
Rev. Abel McEwen — 4 — 44

SPRINGER, Dennis, of Ireland, m. Mary **HUDSON**, of
London, Eng., Oct. [ ], 1667 — 1 — 5

Desire, m. George **ROGERS**, Oct. 7, 1770 — 3 — 85

	Vol.	Page

SPRINGER (cont.)

Grace, d. Dennis & Mary, b Sept. 20, [1672] — 1 — 8

James, m. Rebecca **HARRIS**, July 3, 1796 — 3 — 133

James, s. [James & Rebecca], b. Oct. 8, 1796 — 3 — 133

John, s. Dennis & Mary, b. Apr. 18, [1668] — 1 — 5

Margaret, m. Danyell **RUSSELL**, Jan. 20, [1675] — 1 — 10

Mary, d. Dennis & Mary, b. "ye first week in
August", [1670] — 1 — 7

SQUIRES, SQUIRE, Elizabeth, m. Alanson
BECKWITH, b. of [New London], Feb. 19,
1832, by Rev. Chester Tilden — 4 — 45

Jane, m. Capt. William **CHURCHILL**, Aug. 2,
1852, by Rev. Charles Willett — 4 — 171

Richard, m. Mary **KEENEY**, b. of Lyme, Apr. 18,
1838, by Rev. James M. Macdonald — 4 — 76

STACY, Rebecca, b. June 3, 1769; m. Samuel **CHANEY**,
Jr., Oct. 23, 1791 — 3 — 177

STALLION, Deborah, d. Edward, m. James **AVERY**, Jr.,
s. James, Sr., Feb. 20, [1669] — 1 — 6

Edward, m. Christian **CHAPELL**, Mar. 16, [1692/3] — 1 — 21

Isaack, see under Isaac **FOOTE** — 1 — 44

STALON, Sarah, d. Edward, m. John **EDGECOMBE**, s
Nicholas, of Plymouth, Old England, Feb. 9,
[1673] — 1 — 9

STANDISH, Joseph, m. Matilda **DEGNEW**, b. of [New
London], May 29, 1850, by Rev. Robert A.
Hallam — 4 — 154

STANLEY, James, of Norfolk, Va., m. Marcinda **DART**,
of New London, July 10, 1825, by Rev. Abel
McEwen — 4 — 23

Miranda, m. Franklin **JOHNSON**, b. of New
London, Mar. 21, 1832, by Rev. Abel McEwen — 4 — 46

STANTON, Caroline M., of Norwich, m. M. Jerome
KEENEY, of New London, Jan. 26, 1845, by
Rev. S. Benton — 4 — 116

Edward, m. Charlotte **SPENCER**, b. of New
London, Oct. 16, 1825, by Rev. Abel McEwen — 4 — 24

Eliza, m. Joseph **SMITH**, b. of [New London], Mar.
16, 1849, by Rev. M. P. Alderman — 4 — 145

Mary, d. of Thomas, m. Samuel **ROGERS**, s. of
James, Nov. 17, [1662] — 1 — 3

Mary E., of Brooklyn, Ct., m. William W.
WINCHESTER, of Groton, Apr. 22, 1850, by
Charles A. Clark, Elder — 4 — 153

Mary S., m. Francis **RICHARDS**, Nov. 5, 1809, by
Rev. Abel McEwen — 3 — 241

Prudence, d. Tho[ma]s, late of Groton, decd., m.
Robert **FARGO**, Jr., s. Robert, of New London,
July 1, 1756 — 3 — 2

Theophilus, m. Elizabeth **ROGERS**, Jan. 5, [1698] — 1 — 24

STARK, STARKS, Ann, d. Moses & Deborah, b. May 21,
1749 — 2 — 25

	Vol.	Page

STARK, STARKS (cont.)

	Vol.	Page
Ann, of New London, m. James **MATHERS**, of New York, Nov. 3, 1776	3	23
Ann, d. [Benjamin & Mary], b. Mar. 9, 1798	3	91
Ann, m. William **HAMILTON**, Feb. 8, 1820, by Nehemiah Dodge	3	247
Anna, d. [Daniel Apelton & Electa], b. [ ], in New Boston	3	185
Benajah, s. John & Sarah, b. June 30, 1748	2	23
Benjamin, m. Mary **BLOYD**, May 7, 1782	3	91
Benjamin, s. [Benjamin & Mary], b. Apr. 7, 1783	3	91
Benjamin, m. Charlotte **RICE**, July 5, 1825	3	273
Benjamin, of New Orleans, m. Charlotte **RICE**, of New London, July 5, 1825, by Rev. Abel McEwen	4	23
Charles Lindley, s. [Benjamin & Charlotte], b. June 26, 1837	3	273
Christopher, s. Moses & Deborah, b. May 26, 1751	2	25
Daniel, s. [Daniel Apelton & Electa], b. [ ], in New Boston	3	185
Daniel Appelton, b. July 5, 1761	3	185
Daniel Ap[p]leton, m. Electa **LOVELAND**, of Darby, New Boston, Aug. 22, 1784	3	185
Elizabeth, d. Moses & Deborah, b. Sept. 1, 1747	2	25
Elizabeth, d. [Daniel Apelton & Electa], b. [ ], in Darby, N[ew] Boston	3	185
Elizabeth, d. [Daniel Apelton & Electa], b. [ ], in Darby; d. [ ]	3	185
Jane, m. Joseph **SKINNER**, July 23, 1787	3	101
John Rice, s. [Benjamin & Charlotte], b. Sept. 3, 1832	3	273
Joseph, s. John & Sarah, b. Dec. 17, 1749	2	23
Loveland, s. [Daniel Apelton & Electa], b. [ ], in New Boston	3	185
Lucretia W., of New London, m. William E. **IMLEY**, of Hartford, Sept. 27, 1843, by Rev. Robert A. Hallam	4	106
Mary, d. [Benjamin & Mary], b. Apr. 7, 1796	3	91
Mary, m. George **POTTER**, Jr., b. of New London, Nov. 24, 1824, by Rev. John W. Case	4	20
Mat[t]hew, d*, [Daniel Apelton & Electa], b. [ ], in N[ew] Boston *(Probably a son)	3	185
Moses, of Scarborough, Yorkshire, Old England, m. Deborah **ROGERS**, of New London, d. of John, decd., & grdau. of Joseph Rogers, formerly of New London ,decd., Dec. 6, 1746	2	25
Nicholas Plissam Downer, s. [Daniel Apelton & Electa], b. [ ], in Darby N[ew] Boston	3	185
Nichols, s. [Daniel Apelton & Electa], b. [ ], in New Boston (Entire entry crossed out.)	3	185

	Vol.	Page
STARK, STARKS (cont.)		
Polly, d. [Benjamin & Mary], b. July 18, 1735; d.		
Aug. 24, 1787	3	91
Rachel, d. John & Sarah, b. Aug. 23, 1745	2	23
Richard Robertson, s. [Benjamin & Charlotte], b.		
May 22, 1834	3	273
Truman, s. [Daniel Apelton & Electa], b. [ ],		
in Derby, New Boston	3	185
William, s. [Benjamin & Mary], b. May 18, 1789	3	91
William, s. [Daniel Apelton & Electa], b. [ ],		
in New Boston	3	185
William Wignal, s. [Benjamin & Charlotte], b. Sept.		
4, 1829	3	273
STARR, STAR, Abigail, d. Daniel & Elizabeth, b. Nov.		
12, 1736; d. Feb. 28, 1736/7	2	64
Abigail, d. Daniel & Elizabeth, b. Nov. 12, 1736; d.		
Feb. 28, 1736/7	2	105
Abigail, d. Daniel & Elizabeth, b. Oct. 11, 1750	2	64
Abigail, d. [Jonathan & Elisabeth], b. Feb. 2, 1789	3	84
Abiga[I]ll, d. Daniel & Elizabeth, m. Richard		
DOUGLASS, 2d, Oct. 28, 1790	3	212
Abiga[i]ll, d. William, of Middletown, m. Euclid		
ELLIOTT, May 11, 1794	3	78
Abigail, w. Jared, d. Feb. 12, 1804	3	84
Anna, of Norwich, d. Samuel, m. Stephen		
PRENTICE, of New London, s. Stephen,		
decd., May 31, 1750, by Benj[amin] Lord,		
Clerk	2	119
Anna Morgan, d. [Jonathan, Jr. & Catharine L.], b.		
Feb. 24, 1831	3	272
Benjamin, m. Lydia **LATHAM**, May 20, 1702	1	15
Benjamin, m. Lydia **LATHAM**, May 20, 1702	1	28
Benjamin, s. Benjamin & Lydia, b. Dec. 1, 1702; d.		
Mar. 17, 1702/3	1	28
Benjamin, s. Benjamin & Lydia, b. Dec. 4, 1702	1	15
Benj[amin], s. Daniel & Elizabeth, b. Feb. 20,		
1737/8; d. Apr. 26, 1738	2	64
Benj[amin], s. Jasper & Margaret, b. June 3, 1739	2	103
Caroline, of New London, m. Asa **SPENCER**, of		
Philadelphia, Dec. 6, 1824, by Rev. Abel		
McEwen	4	21
Charles, s. [Jared & Abigail], b. Oct. 28, 1783	3	84
Courtlandt, s. [Richard & Sally], b. Mar. 25, 1809	3	214
Daniel, s. Benjamin, m. Elizabeth **HEMPSTEAD**, d.		
Joshua, b. of New London, Nov. 18, 1735	2	64
Daniel, m. Elizabeth **HEMPSTEAD**, Nov. 18, 1735	2	104
Daniel, s. Daniel & Elizabeth, b. Dec. 26, 1741	2	64
Daniel, Jr., s. Capt. Daniel, m. Lucy **DOUGLASS**, d.		
William, Jan. 5, 1764	3	32
Daniel, s. Daniel, Jr. & Lucy, b. Feb. 22, 1765	3	32
Daniel, Capt., d. June 5, 1780, ae 38	3	32

	Vol.	Page

STARR, STAR (cont.)

Daniel, m. Hannah **WAY**, d. Capt. John Way, Sept. 23, 1796 — 3 — 149

Dominico, of the Rev. Cutter*, m. Angerro C. **DAYTON**, of New London, Nov. 5, [1844], by Rev. J. Blain *(So in the original) — 4 — 115

Eliza, d. Jonathan, m. John **GRIFFING**, Nov. 16, 1803 — 3 — 182

Eliza, m. Martin **LYON**, b. of [New London], June 24, 1847, by Rev. M. P. Alderman — 4 — 132

Elizabeth, d. Jonathan & Elizabeth, b. Aug. 19, 1701 — 1 — 26

Elizabeth, d. Benjamin & Lydia, b. Oct. 4, 1707 — 1 — 15

Elizabeth, d. Mar. 30, 1710 — 1 — 15

Elizabeth, d. Daniel & Elizabeth, b. Aug. 21, 1744 — 2 — 64

Elizabeth, m. James **PENNIMAN**, Sept. 17, 1763 — 3 — 39

Elisabeth, d. [Daniel & Lucy], b. Nov. 21, 1773; d. Dec. 24, 1774 — 3 — 32

Elizabeth, d. [Daniel & Lucy], b. Aug. 10, 1777 — 3 — 32

Elisabeth, d. [Jonathan & Elisabeth], b. Sept. 24, 1783 — 3 — 84

Elizabeth, d. [Jared & Abigail], b. June 20, 1791 — 3 — 84

Elizabeth, d. Daniel, m. Moses **BISHOP**, Mar. 27, 1803 — 3 — 222

Eunice, d. Daniel & Lucy, b. Feb. 28, 1767 — 3 — 32

Eunice, m. Daniel G. **THATCHER**, Oct. 30, 1791 — 3 — 122

Franklin, m. Louisa **DOUGLASS**, b. of [New London], Nov. 16, 1835, by Rev. Abel McEwen — 4 — 64

George, s. [Jared & Abigail], b. June 14, 1787 — 3 — 84

George Burr, s. [John & [E]unis], b. July 3, 1797 — 3 — 201

George E., m. Sarah J. **MALLORY**, b. of New London, Feb. 3, 1851, by Rev. Jabez S. Swan — 4 — 162

Grace, d. Benjamin & Lydia, b. July 1, 1714 — 1 — 42

Grace, m. Robert **FROWD**, Oct. 23, 1734 — 2 — 24

Harriet, of New London, m. Jacob **STOCKMAN**, of Philadelphia, Oct. 28, 1824, by Rev. B. Judd — 4 — 2

Harriet Roosevelt, d. [Jonathan, Jr. & Catharine L.], b. Nov. 7, 1832 — 3 — 272

Henry, s. [Jared & Abigail], b. Dec. 22, 1788 d. Sept. 20, 1789 — 3 — 84

James, s. [Daniel & Lucy], b. July 29, 1780; d. Aug. 30, 1780 — 3 — 32

James, s. [John & [E]unis], b. July 5, 1804 — 3 — 201

Jane W., of [New London], m. Alexander **GARRETT**, of Kentucky, Sept. 29, 1833, by Daniel Huntington — 4 — 54

Jared, m. Mary **COOK**, Jan. 25, 1768, on Long Island — 3 — 84

Jared, s. [Jared & Mary], b. Nov. 1, 1768, on Long Island — 3 — 84

Jared, m. Abigail **HAZARD**, Sept. 11, 1780 — 3 — 84

Jared, m. Esther **NILES**, Mar. 5, 1805 — 3 — 84

Jasper, s. Benjamin & Lydia, b. Mar. 21, 1709/10 — 1 — 15

	Vol.	Page
STARR, STAR (cont.)		
Jasper, s. Jasper & Margaret, b. Feb. 17, 1729, at		
Boston	2	105
Joanna, d. Ben, of New London, m. James **HARRIS**,		
s. Gabriel, of New London, Dec. 11, 1744	2	57
John, s. [Daniel & Lucy], b. July 3, 1771	3	32
John, m. [E]unis **BURR**, d. George, of Hartford, Oct.		
22, 1796	3	201
John, s. [John & [E]unis], b. Nov. 5, 1801	3	201
Jonathan, m. Elizabeth **MORGAN**, Jan. 12, [1698]	1	24
Jonathan, m. Sarah **HALLAM**, Oct. 18, 1770	3	84
Jonathan, s. [Jonathan & Sarah], b. Aug. 12, 1772; d.		
Sept. 15, 1775	3	84
Jonathan, m. Elisabeth **TABER**, Jan. 20, 1780	3	84
Jonathan, s. [Jonathan & Elisabeth], b. Apr. 7, 1781	3	84
Jonathan, Jr., m. Anna **MORGAN**, b. of New		
London, May 30, 1822, by Rev. B. Judd	4	9
Jonathan, Jr., m. Catharine L. **SYTHOFF**, d. Peter,		
of Patterson, N.J., Sept. 10, 1828	3	272
Jonathan, s. [Jonathan, Jr. & Catharine L.], b. Sept. 6,		
1829	3	272
Joshua, s. Daniel & Elizabeth, b. Apr. 28, 1739	2	64
Joshua, Jr., m. Lucy **COLFAX**, d. George, Apr. 19,		
1798	3	193
Joshua, Jr., d. Oct. 1, 1798	3	193
Joshua, s, [Daniel & Hannah], b. Feb. 3, 1803	3	149
Lucinda, d. William, of Groton, m. Dyar **HARRIS**,		
Feb. 3, 1793	3	143
Lucretia Williams, d. Jonathan & Anna, bp. Oct. 19,		
1823, by Rev. B. Judd	3	272
Lucy, d. Benjamin, of New London, m. John		
MILLER, of Wethersfield, s. Joseph, decd.,		
Sept. 27, 1750	2	64
Lucy, d. Samuel, of Norwich, m. Willard		
HUBBARD, s. Benjamin, of Pomfret, July 20,		
1767	3	54
Lucy, d. Daniel & Lucy, b. June 1, 1769	3	32
Lucy, relict, of Joshua **STARR**, & dau. of George		
COLFAX, m. David **MANWARING**, July 28,		
1802	3	86
Lucy Ann, d. [John & [E]unis], b. Feb. 22, 1800	3	201
Lucy Ann P., of New London, m. Henry **BENTON**,		
of Hartford, May 3, 1827, by Rev. Abel		
McEwen	4	30
Lucy Way, d. [Daniel & Hannah], b. Dec. 9, 1800	3	149
Lydia, d. Benjamin & Lydia, b. Oct. 25, 1705	1	15
Lydia, m. John **BOLLES**, Jr., July 20, 1727	2	4
Lydia, d. Ben[jamin], m. John **BOLLES**, Jr., s. John,		
July 20, 1727	2	17
Marcus Aurelius, s. [Richard & Sally], b. Feb. 26,		
1806	3	214

	Vol.	Page

STARR, STAR (cont.)

Marcus Aurelius, m. Elizabeth Starr **GRIFFING**,
Aug. 24, 1829 — 3 — 267

Marcus Aurelius, Jr., s. [Marcus Aurelius &
Elizabeth Starr], b. Aug. 16, 1830 — 3 — 267

Mary, d. Benjamin & Lydia, b. Dec. 26, 1703 — 1 — 15

Mary, d. Jasper & Margret, b. Nov. 6, 1737 — 2 — 103

Mary, w. Jared, d. Sept. 8, 1771, on Long Island — 3 — 84

Mary, d. [Jared & Abigail], b. July 1, 1781 — 3 — 84

Mary, d. Joshua, m. John **PENNIMAN**, Nov. 29,
1792 — 3 — 156

Mary, d. [Joshua, Jr. & Lucy], b. Feb. 3, 1799 — 3 — 193

Mary, d. Jared, m. Samuel **GREEN**, Feb. 14, 1803 — 3 — 162

Mary Ann, d. [Richard & Sally], b. July 4, 1812; d.
Dec. 1, 1820 — 3 — 214

Nancy, d. [Jared & Abigail], b. Jan. 11, 1796 — 3 — 84

Rachel, m. Daniel **DENISON**, Nov. 14, 1726 — 2 — 13

Rebecca, m. Henry **TRUMAN**, June 9, 1776 — 3 — 26

Rebecca, d. [Jonathan & Elisabeth], b. Nov. 7, 1785 — 3 — 84

Rebecca, d. Jonathan & Elizabeth, m. Peter S.
MERCER, Nov. 24, 1815 — 3 — 256

Richard, s. [Daniel & Lucy], b. July 19, 1775 — 3 — 32

Richard, m. Sally **WAY**, d. Capt. John Way, July 8,
1804 — 3 — 214

Richard Douglass, s. [Daniel & Hannah], b. Dec. 10,
1798 — 3 — 149

Robert, s. Jasper & Margaret, b. Aug. 3, 1735 — 2 — 105

Robert, s. [Jared & Abigail], b Aug. 11, 1782; d. Jan.
21, 1808, in Dimarara — 3 — 84

Sally, m. Ephraim **PAULK**, Feb. 1, 1816 — 3 — 242

Samuel, m. Hannah, d. Jon[atha]n **BREWSTER**,
Dec. 23, [1664] — 1 — 4

Samuell, s. Samuel & Hannah, b. Dec. 11, [1665] — 1 — 4

Samuel, s. Jonathan & Elizabeth, b. Nov. 5, 1699 — 1 — 24

Sarah, d. Benj[amin] & Lydia, m. John **DISHON**, s.
Daniel & Ruth, Aug. 25, 1751 — 2 — 1

Sarah, w. Jonathan, d. Mar. 2, 1775 — 3 — 84

Sarah, d. [Jonathan & Elisabeth], b. June 10, 1782 — 3 — 84

Thomas, s. Sam[ue]l & Hannah], b. Sept. 27, 1668 — 1 — 6

Thomas Way, s. [Daniel & Hannah], b. June 13, 1797 — 3 — 149

William, s. Daniel & Elizabeth, b. Apr. 3, 1747 — 2 — 64

STATES, W[illia]m, m. Lucy **HAINES**, b. of [New
London], Nov. 29, 1826, by Rev. Newel S.
Spaulding — 4 — 27

STEBBINS, STEBINS, STEBBENS, Bethya, d. Dan[ie]ll
& Rebecca, b. Apr. 30, [1676] — 1 — 11

Christopher, s. John & Debora[h], b. Sept. 26, [1677] — 1 — 12

Danyell, s. John, of N[ew] London, m. Rebecca, d.
Dan[ie]l **COMSTOCK**, May 31, [1675] — 1 — 10

Deborah, d. Jno. & Deborah, b. Oct. 8, [1664] — 1 — 4

Ebenezer D., m. Lavina **TINKER**, of Waterford,
Nov. 29, 1842, by Henry R. Knapp — 4 — 103

	Vol.	Page
STEBBINS, STEBINS, STEBBENS (cont.)		
Emily L., m. Lorenzo **CRANDALL**, b. of New		
London, Dec. 5 ,1830, by Rev. Abel McEwen	4	39
Emmala, d. [James & Nancy], b. Mar. 9, 1809	3	228
James, m. Nancy **HANCOCK**, d. Thomas, Oct. 12,		
1800	3	228
James, m. Charlotte E. **HAYNES**, b. of New London,		
Apr. 17, 1834, by Chester Tilden	4	56
Jane, d. Jno. & Deborah, b. June 7, 16[ ]	1	67
Joane, d. John & Deborah, b. Sept. 6, [1680]	1	14
John, s. John, m. Deborah [ ], May 8, [1663]	1	4
John, s. John & Debora[h], b. Feb. 11, [1666]	1	5
John, m. Phebe **MINOR**, June 17, 1697	1	23
John, of N[ew] London, m. Rhoda **LEE**, Apr. 6,		
1788, in Lyme, by Andrew Griswold, J.P.	2	123
Joseph, of New London, m. Mary **LESTER**, of		
Lyme, June 2, 1790, by Andrew Griswold, J.P.	2	123
Margaret, d. Jno. & Debora[h], b. Jan. 19, [1674]	1	9
Margaret, w. John, d. Jan. 1, [1678]	1	13
Margaret, d. John & Betharah, b. Nov. 5, [1680]	1	14
Margaret, d. Dan[ie]ll & Bethia, b. [ ], 3, [ ]	1	67
Marthew, d. [James & Nancy], b. June 12, 1802	3	228
Martha, m. Charles **HOBRON**, Apr. 14, 1822, by V.		
R. Osborn	4	7
Mary, d. John & Debora[h], b. Feb. 20, [1671]	1	7
Mary Ann, d. [James & Nancy], b. Oct. 5, 1804	3	228
Nancy, m. William **BROWN**, b. of New London,		
Jan. 9, 1825, by Rev. Daniel Dorchester	4	20
Pasceill, s. Dan[ie]ll & Bethyra*, b. Feb. 24, [1677]		
*(Changed to "Rebecca", by L. B. B.)	1	12
Susan, m. James **BILLINGS**, Sept. 22, 1835, by		
Rev. Alvan Ackley	4	62
Susanna, d. [James & Nancy], b. Aug. 24, 1808	3	228
STEDMAN, Ann, d. Thomas, by his 2d w, h. June l l,		
1(?)0; m Benjamin **LESTER** Testified to by		
Mrs. Elizabeth Trueman & Mrs. Susannah Fox,		
Mar. 4, 1708/9	1	19
Richard Starrett (?), s. Ann, now w. of Benjamin		
LESTER, b. May 24, 1690	1	20
Thomas, m. Hannah **ISBELL**. Testified to by Mrs.		
Elizabeth Trueman & Mrs. Susannah Fox, Mar.		
4, 1708/9	1	19
STEENE, William, m. Elizabeth **SHACKLEFORD**, b. of		
New London, Oct. 1, 1829, by rev. Abel		
McEwen	4	37
STEP, Betsey, m. Providence **FREEMAN**, negroes, [ ],		
179[ ]	3	104
STEPHENS, [see also **STEVENS**], Jane, m. Elias		
AUSTIN, b. of [New London], Dec. 1, 1834,		
by Rev. Ebenezer Blake	4	59
Mary, m. John **HARRIS**, Dec. 1, 1696	1	23

	Vol.	Page

STEPHENS (cont.)

Sophia R., m. Jeremiah **SLATE**, May 14, 1837, by
    Rev. Robert A. Hallam — 4 — 69

William, of Kenellworth, m. Wid. Sarah
    CARPENTER, Nov. 24, 1703 — 1 — 29

STERLING, Hepsibah, of Lyme, m. James **DARROW**,
    Jr. of New London, Nov. 10, 1790 — 3 — 101

STERRY, Nelson, of Groton, m. Prudence M.
    GORDINS, of [New London], Mar. 29, 1836,
    by Rev. Abel McEwen — 4 — 65

Thomas, m. Leona **AMES**, b. of New London, June
    24, 1849, by Rev. Jabez S. Swan — 4 — 146

STEVENS, STEEVENS [see also **STEPHENS**], George,
    s. [Mehitable, a black woman,], b. July 29, 1796 — 3 — 240

Jane, d. [Mehitable, a black woman], b. Mar. 25,
    1798 — 3 — 240

Mary, m. Samuel **FOX**, Mar. 25, 1703 — 1 — 27

Mehitable, a black woman, b. Apr. 30, 1778 — 3 — 240

Meriam, m. Benjamin **BECKLY**, of Wethersfield,
    Nov. 12, 1702 — 1 — 27

Sarah, m. James **ROGERS**, s. Joseph, Mar. 27, 1699 — 1 — 50

STEWARD, [see also **STEWART**], Adoniram Judson, s.
    [Ira R. & Mary], b. Feb. 24, 1828*; d. Oct. 12,
    1831 *(First written "March 29, 1828") — 3 — 206

Asahel, s. [William & Mary], b. June 5, 1773 — 3 — 44

Asahel, m. Lucretia **BECKWITH**, Nov. 6, 1796 — 3 — 134

Asahel, s. [Asahel & Lucretia], b. Apr. 14, 1798 — 3 — 134

Betsey, d. [Elisha & Mary], b. Mar. 19, 1788 — 3 — 3

Charles, s. [Nathan & Drusilla], b. June 2, 1800 — 3 — 126

Daniel, s. [William, Jr. & Lucretia], b. Apr. 25, 1788 — 3 — 17

Elisha, m. Mary **CALKINS**, Jan. 11, 178[7] — 3 — 3

Ethol, s. William & Mary, b. Oct. 5, 1769 — 3 — 44

Eunice, d. [Nathan & Drusilla], b. July 11, 1798 — 3 — 126

Eunice Harris, d. [Ira R. & Mary], b. Apr. 12, 1820 — 3 — 206

Ira R., m. Mary **HARRIS**, Jan. 12, 1819 — 3 — 206

Ira Rogers, s. [Nathan & Drusilla], b. Apr. 3, 1795 — 3 — 126

Jonathan P., m. Nancy **NOYES**, b. of [New London],
    May 24, 1835, by Rev. Alvan Ackley — 4 — 66

Lanson, s. [Ira R. & Mary], b. Sept. 30, 1824 — 3 — 206

Levy, s. [William, Jr. & Lucretia], b. June 17, 1792 — 3 — 17

Lucretia, d. [William, Jr. & Lucretia], b. Dec. 6, 1794 — 3 — 17

Marcus, s. [Nathan & Drusilla], b. June 1, 1796 — 3 — 126

Martha, m. Jethro **BEEBE**, Jan. 14, 1779 — 3 — 12

Mary Drusilla, d. [Ira R. & Mary], b. May 19, 1831 — 3 — 206

Nancy, m. David **BEEBE**, b. of New London, July
    17, 1831, by Rev. Daniel Wildman — 4 — 43

Nathan, m. Drusilla **ROGERS**, Dec. 8, 1793 — 3 — 126

Nathan, of Sag Harbor, N.Y., m. Amelia
    WHITTEMORE, of [New London], June 30,
    1837, by Rev. Abel McEwen — 4 — 72

Oliver, s. [Ira R. & Mary], b. June 16, 1822 — 3 — 206

Polly, m. Jonathan **PEMBER**, Apr. 17, 1788 — 3 — 97

	Vol.	Page
STEWARD (cont.)		
Rebekah, d. [William, Jr. & Lucretia], b. Apr. 29, 1796	3	17
Rebecca, m. Richard **HARRIS**, Dec. 21, 1819	3	171
Sally, d. [William & Mary], b. Mar. 6, 1780	3	44
Silas, s. [Asahel & Lucretia], b. Feb. 26, 1800	3	134
William, Jr., m. Lucretia **ROGERS**, Nov. 7, 1782	3	17
William, d. Sept. 26, 1788, ae 54 y.	3	44
William, s. [William, Jr. & Lucretia], b. Feb. 1, 1798	3	17
STEWART, [see also **STEWARD**], Abigail, d. Matthew & Abigail, b. Oct. 12, 1757	2	73
Alanson, m. Jane **SMITH**, b. of New London, Sept. 20, 1846, by Rev. Jabez S. Swan	4	127
Ann, d. Matthew & Abigail, b. Oct. 19, 1748	2	73
Ann Coles, d. [James & Elizabeth], b. Sept. 8, 1808	3	237
Charles Coles, s. [James & Elizabeth], b. Nov. 17, 1805	3	237
Elizabeth, d. Matthew & Abigail, b. Mar. 6, 1745	2	73
Francis Elizabeth, d. [James & Elizabeth], b. May 27, 1810	3	237
George, s. [James & Elizabeth], b. Sept. 3, 1811	3	237
Hannah, d. Matthew & Abigail, b. Dec. 12, 1746	2	73
Isabella Lydia, d. [James & Elizabeth], b. Nov. 14, 1803	3	237
James, m. Elizabeth **COLES**, d. John, Oct. 10, 1798	3	237
James William, s. [James & Elizabeth], b. June 15, 1816	2	237
Jane, of New London, m. George **LEAVITT**, of New York, Apr. 6, 1847, by Rev. Jabez S. Swan	4	130
Jane S, m. William G. **HODGSON**, b. of [New London], Oct. 26, 1847, by Rev. Robert A. Hallam	4	135
John Carden, s. [James & Elizabeth], b. Sept. 6, 1813	3	237
Lucretia, of Waterford, m. Isaac **HARRISS**, of New London, Dec. 10, 1811	3	191
Mary, d. Matthew & Abigail, b. Feb. 14, 1753	2	73
Mary, d. [James & Elizabeth], b. Nov. 24, 1801	3	237
Mary, m. William H. **SWIFT**, b. of New London, Feb. 2, 1825, by Rev. B. Judd	4	21
Mary, m. Silas **HARRIS**, Sept. 25, 1826, by Rev. Francis Darrow	4	28
Matthew, formerly of Ireland, m. Abigail **GARDINER**, dau. of William & Elizabeth, of Newport, R.I., Oct. 19, 1735, by Rev. Honeyman, of Rhode Island	2	73
Matthew, s. Matthew & Abigail, b. Nov. 5, 1741	2	73
Nancy, d. [William & Jane], b. Oct. 23, 1789	3	100
Oliver, m. Sarah E. **SMITH**, b. of New London, Nov. 3, 1845, by Rev. Jabez S. Swan	4	122
Walter, s. Matthew & Abigail, b. June 17, 1755	2	73
William, s. Matthew & Abigail, b. June 14, 1743	2	73

	Vol.	Page
STEWART (cont.)		
William, m. Jane **WINTHROP**, d. John S., Dec. 6, 1781	3	100
William, d. Sept. 6, 1798	3	100
STICKLAND, [see also **STRICKLAND**], Abigail, d. Jonathan & Joanna, b. Aug. 16, 1757	2	25
Elizabeth, m. Richard **DART**, June 22, [1699]	1	25
Jerome, of New London, m. Hannah **PHILIPS**, of Lyme, Nov. 18, 1792, in Lyme, by Andrew Griswold, J.P.	2	124
Jonathan, s. Samuel, of New London, m. Joanna **HIBBERT**, d. Joseph, of Windham, Oct. 31, 1754	2	25
Joseph, s. Thomas & Prudence, b. Aug. 31, 1770	3	47
Samuel, s. Jonathan & Joanna, b. July 31, 1755	2	25
Tho[ma]s, b. May 10, 1747	3	47
Thomas, s. Peter, m. Prudence **CHAPEL**, d. Jonathan, all of New London, Jan. 12, 1770	3	47
STILLMAN, STILMAN, Albert, of New London, m. Mary Ann **BECKWITH**, of Waterford, Apr. 5, 1835, by Alven Ackley	4	60
Elizabeth, d.Robert, of Norwich, m. William **PRIME**, Apr. 26, 1801	3	35
Elizabeth Ann, m. Franklin **BOLTON**, b. of New London, Nov. 23, 1851, by Rev. Jabez S. Swan	4	172
Sarah A., of [New London], m. Ebon G. **SUTHERLAND**, of Manchester, Vt., Aug. 16, 1835, by Rev. Abel McEwen	4	62
STOCKER, Susanna, d. William & Elizabeth, b. May 21, 1741. Recorded at the request of her mother June 30, 1758	2	105
STOCKMAN, Abbey, d. [Jacob & Susannah], b. June 22, 1805	3	146
Charles Spooner, s. [Jacob & Susannah], b. May 2, 1789	3	146
George, s. [Jacob & Susannah], b. Mar. 1, 1797	3	146
Jacob, of Newport, m. Susannah **SPOONER**, of Newport, July 16, 1786	3	146
Jacob, s. [Jacob & Susannah], b. Mar. 22, 1791	3	146
Jacob, of Philadelphia, m. Harriet **STARR**, of New London, Oct. 28, 1824, by Rev. B. Judd	4	2
Joseph, s. [Jacob & Susannah], b. Jan. 9, 1799	3	146
Mary, d. [Jacob & Susannah], b. Feb. 12, 1795	3	146
Mary, m. Parker H. **SMITH**, b. of New London, June 24, 1827, by Rev. Robert Bowzer	4	31
Nancey, d. [Jacob & Susannah], b. Mar. 10, 1802	3	146
Sally, d. [Jacob & Susannah], b. Dec. 4, 1808	3	146
Sally, m. Nathan **MALLORY**, b. of New London, Dec. [ ], 1827, by Rev. Robert Bowzer	4	32
Susannah, d. [Jacob & Susannah], b. May 22, 1793	3	146
William, s. [Jacob & Susannah], b. June 26, 1787	3	146

	Vol.	Page
STOCKMAN (cont.)		
William, m. Mary T. **POTTER**, Dec. 24, 1820, by		
Rev. Elijah Hedding	4	1
STODDARD, Arabella, of [New London], m. Franklin A.		
PALMER, of Stonington, June 22, 1848, by		
Rev. Abel McEwen	4	140
Charlot[te] Loiza, d. [Ralph & Chralot[te], b. Mar.		
31, 1809	3	206
Charlotte Louisa, of New London, m. George Lyman		
BELLOWS, of Ogdensburg, N.Y., Dec. 10,		
1829, by Rev. Abel McEwen	4	38
Elizabeth, d. [Ralph & Charlot[te], b. June 23, 1813	3	206
Enoch V., m. Mary S. **ALLEN**, d. Lewis Allen, May		
9, 1832	3	181
Enoch V., m. Mary S. **ALLEN**, b. of New London,		
May 9, 1832, by Rev. B. Judd	4	49
Enoch V., m. Sarah A. **ALLEN**, b. of New London,		
Jan. 15, 1849, by Rev. Robert A. Hallam	4	144
Enoch Vine, s. [Enoch V. & Mary S.], b. July 10,		
1840	3	181
George, s. [Enoch V. & Mary S.], b. Jan. 16, 1843	3	181
Harriet, d. [Enoch V. & Mary S.], b. Feb. 7, 1847	3	181
Maria, d. [Ralph & Charlot[te], b. May 5, 1810	3	206
Mary A., m. Henry A. **LATIMER**, b. of [New		
London], Jan. 2, 1844, by Rev. Abel McEwen	4	110
Mary Abby, d. [Ralph & Charlot[te], b. Oct. 10, 1819	3	206
Mary Prudence, d. [Enoch V. & Mary S.], b. Mar. 17,		
1838	3	181
Ralph, m. Charlot[te] **COLFAX**, d. George, Feb. 1,		
1808	3	206
Samuel D., of West Brookfield, Mass., m. Fanny R.		
HARRIS, of [New London], July 3, 1845, by		
Abel McEwen	4	120
Sarah, d. [Ralph & Charlot[te], b. Aug. 21, 1816	3	206
Sarah R., of [New London], b. John S. **CHIPMAN**,		
of Waddington, N.Y., Sept. 25, 1848, by Rev.		
Abel McEwen	4	142
STONE, Abigail, d. [John & Patience], b. Nov. 21, 1767	3	116
Hannah, d. [John & Patience], b. Apr. 17, 1773	3	116
John, m. Patience **EDEY**, Sept. 24, 1769	3	116
John, s. [John & Patience], b. Dec. 13, 1778	3	116
Nathan, s. [John & Patience], b. May 11, 1781	3	116
Oliver, s. [John & Patience], b. Aug. 22, 1770	3	116
Oliver, m. Rebecca **THORP**, d. Nathaniel, Jan. 24,		
1794	3	237
Oliver, s. [Oliver & Rebecca], b. May 5, 1797	3	237
Patty, d. [John & Patience], b. Jan. 1, 1776	3	116
Patty, m. Samuel **MASON**, [ ]	3	36
Rebecca, m. Christopher **CROSBY**, Mar. 8, 1803	3	237
STORY, STORRY, Ephraim, of Groton, s. John, of		
Groton, m. Elizabeth **DARROW**, of New		
London, dau. of Eben[eze]r, Feb. 7 ,1754	2	78

	Vol.	Page
STORY, STORRY (cont.)		
Lydia, d. Eph[rai]m & Elizabeth, b. Apr. 25, 1756, at Lyme	2	78
Peter, s. Clarissa, a black woman, b. Feb. 14, 1819	3	45
Sarah, d. Eph[rai]m & Elizabeth, b. Jan. 10, 1755	2	78
Sarah, d. Eph[rai]m & Elizabeth, b. Mar. 6, 1758	2	78
STOUT, Peter, of Key West, Florida, m. Fanny **BEETS**, of New London, July 30, 1837, by Rev. Robert A. Hallam	4	72
STOW[E], Lucy W., m. Peter **DOUGLASS**, b. of New London, June 10, 1821, by Abel McEwen	4	5
Mary, m. Solloman **COITE**, Dec. 24, 1706	1	32
STRANGE, Anna, m. Daniel **CROCKER**, b. of Norwich, Aug. 22, 1844, by Rev. I. Blain	4	113
STRATFORD, Sarah, d. Clement & Sarah, b. Jan. 24, 1714	1	43
STRATTON, David G, of Millford, m. Elizabeth P. **CLARK**, of New London, June 30, 1844, by Rev. Jabez S. Swan	4	112
STRICKLAND, STRICKLAIN, STRICKLIN, STRICKLING, [see also **STICKLAND**], Charles W, of [New London], m. Frances S. **LESTER**, of Sag Harbor, Sept. 26, 1847, by Rev. T. Edwards	4	134
Frances E., m. John H. **LESTER**, b. of [New London], Sept. 3, 1840, by Rev. Abel McEwen	4	91
Franklin, m. Caroline **PEABODY**, Mar. 27, 1842, by H. R. Knapp	4	101
Leonard, m. Desire A. **COMSTOCK**, b. of [New London], Nov. 1, 1846, by John Howson	4	130
Lucretia, of Montville, m. Thomas I. O. **PENHARLOW**, of New London, Apr. 10, 1842, by Rev. Lemuel Covell	4	99
Margaret, d. Thomas & Ziporah, b. Feb. 21, 1720	1	63
Mary, d. Thomas & Ziporah, b. Aug. 29, 1716	1	62
Mary, d. Thomas, m. Nathaniel **HOLT**, Jr., s. Nath[anie]l, July 29, 1735	2	18
Mary Ann, m. Daniel D. **LATHAM**, May 30, 1849, by Rev. Charles Willett	4	146
Peter, s. Thomas & Ziporah, b. Mar. 12, 1718	1	62
Peter, s. Thomas, m. Sarah **WILLIAMS**, d. Thomas, m. Sarah **WILLIAMS**, d. Thomas, all of New London, May 22, 1745	3	59
Royal N., m. Louisa **HAYDEN**, b. of [New London], Sept. 3, 1839, by Rev. Robert A. Hallam	4	86
Samuel N., m. Eunice L. **JONES**, b. of New London, Nov. 21, 1842, by Eld[er] L. Covell	4	103
Sarah, d. Peter, m. William **ASHCRAFT**, Feb. 12, 1784	3	99
Sarah, of Waterford, m. Asa **COMSTOCK**, 2d, of Montville, Mar. 22, 1833, by Rev. Abel McEwen	4	50

	Vol.	Page

STRICKLAND, STRICKLAIN, STRICKLIN,
STRICKLING (cont.)

	Vol.	Page
Stephen, s. Peter & Sarah, b. Nov. 22, 1760	3	59
Thomas, m. Ziporah **BILLINGS**, Mar. 16, 1714	1	62
Thomas, s. Thomas & Ziporah, b. Sept. 10, 1722	1	63
Zirporah, d. Thomas & Ziporah, b. July 11, 1714	1	62

STROH, Charles, m. Jemima E. **KERSON**, b. of [New
London], Sept. 11, 1851, by Rev. J. M. Eaton — 4 — 165

STRONG, As[a]h[e]l, Rev. of Windham, m. Sarah
RAYMOND, of New London, June 13, 1701/2 — 1 — 26

STROUD, Alice, d. [Richard & Elisabeth], b. Apr. 29,
1783 — 3 — 101

	Vol.	Page
Amanda F., of [New London], m. Daniel **DELARROY**, of Norwich, May 25, 1844, by Rev. Abel McEwen	4	114
Benjamin Billings, s. [Richard & Elisabeth], b .Dec. 17, 1787	3	101
Billings, s. [Richard & Elisabeth], b. Mar. 5, 1793	3	101
Elisabeth, d. [Richard & Elisabeth], b. Oct. 14, 1771	3	101
Fanny, d. [Richard & Elisabeth], b. Apr. 20, 1785	3	101
John, s. [Richard & Elisabeth], b. Dec. 12, 1780	3	101
Mary, d. [Richard & Elisabeth], b. Sept. 15, 1778	3	101
Richard, m. Elisabeth **BILLINGS**, Nov. 25, 1765	3	101
Richard, s. [Richard & Elisabeth], b. July 24, 1774	3	101
Samuel, s. [Richard & Elisabeth], b. Feb. 17, 1791	3	101
Samuel, of New London, m. Lucretia **BEEBE**, of Waterford, May 19, 1822, by Rev. Abel McEwen	4	7
Sophia, d. [Richard & Elisabeth], b. Aug. 14, 1769	3	101
Susannah, d. [Richard & Elisabeth], b. Oct. 11, 1767	3	101
William, s. [Richard & Elisabeth], b. July 21, 1776	3	101

STUBBENS, STUBBINS, STUBENS, Abigail, d.

	Vol.	Page
Christopher & Abigail, b. Aug. 19, 1730	2	102
Abigail, w. Christopher, d. July 22, 1754	2	103
Abigail, d. Jabez & Sarah, b. Feb. 6, 1759	2	103
Ann, d. Christopher & Abigail, b. Mar. 1, 1741/2	2	103
Ann, d. Clement & Sarah, b. July 18, 1743	2	29
Bethiah, d. Christopher & Abigail, b. Dec. 22, 1735	2	102
Christopher, s. Daniel & Bethiah, b. July 7, 1694; m. Abigail **ALLEN**, Dec. 22, 1720	2	102
Christopher, s. John & Phebe, b. June 18, 1713	1	41
Christopher, d. Feb. 27, 1725/6	2	104
Christopher, s. John, d. June 7, 1736	2	104
Christopher, s. Clement & Sarah, b. Jan. 28, 1737/8	2	29
Christopher, s. Christopher & Abigail, b. Sept. 13, 1739	2	102
Christopher, m. Lydia **STUBBENS**, d. of John Stubbens, of New London, Dec. 1, 1754	2	103
Christopher, s. Jabez & Sarah, b. Feb. 8, 1766	2	103
Christopher, d. Feb. 18, 1785; ae 91	3	36
Clement, s. John & Phebe, b. Mar. 8, 1701/2	1	27

	Vol.	Page

STUBBENS, STUBBINS, STUBENS (cont.)

	Vol.	Page
Clement, s. John, of New London, decd., m. Sarah **MINOR**, d. of William, of Lyme, decd., Nov. 25, 1727	2	29
Clement, s. John & Sarah, b. Feb. 21, 1760	2	28
Daniell, m. Lydia **MYNOR**, Dec. 9, 1716	1	47
Deborah, d. Tho[ma]s & Deborah, b. June 10, 1740	2	9
Edward, s. Jabez & Sarah, b. Nov. 16, 1751	2	103
Elisabeth, d. Jos[eph] & Elisabeth, b. May 25, 1765	3	36
Jabez, s. Christopher & Abigail, b. May 17, 1728	2	102
Jabez, s. Chris[tophe]r, of New London, m. Sarah **TURNER**, d. Thomas, of New London, May 19, 1748	2	103
Jabez, s. Jabez & Sarah, b. May 22, 1767	2	103
Joanna, d. Jabez & Sarah, b. Nov. 9, 1749	2	103
John, s. John & Phebe, b. July 18, 1698	1	24
John, d. Mar. 17, 1706/7	2	104
John, s. Clement & Sarah, b. Oct. 16, 1732	2	29
John, s. Clement, of New London, m. Sarah **MINOR**, d. of Joseph, of Lyme, July 18, 1754	2	28
John, s. John & Sarah, b. Mar. 21, 1757; d.	2	28
John, s. John & Sarah, b. July 11, 1764	2	28
Joseph, s. Clement & Sarah, b. Aug. 20, 1740	2	29
Joseph, of New London, s. Clem[en]t, m. Elisabeth **BECKWITH**, of Lyme, d. Jonathan, 2d, of Lyme, May 31, 1764	3	36
Joseph, s. John & Sarah, b. Apr. 22, 1767	2	28
Lucy, d. Thomas & Deborah, b. Jan. 8, 1733/4	2	9
Lucy, d. Thomas & Deborah, b. Jan. 8, 1733/4	2	104
Lucy, d. John & Sarah, b. May 21, 1755	2	28
Lydia, d. John & Phebe, b. May 4, 1709	1	34
Lydia, d. Christopher & Abigail, b. Jan. 8, 1722/3	2	102
Lydia, d. Jabez & Sarah, b. Feb. 14, 1749/50	2	103
Lydia, d. John Stubbens, of New London, m. Christopher **STUBBENS**, Dec. 1, 1754	2	103
Lydia, d. Joseph & Elisabeth, b. Sept. 7, 1766	3	36
Martha, d. John & Phebe, b. Aug. 10, 1706	1	31
Martha, m. Thomas **MINOR**, Nov. 21, 1726	2	67
Mary, d. Paltiah, b. Dec. 24, 1705	1	31
Patience, d. Jabez & Sarah, b. Jan. 27, 1754	2	103
Phebe, d. Thomas & Deborah, b. June 19, 1736	2	9
Ruth, d. Thomas & Deborah, b. Apr. 10, 1732	2	9
Samuel, s. John & Sarah, b. Mar. 19, 1762	2	28
Sarah, d. Clement & Sarah, b. July 25, 1734	2	29
Sarah, d. Jabez & Sarah, b. Apr. 2, 1761	2	103
Sarah, d. Joseph & Elisabeth, b. Feb. 4, 1768	3	36
Sarah, m. Jedediah **BROWN**, [ ]	3	114
Thankfull, d. Thomas & Deborah, b. Jan. 29, 1729/30	2	9
Thankful, d. Thomas & Deborah, b. Jan. 29, 1729/30	2	104
Thomas, s. Jno. & Phebe, b. Aug. 22, 1703	1	29
Thomas, of New London, m. Deborah **GRIMES**, of Wethersfield, May 2, 1727	2	9

	Vol.	Page
STUBBENS, STUBBINS, STUBENS (cont.)		
Thomas, m. Deborah **GRIMES**, May 2, 1727	2	104
STUPUY, Catharine, w. Peter, d. Feb. 14, 1786, ae 26 y.	3	20
Hannah, d. [Peter & Catharine], b. Jan. 9 ,1786; d. Jan. 14, 1786	3	20
Peter, a French gentleman from the W. Indies then residing in New London, m. Catharine **CHADWICK**, of New London, June 20, 1784, by Aaron Kinne, Minister, of Groton	3	20
STYMEL, John, s. John & Mary, of the "Dukedom of Brunswick, City of Gondersine", b. June 28, 1770	3	124
John, m. Wealthy **ROWLEY**, Jan. 28, 1784	3	124
John, s. [John & Wealthy], b. July 28, 1785	3	124
Patty, d. [John & Wealthy], b. June 4, 1789	3	124
SULLIVAN, SULLAVAN, SILLIVAN, Benjamin, m. Patty **NEWDEGATE**, Apr. 3, 1800	3	80
Benjamin, s. [Benjamin & Patty], b. June 8, 1802	3	80
Elisabeth, [d. John, late of Westminster, decd. & Elisabeth], b. Dec. 1, 1773 in Philadelphia, Pa. Recorded June 19, 1794. Witnesses: Tho[ma]s Shaw, W. Stewart, Marvin Wait, Job Taber	3	127
Elizabeth, m. Samuel H. P. **LEE**, Mar. 31, 1794	3	145
Ellen, m. John **SHEEHAN**, June 20, 1852, by Rev. J. Stokes. Witnesses: John Sullivan, Mary Shea	4	171
Jeremiah Chapman, b. Aug. 27, 1768, at Charlestown, S.C.	3	127
John, m. Elizabeth **CHAPMAN**, Feb. 21, 1766, by Mather Byles	2	103
John, m. Mary **FITZGERALD**, July 13, [18]50, [by Peter J. Blenkinsop]. Witnesses: Daniel Sullivan, Alice Fitzgerald	3	306
John, m. Mary **FITZGERALD**, d. July 13, 1850. Witnesses: Daniel Sullivan, Alice Fitzgerald	4	159
John, m. Mary **SULLIVAN**, Mar. 2, 1852, by Rev. J Stokes. Witnesses: John Sullivan, Julia Shea	4	169
Mary, d. [John, late of Westminster, decd. & Elisabeth], b. Nov. 9, 1772, at Philadelphia, Pa. Recorded June 19, 1794. Witnesses: Tho[ma]s Shaw, W. Stewart, Marvin Wait, Job Taber	3	127
Mary, m. John **SULLIVAN**, Mar. 2, 1852, by Rev. J. Stokes. Witnesses: John Sullivan, Julia Shea	4	169
Michael, m. Julia **SHEA**, May 13, 1852, by Rev. J. Stokes. Witnesses: Arthur Hurley, Bridget Casey	4	170
Robert, s. [Benjamin & Patty], b. Feb. 24, 1804	3	80
Sally, d. [Benjamin & Patty], b. Dec. 20, 1800	3	80
SUTHERLAND, Ebon G., of Manchester, Vt., m. Sarah A. **STILLMAN**, of [New London], Aug. 16, 1835, by Rev. Abel McEwen	4	62

	Vol.	Page
SWADDLE, Eliphel, d. Samuel, m. Amasa **MILLER**,		
May 17, 1795	3	236
Theody, d. William, m. Jedidiah **CHAPEL**, Jr., of		
New London, s. Jed[idiah], Jan. 17, 1765	3	33
-----, child of William, d. Oct. 18, [1689], ae 6 y.	1	69
SWAIN, Harriet, m. Elias **WOODWORTH**, of Montville,		
Oct. 13, 1844, by Rev. G. Thompson	4	115
Patience M., m. David O. **MAIN**, Mar. 15, 1840, by		
Caleb I. Allen, J.P.	4	89
SWAN, Ann H., of New London, m. Elsworth C.		
PHELPS, of Stonington, Sept. 21, 1851, by		
Rev. Jabez S. Swan	4	174
Elisha, m. Lydia **DENNIS**, d. John, Mar. 26, 1806	3	37
Elisha, Sr., d. May 27, 1807	3	37
Elisha, s. [Elisha & Lydia], b. Nov. 1, 1807	3	37
Margaret P., of Bristol, R.I., m. Thomas E. **DWYER**,		
of New London, June 16, 1844, by Rev.		
Sanford Benton	4	112
SWANEY, SWAINEY, Abby, of Lyme, m. Elijah		
BOLLES, Jr., of Waterford, July 8, 1832, by		
Rev. Abel McEwen	4	47
Charles D., of Lyme, m. Hannah E. **CROWELL**, of		
Groton, Feb. 18, 1849, by Rev. H. R. Knapp	4	145
SWEENEY, Edmond, m. Johanna **CULLINS**, Feb. 24,		
1852, by Rev. J. Stokes. Witnesses: Garrett		
May, Honora O'Donnelt	4	170
Patrick, m. Catharine **WELCH**, Feb. 11, 1849, by		
Rev. William Logan	4	150
SWEET, Everett L., m. Lucy B. **CARPENTER**, b. of		
Attleborow, Mass., Mar. 6, 1851, by Rev.		
George M. Carpenter	4	160
George, (not American), m. Emeline **GREY**, of		
[New London], Aug. 25, 1844, by Rev. George		
Thompson	4	113
James, of Providence, R.I., m. Margaret P.		
SKINNER, of [New London], Oct. 27, 1833,		
by Rev. Ebenezer Blake	4	52
John G., m. Nancy **ALLEN**, b. of Groton, Apr. 18,		
1823, by Rev. Abel McEwen	4	13
Riley, m. Abba **JEROME**, Apr. 25, 1839, by Rev.		
Abraham Holway	4	85
William, of Providence, R.I., m. Rebecca **SKINNER**,		
of [New London], July 24, 1831, by Rev.		
Alpheus Hayden	4	43
SWIFT, Hannah*, m. Joseph **BRADFORD**, Jr., Mar. [ ],		
1730 *("Probably Henrietta" written in		
pencil)	2	4
William II., m. Mary **STEWART**, b. of New		
London, Feb. 2, 1825, by Rev. B. Judd	4	21
SYTHOFF, Catharine L., d. Peter, of Patterson, N.J., m.		
Jonathan **STARR**, Jr., Sept. 10, 1828	3	272

	Vol.	Page
TABOR, TABER, Amelia, m. Thomas **ALLEN**, Jr., Apr. 23, 1778	3	76
Elizabeth, d. Pardon & Pheebe, b. Aug. 3, 1740; d. Nov. 19, 1743	2	91
Elizabeth, d. Pardon & Elizabeth, b. Mar. 4, 1748	2	91
Elisabeth, m. Jonathan **STARR**, Jan. 20, 1780	3	84
Job, s. Samuel & Naoma, b. May 24, 1748	2	85
Lucy, m. Freeman **CROCKER**, July 26, 1767	3	102
Lydia, d. Philip, m. Charles **HAINES**, s. Jonathan, Apr. 3, 1728	2	16
Lydia, m. Charles **HAINES**, Apr. 3, 1728	2	37
Mary, d. Pardon & Pheebe, b. Mar. 18, 1737/8	2	91
Mary, d. Pardon & Elizabeth, b. May 10, 1750	2	91
Mary, d. Pardon, m. Ebenezer **WAY**, Jr., Nov. 30, 1766	3	147
Naomy, d. Pardon & Pheebe, b. Oct. 27, 1743	2	91
Pardon, s. Philip, m. Phebe **WESCOT**, d. Sam[ue]l, of New London, Dec. 3, 1733	2	32
Pardon, s. Philip & Elizabeth, of New London, m. Pheebe **WESCOAT**, d. Samuel, & Naomy, of New London, Dec. 3, 1733	2	91
Pardon, s. Philip & Elizabeth, m. Elizabeth **HARRIS**, d. Richard & Lucy, May 17, 1747	2	91
Pardon, s. Pardon & Elizabeth, b. Dec. 7, 1751; d. Nov. 6, 1756	2	92
Pardon T., of New London, m. Ama **COLT**, of Lyme, Nov. 26, 1789, by Rev. David Higgins	3	114
Pardon Tillinghast, s. Pardon & Elizabeth, b. Jan. 11, 1756	2	92
Pheebe, d. Pardon & Pheebe, b. Feb. 7, 1733/4	2	91
Phebe, d. Pardon & Phebe, b. Feb. 7, 1734/5	2	32
Philip, s. Pardon & Elizabeth, b. Nov. 3, 1753; d. Nov. 10, 1756	2	92
Samuel, s. Philip, m. Naomi **WESCOTE**, d. Samuel, dec'd., all of New London, July 5, 1747	2	85
Samuel, s. Samuel & Naoma, b. Sept. 29, 1750	2	85
Thomas T., m. Cornelia **CAVERLY**, of Lyme, Apr. 9, 1838, by Rev. James M. Macdonald	4	76
TALMAN, Joanna, testified Apr. 14, 1741, at the desire of Peter Jackson, that Eunice, d. of Hagar, a woman in the service of Madam Eliza Winthrop & reputed wife of Peter **JACKSON**, was b. Feb. [ ], 1729/30	2	50
William, m. Pheebe **CALVERT**, Aug. 14, 1797, by Rev. Charles Seabury	3	129
TANNICK, George, m. Frances **WHEELER**, b. of New London, Apr. 8, 1843, by Jabez Swan, M.G.	4	105
TAPPIN, Peter, Dr., on Oct. 15, 1711, granted freedom to Robert **JACKLIN**, a negro, whom he and his sons had owned 20 y.	1	48

	Vol.	Page
TATE, Elizabeth, formerly w., of Samuel **ROGERS**, had s. Giles Rogers, b. May 22, 1792. Entry recorded at her request	3	175
Robert, s. [William & Elizabeth], b. June 24, 1801	3	175
Robert N., m. Harriet **RUMSEY**, b. of New London, Mar. 21, 1824, by Rev. Abel McEwen	4	17
William, m. Elizabeth **ROGERS**, Aug. 27, 1797	3	175
William, s. [William & Elizabeth], b. Aug. 10, 1799, in Groton	3	175
William, s. W[illia]m Tate & Elizabeth **ROGERS**, b. Aug. 10, 1799, in Groton	3	304
William, s. Mrs. Rebecca **MANIERRE**, b. June 3, 1798* *(First written 1802)	3	193
William, Jr., m. Emeline **CRANNELL**, b. of New London, Oct. 14, 1824, by Rev. B. Judd	4	20
William, m. Virginia **POTTER**, Oct. 17, 1842, by Rev. Boss. Copied from Family Bible, Apr. 23, 1896	3	304
William B., m. Ellen **COMSTOCK**, b. of [New London], [ ] 14, [1847?], by Rev. T. Edwards	4	129
TAYLOR, John, of New London, m. Sarah **ABRAM**, of Haddam, Jan. 15, 1701/2	1	26
John, m. Desire **FULLER**, late of Barnstable, June 11, 1703	1	28
Julius, of Albion, N.Y., m. Frances **EWEN**, of New London, July 16, 1848, by Rev. L. G. Leonard	4	140
Laura, of Colchester, m. Elisha A. **BAKER**, of Groton, Aug. 30, 1825, by Rev. Abel McEwen	4	24
Mary, d. Thomas & Mary, b. Nov. 27, 1730	2	111
Mary, m. James **CROSWELL**, Mar. 25, 1734	2	8
Thomas, m. Mary **PLUMB**, June 25, 1724	2	111
William, s. Thomas & Mary, b. Feb. 3, 1724	2	111
William, of Brooklyn, m. Jane M. **SCOTT**, of Hampton, July 26, 1847, by Frederick M. Walker, J.P.	4	133
TEFFT, TEFT, (see also **TUFTS**), Levy, of New London, m. Abba **NICOLLS**, of Groton, Mar. 27, 1836, by Rev. Squire B. Hascall	4	83
Mary Thankful, m. James **CHAP[P]EL[L]**, b. of New London, Sept. 5, 1830, by Rev. Chester Colton, of Lyme	4	39
TENDEL, Lucinda, of Lebanon, m. Jared **CAGER**, of New London, May 15, 1831, by Rev. Abel McEwen	4	41
THATCHER, Abby Mumford, d. [Anthony & Lucretia], b. June 21, 1821	3	233
Abby S., m. Isaac **SHEPARD**, Aug. 2, 1820	3	152
Abigail Douglass, d. [Daniel G. & Eunice], b. Oct. 21, 1800	3	122
Ann Boradil, d. [Stephen Greenlief & Boradil], b. Aug. 14, 1799	3	195

	Vol.	Page

THATCHER (cont.)

Anthony, m. Lucretia **MUMFORD**, d. John, July 24, 1806* *(The words "Should be February" are written in pencil) — 3 — 233

Charles, s. [Daniel G. & Eunice], b. July 11, 1806; d. June 11, [ ] — 3 — 122

Daniel Anthony, s. [Anthony & Lucretia], b. Sept. 3, 1817 — 3 — 233

Daniel G., m. Eunice **STARR**, Oct. 30, 1791 — 3 — 122

Daniel Starr, s. [Daniel G. & Eunice], b. Aug. 27, 1795 — 3 — 122

George, s. [Daniel G. & Eunice], b. Mar. 17, 1803 — 3 — 122

George, m. Julia **JEPSON**, b. of New London, Apr 11, 1826, by Rev. Isaac Stoddard — 4 — 25

George Thompson, s. [Anthony & Lucretia], b. Jan. 20, 1816 — 3 — 233

Henry Perkins, s. [Anthony & Lucretia], b. Sept. 9, 1819 — 3 — 233

John Christophers, s. [Anthony & Lucretia], b. Feb. 29, 1812 — 3 — 233

Julia H., of [New London], m. James **TOTTEN**, of U. S. Army, Dec. 5, 1843, by Rev. Robert A. Hallam — 4 — 108

Louisa, d. [Anthony & Lucretia], b. Nov. 27, 1813 — 3 — 233

Lucretia M., m. Nathaniel H. **PERRY**, of U. S. Navy, b. of New London, Jan. 27, 1828, by Rev. B. Judd — 4 — 34

Lucretia Mumford, d. [Anthony & Lucretia], b. Sept. 30, 1808 — 3 — 233

Margarett, d. [Stephen Greenlief & Boradil], b. July 14, 1806; d. Sept. 17, 1806 — 3 — 195

Mary Woodbridge, d. [Anthony & Lucretia], b. Apr. 30, 1810 — 3 — 233

Nathaniel Woodbridge, s. [Anthony & Lucretia], b. May 25, 1807 — 3 — 233

Polly, d. [Daniel G. & Eunice], b. July 1, 1793 — 3 — 122

Stephen Greenlief, m. Boradil **COIT**, d. Capt. Nathaniel, Oct. 31, 1798 — 3 — 195

William, s. [Stephen Greenlief & Boradil], b. June 1, 1802 — 3 — 195

William Penniman, s. [Daniel G. & Eunice], b. Mar. 21, 1798 — 3 — 122

THAYER, Elizabeth, of Lynconvill Districk, Me., m. Nathan **JACKSON**, [s. Giles, of Tyringham, Mass.], Sept. 5, 1802 — 3 — 196

THELFEL, James, of New York, m. Elizabeth **ROGERS**, of New London, Apr. 15, 1832, by Rev. B. Judd — 4 — 48

THOMAS, Daniel M., m. Mary L. **BEEBE**, b. of New London, Nov. 28, 1849, by Tryon Edwards — 4 — 149

Elisabeth, d. [John & Elisabeth], b. Aug. 9, 1786 — 3 — 18

Esther, d. [John & Elisabeth], b. Nov. 16, 1788 — 3 — 18

	Vol.	Page
THOMAS (cont.)		
Esther, m. John **PRINCE**, Apr. 4, 1811	3	259
Jane Simbry, d. Bennett, b. June 22, 1780 (See also Jane **SIMBRY**)	3	6
John, m. Elisabeth **GRANT**, Feb. 18, 1786	3	18
Naomi, m. David **MINER**, b. of New London, June 28, 1821, by Rev. Abel McEwen	4	4
Susan, of Waterfrdr, m. Stephen **MAYNARD**, of New London, July 29, 1832, by Chester Tilden	4	47
THOMPKINS, [see under **TOMPKIN**]		
THOMPSON, TOMSON, THOMSIN, Abby Mumford, d. [Dr. Isaac & Catharine], b. Sept. 23, 1807	3	97
Betsey, m. William **DART**, Jr., Jan. 28, 1787	3	8
Catharine E., m. Stanley G. **TROTT**, b. of New London, Oct. 2, 1832	3	233
Catherine E., m. Stanley G. **TROTT**, b. of New London, Oct. 2, 1832, by Rev. Robert A. Hallam	4	57
Catharine Elizabeth, d. [Dr. Isaac & Catharine], b. May 25, 1803	3	97
Charles, of Stratford, m. Hannah **MINER**, of New London, June 30, 1825, by Rev. Abel McEwen	4	23
Elias, s. William & Lucretia, b. Jan. 10, 1772	3	20
Elizabeth Woodbridge, d. [Dr. Isaac & Catharine], b. Apr. 19, 1811	3	97
Ellen Douglass, d. Dr. J. Thompson, of N[ew] London, m. Frederick Lenning **MEECH** (?), of Philadelphia, Apr. 17, 1833, by Rev. J. W. Hallam	4	51
Florimell F., m. Timothy S. **DABOLL**, b. of [New London], Jan. 12, 1846, by Rev. T. Edwards	4	123
Henry M., of Vermont, m. Abby E. **COMSTOCK**, of New London, May 18, 1849, by Rev. Geo[rge] M. Comstock	4	145
Ira, m. Mary L. **CULVER**, Dec. 30, 1845, by Rev. H. R. Knapp	4	122
Isaac, Dr., m. Catharine **MUMFORD**, d. John, of Lyme, Jan. 5, 1800	3	97
Jabez, s. [William & Lucretia], b. Feb. 21, 1775	3	20
James, s. [John & Polly], b. Jan. 2, 1782	3	132
James, m. Harriet **GREEN**, May 20, 1847, by Rev. Robert A. Hallam	4	131
John, of New London, m. Mary **OTIS**, d. Joseph, of New London, Nov. 5, 1724	2	110
John, b. June 3, 1757; m. Polly **GODDARD**, Nov. 11, 1779	3	132
John, s. [John & Polly], b. July 13, 1780	3	132
John Mumford, s. [Dr. Isaac & Catharine], b. July 4, 1801	3	97
Lucina H., of New London, m. George **CHAMPLEN**, of Lebanon, Ct., Apr. 29, 1849, by Rev. Geo[rge] M. Carpenter	4	145

	Vol.	Page
THOMPSON, TOMSON, THOMSIN (cont.)		
Lucretia, relict of James, m. Laban WILLIAMS, July 21, 1807	3	231
Lucretia B., of Norwich, m. Artemas G. DOUGLASS, of N[ew] London, Nov. 16, 1834, by Daniel Huntington	4	60
Lucretia Christopher, d. [Dr. Isaac & Catharine], b. Mar. 24, 1805	3	97
Lydia H., m. Edgar E. FARNHAM, [ ]	3	295
Margaret, m. John ROSSIE, b. of New London, May 31, 1846, by Rev. John Howson	4	126
Margaret F., m. Palmer LESTER, b. of New London, Nov. 25, 1841, by Rev. A. Bois	4	102
Mary, m. Jonathan SIZER, Dec. 3, 1795	3	169
Mary, d. Isaac, m. Andrew DENISON, s. Maj. Robert, b. of New London, [ ]	3	3
Mary Perkins, d. [Dr. Isaac & Catharine], b. Aug. 24, 1809	3	97
Naomi, m. Amos MASON, Feb. 24, 1771	3	117
Otis, s. John & Mary, b. Nov. 3, 1728	2	110
Rachal, m. Samuell WALLER, Aug. 24, 1704	1	30
Rachel, m. Edgecombe LEE, Dec. 7, 1780	3	68
Rachel, m. Edgecombe LEE, Dec. 7, 1780	3	88
Richard, m. Lucretia Van KNAP, Feb. 4, 1830, by Daniel Wildman	4	37
Sarah, d. John & Mary, b. Mar. 8, 1725/6	2	110
William, s. Ezra & Rachel, b. May 25, 1787. Record taken from his indenture to Stephen Bradford signed by his guardian Elijah Herrick	3	117
William, of Provincetown, Mass., m. Mary Ann WALWORTH, of Groton, May 29, 1844, by Rev. Jabez S. Swan	4	112
THOPNE, THORN, Alexander, s. William & Lydia, b. May 8, [1677]	1	11
William, of Dorsetshire, Old England, m. Lydia, widow of Thomas BAYLAY, July 28, [1676]	1	11
THORP, THARP, Amos, m. Naomy MASON, d. Japhet, Dec. 16, 1782	3	182
Amos, s. [Amos & Naomy], b. Oct. 26, 1784	3	182
Catharine, d. Nathaniel & Catharine, b. July 24, 1763	3	130
Catharine, m. Reuben DAVIS, Mar. [ ], 1784	3	130
Daniel, s. [Ezekiel & Rebecca], b. June 20, 1798	3	49
Daniel W., m. Lydia S. HOWARD, Apr. 24, 1851, by Rev. Charles Willett	4	161
Elizabeth, d. [Ezekiel & Rebecca], b. Jan. 27, 1790	3	49
Elizabeth, d. [Nathaniel & Elizabeth], b. Oct. 10, 1790	3	86
Elizabeth, m. Edward M. DARROW, b. of [New London], Sept. 3, 1845, by Rev. Abel McEwen	4	121
[E]unice Teet, d. [Amos & Naomy], b. Jan. 14, 1779	3	182
Ezekiel, m. Rebecca THORP, Jan. 24, 1788	3	49
Fanney, d. [Amos & Naomy], b. Nov. 4, 1787	3	182

	Vol.	Page

THORP, THARP (cont.)

Isaac, m. Catherine **JEFFERY**, d. Moses, Mar. 25, 1798 — 3 — 172

Isaac, s. [Nathaniel & Elizabeth], b. Mar. 15, 1802 — 3 — 86

Japhet Mason, s. [Amos & Naomy], b. Dec. 25, 1793 — 3 — 182

Jeremiah, s. [Nathaniel & Elizabeth], b. June 16, 1798 — 3 — 86

John, s. [Nathaniel & Elizabeth], b. Feb. 26, 1787 — 3 — 86

Lucy Ann, m. Mason **VAN WART**, July 4, 1848, by Rev. Tho[ma]s J. Greenwood — 4 — 140

Mary, d. [Ezekiel & Rebecca], b. Jan. 12, 1792 — 3 — 49

Nancy, d. [Ezekiel & Rebecca], b. May 26, 1796 — 3 — 49

Naomey, d. [Amos & Naomy], b. Nov. 5, 1791 — 3 — 182

Nathaniel, m. Elizabeth **HUSE**, Sept. [ ], 1786 — 3 — 86

Nathaniel, s. [Nathaniel & Elizabeth], b. Dec. 15, 1793 — 3 — 86

Rebecca, m. Ezekiel **THORP**, Jan. 24, 1788 — 3 — 49

Rebecca, d. Nathaniel, m. Oliver **STONE**, Jan. 24, 1794 — 3 — 237

Sally, d. [Ezekiel & Rebecca], b. May 1, 1788 — 3 — 49

Samuel Seabuary, s. [Isaac & Catherine], b. Nov. 28, 1802 — 3 — 172

Susan, d. [Ezekiel & Rebecca], b. Aug. 12, 1800 — 3 — 49

THURSTON, Benjamin B., of Hopkinton, R.I., m. Frances E. **DESHON**, of [New London], Mar. 12, 1834, by Rev. Isaac W. Hallam — 4 — 55

THYERS, Jason, of Groton, m. Katherine **VERNAP**, of New London, Aug. 8, 1824, by Lodowick Fosdick, J.P. — 4 — 18

TIBBITTS, Sarah W., of [New London], m. William T. **ALMY**, of Norwich, Oct. 13, 1851, by Rev. Abel McEwen — 4 — 165

TIFFANY, Marion A., m. Lodowick F. **CROCKER**, June 2, 1850, by Rev. Charles Willett — 4 — 154

TIGHE, Anna, m. Edward **GATELEY**, May 23, 1852, by Rev. J. Stokes. Witnesses: Michael Maxwell, Catharine Murphy — 4 — 170

TILL, Abba, m. Jonathan **KING**, b. of New London, June 1, 1851, by Rev. J. M. Eaton — 4 — 162

TILLER, George, m. Morinda **FANGER**, Feb. 28, 1828, by Rev. La Roy Sunderland — 4 — 33

TILLEY, Elizabeth, d. [James & Mary], b. Apr. 16, 1773; d. Feb. 11, 1791 — 3 — 225

Esther, of New London, m. Henry D. **NOYES**, of Mass., Mar. 30, 1837, by Rev. Squire B. Hascall — 4 — 68

George, s. [James & Elizabeth], b. July 7, 1799 — 3 — 225

James, of New London, s. John, of Edford, County of Devonshire, Great Britain, m. Hannah **SAVEL**, of New London, d. of John, of New London, May 27, 1742 — 2 — 84

James, s. James & Hannah, b. Nov. 24, 1744 — 2 — 84

	Vol.	Page
TILLEY (cont.)		
James, m. Mary **MILLER**, d. Jeremiah, Sept. [ ],		
1771	3	225
James, s. [James & Mary], b. May 28, 1777	3	225
James, m. Elizabeth **MILLER**, d. Jeremiah, Jan. 15,		
1797	3	225
Jeremiah Miller, s. [James & Elizabeth], b. Jan. 6,		
1798	3	225
John, s. James & Hannah, b. Mar. 24, 1749	2	84
Mary, d. James & Hannah, b. Mar. 20, 1742/3	2	84
Mary, d. [James & Mary], b. Oct. 17, 1783	3	225
Mary, w. James, d. Sept. [ ], 1796	3	225
Sarah, d. John, m. John **ROBERTSON**, Nov. 23,		
1806	3	187
William, s. [James & Mary], b. Jan. 7, 1781	3	225
TILLINGHAST, Mary Ann, m. John **FRANCISCO**, b. of		
Norwich, July 24, 1824, by Rev. Abel McEwen	4	19
TILLOTSON, TILOTSON, TILLASON,		
TILLOTTSON, TILLITSON, Almira, m. Orville		
BABCOCK, b. of Lyme, July 3, 1837, by Rev.		
Abel McEwen	4	72
Caroline, m. Zabediah Austin **COBB**, b. of Lyme,		
Feb. 26, 1822, by Rev. B. Judd	4	5
Elizabeth, d. Abraham, of Hebron, m. Isa[i]ah		
BOLLES, July 1, 1776	3	143
Harriet L., of New London, m. John **PRICE**, of New		
York, June 25, 1849, by Rev. Edwin R. Warren	4	148
Jane A., of [New London], m. David **JONES**, of		
Utica, N.Y., Dec. 10, 1848, by Rev. M. P.		
Alderman	4	144
Philenia, m. Washington **DOSETT**, May 17, 1852,		
by Rev. J. M. Eaton	4	168
Sophia, m. Charles H. **PATTISON**, b. of New		
London, Oct. 21, 1849, by Rev. Edwin R.		
Warren	4	149
TINKER, Ann, d. John, of New London, m. John		
ROGERS, s. John, late of New London, decd.,		
Nov. 17, 1748	2	100
Benj[amin], s. Jona[than] & Elizabeth, b. June 23,		
1737	2	112
Catharine, d. [Daniel & Elizabeth], b. Dec. 7, 1795	3	166
Daniel, s. [Daniel & Elizabeth], b. Feb. 5, 1786	3	166
Daniel, s. [Avery & Abigail], b. Nov. 19, 1795	3	3
Daniel, m. Harriet **JACKSON**, b. of New London,		
June 26, 1849, by Rev. Edwin R. Warren	4	148
Daniel, m. Elizabeth **HOLT**, d. Ebenezer, [ ]	3	166
Delight, of Lemster, N.H., m. W[illia]m **GEE**, Jr., of		
Lyme, Mar. 9, 1834, by Chester Tilden	4	54
Edward, s. [Daniel & Elizabeth], b. Dec. 31, 1797	3	166
Eliza, m. Daniel F. **CONKLIN**, June 22, 1823, by		
Thomas W. Tucker, Elder	4	14
Elizabeth, d. Samuel & Elizabeth, b. Nov. 5, 1728	2	111

	Vol.	Page

TINKER (cont.)

	Vol.	Page
Elizabeth, d. [John, 3d, & Mehetable], b. Dec. 9, 1769	3	190
Elisabeth, m. William **ROGERS**, Nov. 20, 1774	3	91
Elizabeth, d. [Daniel & Elizabeth], b. May 14, 1780	3	166
Elisabeth, d. Avery & Abigail, b. Feb. 12, 1793	3	3
Elizabeth, w. Daniel, d. Sept. 29, 1798	3	166
Elizabeth, d. Daniel, m. Samuel **LIT[T]LE**, June 24, 1799	3	166
Elizabeth, m. Levertt G. **LAX**, May 13, 1838, by Rev. James M .Macdonald	4	77
Elizabeth, of [New London], m. William **MINER**, of Lyme, Dec. 18, 1843, by Rev. R. A. G. Thompson	4	109
Emeline, m. Joshua **CRANDALL**, July 20, 1834	3	279
Emeline, m. Joshua **CRANDALL**, b. of [New London], July 20, 1834, by Rev. Ebenezer Blake	4	56
Esther, d. [John, 3d, & Mehetable], b. July 31, 1783	3	190
Ezekiel, m. Elisabeth **BEEBE**, Feb. 19, 1786	3	104
Fanny, m. Antonie **FRANCIS**, b. of [New London], Feb. 7, 1841, by John Lovejoy	4	93
George D., of New York, m. Abby S. **NASON**, of [New London], Nov. 30, 1851, by Rev. Jabez S. Swan	4	172
Grace, of Waterford, m. James **COLLINS**, of New London, Mar. 27, 1814	3	210
Hannah, m. Hezekiah **BEEBE**, Aug. 25, 1729	2	5
Hannah, d. [John, 3d, & Mehetable], b. Aug. 31, 1778	3	190
Hannah, d. [Daniel & Elizabeth], b. Oct. 3, 1793	3	166
Harriet, of N[ew] London, m. William **LESTER**, July 28, 1842, by L. Coyel	2	102
Harris, s. [Daniel & Elizabeth], b. Oct. 14, 1783	3	166
James, s. [John, 3d, & Mehetable], b. Apr. 24, 1772	3	190
Jeremiah, m. Polly **LESTER**, July 3, 1790	3	131
Jeremiah, of New London, m. Mary **LESTER**, of Lyme, July 4, 1790, in Lyme, by Andrew Griswold, J.P.	2	123
Jeremiah, m. Mary **CLARK**, b. of New London, Dec. 19, 1824, by Rev. B. Judd	4	2
John, b. Jan. 30, 1718; m. Elisabeth **DANIELS**, Dec. 19, 1740	3	54
John, 3d, m. Mehetable **ROGERS**, d. James, of Great Neck, June 4, 1767	3	190
John, s. [John, 3d, & Mehetable], b. Nov. 9, 1780	3	190
John, s. [Josiah & Elisabeth], b. Jan. 1, 1791; d. May 27, 1797	3	123
Joseph, s. [Daniel & Elizabeth], b. Mar. 15, 1788	3	166
Josiah, m. Elisabeth **HARRIS**, June 3, 1790	3	123
Judeth, d. Samuel & Elizabeth, b. Mar. 30, 1724	2	111

	Vol.	Page

TINKER (cont.)

Lavina, of Waterford, m. Ebenezer D. **STEBBINS**,
Nov. 29, 1842, by Henry R. Knapp — 4 — 103

Lester, s. [Ezekiel & Elisabeth], b. May 13, 1786 — 3 — 104

Lucretia, d. [Jeremiah & Polly], b. Nov. 13, 1791 — 3 — 131

Lucey, d. [Daniel & Elizabeth], b. Oct. 7, 1781 — 3 — 166

Lucy, d. [Jeremiah & Polly], b. May 8, 1793 — 3 — 131

Lucy, d. Daniel, m. John **CLARKE**, Dec. 31, 1803 — 3 — 210

Lucy, m. Nicholas **DARROW**, Jr., Jan. 10, 1813 — 3 — 214

Lucy, of New London, m. Heman **HATCH**, of
Falmouth, Mass., June 2, 1829, by Rev. Abel
McEwen — 4 — 36

Lucy, of [New London], m. Leonard **COMSTOCK**,
of Montville, Mar. 10, 1833, by James Porter
(Perhaps Lucy **TUCKER**) — 4 — 52

Margaret H., m. George R. **KIMBERLY**, b. of New
London, Nov. 17, 1850, by Rev. Jabez S. Swan — 4 — 157

Mary, m. Elias L. **DARROW**, b. of New London,
Jan. 5, 1845, by Rev. John Blain — 4 — 117

Mary C., m. Andrew J. **COMSTOCK**, b. of New
London, June 6, 1852, by Rev. Jabez S. Swan — 4 — 173

Mehetable, d. [John, 3d, & Mehetable], b. May 8,
1768 — 3 — 190

Merchant, m. Abigail **CHAPMAN**, b. of New
London, Dec. 29, 1825, by Rev. Abel McEwen — 4 — 25

Nathan, of Lyme, Ct., m. Emily **LANPHERE**, of
[New London], Aug. 17, 1848, by Rev. M. P.
Alderman — 4 — 142

Patience, m. Jonathan **LESTER**, May 15, 1729 — 2 — 54

Polly, d. (Jeremiah & Polly), b. Apr. 10, 1795 — 3 — 131

Polly, m. John **HARRIS**, Jr., Dec. 25, 1814 — 3 — 253

Richard, m. Sally **HARRIS**, d. John, Dec. 14, 1798 — 3 — 104

Richard, m. Martha S. **BEEBE**, b. of New London,
May 3, 1846, by Rev. Jabez S. Swan — 4 — 126

Rogers, s. [John, 3d, & Mehetable], b. Sept. 12, 1776 — 3 — 190

Samuel, m. Elizabeth **HARRIS**, Nov. 30, 1720 — 2 — 111

Samuel, s. Samuel & Elizabeth, b. Oct. 28, 1721 — 2 — 111

Sarah, d. [John, 3d, & Mehetable], b. Apr. 10, 1774 — 3 — 190

Sarah, m. Joseph **CHUBB**, Nov. 23, 1779 — 3 — 121

Sarah, d. [John & Elisabeth], b. De[   ] — 3 — 54

William, s. [Richard & Sally], b. Feb. 17, 1802 — 3 — 104

William, m. Emily **CHAPPELL**, Apr. 11, 1825, by
Rev. Francis Darrow — 4 — 22

TENNIE, Braddock M., m. Frances M. **COATS**, b. of
New London, Nov. 23, 1831, by Rev. Abel
McEwen — 4 — 44

TISDALE, Jane, m. John G. **CHAPPEL[L]**, b. of New
London, July 18, 1852, by Rev. Jabez S. Swan — 4 — 175

TITMAN, Benjamin, m. Lucretia **CHIPMAN**, relict of
Samuel Chipman & d. of Samuel **CHESTER**,
Dec. 14, 1799 — 3 — 36

	Vol.	Page

TITMAN (cont.)

Elizabeth, d. [Benjamin & Lucretia], b. Aug. 24,
1801 — 3, 36

Jul[i]a, d. [Benjamin & Lucretia], b. Dec. 11, 1803 — 3, 36

TOREY, Charles B., m. Fanny A. **CALVERT**, b. of [New
London], Mar. 10, 1850, by Rev. Abel McEwen — 4, 152

TOBIN, Robert, m. Catharine **ROWE**, Dec. 25, 1849, by
Rev. W[illia]m Logan — 4, 151

TOMBLING, Thankfull, m. George **SMITH**, June 5,
1720 — 1, 63

TOMLIN, Phebe, m. Nathaniel **HOULT**, Dec. 20, 1706 — 1, 39

[TOMPKIN], THOMPKINS, TOMKIN, Lorenzo D., m.
Eliza **MORGAN**, b. of [New London], Sept.
28, 1847, by Rev. Jabez S. Swan — 4, 134

Mary, d. William, of St. Ann, in Cornhill, Gt. Britain,
m. John **ROGERS**, s. Adam, Dec. 13, 1733 — 2, 94

TONGUE, Anna, d. John & Anna, b. Aug. 15, 1712 — 2, 112

Anna, of New London, m. Joseph **FOLLET**, Mar. 6,
1730/1 — 2, 112

Elizabeth, d. George & Margary, b. Oct. 20, 1652 — 1, 1

Elizabeth, d. John & Anna, b. Oct. 2, 1707 — 2, 112

George, s. George & Margary, b. May 8, [1658] — 1, 3

George, s. John & Anna, b. Sept. 30, 1705; d. May
24, 1729 — 2, 111

Hannah, d. George & Margary, b. July 20, [1654] — 1, 2

James, s. John & Anna, b. Aug. 2, 1719 — 2, 112

John, m. Anna **WHEELER**, b. of New London, Nov.
21, 1701 — 2, 111

John, m. Anna **WHEELER**, Nov. 25, 1702 — 1, 26

John, s. John & Anna, b. Apr. 12, 1704 — 2, 111

Jonathan, s. John & Anna, b. Aug. 16, 1710; d. Oct.
19, 1727 — 2, 112

Joshua, s. John & Anna, b. May 11, 1724 — 2, 112

Lydia, d. John & Anna, b. Feb. 2, 1721/2 — 2, 112

Mary, d. George & Margary, b. Sept. 17, [1657] — 1, 2

Mary, m. John **WICKWARE**, Nov. 6, 1676 — 1, 11

Mary, d. John & Anna, b. Dec. 12, 1714 — 2, 112

Tabitha, d. John & Anna, b. July 23, 1717; d. Sept. 5,
1720 — 2, 112

Tabitha, d. John & Anna, b. Jan. 23, 1727/8 — 2, 112

TOOKER, TOCKER, [see also **TUCKER**], Allyn H., of
Saybrook, m. Eliza **JEPSON**, of New London,
Oct. 17, 1824, by Rev. Abel McEwen — 4, 19

Edah, of Haddam, m. James **CONE**, of New London,
Sept. 25, 1836, by Rev. Squire B. Hascall — 4, 68

Mary, m. John **JONES**, b. of New London, Apr. 9,
1843 — 4, 102

Mary E., of [New London], m. John E. **JAGGAR**,
of New York, [Mar. 1851], by Rev. Abel
McEwen — 4, 161

	Vol.	Page

TOOKER, TOCKER (cont.)
  Michael, of Hartford, m. Elizabeth **TREBY**, of
    N[ew] London, Mar. 22, 1829, by Rev. Amasa
    Taylor — 4 — 51
TOOPY, Catharine, m. Patrick **JINISSAN**, July 20, 1847,
    by Rev. John Brady — 4 — 132
TOPLIFF, Lucina, of Willington, Ct., m. Deac. Robert
    Austin **AVERY**, of Groton, Jan. 7, 1846, by
    Rev. L. Geo[rge] Leonard — 4 — 124
  Marcy, d. [m.] Samuel **WHEELER**, s. Ephraim — 3 — 56
TORRELL, John, m. Mary **ROGERS**, d. Jonathan &
    Sarah, Aug. 11, 1825 — 3 — 209
  Julia, d. [John & Mary], b. Mar. 22, 1828 — 3 — 209
  Mary, d. [John & Mary], b. May 24, 1826 — 3 — 209
TOSSETT, Julia A., m. Stephen **HILL**, b. of [New
    London], May 21, 1847, by Rev. M. P.
    Alderman — 4 — 132
TOTTEN, James, of U. S. Army, m. Julia H.
    THATCHER, of [New London], Dec. 5, 1843,
    by Rev. Robert A. Hallam — 4 — 108
TOWN, George W., m. Sarah B. **HARRIS**, Apr. 29, 1835,
    by Rev. Alvan Ackley — 4 — 166
  Ma[t]thew, of Philadelphia, m. Mary C. **CROCKER**,
    of New London, Apr. 13, 1845, by Rev. Jabez
    S. Swan — 4 — 118
TOY, Amelia, m. Jeremiah H. **GODDARD**, [,
    1851], by Rev. Robert A. Hallam — 4 — 167
TOZER, Richard, of New London, m. Mercy **BEEBE**, of
    New London, Apr. 8, 1702 — 1 — 27
TRACY, TRACEY, Caralina, d. [Isaac & Elizabeth], b.
    July 25, 1801 — 3 — 155
  Catharine, m. Edward L. **BARKER**, b. of New
    London, Apr. 6, 1852, by Rev. Robert A.
    Hallam — 4 — 167
  Eliza, d. [Isaac & Elizabeth], b. Apr. 12, 1798 — 3 — 155
  Harriet Brown, of New London, m. Washington W.
    SHEFFIELD, of N. Stonington, Nov. 28, 1849,
    by Rev. E. R. Warren — 4 — 153
  Isaac, m. Elizabeth **HUNTINGTON**, d. Capt.
    Samuel **CHAMPLIN**, Sept. 23, 1796 — 3 — 155
  Ruth T., of Montville, m. Charles J. **WINTERS**, of
    New London, July 8, 1849, by Rev. Jabez S.
    Swan — 4 — 146
TRASON, Bertrand, m. Honora **LATON**, Aug. 12, 1849,
    by Rev. William Logan — 4 — 150
TREADWAY, Eliza A., of Salem, m. John **WATROUS**,
    of New London, June 11, 1832, by Rev. Abel
    McEwen — 4 — 47
  Frederick W., m. Sarah A. **COIT**, Nov. 4, 1839, by
    James M. Macdonald — 4 — 88
  Henry, m. Eliza **FREEMAN**, b. of [New London],
    July 8, 1838, by Rev. Robert Hallam — 4 — 78

	Vol.	Page
TREAT, Hannah, m. Abel T. **SIZER**, Apr. 25, 1822	3	168
TREBY, TRIBBY, TREBBY, Abby, d. Isaac, m. Asahel		
GROSS, July 16, 1804	3	231
Abigail, d. [Isaac & Lucretia], b. Nov. 17, 1785	3	83
Charlotte, d. [Isaac & Lucretia], b. Mar. 13, 1788	3	83
Charlotte, d. Isaac, m. Ebenezer **GODDARD**, Jr.,		
Oct. 12, 1806	3	198
Charlotet, d. Isaac, m. Ebenezer **GODDARD**, Jr.,		
Oct. 12, 1806	3	233
Elizabeth, of N[ew] London, m. Michael **TOOKER**,		
of Hartford, Mar. 22, 1829, by Rev. Amasa		
Taylor	4	51
George, s. [Isaac & Lucretia], b. Aug. 23, 1791	3	83
Isaac, s. Sam[ue]l & Elizabeth, of Newport, R.I., m.		
Lucretia **HARRIS**, d. Richard & Mary, Jan. 23,		
1783	3	83
Julia, of New London, m. John **SIMMS**, of		
Canterbury, Oct. 30, 1822, by Thomas W.		
Tucker, Elder	4	10
Lucretia, d. [Isaac & Lucretia], b. Nov. 21, 1783	3	83
Margaret, m. Henry **LOOK**, b. of [New London],		
Sept. 10, 1838, by Rev. C. C. Williams	4	79
Mary, b. Aug. [ ], 1783; m. Samuel **SIZER**, May 26,		
1799	3	200
Mehetable, m. Daniel **CHAPMAN**, Dec. 26, 1784	3	174
TRIMBLE, Emeline A., of Newark, N.J., m. William		
H. **LEWIS**, of New London, Jan. 10, 1847, by		
Rev. Frederick Wightman	4	128
TRIPP, Barsheba, of North Kingston, d. of Job, m.		
Richard **SMITH**, of New London, s. John, June		
6, 1741	2	99
TROOP, Ma[r]tha B., of New London, m. Peleg T.		
LOOMIS, of Coventry, Oct. 19, 1826, by Rev.		
Abel McEwen	4	27
TROTT, TROT, Elizabeth, d. [John P. & Louis[e], b.		
Sept. 3, 1798	3	144
Elizabeth C., m. Jirah **ISHAM**, May 28, 1823	3	203
Elizabeth C., m. Genl. Jirah **ISHAM**, b. of New		
London, May 28, 1823, by Rev. B. Judd	4	14
Isaac Thompson, s. [Stanley G. & Catharine E.], b.		
July 26, 1834	3	233
John, s. [John P. & Louis[e], b. June 26, 1797	3	144
John P., m. Louis[e] **CHAPMAN**, d. Capt. Joseph		
Chapman, of Norwich, Dec. 11, 1796	3	144
John Proctor, s. [Thomas P. & Susan], b. Oct. 7, 1824	3	265
Louisa, d. [John P. & Louis[e], b. Aug. 22, 1801	3	144
Lydia, d. [John P. & Louis[e], b. Mar. 12, 1803	3	144
Mary Johnston, d. [John P. & Louis], b. Dec. 29,		
1806	3	144
Nancy Dow, d. [John P. & Louis], b. Dec. 4, 1808	3	144

	Vol.	Page

TROTT, TROT (cont.)

Sarah E., m. George W. **WOODWARD**, b. of
   Wilkesbarre, Pa., Sept. 10, 1832, by Rev. B.
   Judd — 4 — 49

Stanl[e]y, s. [John P. & Louis], b. Aug. 23 ,1804 — 3 — 144

Stanley G., m .Catharine E. **THOMPSON**, b. of New
   London, Oct. 2, 1832 — 3 — 233

Stanley G., m. Catherine E. **THOMPSON**, b. of New
   London, Oct. 2, 1832, by Rev. Robert A.
   Hallam — 4 — 57

Thomas, m. Susan **GRIFFING**, b. of New London,
   Dec. 24, 1823, by Rev. Abel McEwen — 4 — 17

Thomas P., m. Susan **GRIFFING**, d. Christo[pher],
   Dec. 24, 1823 — 3 — 265

Thomas Procter, s. [John P. & Louis], b. Dec. 24,
   1799 — 3 — 144

TRUE, Hannah E., of New London, m. William J.
   SEELEY, of New York, Oct. 19, 1845, by Rev.
   Thoma]s J. Greenwood — 4 — 122

TRUMAN, TRUEMAN, Abigail, d. Jonathan & Abigail,
   b. May 16, 1758 — 2 — 120

Benjamin, s. Joseph & Mary, b. July 11, 1715 — 1 — 46

Clark, s. Eleazer & Mary, b. Sept. 29, 1736 — 2 — 79

Daniell, s. Joseph & Mary, b. Oct. 24, 1717 — 1 — 49

Eleazer, b. Dec. 6, 1705; m. Mary **CLARK**, Oct. 19,
   1727 — 2 — 79

Elizabeth, d. Joseph & Mary, b. Aug. 29, 1704 — 1 — 30

Elizabeth, d. Joseph, Jr. & Mary, b. Jan. 2, 1735/6 — 2 — 112

Elizabeth, d. Jonathan & Abigail, b. Feb. 12, 1765 — 2 — 120

Elizabeth, m. John **GRIFFING**, June 8, 1725 — 2 — 30

Elizabeth, d. Joseph, m. John **GRIFFING**, s.
   Eben[eze]r, b. of New London, June 8, 1725 — 2 — 78

Hannah, d. Eleazer & Mary, b. Aug. 2, 1747 — 2 — 79

Henry, s. Joseph & Mary, b. Apr. 22, 1713 — 1 — 40

Henry, m. Rebecca **STARR**, June 9, 1776 — 1 — 26

Jane, d. Joseph & Mary, b. Dec. 20, 1710 — 1 — 38

Jane, d. Joseph, of New London, m. Samuel **LEE**, s.
   Thomas, of Lyme, June 20, 1733 — 2 — 26

Jane, m. Samuel **LEE**, June 20, 1733 — 2 — 54

John, s. Joseph & Mary, b. Dec. 20, 1708 — 1 — 66

John, s. Eleazer & Mary, b. Sept. 10, 1728 — 2 — 79

John, s. Joseph, d. Mar. 20, 1738/9, at Cow Nick, L.I. — 2 — 113

John, s. Joseph, Jr. & Mary, b. Feb. [ ], 1743/4 — 2 — 113

John Ephraim, s. Jona[than] & Abigail b. Sept. 9,
   [17], in Bakersman, Dutchess County, N.Y. — 2 — 120

Jonathan, s. Eleazer & Mary, b. Oct. 6, 1745 — 2 — 79

Jonathan, of New London, m. Abigail **PIERCE**, of
   Providence, R.I., d. of Nathan, of Providence,
   R.I., Dec. 7, 1751, in Providence, by
   Christopher Harris, J.P. — 2 — 119

Jonathan, s. Jonathan & Abigail, b. June 25, 1763 — 2 — 120

Joseph, m. Mary **SHAPLEY**, Dec. 5, 1701 — 1 — 27

	Vol.	Page
TRUMAN, TRUEMAN (cont.)		
Joseph, s. Joseph & Mary, b. Nov. 20, 1706	1	32
Joseph, Jr., m. Mary **HEMPSTEAD**, Mar. 22, 1733	2	112
Joseph, s. Joseph, Jr. & Mary, b. Apr. 5, 1738	2	112
Mary, m. Benony **HORTON**, Apr. 15, 1700	1	25
Mary, d. Joseph & Mary, b. Oct. 2, 1702	1	28
Mary, [w. Eleazer ?], b. Nov. 15, 1709	2	79
Mary, w. Joseph, d. Aug. 24, 1719	1	58
Mary, m. Peter **HARRIS**, July 3, 1726	2	39
Mary, d. Joseph, Jr. & Mary, b. Feb. 6, 1733/4	2	112
Mary, d. Eleazer & Mary, b. July 25, 1740	2	79
Mary, d. Daniel, b. Apr. 28, 1761; m. Daniel		
CHAPMAN, Dec. 18, 1796	3	174
Nathan, s. Jona[than], & Abi[gail], b. Apr. 11, 1754;		
drowned July 16, 1756	2	120
Nathan, s. Jonathan & Abigail, b. May 7, 1767	2	120
Rebecca, d. [Henry & Rebecca], b. June 2, 1777	3	26
Rebecah, d. Capt. Henry, m. Francis **HAZARD**, July		
2, 1798	3	145
Sarah, d. Joseph, Jr. & Mary, b. Feb. 6, 1739/40	2	113
Sarah, d. Jona[than], & Abigail, b. Apr. 11, 1756	2	120
Susanna, d. Eleazer & Mary, b. Apr. 13, 1742	2	79
Susannah, of Southold, L.I., m. Lester **ROGERS**,		
Apr. 14, 1795	3	45
Susanna, d. Jonathan & Abigail, b. Aug. 4, 17[ ]	2	120
Thomas, s. Jonathan & [Abigail], b. May 16, 1752	2	120
William, s. Eleazer & Mary, b. Apr. 10, 1730	2	79
TUBBS, Dorcas, d. Samuell & Mary, b. Mar. 2, 1688/90	1	19
Elisha, m. Mary **CHAPELL**, d. Isaac, June 1, 1803	3	234
Elisha, d. Jan. 1, 1808	3	234
Joseph, s. Samuel & Mary, b. Sept. 3, 1692	1	21
Mary, of New London, m. Elijah **ABEL**, of Bozrah,		
Oct. 5, 1829, by Rev. Abel McEwen	4	37
Sarah, m. Samuel **BEEBE**, s. William, May 29, 1710	1	52
Sarah, d. Samuel, m. Samuel **BEEBE**, s. William,		
May 29, 1710	2	19
TUCKER, [see also **TOOKER**], Albigence W., of		
Walworth, N.Y., m. Frances E. **ALLEN**, of		
N[ew] London, May 9, 1832, by Rev. B. Judd	4	49
David, m. Mercey **HOLLY,** negroes, Jan. 12, 1809,		
by Elder Samuel West	3	106
Lucy, of [New London], m. Leonard **COMSTOCK**,		
of Montville, Mar. 10, 1833, by James Porter		
(Perhaps Lucy Tinker)	4	52
Mary Bagnall, d. Thomas W. & Polly, b. Jan. 8, 1824	3	194
TUFTS, [see also **TEFFT**], Eldrige, m. Catharine Epes		
COPELAND, Jan. 24, 1848, by Rev. Tho[ma]s		
J. Greenwood	4	137
TULL, Susan, of Groton, m. John **EVANS**, of New		
London, Jan. 8, 1837, by Rev. Squire B. Hascall	4	68
TUMULTY, [see under **TURNULTY**]		

	Vol.	Page
TURNER, Abiga[i]ll, m. Clement **MINOR**, Jr., Jan. 9, 1721/2	2	9
Abiga[I]ll, m. Clement **MINOR**, Jan. 9, 1721/22	1	58
Ann, m. Wanton A. **WEAVER**, Apr. 26, 1818	3	246
Bridgett, d. Jonathan, of New London ,m. William **HARRIS**, of New London, s. W[illia]m, July 15, 1739	2	61
Charles, s. John & Elizabeth, b. Aug. 23, 1754	2	99
Charles, s. Guy, b Dec. 1, 1819	3	180
David, s. Mat[t]hew & Elisabeth, b. Apr. 10, 1776	3	71
Delight, d. Thomas & Patience, b. Feb. 4, 1757	2	91
Dibmore, s. Thomas & Patience, b. Oct. 19, 1731	2	112
Elisha, u. Guy, b. Jan. 20, 1822	3	180
Elizabeth, d. Ezekiel & Susannah, b. Dec. 5, 1696	1	22
Elisebeth, d. Pain & Elinor, b. Dec. 12, 1746	3	10
Elizabeth, d. John & Bathsheba, b. June 16, 1753	2	101
Elizabeth, d. John & Elizabeth, b. May 9, 1757	2	99
Elizabeth, d. Mather & Elizabeth, b. Aug. 2, 1765	2	101
Emma, of New London, m. Lyman **ALLEN**, of Springfield, Mass., June 5, 1825, by Rev. Abel McEwen	4	23
Emy, d. [John & Mary], b. Aug. 31, 1804	3	205
Ezekiel, s. John, of Cittuate, [Mass.], m. Susanna, d. John **KENNEY**, of New London, Dec. 26, [1678]	1	13
Ezekiel, m. Susannah **KEENEY**, Dec. 26, 1678	1	14
Ezekiel, s. John, of Sittuate, m. Susannah, d. Jno. **KEYNEY**, Dec. 26, 1678	1	68
Ezekiel, s. Ezekiel & Susannah, b. Mar. 14, 1699	1	25
Ezekiel, d. Jan. 19, 1703/4	1	29
Grace, of Scituate, m. Richard **CHRISTOPHERS**, Sept. 3, 1691	1	20
Grace, d. Ezekiel & Susannah, b. Aug. 29 ,1692	1	21
Grace, m. Joseph **MINOR**, Jr. Feb. 26, 1712/13	1	39
Hannah, d. Ezekiel & Susannah, b. Sept. 8, 1694	1	22
Hannah, m. Thomas **PEMBER**, Mar. 18, 1712	1	54
Hannah, d. Pain & Ele[a]nor, b. Feb. 26, 1756	3	10
Isaac, s. Mather & Mary, b. Apr. 2, 1754	2	101
Isaac, s. John & Elizabeth, b. Nov. 26, 1759	2	99
James, s. John & Bathsheba, b. June 5, 1757	2	101
James, s. [Matthew & Elisabeth], b. July 13, 1781	3	71
James H., m. Jane W. **CLARK**, Nov. 25, 1841, by Rev. A. Bois	4	102
Jemima, d. Pain & Ele[a]nor, b. Apr. 30, 1758	3	10
John, s. Thomas &Patience, b. July 29, 1728	2	112
John, s. Tho[ma]s, of New London, m. Bathsheba **WHIPPLE**, d. Zachariah, of New London, Nov. 1, 1750	2	101
John, of New London, s. Jonathan, decd., m. Elizabeth **HAINES**, d. Charles, late of New London, decd., Nov. 4, 1750	2	99
John, s. John & Bathsheba, b. Nov. 16, 1751	2	101

	Vol.	Page
TURNER (cont.)		
John, s. Mather &Elizabeth, b. Jan. 19, 1777	2	101
John, m. Mary **NEWSON**, d. Robert, Oct. 2, 1798	3	205
John, lost at sea Sept. [ ], 1804	3	205
Jona[than], s. Pain & Eliner, b. July 24, 1748	3	10
Jonathan, s. Mather & Elizabeth, b. May 20, 1768	2	101
Jonathan T., m. Adelaide D. **RICHARDS**, b. of New London, Nov. 5, 1833, by Rev. Abel McEwen	4	53
Josiah B., m. Julia H. **ISHAM**, July 15, 1822, by Rev. B. Judd	4	10
Lucretia, d. Ezekiel & Susannah, b. Jan. 20, 1701	1	27
Lucretia, m. Joseph **CAULKINS**, Mar. 28, 1721	2	6
Lucretia, d. John, b. Sept. 25, 1768; m. Luther **GALE**, June 21, 1790, by Rev. Henry Channing	3	153
Lydia, d. Ezekiel & Susanna, b. Sept. 5, 1690	1	20
Lydia, m. Joseph **SMITH**, Feb. 20, 1785	3	140
Mary, d. Ezekiel & Susanna, b. May 30, 1686	1	18
Mary, d. Mather & Elizabeth, b. Nov. 22, 1760	2	101
Mary, of New London, m. Francis **CULVENS**, of New Orleans, May 24, 1831, by Rev. Abel McEwen	4	42
Mary L., m. William P. **BENJAMIN**, July 20, 1834, by Rev. Alvan Ackley	4	56
Mather, m. Elizabeth **SMITH**, d. Jona[than], of New London, Feb. 14, 1760	2	101
Mather, s. Mather & Elizabeth, b. June 16, 1773	2	102
Matthew, s. Thomas & Patience, b. Oct. 12, 1733	2	112
Mercy, d. Thomas & Patience, b. Apr. 27, 1740	2	91
Mercy, d. John & Elizabeth, b. Aug. 26, 1751	2	99
Mercy, d. Thomas, of New London, m. Moses **FARGO**, 2d, s. Robert, late of New London, decd., Feb. 14, 1762	3	23
Nancy, m. Marvin **WAIT**, Nov. 15, 1810, at New York	3	42
Pain, s. Jonathan, of New London, m. Eleanor **HAINES**, d. Jona[than], late of New London, decd., Nov. 3, 1745	3	10
Pain, s. Pain & Ele[a]nor, b. May 7, 1754	3	10
Peregreene, s. Mather & Elizabeth, b. Nov. 2, 1762	2	101
Peregrine, of New London, m. Romelia **POTTER**, Apr. 8, 1844, by Rev. G. Thompson	4	111
Peter C., m. Mary L. **MASON**, b. of New London, Dec. 6, 1826, by Rev. Bethel Judd	4	28
Ruth, d. Ezekiel & Susannah, b. Mar. 2, 1688	1	18
Samuel, s. Thomas & Patience, b. Mar. 6, 1741/2	2	91
Samuel R., m. Hannah **BUTLER**, b. of New London, May 16, 1837, by Daniel Huntington	4	70
Sarah, d. Ezekiel & Susannah, b. Oct. 28, 1683	1	17
Sarah, m. Jonathan **CALKINS**, Dec. 11, 1700	1	61
Sarah, d. Thomas & Patience, b. Nov. 15, 1729	2	112

	Vol.	Page

TURNER (cont.)

Sarah, d. Thomas, of New London, m. Jabez
STUBBENS, s. Chris[tophe]r, of New London,
May 19, 1748 — 2, 103

Sarah, d. Pain & Eliner, b. May 24, 1750 — 3, 10

Sarah, d. [Matthew & Elisabeth], b. Aug. 4, 1779 — 3, 71

Sarah, d. John, m. Isaac Van Hook **CRANNALL**,
Dec. 24, 1789 — 3, 165

Susannah, d. Ezekiel & Susannah, b. Jan. 2, 1685 — 1, 17

Susannah, m. Adam **PICKETT**, Nov. 26, 1702 — 1, 27

Susannah, m. Sam[ue]l **FOSDICK**, July 13, 1706 — 1, 62

Susanna, wid., m. Joseph **MINOR**, Aug. 20, 1706 — 1, 52

Thomas, m. Patience **BOLLES**, Nov. 23, 1727 — 2, 112

Thomas, s. John & Bathsheba, b. June 11, 1759 — 2, 101

Tho[ma]s, m. Mercy **WATERHOUSE**, wid. of John,
late of New London, decd., Dec. 8, 1770 — 2, 91

Timothy W., of Uncasville, m. Tabathy
BUD[D]INGTON, of Ledyard, Oct. 11, 1842,
by L. Covel — 4, 103

Zip[p]orah, d. Thomas & Patience, b. Nov. 1, 1743 — 2, 91

TURNULTY*, Mary, m. Michael **FITZMAURICE**, Feb.
11, 1849, by Rev. William Logan   *(Perhaps
"**TUMULTY**") — 4, 150

TUTTLE, TUTHILL, Ann, d. Daniel & Sarah, b. Feb. 25,
1730 — 2, 111

Daniel, m. Sarah **COMSTOCK**, Mar. [ ], 1728 — 2, 111

Elizabeth, d. Daniel & Sarah, b. [ ], 173[ ] — 2, 111

Henrietta A., m. James **CROCKER**, b. of New
London, Apr. 30, 1843, by Rev. Lemuel Covell — 4, 109

Mary, m. Lester **ROGERS**, Jan. 22, 1795 — 3, 134

TYE, Julia, m. Bernard **MILLER**, b. of New London, July
14, 1850, by T. Edwards — 4, 154

TYLER, Charles H., of Springfield, Mass., m. Julia M.
FERGUSON, of Stafford, Ct., June 10, 1852,
by Rev. Thomas Ely — 4, 168

Charlotte A., m. William **HARRIS**, Oct. 1, 1845, by
Rev. Tryon Edwards — 4, 121

UNCAS, Anna, d. John & Hannah, b. Aug. 17, 1749 — 3, 6

Hannah, d. John & Hannah, b. Jan. 20, 1754 — 3, 6

John, d. Apr. 17, 1755 — 3, 6

Joshua, s. John & Hannah, b. June 14, 1747 — 3, 6

Mary Ann, m. William **LITTLE**, b. of New London,
June 5, 1831, by Rev. Abel McEwen — 4, 42

Noah, s. John & Hannah, b. Dec. 17, 1742 — 3, 6

UPDIKE, Est[h]er, m. Thomas **FOSDICK**, June 29, 1720 — 1, 58

UPHIN*, Junies, m. Nancy **HALLADAY**, b. of [New
London], May 13, 1850, by Aaron E. Stone,
J.P.   *(Perhaps "**APHIN**") — 4, 153

UPWARD, John, m. Harriet E. **DART**, b. of [New
London], June 1, 1847, by Rev. Abel McEwen — 4, 132

	Vol.	Page

VAIL, Charles C., of River Head, L.I., N.Y., m. Ellen P.
    HAINES, of Lyme, Sept. 16, 1847, by Rev. L.
    G. Leonard   4   138

VALENTINE, VOLENTINE, Benjamin, m. Nancy
    CORNELL, May 25, 1833, by James Porter   4   50
    Lawrence, of New York, m. Mary **HARRISON**, of
    East Haddam, June 8, 1845, by Rev. Jabez S.
    Swan   4   120
    Samuel M., of New York, m. Elizabeth
    HEMPSTEAD, of [New London], May 13,
    1843, by Rev. Abel McEwen   4   105

VAN COTT, Joshua, of Long Island, m. Nancy
    REYNOLDS, of [New London], Dec. 16,
    1838, by Rev. J. M. Macdonald   4   80
    Nancy, of [New London], m. James E. **HOSKIN**, of
    Philadelphia, June 9, 1840, by Rev. Abel
    McEwen   4   90

VAN DEUSEN, Molly, of [Great Barrington], m. John
    ROGERS, of New London, Sept. 24, 1792, by
    Rev. Gideon Bostwick, of Great Barrington   3   77

VAN KNAP, VANAPS, VAN NAPP, [see also **VANARP**
    and **VERNAP**], Emmeline of New London, m.
    Charles A. **BUNNELL**, of Middlebury, Ohio,
    Sept. 13, 1849, by Rev. T. Edwards   4   147
    Lucretia, m. Richard **THOMPSON**, Feb. 4, 1830, by
    Daniel Wildman   4   37
    Mary Ann, m. Joseph **LEACH**, b. of New London,
    Mar. 20, 1843, by L. Covell   4   101

VANARP, [see also **VAN KNAPP** and **VERNAP**],
    Adam, s. [Frances & Sarah], b. Sept. 10, 1808   3   220
    Catherine, d. [Frances & Sarah], b. Dec. 17, 1810   3   220
    Frances, m. Sarah **FILES**, d. Adam, Dec. 25, 1801   3   220
    Frances, s. [Frances & Sarah], b. Feb. 3, 1805   3   220
    Hannah, d. [Frances & Sarah], b. Aug. 26, 1803   3   220

VANDEVORT, Hannah, of New London, m. George
    DERRY, of East Haddam, Oct. 24, 1825, by
    Rev. Abel McEwen   4   24

VANDERWATER, James B., m. M. D. **HOXIE**, Nov.
    23, 1851, by Rev. James W. Dennis   4   165

VAN WART, Mason, m. Lucy Ann **THORP**, July 4,
    1848, by Rev. Tho[ma]s J. Greenwood   4   140

VARLEY, William, m. Frances C. **WATROUS**, Feb. 16,
    1842, by H. R. Knapp   4   101

VERGUSON, Henry D., m. Sophia **ROGERS**, b. of [New
    London], Mar. 29, 1846, by Rev. L. Geo[rge]
    Leonard   4   125

VERNAP, [see also **VAN KNAP**, and **VANARP**],
    Katherine, of New London, m. Jason
    THYERS, of Groton, Aug. 8, 1824, by
    Lodowick Fosdick, J.P.   4   18

VIBER, Amia, d. John, Jr., b. June 8, 1742   3   3
    Ann, d. John & Johannah, b. Dec. 6, 1729   2   113

	Vol.	Page
VIBER (cont.)		
Catharine, d. John, Jr., b. Nov. 11, 1738	3	3
Joanna, d. John, Jr., b. May 28, 1744	3	3
John, Jr., s. John, m. [ ], b. of New London, Apr. 28, 1737	3	3
John, s. John, Jr., b. June 8, 1740	3	3
Katharine, d. John, of New London, m. Ransford **COMSTOCK**, s. Peter, late of New London, decd., Dec. 13, 1761	3	51
Margaret, d. John & Johannah, b. Nov. 20, 1726	2	113
Obedience, d. John, Jr., b. May [ ], 1748; d. Jan. 28, 175[ ]	3	3
Thomas, s. John & Johannah, b. Nov. 9, 1722	2	113
VINCENT, Frank, of New York, m. Harriet **BARNES**, of [New London], Aug. 11, 1845, by Rev. Abel McEwen	4	120
VINE, Mary, of Old England, m. James **MORGAN**, s. James, "sometime in the month of November", [1666]	1	5
WADE, WAIDE, George, m. Sally A. **COOK**, b. of New London, Mar. 21, 1833, by James Porter	4	50
Jared, m. Ellen **MASON**, Nov. 7, 1847, by Rev. M. P. Alderman	4	135
Lyman, of Lyme, m. Sarah **BECKWITH**, of Waterford, Feb. 21, 1836, by Rev. Squire B. Hascall	4	83
Sally Ann, of [New London], m. Robert **SMITH**, of Philadelphia, June 6, 1842, by Rev. J. W. True	4	102
-----, of Lyme, m. Mercy **PEMBER**, Jan. 8, 1707	1	33
WAIT, Abby Eliza, d. [Samuel & Abigail], b. Feb. 12, 1807	3	178
Alexander Samuel, s. [Samuel & Abigail], b. Apr. 25, 1805	3	178
Eliza*, d. [Marvin & Patty], b. May 4, 1798 *(First written "Patty")	3	42
Hannah, d. [Marvin & Patty], b. Sept. 24, 1789	3	42
Harriot, d. [Marvin & Patty], b. Nov. 27, 1785	3	42
Harriot, m. Leonard D. **RICHARDS**, Nov. 5, 1809, by Rev. Abel McEwen	3	241
John, s. [Samuel & Abigail], b. Feb. 13, 1803	3	178
Marvin, m. Patty **JONES**, b. of New London, Apr. 25, 1779	3	42
Marvin, s. [Marvin & Patty], b. June 22, 1781	3	42
Marvin, m. Har[r]iet **SALTONSTALL**, Apr. 22, 1805	3	42
Marvin, s. [Marvin & Har[r]iet], b. Dec. 10, 1806	3	42
Marvin, m. Nancy **TURNER**, Nov. 15, 1810, at New York	3	42
Oliver, s. [Marvin & Patty], b. Aug. 29, 1791	3	42
Patty Jones, d. [Marvin & Patty], b. Nov. 5, 1782	3	42
Prentice A., m. Esther **MASON**, b. of New London, July 15, 1833, by Chester Tilden	4	52

	Vol.	Page
WAIT (cont.)		
Richard, s. [Marvin & Patty], b. Dec. 20, 1787	3	42
Samuel, m. Abigail **CHADWICK**, d. R[e]uben, of		
Lyme, Apr. 8, 1799	3	178
Seth, s. [Samuel & Abigail], b. Jan. 1, 1801	3	178
Turner, s. [Marvin & Nancy], b. Aug. 27, 1811	3	42
WAKE, Grace, d. John & Mary, b. Mar. 21, 1760	3	15
John, s. John & Mary, b. Apr. 24, 1747	3	15
Lucy, d. John & Mary, b. Sept. 28, 1757	3	15
Samuel, s. John & Mary, b. Oct. 1, 1753	3	15
Sarah, d. John & Mary, b. Oct. 4, 1755	3	15
WALDEN, Amy, d. [William & Ruamini], b. Feb. 4, 1774	2	71
David, s. [William & Ruamini], b. Dec. 4, 1781	2	71
Ebenezer, s. William & Ruamini, b. June 27, 1755	2	71
Edward, s. [William & Ruamini], b. Apr. 31, 1778		
[sic]	2	71
Elizabeth, d. [William & Ruamini], b. June 17, 1759	2	71
Elizabeth, d. [John & Elizabeth], b. May 13, 1798	3	181
John, s. William & Ruamini, b. June 21, 1757	2	71
John, m. Elizabeth **WATROUS**, d. John, Mar. 15,		
1797	3	181
Mary, d. [William & Ruamini], b. Nov. 24, 1771	2	71
Robert, s. [William & Ruamini], b. Nov. 1, 1766	2	71
Sarah, d. [John & Elizabeth], b. June 10, 1802	3	181
Simons, s. [William & Ruamini], b. Sept. 7 ,1768	2	71
William, of Bristol, Gt. Britain, s. William, m.		
Ruamini **SIMONS**, of New London, d.		
Eben[eze]r, of New London, Aug. 5, 1754	2	71
William, s. [William & Ruamini], b. Sept. 13, 1762	2	71
WALES, Perry, of New York, m. Abby **MORRIS**, of		
[New London], (colored), Aug. 12, 1845, by		
Rev. L. Geo[rge] Leonard	4	123
Susan, d. Shub[a]el, m. Jeremiah **KEENEY**, Oct. 21,		
1802	3	177
WALKER, Ann R., of New London, m. Sanford B.		
SMITH, of Ledyard, Nov. 14, 1840, by Rev.		
Jared B. Avery	4	93
Augustus, s. [John & Ann], b. Jan. 13, 1810	3	223
David, s. [John & Mary], b. Nov. 8, 1808	3	40
David, m. Almira **OSBORN**, Aug. 25, 1833, by Rev.		
Abel McEwen	4	53
Deborah, d. [John & Ann], b. Nov. 15, 1796	3	223
Elizabeth, d. [John & Ann], b. Sept. 29, 1804	3	223
Frances Emeline, d. [John & Ann], b. Jan. 21, 1807	3	223
Harriot, d. [John & Ann], b. Dec. 3, 1802	3	223
John, m. Ann **PHILLIPS**, d. Michael, Dec. 24, 1786	3	223
John, s. [John & Ann], b. Sept. 29, 1787	3	223
John, m. Mary **KNAPP**, Dec. 9, 1807	3	40
Lucy, d. [John & Ann], b. Mar. 17, 1793	3	223
Mary, d. [John & Ann], b. Nov. 11, 1794	3	223
Michael Phillips, s. [John & Ann], b. Aug. 15, 1791	3	223
Nancy, d. [John & Ann], b. May 13, 1789	3	223

	Vol.	Page
WALKER (cont.)		
Robert, s. [John & Ann], b. Sept. 7, 1801	3	223
Samuel, s. Richard & Hannah, b. Nov. 13, [1695]	1	22
Sarah, d. [John & Ann], b. Nov. 3, 1798	3	223
WALLER, Ann Spencer, d. [Robert K. & Abby], b. July		
18, 1828	3	217
Robert K., m. Abby **YOUNG**, d. William & Nabby,		
Sept. 20, 1827	3	217
Robert K., m. Abby **YOUNG**, b. of New London,		
Sept. 17, 1827, by Henry Wightman	4	32
Samuell, m. Mary **DANNIELL**, Dec. 26, 1685	1	68
Samuell, m. Rachal **THOMSIN**, Aug. 24, 1704	1	30
William, s. Samuell & Mary, b. Aug. 17, 1686	1	68
WALWORTH, Mary Ann, of Groton, m. William		
THOMPSON, of Provincetown, Mass., May		
29, 1844, by Rev. Jabez S. Swan	4	112
WANT, Ann, d. Philip & Mary, b. Sept. 11, 1733	2	115
Ann, of New London, d. Phillip, decd., m. Patrick		
WARD, of Cork, Ireland, July 27, 1754	3	31
Benjamin, s. Philip & Mary, b. July 28, 1731	2	115
Joseph, s. Philip & Mary, b. Feb. 10, 1738/9	2	116
Joseph, s. Philip, d. Sept. 11, 1740, ae 19 m.	2	116
Martha, d. Philip & Mary, b. Sept. 26, 1725	2	115
Mary, d. Philip & Mary, b. Oct. 6, 1723	2	115
Mary, m. Isaac **FELLOWS**, Sept. 13, 1742	2	26
Philip, m. Mary **COMSTOCK**, May 25, 1721	2	117
Philip, s. Philip & Mary, b. July 20, 1736	2	115
Philip, d. Mar. 7, 1739/40, ae 40 y.	2	116
Thomas, s. Philip & Mary, b. May 4, 1729	2	115
William, s. Philip & Mary, b. Feb. 20, 1721/2	2	117
WANTON, Ann, eldest d. Hon. Joseph & Mary, of		
Newport, b. Dec. 16, 1732, O. S., at Newport;		
m. Winthrop **SALTONSTALL**, eldest		
surviving s. Gurdon & Rebecca, Apr. 17, 1763,		
N.S.	3	63
WARD, Aaron, [s. John & Irene], b. May 7, 1765; d. Sept.		
2, 1765	3	79
Abby A., m. Alonzo **LEWIS**, b. of New London,		
Oct. 9, 1842	4	103
Abigail, d. [John & Irene], b. Apr. 20, 1760; d. Sept.		
8, 1761	3	79
Abraham, twin with Isaac, [s. John & Irene], b. Aug.		
8, 1761; d. Sept. 1, 1761	3	79
Benjamin, s. John & Irene, b. Nov. 14, 1751	2	114
Benjamin, s. [John & Irene], b. Nov. 14, 1751; d. Jan.		
10, 1774	3	79
Benjamin, s. Patrick & Ann, b. May 20, 1754	3	31
Catharine, m. John **REGAN**, May 12, 1849, by Rev.		
William Logan	4	150
Chris[topher], s. John & Irene, b. Oct. 13, 1770	2	114
Christopher, [s. John & Irene], b. Oct. 13, 1770	3	79
Crittenton, s. John & Irene, b. Feb. 14, 1753	2	114

	Vol.	Page

WARD (cont.)

	Vol.	Page
Cruttenden, s. [John & Irene], b. Feb. 15, 1753	3	79
Cruttenden, m. Elisabeth **AMES**, June 25, 1780	3	125
Cruttenden, drowned July 27, 1793	3	125
Edmond, [s. John & Irene], b. Nov. 18, 1766; d. Jan. 22, 1767	3	79
Elizabeth, d. John & Irene, b. Oct. 11, 1754 (twin with Lydia)	2	114
Elisabeth, twin with Lydia, [d. John & Irene], b. Oct. 11, 1754; d. Oct. 25, 1761	3	79
Elisabeth, [w. Cruttenden], d. Aug. 1, 1792	3	125
George, [s. John & Irene], b. Dec. 31, 1763; d. Feb. [ ], 1764	3	79
Irene, [d. John & Irene], b. Feb. 1, 1768; d. Apr. 11, 1768	3	79
Irene, [d. John & Irene], b. Jan. 19, 1772; d. Sept. [ ], 1773	3	79
Isaac, twin with Abraham, [s. John & Irene], b. Aug. 8, 1761; d. Aug. 28, [1761]	3	79
James, s. Patrick & his former wife [ ] **SPRINGER**, b. Sept. 10, 1750. Recorded June 3, 1765, at the desire of Ann Ward	3	31
Jane, m. Michael **MURRAY**, June 22, 1846, by Rev. John Brady	4	127
Jeremiah, s. John & Irene, b. Feb. 1, 1759	2	114
Jeremiah, [s. John & Irene], b. Feb. 1, 1759; d. Sept. 13, 1780	3	79
John, s. John & Elizabeth, b. [ ], 12, 1724	2	116
John, of New London, m. Irene **CRENTTENTON**, of Guilford, Feb. 18, 1747/8	2	114
John, m. Irene **CRUTTENDEN**, Feb. 18, 1748	3	79
John, s. John & Irene, b. July 22, 1749	2	114
John, s. [John & Irene], b. July 22, 1749	3	79
John, drowned Feb. 26, 1771	3	79
John, m. Harriet **WILLIAMS**, May 21, 1841, by John Lovejoy	4	95
Lydia, d. [John & Irene], b. Sept. 25, 1750; d. Oct. 9, following	3	79
Lydia, twin with Elizabeth, d. John & Irene, b. Oct. 11, 1754	2	114
Lydia, twin with Elisabeth, [d. John & Irene], b. Oct. 11, 1754	3	79
Lydia, of [New London], m. James **PERRY**, of Troy, N.Y., Aug. 6, 1843, by Rev. R. A. G. Thompson	4	106
Margaret, m. William **MURRAY**, b. of New London, July 25, 1830, by Rev. Abel McEwen	4	39
Mary, d. John & Irene, b. Feb. 29, 1756	2	114
Mary, [d. John & Irene], b. Feb. 29, 1756	3	79
Mary, m. Nathan **BAILEY**, Jr., Mar. 2, 1777	3	80
Mary, d. [Cruttenden & Elisabeth], b. Feb. 16, 1785	3	125

	Vol.	Page

WARD (cont.)

	Vol.	Page
Patrick, of Cork, Ireland, m. Ann **WANT**, of New London, d. Phillip, decd., July 27, 1754	3	31
Patrick, s. Patrick & Ann, Nov. 13, 1756	3	31
Thomas Cruttenden, s. [Cruttenden & Elisabeth], b. Oct. 7, 1790	3	125
Uriah, s. John & Irene, b. June 2, 1757	2	114
Uriah, [s. John & Irene], b. June 2, 1757; d. Oct. [ ], 1758	3	79
Uriah, [s. John & Irene], b. June 23, 1769; d. Oct. [ ], 1769	3	79
William, s. John & Irene, b. Dec. 11, 1762	2	114
William, [s. John & Irene], b. Dec. 11, 1762	3	79
WARNER, Agness, d. [Hugh & Olive], b. Sept 1, 1791	3	139
Alexander Johnson, s. [Hugh & Olive], b. Sept. 20, 1798	3	139
Elisabeth, d. [Hugh & Olive], b. Jan. 28, 1790; d. Feb. 28, 1796	3	139
Elizabeth, d. [Hugh & Olive], b. Aug. 20, 1800	3	139
George, s. [Hugh & Olive], b. Nov. 26, 1796	3	139
Hugh, b. Aug. 22, 1759; m. Olive **FENK**, May 5, 1789	3	139
Hugh, d. Oct. 22, 1802	3	139
Jacob, s. [Hugh & Olive], b. Mar. 27, 1793	3	139
Olive, m. James **HALL**, Dec. 15, 1802	3	139
Phebe, d. [Hugh & Olive], b. Nov. 27, 1794	3	139
WARRIER, Emily Jane, m. Charles **MINER**, b. of New London, Sept. 29, 1846, by Rev. Jabez S. Swan	4	128
WASHBURN, Henry W., of Sag Harbor, m. Harriet **GREY**, of New London, Apr. 6, 1851, by Rev. James W. Dennis	4	162
WATERHOUSE, Anne, d. of William, of New London, m. Walter **CHAPPELL**, s. George, of New London, Nov. 18, 1756	2	80
Crocker, s. [Nathaniel], b. June 14, 1777	3	33
Daniel, s. Nath[anie]l & Ellzabeth, b. Jan. 2, 1757	2	98
Tudley, s. [John & Elisabeth], b. June 19, 1789	3	51
Eleazer, s. [Elijah & Mary], b. Sept. 22, 1779	3	87
Elijah, s. Joseph, b. May 1, 1741; m. Mary **BISHOP**, d. Sam[ue]l, Jan. 25, 1766	3	87
Elijah, s. [Elijah & Mary], b. Dec. 15, 1776	3	87
Eliza Ann, of Waterford, m. John **JEFFERY**, of New London, Feb. 23, 1825, by Rev. Abel McEwen	4	21
Elizabeth, w. Nathaniel, d. May 6, 1761	2	98
Elisabeth, d. [Elijah & Mary], b. Mar. 11, 1774	3	87
Elizabeth, d. [Nathaniel], b. Nov. 7, 1775	3	33
Elizabeth, d. [John & Elisabeth], b. Oct. 28, 1780	3	51
Eunice, d. [Nathaniel], b. June 10, 1779	3	33
Isaiah, s. [John & Elisabeth], b. May 17, 1778	3	51
Jeremiah, s. [Nathaniel], b. Sept. 22, 1773	3	33
John, s. John, decd., & Mercy, b. Aug. 6, 1751, O.S.	3	51

	Vol.	Page
WATERHOUSE (cont.)		
John, s. [Nathaniel], b. Dec. 20, 1768	3	33
John, m. Elisabeth **MAN[N]**, of Groton, d.		
Timo[thy], Dec. 2, 1770	3	51
John, s. John & Elisabeth, b. Oct. 6, 1771	3	51
Jonathan, s. Nath[anie]ll & Elizabeth, b. June 2, 1758	2	98
Joseph, s. Joseph & Sarah, b. Oct. 15, 1735	2	116
Joseph, s. [Elijah & Mary], b. Sept. 10, 1766	3	87
Joseph, d. May 7, 1785, ae 79 y. 10 m.	3	87
Keturah, d. [Nathaniel], b. Oct. 26, 1784	3	33
Lydia, m. Thomas **MANWARING**, Apr. 14, 1748	3	102
Marsse, d. [Nathaniel], b. Aug. 5, 1781	3	33
Martha, d. [Elijah & Mary], b. Oct. 2, 1772	3	87
Mary, d. [Nathaniel], b. Apr. 25, 1771	3	33
Mercy, wid. of John, late of New London, decd., m.		
Tho[ma]s **TURNER**, Dec. 8, 1770	2	91
Nathan, s. John & Mercy, b. Sept. 15, 1758, N.S.	3	51
Nathan, s. [John & Elisabeth], b. May 24, 1775	3	51
Nathaniel, s. Joseph & Sarah, b. Oct. 19, 1732	2	117
Nathaniel, s. Joseph, of New London, m. Elizabeth		
MORGAN, d. William, of New London, Nov.		
22, 1756	2	98
Nathaniel, m. Mercy **CROCKER**, d. John, late of		
New London, decd., Mar. 22, 1762	2	98
Nathaniel, s. [Nathaniel]. b. June 24, 1766	3	33
Phebe, d. [Elijah & Mary], b. Nov. 23, 1783	3	87
Russel[l], s. John & Elisabeth, b. May 5, 1773	3	51
Samuel, s. [Elijah & Mary], b. June 22, 1769	3	87
Samuel, s. Elijah, m. Anna **BUTLER**, b. of New		
London, Dec. 27, 1787, by Andrew Griswold,		
J.P.	2	123
Sarah, d. Nathaniel & Mercy, b. May 27, 1764	2	98
Sarah, d. [John & Elizabeth], b. Feb. 20, 1783	3	51
William Avery, s. [John & Elisabeth], b. June 20,		
1787	3	51
WATERMAN, Joseph L., of Norwich, m. Betsey B.		
CHURCH, of Montville, Nov. 15, 1844, by		
Rev. Abel McEwen	4	114
Rebecca, of New London, m. John F. **MALLADE**,		
of Montville, May 15, 1831, by Rev. Daniel		
Wildman	4	43
WATROUS, WATERUS, WATEROUS, Ann Elizabeth,		
d. [Elisha & Martha], b. June 18, 1808	3	213
Daniel, m. Ann Maria **LEWIS**, b. of New London,		
Mar. 3, 1842, by Rev. R. W. Allen	4	97
Ebenezer Holt, s. [Stephen & Hannah], b. May 14,		
1788	3	34
Elias Beoller, s. [Elisha & Martha], b. July 30, 1805	3	213
Elisha, m. Martha **GRISWOLD**, d. Andrew, of		
Lyme, Dec. 5, 1795	3	213
Elizabeth, d. John, m. John **WALDEN**, Mar. 15,		
1797	3	181

	Vol.	Page
WATROUS, WATERUS, WATEROUS (cont.)		
Frances C., m. William **VARLEY**, Feb. 16, 1842, by		
H. R. Knapp	4	101
Harriet B., m. Leonard **DART**, Nov. 27, 1827	3	289
Henry, m. Harriet B. **MILLER**, b. of New London ,		
May 12, 1833, by Rev. Edw[ard] Bull	4	51
Hezekiah S., m. Philena A. **SPENCER**, b. of		
Westchester, Ct., Sept. 28, 1847, by Rev. Jabez		
S. Swan	4	134
Jane, d. Isaac, of Lyme, m. Jesse **MINOR**, s. Joseph,		
Nov. 3, 1737	2	33
Jane Maria, d. [Elisha & Martha], b. June 16, 1803	3	213
John, of New London, m. Eliza A. **TREADWAY**, of		
Salem, June 11, 1832, by Rev. Abel McEwen	4	47
John Stephen, s. [Stephen & Hannah], b. June 15,		
1791	3	34
July Ann, d. [Elisha & Martha], b. Jan. 1, 1798, in		
Waterford, N.Y.	3	213
Stephen, m. Hannah **HOLT**, Mar. 9, 1788	3	34
Susan, m. Albert **MILLER**, b. of N[ew] London,		
May 18, 1837, by Rev. Squire B. Hascall	4	69
Warren G., m. Abigail **GETCHEL**, b. of New		
London, Sept. 17, 1832, by Rev. Abel McEwen	4	47
William, m. Ann **PRIM** (?), b. of New London, May		
9, 1833, by James Porter	4	51
William Griswold, s. [Elisha & Martha], b. Apr. 24,		
1801, in Waterford, N.Y.	3	213
WATSON, Abby, m. John **BARBER**, b. of New London,		
June 8, 1845, by Rev. Jabez S. Swan	4	119
Abiga[i]l, m. Charles **JEFFERY**, Nov. 24, 1790	3	223
WAY, Abigail, d. Daniell & Abigail, b. July 2, 1711	1	38
Abigail, d. Daniel, b. Dec. 13, 1726	2	116
Abigail, d. Tho[ma]s & Sarah, b. Aug. 20, 1744	2	69
Agnes, d. George, of Providence, m. Samuel		
HARRIS, o John, of Charlestown, May 14,		
[1679]	1	14
Alfred P., [s. Thomas & Dolly M.], b. June 29, 1820;		
d. Oct. 16, 1821	3	226
Alise, m. George **CHAPPELL**, s. Geo[rge], Oct. 3,		
[1676]	1	11
Ann, d. Ebenezer & Mary, b. Sept. 16, 1722	1	60
Ann, m. William P. **CONE**, b. of New London, Aug.		
17, 1845, by Rev. Jabez S. Swan	4	121
Ann B., d. [Daniel & Theresa], b. Apr. 19, 1816	3	292
Anne, d. Thomas & Anne, b. Jan. 28, 1713	1	41
Azariah, s. William & Mary, b. July 5, 1769	3	44
Caroline B., d. [Daniel & Theresa], b. Oct. 28, 1813	3	292
Charles F., s. [Daniel & Theresa], b. May 20, 1808	3	292
Cynthia, m. Nathaniel **HARRIS**, Dec. 28, 1802	3	244
Daniel, s. Thomas & Anne, b. Dec. 23, [1688]	1	18
Dan[ie]ll, s. Dan[ie]ll & Sarah*, b. Jan. 4, 1722		
*(Perhaps "Abigail"?)	1	60

	Vol.	Page
WAY (cont.)		
Daniel, Jr., s. Daniel, of New London, m. Jerusha		
KIRTLAND, d. Nath[anie]l, of Saybrook,		
decd., May 20, 1763	3	26
Daniel, s. [Daniel, Jr. & Jerusha], b. May 11, 1772	3	26
Daniel, m. Theresa **PALMER**, Oct. 25, 1801	3	292
Daniel, s. [Daniel & Theresa], b. Mar. 2, 1812	3	292
David, s. Thomas & Ann, b. June 20, 1700	1	25
Ebenezer, s. Thomas & Anne, [b.] Oct. 30, [1693]	1	21
Ebenezer, m. Mary **HARRIS**, Nov. 9, 1714	1	44
Ebenezer, s. Eben[eze]r & Mary, b. July 8, 1728	2	116
Ebenezer, Jr., m. Mary **TABER**, d. Pardon Taber,		
Nov. 30, 1766	3	147
Ebenezer, s. [Ebenezer, Jr. & Mary], b. Sept. 29,		
1767; d. Aug. 20, 1784	3	147
Ebenezer, m. Lydia **DORRY**, Dec. 21, 1783	3	147
Ebenezer, s. [Ebenezer & Lydia], b. Sept. 28, 1784	3	147
Ebenezer, Capt. of New London, d. Jan. 28, 1849	3	226
Eliza, d. Ebenezer, m. George W. **CHAMPLIN**,		
Nov. 2, 1794	3	230
Eliza, of [New London], m. William R. H.		
ROCKWELL, Mar. 27, 1831, by Rev.		
Leonard B. Griffing	4	40
Eliza C., d. [Thomas & Dolly M.], b. May 24, 1815;		
d. Mar. 20, 1818	3	226
Elizabeth, d. Thomas & Ann, b. Apr. 20, [1695]	1	22
Elizabeth, m. Jonathan **FAN[N]ING**, May 17, 1714	1	42
Elizabeth, d. Ebenezer & Mary, b. Apr. 23, 1724	1	63
Elizabeth, d. [Ebenezer, Jr. & Mary], b. Jan. 30, 1771	3	147
Elisabeth, m. Josephus **LOVETT**, Jan. 12, 1772	3	22
Elizabeth, d. [Daniel & Theresa], b. Mar. 16, 1806	3	292
Ellen, d. [Thomas & Dolly M.], b. Oct. 14, 1818	3	226
[E]unice, d. Lieut. Thomas Way, m. Clement		
FOSDICK, Oct. 14, 1778	3	105
Hannah, d. Thomas & Ann, b. Jan. 8, 1708/9	1	65
Hannah, d. Eben[eze]r & Mary, b. July 31, 1739	2	116
Hannah, d. Capt. John, m. Daniel **STARR**, Sept. 23,		
1796	3	149
James, s. Thomas & Ann, b. Oct. 3, 1703	1	29
Jerusha E., d. [Daniel & Theresa], b. July 11, 1810	3	292
John, s. Thomas & Anne, b. Apr. 30, 1698	1	24
John, s. Eben[eze]r & Mary, b. Aug. 22, 1731	2	116
John, s. Tho[ma]s & Sarah, b. Oct. 6, 1740	2	69
Joseph, s. William & Mary, b. Nov. 1, 1767	3	44
Lucy, d. Eben[eze]r & Mary, b. Apr. 7, 1735	2	117
Lucy K., d. [Thomas & Dolly M.], b. Dec. 4, 1823	3	226
Lydia, d. Daniell & Abigail, b. Oct. 16, 1712	1	39
Lydia, d. Daniel, b. Jan. 5, 1730/1	2	116
Lydia, d. Daniel, of New London, m. John **HARRIS**,		
s. Henry, late of New London, decd., Jan. 16,		
1755	3	11
Mary, d. Ebenezer & Mary, b. Feb. 25, 1717/18	1	49

	Vol.	Page
WAY (cont.)		
Mary, d. Daniel & Sarah, b. Apr. 19, 1735	2	115
Mary, of New London, d. Daniel, m. John **SMITH**, s.		
John, of Lyme, decd., Feb. 21, 1762	3	52
Mary, d. [Ebenezer, Jr. & Mary], b. Aug. 20, 1769	3	147
Mary, w. Ebenezer, d. Aug. 20, 1771	3	147
May*, s. Thomas & Ann, b. May 15, 1702		
*(Marginal note in pencil says "May" was a		
male and lived in Waterbury)	1	27
Nancy, d. Capt. John, m. Joseph **SISTARE**, Feb. 1,		
1795, by Rev. Henry Channing	3	150
Nathaniel, s. Ebenezer & Mary, b. Sept. 5, 1715	1	46
Nathaniel, s. Daniel & Sarah, b. Feb. 12, 1732/3	2	115
Nathaniel, s. Eben[eze]r & Mary, b. Oct. 23, 1743	2	116
Nathaniel, s. Daniel, Jr. & Jerusha, b. Mar. 14, 1765	3	26
Nathaniel, s. [Daniel & Theresa], b. Oct. 28, 1803	3	292
Peter, s. Daniel, b. July 6, 1724	2	116
Phebe, d. Eben[eze]r & Mary, b. Oct. 12, 1726; d.		
June 2, 1798	2	116
Phebe, d. Dan[ie]l, Jr. & Jerusha, b. Apr. 4, 1763	3	26
Sally, d. Capt. John, m. Richard **STARR**, July 8,		
1804	3	214
Sam[ue]l, s. Daniel & Sarah*, b. Oct. 26, 1718/19		
*(Perhaps "Abigail"? L. B. B.)	1	59
Sarah, d. Daniell & Abigaill, b. Aug. 5, 1716	1	47
Sarah, d. Samuel, of New London, m. William		
HOLT, Jr., s. Nathaniel, of New London, May		
12, 1736	2	59
Sarah, d. Tho[ma]s & Sarah, b. Oct. 14, 1738; d. Feb.		
23, 1738/9	2	69
Sarah, d. Tho[ma]s & Sarah, b. July 26, 1742	2	69
Sarah, d. Dan[ie]ll, [Jr.] & Jerusha, b. Sept. 5, 1766	3	26
Sarah, m. William Clark **BURDICK**, Apr. 5, 1804	3	61
Sarah, d. [Thomas & Dolly M.], b. Mar. 21, 1822	3	226
Sarah, m. Jonathan **STARR**, 2d, b. of New London,		
June 24, 1826, by Rev. Abel McEwen	4	26
Sarah, m. Martin K. **CADY**, b. of [New London],		
Aug. 5, 1841, by Rev. Robert A. Hallam	4	98
Thomas, s. Thomas & Ann, b. Feb. 18, [1690]	1	20
Thomas, s. Daniell & Abigail, b. Aug. 25, 1714	1	44
Tho[ma]s, s. Dan[ie]l, m. Sarah **SAVELL**, d. John, b.		
of New London, Dec. 29, 1737	2	69
Thomas, s. [Ebenezer & Lydia], b. July 31, 1786	3	147
Thomas, s. Eben, m. Dolly M. **HOLT**, d. Jona[than],		
Nov. 26, 1812	3	226
Thomas, s. [Thomas & Dolly M.], b. Nov. 10, 1813	3	226
William, s. Ebenezer & Mary, b. May 15, 1720	1	57
William, of New London, s. Ebenezer, m. Mary		
LOTHROP, of Norwich, d. Nathaniel, May 3,		
1765	3	44
William, s. William & Mary, b. July 3, 1766	3	44

	Vol.	Page
WEAVER, [see also WEBER], Benjamin, s. [William & Abigail], b. May 24, 1780	3	97
Christopher A., m. Sarah A. BROWN, b. of New London, Nov. 24, 1847, by Rev. Jabez S. Swan	4	136
James Harris, s. [William & Abigail], b. Aug. 13, 1784	3	97
John, s. [William & Abigail], b. Mar. 8, 1787	3	97
John, see John WEBER	1	53
Sarah A., m. James NEWCOMB, b. of [New London], Sept. 7, 1847, by Rev. Jabez S. Swan	4	134
Wanton A., m. Ann TURNER, Apr.26, 1818	3	246
William, m. Abigail HARRIS, Nov. 10, 1775 (First written April)	3	97
William, s. [William & Abigail], b. Apr. 27, 1777	3	97
William, of Buffalo, N.Y., m. Ellen ALLEN, of [New London], Sept. 13, 1847, by Rev. Robert A. Hallam (Perhaps William MINER)	4	135
WEBB, Harriet, d. Daniel, m. John H. ALLEN, of New Bedford, Mass., Feb. 11, 1838, by Rev. Daniel Webb	4	75
Nancy D., m. Frederick LESTER, b. of Norwich, Sept. 22, 1840, by Rev. Robert A. Hallam	4	91
WEBER, *Johanna, d. John & Johanna, b. Oct. 31, 1712 *(Perhaps WEAVER)	1	53
John, m. Johannah WILLIAMS, Aug. 9, 1711 (Perhaps John WEAVER)	1	53
John, s. John & Johannah, b. Jan. [ ], 1713/14 (Perhaps WEAVER)	1	53
John, m. Mary ROY, Jan. 10, 1852, by Rev. J. Stokes. Witnesses: Patrick Ward, Elizabeth Roy	4	169
Mary, d. John & Johannah, b. Jan. 9, 1715/16 (Perhaps WEAVER)	1	53
William, s. John & Johannah, b. Sept. 15, 1717 (Perhaps WEAVER)	1	53
WEBSTER, George S., of Island of Cuba, m. Harriet T. ISHAM, of [New London], Nov. 19, 1850, by Rev. Robert A. Hallam	4	160
WEEDEN, WEEDON, Isaac, of Newport, m. Lydia JOHNSTONE, of New London, July 16, 1785	3	44
Isaac Ingraham, s. [Isaac & Lydia], b. May 11, 1793	3	44
John, of Providence, R.I., m. Lucretia BOWICK, of New London, June 1, 1828, by Rev. Abel McEwen	4	34
Lucy Ann, m. Christopher SHAW, b. of [New London], July 13, 1843, by Rev. Abel McEwen	4	106
Lydia, d. [Isaac & Lydia], b. Sept. 29, 1789	3	44
Nancy, d. Isaac & Lydia], b. Apr. 5, 1791	3	44
Sally, d. [Isaac & Lydia], b. Dec. 16, 1786	3	44
Thomas, s. [Isaac & Lydia], b. Mar. 7, 1788	3	44
William Babcock, s. [Isaac & Lydia], b. Jan. 3, 1795	3	44
WEEKS, Abby, m. Thomas WEST, Feb. 8, 1811	3	251

	Vol.	Page
WEEKS (cont.)		
Abigail, d. Joshua & Lemon, b. June 30, 1733	2	108
Abigail, d. [Joseph & Elisabeth], b. Feb. 27, 1774	3	62
Amos, s. Joseph & Mary, b. Nov. 17, 1747	3	30
Amos, m. Rebecca **MORGAN**, Oct. 19, 1768	3	89
Ann, m. William **MELONE**, Oct. 6, 1764	3	64
Anna, d. Eben[eze]r & Eunice, b. Mar. 16, 1766	3	27
Anne, d. Eben[eze]r & Eunice, b. Mar. 13, 1766	3	29
Ebenezer, of New London, s. Eben[eze]r, of Pomfret, m. Eunice **GRISWOLD**, of Lyme, d. Rev. George, Feb. 2, 1764	3	29
Ebenezer, s. Eben[eze]r & Eunice, b. Sept. 24, 1772	3	29
Edward Wells, s. [Joseph & Elisabeth], b. July 11, 1769	3	62
Edward Wells, s. [Joseph & Hannah], b. Apr. 18, 1802	3	153
Elias, s. Joshua & Lemon, b. July 12, 1731	2	108
Elizabeth, d. Joshua & Lemon, b. Apr. 6, 1728	2	108
Elisabeth, d. Ebenezer & [E]unice, b. Nov. 13, 1764	3	27
Elisabeth, d. Eben[eze]r & Eunice, b. Nov. 17, 1764	3	29
Elisabeth, d. Sarah, b. Mar. 25, 1790. Recorded at the desire of her grandmother Mrs. Mary Weeks	3	23
Esther, d. Esther, b. Oct. 25, 1780	3	21
Esther, of New London, m. James **JONES**, of Stratford, June 9, 1799	3	21
Eunice, d. Ebenezer & Eunice, b. Oct. 8, 1767; d Nov. 27, 1767	3	27
Eunice, d. Eben[eze]r & Eunice, b. Oct. 8, [1767]; d Nov. 29, 1767	3	29
Eunice, d. Ebenezer & Eunice, b. Apr. 29, 1774	3	29
Grace, d. [Jethro & Mary], b. Oct. 13, 1782	3	15
Hannah, d. Eben[eze]r & Eunice, b. Apr. 5, 1771	3	29
Hannah, d. [Ebenezer & Eunice], d. June 29, 1777	3	29
Henry, s. [Jethro & Mary], b. Oct. 13, 1778	3	15
Hester, twin with Jonathan, d. Joseph & Mary, b. Sept. 23, 1764	3	30
Jane, d. [Joseph & Elisabeth], b. Dec. 19, 1765	3	62
Jane, m. William **McCARTY**, Dec. 23, 1787	3	20
Jethro, m. Mary **CHAPPEL**, Sept. 10, 1759	3	15
Joanna, d. Jonathan & Ann, b. Jan. 12, 1738/9	2	116
Joanna, d. Jonathan, m. Othniel **BEEBE**, s. William, all of New London, Apr. 2, 1756	2	121
Joanna, d. [Jethro & Mary], b. Feb. 25, 1774	3	15
Jonathan, d. Joshua & Lemon, b. Apr. 26, 1730	2	108
Jonathan, twin with Hester, s. Joseph & Mary, b. Sept. 23, 1764	3	30
Joseph, s. Joseph & Mary, b. Aug. 14, 1750	3	30
Joseph, m. Elisabeth **GRANT**, Nov. 18, 1764	3	62
Joseph, s. Ebenezer & Eunice, b. Apr. 8, 1769	3	29
Joseph, s. [Joseph & Elisabeth], b. May 26, 1771	3	62
Joseph, s. Eben[eze]r & Eunice, d. Mar. 18, 1776	3	29

	Vol.	Page

WEEKS (cont.)

Joseph, m. Hannah **CROCKER**, d. Stephen, Jan. 8,
1801 — 3 — 153

Joseph, m. Mary **BECKWITH** [   ] — 3 — 30

Joseph Holland, s. Eben[eze]r & Eunice, b. May 8,
1776 — 3 — 29

Joshua, m. Lemon **HURLBURT**, b. of New London,
May 16, 1727 — 2 — 108

Martha, d. Joshua & Lemon, b. Nov. 12, 1735 — 2 — 108

Mary, d. Joseph & Mary, b. Nov. 25, 1753 — 3 — 30

Mary, d. [Jethro & Mary], b. Mar. 13, 1765 — 3 — 15

Mary, d. [Joseph & Elisabeth], b. Oct. 16, 1767 — 3 — 62

Mary, m. Daniel **CORY**, Sept. [ ], 1779*   *(First
written 1794) — 3 — 129

Mary, m. Ephraim **SMITH**, Aug. 13, 1786 — 3 — 18

Mary, m. Nathaniel **PECK**, Nov. 23, 1786 — 3 — 111

Nancy, d. [Jethro & Mary], b. July 27, 1785 — 3 — 15

Rebecca, d. [Amos & Rebecca], b. July 3, 1771 — 3 — 89

Sally, d. James, b. July 15, 1773; m. Nicholas
DARROW, [s. Peter], Oct. 9, 1791 — 3 — 154

Sarah, d. [Jethro & Mary], b. Aug. 25, 1771 — 3 — 15

Stephen, s. [Jethro & Mary], b. May 11, 1776 — 3 — 15

WELCH, WELSH, Arthur B., of Canterbury, m. Esther
E. **LESHURE**, of [New London], May 9, 1841,
by Rev. Abel McEwen — 4 — 95

Belinda, of [New London], m. Melvin H.
GARDNER, of Sag Harbour, N.Y., June 5,
1835, by Rev. Abel McEwen — 4 — 61

Betsey, d. [John & Esther], b. July 18, 1801, in Lyme — 3 — 51

Betsey, m. John **MORTON**, b. of New London, June
8, 1831, by Rev. Abel McEwen — 4 — 42

Catharine, m. Patrick **SWEENEY**, Feb. 11, 1849, by
Rev. William Logan — 4 — 150

Catharine, m. John **BURT**, June 7, 1851, by Jno. J.
Brandigee — 4 — 162

Edmund, m. Joanna **PINE**, Oct. 28, 1849, by Rev.
William Logan — 4 — 151

Elizabeth, d. James & Penelope, b. Jan. 25, 1691/2 — 1 — 21

Mary, m. Peter **MASON**, June 27, 1805 — 3 — 68

Mary, m. Thomas **RASBOURN**, Oct. 5, 1829, by
Rev. Francis Darrow — 4 — 37

Stephen, s. [John & Esther], b. Nov. 6, 1803, in Lyme — 3 — 51

Stephen, m. Belinda **DART**, b. of New London, Jan.
10, 1827, by Rev. Abel McEwen — 4 — 28

William, m. M. **LEMMING**, b. of [New London],
Nov. 9, 1834, by Rev. Ebenezer Blake — 4 — 58

William, m. Mary **RYAN**, Feb. 11, 1849, by Rev.
William Logan — 4 — 150

WELLMAN, William F., of Portland, Me., m. Lucy Ann
CLARKE, of [New London], May 23, 1836,
by Rev. Alvan Ackley — 4 — 65

WELLS, Abigaill, d. Ephraim & Abigail, b. Feb. 22, 1697 — 1 — 23

	Vol.	Page

WESTCOTE, WESCOT, WESCOAT, WESCOTE
(cont.)

	Vol.	Page
Samuel, m. Naomy **GOFF**, May [ ], 17[ ]	2	117
Thomas, s. [William & Esther], b. Sept. 18, 1781	3	16
William, b. Aug. 31, 1746; m. Esther **HARRIS**, Jan. 7, 1773	3	16
William, s. [William & Esther], b. Mar. 8, 1775	3	16

WETHERELL, WITHERELL, Danyell, s. William, of Scituate, New England, m. Grace, d. of Jonathan & Grace **BREWSTER**, of New London, Aug. 4, [1659] — 1, 3

	Vol.	Page
Danyel, s. Dan[ie]l & Grace, b. Jan. 26, [1670]	1	7
Daniel, b. Nov. 29, 1630, at the Free School House in Maidstone, County of Kent, Old England; d. Apr. 14, 1719, ae 89 y.	1	51
Hannah, d. Dan[ie]ll & Grace, b. Mar. 21, [1659]	1	3
Hanna[h], d. Danyell, of New London, m. Adam **PICKETT**, of New London, May 26, [1680]	1	14
Mary, d. Dan[ie]l & Grace, b. Oct . 7, [1668]	1	6

WETHERLAKE, Mercy, d. George & Jemima, b. July 5, 1753 — 2, 48

WETMORE, Mary, of Middletown, m. Capt. Andrew **MATHER**, July 7, 1810 — 3, 156

WHALEY, Jonathan, of Montville, m. Mary **LESTER**, of Norwich, July 15, 1831, by Th[omas] S. Perkins, J.P. — 4, 43

	Vol.	Page
Mary A., m. Turner S. **DARROW**, b. of Norwich, Dec. 16, 1847, by Rev. Jabez S. Swan	4	136

WHALIN, Elisabeth, m. Charles **JEFFERY**, Jr., May 16, 1772 — 3, 113

WHEAT, Edwin, s. [Samuel & Sarah], b. May 29, 1796 — 3, 141

	Vol.	Page
Eliza, d. [William & Mary], b. Feb. 26, 1797	3	112
Elizabeth, of New London, m. Richard **COFFIN**, of Nantucket, Mass., Dec. 5, 1825, by Rev. Abel McEwen	4	25
Fanney, d. [William & Mary], b. Feb. 16, 1800	3	112
Fanny B., m. Gurdon **MASON**, b. of New London, Sept. 22, 1822, by Rev. Abel McEwen	4	10
Hannah, d. [William & Mary], b. Nov. 5, 1791	3	112
Harriet, d. [Samuel & Sarah], b. Aug. 19 ,1792	3	141
Mary, d. [Samuel & Sarah], b. Mar. 7, 1787	3	141
Polly, d. [William & Mary], b. May 30, 1789	3	112
Samuel, s. [Samuel & Sarah], b. June 7, 1789	3	141
Sarah, d. [Samuel & Sarah], b. Feb. 7, 1785	3	141
William, m. Mary **SMITH**, Mar. 15, 1789	3	112
William, s. [William & Mary], b. Feb. 8, 1794; d. Oct. 16, 1802	3	112
William Grant, s. [William & Mary], b. Nov. 30, 1802	3	112

WHEELER, WHELOR, Annah, d. Jno. & Elizabeth, b. Jan. 1 ,1687 — 1, 25

	Vol.	Page

WHEELER, WHELOR (cont.)

Anna, m. John **TONGUE**, b. of New London, Nov. 21, 1701 — 2, 111

Anna, m. John **TONGUE**, Nov. 25, 1702 — 1, 26

Bridget, d. Zacheaus & Sarah, b. Apr. 28, 1751 — 2, 58

Cynthia H., m. Russell M. **WELLS**, b. of Waterford, Mar. 22, 1847, by Rev. Jabez S. Swan — 4, 130

David L., of Stonington, m. Mary **HUBBARD**, of New London, Oct. 17, 1831, by Rev. Abel McEwen — 4, 44

Edward, s. Zacheaus & Sarah, b. Aug. 10, 1744; d. Dec. 6, 1744 — 2, 58

Edward, s. Zacheaus & Sarah, b. June 23, 1746 — 2, 58

Elizabeth, d. Jno. & Eliza, b. "the latter end of Feb." [1678] — 1, 13

Elizabeth, m. Nathaniel **BEEBE**, July 2, 1697 — 1, 23

Elizabeth, d. Zacheaus & Sarah, b. July 5, 1737; d. July 13, 1737 — 2, 58

Fanny A. of New London, m. Charles **FAIRFIELD**, of Norwich, May 26, 1850, by Rev. E. R. Warren — 4, 153

Frances, m. George **TANNICK**, b. of New London, Apr. 8, 1843, by Jabez Swan, M.G. — 4, 105

Frederic, s. Zacheaus & Sarah, b. July 28, 1749 — 2, 58

Guy, s. Zacheaus & Sarah, b. May 23, 1753 — 2, 59

Homer, m. Uretta F. **JEFFERY**, b. of New London, July 31, 1842, by Rev. R. W. Allen — 4, 100

Homer, m. Susan Augusta **MINER**, b. of [New London], May 13, 1849, by Rev. Abel McEwen — 4, 145

Homer H., of Stonington, m. Mary Ann **ROBERTS**, of New London, Mar. 26, 1832, by Rev. Abel McEwen — 4, 46

John O., m. Nancy M. **AMES**, b. of [New London], Sept. 9, 1844, by Rev. Abel McEwen — 4, 113

Lucretia, d. Zacheaus & Sarah, b. Aug. 23, 1741 — 2, 58

Lydia, formerly w. of Jesse **EDGECOMBE**, d. Aug. 23, 1787 — 3, 11

Lydia, d. Thomas, of Stonington, m. William **WILLIAMS**, Oct. 16, 1796, in Stonington — 3, 182

Martha, d. John, of East Hampton, N.Y., m. Samuel **BILL**, Jr., s. Sam[ue]l, of New London, May 10, 1737 — 2, 28

Mary, wid. & d. Edward **TINKER**, m. George **ROGERS**, June 15, 1779 — 3, 157

Mercy, wid., d. Col. John **WILLIAMS**, of Stonington, m. Titus **HURLBURT**, Feb. 7, 1770 — 2, 44

Pitt, of Stonington, m. Rebecca A. **ROBERTS**, of New London, May 7, 1830, by Rev. Abel McEwen — 4, 38

Rebecca, d. Zacheaus & Sarah, b. June 23, 1739 — 2, 58

Sally, m. Stedman **DART**, Jan. 20, 1791 — 3, 119

	Vol.	Page

WHEELER, WHELOR (cont.)

Samuel, s. Ephraim & Mary, b. Sept. 17, 1741	2	116
Samuel, s. Ephraim [m.] Mary **TOPLIFF**, d. [ ]	3	56
Sarah, d. Zacheaus & Sarah, b. Jan. 9, 1755	2	59
Zacheas, s. Jno. & Elizabeth, b. June 22, [1675]	1	10
Zacheaus, s. Joshua, of New London, m. Sarah **HARRIS**, d. of William, late of New London, now of Carolina, Sept. 23, 1736	2	58
Zacheaus, s. Zacheaus & Sarah, b. Jan. 11, 1743	2	58

WHIPPLE, Alice, d. Zac[hariah] & Elizabeth, b. Dec. 11,

1734	2	107
Amy Jane, of Waterford, m. John S. **CAPRON**, of Norfolk Va., Oct. 13, 1843, by Rev. Abel McEwen	4	107
Ann, d. [Thomas & Catharine], b. Sept. 12, 1775	3	123
Anne, d. Daniel, of Groton, m. William **ROGERS**, of New London, s. Ichabod, Aug. 20, 1769	3	57
Bathsheba, d. Zac[hariah], & Elizabeth, b. June 6, 1731	2	107
Bathsheba, d. Zachariah, of New London, m. John **TURNER**, s. Tho[ma]s, of New London, Nov. 1, 1750	2	101
Catharine, d. [Thomas & Catharine], b. Jan. 11, 1774	3	123
Charles, s. [Thomas & Catharine], b. Mar. 8, 1779	3	123
Christopher, s. [Thomas & Catharine], b. June 4, 1786	3	123
Content, s. Zac[hariah], & Elizabeth, b. Mar. 27, 1743	2	107
Elizabeth, d. Zachariah & Elizabeth, b. Mar. 15, 1728/9	2	107
Elizabeth, d. Jonathan & Elizabeth, b. Mar. 12, 1729/30	2	115
Elizabeth, w. Zac[hariah], d. Sept. 18, 1751	2	107
Esther, d. [John & Desire], b. Sept. 23, 1803	3	63
Eunice, d. Jona[than] & Elizabeth, b. Dec. 12, 1735	2	115
Eunice, d. [John & Desire], b. May 24, 1800	3	63
Eunice, m. Robert D. **BEEBE**, b. of Waterford, Dec. 19, 1839, by Rev. Abel McEwen	4	88
Frances, m. Asa H. **PAINE**, Aug. 16, 1835, by Rev. Alven Ackley	4	61
Henry Miller, s. [John & Desire], b. Nov. 22, 1790	3	63
Hope, d. Zac[hariah] & Elizabeth, b. Feb. 7, 1740/1	2	107
Isaac, m. Emeline **KEENEY**, b. of New London, Mar. 9, 1851, by Rev. Jabez S. Swan	4	163
James Jeffery, s. [Thomas & Catharine], b. Apr. 6, 1785	3	123
John, s. Zac[hariah], & Elizabeth, b. Feb. 14, 1738	2	107
John, m. Desire **MILLER**, Dec. 31, 1789	3	63
Jonathan, s. David, of New London, m. Elizabeth **DART**, d. of Richard, of New London, Feb. 28, 1726/7	2	115
Jonathan, s. Jonathan & Elizabeth, b. Dec. 24, 1727	2	115

	Vol.	Page
WHIPPLE (cont.)		
Lucy, d. Jonathan &Elizabeth, b. Aug. 22, 1738	2	115
Lucy, m. Isaac **CHAPEL**, Feb. [ ], 1763	3	105
Lucy, d. [John & Desire], b. Aug. 28 ,1792	3	63
Mary, d. [John & Desire], b. Mar. 4, 1795	3	63
Nancy, d. Thomas, m. John **HULL**, May 6, 1794	3	222
Nicholas, s. Jonathan & Elizabeth, b. May 20, 1745	2	115
Patience, d. [Thomas & Catharine], b. Oct. 6, 1781	3	123
Prudance, d. [Thomas & Catharine], b. Nov. 19, 1792	3	123
Sally, d. [Thomas & Catharine], b. June 23, 1795	3	123
Sally A., of New London, m. Samuel s. **ROSE**, of		
Norwich, Jan. 31, 1831, by Rev. Abel McEwen	4	40
Susannah, d. Silas, b. July 21, 1731; m. Eleazer		
BISHOP, Jr., s. Eleazer, Apr. 15, 1750	3	43
Thomas, m. Catharine **JEFFERY**, Sept. 13, 1773	3	123
Thomas, s. [Thomas & Catharine], b. May 21, 1777	3	123
Titus, s. Jona[than] & Elizabeth, b. Feb. 12, 1732/3;		
d. July 28, 1735	2	115
Titus, s. Jonathan & Elizabeth, b. Aug. 15, 1741	2	115
Zachariah, s. Zac[hariah], & Elizabeth, b. June 6,		
1745	2	107
Zethaniah, s. Zac[hariah] & Elizabeth, b. Feb. 3,		
1732/3	2	107
WHITAKER, Chloe, m. Samuel **KEEN[E]Y**, Dec. 25,		
1835, by Rev. Alvan Ackley	4	66
WHITE, Edward, Lieut. of U. S. Army, m. Delia W.		
ADAMS, of New London, Apr. 18, 1832, by		
Rev. B. Judd	4	48
Hannah, m. John **SHEPHERD**, Aug. 2, 1789, by		
Jason Lee, Elder, of Lyme	3	117
James, m. Maria **FLINN**, b. of New London, Nov. 3,		
1844, by Rev. J. Blain	4	115
Lucretia, d. Elihu & Lucretia, b. Jan. 25, 1813, at		
Montville; m. Jonathan **ROGERS**, Jr., [s.		
Jonathan & Sarah], Aug. 14, 1831	3	287
Lucretia, m. Jonathan **ROGERS**, Jr., b. of [New		
London], Aug. 14, 1831, by Rev. Asa Bronson	4	43
Margaret Ann, d. [Mathew & Sarah], b. July 15, 1817	3	219
Mary Jane, m. Harvey F. **DART**, of New London,		
Nov. 29, 1843, by Rev. R. A. G. Thompson	4	109
Ma[t]thew, of North Shields, Eng., m. Sarah		
POTTER, Sept. 1, 1816	3	219
Richard, m. Sarah E. **REYNOLDS**, Jan. 9, 1850, by		
Rev. Jabez S. Swan	4	152
Samuel, m. Martha M. **JORDON**, b. of New		
London, June 9, 1844, by Rev. Jabez S. Swan	4	112
Sarah, [w. Mathew], d. Oct. 1, 1819	3	219
WHITING, Mary Caroline, of E. Greenwich, R.I., m.		
Brayton **WHITTEMORE**, of Killingly, Ct.,		
Dec. 15, 1844, by Rev. Jabez S. Swan	4	115
Nancy, m. Eliphalet **HARRIS**, Jr., Feb. 14, 1790	3	164

	Vol.	Page
WHITING (cont.)		
Philenah, d. Col. John, of New London, m. James		
HOUGHTON, Apr. 28, 1768	2	46
WHITMAN, Hannah, m. Daniel **SMITH**, Jr., Aug. 31,		
1786	3	122
WHITTEMORE, Alvin Fosdick, s. [Samuel & Rhoda], b.		
Aug. 22, 1796	3	183
Amelia, d. [Samuel & Rhoda], b. Sept. 3, 1793; d.		
[ ], 1794	3	183
Amelia, of [New London], m. Nathan **STEWARD**,		
of Sag Harbor, N.Y., June 30, 1837, by Rev.		
Abel McEwen	4	72
Brayton, of Killingly, Ct., m. Mary Caroline		
WHITING, of E. Greenwich, R.I., Dec. 15,		
1844, by Rev. Jabez S. Swan	4	115
Daniel, s. Daniel, of Boston, m. Jane **APPLETON**,		
d. Joshua, of New London, Nov. 5, 1738	2	56
Daniel, s. [Samuel & Rhoda], b. Aug. 6, 1784	3	183
Ebenezer Turell, s. Daniel & Jane, b. Mar. 13 ,1740/1	2	56
Ellen, m. Augustus D. **FORDHAM**, Sept. 1, 1845,		
by Rev. G. Thompson	4	121
George, s. [Samuel & Rhoda], b. Aug. 20, 1786	3	183
Mary, d. Daniel & Jane, b. Aug. 29, 1739; d. May 19,		
1793, and was the first buried in the new		
ground of Melally	2	56
Mary, m. Richard **HARRIS**, Nov. 2, 1760	3	54
Mary, m. Richard **HARRIS**, Nov. 2, 1760	3	79
Mary, d. [Samuel & Rhoda], b. Dec. 18, 1778	3	183
Mary, of [New London], m. Olive R. **DOBBS**, of		
Danbury, Ct., June 28, 1848, by Rev. M. P.		
Alderman	4	140
Nancy, d. [Samuel & Rhoda], b. June 15, 1791	3	183
Philena, m. Edwin H. **SMITH**, of Essex, July 30,		
1845, by Rev. G. Thompson	4	121
Rhoda, d. [Samuel & Rhoda], b. July 25, 1776	3	183
Samuel, m. Rhoda **FOSDICK**, d. Ezekiel, of		
Wethersfield, Nov. 1, 1775	3	138
Samuel, s. [Samuel & Rhoda], b. Feb. 1, 1781; d.		
Dec. 29, 1786	3	183
Samuel, s. [Samuel & Rhoda], b. Feb. 18, 1789	3	183
Sarah T. P., m. Henry **MATHER**, b. of New London,		
Jan. 1, 1851, by Rev. George M. Carpenter	4	158
Sophia, of N[ew] London, m. William H. **HAVENS**,		
of Lyme, Mar. 5, 1837, by Rev. Squire B		
Hascall	4	68
WHITTELSEY, WHITTLECY, Joseph, of Stonington,		
m. Maria A. **CHAPPELL**, of New London,		
Oct. 11, 1831, by Rev. Abel McEwen	4	44
-----, m. Sam[ue]l **COMSTOCK**, May 22, 1705	1	55
WICKS, Jonathan, m. Ann **ROGERS**, Aug. 24, 1732	2	116
WICKWARE, WICKWERE, Ann, d. John & Mary, b.		
Sept. 25, 1697	1	23

	Vol.	Page

WICKWARE, WICKWERE (cont.)

	Vol.	Page
Christopher, s. John & Mary, b. Jan. 8, 1679	1	14
Elizabeth, d. John & Mary, b. Mar. 23, 1688	1	18
Elizabeth, m. Jonas **HAMBL[E]TON**, Sept. 9, 1708	1	33
Elizabeth, m. Jonas **HAMBLETON**, Sept. 9, 1708	2	39
George, s. John & Mary, b. Oct. 4, [1677]	1	12
John, m. Mary **TONGUE**, Nov. 6, 1676	1	11
John, s. John & Mary, b. Dec. 2, 1685	1	18
John, m. Abigail **HAUGHTON**, Dec. 27, 1705	2	58
John, s. Jno. & Abigail, b. May 15, 1708. Recorded July 9, 1739	2	58
Jonathan, s. John & Mary, b. Feb. 19, 1690	1	20
Mary, d. Jno. & Abigail, b. July 7, 1710. Recorded July 9, 1739	2	58
Peter, s. John & Mary, b. Mar. 12, 1694	1	23
Zerviah, d. Jno. & Abigail, b. Dec. 13, 1713. Recorded July 9, 1739	2	58

WIESEMAN, Caroline, d. [William & Mary], b. May 15,

	Vol.	Page
1808	3	190
Mary Burtwell, d. [William & Mary], b. Nov. 3, 1806	3	190
William, m. Mary **ROGERS**, Jan. 26, 1806	3	190

WIGHTMAN, Mary, d. Zerobable, of Bozrah, m. Joshua

	Vol.	Page
HEMPSTE[A]D, 2d, Jan. 31, 1802	3	167

WILBUR, WILBER, Nelson T., m. Sila M. **DOSETT**, b.

	Vol.	Page
of New London, Nov. 7, 1847, by Rev. Jabez S. Swan	4	135
William N., of Stonington, m. Jane O. **EDGCOMB**, of Groton, July 18, 1852, by Rev. Jabez S. Swan	4	175

WILCOX, WILLCOCKS, Dinah, d. of [   ], of

	Vol.	Page
Killingworth, m. Samuel **HARRIS**, s. Samuel, of New London, [ ]	2	80
Julia Ann, m. Elias **DAVIS**, b. of Stonington, Apr. 16, 1850, by Rev. Jabez S. Swan	4	153
Phineas C., m. Augusta C. **SMITH**, Sept. 2, 1845 by Rev. Francis Darrow	4	121

WILKINSON, Mary A. C., of Bath, Me., m. Allen W.

	Vol.	Page
BECKWITH, of New London, Oct. 7, 1851, by Rev. E. R. Warren	4	166

WILLET, WILLETTS, Thomas, s. James, b. Jan. 11,

	Vol.	Page
[1681]	1	15
Valentine, m. Abigail D. **RIDGEWAY**, May 16, 1852, by Rev. Edwin R. Warren	4	168

WILLEY, WILLY, Abell, s. Jno. & Maryann, b. Mar. 3,

	Vol.	Page
[1682]	1	16
Abraham, s. Thomas & Ann, b. Feb. 16, 1711/12	1	39
Allyn, s. John & Maryann, b. Jan. 25, [1681]	1	15
Ann, d. Thomas & Ann, b. Dec. 10, 1718	1	52
Elizabeth, d. Thomas & Anne, b. May 22, 1714	1	42
Isa[a]ck, s. Isa[a]ck* & Merriam, b. Jan. 18, [1671] *(Changed to "John", by L. B. B.)	1	8
Isabell, d. Jno. & Merriam, b. Oct. 21, [1673]	1	9

	Vol.	Page

WILLEY, WILLY (cont.)

John, s. Isa[a]ck, m. Merriam, d. Myles **MOORE**, of
    New London, [ ], 8, [1670]   1   7
John, s. John & Marrian, b. Feb. 24, [1675]   1   10
Mary, m. John **HOLMES**, Feb. 11, 1706/7   1   32
Merrian, d. Jno. & Merrian, b. Nov. 1, [1677]   1   12
Rebecca, d. Hugh, of Wethersfield, m. Thomas
    LATHAM, s. Cary, Oct. 15, [1673]   1   9
Robert, m. Patty **MASON**, b. of New London, Feb.
    11, 1821, by Rev. Nehemiah Dodge   4   4
Thomas, m. Ann **HOUGH**, Dec. 16, 1708   1   34
Thomas, s. Thomas & Ann, b. Feb. 2, 1720/1   1   63
William, s. Thomas & Anne, b. Feb. 26, 1716/17   1   47

WILLIAMS, Aaron, m. Laury **YEOMANS**, b. of
    Norwich, Mar. 13, 1825, by Rev. Abel McEwen   4   21
Abby, d. [Lambert & Mary], b. June 26, 1807   3   224
Ann, of Norwich, m. John **LIBBEE**, of [New
    London], Aug. 4, 1845, by Rev. Abel McEwen   4   120
Benjamin, s. [Coon], b. May 29, 1816   3   242
Betsey, m. Benjamin **BURTON**, b. of New London,
    May 14, 1832, by Rev. Abel McEwen   4   47
Bridget, m. William **SHEFFIELD**, Dec. 10, 1778   3   64
Calvin G., of Stonington, m. Ann **BILLINGS**, of
    [New London], Oct. 25, 1841, by Rev. Abel
    McEwen   4   96
Caroline, of [New London], m. Edwin **ROBBINS**, of
    Groton, July 10, 1839, by Rev. Abel McEwen   4   85
Cecelia, d. [Coon], b. Mar. 10, 1809   3   242
Cynthia, see under Synthia
Cyrus, of New London, m. Caroline **CONGDON**, of
    Lyme, Aug. 22, 1844, by Rev. Rob[er] A.
    Hallam   4   113
David, s. [Owen & Elisabeth], b. Sept. 2, 1786   3   128
David O., s. William & Sally, b. Apr. 5, 1819   3   136
Ebenezer, m. Hannah **BACON**, Apr. 11, 1717   1   48
Ebenezer, s. George & Eunice, b. Nov. 11, 1771   3   73
Eliza, m. Freeman **LATHROP**, b. of New London,
    June 9, 1830, by Rev. B. Judd   4   41
Eliza, of Waterford, m. James **REED**, of [New
    London], June 11, 1848, by Rev. Abel McEwen   4   139
Eliza Pinkham, d. [William & Lydia], b. Jan. 13,
    1801   3   182
Eunice, d. [George & Nancy], b. Mar. 11, 1781   3   73
Eunice, m. Edward **BADETT**, b. of New London,
    Apr. 17, 1842, by Rev. Lemuel Covell   4   99
Frederick, s. [Lambert & Mary], b. Dec. 14, 1803, in
    Groton   3   224
George, s. Geo[rge] & Eunice, m. Nancy
    HEWET[T], d. Israel, of Stonington, Dec. 3,
    1778   3   73

	Vol.	Page

WILLIAMS (cont.)

	Vol.	Page
George H., of Saybrook, m. Sarah Ann **GETCHEL**, of Waterford, Apr. 1, 1844, by Rev. G. Thompson	4	111
Grace, m. Daniell **ROGERS**, Sept. 24, [1702]	1	27
Hannah, d. Jonathan, m. Peras **NAIL**, Sept. [ ], 1793	3	190
Harriet, d. [Thomas W. & Lucretia W.], b. May 28, 1821	3	257
Harriet, m. John **WARD**, May 21, 1841, by John Lovejoy	4	95
Henrietta, d. [Coon], b. Mar. 25, 1814	3	242
James, m. Laura Ann **SIMPSON**, b. of [New London], Mar. 29, 1846, by Rev. Abel McEwen	4	125
James, m. Mary **GAF[F]NEY**, May 12, 1849, by Rev. William Logan	4	150
James M., m. Martha E. **PETTY**, b. of New London, May 12, 1846, by Rev. John Howson	4	126
James M., m. Mary A. **DENNISON**, b. of [New London], May 14, 1848, by Rev. M. P. Alderman	4	139
James S., m. Charlotte **GODDARD**, Jan. 12, 1840, by James M. Macdonald	4	88
James Stephenson, s. [William & Lydia], b. Oct. 2, 1806	3	182
Jesse, s. George & Eunice, b. July 4, 1774	3	73
Johannah, m. John **WEBER***, Aug. 9, 1711 *(Perhaps **WEAVER**)	1	53
John, of Montville, m. Eliza **BROWN**, of New London, Nov. 2, 1825, by W[illia]m P. Cleaveland, J.P.	4	24
John R., m. Betsey **SHAW**, b. of New London, Dec. 30, 1827, by Rev. B. Judd	4	33
John W., s. [William & Lydia], b. Aug. 26, 1799; d. Aug. 19, 1800	3	182
Jonas, of Norwich, m. Lucretia **JEFFERY**, of New London, Jan. 31, 1825, by Rev. Abel McEwen	4	21
Joseph, s. [Owen & Elisabeth], b. Jan. 27, 1794	3	128
Joseph, m. Julia **SATERLEE**, b. of New London, Aug. 9, 1849, by Rev. Edwin R. Warren	4	148
Laban, m. Lucretia **THOMPSON**, relict of James Thompson, July 21, 1807	3	231
Lambert, m. Mary **CHESTER**, d. William, Sept. 29, 1795	3	224
Leonard, s. [Coon], b. May 23, 1811	3	242
Lodewick, s. [Lambert & Mary], b. Feb. 14, 1797, in Groton	3	224
Lucretia, see Lucretia **STARR**	3	272
Lucretia Shaw, d. [Thomas W. & Lucretia W.], b. Feb. 12, 1818	3	257
Lucy Caroline, d. [William & Lydia], b. July 22, 1809	3	182

	Vol.	Page

WILLIAMS (cont.)

Mary, of Stonington, m. Richard **HAMILTON**, of
　New London, July 3, 1822, by Rev. John G.
　Wightman, of Stonington　　3　　156
Mary, of New London, m. Frederick J.
　CHITTENDEN, of Killingworth, Oct. 18,
　1848, by H. Brownson, V.D.M.　　4　　144
Mary Ann, d. [Lambert & Mary], b. Mar. 19, 1800, in
　Groton　　3　　224
Mercy, d. [William & Lydia], b. Oct. 9, 1797, in
　Stonington　　3　　182
Nancy, d. [George & Nancy], b. Sept. 13, 1779　　3　　73
Owen, m. Wid. Elisabeth **NORTON**, formerly
　Elisabeth **SKINNER**, July [ ], 1785　　3　　128
Owen, s. [Owen & Elisabeth], b. Sept. 12, 1790　　3　　128
Rebecca, b. Nov. 15, 1760; m. John **McCARTEY**,
　Nov. 15, 1781　　3　　167
Rhoda Ann, d. [William & Lydia], b. Feb. 15, 1804　　3　　182
Richard H., m. Sarah M. **CLARK**, of Ledward, Ct.,
　July 28, 1841, by Rev. R. W. Allen　　4　　98
Ruth, d. Thomas, b. Sept. 20, 1712. Record
　witnessed by George Richards & Richard Burch　　2　　117
Ruth, m. Joseph **HUNTLEY**, Jan. 7, 1728/9　　2　　37
Sally, d. [Lambert & Mary], b. Aug. 16, 1802, in
　Groton　　3　　224
Samuel, m. Bathshua **CAMP**, July 14, 1713　　1　　41
Sarah, d. Thomas, m. Peter **STRICKLAND**, s.
　Thomas, all of New London, May 22, 1745　　3　　59
Sarah M., m. James D. **SMITH**, b. of New London,
　Oct. 18, 1848, by H. Brownson, V.D.M.　　4　　144
Sevel, m. Elizabeth **FRINK**, b. of [New London],
　Dec. 23, 1838, by Rev. C. C. Williams　　4　　81
Susannah, widow, dau. of [ ] **PENNIMAN**, of
　Braintree, m. Joseph **OWEN**, s. William, of
　Boston, Sept. [ ], 1768　　3　　68
Synthia, d. [George & Nancy], b. Sept. 26, 1782　　3　　73
Thomas W., m. Lucretia W. **PERKINS**, d. Elias &
　Lucretia, May 15, 1817　　3　　257
Thomas W., m. Ann L. **ALLYN**, b. of New London,
　July 14, 1831　　4　　43
Thomas Wheeler Prentice, s. [William & Lydia], b.
　July 1, 1802　　3　　182
William, s. [Owen & Elisabeth], b. Feb. 14, 1796　　3　　128
William, m. Lydia **WHE[E]LOR**, d. Thomas, of
　Stonington, Oct. 16, 1796, in Stonington　　3　　182
William, of Duanesburgh, N.Y., m. Mary **RAY**, of
　New London, Apr. 24, 1825, by Rev. Abel
　McEwen　　4　　22
W[illia]m, of New York, m. Lucretia **GRACE**, of
　New London, Apr. 20, 1845, by Rev. John
　Blain　　4　　119
William Arnold, s. [Coon], b. Nov. 9, 1806　　3　　242

	Vol.	Page
WILLIAMS (cont.)		
William Perkins, s. [Thomas W. & Lucretia W.], b.		
Aug. 17, 1819	3	257
Ziporah, of Norwich, m. Nathaniel **ROGERS**, of		
New London, s. John, late of New London,		
decd., Dec. 6, 1759	3	13
-----, d. John, d. Oct. 23, [1689], ae 2 y.	1	69
WILLIS, J. Franklin, m. Mary Frances **BIRD**, Sept. 1,		
1847, by Rev. Tho[ma]s Greenwood	4	136
Lucy Ann, of New London, m. William **SMITH**, of		
England, May 14, 1846, by Rev. L. Geo[rge]		
Leonard	4	129
William W., m. Cynthia E. **CRANDALL**, b. of New		
London, June 13, 1852, by Rev. Jabez S. Swan	4	174
WILLOUGHBY, WILLOUGHBE, WILLOUBE,		
WILLOUBY, WILLOBE, Abigail, d. William &		
Abigaill, b. Nov. 30, 1700	1	42
Abigail, m. William **CAMPE**, Mar. 26, 1713	1	40
Abigaile, m. Timothy **LESTER**, Aug. 31, 1719	1	51
Abiga[i]ll, m. Ephraim **DATON**, Oct. 27, 1720	1	57
Charles M., of Wintonburg, m. Adeline **JEPSON**,		
Mar. 30, 1831, by Rev. Leonard B. Griffing	4	40
Deliverance, twin with Mary, d. William & Abigaill,		
b. Oct. 22, 1701	1	42
John, s. William & Abigaill, b. Aug. 25, 1703	1	42
Mary, twin with Deliverance, d. William & Abigaill,		
b. Oct. 22, 1701	1	42
Thankfull, d. William & Abigaill, b. Apr. 13, 1708	1	43
William, s. William & Abigaill, b. Nov. 25, 1705	1	43
WILNEY, Charles, m. Elizabeth **SIRLS**, b. of New		
London, June 12, 1831, by Rev. Abel McEwen	4	42
WILSON, WILLSON, Ann P., m. Nathan **BELCHER**,		
Oct. 20, 1841	3	293
Ann P., m. Nathan **BELCHER**, b. of [ ]New		
London], Oct. 20, 1841, by Rev. Abel McEwen	4	97
Ann Peck, d. [Increase & Rachel Wright], b. July 28,		
1816	3	236
Elizabeth, d. Thomas, m. Jonathan **COLFAX**, Dec.		
15, 1783	3	171
Fanny, of Norwich, m. Isaac S. **EWEN**, of New		
London, Dec. 26, 1847, by Rev. L. G. Leonard	4	138
Francis Turner, s. [Increase & Rachel Wright], b.		
Aug. 26, 1827	3	236
George Childs, s. [Increase & Rachel Wright], b.		
May 3, 1814	3	236
Henry G., m. Martha **BUTLER**, b. of [New London],		
Dec. 3, 1843, by Rev. Abel McEwen	4	108
Increase, m. Rachel Wright **FOX**, d. Ezekiel, Jan. 1,		
1810	3	236
Jane, d. [Increase & Rachel Wright], b. May 9, 1824	3	236

	Vol.	Page
WILSON, WILLSON (cont.)		
Jane, of [New London], m. Charles **BELCHER**, of St. Louis, Mo., Oct. 29, 1849, by Rev. Abel McEwen	4	147
John, s. [Increase Rachel Wright], b. June 18, 1811; d. July 29, 1813	3	236
John, m. Jane **SCHYLER**, b. of [New London], June 19, 1838, by Rev. Abel McEwen	4	78
Mary, m. Edw[ar]d **ROBINSON**, s. Geo[rge] & Mary, Nov. 8, 1721	1	59
Mary, m. Samuel P. **FITCH**, May 16, 1798	3	186
Mary, d. [Increase & Rachel Wright], b. Nov. 12, 1818	3	236
Mary, of [New London], m. Christopher M. **NICOLLS**, of Gloucester, Mass., June 19, 1838, by Rev. Abel McEwen	4	78
Sarah, d. Capt. Thomas & Sarah, m. Robert **COLFAX**, s. George & Lucy, [　　　], 1781	3	27
Temperance, m. John **McDONALD**, b. of New London, June 21, 1823, by Christopher Griffing, J.P.	4	14
William, m. Mary **CLAY**, Jan. 27, 1793, by Walter King	3	186
William, d. July [ ], 1795, in Jam[i]ca	3	186
William, s. [Increase Rachel Wright], b. Nov. 24, 1821	3	236
WINANTS, Frances, [w. John], d. June 11, 1809	3	137
John, m. Frances **RICHARDS**, d. Elijah, Jan. [ ], 1789	3	137
Mary, d. [John & Frances], b. May 15, 1793	3	137
WINCHESTER, Lidia, d. Alexander, of Roxbury, m. Nehemyall **SMITH**, s. Nehemia[h], Oct. 24, [1669]	1	6
William, W., of Groton, m. Mary E. **STANTON**, of Brooklyn, Ct., Apr. 22, 1850, by Charles A. Clark, Elder	4	153
WINGROVE, John, m. Sally Ann **HAMLEY**, b. of New London, July 4, 1841, by Rev. R. W. Allen	4	98
Sarah A., m . Robert **GREEN**, b. of New London, Feb. 12, 1851, by Rev. Edwin R. Warren	4	160
WINSLOW, Ann E., m. John **HAMMEL**, b. of [New London], Aug. 29, 1852, by Rev. T. Edwards	4	171
John, of Wiscasset, Maine, m. Nancy **OSBORN**, of [New London], Apr. 23, 1826, by Rev. Isaac Stoddard	4	26
WINTERS, Charles J., of New London, m. Ruth T. **TRACY**, of Montville, July 8, 1849, by Rev. Jabez S. Swan	4	146

	Vol.	Page
WINTHROP, Eliza, Mad. had a servant Eunice, d. of Hagar & reputed w. of Peter **JACKSON**, b. Feb. [ ], 1729/30. Testified to by Sarah Mayhew & Joanna Talman Apr. 14, 1741, at the desire of Peter Jackson	2	50
Elizabeth, Jr. ,m. Jacob **SEBOR**, Apr. 27, 1786	3	80
Francis Bayard, s. [William Henry & Margarett Ann], b. Sept. 18, 1823	3	248
Jane, d. John S., m .William **STEWART**, Dec. 6, 1781	3	100
Jane P., of [New London], m. George F. **CHESTER**, of New York City, Sept. 8, 1852, by Rev. Robert C. Hallam	4	173
Jane Parkin, d. [William Henry & Margarett Ann], b. Apr. 27, 1833	3	248
John Taylor, s. [William Henry & Margarett Ann], b. June 16, 1827; d. July 25, 1829	3	248
Margaret Ann, d. [William Henry & Margarett Ann], b. Nov. 26, 1830	3	248
Mary, m. Richard W. **PARKIN**, July 9, 1786	3	87
Mary, m. William W. **SALTONSTALL**, [ ]	3	267
Rebeckah, d. John, of New London, m. Gurdon **SALTONSTALL**, s. Gurdon, the Gov. of Conn., Mar. 15, 1732/3	2	89
Thomas Parkin, s. [William Henry & Margarett Ann], b. Dec. 6, 1820	3	248
William, Henry, of New York, m. Margarett Ann **PARKIN**, of New London, June 7, 1818, by Rev. Solomon Blakesley, of East Haddam	3	248
William Henry, s. [William Henry & Margarett Ann], b. May 8, 1819	3	248
WIRE, [see also **WYER**], Ann, d. John & Ann, b. July 27, 1739	2	88
John, s. John, of Glasgow, Scotland, m. Ann **RICHARDS**, d. Israel, of New London, Oct. 23, 1734	2	88
John, s. John & Ann, b. Aug. 9, 1737	2	88
Margaret, d. John & Anna, b. Aug. 13, 1735	2	88
Sarah, d. John & Ann, b. Sept. 15, 1742	2	89
WISENBAKER, Catherine, m. Jacob **HOLMES**, b. of New London, Feb. 10, 1823, by Thomas W. Tucker, Elder	4	12
WITTER, Anne, d. Samuel & Sarah, b. Feb. 18, 1749/50	2	18
Elijah, s. Joseph & Elizabeth, b. Sept. 15, 1734	2	117
Elisabeth, m. John **POTTER**, Oct. 24, 1776, in Preston	3	14
Eunice, w. Samuel, d. July 12, 1759	2	18
Ezra, s. Samuel & Sarah, b. Aug. 4, 1754; d. Sept. 18, 1754	2	18
Samuel, s. Samuel & Sarah, b. June 20, 1752	2	18

	Vol.	Page

WITTER (cont.)

Samuel, m. [E]unice **MAPLES**, of New London,
wid. of St.* Maples, Jr., & d. of Thomas **WAY**,
of Lyme, Feb. 9, 1758   *(Perhaps meant for
"Stephen")   2   18

Sarah, w. Samuel, d. Feb. 3, 1757   2   18

WOLCOTT, Frances C., of New London, m. George S.
ROBBINS, of New York, Feb. 19, 1827, by
Rev. Abel McEwen   4   29

Lucretia, d. Dr. Simon Wolcott, m. Richard **LAW**,
Jr., Oct. 28, 1793   3   168

Mary, d. Dr. Simon, m. Christopher **MANWARING**,
Jan. 21, 1807   3   144

WOLF, Anna, d. [Anthony & Anne], b. Nov. 15, 1762   3   2

Anthony, a high German, now resid. in New London,
m. Anne **HEWITSON**, d. John, of New
London, Oct. [ ], 1753, by Rev. Stephen
Gorton   3   2

Anthony, s. Anthony & Anne, b. Mar. 27, 1756   3   2

Elisabeth, d. [Anthony & Anne], b. Mar. 12, 1772   3   2

John, s. Anthony & Anne, b. Sept. 17, 1758   3   2

Lucretia, d. [Anthony & Anne], b. July 22, 1768   3   2

Lucretia, m. Russel[l] **COIT**, Nov. 19, 1791   3   132

Margarett, d. [Anthony & Anne], b. June 18, 1764   3   2

Pegg, m. Rufus **KING**, Jan. 3, 1785   3   96

Richard Dougl[as]*, [s. Anthony & Anne, b.]
*(Entry crossed out.)   3   2

WOOD, Caroline, of New London, m. John F.
CHESTER, of Colchester, Sept. 19, 1825, by
Rev. Abel McEwen   4   24

Elizabeth, of Groton, m. John **BOLLES**, of New
London, May 26, 1736, at her father's house in
Groton, by Joshua Hempstead, J.P.   2   5

Hannah, d. John & Eunice, b. Dec. 20, 1770, in
Groton   3   213

Hannah, d. John, m. Frederick **MINER**, Jan. 18,
1795   3   213

Henry S., of Unedilla, N.Y., m. Caroline N.
NICHOLAS, of New London, June 15, 1843,
by R. A. G. Thompson   4   105

Theodore T., of Morristown, N.J., m. Mary I.
BRANDIGEE, of New London, Oct. 5, 1843,
by Rev. Robert A. Hallam   4   107

Thomas, of R.I., a soldier stationed at Fort Trumbull,
m. Ellenore **CORNELL**, of Griswold, Oct. 9,
1822, at New London, by Lodowick Fosdick,
J.P.   4   10

William, m. Jane **HOPKINS**, d. Benjamin, May 8,
1805   3   228

William, s. [William & Jane], b. Oct. 16, 1806   3   228

WOODBRIDGE, Lucretia Shaw, m. Elias **PERKINS**, b.
of New London, Mar. 14, 1790   3   118

	Vol.	Page
WOODMANCY, Sarah, d. Gabr[ie]ll & Sarah, b. Mar. 16, [1672]	1	8
Thomas, s. Gab[rie]l & Sarah, b. Sept. 17, [1670]	1	6
William, s. Gabriell & Sarah, b. Aug. 3, [1668]	1	5
WOODWARD, WOODARD, Abby, m. Charles **CHAMPLIN**, b. of [New London], Apr. 15, 1852, by Rev. J. M. Eaton	4	167
Abishai, s. [Abishai & Mary], b. Jan. 29, 1788	3	117
Amos, m. Eliza **BAILEY**, d. Nathan, Feb. 26, 1792	3	147
Amos, d. Nov. 2, 1814	3	147
Betsey, d. Abishai, decd., m. George **SHEFFIELD**, s. George, decd., Dec. 26, 1813, at Brooklin, by Rev. J. Whiting	3	240
Eben*, s. [Abiuhai & Mary], b. June 20, 1790 *(First written "Ebenezer")	3	117
Edward, s. [Amos & Eliza], b. Jan. 24, 1799	3	147
Eliza, d. Abisha, m. Samuel **PACKWOOD**, May 1, 1795	3	170
Eliza, d. [Amos & Eliza], b. Oct. 6, 1809 (Twin with John?)	3	147
Eliza S., of New London, m. Joshua Sumner **LEE**, of Ithica, N.Y., June 18, 1823, by Ebenezer Learned, J.P.	4	14
Eliza Terry, d. [Amos & Eliza], b. Mar. 3, 1797	3	147
Emmeline Deborah, d. [Amos & Eliza], b. July 4, 1803	3	147
Eunice, of Hingham, Mass., m. Capt. Norman B. **MINER**, of New London, Oct. 29, 1849, by Rev. Edwin R. Warren	4	149
George N., m. Lydia H. **FOWLER**, b. of [New London], Mar. 31, 1847, by Rev. L. Geo[rge] Leonard	4	129
George W., m. Sarah E. **TROTT**, b. of Wilkesbarre, Pa., Sept. 10, 1832, by Rev. B. Judd	4	49
Gurdon, s. [Abiuhai & Mary], b. Feb. 21, 1795	3	117
Henry, s. [Amos & Eliza], b. Feb. 14, 1795	3	147
Henry M., of Boston, m. Louisa J. **ISHAM**, of [New London], Dec. 10, 1849, by Rev. Robert A. Hallam	4	151
John, s. [Amos & Eliza], b. Feb. 8, 1793; drowned at sea Oct. 1, 1809, ae 16	3	147
John, s. [Amos & Eliza], b. Oct. 6, 1809 (Twin with Eliza?)	3	147
John, of South Hampton, L.I., N.Y., m. Mercy A. **DODGE**, of New London, Aug. 2, 1827, by Rev. Nehemiah Dodge	4	31
Lucretia, m. Albert **LANPHER**, b. of New London, Feb. 9, 1843, by Rev. R. W. Allen	4	104
Nelson, of Lester, Mass., m. Ann W. **ROGERS**, of New London, Mar. 2, 1851, by Rev. Edwin R. Warren	4	160

	Vol.	Page

WOODWARD, WOODARD (cont.)

Phebe, m. William **POTTER**, 2d, s. William, of
England, & Abigail (**DURFEE**) Potter, Aug.
20, 1771, by Rev. Matthew Graves — 3, 207

Richard Giles Bailey, s. [Amos & Eliza], b. Sept. 21,
1805 — 3, 147

William, s. [Abishai & Mary], b. Mar. 16, 1793 — 3, 117

William Amos, s. [Amos & Eliza], b. Mar. 21, 1801 — 3, 147

-----, s. [Abishai & Mary], b. May 24, [1789]; d. June
24, 1789 — 3, 117

WOODWORTH, Charles, of Montville, m. Mary
ARMSTRONG, of Norwich, Feb. 7, 1848, by
Rev. Jabez S. Swan — 4, 137

Charlotte B., d. [William & Asenath], b. Feb. 5, 1806 — 3, 43

Douglass, m. Sibel **HARRIS**, relict of Col. Joseph
Harris, Sept. 11, 1799 — 3, 37

Dudley, of Norwich, m. Lucretia **PAYNE**, of New
London, Mar. 22, 1823, by Rev. Abel McEwen — 4, 13

Elias, of Montville, m. Harriet **SWAIN**, Oct. 13,
1844, by Rev. G. Thompson — 4, 115

Fanny M., of Montville, m. William **PECKHAM**, of
Norwich, Jan. 3, 1848, by Rev. Jabez S. Swan — 4, 136

William, [m.] Asenath, d. John **ANNABLE**, of
Millington, Oct. 3, 1802 — 3, 43

William Stewart, s. [William & Asenath], b. Mar.
19, 1808 — 3, 43

WORKMAN, Abraham George, m. Sarah **SHARKEY**,
Apr. 3, 1853, by Rev. Thomas Ryan — 4, 174

WORTHINGTON, Caroline, d. Hose & Ziba, free
negroes, b. Oct. 10, 1807 — 3, 29

Caroline, m. Peter **LIREM**, b. of New London, Oct.
4, 1823, by Rev. Abel McEwen — 4, 16

Easter, d. Hetty, a negro servant of Winthrop
SALTONSTALL, b. Feb. 5 ,1808 — 3, 176

Eliza, d. Hose & Ziba, free negroes, b. Oct. 18, 1809 — 3, 29

Hose, m. Ziba **PETERS**, free negroes, Oct. 18, 1805 — 3, 29

Joel, of Norwich, m. Susan E. **LANE**, of [New
London], Apr. 7, 1846, by Rev. L. Geo[rge]
Leonard — 4, 125

Nancy, m. Charles **HOVEY**, b. of New London, Apr.
1, 1832, by Rev. Abel McEwen — 4, 46

Sally, m. Jonathan **DOUGLASS**, Apr. 20, 1787 — 3, 143

WORTHYLAKE, Elisabeth, m. John **CLARK**, Nov. 5,
1772 — 3, 79

WRIGHT, Benjamin F., of New York, m. Lucretia H.
FRENCH, of New London, Nov. 28, 1832, by
Rev. J. W. Hallam — 4, 48

David, of New London, m. Martha **HUBBARD**,
Mar. 6, 1786, by Joshua Coit, J.P. — 3, 85

David, s. [David & Martha], b. July 30, 1788 — 3, 85

David, d. Sept. [ ], 1798 — 3, 85

George, m. Mary **SADLER**, Jan. 10, 1716/17 — 1, 47

	Vol.	Page

WRIGHT (cont.)

Martha, d. [David & Martha], b. Dec. 26, 1786 — 3, 85

Mary, [d. William, an Indian, & Hagar, a Negro] b., July 12, 1689 — 1, 31

Mary, m. Robert **JACKLIN**, Oct. 9, 1712 — 1, 47

Mary Hubbard, d. [David & Martha], b. Aug. 19, 1790 — 3, 85

Samuell, [s. William, an Indian, & Hagar, a Negress], b. Nov. 2, 1691 — 1, 31

Sarah, [d. William, an Indian, & Hagar, a Negro], b. June 5, 1686 — 1, 31

Waite, [s. William, an Indian, & Hagar, a Negress], b. Nov. 1, 1697 — 1, 31

William, [s. William, an Indian, & Hagar, a Negress,], b. May 29, 1694 — 1, 31

WYAT[T], John, s. John & Abigaill, b. Nov. 3, 1715 — 1, 49

Richard, m. Hannah **BROMSFIELD**, Dec. 28, 1704 — 1, 30

WYER, [see also **WIRE**], Abraham, of Oyster Bay, Long Island, N.Y., m. Abiah **CULVER**, of Groton, Nov. 25, 1716 — 1, 47

WYYOUGS, Margarette, of Mohegan, m. Benjamin **ONLEY**, of Lyme, Dec. 14, 1851, by Rev. Jabez S. Swan — 4, 172

YENTON, Charlot[te], d. Ezekiel, of Preston, m. John **HO[L]MES**, Mar. 10, 1809 — 3, 225

Elizabeth, d. Ezekiel, m. Nathan **DIXON**, Feb. [ ], 1807 — 3, 225

YEOMANS, Laury, m. Aaron **WILLIAMS**, b. of Norwich, Mar. 13, 1825, by Rev. Abel McEwen — 4, 21

YORK, Michael, m. Harriet E. **BUTLER**, Apr. 21, 1850, by Rev. Charles Willett — 4, 153

YOUNG, Abby, d. [William & Nabby], b. July 5, 1809 — 3, 217

Abby, m. Robert K. **WALLER**, b. of New London, Sept. 17, 1827, by Henry Wightman — 4, 32

Abby, d. William & Nabby, m. Robert K. **WALLER**, Sept. 20, 1827 — 3, 217

Albert Brown, s. William & Nabby, b. Dec. 25, 1802 — 3, 217

Benjamin Holt, s. [William & Nabby], b. Apr. 13, 1799 — 3, 217

Caroline, m. Plympton **MARCY**, b. of Providence, R.I., Feb. 25, 1844, by Rev. S. Benton — 4, 110

Charles, s. [Joseph & Lydia], b. Feb. 10, 1798 — 3, 172

Charles C., of [New London], m. Caroline E. **LEET**, of Chester, Ct., Sept. 19, 1842, by A. Boise — 4, 101

Charles Constant, s. [William & Nabby], b. June 1, 1807 — 3, 217

Elizabeth Holt, d. [William & Nabby], b. Oct. 3, 1811 — 3, 217

Eloisa, of New London, m. William **CHAPPELL**, of Middletown, Mar. 24, 1846, by Rev. L. Geo[rge] Leonard — 4, 125

	Vol.	Page

YOUNG (cont.)

Experience, relict of William, m. John **GORDON**,
[   ]   3   239

Francis Asbury, s. [Joseph & Lydia], b. Dec. 30,
1803   3   172

Henry, m. Lucretia **COIT**, d. Samuel, Oct. 8, 1796   3   61

Henry, s. [Henry & Lucretia], b. Jan. 7, 1804   3   61

Horace Steel, s. [William & Nabby], b. Oct. 17, 1815   3   217

John, s. [Henry & Lucretia], b. May 9, 1801; d. Dec.
[ ], 1802   3   61

John Clark, s. [William & Tabby], b. Jan. 31 ,1801   3   217

Joseph, m. Lydia **BUTLER**, d. Thomas, Aug. 8,
1791   3   172

Joseph, of Wind[h]am, m. Roxy **BECKWITH**, of
[New London], [Jan. , 1836], by Rev. Alvan
Ackley   4   64

Joshua, s. [Joseph & Lydia], b. Apr. 15, 1800   3   172

Louisa, m. John M. **KEENEY**, b. of N[ew] London,
Jan. 20, 1854, by Rev. Abel McEwen   4   54

Mary, d. William, m. Thomas **HOLT**, Jr., Oct. 3,
1791   3   220

Mary, d. [Henry & Lucretia], b. Mar. 11, 1799   3   61

Mary, d. [William & Nabby], b. Oct. 14, 1817   3   217

Mary, m. George **FIELDS**, Nov. 26, 1849, by Rev.
W[illia]m Logan   4   151

Rebakah, of Wethersfield, m. Nathaniel
SALTONSTALL, Sept. 16, 1755   3   161

Samuel, s. [Henry & Lucretia], b. Dec. 17, 1796   3   61

Sarah, of New London, m. Abraham **BLISS**, of
Lebanon, Apr. 29, 1789   3   126

Thomas, s. [Joseph & Lydia], b. Nov. 22, 1795   3   172

William, m. Margaret **HORTON**, Dec. 7, 1715   1   49

William, s. William & Margaret, b. July 26, 1717   1   49

William, s. [Joseph & Lydia], b. Sept. 22 ,1792   3   172

William, m. Nabby **HOLT**, d. Joseph, May 10, 1794   3   217

William H., m. Nancy **CLARK**, b. of New London,
Jan. 22, 1820, by Rev. Nehemiah Dodge   4   2

William Henry, s. [William & Nabby], b. May 15,
1796   3   217

NO SURNAME

Betsey, m. Joseph A. **MOWER**, June 6, 1852, by
Rev. Jabez S. Swan   4   173

Deborah, m. John **STEBBINS**, s. John, May 8,
[1663]   1   4

Ede, m. Stephen **BROOKS**, [   ]   3   63

Ellen, m. Richard **HIGGANS**, Dec. 8, 1850   4   159

Hager, m. Robert **JACKLIN**, Oct. 13, 1713   1   47

Homer, the brickmaker, had a wife who died July 5,
[1689]   1   69

Jane E., of [New London], m. Noyes c. **BARBER**, of
Ovill, N.Y., June 19, 1837, by Rev. Abel
McEwen   4   71

	Vol.	Page
NO SURNAME (cont.)		
Gemima, m. Thomas **DANIELLS**, Dec. 11, 1702		
(Jemima)	1	27
Mary, [m.], Samuel **CONE**, [ ]	3	164
Nathaniell	1	39
Sarah, m. Pardon **LEWIS**, [ ] (Entry		
crossed out)	3	206
NEGROES AND INDIANS		
Ce[a]sar, s. Juno, b. July 27, 1793	3	104
Dicick, m. Dorcas, an Indian woman, July 18, 1707	1	33
Dorcas, an Indian woman, m. Dicick, July 18, 1707	1	33
Hagar, d. Thom & Hagar*, negroes, b. Oct. 4, 1700		
*(Formerly the wife of William **WRIGHT**, an		
Indian)	1	31
Philis, [a black girl], d. Doll, [a slave], b. Oct. [ ],		
1775	3	84
Silva, a black girl, d. Doll, a slave, b. July [ ], 1783	3	84
William, s, Frank & Jemima, b. Nov. 10, 1738		
(Negroes)	2	119